Statistics for Social Science and Public Policy

Advisors:
S.E. Fienberg   W. van der Linden

Statistics for Social Science and Public Policy

Brennan: Generalizability Theory.

Devlin/Fienberg/Resnick/Roeder (Eds.): Intelligence, Genes, and Success: Scientists Respond to *The Bell Curve.*

Finkelstein/Levin: Statistics for Lawyers, Second Edition.

Gastwirth (Ed.): Statistical Science in the Courtroom.

Handcock/Morris: Relative Distribution Methods in the Social Sciences.

Johnson/Albert: Ordinal Data Modeling.

Kolen/Brennan: Test Equating, Scaling, and Linking: Methods and Practices, Second Edition.

Morton/Rolph: Public Policy and Statistics: Case Studies from RAND.

von Davier/Holland/Thayer: The Kernel Method of Test Equating.

Zeisel/Kaye: Prove It with Figures: Empirical Methods in Law and Litigation.

DeBoeck/Wilson: Explanatory Item Response Models: A Generalized Linear and Nonlinear Approach

Michael J. Kolen
Robert L. Brennan

Test Equating, Scaling, and Linking

Methods and Practices

Second Edition

With 63 Illustrations

Michael J. Kolen
College of Education
University of Iowa
Iowa City, IA 52242
USA
michael-kolen@uiowa.edu

Robert L. Brennan
College of Education
University of Iowa
Iowa City, IA 52242
USA
robert-brennan@uiowa.edu

Advisors:

Stephen E. Fienberg
Department of Statistics
Carnegie Mellon University
Pittsburgh, PA 15213
USA

Wim van der Linden
Department of Research Methodology,
 Measurement, and Data Analysis
University of Twente
7500 AE Ens
The Netherlands

Library of Congress Cataloging-in-Publication Data
Kolen, Michael J.
  Test equating, scaling, and linking : methods and practices / Michael J. Kolen, Robert L. Brennan.—2nd ed.
    p. cm. — (Statistics in social sciences and public policy)
  Rev. ed. Of: Test equating. C1995.
  Includes bibliographical references and index.
  ISBN 0-387-40086-9 (alk. paper)
    1. Examinations—Scoring. 2. Examinations—Interpretations. 3. Examinations—Design and construction. 4. Psychological tests—Standards. 5. Educational tests and measurements—Standards. I. Brennan, Robert L. II. Kolen, Michael J. Test equating. III. Title. IV. Series
  LB3060.77.K65   2004
  371.27′1—dc22
                                                                              2004045617

ISBN 0-387-40086-9   Printed on acid-free paper.

© 2004 Springer Science+Business Media, Inc.
All rights reserved. This work may not be translated or copied in whole or in part without the written permission of the publisher (Springer Science+Business Media, Inc., 233 Spring Street, New York, NY 10013, USA), except for brief excerpts in connection with reviews or scholarly analysis. Use in connection with any form of information storage and retrieval, electronic adaptation, computer software, or by similar or dissimilar methodology now know or hereafter developed is forbidden.
The use in this publication of trade names, trademarks, service marks and similar terms, even if the are not identified as such, is not to be taken as an expression of opinion as to whether or not they are subject to proprietary rights.

Printed in the United States of America.   (EB)

9 8 7 6 5 4 3 2 1   SPIN 10929780

Springer-Verlag is a part of *Springer Science+Business Media*

springeronline.com

To Amy, Rachel, and Daniel
  —M.J.K.

To Cicely and Sean
  —R.L.B.

Preface

Prior to 1980, the subject of equating was ignored by most people in the measurement community except for psychometricians, who had responsibility for equating. In the early 1980s, the importance of equating began to be recognized by a broader spectrum of people associated with testing. This increased attention to equating is attributable to at least three developments. First, there continues to be an increase in the number and variety of testing programs that use multiple forms of tests, and the testing professionals responsible for such programs have recognized that scores on multiple forms should be equated. Second, test developers and publishers often have referenced the role of equating in arriving at reported scores to address a number of issues raised by testing critics. Third, the accountability movement in education and issues of fairness in testing have become much more visible. These developments have given equating an increased emphasis among measurement professionals and test users.

In addition to statistical procedures, successful equating involves many aspects of testing, including procedures to develop tests, to administer and score tests, and to interpret scores earned on tests. Of course, psychometricians who conduct equating need to become knowledgeable about all aspects of equating. The prominence of equating, along with its interdependence with so many aspects of the testing process, also suggests that test developers and all other testing professionals should be familiar with the concepts, statistical procedures, and practical issues associated with equating.

Before we published the first edition in 1995, the need for a book on equating became evident to us from our experiences in equating hundreds of test forms in many testing programs, in training psychometricians to conduct equating, in conducting seminars and courses on equating, and in publishing on equating and other areas of psychometrics. Our experience suggested that relatively few measurement professionals had sufficient knowledge to conduct equating. Also, many did not fully appreciate the practical consequences of various changes in testing procedures on equating, such as the consequences of many test-legislation initiatives, the use of performance assessments, and the introduction of computerized test administration. Consequently, we believed that measurement professionals needed to be educated in equating methods and practices; this book is intended to help fulfill this need. Although several general published references on equating existed at the time (e.g., Angoff, 1971; Harris and Crouse, 1993; Holland and Rubin, 1982; Petersen et al., 1989), none of them provided the broad, integrated, in-depth, and up-to-date coverage in the first edition of this book.

After the publication of the first edition in 1995, a large body of new research was published. Much of this work was in technical areas that include smoothing in equipercentile equating, estimation of standard errors of equating, and the use of polytomous item response theory methods in equating. In addition, performance assessments and computer-based tests have recently become more prominent, and these applications create complexities for equating beyond what is typically encountered with paper-and-pencil multiple-choice tests. Thus, updating the material in the first edition was one of the reasons for publishing a second edition.

The first edition briefly considered score scales and test linking. The second edition devotes whole chapters to each of these topics. The development of score scales is an important component of the scaling and equating process. Linking of tests has been of much recent interest, due to various investigations of how to link tests from different test publishers or constructed for different purposes (e.g., Feuer et al., 1999). Because both scaling and linking are closely related to test equating, it seems natural to extend coverage of this book along these lines.

We anticipate that many of the readers of this book will be advanced graduate students, entry-level professionals, or persons preparing to conduct equating, scaling, or linking for the first time. Other readers likely will be experienced professionals in measurement and related fields who will want to use this book as a reference. To address these varied audiences, we make frequent use of examples and stress conceptual issues. This book is not a traditional statistics text. Instead, it is meant for instructional use and as a reference for practical use that is intended to address both statistical and applied issues. The most frequently used methodologies are treated, as well as many practical issues. Although we are unable to cover all of the literature on equating, scaling, and linking, we provide many references so that the interested reader may pursue topics of particular interest.

The principal goals of this book are for the reader to understand the principles of equating, scaling, and linking; to be able to conduct equating, scaling, and linking; and to interpret the results in reasonable ways. After studying this book, the reader should be able to

- Understand the purposes of equating, scaling, and linking and the context in which they are conducted.

- Distinguish between equating, scaling, and linking methodologies and procedures.

- Appreciate the importance to equating of test development and quality control procedures.

- Understand the distinctions among equating properties, equating designs, and equating methods.

- Understand fundamental concepts—including designs, methods, errors, and statistical assumptions.

- Compute equating, scaling, and linking functions and choose among methods.

- Interpret results from equating, scaling, and linking analyses.

- Design reasonable and useful equating, scaling, and linking studies.

- Conduct equating, scaling, and linking in realistic testing situations.

- Identify appropriate and inappropriate uses and interpretations of equating, scaling, and linking results.

We have covered nearly all of the material in this book in a three semester-hour graduate seminar at The University of Iowa. In our course, we supplemented the materials here with general references (Angoff, 1971; Holland and Rubin, 1982; Petersen et al., 1989) so that the students could become familiar with other perspectives and notational schemes. We have used much of the material in this book in training sessions at ACT and at the annual meetings of the National Council on Measurement in Education, the American Educational Research Association, and the American Psychological Association, and in workshops given in Japan, Spain, and Taiwan.

A conceptual overview in Chapter 1 provides a general introduction. In this chapter, we define equating, describe its relationship to test development, and distinguish equating from scaling and linking. We also present properties of equating and equating designs, and introduce the concept of equating error.

In Chapter 2, using the random groups design, we illustrate traditional equating methods, such as equipercentile and linear methods. We also discuss here many of the key concepts of equating, such as properties of converted scores and the influence of the resulting scale scores on the choice of an equating result.

In Chapter 3, we cover smoothing methods in equipercentile equating. We show that the purpose of smoothing is the reduction of error in estimating equating relationships in the population. We describe methods based on log-linear models, cubic splines, and strong true score models.

In Chapter 4, we treat linear equating with nonequivalent groups of examinees. We derive statistical methods and stress the need to disconfound examinee-group and test-form differences. Also, we distinguish observed score equating from true score equating. We continue our discussion of equating with nonequivalent groups in Chapter 5 with our presentation of equipercentile methods.

In Chapter 6, we describe item response theory (IRT) equating methods under various designs. This chapter covers issues that include scaling person and item parameters, IRT true and observed score equating methods, equating using item pools, and equating using polytomous IRT models.

Chapter 7 focuses on standard errors of equating; both bootstrap and analytic procedures are described. We illustrate the use of standard errors to choose sample sizes for equating and to compare the precision in estimating equating relationships for different designs and methods.

In Chapter 8, we describe many practical issues in equating, including the importance of test development procedures, test standardization conditions, and quality control procedures. We stress conditions that are conducive to adequate equating. Also, we discuss comparability issues for performance assessments and computer-based tests.

Chapter 9 is devoted to score scales for tests. We discuss different scaling perspectives. We describe linear and nonlinear transformations that are used to construct score scales, and we consider procedures for enhancing the meaning of scale scores that include incorporating normative, content, and score precision information. We discuss procedures for maintaining score scales and scales for batteries and composites. We conclude with a section on vertical scaling that includes consideration of scaling designs and psychometric methods and a review of research on vertical scaling.

In Chapter 10, we describe linking categorization schemes and criteria and consider equating, vertical scaling, and other related methodologies as a part of these categorization schemes. An extensive example is used to illustrate how the lack of group invariance in concordance relationships can be examined and used as a means for demonstrating some of the limitations of linking methods. We discuss linking in the special circumstances of testing with extended time as well as test translation and adaptation.

Chapter 11 discusses current and future challenges in equating, scaling, and linking. Areas for future developments are highlighted.

We use a random groups illustrative equating example in Chapters 2, 3, and 7; a nonequivalent groups illustrative example in Chapters 4, 5, and 6; a second random groups illustrative example in Chapters 6 and 9; and a single-group illustrative example in Chapter 10. We use data from the administration of a test battery in multiple grades for an illustrative example in Chapter 9, and data from the administration of two different tests for an illustrative example in Chapter 10. Chapters 1–10 each have a set of exercises that are intended to reinforce the concepts and procedures in the chapter. The answers to the exercises are in Appendix A. We describe computer programs and how to obtain them in Appendix B.

We acknowledge the generous contributions that others made to the first edition of this book. We benefitted from interactions with very knowledgeable psychometricians at ACT and elsewhere, and many of the ideas in this book came from conversations and interactions with these people. Specifically, Bradley Hanson reviewed the entire manuscript and made valuable contributions, especially to the statistical presentations. He conducted the bootstrap analyses that are presented in Chapter 7 and, along with Lingjia Zeng, developed much of the computer software used in the examples. Deborah Harris reviewed the entire manuscript, and we thank her especially for her insights on practical issues in equating. Chapters 1 and 8 benefited considerably from her ideas and counsel. Lingjia Zeng also reviewed the entire manuscript and provided us with many ideas on statistical methodology, particularly in the areas of standard errors and IRT equating. Thanks to Dean Colton for his thorough reading of the entire manuscript, Xiaohong Gao for her review and for working through the exercises, and Ronald Cope and Tianqi Han for reading portions of the manuscript.

We are grateful to Nancy Petersen for her in-depth review of a draft of the first edition, her insights, and her encouragement. Bruce Bloxom provided valuable feedback, as did Barbara Plake and her graduate class at the University of Nebraska–Lincoln. We thank an anonymous reviewer, and the reviewer's graduate student, for providing us with their valuable critique. We are indebted to all who have taken our equating courses and training sessions. Amy Kolen deserves thanks for her patience and superb editorial advice. Also, we acknowledge Richard L. Ferguson—President, ACT—and Thomas Saterfiel—Vice President, Research, ACT—for their support in developing the first edition of this book.

The second edition benefitted from published reviews of the first edition by Dorans (1996), Livingston (1996), and van der Linden (1997). We are grateful to Ye Tong for the many hours she spent on electronic typesetting, for all of the errors she found, and for helping with many of the examples and the exercises. We thank Amy Hendrickson for helping to develop the polytomous IRT examples in Chapter 6, Seonghoon Kim for reviewing the additions to Chapter 6 on polytomous IRT and for developing the computer program POLYST, and Ping Yin for her work on Chapters 4 and 10. We acknowledge the work of Zhongmin Cui and Yueh-Mei Chien on the computer programs, and the work of Noo Ree Huh on checking references. We thank the students in our equating and scaling classes at the University of Iowa who discovered many errors and for helping us clarify some confusing portions of earlier drafts. We are grateful to Neil Dorans, Samuel Livingston, and Paul Holland for reviewing portions of the new material. Amy Kolen deserves thanks for her superb editorial advice. We express our appreciation to the Iowa Measurement Research Foundation for providing support to the graduate students who worked with us on this second edition.

Iowa City, IA
May, 2004

Michael J. Kolen
Robert L. Brennan

Contents

Preface   vii

Notation   xxi

1 Introduction and Concepts   1
   1.1 Equating and Related Concepts 1
       1.1.1 Test Forms and Test Specifications 2
       1.1.2 Equating 2
       1.1.3 Processes That Are Related to Equating 3
       1.1.4 Equating and Score Scales 4
       1.1.5 Equating and the Test Score Decline of the 1960s and 1970s 7
   1.2 Equating and Scaling in Practice—A Brief Overview of This Book 7
   1.3 Properties of Equating 9
       1.3.1 Symmetry Property 10
       1.3.2 Same Specifications Property 10
       1.3.3 Equity Properties 10
       1.3.4 Observed Score Equating Properties 12
       1.3.5 Group Invariance Property 13
   1.4 Equating Designs 13
       1.4.1 Random Groups Design 13
       1.4.2 Single Group Design 15
       1.4.3 Single Group Design with Counterbalancing 15

xiv   Contents

	1.4.4 ASVAB Problems with a Single Group Design . . .	17
	1.4.5 Common-Item Nonequivalent Groups Design	19
	1.4.6 NAEP Reading Anomaly—Problems with Common Items	22
1.5	Error in Estimating Equating Relationships	23
1.6	Evaluating the Results of Equating	24
1.7	Testing Situations Considered	25
1.8	Preview	26
1.9	Exercises	27

2 Observed Score Equating Using the Random Groups Design   29

2.1	Mean Equating	30
2.2	Linear Equating	31
2.3	Properties of Mean and Linear Equating	32
2.4	Comparison of Mean and Linear Equating	34
2.5	Equipercentile Equating	36
	2.5.1 Graphical Procedures	39
	2.5.2 Analytic Procedures	43
	2.5.3 Properties of Equated Scores in Equipercentile Equating	46
2.6	Estimating Observed Score Equating Relationships	48
2.7	Scale Scores	52
	2.7.1 Linear Conversions	54
	2.7.2 Truncation of Linear Conversions	55
	2.7.3 Nonlinear Conversions	56
2.8	Equating Using Single Group Designs	62
2.9	Equating Using Alternate Scoring Schemes	63
2.10	Preview of What Follows	64
2.11	Exercises	64

3 Random Groups—Smoothing in Equipercentile Equating   67

3.1	A Conceptual Statistical Framework for Smoothing	68
3.2	Properties of Smoothing Methods	72
3.3	Presmoothing Methods	73
	3.3.1 Polynomial Log-Linear Method	74
	3.3.2 Strong True Score Method	75
	3.3.3 Illustrative Example	77
3.4	Postsmoothing Methods	84
	3.4.1 Illustrative Example	89
3.5	Practical Issues in Equipercentile Equating	91
	3.5.1 Summary of Smoothing Strategies	91
	3.5.2 Equating Error and Sample Size	98
3.6	Exercises	100

4 Nonequivalent Groups—Linear Methods   103
- 4.1 Tucker Method 105
  - 4.1.1 Linear Regression Assumptions 106
  - 4.1.2 Conditional Variance Assumptions 106
  - 4.1.3 Intermediate Results 107
  - 4.1.4 Final Results 108
  - 4.1.5 Special Cases 108
- 4.2 Levine Observed Score Method 109
  - 4.2.1 Correlational Assumptions 109
  - 4.2.2 Linear Regression Assumptions 110
  - 4.2.3 Error Variance Assumptions 110
  - 4.2.4 Intermediate Results 111
  - 4.2.5 General Results 111
  - 4.2.6 Classical Congeneric Model Results 112
- 4.3 Levine True Score Method 115
  - 4.3.1 Results 116
  - 4.3.2 First-Order Equity 118
- 4.4 Illustrative Example and Other Topics 120
  - 4.4.1 Illustrative Example 121
  - 4.4.2 Synthetic Population Weights 124
  - 4.4.3 Mean Equating 125
  - 4.4.4 Decomposing Observed Differences in Means and Variances 125
  - 4.4.5 Relationships Among Tucker and Levine Equating Methods 128
  - 4.4.6 Scale Scores 130
- 4.5 Appendix: Proof $\sigma_s^2(T_X) = \gamma_1^2 \sigma_s^2(T_V)$ Under Classical Congeneric Model 131
- 4.6 Exercises 132

5 Nonequivalent Groups—Equipercentile Methods   135
- 5.1 Frequency Estimation Equipercentile Equating 135
  - 5.1.1 Conditional Distributions 136
  - 5.1.2 Frequency Estimation Method 136
  - 5.1.3 Evaluating the Frequency Estimation Assumption . 138
  - 5.1.4 Numerical Example 139
  - 5.1.5 Estimating the Distributions 142
- 5.2 Braun-Holland Linear Method 144
- 5.3 Chained Equipercentile Equating 145
- 5.4 Illustrative Example 147
  - 5.4.1 Illustrative Results 147
  - 5.4.2 Comparison Among Methods 151
  - 5.4.3 Practical Issues in Equipercentile Equating with Common Items 152
- 5.5 Exercises 153

6 Item Response Theory Methods — 155

- 6.1 Some Necessary IRT Concepts 156
  - 6.1.1 Unidimensionality and Local Independence Assumptions 156
  - 6.1.2 IRT Models 157
  - 6.1.3 IRT Parameter Estimation 160
- 6.2 Transformations of IRT Scales 161
  - 6.2.1 Transformation Equations 162
  - 6.2.2 Demonstrating the Appropriateness of Scale Transformations 162
  - 6.2.3 Expressing A and B Constants 163
  - 6.2.4 Expressing A and B Constants in Terms of Groups of Items and/or Persons 164
- 6.3 Transforming IRT Scales When Parameters Are Estimated 165
  - 6.3.1 Designs 166
  - 6.3.2 Mean/Sigma and Mean/Mean Transformation Methods 167
  - 6.3.3 Characteristic Curve Transformation Methods ... 168
  - 6.3.4 Comparisons Among Scale Transformation Methods 173
- 6.4 Equating and Scaling 175
- 6.5 Equating True Scores 176
  - 6.5.1 Test Characteristic Curves 176
  - 6.5.2 True Score Equating Process 176
  - 6.5.3 The Newton-Raphson Method 177
  - 6.5.4 Using True Score Equating with Observed Scores .. 180
- 6.6 Equating Observed Scores 181
- 6.7 IRT True Score Versus IRT Observed Score Equating 184
- 6.8 Illustrative Example 185
  - 6.8.1 Item Parameter Estimation and Scaling 185
  - 6.8.2 IRT True Score Equating 191
  - 6.8.3 IRT Observed Score Equating 194
  - 6.8.4 Rasch Equating 198
- 6.9 Using IRT Calibrated Item Pools 201
  - 6.9.1 Common-Item Equating to a Calibrated Pool 201
  - 6.9.2 Item Preequating 205
  - 6.9.3 Robustness to Violations of IRT Assumptions 207
- 6.10 Equating with Polytomous IRT 208
  - 6.10.1 Polytomous IRT Models for Ordered Responses ... 209
  - 6.10.2 Scoring Function, Item Response Function, and Test Characteristic Curve 214
  - 6.10.3 Parameter Estimation and Scale Transformation with Polytomous IRT Models 215
  - 6.10.4 True Score Equating 219
  - 6.10.5 Observed Score Equating 219
  - 6.10.6 Example Using the Graded Response Model 220

	6.11	Practical Issues and Caveat 227
	6.12	Exercises 228

7 Standard Errors of Equating — 231

- 7.1 Definition of Standard Error of Equating 232
- 7.2 The Bootstrap 235
  - 7.2.1 Standard Errors Using the Bootstrap 235
  - 7.2.2 Standard Errors of Equating 236
  - 7.2.3 Parametric Bootstrap 238
  - 7.2.4 Standard Errors of Equipercentile Equating with Smoothing 240
  - 7.2.5 Standard Errors of Scale Scores 241
  - 7.2.6 Standard Errors of Equating Chains 242
  - 7.2.7 Mean Standard Error of Equating 243
  - 7.2.8 Caveat 244
- 7.3 The Delta Method 245
  - 7.3.1 Mean Equating Using Single Group and Random Groups Designs 246
  - 7.3.2 Linear Equating Using the Random Groups Design . 247
  - 7.3.3 Equipercentile Equating Using the Random Groups Design 248
  - 7.3.4 Standard Errors for Other Designs 249
  - 7.3.5 Approximations 251
  - 7.3.6 Standard Errors for Scale Scores 253
  - 7.3.7 Standard Errors of Equating Chains 254
  - 7.3.8 Using Delta Method Standard Errors 255
- 7.4 Using Standard Errors in Practice 261
- 7.5 Exercises 263

8 Practical Issues in Equating — 267

- 8.1 Equating and the Test Development Process 269
  - 8.1.1 Test Specifications 269
  - 8.1.2 Characteristics of Common-Item Sets 271
  - 8.1.3 Changes in Test Specifications 272
- 8.2 Data Collection: Design and Implementation 273
  - 8.2.1 Choosing Among Equating Designs 273
  - 8.2.2 Developing Equating Linkage Plans 277
  - 8.2.3 Examinee Groups Used in Equating 285
  - 8.2.4 Sample Size Requirements 288
- 8.3 Choosing from Among the Statistical Procedures 290
  - 8.3.1 Equating Criteria in Research Studies 290
  - 8.3.2 Characteristics of Equating Situations 292
- 8.4 Choosing from Among Equating Results 296
  - 8.4.1 Equating Versus Not Equating 296
  - 8.4.2 Use of Robustness Checks 296

        8.4.3   Choosing from Among Results in the Random Groups
                Design 297
        8.4.4   Choosing from Among Results in the Common-Item
                Nonequivalent Groups Design 298
        8.4.5   Use of Consistency Checks 298
        8.4.6   Equating and Score Scales 300
        8.4.7   Assessing First- and Second-Order Equity for Scale
                Scores 301
   8.5 Importance of Standardization Conditions and Quality Control Procedures 306
        8.5.1   Test Development 307
        8.5.2   Test Administration and Standardization Conditions 307
        8.5.3   Quality Control 309
        8.5.4   Reequating 310
   8.6 Conditions Conducive to Satisfactory Equating 312
   8.7 Comparability Issues in Special Circumstances 312
        8.7.1   Comparability Issues with Computer-Based Tests . . 314
        8.7.2   Comparability of Performance Assessments 320
        8.7.3   Score Comparability with Optional Test Sections . . 323
   8.8 Conclusion 324
   8.9 Exercises 325

9 **Score Scales**   **329**
   9.1 Scaling Perspectives 331
   9.2 Score Transformations 336
   9.3 Incorporating Normative Information 337
        9.3.1   Linear Transformations 337
        9.3.2   Nonlinear Transformations 338
        9.3.3   Example: Normalized Scale Scores 340
        9.3.4   Importance of Norm Group in Setting the Score Scale 344
   9.4 Incorporating Score Precision Information 345
        9.4.1   Rules of Thumb for Number of Distinct Score Points 345
        9.4.2   Linearly Transformed Score Scales with a Given Standard Error of Measurement 348
        9.4.3   Score Scales with Approximately Equal Conditional
                Standard Errors of Measurement 348
        9.4.4   Example: Incorporating Score Precision 351
        9.4.5   Evaluating Psychometric Properties of Scale Scores . 354
        9.4.6   The IRT θ-Scale as a Score Scale 358
   9.5 Incorporating Content Information 358
        9.5.1   Item Mapping 358
        9.5.2   Scale Anchoring 361
        9.5.3   Standard Setting 361
        9.5.4   Numerical Example 364
        9.5.5   Practical Usefulness 366

- 9.6 Maintaining Score Scales ... 366
- 9.7 Scales for Test Batteries and Composites ... 368
  - 9.7.1 Test Batteries ... 368
  - 9.7.2 Composite Scores ... 369
  - 9.7.3 Maintaining Scales for Batteries and Composites ... 371
- 9.8 Vertical Scaling and Developmental Score Scales ... 372
  - 9.8.1 Structure of Batteries ... 373
  - 9.8.2 Type of Domain Being Measured ... 375
  - 9.8.3 Definition of Growth ... 376
  - 9.8.4 Designs for Data Collection for Vertical Scaling ... 377
  - 9.8.5 Test Scoring ... 381
  - 9.8.6 Hieronymus Statistical Methods ... 381
  - 9.8.7 Thurstone Statistical Methods ... 383
  - 9.8.8 IRT Statistical Methods ... 387
  - 9.8.9 Thurstone Illustrative Example ... 393
  - 9.8.10 IRT Illustrative Example ... 401
  - 9.8.11 Statistics for Comparing Scaling Results ... 410
  - 9.8.12 Some Limitations of Vertically Scaled Tests ... 412
  - 9.8.13 Research on Vertical Scaling ... 414
- 9.9 Exercises ... 418

10 Linking   423
- 10.1 Linking Categorization Schemes and Criteria ... 424
  - 10.1.1 Types of Linking ... 427
  - 10.1.2 Mislevy/Linn Taxonomy ... 429
  - 10.1.3 Degrees of Similarity ... 433
- 10.2 Group Invariance ... 437
  - 10.2.1 Statistical Methods Using Observed Scores ... 437
  - 10.2.2 Statistics for Overall Group Invariance ... 441
  - 10.2.3 Statistics for Pairwise Group Invariance ... 443
  - 10.2.4 Example: ACT and ITED Science Tests ... 444
- 10.3 Additional Examples ... 465
  - 10.3.1 Extended Time ... 465
  - 10.3.2 Test Adaptations and Translated Tests ... 467
- 10.4 Discussion ... 469
- 10.5 Exercises ... 470

11 Current and Future Challenges   473
- 11.1 Score Scales ... 473
- 11.2 Equating ... 474
- 11.3 Vertical Scaling ... 475
- 11.4 Linking ... 475
- 11.5 Summary ... 476

References   477

Appendix A: Answers to Exercises 511

Appendix B: Computer Programs 533

Index 535

Notation*

ˆ denotes an estimate	(Chapter 2)
1—population taking Form X	(Chapter 4)
2—population taking Form Y	(Chapter 4)

Arabic Letters

A = slope constant in linear equating and raw-to-scale score transformations	(Chapter 4)
A = slope constant in IRT θ scale transformation	(Chapter 6)
a = item slope parameter in IRT	(Chapter 6)
B = location constant in linear equating and raw-to-scale score transformations	(Chapter 4)
B = location constant in IRT θ scale transformation	(Chapter 6)
b = item location parameter in IRT	(Chapter 6)
b = item or category location parameter in polytomous IRT	(Chapter 6)
b^* = nonlinear transformation of b	(Chapter 9)
$bias$ = bias	(Chapter 3)
C = number of degrees of the polynomial in log-linear smoothing	(Chapter 3)
c = item pseudochance level parameter in IRT	(Chapter 6)
c = item location parameter in Bock's nominal categories model	(Chapter 6)

---

* Chapter where first introduced shown in parentheses.

$constant$ = a constant (Chapter 2)
cov = sampling covariance (Chapter 7)
D = scaling constant in IRT, usually set to 1.7 (Chapter 6)
DTM = Difference That Matters (Chapter 10)
d = category location parameter in generalized
    partial credit model (Chapter 6)
$d_Y(x)$ = expected value of a cubic spline estimator
    of $e_Y(x)$ (Chapter 3)
$d_Y^*(x)$ = average of two splines (Chapter 3)
df = degrees of freedom (Chapter 3)
$\mathbf{E}$ = expected value (Chapter 1)
E = number correct error score (Chapter 4)
e = the equipercentile equating function, such as $e_Y(x)$ (Chapter 2)
$e_Y(x)$ = the Form Y equipercentile equivalent of a
    Form X score (Chapter 1)
$e_X(y)$ = the Form X equipercentile equivalent of a
    Form Y score (Chapter 2)
$effect\ size$ = effect size (Chapter 9)
eq = general equating function, such as $eq_Y(x)$ (Chapter 1)
ew = effective weight (Chapter 9)
$ewMAD$ = equally weighted average of absolute differences (Chapter 10)
$ewMD$ = equally weighted average of differences (Chapter 10)
$ewREMSD$ = equally weighted Root Expected Mean
    Square Difference (Chapter 10)
$\exp$ = exponential (Chapter 6)
$F(x) = Pr(X \leq x)$ is the cumulative distribution for X (Chapter 1)
F^* = cumulative distribution function of $eq_X(y)$ (Chapter 2)
F^{-1} = inverse of function F (Chapter 2)
f = a general function (Chapter 7)
f' = the first derivative of f (Chapter 7)
$f(x) = Pr(X = x)$ is the discrete density for X (Chapter 2)
$f(x,v) = Pr(X = x$ and $V = v)$ is the joint density
    of X and V (Chapter 5)
$f(x|v) = Pr(X = x$ given $V = v)$ is the conditional
    density of x given v (Chapter 5)
$func$ = function solved for in Newton-Raphson iterations (Chapter 6)
$func'$ = first derivative of function solved for in Newton-
    Raphson iterations (Chapter 6)
$G(y) = Pr(Y \leq y)$ is the cumulative distribution for Y (Chapter 1)
G^* = the cumulative distribution function of e_Y (Chapter 1)
G^{-1} = inverse of function G (Chapter 2)
g = item subscript in IRT (Chapter 6)
g = index used to sum over categories in generalized
    partial credit model (Chapter 6)
g = arcsine transformed proportion-correct score (Chapter 9)

$g(y) = Pr(Y = y)$ is the discrete density for Y (Chapter 2)
$g(y,v) = Pr(Y = y$ and $V = v)$ is the joint density
of Y and V (Chapter 5)
$g(y|v) = Pr(Y = y$ given $V = v)$ is the conditional density of
y given v (Chapter 5)
g_{adj} = density adjusted by adding 10^{-6} to each density
and then standardizing (Chapter 2)
H = number of subgroups (Chapter 10)
$Hcrit$ = criterion function for Haebara's method (Chapter 6)
$Hdiff$ = difference function for Haebara's method (Chapter 6)
h = index for summing over categories (Chapter 6)
h = number of scale score points for a confidence interval (Chapter 9)
h = subgroup designator (Chapter 10)
$h(v) = Pr(V = v)$ is the discrete density for V (Chapter 5)
I = IRT scale (Chapter 6)
I = number of scale scores on Test X (Chapter 10)
i and i' = individuals (Chapter 6)
$intercept$ = intercept of an equating function (Chapter 2)
irt = IRT true-score equating function (Chapter 6)
J = IRT scale (Chapter 6)
J = number of scale scores on Test Y (Chapter 10)
j and j' = items (Chapter 6)
K = number of items (Chapter 2)
KR-20 = Kuder-Richardson Formula 20 reliability coefficient (Chapter 9)
KR-21 = Kuder-Richardson Formula 21 reliability coefficient (Chapter 9)
k = Lord's k in the Beta4 method (Chapter 3)
k = categories for an item in polytomous IRT (Chapter 6)
ku = kurtosis, such as $ku(X) = \mathbf{E}[X - \mu(X)]^4/\sigma^4(X)$ (Chapter 2)
$l_Y(x)$ = the Form Y linear equivalent of a Form X score (Chapter 2)
$l_X(y)$ = the Form X linear equivalent of a Form Y score (Chapter 2)
MAD = weighted average of absolute differences (Chapter 10)
MD = weighted average of differences (Chapter 10)
m = number of categories for an item in polytomous IRT (Chapter 6)
$m_Y(x)$ = the mean equating equivalent of a Form X score (Chapter 2)
$m_X(y)$ = the mean equating equivalent of a Form Y score (Chapter 2)
max = maximum score (Chapter 6)
min = minimum score (Chapter 6)
mse = mean squared error (Chapter 3)
N = number of examinees (Chapter 3)
NCE = Normal Curve Equivalent (unrounded) (Chapter 9)
NCE_{int} = Normal Curve Equivalent rounded to an integer (Chapter 9)
$P(x)$ = the percentile rank function for X (Chapter 2)
P^* = a given percentile rank (Chapter 2)
$P^{**} = P/100$ (Chapter 7)
P^{-1} = the percentile function for X (Chapter 2)

xxiv   Notation

p = probability of a correct response in IRT (Chapter 6)
p = category response function in polytomous IRT (Chapter 6)
p^* = cumulative category response function in polytomous IRT (Chapter 6)
p' = first derivative of p (Chapter 6)
pl_{Yh} = parallel linear equating equivalent on Test Y for subgroup h (Chapter 10)
$Q(y)$ = the percentile rank function for Y (Chapter 2)
Q^{-1} = the percentile function for Y (Chapter 2)
R = number of bootstrap replications (Chapter 7)
$REMSD$ = Root Expected Mean Square Difference (Chapter 10)
$RMSD$ = Root Mean Square Difference (Chapter 10)
RP = Response Probability level in item mapping (Chapter 9)
r = index for calculating observed score distribution in IRT (Chapter 6)
r = index for bootstrap replications (Chapter 7)
regression intercept = intercept constant in linear regression (Chapter 5)
regression slope = slope constant in linear regression (Chapter 5)
$rmsel$ = root mean squared error for linking (Chapter 10)
S = smoothing parameter in postsmoothing (Chapter 3)
SC = scale score random variable (Chapter 9)
$SLcrit$ = criterion function for Stocking-Lord method (Chapter 6)
$SLdiff$ = difference function for Stocking-Lord method (Chapter 6)
SMD = Standardized Mean Difference (Chapter 10)
s = synthetic population (Chapter 4)
sc = scale score transformation, such as $sc(y)$ (Chapter 2)
sc_{int} = scale score rounded to an integer (Chapter 2)
se = standard error, such as $se(x)$ is the standard error at score x (Chapter 3)
sem = standard error of measurement (Chapter 7)
sk = skewness, such as $sk(X) = \mathbf{E}[X - \mu(X)]^3/\sigma^3(X)$ (Chapter 2)
slope = slope of equating function (Chapter 2)
st = stanine (unrounded) (Chapter 9)
st = scaling test (Chapter 9)
st_{int} = stanine rounded to an integer (Chapter 9)
T = number correct true score (Chapter 4)
T = normalized score with mean of 50 and standard deviation of 10 (Chapter 9)
T_{int} = normalized score with mean of 50 and standard deviation of 10 rounded to an integer (Chapter 9)
t = realization of number correct true score (Chapter 4)
$t_Y(x)$ = expected value of an alternate estimator of $e_Y(x)$ (Chapter 3)
U = uniform random variable (Chapter 2)
u = standard deviation units (Chapter 7)

V = the random variable indicating raw score on Form V (Chapter 4)
v = spline coefficient (Chapter 3)
v = a realization of V (Chapter 4)
v = subgroup weight for a particular score (Chapter 10)
var = sampling variance (Chapter 3)
w = weight for synthetic group (Chapter 4)
w = nominal weight (Chapter 9)
w = subgroup weight (Chapter 10)
X = the random variable indicating raw score on Form X (Chapter 1)
X = random variable indicating scale score on Test X (Chapter 10)
$X^* = X + U$ used in the continuization process (Chapter 2)
x = a realization of X (Chapter 1)
x^* = integer closest to x such that $x^* - .5 \leq x < x^* + .5$ (Chapter 2)
x^* = Form X_2 score equated to the Form X_1 scale (Chapter 7)
x_{high} = upper limit in spline calculations (Chapter 3)
x_L^* = the largest integer score with a cumulative percent less than P^* (Chapter 2)
x_{low} = lower limit in spline calculations (Chapter 3)
x_U^* = the smallest integer score with a cumulative percent greater than P^* (Chapter 2)
Y = the random variable indicating raw score on Form Y (Chapter 1)
Y = random variable indicating scale score on Test Y (Chapter 10)
y = a realization of Y (Chapter 1)
y_i^* = largest tabled raw score less than or equal to $e_Y(x)$ in finding scale scores (Chapter 2)
y_L^* = the largest integer score with a cumulative percent less than Q^* (Chapter 2)
y_U^* = the smallest integer score with a cumulative percent greater than Q^* (Chapter 2)
Z = the random variable indicating raw score on Form Z (Chapter 4)
z = a realization of Z (Chapter 4)
z = unit normal variable (Chapter 7)
z = normalized score (Chapter 9)
z^* = selected set of normalized scores in Thurstone scaling (Chapter 9)
z_γ = unit normal score associated with a $100\gamma\%$ confidence interval (Chapter 9)

Greek Letters

$\alpha(X|V)$ and $\alpha(Y|V)$ = linear regression slopes (Chapter 4)
$\beta(X|V)$ and $\beta(Y|V)$ = linear regression intercepts (Chapter 4)
χ^2 = chi-square test statistic (Chapter 3)
δ = location parameter in congeneric models (Chapter 4)
ϕ = normal ordinate (Chapter 7)

Notation

γ = expansion factor in linear equating with the common-item nonequivalent groups design	(Chapter 4)
γ = confidence coefficient	(Chapter 9)
λ = effective test length in congeneric models	(Chapter 4)
μ = mean as in $\mu(X)$ and $\mu(Y)$	(Chapter 2)
ν = weight for a pair of subgroups and a particular score	(Chapter 10)
Φ = inverse normal transformation	(Chapter 9)
Θ = parameter used in developing the delta method	(Chapter 7)
θ = ability in IRT	(Chapter 6)
θ^+ = new value in Newton-Raphson iterations	(Chapter 6)
θ_- = initial value in Newton-Raphson iterations	(Chapter 6)
θ^* = nonlinear transformation of θ	(Chapter 9)
ρ = correlation, such as $\rho(X,V)$	(Chapter 4)
$\rho(X,X')$ = reliability	(Chapter 4)
$\sigma(X,V)$ and $\sigma(Y,V)$ = covariance	(Chapter 4)
σ^2 = variance such as $\sigma^2(X) = \mathbf{E}[X - \mu(X)]^2$	(Chapter 2)
σ_{ij} = covariance between variables i and j	(Chapter 9)
τ = true score	(Chapter 1)
τ^* = true score outside of range of possible true scores	(Chapter 6)
$\hat{\tau}$ = estimated true scores	(Chapter 9)
ω = weight in log-linear smoothing	(Chapter 3)
Ψ = function that relates true scores	(Chapter 4)
ψ = distribution of a latent variable	(Chapter 3)
∂ = partial derivative	(Chapter 7)

1
Introduction and Concepts[1]

This chapter provides a general overview of equating and briefly considers important concepts. The concept of equating is described, as is why it is needed, and how to distinguish it from other related processes. Equating properties and designs are considered in detail, because these concepts provide the organizing themes for addressing the statistical methods treated in subsequent chapters. Some issues in evaluating equating are also considered. The chapter concludes with a preview of subsequent chapters.

1.1 Equating and Related Concepts

Scores on tests often are used as one piece of information in making important decisions. Some of these decisions focus at the *individual level*, such as when a student decides which college to attend or on a course in which to enroll. For other decisions the focus is more at an *institutional level*. For example, an agency or institution might need to decide what test score is required to certify individuals for a profession or to admit students into a college, university, or the military. Still other decisions are made at the *public policy level*, such as addressing what can be done to improve education in the United States and how changes in educational practice can be evaluated. Regardless of the type of decision that is to be made, it should

---

[1] Some of the material in this chapter is based on Kolen (1988).

be based on the most accurate information possible. All other things being equal, *the more accurate the information, the better the decision.*

Making decisions in many of these contexts requires that tests be administered on multiple occasions. For example, college admissions tests typically are administered on particular days, referred to as *test dates*, so examinees can have some flexibility in choosing when to be tested. Tests also are given over many years to track educational trends over time. If the same test questions were routinely administered on each test date, then examinees might inform others about the test questions. Or, an examinee who tested twice might be administered the same test questions on the two test dates. In these situations, a test might become more of a measure of exposure to the specific questions that are on the test than of the construct that the test is supposed to measure.

1.1.1 Test Forms and Test Specifications

These test security problems can be addressed by administering a different collection of test questions, referred to as a *test form*, to examinees who test on different test dates. A test form is a set of test questions that is built according to content and statistical *test specifications* (Millman and Greene, 1989). Test specifications provide guidelines for developing the test. Those responsible for constructing the test, the *test developers*, use these specifications to ensure that the test forms are as similar as possible to one another in content and statistical characteristics.

1.1.2 Equating

The use of different test forms on different test dates leads to another concern: the forms might differ somewhat in difficulty. *Equating is a statistical process that is used to adjust scores on test forms so that scores on the forms can be used interchangeably.* Equating adjusts for differences in difficulty among forms that are built to be similar in difficulty and content.

The following situation is intended to develop further the concept of equating. Suppose that a student takes a college admissions test for the second time and earns a higher reported score than on the first testing. One explanation of this difference is that the reported score on the second testing reflects a higher level of achievement than the reported score on the first testing. However, suppose that the student had been administered exactly the same test questions on both testings. Rather than indicating a higher level of achievement, the student's reported score on the second testing might be inflated because the student had already been exposed to the test items. Fortunately, a new test form is used each time a test is administered for most college admissions tests. Therefore, a student would not likely be administered the same test questions on any two test dates.

The use of different test forms on different test dates might cause another problem, as is illustrated by the following situation. Two students apply for the same college scholarship that is based partly on test scores. The two students take the test on different test dates, and Student 1 earns a higher reported score than Student 2. One possible explanation of this difference is that Student 1 is higher achieving than Student 2. However, if Student 1 took an easier test form than Student 2, then Student 1 would have an unfair advantage over Student 2. In this case, the difference in scores might be due to differences in the difficulty of the test forms rather than in the achievement levels of the students. To avoid this problem, equating is used with most college admissions tests. If the test forms are successfully equated, then the difference in equated scores for Student 1 and Student 2 is not attributable to Student 1's taking an easier form.

The process of equating is used in situations where such *alternate forms* of a test exist and scores earned on different forms are compared to each other. Even though test developers attempt to construct test forms that are as similar as possible to one another in content and statistical specifications, the forms typically differ somewhat in difficulty. Equating is intended to adjust for these difficulty differences, allowing the forms to be used interchangeably. *Equating adjusts for differences in difficulty, not for differences in content.* After successful equating, for example, examinees who earn an equated score of, say, 26 on one test form could be considered, on average, to be at the same achievement level as examinees who earn an equated score of 26 on a different test form.

1.1.3 Processes That Are Related to Equating

There are processes that are similar to equating, which may be more properly referred to as *scaling to achieve comparability*, in the terminology of the *Standards for Educational and Psychological Testing* (AERA, APA, NCME, 1999), or *linking*, in the terminology of Linn (1993) and Mislevy (1992). One of these processes is *vertical scaling* (frequently referred to as vertical "*equating*"), which often is used with elementary school achievement test batteries. In these batteries, students often are administered questions that test content matched to their current grade level. This procedure allows developmental scores (e.g., grade equivalents) of examinees at different grade levels to be compared. Because the content of the tests administered to students at various educational levels is different, however, scores on tests intended for different educational levels cannot be used interchangeably. Other examples of linking include relating scores on one test to those on another, and scaling the tests within a battery so that they all have the same distributional characteristics. As with vertical scaling, solutions to these problems do not allow test scores to be used interchangeably, because the content of the tests is different.

Although similar statistical procedures often are used in linking and equating, their purposes are different. Whereas tests that are purposefully built to be different are linked, equating is used to adjust scores on test forms that are built to be as similar as possible in content and statistical characteristics. When equating is successful, scores on alternate forms can be used interchangeably. Issues in linking tests that are not built to the same specifications are considered further in Chapters 9 and 10.

1.1.4 Equating and Score Scales

On a multiple-choice test, the *raw score* an examinee earns is often the number of items the examinee answers correctly. Other raw scores might involve penalties for wrong answers or weighting items differentially. On tests that require ratings by judges, a raw score might be the sum of the numerical ratings made by the judges.

Raw scores often are transformed to *scale scores*. The *raw-to-scale score transformation* can be chosen by test developers to enhance the interpretability of scores by incorporating useful information into the score scale (Petersen et al., 1989). Information based on a nationally representative group of examinees, referred to as a *national norm group*, sometimes is used as a basis for establishing score scales. For example, the number-correct scores for the four tests of the initial form of a revised version of the ACT Assessment were scaled (Brennan, 1989) to have a mean scale score of 18 for a nationally representative sample of college-bound 12th graders. Thus, an examinee who earned a scale score of 22, for example, would know that this score was above the mean scale score for the nationally representative sample of college-bound 12th graders used to develop the score scale. One alternative to using nationally representative norm groups is to base scale score characteristics on a *user norm group*, which is a group of examinees that is administered the test under operational conditions. For example, a rescaled SAT scale was established for use beginning in 1995 by setting the mean score equal to 500 for the group of SAT examinees that graduated from high school in 1990 (Cook, 1994; Dorans, 2002).

Scaling and Equating Process

Equating can be viewed as an aspect of a more general *scaling and equating process*. Score scales typically are established using a single test form. For subsequent test forms, the scale is maintained through an equating process that places raw scores from subsequent forms on the established score scale. In this way, a scale score has the same meaning regardless of the test form administered or the group of examinees tested. Typically, raw scores on the new form are equated to raw scores on the old form, and these equated raw scores are then converted to scale scores using the raw-to-scale score transformation for the old form.

TABLE 1.1. Hypothetical Conversion Tables for Test Forms.

Scale	Form Y Raw	Form X_1 Raw	Form X_2 Raw
•	•	•	•
•	•	•	•
•	•	•	•
13	26	27	28
14	27	28	29
14	28	29	30
15	29	30	31
15	30	31	32
•	•	•	•
•	•	•	•
•	•	•	•

Example of the Scaling and Equating Process

The hypothetical conversions shown in Table 1.1 illustrate the scaling and equating process. The first two columns show the relationship between Form Y raw scores and scale scores. For example, a raw score of 28 on Form Y converts to a scale score of 14. (At this point there is no need to be concerned about what particular method was used to develop the raw-to-scale score transformation.) The relationship between Form Y raw scores and scale scores shown in the first two columns involves scaling—not equating, because Form Y is the only form that is being considered so far.

Assume that an equating process indicates that Form X_1 is 1 point easier than Form Y throughout the score scale. A raw score of 29 on Form X_1 would thus reflect the same level of achievement as a raw score of 28 on Form Y. This relationship between Form Y raw scores and Form X_1 raw scores is displayed in the second and third columns in Table 1.1. What scale score corresponds to a Form X_1 raw score of 29? A scale score of 14 corresponds to this raw score, because a Form X_1 raw score of 29 corresponds to a Form Y raw score of 28, and a Form Y raw score of 28 corresponds to a scale score of 14.

To carry the example one step further, assume that Form X_2 is found to be uniformly 1 raw score point easier than Form X_1. Then, as illustrated in Table 1.1, a raw score of 30 on Form X_2 corresponds to a raw score of 29 on Form X_1, which corresponds to a raw score of 28 on Form Y, which corresponds to a scale score of 14. Later, additional forms could be converted to scale scores by a similar chaining process. The result of a successful scaling and equating process is that scale scores on all forms can be used interchangeably.

Possible Alternatives to Equating

Equating has the potential to improve score reporting and interpretation of tests that have alternate forms when examinees administered different forms are evaluated at the same time, or when score trends are to be evaluated over time. When at least one of these characteristics is present, at least two possible, but typically unacceptable, alternatives to equating exist. One alternative is to report raw scores regardless of the form administered. As was the case with Students 1 and 2 considered earlier, this approach could cause problems because examinees who were administered an easier form are advantaged and those who were administered a more difficult form are disadvantaged. As another example, suppose that the mean score on a test increased from 27 one year to 30 another year, and that different forms of the test were administered in the two years. Without additional information, it is impossible to determine whether this 3-point score increase is attributable to differences in the difficulty of the two forms, differences in the achievement level of the groups tested, or some combination of these two factors.

A second alternative to equating is to convert raw scores to other types of scores so that certain characteristics of the score distributions are the same across all test dates. For example, for a test with two test dates per year, say in February and August, the February raw scores might be converted to scores having a mean of 50 among the February examinees, and the August raw scores might be converted to have a mean of 50 among the August examinees. Suppose, given this situation, that an examinee somehow knew that August examinees were higher achieving, on average, than February examinees. In which month should the examinee take the test to earn the highest score? Because the August examinees are higher achieving, a high converted score would be more difficult to get in August than in February. Examinees who take the test in February, therefore, would be advantaged. Under these circumstances, examinees who take the test with a lower achieving group are advantaged, and examinees who take the test with a higher achieving group are disadvantaged. Furthermore, trends in average examinee performance cannot be addressed using this alternative because the average converted scores are the same regardless of the achievement level of the group tested.

Successfully equated scores are not affected by the problems that occur with these two alternatives. Successful equating adjusts for differences in the difficulty of test forms; the resulting equated scores have the same meaning regardless of when or to whom the test was administered.

1.1.5 Equating and the Test Score Decline of the 1960s and 1970s

The importance of equating in evaluating trends over time is illustrated by issues surrounding the substantial decline in test scores in the 1960s and 1970s. A number of studies were undertaken to try to understand the causes for this decline. (See, for example, Advisory Panel on the Scholastic Aptitude Test Score Decline, 1977; Congressional Budget Office, 1986; Harnischfeger and Wiley, 1975). One of the potential causes that was investigated was whether the decline was attributable to inaccurate equating. The studies concluded that the equating was adequate. Thus, the equating procedures allowed the investigators to rule out changes in test difficulty as being the reason for the score decline. Next the investigators searched for other explanations. These explanations included changes in how students were being educated, changes in demographics of test takers, and changes in social and environmental conditions. It is particularly important to note that the search for these other explanations was made possible because equating ruled out changes in test difficulty as the reason for the score decline.

1.2 Equating and Scaling in Practice—A Brief Overview of This Book

So far, what equating is and why it is important have been described in general terms. Clearly, equating involves the implementation of statistical procedures. In addition, as has been stressed, equating requires that all test forms be developed according to the same content and statistical specifications. Equating also relies on adequate test administration procedures, so that the collected data can be used to judge accurately the extent to which the test forms differ statistically. In our experience, the most challenging part of equating often is ensuring that the test development, test administration, and statistical procedures are coordinated. The following is a list of steps for implementing equating (the order might vary in practice):

1. *Decide on the purpose for equating.*

2. *Construct alternate forms.* Alternate test forms are constructed in accordance with the same content and statistical specifications.

3. *Choose a design for data collection.* Equating requires that data be collected for providing information on how the test forms differ statistically.

4. *Implement the data collection design.* The test is administered and the data are collected as specified by the design.

5. *Choose one or more operational definitions of equating.* Equating requires that a choice be made about what types of relationships between forms are to be estimated. For example, this choice might involve deciding on whether to implement linear or nonlinear equating methods.

6. *Choose one or more statistical estimation methods.* Various procedures exist for estimating a particular equating relationship. For example, in Chapter 4, linear equating relationships are estimated using the Tucker and Levine methods.

7. *Evaluate the results of equating.* After equating is conducted, the results need to be evaluated. Some evaluation procedures are discussed along with methods described in Chapters 2–6. The test development process, test administration, statistical procedures, and properties of the resulting equating are all components of the evaluation, as is discussed in Chapter 8.

As these steps in the equating process suggest, individuals responsible for conducting equating make choices about designs, operational definitions, statistical techniques, and evaluation procedures. In addition, various practical issues in test administration and quality control are often vital to successful equating.

In practice, equating requires considerable judgment on the part of the individuals responsible for conducting equating. General experience and knowledge about equating, along with experience in equating for tests in a testing program, are vital to making informed judgments. As a statistical process, equating also requires the use of statistical techniques. Therefore, conducting equating involves a mix of practical issues and statistical knowledge. This book treats both practical issues and statistical concepts and procedures.

This book is intended to describe the concept of test form equating, to distinguish equating from other similar processes, to describe techniques used in equating, and to describe various practical issues involved in conducting equating. These purposes are addressed by describing information, techniques, and resources that are necessary to understand the principles of equating, to design and conduct an informed equating, and to evaluate the results of equating in reasonable ways.

This book also is intended to describe the concept of test scaling in detail. Test scaling is distinguished from test form equating. Techniques and practical issues involved in scaling are developed that are necessary for understanding how tests are scaled and to evaluate the results of scaling techniques. Linking methods are also discussed by presenting conceptual frameworks for linking and discussing some prominent examples of linking as it is used in practice.

Many of the changes that have taken place in the literature on equating, scaling, and linking in recent years are reflected in this book. Although the vast literature that has developed is impossible to review in a single volume, this book provides many references that should help the reader access the literature. We recommend that the classic work by Angoff (1971) be consulted as a supplement to this book for its treatment of many of the issues in traditional equating. scaling, and linking methods and for its perspective on equating and scaling. Works by Harris (1993), Harris and Crouse (1993), Holland and Rubin (1982), Linn (1993), Mislevy (1992), and Petersen et al. (1989) also should be consulted as supplements.

Subsequent sections of this chapter focus on equating properties and equating designs, which are required concepts for Chapters 2–6. Equating error and evaluation of equating methods also are briefly discussed. Specific operational definitions and statistical estimation methods are the focus of Chapters 2–6. Equating error is described in Chapters 7 and 8. Practical issues in equating, along with new directions, are also discussed in Chapter 8. Score scales are discussed in Chapter 9 and linking in Chapter 10.

1.3 Properties of Equating

Various desirable properties of equating relationships have been proposed in the literature (Angoff, 1971; Harris and Crouse, 1993; Lord, 1980; Petersen et al., 1989). Some properties focus on individuals' scores, others on distributions of scores. At the individual level, ideally, an examinee taking one form would earn the same reported score regardless of the form taken. At the distribution level, for a group of examinees, the same proportion would earn a reported score at or below, say, 26 on Form X as they would on Form Y. These types of properties have been used as the principal basis for developing equating procedures.

Some properties focus on variables that cannot be directly observed, such as *true scores* in *classical test theory* (Lord and Novick, 1968) and *latent abilities* in *item response theory* (*IRT*) (Lord, 1980). True scores and latent abilities are scores that an examinee would have earned had there been no measurement error. For example, in classical test theory the score that an examinee earns, the examinee's *observed score*, is viewed as being composed of the examinee's true score and measurement error. It is assumed that if the examinee could be measured repeatedly, then measurement error would, on average, equal zero. Statistically, the true score is the expected score over replications. Because the examinee is not measured repeatedly in practice, the examinee's true score is not directly observed. Instead, the true score is modeled using a test theory model.

Other equating properties focus on observed scores. Observed score properties of equating do not rely on test theory models.

1.3.1 Symmetry Property

The *symmetry property* (Lord, 1980), which requires that equating transformations be symmetric, is required for a relationship to be considered an equating relationship. This property requires that the function used to transform a score on Form X to the Form Y scale be the inverse of the function used to transform a score on Form Y to the Form X scale. For example, this property implies that if a raw score of 26 on Form X converts to a raw score of 27 on Form Y, then a raw score of 27 on Form Y must convert to a raw score of 26 on Form X. This symmetry property rules out regression as an equating method, because the regression of Y on X is, in general, different from the regression of X on Y. As a check on this property, an equating of Form X to Form Y and an equating of Form Y to Form X could be conducted. If these equating relationships are plotted, then the symmetry property requires that these plots be indistinguishable. Symmetry is considered again in Chapter 2.

1.3.2 Same Specifications Property

As indicated earlier, test forms must be built to the same content and statistical specifications if they are to be equated. Otherwise, regardless of the statistical procedures used, the scores can not be used interchangeably. This *same specifications property* is essential if scores on alternate forms are to be considered interchangeable.

1.3.3 Equity Properties

Lord (1980, p. 195) proposed *Lord's equity property* of equating, which is based on test theory models. For Lord's equity property to hold, it must be a matter of indifference to each examinee whether Form X or Form Y is administered.

Lord defined this property specifically. Lord's equity property holds if examinees with a given true score have the same distribution of converted scores on Form X as they would on Form Y. To make the description of this property more precise, define

τ as the true score;

Form X as the new form—let X represent the random variable score on Form X, and let x represent a particular score on Form X (i.e., a realization of X);

Form Y as the old form—let Y represent the random variable score on Form Y, and let y represent a particular score on Form Y (i.e., a realization of Y);

G as the cumulative distribution of scores on Form Y for the population of examinees;

eq_Y as an equating function that is used to convert scores on Form X to the scale of Form Y; and

G^* as the cumulative distribution of eq_Y for the same population of examinees.

Lord's equity property holds in the population if

$$G^*[eq_Y(x)|\tau] = G(y|\tau), \quad \text{for all } \tau. \tag{1.1}$$

This property implies that examinees with a given true score would have identical observed score means, standard deviations, and distributional shapes of converted scores on Form X and scores on Form Y. In particular, the identical standard deviations imply that the conditional standard error of measurement at any true score are equal on the two forms. If, for example, Form X measured somewhat more precisely at high scores than Form Y, then Lord's equity property would not be met.

Lord (1980) showed that, under fairly general conditions, Lord's equity property specified in equation (1.1) is possible only if Form X and Form Y are essentially identical. However, identical forms typically cannot be constructed in practice. Furthermore, if identical forms could be constructed, then there would be no need for equating. Thus, using Lord's equity property as the criterion, equating is either impossible or unnecessary.

Morris (1982) suggested a less restrictive version of Lord's equity property that might be more readily achieved, which is referred to as the *first-order equity property* or *weak equity property* (also see Yen, 1983). Under the first-order equity property, examinees with a given true score have the same mean converted score on Form X as they have on Form Y. Defining **E** as the expectation operator, an equating achieves the first-order equity property if

$$\mathbf{E}[eq_Y(X)|\tau] = \mathbf{E}(Y|\tau) \quad \text{for all } \tau. \tag{1.2}$$

The first-order equity property implies that examinees are expected to earn the same equated score on Form X as they would on Form Y. Suppose examinees with a given true score earn, on average, a score of 26 on Form Y. Under the first-order equity property, these examinees also would earn, on average, an equated score of 26 on Form X.

As is described in Chapter 4, linear methods have been developed that are consistent with the first-order equity property. Also, the IRT true score methods that are discussed in Chapter 6 are related to this equity property. The equating methods that are based on equity properties are closely related to other psychometric procedures, such as models used to estimate reliability. These methods make explicit the requirement that the two forms measure the same achievement through the true score.

1.3.4 Observed Score Equating Properties

In observed score equating, the characteristics of score distributions are set equal for a specified *population of examinees* (Angoff, 1971). For the *equipercentile equating property*, the converted scores on Form X have the same distribution as scores on Form Y. More explicitly, this property holds, for the *equipercentile equating function*, e_Y, if

$$G^*[e_Y(x)] = G(y), \qquad (1.3)$$

where G^* and G were defined previously. The equipercentile equating property implies that the cumulative distribution of equated scores on Form X is equal to the cumulative distribution of scores on Form Y.

Suppose a passing score was set at a *scale score* of 26. If the equating of the forms achieved the equipercentile equating property, then the proportion of examinees in the population earning a scale score below 26 on Form X would be the same as the proportion of examinees in the population earning a scale score below 26 on Form Y. In addition, in the population, the same proportion of examinees would score below any particular scale score, regardless of the form taken. For example, if a scale score of 26 was chosen as a passing score, then the same proportion of examinees in the population would pass using either Form X or Form Y.

The equipercentile equating property is the focus of the equipercentile equating methods described in Chapters 2, 3, and 5 and the IRT observed score equating method described in Chapter 6. Two other observed score equating properties also may be used sometimes. Under the *mean equating property*, converted scores on the two forms have the same mean. This property is the focus of the mean observed score equating methods described in Chapter 2. Under the *linear equating property*, converted scores on the two forms have the same mean and standard deviation. This property is the focus of the linear observed score methods described in Chapters 2, 4, and 5. When the equipercentile equating property holds, the linear and mean equating properties must also hold. When the linear equating property holds, the mean equating property also must hold.

Observed score equating methods associated with the observed score properties of equating predate other methods, which partially explains why they have been used more often. Observed score methods do not directly consider true scores or other unobservable variables, and in this way they are less complicated. As a consequence, however, nothing in the statistical machinery of observed score equating requires that test forms be built to the same specifications. This requirement is added so that results from equating may be reasonably and usefully interpreted.

1.3.5 Group Invariance Property

Under the *group invariance property*, the equating relationship is the same regardless of the group of examinees used to conduct the equating. For example, if the group invariance property holds, the same equating relationship would be found for females and males. Lord and Wingersky (1984) indicated that methods based on observed score properties of equating are not strictly group invariant. This observation was further discussed by van der Linden (2000). However, research on the group invariance property conducted by Angoff and Cowell (1986) and Harris and Kolen (1986) suggested that the conversions are very similar across various examinee groups, at least in those situations where carefully constructed alternate forms are equated. Lord and Wingersky (1984) indicated that, under certain theoretical conditions, which were stated explicitly by van der Linden (2000), true score equating methods are group invariant. However, group invariance does not necessarily hold for these methods when observed scores are substituted for true scores. Dorans and Holland (2000) developed procedures and statistics for investigating group invariance. Because group invariance cannot be assumed to exist in the strictest sense, the population of examinees on which the equating relationship is developed should be clearly stated and representative of the group of examinees who are administered the test.

1.4 Equating Designs

A variety of designs can be used for collecting data for equating. The group of examinees included in an equating study should be reasonably representative of the group of examinees who will be administered the test under typical test administration conditions. The choice of a design involves both practical and statistical issues. Three commonly used designs are illustrated in Figure 1.1. Assume that a conversion from Form Y to scale scores has been developed, and that Form X is a new form to be equated to Form Y.

1.4.1 Random Groups Design

The *random groups design* is the first design shown in Figure 1.1. In this design, examinees are randomly assigned the form to be administered.

A *spiraling* process is one procedure that can be used to randomly assign forms using this design. In one method for spiraling, Form X and Form Y are alternated when the test booklets are packaged. When the booklets are handed out, the first examinee receives Form X, the second examinee Form Y, the third examinee Form X, and so on. This spiraling process typically leads to comparable, *randomly equivalent* groups taking Form X and Form Y. When using this design, the difference between group-level performance

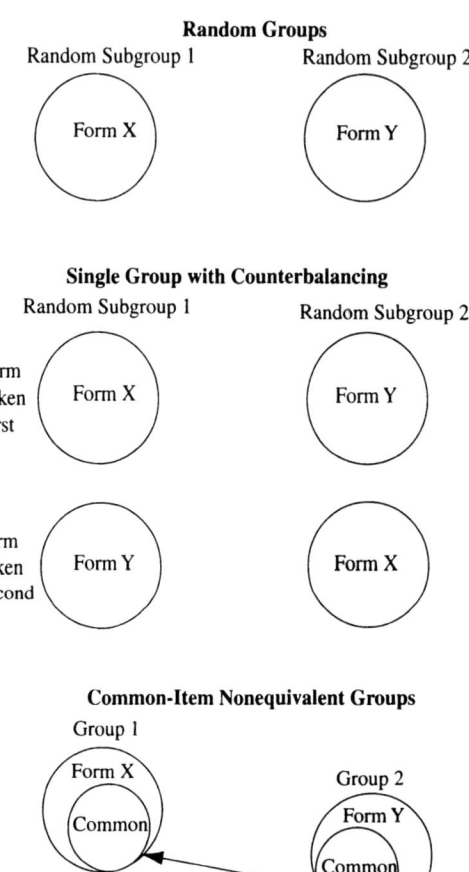

FIGURE 1.1. Illustration of three data collection designs.

on the two forms is taken as a direct indication of the difference in difficulty between the forms.

For example, suppose that the random groups design is used to equate Form X to Form Y using large representative examinee groups. Suppose also that the mean for Form Y is 77 raw score points and the mean for Form X is 72 raw score points. Because the mean for Form Y is 5 points higher than the mean for Form X, Form Y is 5 raw score points easier, on average, than Form X. This example is a simplification of equating in practice. More complete methods for equating using the random groups design are described in detail in Chapter 2.

One practical feature of the random groups design is that each examinee takes only one form of the test, thus minimizing testing time relative to a design in which examinees take more than one form. In addition, more than one new form can be equated at the same time by including the additional new forms in the spiraling process. The random groups design requires that all the forms be available and administered at the same time, which might be difficult in some situations. If there is concern about test form security, administering more than one form could exacerbate these concerns. Because different examinees take the forms to be equated, large sample sizes are typically needed.

When spiraling is used for random assignment, certain practical issues should be considered. First, examinees should not be seated in a way that would defeat the process. For example, if examinees were systematically seated boy—girl, boy—girl, then the boys might all be administered Form X and the girls Form Y. Also, suppose that there were many testing rooms. If the first examinee in each room was administered Form X, then more Form X booklets would be administered than Form Y booklets in those rooms with an odd number of examinees.

1.4.2 Single Group Design

In the *single group design* (not shown in Figure 1.1) the same examinees are administered both Form X and Form Y. What if Form X was administered first to all examinees followed by Form Y? If fatigue was a factor in examinee performance, then Form Y could appear relatively more difficult than Form X because examinees would be tired when administered Form Y. On the other hand, if familiarity with the test increased performance, then Form Y could appear to be easier than Form X. Because these *order effects* are typically present, and there is no reason to believe they cancel each other out, this design is rarely used in practice.

1.4.3 Single Group Design with Counterbalancing

Counterbalancing the order of administration of the forms is one way to deal with order effects in the single group design. In one method for coun-

TABLE 1.2. Means for Two Forms of a Hypothetical Test Administered Using the Single Group Design with Counterbalancing.

	Subgroup 1	Subgroup 2
Form taken first	Form X 72	Form Y 77
Form taken second	Form Y 75	Form X 71

terbalancing, test booklets are constructed that contain Form X and Form Y. One-half of the test booklets are printed with Form X following Form Y, and the other half are printed with Form Y following Form X. In packaging, test booklets having Form X first are alternated with test booklets having Form Y first. When the test booklets are handed out, the first examinee takes Form X first, the second examinee takes Form Y first, the third examinee takes Form X first, and so on. When the booklets are administered, the first and second forms are separately timed. This spiraling process helps to ensure that the examinee group receiving Form Y first is comparable to the examinee group receiving Form X first.

Figure 1.1 provides an illustration of the *single group design with counterbalancing*. The portion of the design labeled "Form Taken First" is identical to the random groups design shown in Figure 1.1. Therefore, Form X could be equated to Form Y using only the data from the form taken first (i.e., Form X data from Subgroup 1 and Form Y data from Subgroup 2). To take full advantage of this design, however, the data from the "Form Taken Second" also could be used. Assume that examinees typically take only one form of the test when the test is later administered operationally to examinees. In this case, the equating relationship of interest would be the relationship between the forms when the forms are administered first. If the effect of taking Form X after taking Form Y is the same as the effect of taking Form Y after taking Form X, then the equating relationship will be the same between the forms taken first as it is between the forms taken second. Otherwise, a *differential order effect* is said to have occurred, and the equating relationships would differ. In this case, the data for the form that is taken second might need to be disregarded, which could lead to instability in the equating (see Chapter 7 for a discussion of equating error) and a waste of examinee time.

As an example, Table 1.2 presents a situation in which the effect of taking Form X after taking Form Y differs from the effect of taking Form Y after taking Form X. In this example, alternate forms of a test are to be equated by the single group design with counterbalancing using very large groups of examinees. The raw score means for the form that was taken first are shown in the first line of the table. Subgroup 2 had a mean of 77 on Form Y, which is 5 points higher than the mean of 72 earned by the randomly equivalent Subgroup 1 on Form X. Thus, using only data from the form that was taken first, Form Y appears to be 5 points easier, on average, than Form X. The means for the form that was taken second are shown in the second line of the table. Subgroup 1 had a mean of 75 on Form Y, which is 4 points higher than the mean of 71 earned by randomly equivalent Subgroup 2 on Form X. Thus, using data from the form taken second, Form Y is 4 points easier, on average, than Form X. Because the sample size is very large, this 4- versus 5-point difference suggests that there is a differential order effect. When a differential order effect like this one is present, the data from the form taken second might need to be disregarded. These issues are discussed further in Chapter 2.

In addition to the need to control for differential order effects, other practical problems can restrict the usefulness of the single group design with counterbalancing. Because two forms must be administered to the same students, testing time needs to be doubled, which often is not practically feasible. If fatigue and practice are effectively controlled by counterbalancing and differential order effects are not present, then the primary benefit in using the single group design with counterbalancing is that it typically has smaller sample size requirements than the random groups design, because, by taking both of the forms, each examinee serves as his or her own control.

In practice, the single group design with counterbalancing might be used instead of the random groups design when (1) administering two forms to examinees is operationally possible, (2) differential order effects are not expected to occur, and (3) it is difficult to obtain participation of a sufficient number of examinees in an equating study that uses the random groups design. Relative sample size requirements for these two designs are discussed in Chapter 7.

1.4.4 ASVAB Problems with a Single Group Design

The Armed Services Vocational Aptitude Battery (ASVAB) is a battery of ability tests that is used in the process of selecting individuals for the military. In 1976, new forms of the ASVAB were introduced. Scores on these forms were to be reported on the scale of previous forms through the use of a scaling process. (Because the content of the new forms differed somewhat from the content of the previous forms, the process used to convert scores to the scale of the previous forms is referred to here as scaling rather than as equating.) Maier (1993) indicated that problems occurred in the scaling process, with the result that many individuals entered the military who were actually not eligible to enter under the standards that were intended to be in effect at the time. As a result, Maier estimated that between January 1, 1976, and September 30, 1980, over 350,000 individuals entered the military who should have been judged ineligible. Maier reported

18   1. Introduction and Concepts

that a complicated set of circumstances led to these problems. Most of the problems were a result of how the scaling study was designed and carried out. The effects of one of these problems are discussed here.

The examinees included in the study were applying to the military. In the scaling process, each examinee was administered both the old and new forms. (Supposedly, the order was counterbalanced—see Maier, 1993, for a discussion.) The scores on the old form were used for selection. No decisions about the examinees were made using the scores on the new form. Many examinees were able to distinguish between the old and the new forms. (For example, the content differed and the printing quality of the old form was better than that for the new form.) Also, many examinees knew that only the scores on the old form were to be used for selection purposes. Because the scores on the old form were to be used in the process of making selection decisions, the examinees were likely more motivated when taking the old form than they were when taking the new form. It seems reasonable to assume that scores under conditions of greater motivation would be higher than they would be under lower motivation conditions.

The following hypothetical example demonstrates how this motivation difference might be reflected in the scale scores. Suppose that the following conditions hold:

1. A raw score of 10 on the old form corresponds to a raw score of 10 on the new form under conditions of high motivation.

2. A raw score of 8 on the old form corresponds to a raw score of 8 on the new form under conditions of high motivation.

3. A raw score of 10 on each form corresponds to a scale score of 27 under the conditions of high motivation.

4. A raw score of 8 on each form corresponds to a scale score of 25 under the conditions of high motivation.

5. When either of the forms is administered under conditions of lower motivation the raw scores are depressed by 2 points.

Conditions 1 and 2 imply that the old and new forms are equally difficult at a raw score of 10 under high motivation conditions. The same is true at a raw score of 8.

What would happen in a scaling study if the old form was administered under high motivation and the new form under low motivation, and the motivation differences were not taken into account? In this case, a score of 8 on the new form would appear to correspond to a score of 10 on the old form, because the new form score would be depressed by 2 points. In the scaling process, an 8 on the new form would be considered to be equivalent to a 10 on the old form and to a scale score of 27. That is, an 8 on the new form would correspond to a scale score of 27 instead of the correct scale score of 25. Thus, when the new form is used later under high motivation conditions, scale scores on the new form would be too high.

Reasoning similar to that in this hypothetical example led Maier (1993) to conclude that motivation differences caused the scale scores on the new form to be too high when the new form was used to make selection decisions for examinees. The most direct effect of these problems was that the military selected many individuals using scores on the new form whose skill levels were lower than the intended standards. After the problem was initially detected in 1976, it took until October of 1980 to sort out the causes for the problems and to build new tests and scales that were judged to be sound. It took much effort to resolve the ASVAB scaling problem, including conducting a series of research studies, hiring a panel of outside testing experts, and significantly improving the quality control and oversight procedures for the ASVAB program.

1.4.5 Common-Item Nonequivalent Groups Design

The last design shown in Figure 1.1 is the *common-item nonequivalent groups design*. This design often is used when more than one form per test date cannot be administered because of test security or other practical concerns. In this design, Form X and Form Y have a set of items in common, and different groups of examinees are administered the two forms. For example, a group tested one year might be administered Form X and a group tested another year might be administered Form Y. This design has two variations. When the score on the set of common items contributes to the examinee's score on the test, the set of common items is referred to as *internal*. The internal common items are chosen to represent the content and statistical characteristics of the old form. For this reason, internal common items typically are interspersed among the other items in the test form. When the score on the set of common items does *not* contribute to the examinee's score on the test form, the set of common items is referred to as *external*. Typically, external common items are administered as a separately timed section.

To reflect group differences accurately, the set of common items should be proportionally representative of the total test forms in content and statistical characteristics. That is, the common-item set should be a "mini version" of the total test form. The common items also should behave similarly in the old and new forms. To help ensure similar behavior, each common item should occupy a similar location (item number) in the two forms. In addition, the common items should be exactly the same (e.g., no wording changes or rearranging of alternatives) in the old and new forms. Additional ways to help ensure adequate equating using the common-item nonequivalent groups design are described in Chapter 8.

In this design, the group of examinees taking Form X is *not* considered to be equivalent to the group of examinees taking Form Y. Differences

TABLE 1.3. Means for Two Forms of a Hypothetical 100-Item Test with an Internal Set of 20 Common Items.

Group	Form X (100 items)	Form Y (100 items)	Common Items (20 items)
1	72	—	13 (65%)
2	—	77	15 (75%)

between means (and other score distribution characteristics) on Form X and Form Y can result from a combination of examinee group differences and test form differences. The central task in equating using this design is to separate group differences from form differences.

The hypothetical example in Table 1.3 illustrates how differences might be separated. Form X and Form Y each contain 100 multiple-choice items that are scored number correct, and there is an internal set of 20 items in common between the two forms. The means on the common items suggest that Group 2 is higher achieving than Group 1, because members of Group 2, on average, correctly answered 75% of the common items, whereas members of Group 1 correctly answered only 65% of the common items. That is, on average, Group 2 correctly answered 10% more of the common items than did Group 1.

Which of the two forms is easier? To provide one possible answer, consider the following question: What would have been the mean on Form X for Group 2 had Group 2 taken Form X? Group 2 correctly answered 10% more of the common items than did Group 1. Therefore, Group 2 might be expected to answer 10% more of the Form X items correctly than would Group 1. Using this line of reasoning (and using the fact that Form X contains 100 items), the mean for Group 2 on Form X would be expected to be $82 = 72 + 10$. Because Group 2 earned a mean of 77 on Form Y and has an expected mean of 82 on Form X, Form X appears to be 5 points easier than Form Y.

This example is an oversimplification of how equating actually would be accomplished, and these results would hold only under very stringent conditions. The equating methods discussed in Chapters 4–6 might even lead to the opposite conclusion about which form is more difficult. This example is intended to illustrate that a major task in conducting equating with the nonequivalent groups design is to separate group and form differences.

As indicated earlier, for this design to function well the common items need to represent the content and statistical characteristics of the total test. Table 1.4 provides data for a hypothetical test that is intended to illustrate the need for the set of common items to be content representative. In this example, Group 1 and Group 2 are again nonequivalent groups of examinees. The test consists of items from two content areas, Content I and Content II. As shown near the top of Table 1.4, on average, Group 1

TABLE 1.4. Percent Correct for Two Groups on a Hypothetical Test.

	Group 1	Group 2
Content		
I	70%	80%
II	80%	70%
For Total Test	75% =	75% =
$\frac{1}{2}$(Content I) + $\frac{1}{2}$(Content II)	$\frac{1}{2}$(70%) + $\frac{1}{2}$(80%)	$\frac{1}{2}$(80%) + $\frac{1}{2}$(70%)
For Common Items	72.5% =	77.5% =
$\frac{3}{4}$(Content I) + $\frac{1}{4}$(Content II)	$\frac{3}{4}$(70%) + $\frac{1}{4}$(80%)	$\frac{3}{4}$(80%) + $\frac{1}{4}$(70%)

correctly answered 70% of the Content I items and 80% of the Content II items. Group 2 correctly answered 80% of the Content I items and 70% of the Content II items. If the total test contains one-half Content I items and one-half Content II items, then, as illustrated near the middle of Table 1.4, both Group 1 and Group 2 will earn an average score of 75% correct on the whole test. Thus, the two groups have the same average level of achievement for the total test, consisting of one-half Content I and one-half Content II items.

Assume that two forms of the test are to be equated. If, as illustrated near the bottom of Table 1.4, the common-item set contains three-fourths Content I items and one-fourth Content II items, Group 1 will correctly answer 72.5% of the common items, and Group 2 will correctly answer 77.5% of the common items. Thus, for this set of common items, Group 2 appears to be higher achieving than Group 1, even though the two groups are at the same level on the total test. This example illustrates that common items need to be content representative if they are to portray group differences accurately and lead to a satisfactory equating. (See Klein and Jarjoura, 1985, for an illustration of the need for content representativeness for an actual test.)

The common-item nonequivalent groups design is widely used. A major reason for its popularity is that this design requires that only one test form be administered per test date, which is how test forms usually are administered in operational settings. In contrast, the random groups design typically requires different test forms to be administered to random subgroups of examinees, and the single group design requires that more than one form be administered to each examinee. Another advantage of the common-item nonequivalent groups design is that, with external sets of common items, it might be possible for all items that contribute to an examinee's score (the noncommon items) to be disclosed following the test date. The ability to disclose items is important for some testing programs, because some states have mandated disclosure for certain tests, and some test publishers have opted for disclosure. However, common items should not be disclosed if they are to be used to equate subsequent forms. (See Chapter 8 for further discussion.)

The administrative flexibility offered by the use of nonequivalent groups is gained at some cost. As is described in Chapters 4–6, strong statistical assumptions are required to separate group and form differences. The larger the differences between examinee groups, the more difficult it becomes for the statistical methods to separate the group and form differences. The only link between the two groups is the common items, so the content and statistical representativeness of the common items are especially crucial when the groups differ. Although a variety of statistical equating methods have been proposed for the common-item nonequivalent groups design, no method has been found that provides completely appropriate adjustments when the examinee groups are very different.

1.4.6 NAEP Reading Anomaly—Problems with Common Items

The National Assessment of Educational Progress (NAEP) is a congressionally mandated survey of the educational achievement of students in American schools. NAEP measures performance trends in many achievement areas, based on representative samples at three grade/age levels. The preliminary results from the 1986 NAEP Assessment in Reading indicated that the reading results "showed a surprisingly large decrease from 1984 at age 17 and, to a lesser degree, at age 9.... Such large changes in reading proficiency were considered extremely unlikely to have occurred in just two years without the awareness of the educational community." (Zwick, 1991, p. 11).

A series of inquiries were conducted to better understand the reasons for the decline. One potential cause that was investigated was the manner in which common items were used in linking the 1984 and 1986 assessments. Zwick (1991) indicated that the following differences existed between the administrations:

1. In 1984, the test booklets administered to examinees contained reading and writing sections. In 1986, the booklets administered to examinees contained reading, mathematics, and/or science sections at ages 9 and 13. In 1986, the booklets contained reading, computer science, history, and/or literature at age 17.

2. The composition of the reading sections differed in 1984 and 1986. Items that were common to the two years appeared in different orders, and the time available to complete the common items differed in the two years.

The investigations concluded that these differences in the context in which the common items appeared in the two years, rather than changes in reading achievement, were responsible for much of the difference that was observed (Zwick, 1991). This so-called NAEP reading anomaly illustrates the importance of administering common items in the same context in the old and new forms. Otherwise, context effects can lead to very misleading results.

1.5 Error in Estimating Equating Relationships

Estimated equating relationships typically contain estimation error. A major goal in designing and conducting equating is to minimize such equating error.

Random equating error is present whenever samples from populations of examinees are used to estimate parameters (e.g., means, standard deviations, and percentile ranks) that are involved in estimating an equating relationship. Random error is typically indexed by the standard error of equating, which is the focus of Chapter 7. Conceptually, the *standard error of equating* is the standard deviation of score equivalents over replications of the equating procedure. The following situation illustrates the meaning of the standard error of equating when estimating the Form Y score equivalent of a Form X score.

1. Draw a random sample of size 1,000 from a population of examinees.

2. Find the Form Y score equivalent of a Form X score of 75 using data from this sample and a given equating method.

3. Repeat steps 1 and 2 a large number of times, which results in a large number of estimates of the Form Y score equivalent of a Form X score of 75.

4. The standard deviation of these estimates is an estimate of the standard error of equating for a Form X score of 75.

As these steps illustrate, the standard error of equating is defined separately for each score on Form X.

As the sample size becomes larger, the standard error of equating becomes smaller, and it becomes inconsequential for very large sample sizes (assuming very large populations, as discussed in Chapter 7). Random error can be controlled by using large samples of examinees, by choosing an equating design that reduces such error, or both. Random error is especially troublesome when practical issues dictate the use of small samples of examinees.

24   1. Introduction and Concepts

Systematic equating error results from violations of the assumptions and conditions of equating. For example, in the random groups design, systematic error results if a particular spiraling process is inadequate for achieving group comparability. In the single group design with counterbalancing, failure to control adequately for differential order effects can be a major source of systematic error. In the common-item nonequivalent groups design, systematic error results if the assumptions of statistical methods used to separate form and group differences are not met. These assumptions can be especially difficult to meet under the following conditions: the groups differ substantially, the common items are not representative of the total test form in content and statistical characteristics, or the common items function differently from one administration to the next. A major problem with this design is that sufficient data typically are not available to estimate or adjust for systematic error.

Over time, after a large number of test forms are involved in the scaling and equating process, both random and systematic errors tend to accumulate. Although the amount of random error can be quantified readily using the standard error of equating, systematic error is much more difficult to quantify. In conducting and designing equating studies, both types of error should be minimized to the extent possible. In some practical circumstances the amount of equating error might be so large that equating would add more error into the scores than if no equating had been done. Thus, equating is not always defensible. This issue is described further in Chapter 8.

1.6 Evaluating the Results of Equating

In addition to designing an equating study, an operational definition of equating and a method for estimating an equating relationship need to be chosen. Then, after the equating is conducted, the results should be evaluated. As indicated by Harris and Crouse (1993), such evaluation requires that criteria for equating be identified. Estimating random error using standard errors of equating can be used to develop criteria. Criteria for evaluating equating also can be based on consistency of results with previous results.

The properties of equating that were described earlier also can be used to develop evaluative criteria. The symmetry and same specifications properties always must be achieved. Some aspects of Lord's equity property can be evaluated. For example, procedures are discussed in Chapter 8 that indicate the extent to which examinees can be expected to earn approximately the same score, regardless of the form that they take. Procedures are also considered that can be used to evaluate the extent to which examinees are measured with equal precision across forms. Observed score equating properties are especially important when equating is evaluated from an institutional perspective. An institution that is admitting students needs to know that the particular test form administered would not affect the numbers of students who would be admitted. The group invariance property is important from the perspective of treating subgroups of examinees equitably. The equating relationship should be very similar across subgroups. As a check on the group invariance property, the equating can be conducted on various important subgroups. Procedures for evaluating equating are discussed more fully in Chapter 8.

1.7 Testing Situations Considered

In this chapter, equating has been described for testing programs in which alternate forms of tests are administered on various test dates. Equating is very common in this circumstance, especially when tight test security is required, such as when equating professional certification, licensure, and college admissions tests. Another common circumstance is for two or more forms of a test to be developed and equated at one time. The equated forms then are used for a period of years until the content becomes dated. Alternate forms of elementary achievement level batteries, for example, often are administered under these sorts of conditions. The procedures described in this book pertain directly to equating alternate forms of tests under either of these circumstances.

In recent years, test administration on the computer has become common. Computer administration is often done by selecting test items to be administered from a pool of items, with each examinee being administered a different set of items. In this case, a clear need exists to use processes to ensure that scores earned by different examinees are comparable to one another. However, as discussed in Chapter 8, such procedures often are different from the equating methods to be discussed in Chapters 2 through 7 of this book.

In this book, equating is presented mainly in the context of dichotomously (right versus wrong) scored tests. Recently, there has been considerable attention given to performance tests, which require judges or a computer to score tasks or items. Many of the concepts of equating for multiple-choice tests also pertain to performance tests. However, the use of judges along with difficulties in representing the domain of content complicate equating for performance tests. Chapter 8 discusses when and how the methods treated in this book can be applied to performance tests.

The procedures used to calculate raw scores on a test affect how equating procedures are implemented. In this book, tests typically are assumed to be scored number-correct, with scores ranging from zero to the number of items on the test. Many of the procedures described can be adapted to other

26   1. Introduction and Concepts

types of scoring, however, such as scores that are corrected for guessing. For example, a generalization of equipercentile equating to scoring which produces scores that are not integers is described in Chapter 2. In Chapter 3, smoothing techniques are referenced which can be used with scores that are not integers. Many of the techniques in Chapters 4 and 5 can be adapted readily to other scoring schemes. In Chapter 6, noninteger IRT scoring is discussed. Issues in performance assessments are described in Chapter 8. To simplify exposition, unless noted otherwise, assume that alternate forms of dichotomously scored tests are being equated. Scores on these tests range from zero to the number of items on the test.

1.8   Preview

This chapter has discussed equating properties and equating designs. Chapter 2 treats equating using the random groups design, which, compared to other designs, requires very few statistical assumptions. For this reason, the random groups design is ideal for presenting many of the statistical concepts in observed score equating. Specifically, the mean, linear, and equipercentile equating methods are considered. The topic of Chapter 3 is smoothing techniques that are used to reduce total error in estimated equipercentile relationships.

Linear methods appropriate for the common-item nonequivalent groups design are described in Chapter 4. In addition to considering observed score methods, methods based on test theory models are introduced in Chapter 4. Equipercentile methods for the common-item nonequivalent groups design are presented in Chapter 5.

IRT methods, which are also test theory-based methods, are the topic of Chapter 6. IRT methods are presented that can be used with the equating designs described in this chapter. In addition, IRT methods appropriate for equating using item pools are described.

Equating procedures are all statistical techniques that are subject to random error. Procedures for estimating the standard error of equating are described in Chapter 7 along with discussions of sample sizes required to attain desired levels of equating precision. Chapter 8 focuses on various practical issues in equating. These topics include evaluating the results of equating and choosing among equating methods and results. In addition, current topics, such as linking performance assessments and linking computerized tests, are considered.

Chapter 9 considers issues associated with developing score scales for individual tests and test batteries. In addition, vertical scaling processes that are often used with elementary level achievement test batteries are considered in detail. Linking of tests is the topic of Chapter 10. Chapter 11 discusses current and future challenges, and areas for future developments are highlighted.

1.9 Exercises

Exercises are presented at the end of each chapter of this book, Some of the exercises are intended to reinforce important concepts and consider practical issues; others are intended to facilitate learning how to apply statistical techniques. Answers to the exercises are provided in Appendix A.

1.1. A scholarship test is administered twice per year, and different forms are administered on each test date. Currently, the top 1% of the examinees on each test date earn scholarships.

   a. Would equating the two forms affect who was awarded a scholarship? Why or why not?

   b. Suppose the top 1% who took the test during the year (rather than at each test date) were awarded scholarships. Would the use of equating affect who was awarded a scholarship? Why or why not?

1.2. Refer to the example in Table 1.1. Suppose that a new form, Form X_3, was found to be uniformly 1 point easier than Form X_2. What scale score would correspond to a Form X_3 raw score of 29?

1.3. A state passes a law that all items which contribute to an examinee's score on a test will be released to that examinee, on request, following the test date. Assume that the test is to be secure. Which of the following equating designs could be used in this situation: random groups, single group with counterbalancing, common-item nonequivalent groups with an internal set of common items, common-item nonequivalent groups with an external set of common items? Briefly indicate how equating would be accomplished using this (these) design(s).

1.4. Equating of forms of a 45-minute test is to be conducted by collecting data on a group of examinees who are being tested for the purpose of conducting equating. Suppose that it is relatively easy to get large groups of examinees to participate in the study, but it is difficult to get any student to test for more than one 50-minute class period, where 5 minutes are needed to hand out materials, give instructions, and collect materials. Would it be better to use the random groups design or the single group design with counterbalancing in this situation? Why?

1.5. Suppose that only one form of a test can be administered on any given test date. Of the designs discussed, which equating design(s) can be used?

1.6. Refer to the data shown in Table 1.4.

   a. Which group would appear to be higher achieving on a set of common items composed only of Content I items?

   b. Which group would appear to be higher achieving on a set of common items composed only of Content II items?

   c. What is the implication of your answers to a and b?

1.7. Consider the following statements for equated Forms X and Y:

   I. "Examinees A and B are at the same level of achievement, because A scored at the 50th percentile nationally on Form X and B scored at the 50th percentile nationally on Form Y."

   II. "Examinees A and B are at the same level of achievement, because the expected equated score of A on Form X equals the expected score of B on Form Y."

   Which of these statements is consistent with an observed score property of equating? Which is consistent with Lord's equity property of equating?

1.8. If a very large group of examinees is used in an equating study, which source of equating error would almost surely be small, random or systematic? Which source of equating error could be large if the very large group of examinees used in the equating were not representative of the examinees that are to be tested, random or systematic?

2
Observed Score Equating Using the Random Groups Design

As was stressed in Chapter 1, the same specifications property is an essential property of equating, which means that the forms to be equated must be built to the same content and statistical specifications. We also stressed that the symmetry property is essential for any equating relationship. The focus of the present chapter is on methods that are designed to achieve the observed score equating property, along with the same specifications and symmetry properties. As was described in Chapter 1, these observed score equating methods are developed with the goal that, after equating, converted scores on two forms have at least some of the same score distribution characteristics in a population of examinees.

In this chapter, these methods are developed in the context of the random groups design. Of the designs discussed thus far, the assumptions required for the random groups design are the least severe and most readily achieved. Thus, very few sources of systematic error are present with the random groups design. Because of the minimal assumptions required with the random groups design, this design is ideal for use in presenting the basic statistical methods in observed score equating, which is the focus of the present chapter.

The definitions and properties of mean, linear, and equipercentile equating methods are described in this chapter. These methods are presented, initially, in terms of population parameters (e.g., population means and standard deviations) for a specific population of examinees. We also discuss the process of estimating equating relationships, which requires that statistics (e.g., sample means and sample standard deviations) be substituted in place of the parameters. The methods then are illustrated using a real data example. Following the presentation of the methods, issues in using scale scores are described and illustrated. We then briefly discuss equating using the single group design.

An important practical challenge in using the random groups design is to obtain large enough sample sizes so that random error (see Chapter 7 for a discussion of standard errors) is at an acceptable level (rules of thumb for appropriate sample sizes are given in Chapter 8). For the equipercentile equating method, in Chapter 3 we describe statistical smoothing methods that often are used to help reduce random error when conducting equipercentile equating using the random groups design.

For simplicity, the statistical methods in this chapter are developed using a testing situation in which tests consist of test items that are scored correct (1) or incorrect (0), and where the total score is the number of items answered correctly. Near the end of the chapter, a process for equating tests that are scored using other scoring schemes is described.

2.1 Mean Equating

In mean equating, Form X is considered to differ in difficulty from Form Y by a constant amount along the score scale. For example, under mean equating, if Form X is 2 points easier than Form Y for high-scoring examinees, it is also 2 points easier than Form Y for low-scoring examinees. Although a constant difference might be overly restrictive in many testing situations, mean equating is useful for illustrating some important equating concepts.

As was done in Chapter 1, define Form X as the new form, let X represent the random variable score on Form X, and let x represent a particular score on Form X (i.e., a realization of X); and define Form Y as the old form, let Y represent the random variable score on Form Y, and let y represent a particular score on Form Y (i.e., a realization of Y). Also, define $\mu(X)$ as the mean on Form X and $\mu(Y)$ as the mean on Form Y for a population of examinees. In mean equating, scores on the two forms that are an equal (signed) distance away from their respective means are set equal:

$$x - \mu(X) = y - \mu(Y). \tag{2.1}$$

Then solve for y and obtain

$$m_Y(x) = y = x - \mu(X) + \mu(Y). \tag{2.2}$$

In this equation, $m_Y(x)$ refers to a score x on Form X transformed to the scale of Form Y using mean equating.

As an illustration of how to apply this formula, consider the situation discussed in Chapter 1, in which the mean on Form X was 72 and the mean on Form Y was 77. Based on this example, equation (2.2) indicates that 5 points would need to be added to a Form X score to transform a score on Form X to the Form Y scale. That is,

$$m_Y(x) = x - 72 + 77 = x + 5.$$

For example, using mean equating, a score of 72 on Form X is considered to indicate the same level of achievement as a score of 77 ($77 = 72 + 5$) on Form Y. And, a score of 75 on Form X is considered to indicate the same level of achievement as a score of 80 on Form Y. Thus, mean equating involves the addition of a constant (which might be negative) to all raw scores on Form X to find equated scores on Form Y.

2.2 Linear Equating

Rather than considering the differences between two forms to be a constant, linear equating allows for the differences in difficulty between the two test forms to vary along the score scale. For example, linear equating allows Form X to be more difficult than Form Y for low-achieving examinees but less difficult for high-achieving examinees.

In linear equating, scores that are an equal (signed) distance from their means in standard deviation units are set equal. Thus, linear equating can be viewed as allowing for the scale units, as well as the means, of the two forms to differ. Define $\sigma(X)$ and $\sigma(Y)$ as the standard deviations of Form X and Form Y scores, respectively. The linear conversion is defined by setting standardized deviation scores (z-scores) on the two forms to be equal such that

$$\frac{x - \mu(X)}{\sigma(X)} = \frac{y - \mu(Y)}{\sigma(Y)}. \tag{2.3}$$

If the standard deviations for the two forms were equal, equation (2.3) could be simplified to equal the mean equating equation (2.2). Thus, if the standard deviations of the two forms are equal, then mean and linear equating produce the same result. Solving for y in equation (2.3),

$$l_Y(x) = y = \sigma(Y)\left[\frac{x - \mu(X)}{\sigma(X)}\right] + \mu(Y), \tag{2.4}$$

where $l_Y(x)$ is the linear conversion equation for converting observed scores on Form X to the scale of Form Y. By rearranging terms, an alternate expression for $l_Y(x)$ is

$$l_Y(x) = y = \frac{\sigma(Y)}{\sigma(X)}x + \left[\mu(Y) - \frac{\sigma(Y)}{\sigma(X)}\mu(X)\right]. \tag{2.5}$$

This expression is a linear equation of the form $slope\ (x) + intercept$ with

$$slope = \frac{\sigma(Y)}{\sigma(X)}, \quad \text{and} \quad intercept = \mu(Y) - \frac{\sigma(Y)}{\sigma(X)}\mu(X). \quad (2.6)$$

What if the standard deviations in the mean equating example were $\sigma(X) = 10$ and $\sigma(Y) = 9$? The slope is $9/10 = .9$, and the intercept is $77 - (9/10)72 = 12.2$. The resulting conversion equation is $l_Y(x) = .9x + 12.2$. What is $l_Y(x)$ if $x = 75$?

$$l_Y(75) = .9(75) + 12.2 = 79.7.$$

How about if $x = 77$ or $x = 85$?

$$\begin{aligned} l_Y(77) &= .9(77) + 12.2 = 81.5, \text{ and} \\ l_Y(85) &= .9(85) + 12.2 = 88.7. \end{aligned}$$

These equated values illustrate that the difference in test form difficulty varies with score level. For example, the difference in difficulty between Form X and Form Y for a Form X score of 75 is 4.7(79.7 − 75), whereas the difference for a Form X score of 85 is 3.7(88.7 − 85).

2.3 Properties of Mean and Linear Equating

In general, what are the properties of the equated scores? From Chapter 1, **E** is the expectation operator. The mean of a variable is found by taking the expected value of that variable. Using equation (2.2), the mean converted score $m_Y(x)$, for mean equating is

$$\mathbf{E}[m_Y(X)] = \mathbf{E}[X - \mu(X) + \mu(Y)] = \mu(X) - \mu(X) + \mu(Y) = \mu(Y). \quad (2.7)$$

That is, for mean equating the mean of the Form X scores equated to the Form Y scale is equal to the mean of the Form Y scores. In the example described earlier, the mean of the equated Form X scores is 77 [recall that $m_Y(x) = x + 5$ and $\mu(X) = 72$], the same value as the mean of the Form Y scores. Note that standard deviations were not shown in equation (2.7). What would be the standard deviation of Form X scores converted using the mean equating equation (2.2)? Because the Form X scores are converted to Form Y by adding a constant, the standard deviation of the converted scores would be the same as the standard deviation of the scores prior to conversion. That is, under mean equating, $\sigma[m_Y(X)] = \sigma(X)$.

Using equation (2.5), the mean equated score for linear equating can be found as follows:

$$\mathbf{E}[l_Y(X)] = \mathbf{E}\left[\frac{\sigma(Y)}{\sigma(X)}X + \mu(Y) - \frac{\sigma(Y)}{\sigma(X)}\mu(X)\right]$$

$$= \frac{\sigma(Y)}{\sigma(X)} \mathbf{E}(X) + \mu(Y) - \frac{\sigma(Y)}{\sigma(X)} \mu(X)$$
$$= \mu(Y), \qquad (2.8)$$

because $\mathbf{E}(X) = \mu(X)$.

The standard deviation of the equated scores is found by first substituting equation (2.5) for $l_Y(X)$ as follows:

$$\sigma[l_Y(X)] = \sigma\left[\frac{\sigma(Y)}{\sigma(X)}X + \mu(Y) - \frac{\sigma(Y)}{\sigma(X)}\mu(X)\right]$$

To continue, the standard deviation of a score plus a constant is equal to the standard deviation of the score. That is, $\sigma(X + constant) = \sigma(X)$. By recognizing in the linear equating equation that the terms to the right of the addition sign are a constant, the following holds:

$$\sigma[l_Y(X)] = \sigma\left[\frac{\sigma(Y)}{\sigma(X)}X\right].$$

Also note that the standard deviation of a score multiplied by a constant equals the standard deviation of the score multiplied by the constant. That is, $\sigma(constant\ X) = constant\ \sigma(X)$. Noting that the ratio of standard deviations in the large parentheses is also a constant that multiplies X,

$$\sigma[l_Y(X)] = \frac{\sigma(Y)}{\sigma(X)}\sigma(X) = \sigma(Y). \qquad (2.9)$$

Therefore, the mean and standard deviation of the Form X scores equated to the Form Y scale are equal to the mean and standard deviation, respectively, of the Form Y scores. In the example described earlier for linear equating, the mean of the equated Form X scores is 77 and the standard deviation is 9; these are the same values as the mean and standard deviation of the Form Y scores.

Consider the equation for mean equating, equation (2.2), and the equation for linear equating (2.5). If either of the equations were solved for x, rather than for y, the equation for equating Form Y scores to the scale of Form X would result. These conversions would be symbolized by $m_X(y)$ and $l_X(y)$, respectively. Equating relationships are defined as being *symmetric* because the equation used to convert Form X scores to the Form Y scale is the inverse of the equation used to convert Form Y scores to the Form X scale.

The equation for linear equating (2.5) is deceptively like a linear regression equation. The difference is that, for linear regression, the $\sigma(Y)/\sigma(X)$ terms are multiplied by the correlation between X and Y However, a linear regression equation does not qualify as an equating function because the regression of X on Y is different from the regression of Y on X, unless the correlation coefficient is 1. For this reason, regression equations cannot, in

34   2. Observed Score Equating Using the Random Groups Design

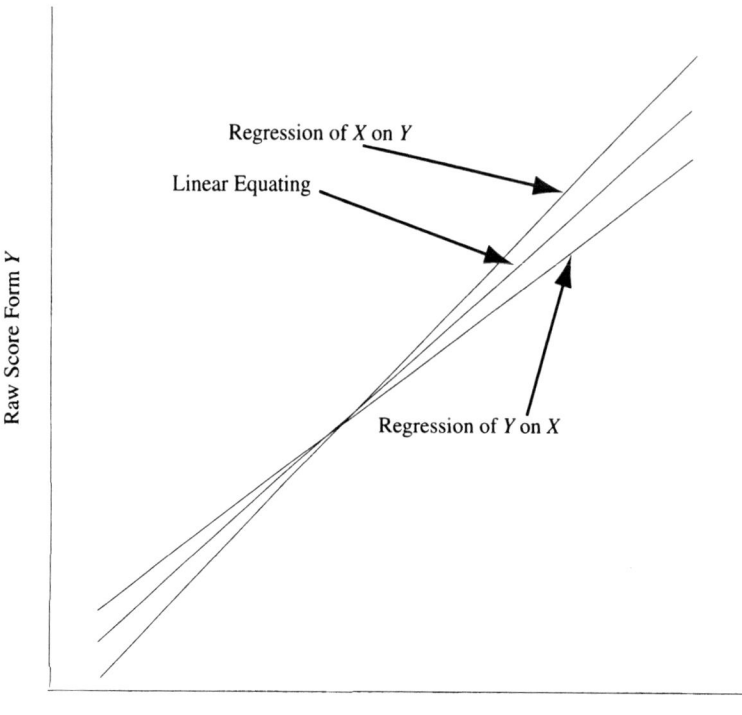

FIGURE 2.1. Comparison of linear regression and linear equating.

general, be used as equating functions. The comparison between linear regression and linear equating is illustrated in Figure 2.1. The regression of Y on X is different from the regression of X on Y. Also note that there is only one linear equating relationship graphed in the figure. This relationship can be used to transform Form X scores to the Form Y scale, or to transform Form Y scores to the Form X scale.

2.4 Comparison of Mean and Linear Equating

Figure 2.2 illustrates the equating of Form X and Form Y using the hypothetical test forms already discussed. The equations for equating scores on Form X to the Form Y scale are plotted in this figure.

Also plotted in this figure are the results from the "identity equating." In the *identity equating*, a score on Form X is considered to be equivalent to the identical score on Form Y; for example, a 40 on Form X is considered to be equivalent to a 40 on Form Y. Identity equating would be the same as mean and linear equating if the two forms were identical in difficulty all along the score scale.

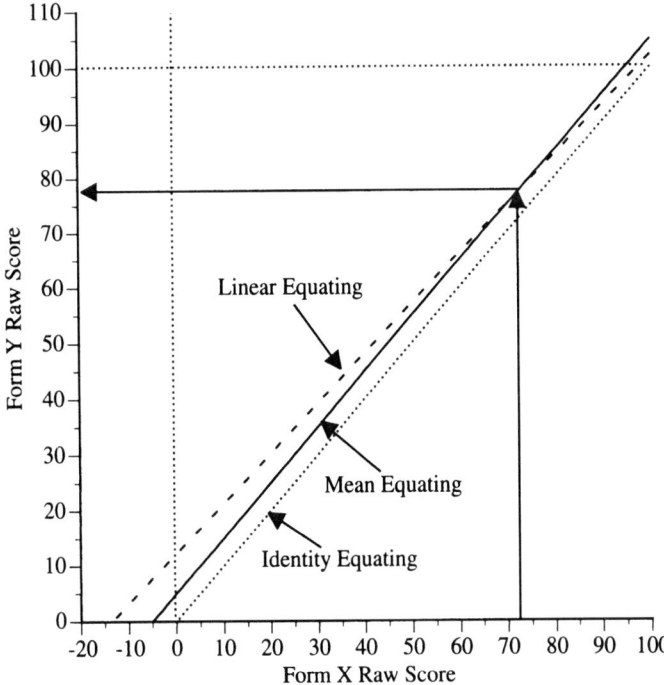

FIGURE 2.2. Graph of mean and linear equating for a hypothetical 100-item test.

To find a Form Y equivalent of a Form X score using the graph, find the Form X value of interest on the horizontal axis, go up to the function, and then go over to the vertical axis to read off the Form Y equivalent.

How to find the Form Y equivalent of a Form X score of 72 is illustrated in the figure using the arrows. This equivalent is 77, using either mean or linear equating. The score 72 is the mean score on Form X. As indicated earlier, both mean and linear equating will produce the same result at the mean.

Now refer to the identity equating line in the figure, and note that the line for mean equating is parallel to the line for the identity equating. The lines for these two methods will always be parallel. As can be seen, the line for mean equating is uniformly 5 points vertically above the line for the identity equating, because Form Y is, on average, 5 points less difficult than Form X. Refer to the line for linear equating. This line is not parallel to the identity equating line. The linear equating line is further above the identity equating line at the low scores than at the high scores. This observation is consistent with the earlier discussion in which the difference in difficulty between Form X and Form Y was shown to be greater at the lower scores than at the higher scores.

Assume that the test in this example is scored number-correct. Number-correct scores for this 100-item test can range from 0 to 100. Figure 2.2 illustrates that equated scores from mean and linear equating can sometimes be out of the range of possible observed scores. The dotted lines at 0 on Form X and at 100 illustrate the boundaries of possible observed scores. For example, using linear equating, a score of 100 on Form X equates to a score of approximately 102 on Form Y. Also, using linear equating, a score of 0 on Form Y equates to a score of approximately −14 on Form X. There are a variety of ways to handle this problem. One way is to allow the top and bottom to "float." For example, the highest equated score might be allowed to exceed the highest raw score. An alternative is to truncate the conversion at the highest and lowest scores. In the example, truncation involves setting all converted scores greater than 100 equal to 100 and setting all converted scores less than 0 equal to 0. That is, all Form Y scores that equate to Form X scores below 0 would be set to 0 and all Form X scores that equate to Form Y scores above 100 would be set to 100. In practice, the decision about how to handle equated scores outside the range typically interacts with the score scale that is used for reporting scores. Sometimes this issue is effectively of no consequence, because no one achieves the extreme raw scores on Form X that equate to unobtainable scores on Form Y.

In summary, in mean equating the conversion is derived by setting the deviation scores on the two forms equal, whereas in linear equating the standardized deviation scores (z-scores) on the two forms are set equal. In mean equating, scores on Form X are adjusted by a constant amount that is equal to the difference between the Form Y and Form X means. In linear equating, scores on Form X are adjusted using a linear equation that allows for the forms to be differentially difficult along the score scale. In mean equating, the mean of the Form X scores equated to the Form Y scale is equal to the mean of the Form Y scores; whereas in linear equating, the standard deviation as well as the mean are equal. In general, mean equating is less complicated than linear equating, but linear equating provides for more flexibility in the conversion than does mean equating.

2.5 Equipercentile Equating

In equipercentile equating, a curve is used to describe form-to-form differences in difficulty, which makes equipercentile equating even more general than linear equating. Using equipercentile equating, for example, Form X could be more difficult than Form Y at high and low scores, but less difficult at the middle scores.

The equating function is an equipercentile equating function if the distribution of scores on Form X converted to the Form Y scale is equal to the distribution of scores on Form Y in the population. The equipercentile equating function is developed by identifying scores on Form X that have the same percentile ranks as scores on Form Y.

The definition of equipercentile equating developed by Braun and Holland (1982) is adapted for use here. Consider the following definitions of terms, some of which were presented previously:

X is a random variable representing a score on Form X, and x is a particular value (i.e., a realization) of X.

Y is a random variable representing a score on Form Y, and y is a particular value (i.e., a realization) of Y.

F is the cumulative distribution function of X in the population.

G is the cumulative distribution function of Y in the same population.

e_Y is a symmetric equating function used to convert scores on Form X to the Form Y scale.

G^* is the cumulative distribution function of e_Y in the same population. That is, G^* is the cumulative distribution function of scores on Form X converted to the Form Y scale.

The function e_Y is defined to be the equipercentile equating function in the population if

$$G^* = G. \tag{2.10}$$

That is, the function e_Y is the equipercentile equating function in the population if the cumulative distribution function of scores on Form X converted to the Form Y scale is equal to the cumulative distribution function of scores on Form Y.

Braun and Holland (1982) indicated that the following function is an equipercentile equating function when X and Y are continuous random variables:

$$e_Y(x) = G^{-1}[F(x)], \tag{2.11}$$

where G^{-1} is the inverse of the cumulative distribution function G.

As previously indicated, to be an equating function, e_Y must be symmetric. Define

e_X as a symmetric equating function used to convert scores on Form Y to the Form X scale, and

F^* as the cumulative distribution function of e_X in the population. That is, F^* is the cumulative distribution function of scores on Form Y converted to the Form X scale.

By the symmetry property,

$$e_X^{-1}(x) = e_Y(x) \text{ and } e_Y^{-1}(y) = e_X(y). \tag{2.12}$$

Also,

$$e_X(y) = F^{-1}[G(y)], \tag{2.13}$$

is the equipercentile equating function for converting Form Y scores to the Form X scale. In this equation, F^{-1} is the inverse of the cumulative distribution function F.

Following the definitions in equations (2.10)–(2.13), an equipercentile equivalent for the population of examinees can be constructed in the following manner: For a given Form X score, find the percentage of examinees earning scores at or below that Form X score. Next, find the Form Y score that has the same percentage of examinees at or below it. These Form X and Form Y scores are considered to be equivalent. For example, suppose that 20% of the examinees in the population earned a Form X score at or below 26 and 20% of the examinees in the population earned a Form Y score at or below 27. Then a Form X score of 26 would be considered to represent the same level of achievement as a Form Y score of 27. Using equipercentile equating, a Form X score of 26 would be equated to a Form Y score of 27.

The preceding discussion was based on an assumption that test scores are continuous random variables. Typically, however, test scores are discrete. For example, number-correct scores take on only integer values. With discrete test scores, the definition of equipercentile equating is more complicated than the situation just described. Consider the following situation. Suppose that a test is scored number-correct and that the following is true of the population distributions:

1. 20% of the examinees score at or below 26 on Form X.

2. 18% of the examinees score at or below 27 on Form Y.

3. 23% of the examinees score at or below 28 on Form Y.

What is the Form Y equipercentile equivalent of a Form X score of 26? No Form Y score exists that has precisely 20% of the scores at or below it. Strictly speaking, no Form Y equivalent of a Form X score of 26 exists. Thus, the goal of equipercentile equating stated in equation (2.10) cannot be met strictly when test scores are discrete.

How can equipercentile equating be conducted when scores are discrete? A tradition exists in educational and psychological measurement to view discrete test scores as being continuous by using percentiles and percentile ranks as defined in many educational and psychological measurement textbooks (e.g., Blommers and Forsyth, 1977; Ebel and Frisbie, 1991). In this approach, an integer score of 28, for example, is considered to represent scores in the range 27.5–28.5. Examinees with scores of 28 are considered to be uniformly distributed in this range. The percentile rank of a score of 28 is defined as being the percentage of scores *below* 28. However, because only 1/2 of the examinees who score 28 are considered to be below 28 (the remainder being between 28 and 28.5), the percentile rank of 28 is the percentage of examinees who earned integer scores of 27 and below, plus 1/2 the percentage of examinees who earned an integer score of 28. Placing the preceding example in the context of percentile ranks, 18% of the examinees earned a Form Y score below 27.5 and 5% (23–18%) of the examinees earned a score between 27.5 and 28.5. So the percentile rank of a Form Y score of 28 would be 18% + 1/2(5%) = 20.5%. In the terminology typically used, the percentile rank of an integer score is the percentile rank at the midpoint of the interval that contains that score.

Holland and Thayer (1989) presented a statistical justification for using percentiles and percentile ranks. In their approach, they use what they refer to as a *continuization* process. Given a discrete integer-valued random variable X and a random variable U that is uniformly distributed over the range $-1/2$ to $+1/2$, they define a new random variable

$$X^* = X + U.$$

This new random variable is continuous. The cumulative distribution function of this new random variable corresponds to the percentile rank function. The inverse of the cumulative distribution of this new function exists and is the percentile function. Holland and Thayer (1989) also generalized their approach to incorporate continuization processes that are based on distributions other than the uniform. This approach was developed further by von Davier et al. (2003)

In the present chapter, the traditional approach to percentiles and percentile ranks is followed. Holland and Thayer (1989) and von Davier et al. (2003) should be consulted if a more in-depth discussion of continuization approaches is desired.

The equipercentile methods presented next assume that the observed scores on the tests to be equated are integer scores that range from zero through the number of items on the test, as would be true of tests scored number-correct. Generalizations to other scoring schemes are discussed as well.

2.5.1 Graphical Procedures

Equipercentile equating using graphical methods provides a conceptual framework for subsequent consideration of analytic methods. A hypothetical four-item test is used to illustrate the graphical process for equipercentile equating. Data for Form X are presented in Table 2.1.

In this table, x refers to test score and $f(x)$ to the proportion of examinees earning the score x. For example, the proportion of examinees earning a score of 0 is .20. $F(x)$ is the cumulative proportion at or below x. For example, the proportion of examinees scoring 3 or below is .9. $P(x)$ refers to the percentile rank, and for an integer score it equals the percentage of examinees below x plus 1/2 the percentage of examinees at x—i.e., for integer score x, $P(x) = 100[F(x-1) + f(x)/2]$.

TABLE 2.1. Form X Score Distribution for a Hypothetical Four-Item Test.

x	$f(x)$	$F(x)$	$P(x)$
0	.2	.2	10
1	.3	.5	35
2	.2	.7	60
3	.2	.9	80
4	.1	1.0	95

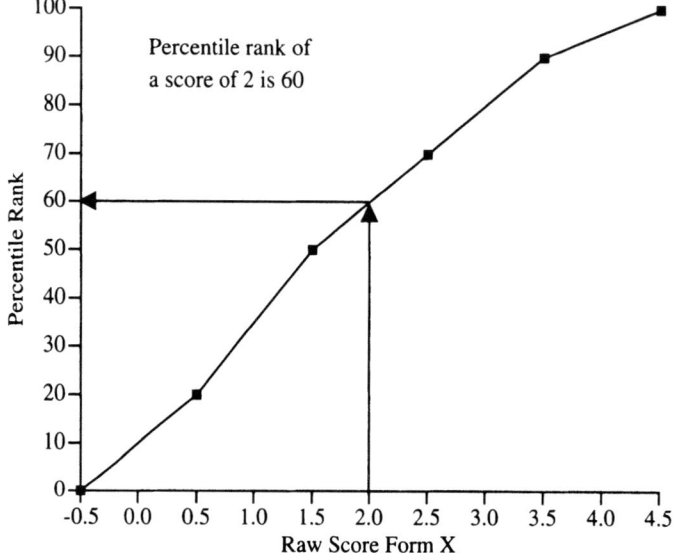

FIGURE 2.3. Form X percentile ranks on a hypothetical four-item test.

To be consistent with traditional definitions of percentile ranks, the percentile rank function is plotted as points at the upper limit of each score interval. For example, the percentile rank of a score of 3.5 is 90, which is 100 times the cumulative proportion at or below 3. Therefore, to plot the percentile ranks, plot the percentile ranks at each integer score plus .5. The percentile ranks at an integer score plus .5 can be found from Table 2.1 by taking the cumulative distribution function values, $F(x)$, at an integer and multiplying them by 100 to make them percentages. Figure 2.3 illustrates how to plot the percentile rank distribution for Form X.

A percentile rank of 0 is also plotted at a Form X score of $-.5$. The points are then connected with straight lines. An example is presented for finding the percentile rank of a Form X integer score of 2 using the arrows in Figure 2.3. As can be seen, the percentile rank of a score of 2 is 60, which is the same result found in Table 2.1.

TABLE 2.2. Form X and Form Y Distributions for a Hypothetical Four-Item Test.

y	g(y)	G(y)	Q(Y)	x	f(x)	F(x)	P(x)
0	.1	.1	5	0	.2	.2	10
1	.2	.3	20	1	.3	.5	35
2	.2	.5	40	2	.2	.7	60
3	.3	.8	65	3	.2	.9	80
4	.2	1.0	90	4	.1	1.0	95

In Figure 2.3, percentile ranks of scores between $-.5$ and 0.0 are greater than zero. These nonzero percentile ranks result from using the traditional definition of percentile ranks, in which scores of 0 are assumed to be uniformly distributed from $-.5$ to $.5$. Also, scores of 4 are considered to be uniformly distributed between 3.5 to 4.5, so that scores above 4 have percentile ranks less than 100. Under this conceptualization, the range of possible scores is treated as being between $-.5$ and the highest integer score $+.5$.

Data from Form Y also need to be used in the equating process. The data for Form Y are presented along with the Form X data in Table 2.2. In this table, y refers to Form Y scores, $g(y)$ to the proportion of examinees at each score, $G(y)$ to the proportion at or below each score, and $Q(y)$ to the percentile rank at each score. Percentile ranks for Form Y are plotted in the same manner as they were for Form X. To find the equipercentile equivalent of a particular score on Form X, find the Form Y score with the same percentile rank. Figure 2.4 illustrates this process for finding the equipercentile equivalent of a Form X score of 2. As indicated by the arrows, a Form X score of 2 has a percentile rank of 60. Following the arrows, it can be seen that the Form Y score of about 2.8 (actually 2.83) is equivalent to the Form X score of 2.

The equivalents can also be plotted. To construct such a graph, plot, as points, Form Y equivalents of Form X scores at each integer plus .5. Then plot Form X equivalents of Form Y scores at each integer plus .5. To handle scores below the lowest integer scores $+.5$, a point is plotted at the (x, y) pair $(-.5, -.5)$. The plotted points are then connected by straight lines. This process is illustrated for the example in Figure 2.5. As indicated by the arrows in the figure, a Form X score of 2 is equivalent to a Form Y score of 2.8 (actually 2.83), which is consistent with the result found earlier. This plot of equivalents displays the Form Y equivalents of Form X scores.

In summary, the graphical process of finding equipercentile equivalents is as follows: Plot percentile ranks for each form on the same graph. To find a Form Y equivalent of a Form X score, start by finding the percentile rank of the Form X score. Then find the Form Y score that has that same percentile

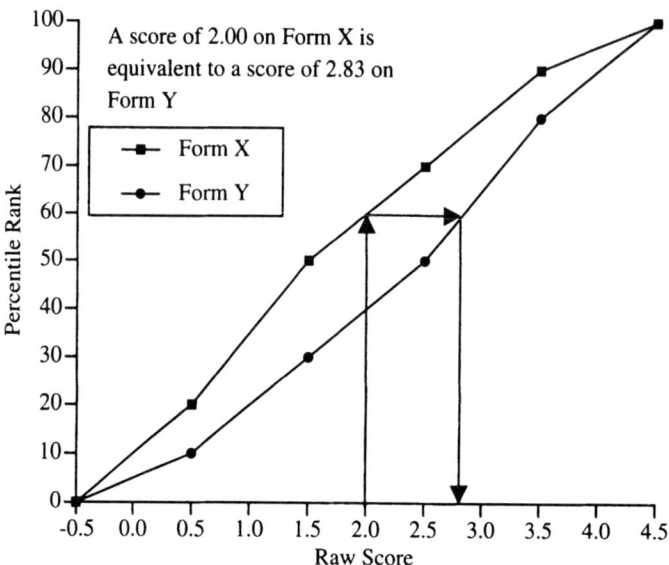

FIGURE 2.4. Graphical equipercentile equating for a hypothetical four-item test.

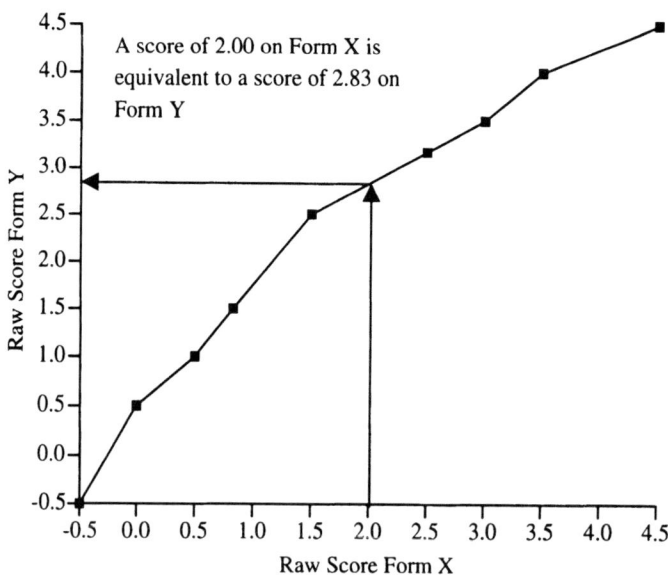

FIGURE 2.5. Equipercentile equivalents for a hypothetical four-item test.

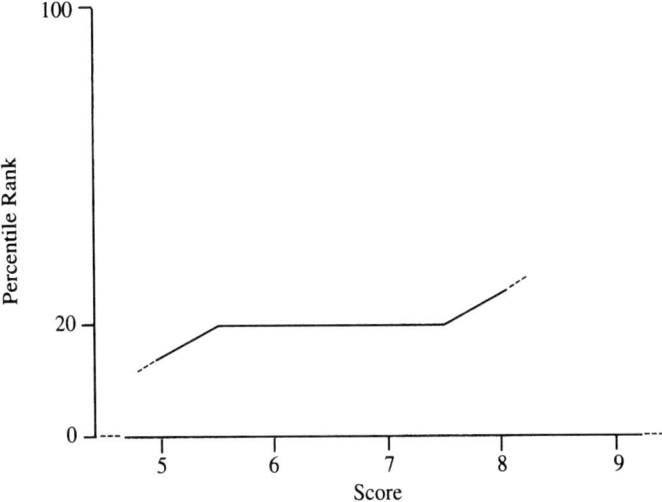

FIGURE 2.6. Illustration of percentile ranks when no examinees earn a particular score.

rank. Equivalents can be plotted in a graph that shows the equipercentile relationship between the two forms.

One issue that arises in equipercentile equating is how to handle situations in which no examinees earn a particular score. When this occurs, the score that corresponds to a particular percentile rank might not be unique. Suppose for example that x has a percentile rank of 20. To find the equipercentile equivalent, the Form Y score that has a percentile rank of 20 needs to be found. Suppose, however, that there is no unique score on Form Y that has a percentile rank of 20, as illustrated in Figure 2.6.

The percentile ranks shown in Figure 2.6 could occur if no examinees earned scores of 6 and 7. In this case, the graph indicates that scores in the range 5.5 to 7.5 all have percentile ranks of 20. The choice of the Form Y score that has a percentile rank of 20 is arbitrary. In this situation, usually the middle score would be chosen. So, in the example the score with a percentile rank of 20 would be designated as 6.5. Choosing the middle score is arbitrary, technically, but doing so seems sensible.

2.5.2 Analytic Procedures

The graphical method discussed in the previous section is not likely to be viable for equating a large number of real forms in real time. In addition, equating using graphical procedures can be inaccurate. What is needed are formulas that provide more formal definitions of percentile ranks and equipercentile equivalents. The following discussion provides such formulas. The result of applying these formulas is to produce percentile ranks and equipercentile equivalents that are equal to those that would result using the graphical procedures.

To define percentile ranks, let K_X represent the number of items on Form X of a test. Define X as a random variable representing test scores on Form X that can take on the integer values $0, 1, \ldots, K_X$. Define $f(x)$ as the discrete density function for $X = x$. That is,

$$f(x) \geq 0 \text{ for integer scores } x = 0, 1, \ldots, K_X;$$
$$f(x) = 0 \text{ otherwise; and}$$
$$\sum f(x) = 1.$$

Define $F(x)$ as the discrete cumulative distribution function. That is, $F(x)$ is the proportion of examinees in the population earning a score *at or below* x. Therefore,

$$0 \leq F(x) \leq 1 \text{ for } x = 0, 1, \ldots, K_X;$$
$$F(x) = 0 \text{ for } x < 0; \text{ and}$$
$$F(x) = 1 \text{ for } x > K_X.$$

Consider a possible noninteger value of x. Define x^* as that integer that is closest to x such that $x^* - .5 \leq x < x^* + .5$. For example, if $x = 5.7$, $x^* = 6$; if $x = 6.4$, $x^* = 6$; and if $x = 5.5$, $x^* = 6$. The percentile rank function for Form X is

$$\begin{aligned} P(x) &= 100\{F(x^* - 1) + [x - (x^* - .5)][F(x^*) - F(x^* - 1)]\}, \\ & \quad -.5 \leq x < K_X + .5, \\ &= 0, \qquad x < -.5, \\ &= 100, \qquad x \geq K_x + .5. \end{aligned} \qquad (2.14)$$

To illustrate how this equation functions, consider the following example based on the data in Table 2.1. Calculate the percentile rank for a score of $x = 1.3$, using equation (2.14):

$$\begin{aligned} P(1.3) &= 100\{F(0) + [1.3 - (1 - .5)][F(1) - F(0)]\} \\ &= 100\{.2 + [.8][.5 - .2]\} = 100\{.2 + .24\} = 44. \end{aligned}$$

In this case, $x^* = 1.0$, because 1 is the integer score that is closest to 1.3. The term $[F(1) - F(0)] = .5 - .2 = .3$ represents the proportion of examinees earning a score of 1. These scores are considered to range from .5 to 1.5. The term $[1.3 - (1 - .5)] = .8$ indicates that the score of 1.3 is, proportionally, .8 of the distance between .5 and 1.5. So, $[.8][.3] = .24$ represents the probability of scoring between .5 and 1.3. The probability of scoring below .5 is represented by $F(0) = .2$. Therefore, the percentile rank of a score of 1.3 equals 44.

The inverse of the percentile rank function, which often is referred to as the percentile function, is symbolized as P^{-1}. Two alternate percentile functions are given as follows. These functions produce the same result, unless some of the probabilities are zero. Given a percentile rank (e.g., the 10th percentile rank), this inverse function is used to find the score corresponding to that percentile rank. To find this function, solve equation (2.14) for x. Specifically, for a given percentile rank P^*, the percentile is

$$x_U(P^*) = P^{-1}[P^*] = \frac{P^*/100 - F(x_U^* - 1)}{F(x_U^*) - F(x_U^* - 1)} + (x_U^* - .5), \quad 0 \leq P^* < 100,$$

$$= K_X + .5, \qquad P^* = 100. \quad (2.15)$$

In equation (2.15), for $0 \leq P^* < 100$, x_U^* is the *smallest* integer score with a cumulative percent $[100F(x)]$ that is *greater than* P^*. An alternate expression for the percentile is

$$x_L(P^*) = P^{-1}[P^*] = \frac{P^*/100 - F(x_L^*)}{F(x_L^* + 1) - F(x_L^*)} + (x_L^* + .5), \quad 0 < P^* \leq 100,$$

$$= -.5, \qquad P^* = 0. \quad (2.16)$$

In equation (2.16), for $0 < P^* \leq 100$, x_L^* is the *largest* integer score with a cumulative percent $[100F(x)]$ that is *less than* P^*. If the $f(x)$ are nonzero at all score points $0, 1, \ldots, K_X$, then $x = x_U = x_L$, and either expression can be used. If some of the $f(x)$ are zero, then $x_U \neq x_L$ for at least some percentile ranks. In this case, the convention $x = (x_U + x_L)/2$ is used. This convention produces the same results as the one described in association with Figure 2.6 using the graphical procedures. In most situations, it seems reasonable to assume that the $f(x)$ are all nonzero over the integer score range $0, 1, \ldots, K_X$. For this reason, and to simplify issues, when considering population distributions in the following discussion, only equation (2.15) is used with $x_U = x$. When considering estimates of population distributions, estimated probabilities of zero are often encountered (i.e., when no examinees in a sample earn a particular score).

As an example of how to use equation (2.15), find the score corresponding to a percentile rank of 62 using the inverse of the percentile rank function using the data in Table 2.1. In this case $x_U^* = 2$ because, in Table 2.1, it is the *smallest* integer score with $F(x)$ that is *greater than* .62. Then

$$P^{-1}(62) = \frac{62/100 - F(1)}{F(2) - F(1)} + (2 - .5)$$

$$= \frac{.62 - .5}{.7 - .5} + (2 - .5) = .12/.20 + 1.5 = .60 + 1.5 = 2.1.$$

In equipercentile equating, the interest is in finding a score on Form Y that has the same percentile rank as a score on Form X. Referring to y as a score on Form Y, let K_Y refer to the number of items on Form Y, let $g(y)$

refer to the discrete density of y, let $G(y)$ refer to the discrete cumulative distribution of y, let $Q(y)$ refer to the percentile rank of y, and let Q^{-1} refer to the inverse of the percentile rank function for Form Y. Then the Form Y equipercentile equivalent of score x on Form X is

$$e_Y(x) = y = Q^{-1}[P(x)], \qquad -.5 \leq x \leq K_X + .5. \qquad (2.17)$$

This equation indicates that, to find the equipercentile equivalent of score x on the scale of Form Y, first find the percentile rank of x in the Form X distribution. Then find the Form Y score that has that same percentile rank in the Form Y distribution. Equation (2.17) is symmetric. That is, to find the Form X equivalent of a Form Y score, equation (2.17) is solved for y, giving $e_X(y) = P^{-1}[Q(y)]$.

Analytically, to find $e_Y(x)$ given by equation (2.17), use the analog of equation (2.15) for the Form Y distribution. That is, use

$$\begin{aligned} e_Y(x) &= Q^{-1}[P(x)] \\ &= \frac{P(x)/100 - G(y_U^* - 1)}{G(y_U^*) - G(y_U^* - 1)} + (y_U^* - .5), \qquad 0 \leq P(x) < 100, \\ &= K_Y + .5, \qquad\qquad\qquad\qquad\qquad\qquad P(x) = 100. \quad (2.18) \end{aligned}$$

[Note that, to use this equation when some Form Y scores have zero probabilities, it also is necessary to use y_L^* as described in the discussion following equation (2.16).] Refer to Table 2.2. As an example of finding equipercentile equivalents, find the Form Y equipercentile equivalent of a Form X score of 2. The percentile rank of a Form X score of 2 is $P(2) = 60$, as is shown in Table 2.2. To find the equipercentile equivalent, the Form Y score that has a percentile rank of 60 must be found. Because 3 is the score with the smallest $G(y)$ that is *greater than* .60, $y_U^* = 3$. Thus, using equation (2.18),

$$e_Y(x) = Q^{-1}[60] = \frac{60/100 - .5}{.8 - .5} + (3 - .5) = .1/.3 + 2.5 = 2.8333.$$

The raw score equipercentile equivalents that result typically are noninteger. Noninteger scores arise through the continuization process used to define percentiles and percentile ranks. Issues related to rounding to integers are considered later in the discussion of scale scores.

2.5.3 Properties of Equated Scores in Equipercentile Equating

Conducting equipercentile equating using equation (2.18) always results in equated scores in the range $-.5 \leq e_Y(x) \leq K_Y + .5$. Thus, equipercentile equating has the desirable property that the equated scores will always be within the range of possible scores under the traditional conceptualization of percentiles and percentile ranks. The problem of having equated scores

TABLE 2.3. Form Y Equivalents of Form X
Scores for a Hypothetical Four-Item Test.

x	$f(x)$	$e_Y(x)$
0	.2	.50
1	.3	1.75
2	.2	2.8333
3	.2	3.50
4	.1	4.25

TABLE 2.4. Moments for Equating Form X and Form Y of a Hypothetical Four-Item Test.

Score	μ	σ	sk	ku
y	2.3000	1.2689	$-.2820$	1.9728
x	1.7000	1.2689	.2820	1.9728
$e_Y(x)$	2.3167	1.2098	$-.0972$	1.8733

that are out of the range of possible scores which occur with mean and linear equating does not occur with equipercentile equating.

Ideally, in equipercentile equating the equated scores on Form X would have the same distribution as the scores on Form Y. As was previously indicated, if test scores were continuous, then these distributions would be the same. However, test scores are discrete. A continuization process involving percentiles and percentile ranks was used to render the problem mathematically tractable. However, when the results of equating are applied to discrete scores, the equated Form X score distribution will differ from the Form Y distribution.

Consider the following illustration. Using the hypothetical four-item test from Table 2.2, Table 2.3 provides the Form Y equivalents of scores resulting from the use of equation (2.18). The moments that result are shown in Table 2.4, where skewness and kurtosis are defined for Form X, respectively, as

$$sk(X) = \frac{\mathrm{E}[X - \mu(X)]^3}{[\sigma(X)]^3}, \text{ and} \qquad (2.19)$$

$$ku(X) = \frac{\mathrm{E}[X - \mu(X)]^4}{[\sigma(X)]^4}. \qquad (2.20)$$

Central moments for other variables are defined similarly. To arrive at the moments of the equated scores, $e_Y(x)$, in Table 2.4, the Form X scores were equated to Form Y scores. For example, as indicated in Table 2.3, the proportion of examinees earning an $e_Y(x)$ of .50 is .20.

Moments of these equated scores then were found. Ideally, the moments for $e_Y(x)$ in Table 2.4 would be equal to those for y. As can be seen, however, there are departures. These departures are a result of the discreteness of the scores. The departures in Table 2.4 are relatively large because the test is so short. Departures likely would be considerably less with longer, more realistic tests. For tests of realistic lengths, not being able to achieve the equal distribution goal precisely often is more of a theoretical concern than a practical one.

2.6 Estimating Observed Score Equating Relationships

So far, the methods have been described using population parameters. In practice, sample statistics are all that are available, and these sample statistics are substituted for the parameters in the preceding equations.

One estimation problem that occurs in equipercentile equating is how to calculate the function P^{-1} when the frequency at some score points is zero. The conventions associated with equations (2.15) and (2.16) for averaging the results is one procedure for producing a unique result. Another procedure is to add a very small relative frequency to each score, and then adjust the relative frequencies so they sum to one. If adj is taken as this small quantity, then the adjusted relative frequencies on Form Y are

$$\hat{g}_{adj}(y) = \frac{\hat{g}(y) + adj}{1 + (K_Y + 1) \cdot adj},$$

where $\hat{g}(y)$ is the relative frequency that was observed. For example, if $K_Y = 10$, $adj = 10^{-6}$, and $\hat{g}(2) = .02$, then

$$\hat{g}_{adj}(2) = \frac{.02 + 10^{-6}}{1 + (10 + 1) \cdot 10^{-6}} = .02000078.$$

A similar procedure could be used for Form X. The equating then can be done using the adjusted relative frequencies. Experience has shown that a value around $adj = 10^{-6}$ can be used without creating a serious bias in the equating. A third solution to the zero frequency problem is to use smoothing methods, which are the subject of Chapter 3.

Data for an example of an equating of Form X and Form Y of the original ACT Mathematics test are presented in Table 2.5. This test contains 40 multiple-choice items scored incorrect (0) or correct (1). Form X was administered to 4,329 examinees and Form Y to 4,152 examinees in a spiral administration, which resulted in random groups of examinees being administered Form X and Form Y. The sample sizes for the two forms differ, in part, because Form X always preceded Form Y in the distribution of

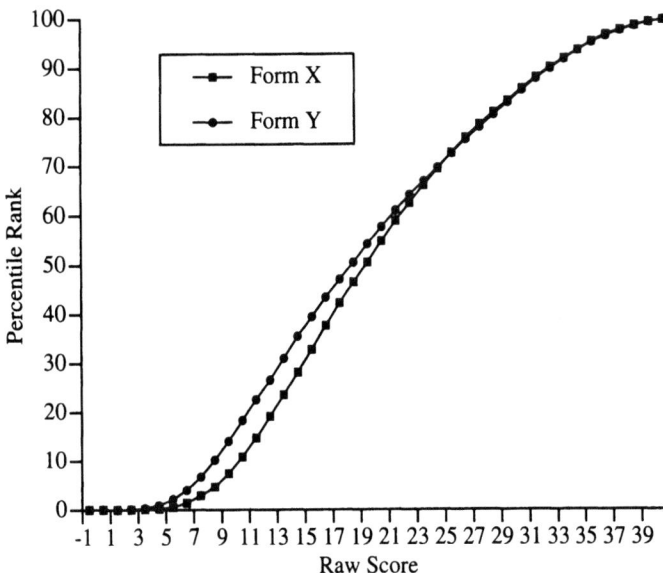

FIGURE 2.7. Percentile ranks for equating Form X and Form Y of the original ACT Mathematics test.

booklets in each testing room. Thus, one more Form X than Form Y booklet was administered in some testing rooms. In the table, a "^" is used to indicate an estimate of a population parameter, and N_X and N_Y refer to sample sizes for the forms. Consider, for example, a score of 10 on Form Y. From Table 2.5, 194 examinees earned a score of 10, and 857 examinees earned a score of 10 or below; the proportion of examinees earning a score of 10 is .0467, the proportion of examinees at or below a score of 10 is .2064, and the estimated percentile rank of a score of 10 is 18.30.

Percentile ranks for Forms X and Y are plotted in Figure 2.7. The percentile ranks are plotted for each score point plus .5. Form X appears to be somewhat easier than Form Y, because the Form X distribution is shifted to the right. The relative frequency distributions are shown in Figure 2.8.

Both score distributions are positively skewed, and Form X again appears to be somewhat easier than Form Y. Estimates of central moments for Form X and Form Y are given in the upper portion of Table 2.6. Both forms have means, $\hat{\mu}$, less than 20 (which is 50% of the 40 items), so it appears that the tests are somewhat difficult for these examinees. Form X is, on average, nearly 1 point easier than Form Y. Based on the standard deviations, $\hat{\sigma}$, the distribution for Form X is less variable than the distribution for Form Y. As indicated by the skewness values, $\widehat{sk}$ the distributions are positively skewed, where skewness for the population is defined in equation (2.19). Based on the kurtosis estimates, $\widehat{ku}$, the distributions have lower kurtosis

2. Observed Score Equating Using the Random Groups Design

TABLE 2.5. Data for Equating Form X and Form Y of the Original ACT Mathematics Test.

	Form Y					Form X				
Raw Score	$N_Y \cdot \hat{g}(y)$	$N_Y \cdot \hat{G}(y)$	$\hat{g}(y)$	$\hat{G}(y)$	$\hat{Q}(y)$	$N_X \cdot \hat{f}(x)$	$N_X \cdot \hat{F}(x)$	$\hat{f}(x)$	$\hat{F}(x)$	$\hat{P}(x)$
0	0	0	.0000	.0000	.00	0	0	.0000	.0000	.00
1	1	1	.0002	.0002	.01	1	1	.0002	.0002	.01
2	3	4	.0007	.0010	.06	1	2	.0002	.0005	.03
3	13	17	.0031	.0041	.25	3	5	.0007	.0012	.08
4	42	59	.0101	.0142	.92	9	14	.0021	.0032	.22
5	59	118	.0142	.0284	2.13	18	32	.0042	.0074	.53
6	95	213	.0229	.0513	3.99	59	91	.0136	.0210	1.42
7	131	344	.0316	.0829	6.71	67	158	.0155	.0365	2.88
8	158	502	.0381	.1209	10.19	91	249	.0210	.0575	4.70
9	161	663	.0388	.1597	14.03	144	393	.0333	.0908	7.42
10	194	857	.0467	.2064	18.30	149	542	.0344	.1252	10.80
11	164	1021	.0395	.2459	22.62	192	734	.0444	.1696	14.74
12	166	1187	.0400	.2859	26.59	192	926	.0444	.2139	19.17
13	197	384	.0474	.3333	30.96	192	1118	.0444	.2583	23.61
14	177	561	.0426	.3760	35.46	201	1319	.0464	.3047	28.15
15	158	1719	.0381	.4140	39.50	204	1523	.0471	.3518	32.83
16	169	1888	.0407	.4547	43.44	217	1740	.0501	.4019	37.69
17	132	2020	.0318	.4865	47.06	181	1921	.0418	.4438	42.28
18	158	2178	.0381	.5246	50.55	184	2105	.0425	.4863	46.50
19	151	2329	.0364	.5609	54.28	170	2275	.0393	.5255	50.59
20	134	2463	.0323	.5932	57.71	201	2476	.0464	.5720	54.87
21	137	2600	.0330	.6262	60.97	147	2623	.0340	.6059	58.89
22	122	2722	.0294	.6556	64.09	163	2786	.0377	.6436	62.47
23	110	2832	.0265	.6821	66.88	147	2933	.0340	.6775	66.05
24	116	2948	.0279	.7100	69.61	140	3073	.0323	.7099	69.37
25	132	3080	.0318	.7418	72.59	147	3220	.0340	.7438	72.68
26	104	3184	.0250	.7669	75.43	126	3346	.0291	.7729	75.84
27	104	3288	.0250	.7919	77.94	113	3459	.0261	.7990	78.60
28	114	3402	.0275	.8194	80.56	100	3559	.0231	.8221	81.06
29	97	3499	.0234	.8427	83.10	106	3665	.0245	.8466	83.44
30	107	3606	.0258	.8685	85.56	107	3772	.0247	.8713	85.90
31	88	3694	.0212	.8897	87.91	91	3863	.0210	.8924	88.18
32	80	3774	.0193	.9090	89.93	83	3946	.0192	.9115	90.19
33	79	3853	.0190	.9280	91.85	73	4019	.0169	.9284	92.00
34	70	3923	.0169	.9448	93.64	72	4091	.0166	.9450	93.67
35	61	3984	.0147	.9595	95.22	75	4166	.0173	.9623	95.37
36	48	4032	.0116	.9711	96.53	50	4216	.0116	.9739	96.81
37	47	4079	.0113	.9824	97.68	37	4253	.0085	.9824	97.82
38	29	4108	.0070	.9894	98.59	38	4291	.0088	.9912	98.68
39	32	4140	.0077	.9971	99.33	23	4314	.0053	.9965	99.39
40	12	4152	.0029	1.0000	99.86	15	4329	.0035	1.000	99.83

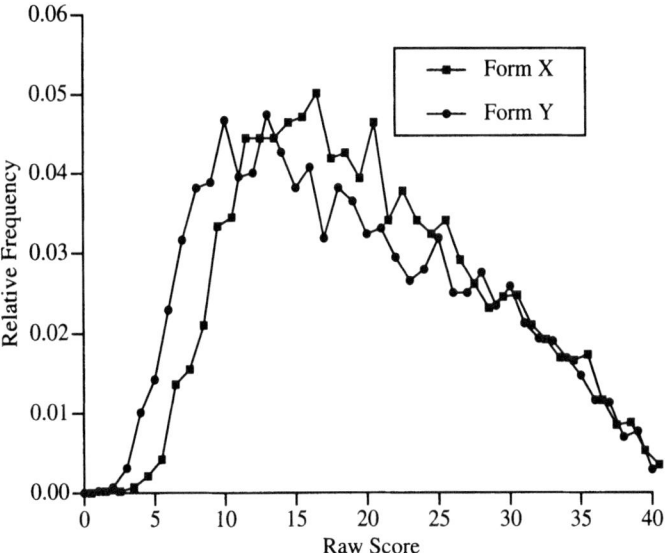

FIGURE 2.8. Relative frequency distributions for Form X and Form Y of the original ACT Mathematics test.

than a normal distribution, which would have a kurtosis value of 3, where kurtosis for the population is defined in equation (2.20).

The conversions for mean, linear, and equipercentile equating are shown in Table 2.7 and are graphed in Figure 2.9. The linear and equipercentile results were calculated using the *RAGE-RGEQUATE* computer program described in Appendix B. The moments for converted scores are shown in the bottom portion of Table 2.6. As expected, the mean converted scores for mean equating are the same as the mean for Form Y. For linear equating, the mean and standard deviation of the converted scores agree with the mean and standard deviation of Form Y. The first four moments of converted scores for equipercentile equating are very similar to those for Form Y. In Table 2.7, it can be seen that mean and linear equating produce results that are outside the range of possible raw scores. Because of the large number of values in Table 2.7 and the considerable similarity of equating functions in Figure 2.9, differences between the functions are difficult to ascertain.

The use of considerably larger graph paper would help in such a comparison. Alternatively, difference-type plots can be used, as in Figure 2.10. In this graph, the difference between the results for each method and the results for the identity equating are plotted. To find the Form Y equivalent of a Form X score, just add the vertical axis value to the horizontal axis value. For example, for equipercentile equating a Form X score of 10 has a vertical axis value of approximately −1.8. Thus, the Form Y equivalent of a Form X score of 10 is approximately $8.2 = 10 - 1.8$. This value is the

TABLE 2.6. Moments for Equating Form X and Form Y.

Test Form	$\hat{\mu}$	$\hat{\sigma}$	$\widehat{sk}$	$\widehat{ku}$
Form Y	18.9798	8.9393	.3527	2.1464
Form X	19.8524	8.2116	.3753	2.3024
Form X Equated to Form Y Scale for Various Methods				
Mean	18.9798	8.2116	.3753	2.3024
Linear	18.9798	8.9393	.3753	2.3024
Equipercentile	18.9799	8.9352	.3545	2.1465

same as the one indicated in Table 2.7 (8.1607), apart from error inherent in trying to read values from a graph.

In Figure 2.10, the horizontal line for the identity equating is at a vertical axis value of 0, which will always be the case with difference plots constructed in the manner of Figure 2.10. The results for mean equating are displayed by a line that is parallel to, but nearly 1 point below, the line for the identity equating. The line for linear equating crosses the identity equating and mean equating lines. The equipercentile equating relationship appears to be definitely nonlinear. Referring to the equipercentile relationship, Form X appears to be nearly 2 points easier around a Form X score of 10, and the two forms appear to be similar in difficulty at scores in the range of 25 to 40.

The plot in Figure 2.10 for equipercentile equating is somewhat irregular (bumpy). These irregularities are a result of random error in estimating the equivalents. Smoothing methods are introduced in Chapter 3, which lead to more regular plots and less random error.

2.7 Scale Scores

When equating is conducted in practice, raw scores typically are converted to scale scores. As described in Chapter 9, scale scores are constructed to facilitate score interpretation, often by incorporating normative or content information. For example, scale scores might be constructed to have a particular mean in a nationally representative group of examinees. The effects of equating on scale scores are crucial to the interpretation of equating results, because scale scores are the scores typically reported to examinees. A further discussion of methods for developing score scales is provided in Chapter 9. The use of scale scores in the equating context is described next.

TABLE 2.7. Raw-to-Raw Score Conversion Tables.

Form X Score	Form Y Equivalent Using Equating Method		
	Mean	Linear	Equipercentile
0	−.8726	−2.6319	.0000
1	.1274	−1.5432	.9796
2	1.1274	−.4546	1.6462
3	2.1274	.6340	2.2856
4	3.1274	1.7226	2.8932
5	4.1274	2,8112	3.6205
6	5.1274	3.8998	4.4997
7	6.1274	4.9884	5.5148
8	7.1274	6.0771	6.3124
9	8.1274	7.1657	7.2242
10	9.1274	8.2543	8.1607
11	10.1274	9.3429	9.1827
12	11.1274	10.4315	10.1859
13	12.1274	11.5201	11.2513
14	13.1274	12.6088	12.3896
15	14.1274	13.6974	13.3929
16	15.1274	14.7860	14.5240
17	16.1274	15.8746	15.7169
18	17.1274	16.9632	16.8234
19	18.1274	18.0518	18.0092
20	19.1274	19.1405	19.1647
21	20.1274	20.2291	20.3676
22	21.1274	21.3177	21.4556
23	22.1274	22.4063	22.6871
24	23.1274	23.4949	23.9157
25	24.1274	24.5835	25.0292
26	25.1274	25.6722	26.1612
27	26.1274	26.7608	27.2633
28	27.1274	27.8494	28.1801
29	28.1274	28.9380	29.1424
30	29.1274	30.0266	30.1305
31	30.1274	31.1152	31.1297
32	31.1274	32.2039	32.1357
33	32.1274	33.2925	33.0781
34	33.1274	34.3811	34.0172
35	34.1274	35.4697	35.1016
36	35.1274	36.5583	36.2426
37	36.1274	37.6469	37.1248
38	37.1274	38.7355	38.1321
39	38.1274	39.8242	39.0807
40	39.1274	40.9128	39.9006

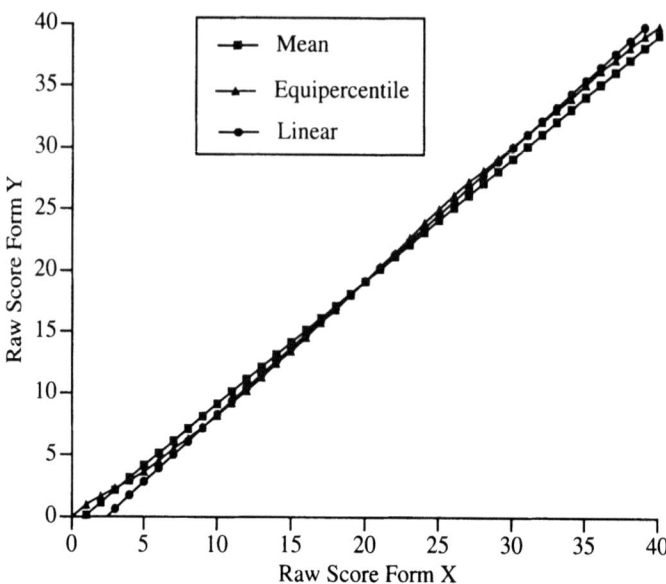

FIGURE 2.9. Results for equating Form X and Form Y of the original ACT Mathematics test.

2.7.1 Linear Conversions

The least complicated raw-to-scale score transformations that typically are used in practice are linear in form. For example, suppose that a national norming study was conducted using Form Y of the 100-item test that was used earlier in this chapter to illustrate mean and linear equating. Assume that the mean raw score, $\mu(Y)$, was 70 and the standard deviation, $\sigma(Y)$, was 10 for the national norm group. Also assume that the mean scale score, $\mu(sc)$, was intended to be 20 and the standard deviation of the scale scores, $\sigma(sc)$, 5. Then the raw-to-scale score transformation (sc) for converting raw scores on the old form, Form Y, to scale scores is

$$sc(y) = \frac{\sigma(sc)}{\sigma(Y)} y + \left[\mu(sc) - \frac{\sigma(sc)}{\sigma(Y)} \mu(Y)\right]. \quad (2.21)$$

Substituting we have

$$\begin{aligned} sc(y) &= \frac{5}{10} y + \left[20 - \frac{5}{10} 70\right] \\ &= .5y - 15. \end{aligned}$$

Now assume that scores on Form X are to be converted to scale scores based on the equating used in the earlier linear equating example. As was found

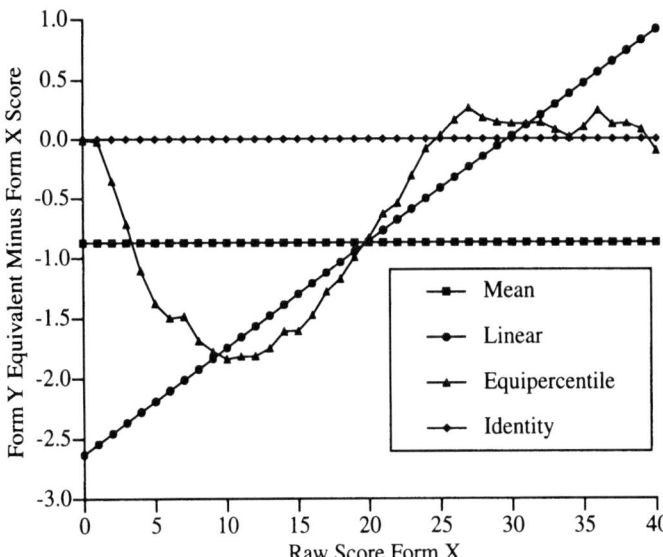

FIGURE 2.10. Results expressed as differences for equating Form X and Form Y of the original ACT Mathematics test.

earlier, the linear conversion equation for equating raw scores on Form X to raw scores on Form Y was $l_Y(x) = .9x + 12.2$. To find the raw-to-scale score transformation for Form X, substitute $l_Y(x)$ for y in the raw-to-scale score transformation for Form Y. This gives

$$
\begin{aligned}
sc[l_Y(x)] &= .5[l_Y(x)] - 15 \\
&= .5[.9x + 12.2] - 15 \\
&= .45x - 8.9.
\end{aligned}
$$

For example, a raw score of 74 on Form X converts to a scale score of $.45(74) - 8.9 = 24.4$. In this manner, raw-to-scale score conversions for all Form X raw scores can be found. When another new form is constructed and equated to Form X, a similar process can be used to find the scale score equivalents of scores on this new form.

2.7.2 Truncation of Linear Conversions

When linear transformations are used as scaling transformations, the score scale transformation often needs to be truncated at the upper and/or lower extremes. For example, the Form Y raw-to-scale score transformation, $sc(y) = .5y - 15$, produces scale scores below 1 for raw scores below 32. Suppose that scale scores are intended to be 1 or greater. The transformation for this form then would be as follows:

$$sc(y) = .5y - 15, \quad y \geq 32,$$

56   2. Observed Score Equating Using the Random Groups Design

$$= 1, \qquad y < 32.$$

Also, a raw score of 22 on Form X is equivalent to a raw score of $32 = .9(22) + 12.2$ on Form Y. So, the raw-to-scale score conversion for Form X is

$$\begin{aligned} sc[l_Y(x)] &= .45x - 8.9, & x \geq 22, \\ &= 1, & x < 22. \end{aligned}$$

Truncation can also occur at the top end. For example, truncation would be needed at the top end for Form X but not for Form Y if the highest scale score was set to 35 on this 100-item test (the reader should verify this fact).

Scale scores are typically rounded to integers for reporting purposes. Define sc_{int}, as the scale score rounded to an integer. Then, for example, $sc_{int}[l_Y(x = 74)] = 24$, because a scale score of 24.4 rounds to a scale score of 24.

2.7.3 Nonlinear Conversions

Nonlinear raw-to-scale score transformations are often used in practice. Examples of nonlinear transformations include the following: normalized scales, grade equivalents, and scales constructed to stabilize measurement error variability (see Chapter 9). The use of nonlinear transformations complicates the process of converting raw scores to scale scores. The nonlinear function could be specified as a continuous function. However, when using discrete test scores (e.g., number-correct scores) the function is often defined at selected raw score values, and linear interpolation is used to compute scale score equivalents at other raw score values. The scheme for nonlinear raw-to-scale score transformations that is presented here is designed to be consistent with the definitions of equipercentile equating described earlier.

The first step in describing the process is to specify $sc(y)$, the raw-to-scale score function for Form Y. In the present approach, the conversions of Form Y raw scores to scale scores are specified at Form Y raw scores of $-.5$, $K_Y + .5$, and all integer score points through and including 0 to K_Y. The first two columns of Table 2.8 present an example. As can be seen, each integer raw score on Form Y has a scale score equivalent. For example, the scale score equivalent of a Form Y raw score of 24 is 22.3220. These equivalents resulted from an earlier equating of Form Y.

When Form X is equated to Form Y, the Form Y equivalents are typically noninteger. These noninteger equivalents need to be converted to scale scores, so a procedure is needed to find scale score equivalents of noninteger scores on Form Y. Linear interpolation is used in the present approach. For example, to find the scale score equivalent of a Form Y score of 24.5

TABLE 2.8. Raw-to-Scale Score Conversion Tables.

Raw Score	Form Y Scale Scores		Form X Scale Scores					
			Mean Equating		Linear Equating		Equipercentile	
	sc	sc_{int}	sc	sc_{int}	sc	sc_{int}	sc	sc_{int}
−.5	.5000	1	.5000	1	.5000	1	.5000	1
0	.5000	1	.5000	1	.5000	1	.5000	1
1	.5000	1	.5000	1	.5000	1	.5000	1
2	.5000	1	.5000	1	.5000	1	.5000	1
3	.5000	1	.5000	1	.5000	1	.5000	1
4	.5000	1	.5000	1	.5000	1	.5000	1
5	.6900	1	.5242	1	.5000	1	.5000	1
6	1.6562	2	.8131	1	.5000	1	.5949	1
7	3.1082	3	1.8412	2	.6878	1	1.1874	1
8	4.6971	5	3.3106	3	1.7681	2	2.1098	2
9	6.1207	6	4.8784	5	3.3715	3	3.4645	3
10	7.4732	7	6.2930	6	5.0591	5	4.9258	5
11	8.9007	9	7.6550	8	6.5845	7	6.3678	6
12	10.3392	10	9.0839	9	8.0892	8	7.7386	8
13	11.6388	12	10.5047	11	9.6489	10	9.2622	9
14	12.8254	13	11.7899	12	11.1303	11	10.8456	11
15	14.0157	14	12.9770	13	12.4663	12	12.1050	12
16	15.2127	15	14.1682	14	13.7610	14	13.4491	13
17	16.3528	16	15.3579	15	15.0626	15	14.8738	15
18	17.3824	17	16.4839	16	16.3109	16	16.1515	16
19	18.3403	18	17.5044	18	17.4321	17	17.3912	17
20	19.2844	19	18.4606	18	18.4729	18	18.4958	18
21	20.1839	20	19.3990	19	19.4905	19	19.6151	20
22	20.9947	21	20.2872	20	20.4415	20	20.5533	21
23	21.7000	22	21.0845	21	21.2813	21	21.4793	21
24	22.3220	22	21.7792	22	22.0078	22	22.2695	22
25	22.9178	23	22.3979	22	22.6697	23	22.9353	23
26	23.5183	24	22.9943	23	23.3214	23	23.6171	24
27	24.1314	24	23.5964	24	23.9847	24	24.2949	24
28	24.7525	25	24.2105	24	24.6590	25	24.8496	25
29	25.2915	25	24.8212	25	25.2581	25	25.3538	25
30	25.7287	26	25.3472	25	25.7400	26	25.7841	26
31	26.1534	26	25.7828	26	26.2104	26	26.2176	26
32	26.6480	27	26.2164	26	26.7684	27	26.7281	27
33	27.2385	27	26.7232	27	27.4343	27	27,2908	27
34	27.9081	28	27.3238	27	28.2070	28	27.9216	28
35	28.6925	29	28.0080	28	29.1886	29	28.7998	29
36	29.7486	30	28.8270	29	30.5595	31	30.1009	30
37	31.2010	31	29.9336	30	32.1652	32	31.3869	31
38	32.6914	33	31.3908	31	33.7975	34	32.8900	33
39	34.1952	34	32.8830	33	35.2388	35	34.2974	34
40	35.4615	35	34.3565	34	36.5000	36	35.3356	35
40.5	36.5000	36	34.9897	35	36.5000	36	36.5000	36

58   2. Observed Score Equating Using the Random Groups Design

in Table 2.8, find the scale score that is halfway between the scale score equivalents of Form Y raw scores of 24 (22.3220) and 25 (22.9178). The reader should verify that this value is 22.6199.

Note that scale score equivalents are provided in the table for raw scores of $-.5$ and 40.5. These values provide minimum and maximum scale scores when equipercentile equating is used. (As was indicated earlier, the minimum equated raw score in equipercentile equating is $-.5$ and the maximum is $K_Y + .5$.)

To make the specification of conversion for Form Y to scale scores more explicit, let y_i refer to the i-th point that is tabled. For $-.5 \leq y \leq K_Y + .5$, define y_i^* as the tabled raw score that is the *largest* among the tabled scores that are *less than or equal* to y. In this case, the linearly interpolated raw-to-scale score transformation is defined as

$$\begin{aligned} sc(y) &= sc(y_i^*) + \frac{y - y_i^*}{y_{i+1}^* - y_i^*}[sc(y_{i+1}^*) - sc(y_i^*)], \quad -.5 \leq y \leq K_Y + .5, \\ &= sc(-.5), \quad\quad\quad\quad\quad\quad\quad\quad\quad\quad\quad\quad y < -.5, \\ &= sc(K_Y + .5), \quad\quad\quad\quad\quad\quad\quad\quad\quad\quad y > Ky + .5, \quad (2.22) \end{aligned}$$

where y_{i+1}^* is the *smallest* tabled raw score that is *greater than or equal* to y_i^*. Note that $sc(-.5)$ is the minimum scale score and that $sc(K_Y + .5)$ is the maximum scale score.

To illustrate how this equation works, refer again to Table 2.8. How would the scale score equivalent of a raw score of $y = 18.3$ be found using equation (2.22)? Note that $y_i^* = 18$, because this score is the *largest* tabled score that is *less than or equal* to y. Using equation (2.22),

$$\begin{aligned} sc(y) &= sc(18) + \frac{18.3 - 18}{19 - 18}[sc(19) - sc(18)] \\ &= 17.3824 + \frac{18.3 - 18}{19 - 18}[18.3403 - 17.3824] \\ &= 17.6698. \end{aligned}$$

To illustrate that equation (2.22) is a linear interpolation expression, note that the scale score equivalent of 18 is 17.3824. The scale score 18.3 is, proportionally, .3 of the way between 18 and 19. This .3 value is multiplied by the difference between the scale score equivalents at 19 (18.3403) and at 18 (17.3824). Then .3 times this difference is $.3[18.3403 - 17.3824] = .2874$. Adding .2874 to 17.3824 gives 17.6698.

Typically, the tabled scores used to apply equation (2.22) will be integer raw scores along with $-.5$ and $K_Y + .5$. Equation (2.22), however, allows for more general schemes. For example, scale score equivalents could be tabled at each half raw score, such as $-.5, .0, .5, 1.0$, etc.

In practice, integer scores, which are found by rounding $sc(y)$, are reported to examinees. The third column of the table provides these integer scale score equivalents for integer raw scores (sc_{int}). A raw score of $-.5$

was set equal to a scale score value of .5 and a raw score of 40.5 was set equal to a scale score value of 36.5. These values were chosen so that the minimum possible rounded scale score would be 1 and the maximum 36. In rounding, a convention is used where a scale score that precisely equals an integer score plus .5 rounds up to the next integer score. The exception to this convention is that the scale score is rounded down for the highest scale score, so that 36.5 rounds to 36.

To find the scale score equivalents of the Form X raw scores, the raw scores on Form X are first equated to raw scores on Form Y using equation (2.18). Then, substituting $e_Y(x)$ for y in equation (2.22),

$$sc[e_Y(x)] = sc(y_i^*) + \frac{e_Y(x) - y_i^*}{y_{i+1}^* - y_i^*}[sc(y_{i+1}^*) - sc(y_i^*)], -.5 \leq e_Y(x) \leq K_X + .5. \quad (2.23)$$

In this equation, y_i^* is defined as the *largest* tabled raw score that is *less than or equal to* $e_Y(x)$. This definition of y_i^* as well as the definition of y_{i+1}^* are consistent with their definitions in equation (2.22). The transformation is defined only for the range of Form X scores, $-.5 \leq x \leq K_X + .5$. There is no need to define this function outside this range, because $e_Y(x)$ is defined only in this range in equation (2.17). The minimum and maximum scale scores for Form X are identical to those for Form Y, which occur at $sc[e_Y(x = -.5)]$ and at $sc[e_Y(x = K_X + .5)]$, respectively.

As an example, equation (2.23) is used with the ACT Mathematics equating example. Suppose that the scale score equivalent of a Form X raw score of 24 is to be found using equipercentile equating. In Table 2.7, a Form X raw score of 24 is shown to be equivalent to a Form Y raw score of 23.9157. To apply equation (2.22), note that the largest Form Y raw score in Table 2.8 that is less than 23.9157 is 23. So, $y_i^* = 23$, and $y_{i+1}^* = 24$. From Table 2.8, $sc(23) = 21.7000$ and $sc(24) = 22.3220$. Applying equation (2.22),

$$\begin{aligned}
sc[e_Y(x = 24)] &= sc(23.9157) \\
&= sc(23) + \frac{23.9157 - 23}{24 - 23}[sc(24) - sc(23)] \\
&= 21.7000 + \frac{23.9157 - 23}{24 - 23}[22.3220 - 21.7000] \\
&= 22.2696.
\end{aligned}$$

For a Form X raw score of 24, this value agrees with the value using equipercentile equating in Table 2.8, apart from rounding. Rounding to an integer, $sc_{int}[e_Y(x = 24)] = 22$.

Mean and linear raw score equating results can be converted to nonlinear scale scores by substituting $m_Y(x)$ or $l_Y(x)$ for y in equation (2.22). The raw score equivalents from either the mean or linear methods might fall outside the range of possible Form Y scores. This problem is handled in

TABLE 2.9. Scale Score Moments.

Test Form	$\hat{\mu}_{sc}$	$\hat{\sigma}_{sc}$	$\widehat{sk}_{sc}$	$\widehat{ku}_{sc}$
Form Y				
unrounded	16.5120	8.3812	−.1344	2.0557
rounded	16.4875	8.3750	−.1025	2.0229
Form X Equated to Form Y Scale for Various Methods				
Mean				
unrounded	16.7319	7.6474	−.1868	2.1952
rounded	16.6925	7.5965	−.1678	2.2032
Linear				
unrounded	16.5875	8.3688	−.1168	2.1979
rounded	16.5082	8.3065	−.0776	2.1949
Equipercentile				
unrounded	16.5125	8.3725	−.1300	2.0515
rounded	16.4324	8.3973	−.1212	2.0294

equation (2.22) by truncating the scale scores. For example, if $l_Y(x) < -.5$, then $sc(y) = sc(-.5)$ by equation (2.22). The unrounded and rounded raw-to-scale score conversions for the mean and linear equating results are presented in Table 2.8.

Inspecting the central moments of scale scores can be useful in judging the accuracy of equating. Ideally, after equating, the scale score moments for converted Form X scores would be identical to those for Form Y. However, the moments typically are not identical, in part because the scores are discrete. If equating is successful, then the scale score moments for converted Form X scores should be very similar (say, agree, to at least one decimal place) to the scale score moments for Form Y. Should the Form X moments be compared to the rounded or unrounded Form Y moments? The answer is not entirely clear. However, the approach taken here is to compare the Form X moments to the Form Y unrounded moments. The rationale for this approach is that the unrounded transformation for Form Y most closely defines the score scale for the test, whereas rounding is used primarily to facilitate score interpretability. Following this logic, the use of Form Y unrounded moments for comparison purposes should lead to greater score scale stability when, over time, many forms become involved in the equating process.

Moments are shown in Table 2.9 for Form Y and for Form X using mean, linear, and equipercentile equating. Moments are shown for the unrounded (sc) and rounded (sc_{int}) score transformations. Note that the process of rounding affects the moments for Form Y. Also, the Form X scale score mean for mean equating (both rounded and unrounded) is much larger than the unrounded scale score mean for Form Y. Presumably, the use of a nonlinear raw-to-scale score transformation for Form Y is responsible. When the raw-to-scale score conversion for Form Y is nonlinear, the mean scale score for Form X is typically not equal to the mean scale score for Form Y for mean and linear equating. Similarly, when the raw-to-scale score conversion for Form Y is nonlinear, the standard deviation of the Form X scale scores typically is not equal to the standard deviation of Form Y scale scores for linear equating.

For equipercentile equating, the unrounded moments for Form X are similar to the unrounded moments for Form Y. The rounding process results in the mean of Form X being somewhat low. Is there anything that can be done to raise the mean of the rounded scores? Refer to Table 2.8. In this table, a raw score of 23 converts to an unrounded scale score of 21.4793 and a rounded scale score of 21. If the unrounded converted score had been only .0207 points higher, then the rounded converted score would have been 22. This observation suggests that the rounded conversion might be adjusted to make the moments more similar. Consider adjusting the conversion so that a raw score of 23 converts to a scale score of 22 (instead of 21) and a raw score of 16 converts to a scale score of 14 (instead of 13). The moments for the adjusted conversion are as follows: $\hat{\mu}_{sc} = 16.5165$, $\hat{\sigma}_{sc} = 8.3998$, $\widehat{sk}_{sc} = -.1445$, and $\widehat{ku}_{sc} = 2.0347$. Overall, the moments of the adjusted conversion seem closer to the moments of the original unrounded conversion. For this reason, the adjusted conversion might be used in practice.

Should the rounded conversions actually be adjusted in practice? To the extent that moments for the Form X rounded scale scores are made more similar to the unrounded scale score moments for Form Y, adjusting the conversions would seem advantageous. However, adjusting the conversions might lead to greater differences between the cumulative distributions of scale scores for Form X and Form Y at some scale score points. That is, adjusted conversions lead to less similar percentile ranks of scale scores across the two forms. In addition, adjusted conversions affect the scores of individual examinees.

Because adjusting can lead to less similar scale score distributions, and because it adds a subjective element into the equating process, we typically take a conservative approach to adjusting conversions. A rule of thumb that we often follow is to consider adjusting the conversions only if the moments are closer after adjusting than before adjusting, and the unrounded conversion is within .1 point of rounding to the next higher or lower value (e.g., 21.4793 in the example is within .1 point of rounding to 22). Smoothing methods are considered in Chapter 3, which might eliminate the need to consider subjective adjustments.

In the examples, scale score equivalents of integer raw scores were specified and linear interpolation was used between the integer scores. If more precision is desired, scale score equivalents of fractional raw scores could be specified. The procedures associated with equations (2.22) and (2.23) are expressed in sufficient generality to handle this additional precision. Procedures using nonlinear interpolation also could be developed, although linear interpolation is likely sufficient for practical purposes.

When score scales are established, the highest and lowest possible scale scores are often fixed at particular values. For example, the ACT score scale is said to range from 1 to 36. The approach taken here to scaling when using nonlinear conversions is to fix the ends of the score scale at specific points. Over time, if forms become easier or more difficult, the end points could be adjusted. However, such adjustments would require careful judgment. An alternative procedure involves leaving enough room at the top and bottom of the score scale to handle these problems. For example, suppose that the rounded score scale for an original form is to have a high score of 36 for the first form developed. However, there is a desire to allow scale scores on subsequent forms to go as high as 40 if the forms become more difficult. For the initial Form Y, a scale score of 36 could be assigned to a raw score equal to K_Y and a scale score of 40.5 could be assigned to a raw score equal to $K_Y + .5$. If subsequent forms are more difficult than Form Y, the procedures described here could lead to scale scores as high as 40.5. Of course, alternate interpolation rules could lead to different properties. Rules for nonlinear scaling and equating also might be developed that would allow the highest and lowest scores to float without limit. The approach taken here is to provide a set of equations to be used for nonlinear equating and scaling that can adequately handle, in a consistent manner, many of the situations we have encountered in practice.

One practical problem sometimes occurs when the highest possible raw score does not equate to the highest possible scale score. For the ACT, for example, the highest possible raw score is assigned a scale score value of 36, regardless of the results of the equating. For the SAT (Donlon, 1984, p. 19), the highest possible raw score is assigned a scale score value of 800, and other converted scores are sometimes adjusted, as well.

2.8 Equating Using Single Group Designs

If practice, fatigue, and other order effects do not have an effect on scores, then the statistical process for mean, linear, and equipercentile equating using the single group design (without counterbalancing) is essentially the same as with the random groups design. However, order typically has an affect, and for this reason the single group design (without counterbalancing) is not recommended.

When the single group design with counterbalancing is used, the following four equatings can be conducted:

1. Equate Form X and Form Y using the random groups design for examinees who were administered Form X first and Form Y first.

2. Equate Form X and Form Y using the random groups design for examinees who were administered Form X second and Form Y second.

3. Equate Form X and Form Y using the single group design for examinees who were administered Form X first and Form Y second.

4. Equate Form X and Form Y using the single group design for examinees who were administered Form X second and Form Y first.

Compare equatings 1 and 2. Standard errors of equating described in Chapter 7 can be used as a baseline for comparing the equatings. If the equatings give different results, apart from sampling error, then Forms X and Y are differentially affected by appearing second. In this case, only the first equating should be used. Note that the first equating is a random groups equating, so it is unaffected by order. The problem with using the first equating only is that the sample size might be quite small. However, when differential order effects occur, then equating 1 might be the only equating that would not be biased.

If equatings 1 and 2 give the same results, apart from sampling error, then Forms X and Y are similarly affected by appearing second. In this case, all of the data can be used. One possibility would be to pool all of the Form X data and all of the Form Y data, and equate the pooled distributions. Angoff (1971) and Petersen et al. (1989) provide procedures for linear equating. Holland and Thayer (1990) and von Davier et al. (2003) presented a systematic scheme that is based on statistical tests using log-linear models for equipercentile equating under the single group counterbalanced design.

2.9 Equating Using Alternate Scoring Schemes

The presentation of equipercentile equating and scale scores assumed that the tests to be equated are scored number-correct, with the observed scores ranging from 0 to the number of items. Although this type of scoring scheme is the one that is used most often with educational tests, alternative scoring procedures are becoming much more popular, and the procedures described previously can be generalized to other scoring schemes. For example, whenever raw scores are integer scores that range from 0 to a positive integer value, the procedures can be used directly by defining K as the maximum score on a form, rather than as the number of items on a form as has been done.

Some scoring schemes might produce discrete scores that are not necessarily integers. For example, when tests are scored using a correction for guessing, a fractional score point often is subtracted from the total score whenever an item is answered incorrectly. In this case, raw scores are not integers. However, the discrete score points that can possibly occur are specifiable and equally spaced. One way to conduct equating in this situation is to transform the raw scores. The lowest possible raw score is transformed to a score of 0, the next lowest raw score is transformed to a score of 1, and so on through K, which is defined as the transformed value of the highest possible raw score. The procedures described in this chapter then can be applied and the scores transformed back to their original units.

Equipercentile equating also can be conducted when the scores are considered to be continuous, which might be the case when equating forms of a computerized adaptive test. In many ways, equating in this situation is more straightforward than with discrete scores, because the definitional problems associated with continuization do not need to be considered. Still, difficulties might arise in trying to define score equivalents in portions of the score scale where few examinees earn scores. In addition, even if the range of scores is potentially infinite, the range of scores for which equipercentile equivalents are to be found needs to be considered.

2.10 Preview of What Follows

In this chapter, we described many of the issues associated with observed score equating using the random groups design, including defining methods, describing their properties, and estimating the relationships. We also discussed the relationships between equating and score scales. One of the major relevant issues not addressed in this chapter is the use of smoothing methods to reduce random error in estimating equipercentile equivalents. Smoothing is the topic of Chapter 3. Also, as we show in Chapters 4 and 5, the implementation of observed score equating methods becomes much more complicated when the groups administered the two forms are not randomly equivalent. Observed score methods associated with IRT are described in Chapter 6. Estimating random error in observed score equating is discussed in detail in Chapter 7, and practical issues are discussed in Chapter 8. Scaling and linking are discussed in Chapters 9 and 10

2.11 Exercises

2.1. From Table 2.2 find $P(2.7)$, $P(.2)$, $P^{-1}(25)$, $P^{-1}(97)$.

2.2. From Table 2.2, find the linear and mean conversion equation for converting scores on Form X to the Form Y scale.

2.3. Find the mean and standard deviation of the Form X scores converted to the Form Y scale for the equipercentile equivalents shown in Table 2.3.

2.4. Fill in Table 2.10 and Table 2.11.

TABLE 2.10. Score Distributions for Exercise 2.4.

x	$f(x)$	$F(x)$	$P(x)$	y	$g(y)$	$G(y)$	$Q(y)$
0	.00			0	.00		
1	.01			1	.02		
2	.02			2	.05		
3	.03			3	.10		
4	.04			4	.20		
5	.10			5	.25		
6	.20			6	.20		
7	.25			7	.10		
8	.20			8	.05		
9	.10			9	.02		
10	.05			10	.01		

TABLE 2.11. Equated Scores for Exercise 2.4.

x	$m_Y(x)$	$l_Y(x)$	$e_Y(x)$
0			
1			
2			
3			
4			
5			
6			
7			
8			
9			
10			

2.5. If the standard deviations on Form X and Y are equal, which methods, if any, among mean, linear, and equipercentile will produce the same results? Why?

2.6. Suppose that a raw score of 20 on Form W was found to be equivalent to a raw score of 23.15 on Form X. What would be the scale score

2. Observed Score Equating Using the Random Groups Design

equivalent of a Form W raw score of 20 using the Form X equipercentile conversion shown in Table 2.8?

2.7. Suppose that the linear raw-to-scale score conversion equation for Form Y was $sc(y) = 1.1y + 10$. Also suppose that the linear equating of Form X to Form Y was $l_Y(x) = .8x + 1.2$. What is the linear conversion of Form X scores to scale scores?

2.8. In general, how would the shape of the distribution of Form X raw scores equated to the Form Y raw scale compare to the shape of the original Form X raw score distribution using mean, linear, and equipercentile equating?

3
Random Groups—Smoothing in Equipercentile Equating

As described in Chapter 2, sample statistics are used to estimate equating relationships. For mean and linear equating, the use of sample means and standard deviations in place of the parameters typically leads to adequate equating precision, even when the sample size is fairly small. However, when sample percentiles and percentile ranks are used to estimate equipercentile relationships, equating often is not sufficiently precise for practical purposes because of sampling error.

One indication that considerable error is present in estimating equipercentile equivalents is that score distributions and equipercentile relationships appear irregular when graphed. For example, the equating shown in Figure 2.10 was based on over 4,000 examinees per form. Even with these large sample sizes, the equipercentile relationship is somewhat irregular. Presumably, if very large sample sizes or the entire population were available, score distributions and equipercentile relationships would be reasonably smooth.

Smoothing methods have been developed that produce estimates of the empirical distributions and the equipercentile relationship which will have the smoothness property that is characteristic of the population. In turn, it is hoped that the resulting estimates will be more precise than the unsmoothed relationships. However, the danger in using smoothing methods is that the resulting estimates of the population distributions, even though they are smooth, might be poorer estimates of the population distributions or equating relationship than the unsmoothed estimates. The quality of analytic smoothing methods is an empirical issue and has been the focus of research (Cope and Kolen, 1990; Little and Rubin, 1994; Fairbank,

1987; Hanson et al., 1994; Kolen, 1984). Also, when there are very few score points, the equating relationships can appear irregular, even after smoothing, because of the discreteness issues discussed in Chapter 2. Two general types of smoothing can be conducted: In *presmoothing*, the score distributions are smoothed; in *postsmoothing*, the equipercentile equivalents are smoothed. Smoothing can be conducted by hand or by using analytical methods. Various analytic smoothing techniques are described in this chapter. In addition, we consider various practical issues in choosing among various equating relationships.

3.1 A Conceptual Statistical Framework for Smoothing

A conceptual statistical framework is developed in this section which is intended to provide a framework for distinguishing random error in equipercentile equating from systematic error that is introduced by smoothing. The following discussion considers different sources of equating errors. To be clear that the focus is on a Form X raw score, define x_i as a particular score on Form X. Define $e_Y(x_i)$ as the population equipercentile equivalent at that score, and define $\hat{e}_Y(x_i)$ as the sample estimate. Also assume that $E[\hat{e}_Y(x_i)] = e_Y(x_i)$, where $\mathbf{E}$ is the expectation over random samples. Equating error at a particular score is defined as the difference between the sample equipercentile equivalent and the population equipercentile equivalent. That is, equating error at score x_i for a given equating is

$$[\hat{e}_Y(x_i) - e_Y(x_i)]. \qquad (3.1)$$

Conceive of replicating the equating a large number of times; for each replication the equating is based on two random samples of examinees from a population of examinees who take Form X and Form Y, respectively. Equating error variance at score point x_i is

$$var[\hat{e}_Y(x_i)] = \mathbf{E}[\hat{e}_Y(x_i) - e_Y(x_i)]^2, \qquad (3.2)$$

where the variance is taken over replications. The standard error of equating is defined as the square root of the error variance,

$$se[\hat{e}_Y(x_i)] = \sqrt{var[\hat{e}_Y(x_i)]} = \sqrt{\mathbf{E}[\hat{e}_Y(x_i) - e_Y(x_i)]^2}. \qquad (3.3)$$

The error indexed in equations (3.1)–(3.3) is random error that is due to the sampling of examinees to estimate the population quantity.

A graphic depiction is given in Figure 3.1. In this figure, the Form Y equivalents of Form X scores, indicated by $e_Y(x)$, are graphed. Also, a particular score, x_i, is shown on the horizontal axis. Above x_i, a distribution

A Conceptual Statistical Framework for Smoothing   69

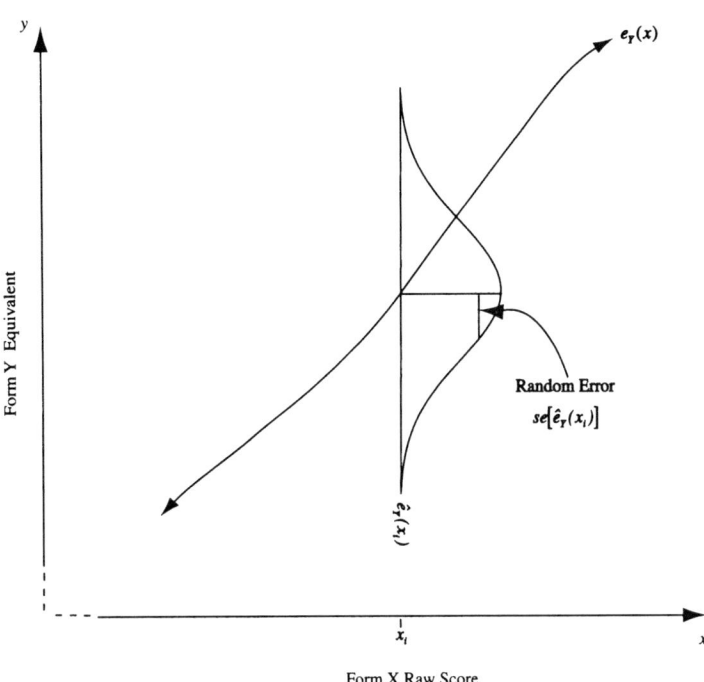

FIGURE 3.1. Schematic plot illustrating random equating error in unsmoothed equipercentile equating.

is plotted that represents estimated Form Y equivalents of x_i over replications of the equating. As can be seen, the mean equivalent falls on the $e_Y(x)$ curve. Random variability, due to the sampling of examinees, is indexed by $se[\hat{e}_Y(x_i)]$. Smoothing methods often can be used to reduce the error variability. Define $\hat{t}_Y(x_i)$ as an alternative estimator of $e_Y(x_i)$ that results from using a smoothing method. Define

$$t_Y(x_i) = \mathbf{E}[\hat{t}_Y(x_i)], \tag{3.4}$$

which is the expected value over replications of the smoothed equating. Defining total error at score x_i as $\hat{t}_Y(x_i) - e_Y(x_i)$, the mean-squared error (mse) in equating at score x_i using the smoothing method is

$$mse[\hat{t}_Y(x_i)] = \mathbf{E}[\hat{t}_Y(x_i) - e_Y(x_i)]^2. \tag{3.5}$$

Random error variability in the smoothed equating relationships is indexed by

$$var[\hat{t}_Y(x_i)] = \mathbf{E}[\hat{t}_Y(x_i) - t_Y(x_i)]^2, \tag{3.6}$$

and

$$se[\hat{t}_Y(x_i)] = \sqrt{var[\hat{t}_Y(x_i)]}.$$

Systematic error, or bias, in equating using smoothing is defined as

$$bias[t_Y(x_i)] = t_Y(x_i) - e_Y(x_i). \tag{3.7}$$

Total error can be partitioned into random error and systematic error components as follows:

$$\begin{array}{rl} \hat{t}_Y(x_i) - e_Y(x_i) = & [\hat{t}_Y(x_i) - t_Y(x_i)] + [t_Y(x_i) - e_Y(x_i)]. \\ \{\text{Total Error}\} & \{\text{Random Error}\} \quad \{\text{Systematic Error}\} \end{array}$$

In terms of squared quantities,

$$\begin{aligned} mse[\hat{t}_Y(x_i)] &= var[\hat{t}_Y(x_i)] + \{bias[t_Y(x_i)]\}^2 \\ &= \mathbf{E}[\hat{t}_Y(x_i) - t_Y(x_i)]^2 + [t_Y(x_i) - e_Y(x_i)]^2. \end{aligned} \tag{3.8}$$

Thus, when using a smoothing method, total error in equating is the sum of random error and systematic error components. Smoothing methods are designed to produce smooth functions which contain less random error than that for unsmoothed equipercentile equating. However, smoothing methods can introduce systematic error. The intent in using a smoothing method is for the increase in systematic error to be more than offset by the decrease in random error. Then the total error using the smoothing method is less than that for the unsmoothed equivalents. That is, smoothing at score point x_i is useful to the degree that $mse[\hat{t}_Y(x_i)]$ is less than $var[\hat{e}_Y(x_i)]$.

Refer to Figure 3.2 for a graphic description. In this figure, the Form Y equivalents of Form X scores, indicated by $e_Y(x)$, are graphed as they were

A Conceptual Statistical Framework for Smoothing 71

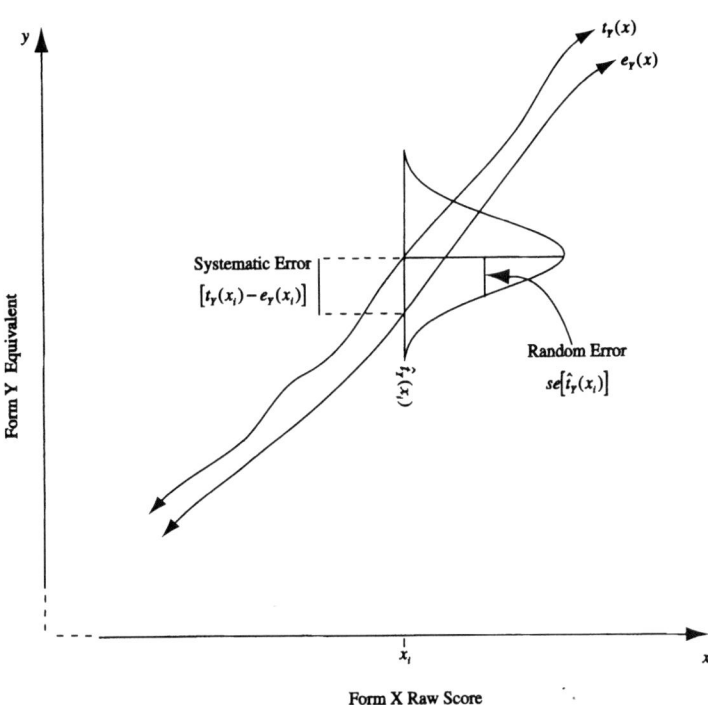

FIGURE 3.2. Schematic plot illustrating systematic and random equating error in smoothed equipercentile equating.

in Figure 3.1. Also, $t_Y(x)$ is graphed and differs from $e_Y(x)$. This difference at x_i is referred to as "Systematic Error" in the graph. The distribution plotted above x_i represents Form Y equivalents of x_i over replications of the smoothed equating. The random variability due to sampling of examinees is indexed by $se[\hat{t}_Y(x_i)]$. Compare the random error component in Figure 3.2 to that in Figure 3.1, which presents random equating error without smoothing. This comparison suggests that the smoothing method results in less random equating error at score x_i than does the unsmoothed equipercentile equating. Thus, the smoothing method reduces random error but introduces systematic error.

The preceding discussion focused on equating error at a single score point. Overall indexes of error can be obtained by summing each of the error components over score points. In this case, the goal of smoothing can be viewed as reducing mean-squared (total) error in estimating the population equipercentile equivalents over score points.

3.2 Properties of Smoothing Methods

Mean and linear equating methods can be viewed as smoothing methods that estimate the equipercentile relationship. In some situations, these methods can lead to less total error in estimating the equipercentile equivalents than equipercentile equating. For example, what if the score distributions for Form X and Form Y are identical in shape (i.e., they differ only in mean and standard deviation)? In this case, the population linear equating and equipercentile equating relationships are identical. For samples of typical size, linear equating will produce less total error in estimating equipercentile equivalents than equipercentile equating when the distributions are the same shape, because less random error is associated with linear equating than with equipercentile equating (see Chapter 7). Even if the distribution shapes are only similar, linear methods might still produce less total error in estimating equipercentile equivalents than equipercentile equating for small samples.

A smoothing method should possess certain desirable characteristics for it to be useful in practice. First, the method should produce *accurate* estimates of the population distributions or equipercentile equivalents. That is, the method should not systematically distort the relationship in a manner that has negative practical consequences. Second, the method should be *flexible* enough to handle the variety of distributions and equipercentile relationships that are found in practice. Third, there should be a *statistical framework* for studying fit. Fourth, the method should improve estimation, as shown by an *empirical research* base. Fortunately, there are analytic smoothing methods that share these characteristics.

Three types of presmoothing methods have been considered for use in equating. One type of method estimates the relative frequency at a score point by averaging the relative frequency at a score point with relative frequencies at surrounding score points. These *rolling average* or *kernel methods* were reviewed by Kolen (1991) and include the Cureton and Tukey (1951) method. Kolen (1991) indicated that these methods often lead to estimated distributions that appear bumpy or are systematically distorted. Although these methods have been found to improve estimation, the improvement is less than for some other methods. For these reasons, rolling average methods are not described further here. Rather, a *log-linear* method and a *strong true score method* for presmoothing are described next. As will be described later in this chapter, these methods have been studied empirically through simulation and have been shown to improve estimation of test score distributions (Kolen, 1991). A postsmoothing method that uses *cubic splines* is also described. The postsmoothing method also has been shown, empirically, to improve estimation (Fairbank, 1987; Kolen, 1984). In addition, Hanson et al. (1994) demonstrated, empirically, that the presmoothing and postsmoothing methods described here improve estimation of equipercentile equivalents to a similar extent. The methods that are described possess the four characteristics of smoothing methods that were described earlier: they have been shown to produce accurate results, they are flexible, they are associated with a statistical framework for studying fit, and they can improve estimation as shown by an empirical research base.

3.3 Presmoothing Methods

In presmoothing methods, the score distribution is smoothed. In smoothing the distributions, accuracy in estimating the distributions is crucial. One important property that relates closely to accuracy is *moment preservation*. In moment preservation, the smoothed distribution has at least some of the same central moments as the observed distribution. For example, a method preserves the first two central moments if the mean and standard deviation of the smoothed distribution are the same as the mean and standard deviation of the unsmoothed distribution.

One presmoothing method uses a polynomial log-linear model with polynomial contrasts to smooth score distributions. The second method is a strong true score model. In strong true score models, a general distributional form is specified for true scores. A distributional form is also specified for error given true score. For both methods, after the distributions are smoothed, Form X is equated to Form Y using the smoothed distributions and equipercentile equating. This equating relationship along with

74   3. Random Groups—Smoothing in Equipercentile Equating

the raw-to-scale score transformation for Form Y are used to convert Form X scores to scale scores.

3.3.1 Polynomial Log-Linear Method

Log-linear models that take into account the ordered property of test scores can be used to estimate test score distributions. The method considered here fits polynomial functions to the log of the sample density. This model was described by Darroch and Ratcliff (1972), Haberman (1974a,b, 1978), and Rosenbaum and Thayer (1987). Holland and Thayer (1987, 2000) presented a thorough description of this model including algorithms for estimation, properties of the estimates, and applications to fit test score distributions. The polynomial log-linear method fits a model of the following form to the distribution:

$$\log[N_X f(x)] = \omega_0 + \omega_1 x + \omega_2 x^2 + \cdots + \omega_C x^C. \quad (3.9)$$

In this equation, the log of the density is expressed as a lower-order polynomial of degree C. For example, if $C = 2$, then $\log[N_X]f(x) = \omega_0 + \omega_1 x + \omega_2 x^2$, and the model is a polynomial of degree 2 (quadratic). The ω parameters in the model can be estimated by the method of maximum likelihood. Note that the use of logarithms allows for log-linear models to be additive as in equation (3.9).

The resulting fitted distribution has the moment preservation property that the first C moments of the fitted distribution are identical to those of the sample distribution. For example, if $C = 2$, then the mean and standard deviation of the fitted distribution are identical to the mean and standard deviation of the sample distribution. Holland and Thayer (1987) described algorithms for maximum likelihood estimation with this method. Some statistical packages for log-linear models (e.g., the LOGLINEAR procedure of SPSS-X) can also be used. The *RAGE-RGEQUATE* computer program described in Appendix B also can be used.

The choice of C is an important consideration when using this method. The fitted distribution can be compared, subjectively, to the empirical distribution. Because this method uses a log-linear model, the statistical methods that have been developed for assessing the fit of these models also can be used. In one procedure, likelihood ratio chi-square goodness-of-fit statistics are calculated for each C that is fit and can be tested for significance. In addition, because the models are hierarchical, likelihood ratio difference chi-squares can be tested for significance. For example, the difference between the overall likelihood ratio chi-square statistics for $C = 2$ and $C = 3$ can be compared to a chi-square table with one degree of freedom. A significant difference would suggest that the model with more terms (e.g., $C = 3$) fits the data better than the model with fewer terms (e.g., $C = 2$). In model selection, preference might be given to the simplest model that adequately fits the distribution, under the presumption that models which are more complicated than necessary might lead to excess equating error. A structured procedure that uses the likelihood ratio difference chi-squares to choose C is described by Haberman (1974a) and Hanson (1990). Holland and Thayer (2000) provide other statistical procedures that can be used to assess the fit of the log-linear method.

Because multiple significance tests are involved, these procedures should be used in combination with the inspection of graphs and central moments, and previous experience in choosing a degree of smoothing. When inspecting graphs, the investigator tries to judge whether the fitted distribution is smooth and does not depart too much from the empirical distribution. Refer to Bishop et al. (1975) for a general description of model fitting procedures for log-linear models.

3.3.2 Strong True Score Method

Unlike the log-linear method, strong true score methods require the use of a parametric model for true scores. Lord (1965) developed a procedure, referred to here as the *beta4 method*, to estimate the distribution of true scores. This procedure also results in a smooth distribution of observed scores, which is the primary reason that Lord's (1965) method is of interest here. In the development of the beta4 procedure, a parametric form is assumed for the population distribution of proportion-correct true scores, $\psi(\tau)$. Also, a conditional parametric form is assumed for the distribution of observed score given true score, $f(x|\tau)$. Then the observed score distribution can be written as follows:

$$f(x) = \int_0^1 f(x|\tau)\psi(\tau)\,d\tau. \qquad (3.10)$$

In the beta4 method proposed by Lord (1965) the true score distribution, $\psi(\tau)$, was assumed to be four-parameter beta. The four-parameter beta has two parameters that allow for a wide variety of shapes for the distribution. For example, the four-parameter beta can be skewed positively or negatively, and it can even be U-shaped. The four-parameter beta also has parameters for the high- and low–proportion-correct true scores that are within the range of zero to one. The conditional distribution of observed score given true score, $f(x|\tau)$, was assumed by Lord (1965) to be either binomial or compound binomial. Lord (1965) provided a two-term approximation to the compound binomial method that is usually used in implementing the method. The score distribution, $f(x)$, that results from the use of equation (3.10) in combination with the model assumptions just described is referred to as the *four-parameter beta compound binomial distribution* or the *beta4 distribution*. This distribution can take on a wide variety of forms.

Lord (1965) presented a procedure for estimating this distribution and the associated true score distribution by the method of moments. This estimation procedure uses the number of items, the first four central moments (mean, standard deviation, skewness, and kurtosis) of the sample distribution, and a parameter Lord referred to as k. Lord's k can be estimated directly from the coefficient alpha reliability coefficient. Hanson (1991b) also described the estimation procedure in detail. He described situations in which the method of moments leads to invalid parameter values, such as an upper limit for proportion-correct true scores above 1, and provided procedures for dealing with them.

One important property of this method is that the first four central moments of the fitted distribution agree with those of the sample distribution, provided there are no invalid parameter estimates. Otherwise, fewer than four central moments agree. For example, suppose that the method of moments using the first four central moments produces invalid parameter values. Then the method described by Hanson (1991b) fits the distribution using the method of moments so that the first three central moments agree, and the fourth moment of the fitted distribution is as close as possible to the fourth moment of the observed distribution.

As with the log-linear model, the fit of the model can be evaluated by comparing plots and central moments of the sample and fitted distributions. Statistical methods also can be used. A standard chi-square goodness-of-fit statistic can be calculated, as suggested by Lord (1965). Assuming that all score points are included in the calculation of the chi-square statistic, the degrees of freedom are the number of score points ($K + 1$, to account for a score of 0), minus 1, minus the number of parameters fit. For the beta4 method, the degrees of freedom are $K - 4 = (K + 1) - 1 - 4$.

There are some other strong true score methods that are related to the beta4 method. One simplification of the beta4 method is the *beta-binomial* or *negative hypergeometric distribution* described by Keats and Lord (1962). One difference between this model and the Lord (1965) model is that the two-parameter beta distribution is used for true scores. The two-parameter beta distribution is identical to a four-parameter beta distribution with the highest and lowest proportion-correct true scores set at 1 and 0, respectively. The beta-binomial model uses a binomial distribution for the distribution of observed score given true score. The beta-binomial distribution fits a narrower range of distributions than the beta4 distribution. For example, the beta-binomial distribution cannot be negatively skewed if the mean is less than one-half the items correct. Kolen (1991) concluded that the beta-binomial is not flexible enough to be used in typical equating applications. Carlin and Rubin (1991) studied a special case of the beta4 method that fits three moments, and found that it fit considerably better than the beta-binomial model. Little and Rubin (1994) studied and extend beta binomial model and found that it and the log-linear method improved estimation.

Lord (1969) generalized the beta4 distribution. In this generalization, the parametric form of the true score distribution was not specified. Lord (1969, 1980) referred to the resulting procedure as *Method 20*. Method 20 is more flexible than the beta4 method. For example, Method 20 can produce a variety of multimodal distributions. However, Lord (1969) indicated that Method 20 requires sample sizes of at least 10,000 examinees per form, which makes it impractical in most equating situations.

Another related approach fits continuous distributions to discrete test score distributions. Brandenburg and Forsyth (1974) fit a (continuous) four-parameter beta distribution directly to sample observed test score distributions and concluded that it fit very well. Use of this procedure eliminates further need for a continuization step in equipercentile equating. Although not presented in detail here, fitting of continuous distributions in equating deserves further investigation.

3.3.3 Illustrative Example

The ACT Mathematics example that was considered in the previous chapter is used to illustrate the presmoothing methods. The computer program *RAGE-RGEQUATE* described in Appendix B was used to conduct the equating. The first step in applying these methods is to fit the raw score distributions. The smoothed distributions (indicated by solid symbols) for Form Y are shown in Figure 3.3 along with the unsmoothed distributions. The distributions for Form X are shown in Figure 3.4. The beta4 and selected log-linear smoothed distributions are shown. In fitting the beta4 method for Form X, fitting all 4 moments resulted in invalid parameter estimates, so only the first 3 moments were fit. The beta4 model was fit setting Lord's $k = 0$.

Visual inspection suggests that the beta4 method fits the distributions of both forms very well. The log-linear method with $C = 2$ appears to fit both distributions poorly. For Form X and Form Y, $C = 6$ appears to fit the distributions well. The $C = 10$ smoothings appear to slightly overfit the distributions for both forms in the score range of 23–30, in that the fitted distributions are a bit irregular. These irregularities, along with the observation that the statistical tests indicate that values of C greater than 6 do not improve the fit, suggest that $C = 10$ might be fitting aspects of the distributions that are due to sampling error.

Summary statistics for the fitted distributions are shown in Table 3.1 for Form Y and Form X. Because of the moment preservation property of the beta4 method, the first 3 or 4 moments of the fitted distribution for this method agree with those for the sample distribution. Only 3 moments could be fit using the beta4 method with Form X, so the kurtosis for the beta4 method differs from the kurtosis for the sample data. However, this difference in kurtosis values is small (2.3024 for the sample distribution and 2.2806 for the fitted distribution). For both distributions, the chi-square

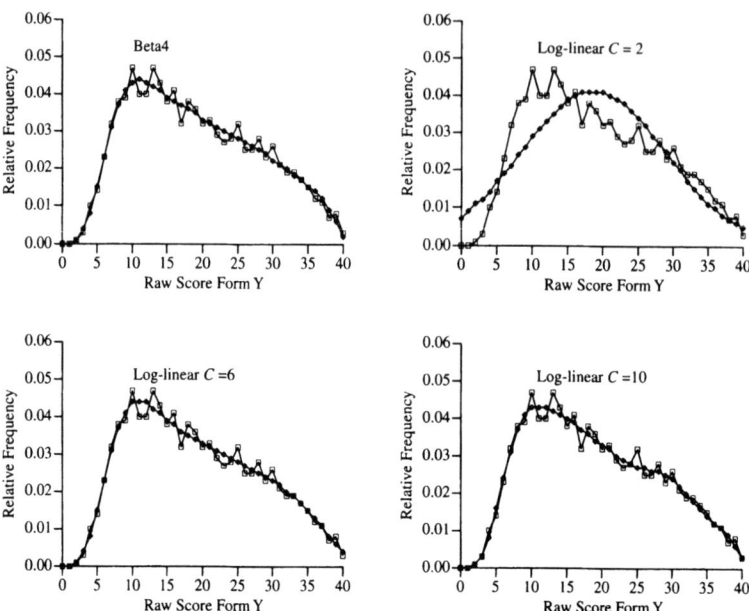

FIGURE 3.3. Presmoothing Form Y distribution.

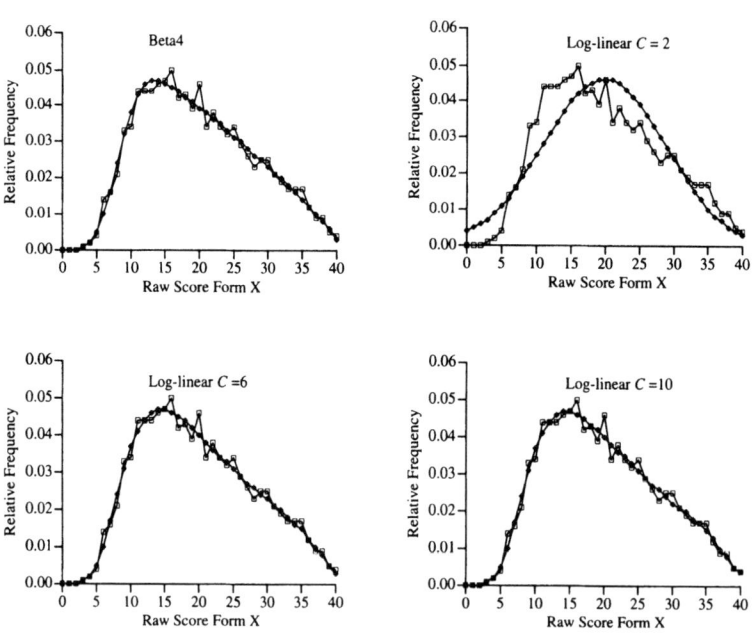

FIGURE 3.4. Presmoothing Form X distribution.

TABLE 3.1. Moments and Fit Statistics for Presmoothing.

Form	Method	$\hat{\mu}$	$\hat{\sigma}$	$\hat{sk}$	$\hat{ku}$	$\chi^2(df)$	$\chi^2_C - \chi^2_{C+1}$
Y	Sample	18.9798	8.9393	.3527	2.1464		
	Beta4	18.9798	8.9393	.3527	2.1464	31.64(36)	
	Log-linear						
	$C = 10$	18.9798	8.9393	.3527	2.1464	25.92(30)	
	$C = 9$	18.9798	8.9393	.3527	2.1464	26.38(31)	.46
	$C = 8$	18.9798	8.9393	.3527	2.1464	27.00(32)	.62
	$C = 7$	18.9798	8.9393	.3527	2.1464	28.30(33)	1.30
	$C = 6$	18.9798	8.9393	.3527	2.1464	29.45(34)	1.15
	$C = 5$	18.9798	8.9393	.3527	2.1464	39.31(35)	9.86
	$C = 4$	18.9798	8.9393	.3527	2.1464	61.53(36)	22.22
	$C = 3$	18.9798	8.9393	.3527	2.5167	318.66(37)	257.13
	$C = 2$	18.9798	8.9393	.0709	2.3851	489.47(38)	170.81
	$C = 1$	18.9798	11.8057	.1037	1.8134	1579.99(39)	1090.52
X	Sample	19.8524	8.2116	.3753	2.3024		
	Beta4[a]	19.8524	8.2116	.3753	2.2806	33.97(37)	
	Log-linear						
	$C = 10$	19.8524	8.2116	.3753	2.3024	29.68(30)	
	$C = 9$	19.8524	8.2116	.3753	2.3024	29.91(31)	.23
	$C = 8$	19.8524	8.2116	.3753	2.3024	29.94(32)	.03
	$C = 7$	19.8524	8.2116	.3753	2.3024	30.40(33)	.46
	$C = 6$	19.8524	8.2116	.3753	2.3024	30.61(34)	.20
	$C = 5$	19.8524	8.2116	.3753	2.3024	35.78(35)	5.18
	$C = 4$	19.8524	8.2116	.3753	2.3024	40.80(36)	5.01
	$C = 3$	19.8524	8.2116	.3753	2.6565	212.82(37)	172.02
	$C = 2$	19.8524	8.2116	.0082	2.5420	445.19(38)	232.36
	$C = 1$	19.8524	11.8316	.0150	1.7989	2215.02(39)	1769.83

[a] Only 3 moments could be fit using the beta4 method with Form X.

statistic, $\chi^2(df)$ for the beta4 method is less than its degrees of freedom, indicating a reasonable fit.

The log-linear method was fit using values of C ranging from 1 to 10 for both forms. Because of the moment preservation property of the log-linear method, the first 4 moments of the fitted distribution for $C \geq 4$ agree with those for the sample distribution, 3 moments agree for $C = 3$, and fewer moments agree for lower values of C.

Two likelihood ratio χ^2 statistics are presented in the table. The model selection strategy here is to use the significance tests to rule out models. Models that are not ruled out by any of the significance tests then are considered further. Preference is given to the simplest model that is not ruled out, under the presumption that the simplest model which adequately fits the distribution leads to less estimation error than more complicated models. The inspection of plots of the smoothed distributions also is considered in the process of choosing models for further consideration. In model fitting situations such as those considered here, significance tests are viewed more as providing a guide for choosing a model than as a means for providing a definitive decision rule.

The difference statistic, $\chi^2_C - \chi^2_{C+1}$, is a one degree of freedom χ^2 that is the difference between the overall χ^2 at C and the overall χ^2 at $C+1$. A significant difference suggests that the model with parameter $C+1$ improves the fit over the model with parameter C. This type of difference χ^2 often is used in fitting hierarchical log-linear models like the one described here. In using the $\chi^2_C - \chi^2_{C+1}$ statistic, a value of C is chosen that is one greater than the largest value of C that has a significant χ^2. For both distributions, using a nominal .05 level, the value at $C = 5$ is the highest value with a significant χ^2 (i.e., $\chi^2 > 3.84$), suggesting that $C \geq 6$ should be considered further. Note that, according to Haberman (1974), the experiment-wise significance level over 9 significance tests with a nominal .05 level is less than or equal to $.3698 = 1 - (1 - .05)^9$.

The term $\chi^2(df)$ test is an overall goodness-of-fit test that compares the fitted model to the empirical distribution. A significant χ^2 suggests that the model does not fit the observed data. For Form Y, the overall χ^2 is significant at the nominal .05 level for $C \leq 4$, suggesting that $C \geq 5$ should be considered further. For Form X, the overall χ^2 is significant at the .05 level for $C \leq 3$, suggesting that $C \geq 4$ should be considered further. (Note that, at the .05 level, the χ^2 critical values range from 43.8 to 54.6, approximately.)

The fit for $C = 6$ is the minimum value of C (the simplest model) that appears to meet both of the significance test criteria for both Form X and Form Y. The smoothed distributions shown in Figures 3.3 and 3.4 for $C = 6$ also appear to fit well. The models using $C = 6$ for Form X and $C = 6$ for Form Y are examined further.

After fitting the distributions, equipercentile methods are used to equate Form X and Form Y. The equipercentile relationships are presented in Table 3.2 and are graphed in Figure 3.5 for the beta4 method and the log-linear method with $C = 6$ in the same format that was used in Figure 2.10. Figure 3.5 also shows the identity equating and unsmoothed relationships. In addition, ±1 standard error bands are shown. These bands were calculated using standard errors of unsmoothed equipercentile equating that are described in Chapter 7. The upper part of the bands were formed by adding one standard error of equipercentile equating to the unsmoothed relationship. The lower part of the bands were formed by subtracting one standard error. For equating to be adequate, a sensible standard is that the smoothed relationship should lie predominantly within the standard error band.

The equipercentile relationship shown for the beta4 method falls within the standard error band except at Form X raw scores of 1, 2, 7, and 39. These scores are extreme, with few examinees earning any of the scores.

TABLE 3.2. Raw-to-Raw Score Conversions for Presmoothing.

Form X Score	Standard Error	Form Y Equivalent Using Equating Method		
		Unsmoothed	Beta4	Log-Linear $C = 6$
0	1.9384	.0000	−.4581	.4384
1	.8306	.9796	.1063	.1239
2	.5210	1.6462	.8560	.9293
3	.8210	2.2856	1.7331	1.8264
4	.2950	2.8932	2.6380	2.7410
5	.1478	3.6205	3.5517	3.6573
6	.2541	4.4997	4.4434	4.5710
7	.1582	5.5148	5.3311	5.4725
8	.1969	6.3124	6.2572	6.3577
9	.1761	7.2242	7.2121	7.2731
10	.1731	8.1607	8.1931	8.2143
11	.1952	9.1827	9.2010	9.1819
12	.1800	10.1859	10.2367	10.1790
13	.2311	11.2513	11.3003	11.2092
14	.2431	12.3896	12.3892	12.2750
15	.2138	13.3929	13.4985	13.3764
16	.2764	14.5240	14.6263	14.5111
17	.2617	15.7169	15.7633	15.6784
18	.3383	16.8234	16.9047	16.8638
19	.2826	18.0092	18.0470	18.0566
20	.2947	19.1647	19.1880	19.2469
21	.3299	20.3676	20.3258	20.4262
22	.3183	21.4556	21.4589	21.5911
23	.3865	22.6871	22.5890	22.7368
24	.3555	23.9157	23.7131	23.8595
25	.3013	25.0292	24.8287	24.9594
26	.3683	26.1612	25.9347	26.0374
27	.3532	27.2633	27.0296	27.0954
28	.3069	28.1801	28.1124	28.1357
29	.3422	29.1424	29.1817	29.1606
30	.2896	30.1305	30.2362	30.1729
31	.3268	31.1297	31.2743	31.1749
32	.3309	32.1357	32.2945	32.1691
33	.3048	33.0781	33.2951	33.1576
34	.3080	34.0172	34.2741	34.1424
35	.3044	35.1016	35.2296	35.1250
36	.3240	36.2426	36.1603	36.1064
37	.2714	37.1248	37.0669	37.0873
38	.3430	38.1321	37.9553	38.0676
39	.2018	39.0807	38.8442	39.0462
40	.2787	39.9006	39.7984	40.0202

82 3. Random Groups—Smoothing in Equipercentile Equating

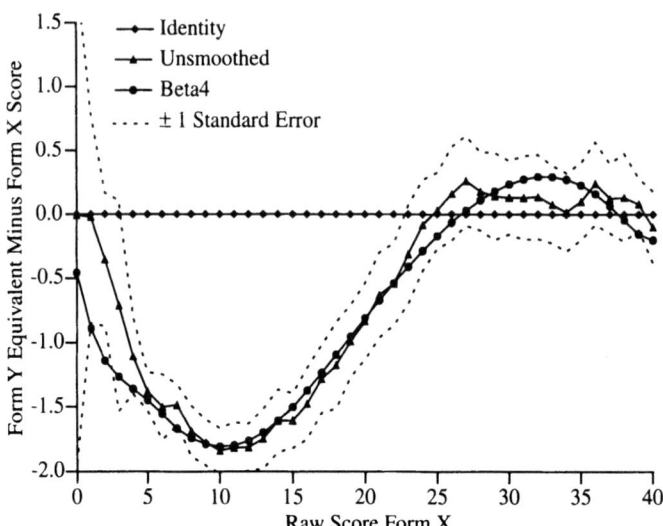

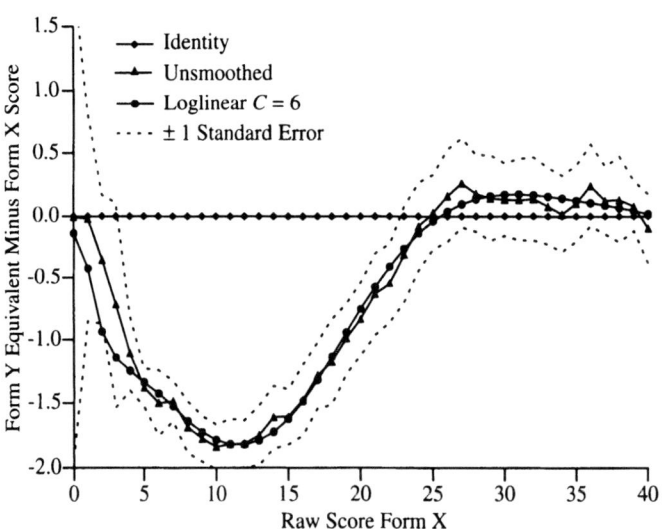

FIGURE 3.5. Raw-to-raw score equivalents for presmoothing.

TABLE 3.3. Raw Score Moments for Presmoothing.

Test Form	$\hat{\mu}$	$\hat{\sigma}$	$\widehat{sk}$	$\widehat{ku}$
Form Y	18.9798	8.9393	.3527	2.1464
Form X	19.8524	8.2116	.3753	2.3024
Form X Equated to Form Y Scale				
Unsmoothed	18.9799	8.9352	.3545	2.1465
Beta4	18.9805	8.9307	.3556	2.1665
Log-linear $C = 6$	18.9809	8.9354	.3541	2.1464

Because there are few examinees at these scores, and standard errors of equipercentile equating are poorly estimated at the extremes, these scores can be disregarded and the fit for the beta4 method appears to be adequate. The equipercentile relationship shown for the log-linear method with $C = 6$ is within the standard error band at all scores except at a Form X raw score of 2. The log-linear equivalents are, in general, closer to the unsmoothed relationship than those for the beta4 method. Because the log-linear method results in a smooth curve that is closer to the unsmoothed relationship, it might be viewed as somewhat superior to that for the beta4 method in this case. Because the relationship for both methods appears smooth without departing too far from the unsmoothed relationship, equating using either method seems adequate.

Summary statistics for the raw-to-raw equipercentile equating using these two presmoothing methods are presented in Table 3.3. The moments for the two smoothed methods are very similar to those for Form Y, again suggesting that both of the smoothings were adequate.

The next step in equating is to convert the raw scores on Form X to scale scores, as was done in Table 2.8. Scale score moments are shown in Table 3.4, and the raw-to-scale score conversions are shown in Table 3.5. The unsmoothed moments and equivalents are identical to the values shown previously in Chapter 2. The moments for the unrounded scale scores all appear to be very similar to those for the unrounded scale scores for Form Y. Also, the moments for the rounded scale scores for the beta4 method appear to be similar to those for the unrounded scale scores for Form Y. However, the mean for the rounded log-linear method (16.5461) appears to be somewhat larger than the mean for the Form Y unrounded equivalents (16.5120). This observation suggests that it might be desirable to consider adjusting the rounded raw-to-scale score conversion for the log-linear method, as was done in Chapter 2. Refer to Table 3.5. For the log-linear method, a raw score of 23 converts to a scale score of 21.5143, which rounds to a 22. If the raw score of 23 is converted to a scale score of 21 instead of a scale score of 22, then the moments are as follows: $\hat{\mu}_{sc} = 16.5121$,

TABLE 3.4. Scale Score Moments for Presmoothing.

Test Form	$\hat{\mu}_{sc}$	$\hat{\sigma}_{sc}$	$\widehat{sk}_{sc}$	$\widehat{ku}_{sc}$
Form Y				
unrounded	16.5120	8.3812	−.1344	2.0557
rounded	16.4875	8.3750	−.1025	2.0229
Form X Equated to Form Y Scale				
Unsmoothed				
unrounded	16.5125	8.3725	−.1300	2.0515
rounded	16.4324	8.3973	−.1212	2.0294
Beta4				
unrounded	16.5230	8.3554	−.1411	2.0628
rounded	16.4999	8.3664	−.1509	2.0549
Log-linear $C = 6$				
unrounded	16.5126	8.3699	−.1294	2.0419
rounded	16.5461	8.3772	−.1289	2.0003

$\hat{\sigma}_{sc} = 8.3570$, $\widehat{sk}_{sc} = -.1219$, and $\widehat{ku}_{sc} = 2.0142$. After adjustment, the mean is closer to the unrounded mean for Form Y. However, the standard deviation and skewness are farther away. Because the mean is more often given primary attention and the other moments are still reasonably close to the Form Y unrounded moments, the adjustment appears to improve the equating. However, the results without adjustment also appear to be acceptable. As was indicated in Chapter 2, adjustment of conversions should be done conservatively, because it affects score distributions and individual scores.

3.4 Postsmoothing Methods

In postsmoothing methods, the equipercentile equivalents, $\hat{e}_Y(x)$, are smoothed directly. Postsmoothing methods fit a curve to the equipercentile relationship. In implementing postsmoothing methods, the smoothed relationship should appear smooth without departing too much from the observed relationship. The method to be described was presented by Kolen (1984) and makes use of cubic smoothing splines described by Reinsch (1967). The spline fitting algorithm was also described by de Boor (1978, pp. 235–243). Polynomials also could be used, but cubic splines are used instead because they appear to provide greater flexibility.

TABLE 3.5. Raw-to-Scale Score Conversions for Presmoothing.

Raw Score	Form Y Scale Scores		Form X Scale Scores					
			Unsmoothed		Beta4		Log-linear $C = 6$	
	sc	sc_{int}	sc	sc_{int}	sc	sc_{int}	sc	sc_{int}
−.5	.5000	1	.5000	1	.5000	1	.5000	1
0	.5000	1	.5000	1	.5000	1	.5000	1
1	.5000	1	.5000	1	.5000	1	.5000	1
2	.5000	1	.5000	1	.5000	1	.5000	1
3	.5000	1	.5000	1	.5000	1	.5000	1
4	.5000	1	.5000	1	.5000	1	.5000	1
5	.6900	1	.5000	1	.5000	1	.5000	1
6	1.6562	2	.5949	1	.5842	1	.6084	1
7	3.1082	3	1.1874	1	1.0100	1	1.1465	1
8	4.6971	5	2.1098	2	2.0296	2	2.1756	2
9	6.1207	6	3.4645	3	3.4451	3	3.5421	4
10	7.4732	7	4.9258	5	4.9720	5	5.0022	5
11	8.9007	9	6.3678	6	6.3925	6	6.3667	6
12	10.3392	10	7.7386	8	7.8111	8	7.7287	8
13	11.6388	12	9.2622	9	9.3327	9	9.2016	9
14	12.8254	13	10.8456	11	10.8450	11	10.6965	11
15	14.0157	14	12.1050	12	12.2303	12	12.0855	12
16	15.2127	15	13.4491	13	13.5709	14	13.4337	13
17	16.3528	16	14.8738	15	14.9294	15	14.8277	15
18	17.3824	17	16.1515	16	16.2441	16	16.1975	16
19	18.3403	18	17.3912	17	17.4274	17	17.4367	17
20	19.2844	19	18.4958	18	18.5178	19	18.5734	19
21	20.1839	20	19.6151	20	19.5775	20	19.6678	20
22	20.9947	21	20.5533	21	20.5560	21	20.6631	21
23	21.7000	22	21.4793	21	21.4101	21	21.5143	22
24	22.3220	22	22.2695	22	22.1436	22	22.2346	22
25	22.9178	23	22.9353	23	22.8158	23	22.8936	23
26	23.5183	24	23.6171	24	23.4791	23	23.5412	24
27	24.1314	24	24.2949	24	24.1498	24	24.1906	24
28	24.7525	25	24.8496	25	24.8131	25	24.8256	25
29	25.2915	25	25.3538	25	25.3710	25	25.3617	25
30	25.7287	26	25.7841	26	25.8290	26	25.8021	26
31	26.1534	26	26.2176	26	26.2891	26	26.2399	26
32	26.6480	27	26.7281	27	26.8219	27	26.7479	27
33	27.2385	27	27.2908	27	27.4361	27	27.3441	27
34	27.9081	28	27.9216	28	28.1230	28	28.0198	28
35	28.6925	29	28.7998	29	28.9350	29	28.8245	29
36	29.7486	30	30.1009	30	29.9815	30	29.9032	30
37	31.2010	31	31.3869	31	31.3006	31	31.3312	31
38	32.6914	33	32.8900	33	32.6247	33	32.7931	33
39	34.1952	34	34.2974	34	33.9609	34	34.2539	34
40	35.4615	35	35.3356	35	35.2062	35	35.4871	35
40.5	36.5000	36	36.5000	36	36.5000	36	36.5000	36

3. Random Groups—Smoothing in Equipercentile Equating

For integer scores, x_i, the spline function is,

$$\hat{d}_Y(x) = v_{0i} + v_{1i}(x - x_i) + v_{2i}(x - x_i)^2 + v_{3i}(x - x_i)^3,$$
$$x_i \le x < x_i + 1. \quad (3.11)$$

The weights $(v_{0i}, v_{1i}, v_{2i}, v_{3i})$ change from one score point to the next, so that there is a different cubic equation defined between each integer score. At each score point, x_i, the cubic spline is continuous (continuous second derivatives). The spline is fit over the range of scores x_{low} to x_{high}, $0 \le x_{low} \le x \le x_{high} \le K_X$, where x_{low} is the lower integer score in the range and x_{high} is the upper integer score in the range.

The function, over score points, is minimized subject to having minimum curvature and satisfying the following constraint:

$$\frac{\sum_{i=low}^{high} \left[\frac{\hat{d}_Y(x_i) - \hat{e}_Y(x_i)}{\widehat{se}[\hat{e}_Y(x_i)]}\right]^2}{x_{high} - x_{low} + 1} \le S. \quad (3.12)$$

In this equation, the summation is over those points for which the spline is fit. The term $\widehat{se}[\hat{e}_Y(x_i)]$ is the estimated standard error of equipercentile equating, which is defined specifically in Chapter 7. The standard error of equating is used to standardize the differences between the unsmoothed and smoothed relationships. The use of the standard error results in the smoothed and unsmoothed relationships being closer where the standard error is small, and allows them to be farther apart when the standard error is large. The parameter S (where $S \ge 0$) is set by the investigator and controls the degree of smoothing. Several values of S typically are tried and the results compared.

If $S = 0$, then the fitted spline equals the unsmoothed equivalents at all integer score points. If S is very large, then the spline function is a straight line. Intermediate values of S produce a nonlinear function that deviates from the unsmoothed equipercentile relationship by varying degrees. If $S = 1$ then the average squared standardized difference between the smoothed and unsmoothed equivalents is 1.0. Values of S between 0 and 1 have been found to produce adequate results in practice.

The spline is fit over a restricted range of score points so that scores with few examinees and large or poorly estimated standard errors do not unnecessarily influence the spline function. Kolen (1984) recommended that x_{low} and x_{high} be chosen to exclude score points with percentile ranks below .5 and above 99.5.

A linear interpolation procedure that is consistent with the definition of equipercentile equating in Chapter 2 can be used to obtain equivalents outside the range of the spline function. The following equations can be used for linear interpolation outside the range:

$$\hat{d}_Y(x) = \left\{\frac{[\hat{d}_Y(x_{low}) + .5]}{x_{low} + .5}\right\}x$$

$$+ \left\{-.5 + \frac{.5[\hat{d}_Y(x_{low}) + .5]}{x_{low} + .5}\right\}, \quad -.5 \leq x < x_{low},$$

$$\hat{d}_Y(x) = \left\{\frac{[\hat{d}_Y(x_{high}) - (K_Y + .5)]}{x_{high} - (K_X + .5)}\right\}x$$

$$+ \left\{\hat{d}_Y(x_{high}) - \frac{x_{high}[\hat{d}_Y(x_{high}) - (K_Y + .5)]}{x_{high} - (K_X + .5)}\right\},$$

$$x_{high} < x \leq (K_X + .5). \quad (3.13)$$

At the lower end, linear interpolation is between the point $(-.5, -.5)$ and $[x_{low}, \hat{d}_Y(x_{low})]$. At the upper end, linear interpolation is between the point $[x_{high}, \hat{d}_Y(x_{high})]$ and $(K_X + .5, K_Y + .5)$.

Table 3.6 illustrates a cubic spline function that was fit to the ACT Mathematics data using $S = .20$. For this example, the spline function is defined over the Form X raw score range from 5 to 39. The second column shows the spline conversion at Form X integer scores. Equation (3.11) is used to find smoothed values at noninteger scores that are needed for equating. For example, to find the estimated Form Y equivalent of a Form X score of 6.3, note that $x_i = 6$ and $(x - x_i) = (6.3 - 6.0) = .3$. Then,

$$\hat{d}_Y(6.3) = 4.4379 + .9460(.3) + .0013(.3)^2 + .0005(.3)^3 = 4.7218.$$

To illustrate that the spline is continuous, note that the tabled value for a score of $x_i = 7$ is 5.3857. This spline function at 7 also can be obtained using $x = 7$ and $x_i = 6$ as follows. In this case, $(x - x_i) = (7 - 6) = 1$. Applying the cubic equation,

$$\hat{d}_Y(7) = 4.4379 + .9460(1) + .0013(1) + .0005(1) = 5.3857,$$

which equals the tabled value for $x_i = 7$. Also, the sum of the coefficients in any row equals the value of $\hat{d}_Y(x_i)$ shown in the next row. This equality property is necessary if the spline is to be continuous.

In addition, the spline has continuous second derivatives evaluated at all score points. The second derivative of the spline function evaluated at x in equation (3.11) can be shown to equal $2v_{2i} + 6v_{3i}(x - x_i)$. The second derivative evaluated at a score of 7 using the coefficients at $x_i = 6$ is

$$2(.0013) + 6(.0005)(7 - 6) = .0056.$$

The second derivative evaluated at a score of 7 using the coefficients at $x_i = 7$ is

$$2(.0028) + 6(.0009)(7 - 7) = .0056.$$

TABLE 3.6. Spline Coefficients for Converting Form X Scores to the Form Y Scale for $S = .20$.

x	$\hat{d}_Y(x) = \hat{v}_0$	$\hat{v}_1$	$\hat{v}_2$	$\hat{v}_3$	$\widehat{se}[\hat{e}_Y(x)]$	$\left[\dfrac{\hat{d}_Y(x)-\hat{e}_Y(x)}{\widehat{se}[\hat{e}_Y(x)]}\right]^2$
5	3.4927	.9447	.0000	.0004	.1478	.7418
6	4.4379	.9460	.0013	.0005	.2541	.0597
7	5.3857	.9502	.0028	.0009	.1582	.6680
8	6.3397	.9585	.0055	.0008	.1969	.0198
9	7.3046	.9721	.0081	.0006	.1761	.2095
10	8.2854	.9902	.0100	.0003	.1731	.5165
11	9.2859	1.0112	.0110	.0001	.1952	.2779
12	10.3082	1.0336	.0114	−.0001	.1800	.4609
13	11.3531	1.0560	.0110	−.0003	.2311	.1952
14	12.4197	1.0770	.0101	−.0003	.2431	.0149
15	13.5066	1.0963	.0091	−.0005	.2138	.2823
16	14.6114	1.1129	.0076	−.0006	.2764	.1000
17	15.7313	1.1263	.0058	−.0006	.2617	.0030
18	16.8627	1.1359	.0039	−.0006	.3383	.0138
19	18.0019	1.1419	.0020	−.0006	.2826	.0006
20	19.1451	1.1439	.0001	−.0006	.2947	.0046
21	20.2885	1.1423	−.0018	−.0006	.3299	.0581
22	21.4285	1.1370	−.0035	−.0005	.3183	.0075
23	22.5615	1.1285	−.0051	−.0005	.3865	.1054
24	23.6844	1.1169	−.0065	−.0003	.3555	.4244
25	24.7945	1.1028	−.0076	−.0002	.3013	.6057
26	25.8895	1.0872	−.0080	.0000	.3683	.5434
27	26.9687	1.0712	−.0080	.0002	.3532	.6943
28	28.0321	1.0557	−.0075	.0003	.3069	.2322
29	29.0806	1.0416	−.0066	.0003	.3422	.0322
30	30.1159	1.0294	−.0056	.0003	.2896	.0024
31	31.1401	1.0192	−.0046	.0003	.3268	.0010
32	32.1551	1.0111	−.0036	.0003	.3309	.0033
33	33.1630	1.0050	−.0026	.0003	.3048	.0778
34	34.1657	1.0006	−.0018	.0001	.3080	.2331
35	35.1646	.9974	−.0014	.0001	.3044	.0423
36	36.1607	.9949	−.0011	.0001	.3240	.0645
37	37.1547	.9931	−.0007	.0001	.2714	.0120
38	38.1473	.9921	−.0003	.0001	.3430	.0020
39	39.1392				.2018	.0832

The equality of these two expressions illustrates the continuous second derivative property of the cubic spline. This property can be shown to hold at the other score points as well.

The rightmost column in Table 3.6 shows the squared standardized difference at each score point. The mean of the values in this column is .20, because $S = .20$.

One problem with the spline expression in equations (3.11) and (3.12) is that it is a regression function, so it is not symmetric. That is, the spline that is used for converting Form X to Form Y is different from the spline that is used for converting Form Y to Form X. To arrive at a function that is more nearly symmetric, define $\hat{d}_X(y)$ as the spline function that converts Form Y scores to Form X scores using the same procedures and the same value of S. Assuming that the inverse function exists, define the inverse of this function as $\hat{d}_X^{-1}(x)$. (Note that the inverse is not guaranteed to exist, although the lack of an inverse has not been known to cause problems in practice.) This inverse can be used to transform Form X scores to the Form Y scale. A more nearly symmetric equating function then can be defined as the average of two splines: the spline developed for converting Form X to the Form Y scale and the inverse of the spline developed for converting Form Y to the Form X scale. For a particular S, define this quantity as

$$\hat{d}_Y^*(x) = \frac{\hat{d}_Y(x) + \hat{d}_X^{-1}(x)}{2}, -.5 \leq x \leq K_X + .5. \quad (3.14)$$

The expression in equation (3.14) is the final estimate of the equipercentile equating function. (See Wang and Kolen, 1996, for a further discussion of symmetry and for an alternative postsmoothing method to the one described here.)

To implement the method, the equating is conducted using a variety of values of S. Graphs of the resulting equivalents can be examined for smoothness and compared to the unsmoothed equivalents. Standard errors of equating can be very useful for evaluating various degrees of smoothing. Ideally, the procedure results in a smooth function that does not depart too much from the unsmoothed equivalents. In addition, the central moments for the Form X scores equated to the Form Y scale using smoothing should be compared to those for the Form Y scores. Central moments for the scale scores that result from the equating also should be inspected.

3.4.1 Illustrative Example

Because there are no statistical tests associated with the postsmoothing method described here, inspection of graphs and moments is even more crucial for choosing a degree of smoothing than in the presmoothing methods. For the ACT Mathematics example, equating was conducted using eight different values for S ranging from .01 to 1.0. The *RAGE-RGEQUATE* computer program described in Appendix B was used to conduct the analyses. The equipercentile relationships using these methods are presented in Table 3.7 and graphed in Figures 3.6 and 3.7.

As can be seen in the figures, the equivalents deviate more from the unsmoothed equivalents as the values of S increase. For $S = .01$, the smoothed and unsmoothed equivalents are very close, and the smoothed equivalents appear to be bumpy. However, the smoothed equivalents are within the standard error bands. For $S = .05$, the equivalents appear to be smooth and are within the standard error bands at all points. As S increases, the smoothed relationship continues to deviate more from the unsmoothed relationship. For $S \geq .75$, the smoothed relationship is outside the standard error bands at many score points. The relationship for $S = .05$ appears to be the one for which there is the least amount of smoothing required to achieve a smooth function of the values tried. The relationship for $S = .10$ also seems acceptable.

Moments for the smoothed relationships are shown in Table 3.8. As S increases, the moments for the smoothed equipercentile equating depart more from the Form Y moments. This result suggests that lower values of S are to be preferred for this example.

Now consider Form X scale score equivalents. Scale score moments are shown in Table 3.9 for the scale score equivalents shown in Tables 3.10 and 3.11. An asterisk indicates the moment that is closest, among the smoothed results, to the Form Y unrounded equivalents. The rounded mean and standard deviation are closest for the $S = .05$ conversion, and the other moments also are fairly close.

As indicated in Chapter 2, scale scores that are reported to examinees are rounded. The rounded conversion is shown in Table 3.11. Asterisks in this table indicate score points where adjacent smoothing values convert to different scale scores. For example, a Form X raw score of 9 converts to a scale score of 3 for $S = .01$ and to a scale score of 4 for $S = .05$. As can be seen, this is the only difference in the rounded conversions between these two degrees of smoothing. Sometimes, there are gaps in the conversion table that can be removed by adjusting the conversion. Other times, adjustments can be used to improve the scale score moments. In this example, adjustment of conversions does not seem warranted.

All things considered, the results from these procedures suggest that $S = .05$ is the most appropriate of the values tried. However, this example should not be overgeneralized. The smallest smoothing values do not always appear to produce the most adequate equating. Especially for the rounded conversions, higher values of S often lead to more adequate results. There is no single statistical criterion that can be used. Instead, various values of S need to be tried and the results compared.

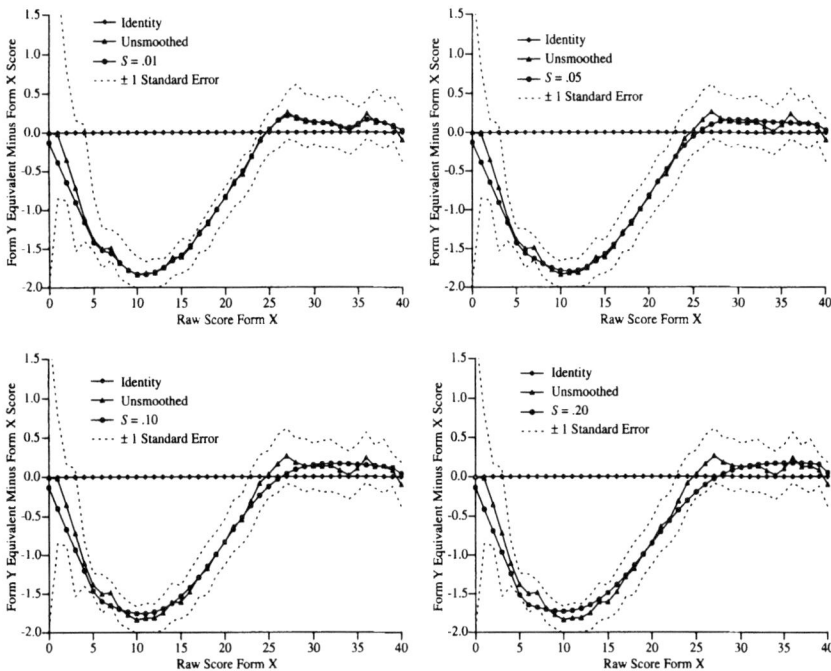

FIGURE 3.6. Raw-to-raw equivalents for postsmoothing, $S = .01, .05, .10, .20$.

3.5 Practical Issues in Equipercentile Equating

As was indicated earlier, the purpose of smoothing in equipercentile equating is to reduce equating error. However, there is a danger that smoothing will introduce equating error. Provided next are guidelines to help ensure that smoothing improves the equating process. Guidelines for the sample sizes needed to produce adequate equating are considered subsequently.

3.5.1 Summary of Smoothing Strategies

The strategies for presmoothing and postsmoothing that were illustrated in this chapter have much in common, although the strategies differ. The focus in presmoothing is on finding a method for smoothing score distributions, whereas the focus in postsmoothing is on choosing among degrees of smoothing of the equipercentile relationship. Another difference is that statistical tests can be used with the presmoothing method, whereas no statistical tests exist for the postsmoothing method. The following are the steps in the smoothing strategies that have been discussed. Step 1 is used only with presmoothing. Differences between presmoothing and postsmoothing strategies are highlighted.

TABLE 3.7. Raw-to-Raw Score Conversions for Postsmoothing.

Form X Score	No Smooth	Form Y Equivalent							
		$S=.01$	$S=.05$	$S=.10$	$S=.20$	$S=.30$	$S=.50$	$S=.75$	$S=1.00$
0	.000	−.129	−.129	−.133	−.138	−.141	−.146	−.150	−.154
1	.980	.614	.612	.600	.586	.577	.563	.550	.539
2	1.646	1.356	1.353	1.333	1.311	1.295	1.272	1.250	1.232
3	2.286	2.098	2.094	2.067	2.035	2.013	1.981	1.950	1.925
4	2.893	2.841	2.835	2.800	2.759	2.731	2.690	2.650	2.618
5	3.620	3.583	3.576	3.534	3.484	3.449	3.398	3.350	3.311
6	4.500	4.480	4.440	4.400	4.354	4.322	4.273	4.225	4.185
7	5.515	5.443	5.372	5.349	5.323	5.305	5.277	5.249	5.226
8	6.312	6.324	6.306	6.302	6.296	6.292	6.284	6.276	6.269
9	7.224	7.218	7.252	7.265	7.278	7.286	7.297	7.306	7.313
10	8.161	8.168	8.216	8.243	8.271	8.290	8.317	8.342	8.362
11	9.183	9.166	9.205	9.241	9.281	9.308	9.347	9.385	9.415
12	10.186	10.195	10.221	10.262	10.309	10.342	10.390	10.436	10.474
13	11.251	11.260	11.266	11.307	11.357	11.392	11.445	11.496	11.538
14	12.390	12.345	12.338	12.375	12.424	12.460	12.513	12.565	12.607
15	13.393	13.419	13.434	13.467	13.511	13.544	13.594	13.642	13.683
16	14.524	14.541	14.553	14.579	14.616	14.643	14.686	14.728	14.763
17	15.717	15.695	15.692	15.710	15.736	15.756	15.788	15.820	15.848
18	16.823	16.846	16.846	16.855	16.868	16.879	16.898	16.918	16.936
19	18.009	18.005	18.011	18.010	18.008	18.009	18.013	18.020	18.026
20	19.165	19.171	19.183	19.170	19.153	19.143	19.132	19.123	19.118
21	20.368	20.337	20.356	20.330	20.298	20.278	20.251	20.228	20.211
22	21.456	21.499	21.525	21.485	21.439	21.409	21.368	21.331	21.303
23	22.687	22.695	22.685	22.630	22.572	22.534	22.480	22.432	22.393
24	23.916	23.890	23.826	23.761	23.694	23.650	23.586	23.528	23.481
25	25.029	25.045	24.945	24.873	24.802	24.754	24.685	24.619	24.566
26	26.161	26.160	26.037	25.966	25.894	25.846	25.774	25.704	25.648
27	27.263	27.214	27.101	27.038	26.971	26.924	26.853	26.783	26.725
28	28.180	28.197	28.140	28.091	28.033	27.990	27.922	27.855	27.798
29	29.142	29.161	29.160	29.127	29.080	29.042	28.982	28.920	28.867
30	30.130	30.138	30.166	30.150	30.115	30.084	30.033	29.979	29.932
31	31.130	31.126	31.162	31.162	31.139	31.117	31.076	31.032	30.994
32	32.136	32.107	32.154	32.166	32.156	32.141	32.113	32.081	32.052
33	33.078	33.075	33.144	33.165	33.166	33.160	33.144	33.125	33.108
34	34.017	34.065	34.136	34.161	34.171	34.173	34.171	34.167	34.161
35	35.102	35.112	35.130	35.155	35.174	35.183	35.195	35.205	35.213
36	36.243	36.165	36.126	36.148	36.174	36.191	36.217	36.242	36.263
37	37.125	37.156	37.120	37.140	37.172	37.197	37.237	37.278	37.313
38	38.132	38.125	38.114	38.131	38.169	38.202	38.256	38.313	38.362
39	39.081	39.092	39.103	39.117	39.155	39.188	39.243	39.297	39.341
40	39.901	40.031	40.034	40.039	40.052	40.063	40.081	40.099	40.114

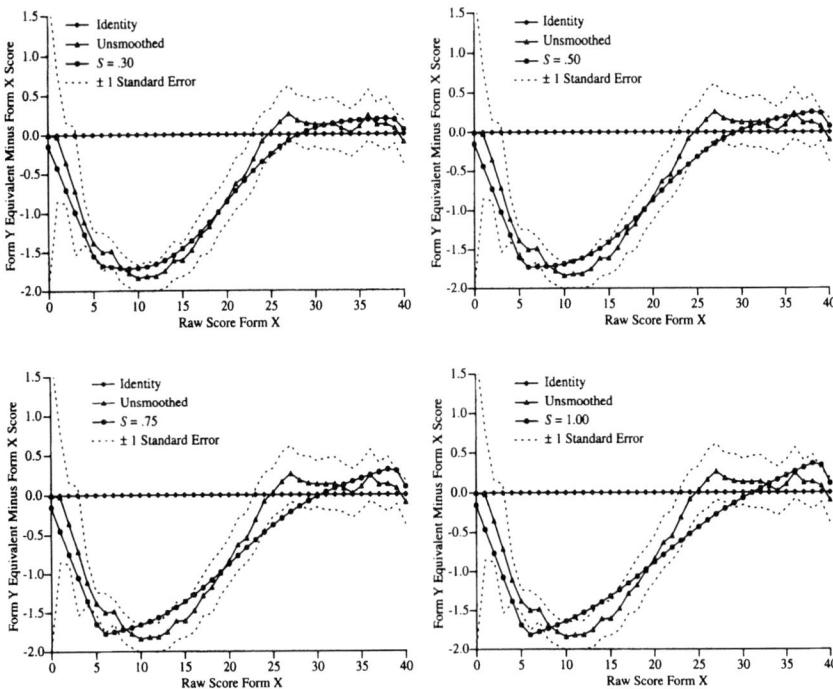

FIGURE 3.7. Raw-to-raw equivalents for postsmoothing, $S = .30, .50, .75, 1.00$.

Step 1. Fit the score distributions (presmoothing only). The strategy used for fitting the score distributions involves both graphic inspection and the use of statistical indices. For the log-linear method

(a) Examine graphs of the fitted versus the sample distribution. For an adequate fit, the fitted distribution should be smooth without departing more than necessary from the sample distribution.

(b) Examine $\chi_C^2 - \chi_{C+1}^2$. Choose a degree among those that are fit which is larger than the largest value of C that has a significant χ^2.

(c) Examine the overall χ^2 fit statistic. The degree chosen should not be significant.

Ideally, a degree of smoothing would be chosen that meets all of these criteria. When fitting the beta4 method, only (a) and (c) are used. Also, when the sample size is very large, minor differences between models might be significant. This issue needs to be considered when setting the overall significance level. This model selection strategy needs to be applied with caution and not followed too rigidly in practice. More than one acceptable set of values for C for the log-linear model can be chosen and evaluated in subsequent steps.

94   3. Random Groups—Smoothing in Equipercentile Equating

TABLE 3.8. Raw Score Moments for Postsmoothing.

Test Form	$\hat{\mu}$	$\hat{\sigma}$	$\widehat{sk}$	$\widehat{ku}$
Form Y	18.9798	8.9393	.3527	2.1464
Form X	19.8524	8.2116	.3753	2.3024
Form X Equated to Form Y Scale				
Unsmoothed	18.9799	8.9352	.3545	2.1465
$S = .01$	18.9789*	8.9393*	.3533*	2.1488*
$S = .05$	18.9767	8.9313	.3561	2.1587
$S = .10$	18.9743	8.9172	.3603	2.1738
$S = .20$	18.9717	8.8987	.3644	2.1922
$S = .30$	18.9699	8.8852	.3670	2.2054
$S = .50$	18.9676	8.8643	.3704	2.2258
$S = .75$	18.9656	8.8439	.3733	2.2457
$S = 1.00$	18.9642	8.8271	.3756	2.2624

*Indicates moment closest to Form Y moment among smoothed estimates.

Step 2. Construct the raw-to-raw equivalents. For presmoothing, construct the equipercentile equivalents for the models from Step 1. For postsmoothing, construct the equipercentile equivalents for the degrees of smoothing that are to be evaluated.

(a) Examine the graphs of the raw-to-raw equivalents. For smoothing to be adequate, the relationship should be smooth without departing too much from the unsmoothed equivalents, as indicated by the standard error bands.

(b) Examine the moments of the equated raw scores. The moments of the Form X equated raw scores should be close to those for Form Y.

Models that are judged to produce adequate results are considered further.

Step 3. Construct the raw-to-scale score equivalents.. For presmoothing, construct the equivalents for the methods chosen in Step 1. For postsmoothing, construct the equivalents for various degrees of smoothing that are to be considered further.

(a) Examine the moments for the unrounded scale scores. The moments for the Form X scale scores should not be too different from the moments for the Form Y scale scores.

(b) Examine the moments for the rounded Form X scale scores. The moments for the Form X rounded scale scores should be similar to the moments for the unrounded Form Y scales scores.

TABLE 3.9. Scale Score Moments for Postsmoothing.

Test Form	$\hat{\mu}_{sc}$	$\hat{\sigma}_{sc}$	$\widehat{sk}_{sc}$	$\widehat{ku}_{sc}$
Form Y				
unrounded	16.5120	8.3812	−.1344	2.0557
rounded	16.4875	8.3750	−.1025	2.0229
Form X Equated to Form Y Scale for				
Unsmoothed				
unrounded	16.5125	8.3725	−.1300	2.0515
rounded	16.4324	8.3973	−.1212	2.0294
$S = .01$				
unrounded	16.5120*	8.3758*	−.1303*	2.0543*
rounded	16.4823	8.4164	−.1308*	2.0334
$S = .05$				
unrounded	16.5158	8.3638	−.1302	2.0606
rounded	16.5156*	8.3648*	−.1164	2.0262
$S = .10$				
unrounded	16.5236	8.3475	−.1294	2.0737
rounded	16.5366	8.3223	−.1308	2.0597*
$S = .20$				
unrounded	16.5336	8.3284	−.1289	2.0908
rounded	16.5345	8.2576	−.1103	2.0859
$S = .30$				
unrounded	16.5409	8.3152	−.1287	2.1034
rounded	16.5345	8.2576	−.1103	2.0859
$S = .50$				
unrounded	16.5523	8.2956	−.1288	2.1229
rounded	16.5551	8.2288	−.0907	2.1525
$S = .75$				
unrounded	16.5635	8.2770	−.1292	2.1423
rounded	16.5211	8.2165	−.0804	2.1632
$S = 1.00$				
unrounded	16.5731	8.2619	−.1297	2.1586
rounded	16.5211	8.2165	−.0804	2.1632

* Indicates moment closest to unrounded for Form Y among smoothed estimates.

TABLE 3.10. Unrounded Raw-to-Scale Score Conversions for Postsmoothing.

Form X Score	No Smooth	Form Y Equivalent $S=.01$	$S=.05$	$S=.10$	$S=.20$	$S=.30$	$S=.50$	$S=.75$	$S=1.00$
0	.500	.500	.500	.500	.500	.500	.500	.500	.500
1	.500	.500	.500	.500	.500	.500	.500	.500	.500
2	.500	.500	.500	.500	.500	.500	.500	.500	.500
3	.500	.500	.500	.500	.500	.500	.500	.500	.500
4	.500	.500	.500	.500	.500	.500	.500	.500	.500
5	.500	.500	.500	.500	.500	.500	.500	.500	.500
6	.595	.591	.584	.576	.567	.561	.552	.543	.535
7	1.187	1.118	1.049	1.027	1.002	.985	.958	.931	.908
8	2.110	2.126	2.101	2.095	2.087	2.080	2.069	2.057	2.046
9	3.464	3.455	3.508	3.529	3.550	3.562	3.579	3.595	3.606
10	4.926	4.936	5.004	5.043	5.084	5.110	5.148	5.184	5.213
11	6.368	6.346	6.398	6.447	6.501	6.537	6.591	6.641	6.682
12	7.739	7.752	7.789	7.847	7.914	7.961	8.030	8.095	8.149
13	9.262	9.274	9.284	9.342	9.414	9.465	9.541	9.614	9.674
14	10.846	10.787	10.778	10.827	10.891	10.937	11.006	11.073	11.129
15	12.105	12.136	12.154	12.193	12.246	12.284	12.343	12.401	12.449
16	13.449	13.469	13.484	13.515	13.559	13.591	13.642	13.692	13.734
17	14.874	14.848	14.844	14.866	14.897	14.920	14.959	14.997	15.030
18	16.152	16.177	16.178	16.188	16.202	16.215	16.236	16.259	16.279
19	17.391	17.387	17.393	17.392	17.390	17.391	17.395	17.401	17.408
20	18.496	18.501	18.513	18.501	18.485	18.476	18.465	18.457	18.452
21	19.615	19.588	19.605	19.582	19.552	19.534	19.510	19.489	19.474
22	20.553	20.588	20.610	20.577	20.539	20.515	20.482	20.452	20.429
23	21.479	21.485	21.477	21.439	21.398	21.371	21.333	21.299	21.272
24	22.270	22.254	22.214	22.173	22.131	22.104	22.065	22.028	21.999
25	22.935	22.945	22.885	22.842	22.800	22.771	22.730	22.691	22.659
26	23.617	23.616	23.541	23.498	23.455	23.426	23.382	23.341	23.307
27	24.295	24.264	24.194	24.155	24.114	24.085	24.041	23.998	23.963
28	24.850	24.859	24.828	24.802	24.770	24.746	24.704	24.662	24.627
29	24.354	25.362	25.361	25.347	25.326	25.310	25.282	25,248	25.220
30	25.784	25.787	25.799	25.792	25.777	25.764	25.743	25.719	25.699
31	26.218	26.216	26.234	26.233	26.222	26.211	26.191	26.169	26.151
32	26.728	26.711	26.739	26.746	26.740	26.731	26.715	26.696	26.679
33	27.291	27.289	27.335	27.349	27.350	27.345	27.335	27.322	27.311
34	27.922	27.959	28.015	28.034	28.042	28.044	28.043	28.039	28.034
35	28.800	28.811	28.830	28.856	28.876	28.886	28.899	28.909	29.917
36	30.101	29.988	29.931	29.964	30.001	30.026	30.064	30.100	30.131
37	31.387	31.433	31.380	31.410	31.457	31.494	31.554	31.615	31.667
38	32.890	32.879	32.863	32.889	32.946	32.995	33.076	33.161	33.235
39	34.297	34.311	34.326	34.343	34.391	34.434	34.503	34.571	34.627
40	35.336	35.525	35.533	35.542	35.569	35.592	35.630	35.667	35.698

TABLE 3.11. Rounded Raw-to-Scale Score Conversions for Postsmoothing.

Form X Score	Form Y Equivalent								
	No Smooth	$S = .01$	$S = .05$	$S = .10$	$S = .20$	$S = .30$	$S = .50$	$S = .75$	$S = 1$
0	1	1	1	1	1	1	1	1	1
1	1	1	1	1	1	1	1	1	1
2	1	1	1	1	1	1	1	1	1
3	1	1	1	1	1	1	1	1	1
4	1	1	1	1	1	1	1	1	1
5	1	1	1	1	1	1	1	1	1
6	1	1	1	1	1	1	1	1	1
7	1	1	1	1	1	1	1	1	1
8	2	2	2	2	2	2	2	2	2
9	3	3*	4	4	4	4	4	4	4
10	5	5	5	5	5	5	5	5	5
11	6	6	6	6*	7	7	7	7	7
12	8	8	8	8	8	8	8	8	8
13	9	9	9	9	9	9*	10	10	10
14	11	11	11	11	11	11	11	11	11
15	12	12	12	12	12	12	12	12	12
16	13	13	13*	14	14	14	14	14	14
17	15	15	15	15	15	15	15	15	15
18	16	16	16	16	16	16	16	16	16
19	17	17	17	17	17	17	17	17	17
20	18*	19	19	19*	18	18	18	18	18
21	20	20	20	20	20	20	20*	19	19
22	21	21	21	21	21	21*	20	20	20
23	21	21	21	21	21	21	21	21	21
24	22	22	22	22	22	22	22	22	22
25	23	23	23	23	23	23	23	23	23
26	24	24	24*	23	23	23	23	23	23
27	24	24	24	24	24	24	24	24	24
28	25	25	25	25	25	25	25	25	25
29	25	25	25	25	25	25	25	25	25
30	26	26	26	26	26	26	26	26	26
31	26	26	26	26	26	26	26	26	26
32	27	27	27	27	27	27	27	27	27
33	27	27	27	27	27	27	27	27	27
34	28	28	28	28	28	28	28	28	28
35	29	29	29	29	29	29	29	29	29
36	30	30	30	30	30	30	30	30	30
37	31	31	31	31	31	31	32	32	32
38	33	33	33	33	33	33	33	33	33
39	34	34	34	34	34	34*	35	35	35
40	35*	36	36	36	36	36	36	36	36

* Indicates a different conversion obtained for adjacent methods.

98   3. Random Groups—Smoothing in Equipercentile Equating

(c) Consider adjusting the rounded raw-to-scale score equivalents for Form X. If the moments for the Form X rounded scale scores are not close enough to the moments for the unrounded Form Y scale scores, then different adjustments of the conversion should be considered.

The strategy described might result in more than one method or degree of smoothing being adequate, and various subjective judgments could be made. Such judgments are necessarily dependent on the testing program in which the equating is being done. General rules of thumb do not seem possible, because testing programs vary so much in their sample sizes, distribution shapes, numbers of items, and other relevant characteristics. However, rules of thumb for a particular testing program often can be developed after some experience with the program.

3.5.2 Equating Error and Sample Size

Holland et al. (1989) and von Davier et al. (2003) developed standard error formulas for equipercentile equating using log-linear presmoothing. Standard error formulas have not been derived for the other smoothing methods, although the bootstrap methods (Efron and Tibshirani, 1993) (to be described in Chapter 7) can be used. There is no general analytic procedure for estimating systematic error. Technically, the estimation of both types of error is necessary to thoroughly evaluate the effects of smoothing.

Hanson et al. (1994) conducted an empirical comparison of the presmoothing and postsmoothing methods that are presented here. In this study, empirical score distributions were smoothed. The smoothed distributions were assumed to be the population distributions. Random samples of a given size then were drawn from the population distributions. Equipercentile equivalents were estimated from these random samples using both presmoothing and postsmoothing methods. Because the population distributions were known, random and systematic error components could be estimated separately. Note that the use of smoothed distributions as population distributions helps ensure that the distributions are realistic. Still, the Hanson et al. (1994) study is but one simulation.

Mean-squared errors for a portion of the Hanson et al. (1994) study are presented in Table 3.12 for the enhanced ACT Assessment English and Science Reasoning tests. The values in the table are estimates of the total error of equation (3.8). Larger values indicate more total equating error. The first row in the upper and lower portions of the table is for the identity equating. Note the relatively large value for ACT English compared to that for ACT Science Reasoning. This difference occurs because the two English forms are quite different from one another, whereas the two Science Reasoning forms are very similar. The sample sizes in the table are per form. For the English test with $N = 100$, the identity equating results in less error than some of the smoothing methods. For the Science Reasoning test with

TABLE 3.12. Mean-Squared Equating Error from Hanson et al. (1994) Study.

Test	Equating Method	N=100	N=250	N=500	N=1000	N=3000
ACT	Identity	5.76	5.76	5.76	5.76	5.76
English	Linear	6.15	3.65	2.80	2.33	2.00
($K = 75$)	Unsmoothed	6.60	2.83	1.50	.75	.25
	Beta4	5.28	2.24	1.22	.63	.24
	Log-linear $C = 3$	5.20	2.30	1.29	.71	.35
	Log-linear $C = 4$	5.66	2.47	1.39	.77	.36
	Log-linear $C = 6$	6.09	2.55	1.33	.67	.23
	Postsmoothing $S = .10$	5.98	2.55	1.33	.67	.22
	Postsmoothing $S = .25$	5.57	2.34	1.23	.62	.21
	Postsmoothing $S = .50$	5.17	2.19	1.17	.59	.21
ACT	Identity	.51	.51	.51	.51	.51
Science	Linear	1.03	.46	.20	.11	.05
Reasoning	Unsmoothed	1.62	.70	.32	.17	.06
($K = 40$)	Beta4	1.28	.55	.24	.12	.04
	Log-linear $C = 3$	1.17	.51	.22	.12	.04
	Log-linear $C = 4$	1.34	.57	.25	.13	.04
	Log-linear $C = 6$	1.52	.63	.28	.14	.05
	Postsmoothing $S = .10$	1.42	.63	.28	.14	.05
	Postsmoothing $S = .25$	1.32	.56	.24	.12	.04
	Postsmoothing $S = .50$	1.26	.51	.22	.11	.04

$N = 100$, the identity equating results in the least amount of error of all of the methods. For the English test, one of the smoothed equipercentile methods (postsmoothing $S = .50$) produces the lowest mean-squared error for all sample sizes. For the Science Reasoning test, only at a sample size of 3,000 do all of the smoothing methods have mean-squared error values equal to or lower than the value for linear equating.

In comparing the smoothing results to one another, there is no method that appears to be clearly superior to the others. For the English test, the mean-squared error for the best smoothing method is approximately 80% of that of the unsmoothed equipercentile method. For the Science Reasoning test, the mean-squared error for the best smoothing method is approximately 70% of that of the unsmoothed equipercentile method. Thus, smoothed equipercentile equating produces a modest reduction in error compared to unsmoothed equipercentile equating. These results are for equating error averaged over all score points. More detailed results presented by Hanson et al. (1994) indicate that the smoothing reduces error, even at extreme scores.

The results from the Hanson et al. (1994) study as well as practical experience with these methods suggest the use of the following guidelines:

- Use of the identity equating can be preferable to using one of the other equating methods, especially with sample sizes at or below 100 examinees per test form. The use of equipercentile equating with fewer than 250 examinees per form might even introduce error.

- Smoothing in equipercentile equating can be expected to produce a modest decrease in mean-squared equating error when compared to unsmoothed equipercentile equating.

No clear method exists for choosing whether to use presmoothing versus postsmoothing. One positive characteristic of the presmoothing methods is that there are statistical tests that can be readily used. Such tests do not exist for the postsmoothing method. In addition, the postsmoothing method described here requires averaging two splines, and there is no compelling theoretical reason for doing so other than to produce a symmetric relationship. However, postsmoothing directly smoothes the equipercentile relationship, which is more direct than smoothing the distributions, as is done with the presmoothing methods. The presmoothing and postsmoothing methods have been used in practice in testing programs with good results. Research evidence suggests that both types of methods can produce results which have the potential to improve equating accuracy. Thus, either type of method can function adequately in operational testing programs.

3.6 Exercises

3.1. Suppose that, in the population, the Form Y equipercentile equivalent of a Form X score of 26 is 28.3. Also, suppose that the expected (over a large number of random samples) equivalent using a smoothing method is 29.1. Based on a sample, the unsmoothed equivalent is estimated to be 31.1 and the smoothed equipercentile equivalent is estimated to be 31.3. Answer the following questions about finding the Form Y equipercentile equivalent of a Form X score of 26. Indicate if the question cannot be answered from the information given.

    a. What is the systematic error in using the smoothing method?

    b. What is the error in estimating the equipercentile equivalent using the unsmoothed equipercentile method in the sample?

    c. What is the error in estimating the equipercentile equivalent using the smoothed equipercentile method in the sample?

    d. What is the standard error of equating using the unsmoothed equipercentile method?

    e. Which method (smoothed or unsmoothed) was more accurate in the sample?

Exercises 101

   f. Which method (smoothed or unsmoothed) would be better over a large number of replications?

3.2. If $C = 3$ in the log-linear method, which of the following would be the same for the observed distribution and smoothed distribution: mean, standard deviation, skewness, kurtosis?

3.3. Suppose a nominal alpha level of 30 had been used. In Table 3.1, what values of C would have been eliminated using the single degree of freedom difference χ^2 statistics for Form X and for Form Y? (The significance level is 1.07.)

3.4. What would be the cubic spline equivalent of a score on x of 28.6 using the data shown in Table 3.6?

3.5. In Table 3.11, which pairs of conversions are identical? Are there any circumstances under which it would matter whether one or the other of the identical conversions was chosen?

3.6. In Figures 3.6 and 3.7, ±1 standard error bands are presented. If ±2 standard error bands had been used, which S parameters would have had relationships that fell within the band? How about the relationship for the identity equating?

3.7. In Table 3.12, under what conditions in the studies presented was it better to use the identity equating than to use any of the methods studied? What factor do you think could have made the identity equating appear to be relatively better with small samples for the Science Reasoning test than for the English test? Can you think of a situation in which the identity equating would always be better than one of the other equating methods?

4
Nonequivalent Groups—Linear Methods

Chapter 1 introduced the common-item nonequivalent groups design. For this design, two groups of examinees from different populations are each administered different test forms that have a set of items in common. This design often is used when only one form of a test can be administered on a given test date. As discussed in Chapter 1, the set of common items should be as similar as possible to the full-length forms in both content and statistical characteristics.

There are two special cases of the common-item nonequivalent groups design. The common item set is said to be *internal* when scores on the common items contribute to the total scores for both forms. By contrast, the common items are said to be *external* when their scores do not contribute to total scores. Notationally, denote the new test form and the random variable score on that form as X, the old form and the random variable score on that form as Y, and the common-item set and the random variable score on the common-item set as V. Assume that X and V are taken by a group of examinees from Population 1, and Y and V are taken by a group of examinees from Population 2. If V is an internal set of common items, then X and Y include scores on V. If V is external, then X and Y do not include scores on V. For example, consider an examinee who got 10 common items correct and 40 noncommon items correct. If V is an internal set of common items, then $x = 50$. If V is an external set, then $x = 40$.

In general, the common items are used to adjust for population differences. Doing so requires strong statistical assumptions because each examinee comes from only one population and takes only one form. The various

104   4. Nonequivalent Groups—Linear Methods

methods for performing equating under the common-item nonequivalent groups design are distinguished in terms of their statistical assumptions.

Even though the design under consideration here involves two populations, an equating function is typically viewed as being defined for a single population. Therefore, Populations 1 and 2 must be combined to obtain a single population for defining an equating relationship. To address this issue Braun and Holland (1982) introduced the concept of a *synthetic population* in which Populations 1 and 2 are weighted by w_1 and w_2, respectively, where $w_1 + w_2 = 1$ and $w_1, w_2 \geq 0$.

The equating methods considered in this chapter are all linear. The first two methods are called *observed score* equating methods because observed scores on X are transformed to observed scores on the scale of Y. The third method is called a *true score* method because it relates true scores on X to the scale of true scores on Y. All of these methods are described by Angoff (1971) and Petersen et al. (1989). However, the presentation here more closely parallels a combination of Kolen and Brennan (1987) and Brennan (1990). Other authors who have provided derivations of one or more of these methods include MacCann (1990) and Woodruff (1986, 1989).

As discussed in Chapter 2, the linear conversion is defined by setting standardized deviation scores (z-scores) equal for the two forms. For the common-item nonequivalent groups design, this results in the following linear equation for equating observed scores on X to the scale of observed scores on Y:

$$l_{Y_S}(x) = \frac{\sigma_s(Y)}{\sigma_s(X)}[x - \mu_s(X)] + \mu_s(Y), \qquad (4.1)$$

where s indicates the synthetic population. The four synthetic population parameters in equation (4.1) can be expressed in terms of parameters for Populations 1 and 2 as follows:

$$\mu_s(X) = w_1\mu_1(X) + w_2\mu_2(X), \qquad (4.2)$$

$$\mu_s(Y) = w_1\mu_1(Y) + w_2\mu_2(Y), \qquad (4.3)$$

$$\sigma_s^2(X) = w_1\sigma_1^2(X) + w_2\sigma_2^2(X) + w_1w_2[\mu_1(X) - \mu_2(X)]^2, \qquad (4.4)$$

and

$$\sigma_s^2(Y) = w_1\sigma_1^2(Y) + w_2\sigma_2^2(Y) + w_1w_2[\mu_1(Y) - \mu_2(Y)]^2, \qquad (4.5)$$

where the subscripts 1 and 2 refer to Populations 1 and 2, respectively.

For the common-item nonequivalent groups design, X is not administered to examinees in Population 2, and Y is not administered to examinees in Population 1. Therefore, $\mu_2(X)$, $\sigma_2^2(X)$, $\mu_1(Y)$, and $\sigma_1^2(Y)$ in equations (4.2)–(4.5) cannot be estimated directly. The Tucker and Levine observed score methods considered next make different statistical assumptions in order to express these four parameters as functions of directly estimable parameters. Throughout this chapter, all results are reported in terms of

Parameters Estimated from Data

Form X Administered in Population 1: $\mu_1(X)$ and $\sigma_1^2(X)$	Form Y Administered in Population 2: $\mu_2(Y)$ and $\sigma_2^2(Y)$

Parameters Estimated from Assumptions

Form X Moments in Population 2: $\boldsymbol{\mu_2(X)}$ and $\boldsymbol{\sigma_2^2(X)}$	Form Y Moments in Population 1: $\boldsymbol{\mu_1(Y)}$ and $\boldsymbol{\sigma_1^2(Y)}$

Parameters for Synthetic Population

$$\mu_S(X) = w_1\mu_1(X) + w_2\boldsymbol{\mu_2(X)}$$
$$\mu_S(Y) = w_1\boldsymbol{\mu_1(Y)} + w_2\mu_2(Y)$$
$$\sigma_S^2(X) = w_1\sigma_1^2(X) + w_2\boldsymbol{\sigma_2^2(X)} + w_1w_2\left[\mu_1(X) - \boldsymbol{\mu_2(X)}\right]^2$$
$$\sigma_S^2(Y) = w_1\boldsymbol{\sigma_1^2(Y)} + w_2\sigma_2^2(Y) + w_1w_2\left[\boldsymbol{\mu_1(Y)} - \mu_2(Y)\right]^2$$

FIGURE 4.1. Linear equating parameters for the common-item nonequivalent groups design.

parameters, some of which are directly estimable [e.g., $\mu_1(X)$], while others are not [e.g., $\mu_2(X)$]. In practice, of course, the results are used by replacing all parameters with estimates. The parameters estimated from the data and from assumptions are distinguished in Figure 4.1.

4.1 Tucker Method

The Tucker method was described by Gulliksen (1950, pp. 299–301), who attributed it to Ledyard Tucker. This method makes two types of assumptions in order to estimate the parameters in equations (4.2)–(4.5) that cannot be estimated directly. The first type of assumption concerns the regressions of total scores on common-item scores. The second type of assumption concerns the conditional variances of total scores given common-item scores. Basically, these are the assumptions of univariate selection theory (see Gulliksen, 1950, pp. 131,132).

4.1.1 Linear Regression Assumptions

First, the regression of X on V is assumed to be the same linear function for both Populations 1 and 2. A similar assumption is made for Y on V. Letting α represent a regression slope and β a regression intercept,

$$\alpha_1(X|V) = \sigma_1(X,V)/\sigma_1^2(V) \tag{4.6}$$

and

$$\beta_1(X|V) = \mu_1(X) - \alpha_1(X|V)\mu_1(V) \tag{4.7}$$

are the slope and intercept, respectively, for the regression of X on V in Population 1. These two quantities are directly observed. In Population 2, the slope and intercept are

$$\alpha_2(X|V) = \sigma_2(X,V)/\sigma_2^2(V) \tag{4.8}$$

and

$$\beta_2(X|V) = \mu_2(X) - \alpha_2(X|V)\mu_2(V). \tag{4.9}$$

These two quantities are not directly observed. For X and V, then, the regression assumption is

$$\alpha_2(X|V) = \alpha_1(X|V) \tag{4.10}$$

and

$$\beta_2(X|V) = \beta_1(X|V), \tag{4.11}$$

where the quantities to the left of the equal sign are not directly observable. Similarly, for Y and V, the regression assumption is

$$\alpha_1(Y|V) = \alpha_2(Y|V)$$

and

$$\beta_1(Y|V) = \beta_2(Y|V).$$

4.1.2 Conditional Variance Assumptions

Also, for the Tucker method, the conditional variance of X given V is assumed to be the same for Populations 1 and 2. A similar statement holds for Y given V. Stated explicitly, these assumptions are

$$\sigma_2^2(X)\left[1 - \rho_2^2(X,V)\right] = \sigma_1^2(X)\left[1 - \rho_1^2(X,V)\right] \tag{4.12}$$

and

$$\sigma_1^2(Y)\left[1 - \rho_1^2(Y,V)\right] = \sigma_2^2(Y)\left[1 - \rho_2^2(Y,V)\right],$$

where ρ is a correlation and the quantities that are not directly observable are to the left of the equalities.

4.1.3 Intermediate Results

The above assumptions are sufficient to solve for $\mu_2(X)$, $\sigma_2(X)$, $\mu_1(Y)$, and $\sigma_1(Y)$ in terms of observable quantities. Consider, for example, $\mu_2(X)$. Because the regression of X on V is assumed to be linear,

$$\mu_2(X) = \beta_2(X|V) + \alpha_2(X|V)\mu_2(V).$$

Using equations (4.10) and (4.11),

$$\mu_2(X) = \beta_1(X|V) + \alpha_1(X|V)\mu_2(V).$$

Now, using equation (4.7),

$$\begin{aligned}\mu_2(X) &= \big[\mu_1(X) - \alpha_1(X|V)\mu_1(V)\big] + \alpha_1(X|V)\mu_2(V)\\ &= \mu_1(X) - \alpha_1(X|V)\big[\mu_1(V) - \mu_2(V)\big].\end{aligned} \quad (4.13)$$

Following a similar approach,

$$\mu_1(Y) = \mu_2(Y) + \alpha_2(Y|V)\big[\mu_1(V) - \mu_2(V)\big]. \quad (4.14)$$

To obtain $\sigma_2^2(X)$, begin by noting that

$$\rho_1(X,V) = \sigma_1(X,V)/\big[\sigma_1(X)\sigma_1(V)\big],$$

where $\sigma_1(X,V)$ is a covariance. Rearranging terms in equation (4.6),

$$\sigma_1(X,V) = \alpha_1(X|V)\sigma_1^2(V).$$

Therefore,

$$\rho_1(X,V) = \alpha_1(X|V)\sigma_1(V)/\sigma_1(X)$$

and, with a little bit of algebra,

$$\sigma_1^2(X)\big[1 - \rho_1^2(X,V)\big] = \sigma_1^2(X) - \alpha_1^2(X|V)\sigma_1^2(V).$$

Similarly,

$$\sigma_2^2(X)\big[1 - \rho_2^2(X,V)\big] = \sigma_2^2(X) - \alpha_2^2(X|V)\sigma_2^2(V).$$

Now, using equation (4.12),

$$\sigma_2^2(X) - \alpha_2^2(X|V)\sigma_2^2(V) = \sigma_1^2(X) - \alpha_1^2(X|V)\sigma_1^2(V).$$

Because $\alpha_2(X|V) = \alpha_1(X|V)$ by assumption,

$$\sigma_2^2(X) = \sigma_1^2(X) - \alpha_1^2(X|V)\big[\sigma_1^2(V) - \sigma_2^2(V)\big]. \quad (4.15)$$

A similar derivation gives,

$$\sigma_1^2(Y) = \sigma_2^2(Y) + \alpha_2^2(Y|V)\big[\sigma_1^2(V) - \sigma_2^2(V)\big]. \quad (4.16)$$

4.1.4 Final Results

Given the results in equations (4.13)–(4.16), the synthetic population means and variances in equations (4.2)–(4.5) can be shown to be

$$\mu_s(X) = \mu_1(X) - w_2\gamma_1[\mu_1(V) - \mu_2(V)], \quad (4.17)$$
$$\mu_s(Y) = \mu_2(Y) + w_1\gamma_2[\mu_1(V) - \mu_2(V)], \quad (4.18)$$

$$\sigma_s^2(X) = \sigma_1^2(X) - w_2\gamma_1^2[\sigma_1^2(V) - \sigma_2^2(V)] + w_1 w_2 \gamma_1^2 [\mu_1(V) - \mu_2(V)]^2, \quad (4.19)$$

and

$$\sigma_s^2(Y) = \sigma_2^2(Y) + w_1\gamma_2^2[\sigma_1^2(V) - \sigma_2^2(V)] + w_1 w_2 \gamma_2^2 [\mu_1(V) - \mu_2(V)]^2, \quad (4.20)$$

where the γ-terms are the regression slopes

$$\gamma_1 = \alpha_1(X|V) = \sigma_1(X, V)/\sigma_1^2(V) \quad (4.21)$$

and

$$\gamma_2 = \alpha_2(X|V) = \sigma_2(X, V)/\sigma_2^2(V), \quad (4.22)$$

and the parameters to the right of the equal signs can be estimated directly from the data. The Tucker linear equating function is obtained by using the results from equations (4.17)–(4.22) in equation (4.1).

It is evident from the form of equations (4.17)–(4.20) that the synthetic population means and variances for X and Y can be viewed as adjustments to directly observable quantities. The adjustments are functions of differences in means and variances for the common items. If $\mu_1(V) = \mu_2(V)$ and a $\sigma_1^2(V) = \sigma_2^2(V)$, then the synthetic population parameters would equal observable means and variances.

Note that the foregoing derivation does not require specifying whether the common-item set is an internal scored set of items or an external unscored set. Consequently, the results apply to both possibilities, provided, of course, that X is correctly specified as the total set of items that directly contribute to an examinee's score. That is, scores on X include scores on V if V is an internal common-item set, and scores on X do not include scores on V if V is an external common-item set.

4.1.5 Special Cases

Equations (4.17)–(4.22) apply for any set of nonnegative weights, w_1 and w_2, provided that $w_1 + w_2 = 1$. At least three special cases are sometimes considered. First, Gulliksen's (1950, pp. 299–301) initial presentation of the Tucker method can be obtained by setting $w_1 = 1$ and $w_2 = 0$, in which case the synthetic population is the population that took the new form. Second, Angoff (1971, p. 580) provides formulas for the Tucker method based on weights that are proportional to sample sizes—i.e., $w_1 = N_1/(N_1 + N_2)$ and

$w_2 = N_2/(N_1+N_2)$ where N_1 and N_2 are the sample sizes from Populations 1 and 2, respectively. Third, the weights are sometimes set equal (i.e., $w_1 = w_2 = .5$), reflecting an a priori judgment that both Populations 1 and 2 are equally relevant for the investigator's conception of the synthetic population.

4.2 Levine Observed Score Method

The assumptions of the Tucker method involve only observable quantities. No reference is made to true scores. Yet, it would seem that for equating to be sensible, true scores must be functionally related. Otherwise, it would not be sensible to talk about scores being interchangeable. This argument per se does not render the Tucker method inappropriate, but it does suggest that there may be merit in deriving equating results based on assumptions about true scores. One such method is discussed in this section.

The Levine observed score method was originally developed by Levine (1955), although he did not explicitly consider the concept of a synthetic population. Consequently, the present development is more general than Levine's (1955). This method is an observed score equating method in the sense that it uses equation (4.1) to relate *observed* scores on X to the scale of *observed* scores on Y. However, the assumptions for this method pertain to true scores T_X, T_Y, and T_V which are assumed to be related to observed scores according to the classical test theory model (see Feldt and Brennan, 1989):

$$X = T_X + E_X, \qquad (4.23)$$
$$Y = T_Y + E_Y, \qquad (4.24)$$

and

$$V = T_V + E_V, \qquad (4.25)$$

where E_X, E_Y, and E_V are errors that have zero expectations and are uncorrelated with true scores.

4.2.1 Correlational Assumptions

The Levine method assumes that X, Y, and V are all measuring the same thing in the sense that T_X and T_V as well as T_Y and T_V correlate perfectly in both Populations 1 and 2:

$$\rho_1(T_X, T_V) = \rho_2(T_X, T_V) = 1 \qquad (4.26)$$

and

$$\rho_1(T_Y, T_V) = \rho_2(T_Y, T_V) = 1. \qquad (4.27)$$

Note that equations (4.26) and (4.27) imply that T_X and T_Y are functionally related in both populations.

4.2.2 Linear Regression Assumptions

Also for the Levine method, the regression of T_X on T_V is assumed to be the same linear function for both Populations 1 and 2, and a similar assumption is made for the regression of T_Y on T_V.

The slope of T_X on T_V is $\alpha_1(T_X|T_V) = \rho_1(T_X, T_V)\sigma_1(T_X)/\sigma_1(T_V)$, by definition. Since $\rho_1(T_X, T_V) = 1$ from the correlational assumption in equation (4.26), $\alpha_1(T_X|T_V) = \sigma_1(T_X)/\sigma_1(T_V)$. Similarly, $\alpha_2(T_X|T_V) = \sigma_2(T_X)/\sigma_2(T_V)$. Consequently, the assumption of equal true score regression slopes for T_X on T_V in Populations 1 and 2 is effectively

$$\frac{\sigma_2(T_X)}{\sigma_2(T_V)} = \frac{\sigma_1(T_X)}{\sigma_1(T_V)}. \tag{4.28}$$

By an analogous derivation,

$$\frac{\sigma_1(T_Y)}{\sigma_1(T_V)} = \frac{\sigma_2(T_Y)}{\sigma_2(T_V)}. \tag{4.29}$$

For each of the classical test theory model equations (4.23)–(4.25), the mean of observed scores equals the mean of true scores. Consequently, the assumption of equal true score regression intercepts for T_X on T_V in Populations 1 and 2 is

$$\mu_2(X) - \frac{\sigma_2(T_X)}{\sigma_2(T_V)}\mu_2(V) = \mu_1(X) - \frac{\sigma_1(T_X)}{\sigma_1(T_V)}\mu_1(V). \tag{4.30}$$

Similarly, for the intercepts of T_Y on T_V,

$$\mu_1(Y) - \frac{\sigma_1(T_Y)}{\sigma_1(T_V)}\mu_1(V) = \mu_2(Y) - \frac{\sigma_2(T_Y)}{\sigma_2(T_V)}\mu_2(V). \tag{4.31}$$

4.2.3 Error Variance Assumptions

The Levine method also assumes that the measurement error variance for X is the same for Populations 1 and 2. A similar assumption is made for Y and V. Because true scores and errors are uncorrelated under the classical test theory model, error variance is the difference between observed score variance and true score variance. Therefore, the error variance assumptions are

$$\begin{aligned} \sigma_2^2(X) - \sigma_2^2(T_X) &= \sigma_1^2(X) - \sigma_1^2(T_X), \\ \sigma_1^2(Y) - \sigma_1^2(T_Y) &= \sigma_2^2(Y) - \sigma_2^2(T_Y), \end{aligned} \tag{4.32}$$

and

$$\sigma_1^2(V) - \sigma_1^2(T_V) = \sigma_2^2(V) - \sigma_2^2(T_V). \tag{4.33}$$

4.2.4 Intermediate Results

Recall that expressions for $\mu_2(X)$, $\sigma_2(X)$, $\mu_1(Y)$, and $\sigma_1(Y)$ are needed in order to obtain the synthetic population means and variances in equations (4.2)–(4.5).

By rearranging terms in equation (4.30) and then using equation (4.28),

$$\mu_2(X) = \mu_1(X) - \frac{\sigma_1(T_X)}{\sigma_1(T_V)}\left[\mu_1(V) - \mu_2(V)\right]. \tag{4.34}$$

Similarly, using equations (4.31) and (4.29),

$$\mu_1(Y) = \mu_2(Y) + \frac{\sigma_2(T_Y)}{\sigma_2(T_V)}\left[\mu_1(V) - \mu_2(V)\right]. \tag{4.35}$$

From equation (4.32) an expression for $\sigma_2^2(X)$ is

$$\sigma_2^2(X) = \sigma_1^2(X) - \sigma_1^2(T_X) + \sigma_2^2(T_X).$$

From equation (4.28), $\sigma_2(T_X) = \sigma_1(T_X)\sigma_2(T_V)/\sigma_1(T_V)$. It follows that

$$\begin{aligned}\sigma_2^2(X) &= \sigma_1^2(X) - \sigma_1^2(T_X)\left[1 - \sigma_2^2(T_V)/\sigma_1^2(T_V)\right] \\ &= \sigma_1^2(T_X) - \frac{\sigma_1^2(T_X)}{\sigma_1^2(T_V)}\left[\sigma_1^2(T_V) - \sigma_2^2(T_V)\right].\end{aligned}$$

Using equation (4.33),

$$\sigma_2^2(X) = \sigma_1^2(X) - \frac{\sigma_1^2(T_X)}{\sigma_1^2(T_V)}\left[\sigma_1^2(V) - \sigma_2^2(V)\right]. \tag{4.36}$$

Similarly,

$$\sigma_1^2(Y) = \sigma_2^2(Y) + \frac{\sigma_2^2(T_Y)}{\sigma_2^2(T_V)}\left[\sigma_1^2(V) - \sigma_2^2(V)\right]. \tag{4.37}$$

4.2.5 General Results

Given the results in equations (4.34)–(4.37), it can be shown algebraically that the synthetic population means and variances in equations (4.2)–(4.5) are given by equations (4.17)–(4.20) with

$$\gamma_1 = \sigma_1(T_X)/\sigma_1(T_V) \tag{4.38}$$

and

$$\gamma_2 = \sigma_2(T_Y)/\sigma_2(T_V). \tag{4.39}$$

That is, under the Levine assumptions, the γ-terms are ratios of true score standard deviations. Note that the derivation of these results did not require specifying whether V was an internal or external set of common items.

The expressions for the γ-terms in equations (4.38) and (4.39) are not immediately usable because they are ratios of true score standard deviations, which are not directly observed. Given the assumptions of classical test theory, and letting $\rho(X, X') = \sigma^2(T_X)/\sigma^2(X)$ denote the reliability of X, it follows that $\sigma(T_X) = \sigma(X)\sqrt{\rho(X, X')}$. Similarly, $\sigma(T_Y) = \sigma(Y)\sqrt{\rho(Y, Y')}$ and $\sigma(T_V) = \sigma(V)\sqrt{\rho(V, V')}$. Consequently, the γ-terms can be expressed as

$$\gamma_1 = \frac{\sigma_1(X)\sqrt{\rho_1(X, X')}}{\sigma_1(V)\sqrt{\rho_1(V, V')}} \quad (4.40)$$

and

$$\gamma_2 = \frac{\sigma_2(Y)\sqrt{\rho_2(Y, Y')}}{\sigma_2(V)\sqrt{\rho_2(V, V')}}. \quad (4.41)$$

In principle, any defensible estimates of the reliabilities in equations (4.40) and (4.41) could be used to estimate γ_1 and γ_2. In practice, the most frequently used equations for the Levine method can be shown to result from applying what will be called the "classical congeneric" test theory model (see Feldt and Brennan, 1989, pp. 111,112). [Note that Levine's 1955 derivation effectively stopped with equations (4.40) and (4.41).]

4.2.6 Classical Congeneric Model Results

In this section, unless otherwise noted, the classical congeneric model is assumed for X and V, and for a single population. It is straightforward to extend the results presented here to Y and V, and to Populations 1 and 2.

Recall from equations (4.23) and (4.25) that for the classical model $X = T_X + E_X$ and $V = T_V + E_V$, where E_X and T_X, as well as E_V and T_V, are assumed to be uncorrelated. The congeneric model goes one step further in specifying that T_X and T_V are linearly related, which is consistent with the assumption in equation (4.26) that T_X and T_V are perfectly correlated.

For our present purposes, a convenient way to represent that T_X and T_V are linearly related is to set $T_X = \lambda_X T + \delta_X$ and $T_V = \lambda_V T + \delta_V$, where the λ's are slopes and the δ's are constant intercepts (see Feldt and Brennan, 1989, pp. 110,111). This implies that $T_X = (\lambda_X/\lambda_V)T_V + [\delta_X - (\lambda_X/\lambda_V)\delta_V]$, although this expression is not required in the subsequent derivation. Under the congeneric model, then, the equations for X and V can be expressed as

$$X = T_X + E_X = (\lambda_X T + \delta_X) + E_X \quad (4.42)$$

and

$$V = T_V + E_V = (\lambda_V T + \delta_V) + E_V. \quad (4.43)$$

The classical congeneric model adds the assumptions that

$$\sigma^2(E_X) = \lambda_X \sigma^2(E) \quad (4.44)$$

and
$$\sigma^2(E_V) = \lambda_V \sigma^2(E). \tag{4.45}$$

In classical test theory, error variances are proportional to test length. Here, error variances are proportional to λ_X and λ_V which are called "effective" test lengths. Note also that the ratio $\sigma^2(E_X)/\sigma^2(E_V)$ is simply λ_X/λ_V.

Given equations (4.42)–(4.45), the following can be shown relatively easily:

$$\sigma^2(X) = \lambda_X^2 \sigma^2(T) + \lambda_X \sigma^2(E), \tag{4.46}$$
$$\sigma^2(V) = \lambda_V^2 \sigma^2(T) + \lambda_V \sigma^2(E), \tag{4.47}$$

and
$$\sigma(X,V) = \lambda_X \lambda_V \sigma^2(T) + \sigma(E_X, E_V). \tag{4.48}$$

Here, we make use of the classical congeneric model to obtain an expression for $\sigma(T_X)/\sigma(T_V)$, which is the γ-term in equation (4.38). From equations (4.42) and (4.43),

$$\gamma = \frac{\sigma(T_X)}{\sigma(T_V)} = \frac{\lambda_X \sigma(T)}{\lambda_V \sigma(T)} = \frac{\lambda_X}{\lambda_V}, \tag{4.49}$$

which means that γ can be interpreted as the ratio of effective test lengths for X and V, respectively. Two cases need to be considered: (a) an internal anchor in which all items in V are included in X, and (b) an external anchor in which V and X consist of entirely different sets of items. These two cases can be distinguished in terms of the error covariance $\sigma(E_X, E_V)$ in equation (4.48).

Internal Anchor

When V is included in X, the full-length test is X. Now, let A be the noncommon part of X such that $X = A + V$. Under the congeneric model, the covariance between the errors for A and V is assumed to be 0 because these two parts of X consist of entirely different items. Consequently,

$$\sigma(E_X, E_V) = \sigma(E_{A+V}, E_V) = \sigma(E_V, E_V) = \sigma^2(E_V) = \lambda_V \sigma^2(E). \tag{4.50}$$

That is, the covariance between E_X and E_V is simply the variance of E_V.

Using equation (4.50) in (4.48) gives

$$\begin{aligned}\sigma(X,V) &= \lambda_X \lambda_V \sigma^2(T) + \lambda_V \sigma^2(E) \\ &= \lambda_V \left[\lambda_X \sigma^2(T) + \sigma^2(E)\right].\end{aligned} \tag{4.51}$$

After rewriting equation (4.46) as

$$\sigma^2(X) = \lambda_X \left[\lambda_X \sigma^2(T) + \sigma^2(E)\right],$$

it is evident from equation (4.51) and the above expression for $\sigma^2(X)$ that γ in equation (4.49) is

$$\gamma = \lambda_X/\lambda_V = \sigma^2(X)/\sigma(X,V) = 1/\alpha(V|X). \tag{4.52}$$

Therefore, for the internal anchor case, the results for Levine's observed score method under the classical congeneric model are obtained by using

$$\gamma_1 = 1/\alpha_1(V|X) = \sigma_1^2(X)/\sigma_1(X,V) \tag{4.53}$$

and

$$\gamma_2 = 1/\alpha_2(V|Y) = \sigma_2^2(Y)/\sigma_2(Y,V). \tag{4.54}$$

That is, with an internal anchor, the γ-terms in equations (4.17)–(4.20) under the classical congeneric model are the inverses of the regression slopes of V on X and V on Y.

External Anchor

When X and V contain no items in common, under the congeneric model,

$$\sigma(E_X, E_V) = 0. \tag{4.55}$$

Using equation (4.55) in (4.48) gives

$$\sigma(X,V) = \lambda_X \lambda_V \sigma^2(T). \tag{4.56}$$

From equations (4.46) and (4.56),

$$\sigma^2(X) + \sigma(X,V) = \lambda_X\big[(\lambda_X + \lambda_V)\sigma^2(T) + \sigma^2(E)\big].$$

Similarly, using equations (4.47) and (4.56),

$$\sigma^2(V) + \sigma(X,V) = \lambda_V\big[(\lambda_X + \lambda_V)\sigma^2(T) + \sigma^2(E)\big].$$

It follows that γ in equation (4.49) is

$$\gamma = \frac{\lambda_X}{\lambda_V} = \frac{\sigma^2(X) + \sigma(X,V)}{\sigma^2(V) + \sigma(X,V)}. \tag{4.57}$$

Therefore, for the external anchor case, the results for Levine's observed score method under the classical congeneric model are obtained by using

$$\gamma_1 = \frac{\sigma_1^2(X) + \sigma_1(X,V)}{\sigma_1^2(V) + \sigma_1(X,V)} \tag{4.58}$$

and

$$\gamma_2 = \frac{\sigma_2^2(Y) + \sigma_2(Y,V)}{\sigma_2^2(V) + \sigma_2(Y,V)} \tag{4.59}$$

in equations (4.17)–(4.20).

TABLE 4.1. Classical Congeneric Model Results.

Quantity	Anchor Internal	Anchor External
$\gamma = \dfrac{\lambda_X}{\lambda_V}$	$\dfrac{1}{\alpha(V\|X)} = \dfrac{\sigma^2(X)}{\sigma(X,V)}$	$\dfrac{\sigma^2(X) + \sigma(X,V)}{\sigma^2(V) + \sigma(X,V)}$
$\sigma^2(T_X)$	$\dfrac{\gamma^2[\sigma(X,V) - \sigma^2(V)]}{\gamma - 1}$	$\gamma\sigma(X,V)$
$\sigma^2(T_V)$	$\dfrac{\sigma(X,V) - \sigma^2(V)}{\gamma - 1}$	$\dfrac{\sigma(X,V)}{\gamma}$
$\sigma^2(E_X)$	$\dfrac{\gamma^2\sigma^2(V) - \gamma\sigma(X,V)}{\gamma - 1}$	$\sigma^2(X) - \gamma\sigma(X,V)$
$\sigma^2(E_V)$	$\dfrac{\gamma\sigma^2(V) - \sigma(X,V)}{\gamma - 1}$	$\sigma^2(V) - \dfrac{\sigma(X,V)}{\gamma}$
$\rho(X,X')$	$\dfrac{\gamma^2[\sigma(X,V) - \sigma^2(V)]}{(\gamma - 1)\sigma^2(X)}$	$\dfrac{\gamma\sigma(X,V)}{\sigma^2(X)}$
$\rho(V,V')$	$\dfrac{\sigma(X,V) - \sigma^2(V)}{(\gamma - 1)\sigma^2(V)}$	$\dfrac{\sigma(X,V)}{\gamma\sigma^2(V)}$

Note: Here, the population subscript "1" has been suppressed.

Comments

Under the assumption that $w_1 = N_1/(N_1+N_2)$ and $w_2 = N_2/(N_1+N_2)$, the results for Levine's observed score method and a classical congeneric model are identical to those reported by Angoff (1971), although the derivation is different. Angoff's (1971) results are sometimes called the Levine-Angoff method, or described as "Levine's method using Angoff error variances." The error variances are those in Angoff (1953), which are also reported by Petersen et al. (1989, p. 254). Brennan (1990) has shown that Angoff's error variances are derivable from the classical congeneric model. Table 4.1 reports these error variances along with other results for the classical congeneric model that can be used to express the quantities illustrated in Figure 4.1.

4.3 Levine True Score Method

Levine (1955) also derived results for a true score equating method using the same assumptions about true scores discussed in the previous section. The principal difference between the observed score and true score methods

116   4. Nonequivalent Groups—Linear Methods

is that the observed score method uses equation (4.1) to equate observed scores on X to the scale of observed scores on Y, whereas the true score method equates true scores. Specifically, the following equation is used to equate true scores on X to the scale of true scores on Y:

$$l_{Y_S}(t_X) = \frac{\sigma_s(T_Y)}{\sigma_s(T_X)}[t_X - \mu_s(T_X)] + \mu_s(T_Y).$$

In classical theory, observed score means equal true score means. Therefore,

$$l_{Y_S}(t_X) = \frac{\sigma_s(T_Y)}{\sigma_s(T_X)}[t_X - \mu_s(X)] + \mu_s(Y). \tag{4.60}$$

4.3.1 Results

Equations (4.2) and (4.3) are still appropriate for $\mu_s(X)$ and $\mu_s(Y)$, respectively. Also, under Levine's assumptions, equations (4.34) and (4.35) still apply for $\mu_2(X)$ and $\mu_1(Y)$, respectively. Consequently, equations (4.17) and (4.18) for $\mu_s(X)$ and $\mu_s(Y)$ are valid for both the Levine observed score and the Levine true score methods, with the γ-terms given by equations (4.38) and (4.39). For ease of reference, these results are repeated below:

$$\mu_s(X) = \mu_1(X) - w_2\gamma_1[\mu_1(V) - \mu_2(V)], \tag{4.17}$$

and

$$\mu_s(Y) = \mu_2(Y) + w_1\gamma_2[\mu_1(V) - \mu_2(V)], \tag{4.18}$$

where

$$\gamma_1 = \sigma_1(T_X)/\sigma_1(T_V) \tag{4.38}$$

and

$$\gamma_2 = \sigma_2(T_Y)/\sigma_2(T_V). \tag{4.39}$$

Using Levine's true score assumptions, the derivation of expressions for the variance of T_X and T_Y for the synthetic population is tedious (see Appendix), although the results are simple:

$$\sigma_s^2(T_X) = \gamma_1^2\sigma_s^2(T_V) \tag{4.61}$$

and

$$\sigma_s^2(T_Y) = \gamma_2^2\sigma_s^2(T_V), \tag{4.62}$$

where

$$\sigma_s^2(T_V) = w_1\sigma_1^2(T_V) + w_2\sigma_2^2(T_V) + w_1w_2[\mu_1(V) - \mu_2(V)]^2.$$

From equations (4.61) and (4.62), the slope of the equating relationship $l_{Y_S}(t_X)$ in equation (4.60) is

$$\sigma_s(T_Y)/\sigma_s(T_X) = \gamma_2/\gamma_1, \tag{4.63}$$

where the γ-terms are given by equations (4.38) and (4.39).

These results are quite general, but they are not directly usable without expressions for the true score standard deviations $\sigma_1(T_X)$, $\sigma_2(T_Y)$, $\sigma_1(T_V)$, and $\sigma_2(T_V)$, which are incorporated in γ_1 and γ_2. As with the Levine observed score method, $\sigma_1(X)\sqrt{\rho_1(X,X')}$ can be used for $\sigma_1(T_X)$, and corresponding expressions can be used for the other true score standard deviations. Then, given estimates of the required reliabilities, the linear equating relationship $l_{Y_S}(t_X)$ in equation (4.60) can be determined.

One counterintuitive property of the Levine true score method is that the slope and intercept do not depend on the synthetic population weights w_1 and w_2. Clearly, this is true for the slope in equation (4.63). From equations (4.60) and (4.63), the intercept is

$$\mu_s(Y) - (\gamma_2/\gamma_1)\mu_s(X),$$

and, using equations (4.17) and (4.18), it can be expressed as

$$\mu_2(Y) + w_1\gamma_2[\mu_1(V) - \mu_2(V)] - (\gamma_2/\gamma_1)\{\mu_1(X) - w_2\gamma_1[\mu_1(V) - \mu_2(V)]\}$$
$$= \mu_2(Y) - (\gamma_2/\gamma_1)\mu_1(X) + \gamma_2(w_1 + w_2)[\mu_1(V) - \mu_2(V)]$$
$$= \mu_2(Y) - (\gamma_2/\gamma_1)\mu_1(X) + \gamma_2[\mu_1(V) - \mu_2(V)], \quad (4.64)$$

which does not depend on the weights w_1 and w_2.

Given the slope and intercept in equations (4.63) and (4.64), respectively, the linear equating relationship for Levine's true score method can be expressed as

$$l_Y(t_X) = (\gamma_2/\gamma_1)[t_X - \mu_1(X)] + \mu_2(Y) + \gamma_2[\mu_1(V) - \mu_2(V)], \quad (4.65)$$

which gives the same Form Y equivalents as equation (4.60). Note, however, that s does not appear as a subscript of l in equation (4.65) because this expression for Levine's true score method does not involve a synthetic population. In short, Levine's true score method does not require the conceptual framework of a synthetic population and is invariant with respect to the weights w_1 and w_2.

Classical Congeneric Model

Results for Levine true score equating under the classical congeneric model with an internal anchor are obtained simply by using equations (4.53) and (4.54) for γ_1 and γ_2, respectively. For an external anchor, equations (4.58) and (4.59) are used.

Using Levine's True Score Method with Observed Scores

Equations (4.60) and (4.65) were derived for true scores, not observed scores. Even so, in practice, observed scores are used in place of true scores.

That is, observed scores on X are assumed to be related to the scale of observed scores on Y by the equation

$$l_Y(x) = (\gamma_2/\gamma_1)[x - \mu_1(X)] + \mu_2(Y) + \gamma_2[\mu_1(V) - \mu_2(V)]. \quad (4.66)$$

Although replacing true scores with observed scores may appear sensible, there is no seemingly compelling logical basis for doing so. Note, in particular, that the transformed observed scores on X [i.e., $l_Y(x)$] typically do not have the same standard deviation as either the true scores on Y or the observed scores on Y. However, as will be discussed next, Levine's true score method applied to observed scores has an interesting property.

4.3.2 First-Order Equity

Although the logic of using observed scores in Levine's true score equating function appears somewhat less than compelling, Hanson (1991a) has shown that using observed scores in Levine's true score equating function for the common-item nonequivalent groups design results in first-order equity (see Chapter 1) of the equated test scores under the classical congeneric model. Hanson's (1991a) result gives Levine's true score equating method applied to observed scores a well-grounded theoretical justification. In general, his result means that, for the population of persons with a particular true score on Y, the expected value of the linearly transformed scores on X [equation (4.66)] equals the expected value of the scores on Y, and this statement holds for all true scores on Y. In formal terms, first-order equity means that

$$\mathbf{E}[l_Y(X)|\psi(T_X) = \tau] = \mathbf{E}[Y|T_Y = \tau] \quad \text{for all } \tau, \quad (4.67)$$

where ψ is a function that relates true scores on X to true scores on Y, and X is capitalized in $l_Y(X)$ to emphasize that interest is focused here on the variable X rather than on a realization x.

Before treating the specific case of the common-item nonequivalent groups design, it is shown next that first-order equity holds whenever there exists a population such that Forms X and Y are congeneric and true scores are replaced by observed scores. As was discussed previously, for the congeneric model,

$$X = T_X + E_X = (\lambda_X T + \delta_X) + E_X \text{ and } Y = T_Y + E_Y = (\lambda_Y T + \delta_Y) + E_Y.$$

To convert true scores on X to the scale of true scores on Y, it can be shown that

$$T_Y = \Psi(T_X) = \frac{\lambda_Y}{\lambda_X}(T_X - \delta_X) + \delta_Y.$$

Substituting X for T_X gives

$$l_Y(X) = \frac{\lambda_Y}{\lambda_X}(X - \delta_X) + \delta_Y. \tag{4.68}$$

In congeneric theory, the expected value of errors is 0. Thus,

$$\mathbf{E}(X|T=\tau) = \mathbf{E}\big[\lambda_X T + \delta_X + E_X\big] = \lambda_X T + \delta_X \text{ and}$$
$$\mathbf{E}(Y|T=\tau) = \mathbf{E}\big[\lambda_Y T + \delta_Y + E_Y\big] = \lambda_Y T + \delta_Y.$$

First-order equity holds for $l_Y(X)$ because the expected value of $l_Y(X)$ given $\Psi(T_X) = \tau$ equals the expected value of Y given $T_Y = \tau$:

$$\mathbf{E}\left[\frac{\lambda_Y}{\lambda_X}(X - \delta_X) + \delta_Y | \Psi(T_X) = \tau\right]$$
$$= \mathbf{E}\left[\frac{\lambda_Y}{\lambda_X}(\lambda_X T + \delta_X + E_X - \delta_X) + \delta_Y | T_Y = \tau\right]$$
$$= \lambda_Y T + \delta_Y = \mathbf{E}[Y|T_Y = \tau],$$

as was previously indicated.

For the common-item nonequivalent groups design, one parameterization of the classical congeneric model is

$$\left.\begin{aligned}
X_1 &= (\lambda_X T_1 + \delta_X) + E_{X_1}, & \sigma_1^2(E_X) &= \lambda_X \sigma_1^2(E), \\
Y_2 &= (\lambda_Y T_2 + \delta_Y) + E_{Y_2}, & \sigma_2^2(E_Y) &= \lambda_Y \sigma_2^2(E), \\
V_1 &= (\lambda_V T_1 + \delta_V) + E_{V_1}, & \sigma_1^2(E_V) &= \lambda_V \sigma_1^2(E), \\
V_2 &= (\lambda_V T_2 + \delta_V) + E_{V_2}, & \sigma_2^2(E_V) &= \lambda_V \sigma_2^2(E),
\end{aligned}\right\} \tag{4.69}$$

where the subscripts 1 and 2 designate the populations. This parameterization is different from that in Hanson (1991a), but it is consistent with the parameterization introduced previously.

Given the parameterization in equation set (4.69),

$$\left.\begin{aligned}
\mu_1(X) &= \lambda_X \mu_1(T) + \delta_X, & \mu_2(Y) &= \lambda_Y \mu_2(T) + \delta_Y, \\
\mu_1(V) &= \lambda_V \mu_1(T) + \delta_V, & \mu_2(V) &= \lambda_V \mu_2(T) + \delta_V, \\
\sigma_1^2(X) &= \lambda_X^2 \sigma_1^2(T) + \lambda_X \sigma_1^2(E), & \sigma_2^2(Y) &= \lambda_Y^2 \sigma_2^2(T) + \lambda_Y \sigma_2^2(E), \\
\sigma_1^2(V) &= \lambda_V^2 \sigma_1^2(T) + \lambda_V \sigma_1^2(E), & \sigma_2^2(V) &= \lambda_V^2 \sigma_2^2(T) + \lambda_V \sigma_2^2(E), \\
\sigma_1(X,V) &= \lambda_X \lambda_V \sigma_1^2(T) & \sigma_2(X,V) &= \lambda_Y \lambda_V \sigma_2^2(T) \\
&\quad + \sigma_1(E_X, E_V), & &\quad + \sigma_2(E_Y, E_V).
\end{aligned}\right\} \tag{4.70}$$

From equation (4.50), for the internal case, $\sigma_1(E_X, E_V) = \lambda_V \sigma_1^2(E)$; similarly, $\sigma_2(E_Y, E_V) = \lambda_V \sigma_2^2(E)$. From equation (4.55), for the external case, $\sigma_1(E_X, E_V) = 0$; similarly, $\sigma_2(E_Y, E_V) = 0$.

To prove that first-order equity holds for Levine's true score method applied to observed scores, it is sufficient to show that the slope and intercept in the Levine equation (4.66) equal the slope and intercept, respectively, in equation (4.68).

To prove the equality of slopes, it is necessary to show that

$$\gamma_2/\gamma_1 = \lambda_Y/\lambda_X.$$

For the internal case, from equation (4.53),

$$\begin{aligned}\gamma_1 &= \sigma_1^2(X)/\sigma_1(X,V) \\ &= \frac{\lambda_X^2 \sigma_1^2(T) + \lambda_X \sigma_1^2(E)}{\lambda_X \lambda_V \sigma_1^2(T) + \lambda_V \sigma_1^2(E)} \\ &= \lambda_X/\lambda_V.\end{aligned}$$

Similarly,

$$\gamma_2 = \lambda_Y/\lambda_V \qquad (4.71)$$

and, consequently,

$$\gamma_2/\gamma_1 = \lambda_Y/\lambda_X. \qquad (4.72)$$

The external case is left as an exercise for the reader.

To prove the equality of intercepts, it is necessary to show that

$$\mu_2(Y) - (\gamma_2/\gamma_1)\mu_1(X) + \gamma_2\big[\mu_1(V) - \mu_2(V)\big] = \delta_Y - (\lambda_Y/\lambda_X)\delta_X.$$

For the internal case, from equations (4.71) and (4.72), the intercept is

$$\begin{aligned}&\mu_2(Y) - (\lambda_Y/\lambda_X)\mu_1(X) + (\lambda_Y/\lambda_V)\big[\mu_1(V) - \mu_2(V)\big] \\ &= \big[\lambda_Y \mu_2(T) + \delta_Y\big] - (\lambda_Y/\lambda_X)\big[\lambda_X \mu_1(T) + \delta_X\big] \\ &\quad + (\lambda_Y/\lambda_V)\big[\lambda_V \mu_1(T) + \delta_V - \lambda_V \mu_2(T) - \delta_V\big] \\ &= \lambda_Y\big[\mu_2(T) - \mu_1(T)\big] + \big[\delta_Y - (\lambda_Y/\lambda_X)\delta_X\big] + \lambda_Y\big[\mu_1(T) - \mu_2(T)\big] \\ &= \delta_Y - (\lambda_Y/\lambda_X)\delta_X.\end{aligned}$$

The external case is left as an exercise for the reader.

4.4 Illustrative Example and Other Topics

Table 4.2 provides the principal computational equations for the three linear equating methods that have been developed in this chapter. Note that terms containing w_2 in equations (4.17)–(4.20) in Table 4.2 are slightly separated from the other terms. Doing so more clearly reveals the simplifications in synthetic population means and variances when $w_1 = 1$ and $w_2 = 0$. In this section, all references to Levine methods (except for parts of Table 4.2) assume the classical congeneric model.

4.4.1 Illustrative Example

Table 4.3 provides statistics for a real data example that employs two 36-item forms, Form X and Form Y, in which every third item in both forms is a common item. Therefore, items 3, 6, 9, ..., 36 constitute the 12-item common set V. Scores on V are contained in X, so V is an internal set of items. Form X was administered to 1,655 examinees, and Form Y was administered to 1,638 examinees. Method of moments estimates of directly observable parameters are presented in Table 4.3. The Tucker and Levine observed score analyses were conducted using the *CIPE* computer program described in Appendix B.

To simplify computations, let $w_1 = 1$ and $w_2 = 1 - w_1 = 0$ for the Tucker and Levine observed score methods. For this synthetic population, using equations (4.17) and (4.19),

$$\hat{\mu}_s(X) = \hat{\mu}_1(X) = 15.8205$$

and

$$\hat{\sigma}_s(X) = \hat{\sigma}_1(X) = 6.5278.$$

Now, for the Tucker method, using equation (4.22),

$$\hat{\gamma}_2 = \hat{\sigma}_2(Y, V)/\hat{\sigma}_2^2(V) = 14.7603/2.4515^2 = 2.4560.$$

Using this value in equations (4.18) and (4.20) gives

$$\hat{\mu}_s(Y) = 18.6728 + 2.4560(5.1063 - 5.8626) = 16.8153$$

and

$$\hat{\sigma}_s(Y) = \sqrt{6.8784^2 + 2.4560^2(2.3760^2 - 2.4515^2)} = 6.7167.$$

Applying these results in equation (4.1) gives

$$\begin{align} \hat{l}_{Y_s}(x) &= (6.7167/6.5278)(x - 15.8205) + 16.8153 \\ &= .5370 + 1.0289x. \end{align} \quad (4.73)$$

For the Levine observed score method, with $w_1 = 1$, $\hat{\mu}_s(X) = 15.8205$ and $\hat{\sigma}_s(X) = 6.5278$, as for the Tucker method. However, for the Levine method under the classical congeneric model, using equation (4.54),

$$\hat{\gamma}_2 = \hat{\sigma}_2^2(Y)/\hat{\sigma}_2(Y, V) = 6.8784^2/14.7603 = 3.2054 \quad (4.74)$$

Then, using equations (4.18) and (4.20),

$$\hat{\mu}_s(Y) = 18.6728 + 3.2054(5.1063 - 5.8626) = 16.2486,$$

and

$$\hat{\sigma}_s(Y) = \sqrt{6.8784^2 + 3.2054^2(2.3760^2 - 2.4515^2)} = 6.6006.$$

TABLE 4.2. Computational Formulas and Equations for Linear Equating Methods with the Common-Item Nonequivalent Groups Design.

Tucker and Levine Observed Score Methods

$$l_{Y_S}(x) = [\sigma_s(Y)/\sigma_s(X)][x - \mu_s(X)] + \mu_s(Y) \qquad (4.1)$$

Levine True Score Method Applied to Observed Scores

$$l_Y(x) = (\gamma_2/\gamma_1)[x - \mu_1(X)] + \mu_2(Y) + \gamma_2[\mu_1(V) - \mu_2(V)] \qquad (4.66)$$

$$\mu_s(X) = \mu_1(X) - w_2\gamma_1[\mu_1(V) - \mu_2(V)] \qquad (4.17)$$

$$\mu_s(Y) = \mu_2(Y) + w_1\gamma_2[\mu_1(V) - \mu_2(V)] \qquad (4.18)$$

$$\sigma_s^2(X) = \sigma_1^2(X) - w_2\gamma_1^2[\sigma_1^2(V) - \sigma_2^2(V)] + w_1w_2\gamma_1^2[\mu_1(V) - \mu_2(V)]^2 \qquad (4.19)$$

$$\sigma_s^2(Y) = \sigma_2^2(Y) + w_1\gamma_2^2[\sigma_1^2(V) - \sigma_2^2(V)] + w_1w_2\gamma_2^2[\mu_1(V) - \mu_2(V)]^2 \qquad (4.20)$$

Tucker Observed Score Method

$$\gamma_1 = \alpha_1(X|V) = \sigma_1(X,V)/\sigma_1^2(V) \quad \text{internal anchor} \qquad (4.21)$$
$$\text{and}$$
$$\gamma_2 = \alpha_2(Y|V) = \sigma_2(Y,V)/\sigma_2^2(V) \quad \text{external anchor} \qquad (4.22)$$

Levine Methods Under a Classical Congeneric Model

$$\gamma_1 = 1/\alpha_1(V|X) = \sigma_1^2(X)/\sigma_1(X,V) \quad \Big\} \text{ internal anchor} \qquad (4.53)$$
$$\gamma_2 = 1/\alpha_2(V|Y) = \sigma_2^2(Y)/\sigma_2(Y,V) \qquad (4.54)$$

$$\gamma_1 = \frac{\sigma_1^2(X) + \sigma_1(X,V)}{\sigma_1^2(V) + \sigma_1(X,V)} \qquad (4.58)$$
$$\Big\} \text{ external anchor}$$
$$\gamma_2 = \frac{\sigma_2^2(Y) + \sigma_2(Y,V)}{\sigma_2^2(V) + \sigma_2(Y,V)} \qquad (4.59)$$

$$\gamma_1 = \frac{\sigma_1(X)\sqrt{\rho_1(X,X')}}{\sigma_1(V)\sqrt{\rho_1(V,V')}} \quad \text{and} \quad \gamma_2 = \frac{\sigma_2(Y)\sqrt{\rho_2(Y,Y')}}{\sigma_2(V)\sqrt{\rho_2(V,V')}}.$$

TABLE 4.3. Directly Observable Statistics for an Illustrative Example of Equating Forms X and Y Using the Common-Item Nonequivalent Groups Design.

Group	Score	$\hat{\mu}$	$\hat{\sigma}$	Covariance	Correlation
1	X	15.8205	6.5278	13.4088	.8645
1	V	5.1063	2.3760		
2	Y	18.6728	6.8784	14.7603	.8753
2	V	5.862	2.4515		

Note: $N_1 = 1,655$ and $N_2 = 1,638$.

Applying these results in equation (4.1) gives

$$\hat{l}_{Y_s}(x) = (6.6006/6.5278)(x - 15.8205) + 16.2486$$
$$= .2517 + 1.0112x. \qquad (4.75)$$

For the Levine true score method applied to observed scores, $\hat{\gamma}_2 = 3.2054$ in equation (4.74) still applies and, using equation (4.53),

$$\hat{\gamma}_1 = \hat{\sigma}_1^2(X)/\hat{\sigma}_1(X,V) = 6.5278^2/13.4088 = 3.1779.$$

Therefore, equation (4.66) gives

$$\hat{l}_Y(x) = (3.2054/3.1779)(x - 15.8205) + 18.6728$$
$$+ 3.2054(5.1063 - 5.8626)$$
$$= .2912 + 1.0087x. \qquad (4.76)$$

These results are summarized in Table 4.4. The slight discrepancies in slopes and intercepts in equations (4.73), (4.75), and (4.76) compared to those in Table 4.4 are due to rounding error, the results in Table 4.4 are more accurate. In practice, it is generally advisable to perform computations with more decimal digits than presented here for illustrative purposes, especially for accurate estimates of intercepts.

The similarity of slopes and intercepts for the three methods suggests that the Form Y equivalents will be about the same for all three methods. This finding is illustrated by the results provided in Table 4.5. The Form Y equivalents for the three methods are very similar, although there is a greater difference between the equivalents for the Tucker method and either Levine method than between the equivalents for the two Levine methods. The new Form X is more difficult than the old Form Y for very high achieving examinees, as suggested in Table 4.5, where, for all three methods, the Form Y equivalent of $x = 36$ is a score greater than the maximum possible score of 36.

As was discussed in Chapter 2, raw score equivalents that are out of the range of possible scores can be problematic. Sometimes, equivalents

TABLE 4.4. Linear Equating Results for the Illustrative Example in Table 4.3 Using the Classical Congeneric Model with Levine's Methods.

w_1	Method	$\hat{\gamma}_1$	$\hat{\gamma}_2$	$\hat{\mu}_s(X)$	$\hat{\mu}_s(Y)$	$\hat{\sigma}_s(X)$	$\hat{\sigma}_s(Y)$	$\widehat{int}$	$\widehat{slope}$
1	Tucker	(a)	2.4560	15.8205	16.8153	6.5278	6.7168	.5368	1.0289
	Lev Obs. Sc.	(a)	3.2054	15.8205	16.2485	6.5278	6.6007	.2513	1.0112
.5	Tucker	2.3751	2.4560	16.7187	17.7440	6.6668	6.8612	.5378	1.0292
	Lev Obs. Sc.	3.1779	3.2054	17.0223	17.4607	6.7747	6.8491	.2514	1.0110
.5026[c]	Tucker	2.3751	2,4560	16.7141	17.7392	6.6664	6.8608	.5378	1.0292
	Lev Obs. Sc.	3.1779	3.2054	17.0161	17.4544	6.7740	6.8484	.2514	1.0110
—	Lev True Sc.	3.1779	3.2054	15.8205	16.2485	(b)	(b)	.2914	1.0086

[a] Not required when $w_1 = 1$.
[b] Not required for Levine true score equating.
[c] Proportional to sample size [i.e., $w_1 = N_1/(N_1 + N_2) = .5026$].

TABLE 4.5. Selected Form Y Equivalents for Illustrative Example with $w_1 = 1$.

x	Tucker	Levine Observed Score	Levine True Score
0	.54	.25	.29
10	10.83	10.36	10.38
20	21.12	20.47	20.46
30	31.41	30.59	30.55
36	37.58	36.65	36.60

greater than the maximum observable raw score are set to this maximum score. In other cases, this problem is handled through the transformation to scale scores. In most cases, doing so has little practical importance, but this issue could be consequential when various test forms are used for scholarship decisions. The occasional need to truncate Form Y equivalents is a limitation of linear equating procedures. This issue will be discussed further in Chapter 8.

4.4.2 Synthetic Population Weights

As noted previously, the synthetic population weights (w_1 and $w_2 = 1 - w_1$) have no bearing on Levine's true score method. That is why the results for this method appear on a separate line in Table 4.4. For the Tucker and Levine observed score methods, however, the weights do matter, in the sense that they are required to derive the results. From a practical perspective, however, the weights seldom make much difference in the Form Y equivalents. This observation is illustrated in Table 4.4 by the fact that the intercepts and slopes for Tucker equating are almost identical under very different weighting schemes (e.g., $w_1 = 1$ and $w_1 = .5$), and the same is true for Levine observed score equating.

Although the choice of weights makes little practical difference in the vast majority of real equating contexts, many equations are simplified considerably by choosing $w_1 = 1$ and $w_2 = 0$. This observation is evident from examining equations (4.17)–(4.20) in Table 4.2. Furthermore, setting $w_1 = 1$ means that the synthetic group is simply the new population, which is often the only population that will take the new form under the nonequivalent groups design. Therefore, using $w_1 = 1$ often results in some conceptual simplifications. For these reasons, setting $w_1 = 1$ appears to have merit. However, the choice of synthetic population weights ultimately is a judgment that should be based on an investigator's conceptualization of the synthetic population. It is not the authors' intent to suggest that $w_1 = 1$ be used routinely or thoughtlessly. (See Angoff, 1987; Kolen and Brennan, 1987; Brennan and Kolen, 1987a, for further discussion and debate about choosing w_1 and w_2.)

4.4.3 Mean Equating

If sample sizes are quite small (say, less than 100), the standard errors of linear equating (as will be discussed in Chapter 7) may be unacceptably large. In such cases, mean equating might be considered. Form Y equivalents for mean equating under the Tucker and Levine observed score methods are obtained by setting $\sigma_s(Y)/\sigma_s(X) = 1$ in equation (4.1), which gives

$$m_{Y_s}(x) = [x - \mu_s(X)] + \mu_s(Y), \qquad (4.77)$$

where $\mu_s(X)$ and $\mu_s(Y)$ are given by equations (4.17) and (4.18). Effectively, the Form Y equivalent of a Form X score is obtained by adding the same constant, $\mu_s(Y) - \mu_s(x)$, to all scores on Form X.

Form Y equivalents under Levine's true score method are obtained by setting $\gamma_2/\gamma_1 = 1$ in equation (4.66), which gives

$$m_Y(x) = [x - \mu_1(X)] + \{\mu_2(Y) + \gamma_2[\mu_1(V) - \mu_2(V)]\}. \qquad (4.78)$$

Note that, if $w_1 = 1$, equations (4.77) and (4.78) are identical because $\mu_s(X) = \mu_1(X)$ and $\mu_s(Y)$ is given by the term in braces in equation (4.78). Since γ_2 is the same for both of Levine's methods, this implies that, when $w_1 = 1$, mean equating results are identical for Levine's observed score and true score methods.

4.4.4 Decomposing Observed Differences in Means and Variances

In the common-item nonequivalent groups design, differences in the observable means $\mu_1(X) - \mu_2(Y)$ and observable variances $\sigma_1^2(X) - \sigma_2^2(Y)$ are due to the confounded effects of group and form differences. Since estimates of these parameters are directly observed, a natural question is, "How much of the observed difference in means (or variances) is attributable to group differences, and how much is attributable to form differences?" An answer to this question is of some consequence to both test developers and psychometricians responsible for equating. There is nothing a test developer can do about group differences; but in principle, if form differences are known to be relatively large, test developers can take steps to create more similar forms in the future. Furthermore, if a psychometrician notices that group differences or form differences are very large, this should alert him or her to the possibility that equating results may be suspect.

One way to answer the question posed in the previous paragraph is discussed by Kolen and Brennan (1987). Their treatment is briefly summarized here.

Decomposing Differences in Means

Begin with the tautology

$$\mu_1(X) - \mu_2(Y) = \mu_s(X) - \mu_s(Y) + \{[\mu_1(X) - \mu_s(X)] - [\mu_2(Y) - \mu_s(Y)]\}. \tag{4.79}$$

Note that $\mu_s(X) - \mu_s(Y)$ is the mean difference for the two forms for the synthetic population. Since the synthetic population is constant, the difference is entirely attributable to forms and will be called the *form difference factor*. The remaining terms in braces will be called the *population difference factor*. [Note that, since equation (4.79) involves a synthetic population, it does not apply to Levine's true score procedure.]

After replacing equations (4.2) and (4.3) in equation (4.79), it can be shown that

$$\begin{aligned}
\mu_1(X) - \mu_2(Y) &= w_1\{\mu_1(X) - \mu_1(Y)\} && \text{Form difference for Population 1} \\
&+ w_2\{\mu_2(X) - \mu_2(Y)\} && \text{Form difference for Population 2} \\
&+ w_2\{\mu_1(X) - \mu_2(X)\} && \text{Population difference on } X \text{ scale} \\
&+ w_1\{\mu_1(Y) - \mu_2(Y)\} && \text{Population difference on } Y \text{ scale},
\end{aligned} \tag{4.80}$$

where the descriptions on the right describe the mathematical terms in braces (i.e., excluding the w_1 and w_2 weights). This expression states that $\mu_1(X) - \mu_2(Y)$ is a function of two weighted form difference factors (one for each population) and two weighted population difference factors (one for each scale). Since this result is rather complicated, it is probably of little practical value in most circumstances.

Equation (4.80) simplifies considerably, however, if $w_1 = 1$. Then

$$\begin{aligned}
\mu_1(X) - \mu_2(Y) &= \{\mu_1(X) - \mu_1(Y)\} && \text{Form difference for Population 1} \\
&+ \{\mu_1(Y) - \mu_2(Y)\} && \text{Population difference on } Y \text{ scale.}
\end{aligned} \tag{4.81}$$

Illustrative Example and Other Topics   127

When $w_1 = 1$ in equation (4.18),

$$\mu_s(Y) = \mu_1(Y) = \mu_2(Y) + \gamma_2[\mu_1(V) - \mu_2(V)].$$

Therefore, equation (4.81) results in

$$\mu_1(X) - \mu_2(Y) = \{\mu_1(X) - \mu_2(Y) \\ - \gamma_2[\mu_1(V) - \mu_2(V)]\} \quad \text{Form difference for Population 1} \\ + \{\gamma_2[\mu_1(V) - \mu_2(V)]\} \quad \text{Population difference on } Y \text{ scale.} \tag{4.82}$$

Note that equation (4.82) applies to the Tucker method as well as both the Levine observed score and the Levine true score methods. As was discussed previously, the choice of synthetic population weights generally has little effect on Form Y equivalents. Consequently, equation (4.82) should be adequate for practical use in partitioning $\mu_1(X) - \mu_2(Y)$ into parts attributable to group and form differences.

Refer again to the example in Table 4.3 and the associated results in Table 4.4. For the Tucker method, equation (4.82) gives

$$15.8205 - 18.6728 = \{15.8205 - 18.6728 - 2.4560(5.1063 - 5.8626)\} \\ + \{2.4560(5.1063 - 5.8626)\},$$

which simplifies to

$$-2.85 = -.99 - 1.86. \tag{4.83}$$

This result means that, on average: (a) the new group (Population 1) is lower achieving than the old group (Population 2) by 1.86 units on the Form Y scale; and (b) for the new group, the new Form X is more difficult than the old Form Y by .99 unit.

The corresponding result for both of the Levine methods under the classical congeneric model is obtained by using $\gamma_2 = 3.2054$ (rather than $\gamma_2 = 2.4560$) in equation (4.82), which gives

$$-2.85 = -.43 - 2.42. \tag{4.84}$$

Under the Levine assumptions, population mean differences on the Form Y scale are greater than under the Tucker assumptions by $2.42 - 1.86 = .56$ unit.

Decomposing Differences in Variances

As has been shown by Kolen and Brennan (1987), decomposing $\sigma_1^2(X) - \sigma_2^2(Y)$ is considerably more complicated, in general. However, for all three equating methods discussed in this chapter, when $w_1 = 1$ the result is quite simple:

$$\sigma_1^2(X) - \sigma_2^2(Y) = \{\sigma_1^2(X) - \sigma_2^2(Y) \\ - \gamma_2^2[\sigma_1^2(V) - \sigma_2^2(V)]\} \quad \text{Form difference for Population 1} \\ + \{\gamma_2^2[\sigma_1^2(V) - \sigma_2^2(V)]\}. \quad \text{Population difference on } Y \text{ scale.} \tag{4.85}$$

The form of equation (4.85) parallels that of equation (4.82) for decomposing the difference in means.

For the example in Tables 4.3 and 4.4, under Tucker assumptions, using equation (4.85),

$$6.5278^2 - 6.8784^2 = \{6.5278^2 - 6.8784^2 - [2.4560^2(2.3760^2 - 2.4515^2)]\} \\ + \{2.4560^2(2.3760^2 - 2.4515^2)\},$$

which gives approximately

$$-4.70 = -2.50 - 2.20,$$

where -2.50 is the form difference factor, and -2.20 is the population difference factor. This result means that, on average: (a) on the old Form Y scale, the new group (Population 1) has smaller variance than the old group by 2.20 units; and (b) for the new group, the new Form X has smaller variance than the old Form Y by 2.50 units.

The reader can verify that the corresponding result for both Levine methods under the classical congeneric model is

$$-4.70 = -.96 - 3.74.$$

Under the Levine assumptions, population differences in variances on the Form Y scale are greater than under the Tucker assumptions by $3.74 - 2.20 = 1.54$ units.

4.4.5 Relationships Among Tucker and Levine Equating Methods

Kolen and Brennan (1987) show that, for both an internal and external anchor, if $\sigma_1(X, V) > 0$, then γ_1 for the Levine methods under a classical congeneric model is larger than γ_1 for the Tucker method. A similar result holds for the γ_2-terms. As is evident from equations (4.17)–(4.20) for the observed score methods and from equation (4.66) for the Levine true score method, the γ-terms are "expansion factors" in the sense that they multiply the group differences $\mu_1(V) - \mu_2(V)$ and $\sigma_1^2(V) - \sigma_2^2(V)$. This relationship is also evident from the form of equations (4.82) and (4.85). Therefore, because the Levine γ's are larger than the Tucker γ's, population differences under the Levine assumptions are greater than under the Tucker assumptions, as is illustrated by the example results for the decompositions of observed means and variances. This may be one reason why the Levine methods sometimes are said to be more appropriate than the Tucker method when groups are rather dissimilar. Although this ad hoc reasoning is by no means definitive, it does suggest that an investigator might choose one of the Levine methods when it is known, or strongly suspected, that populations differ substantially. This logic is especially compelling if there is also reason to believe that the forms are quite similar, because in that case the true score assumptions of the Levine methods are plausible. However, if the populations are too dissimilar, any equating is suspect.

Along a similar line of reasoning, if the forms are known or suspected to be dissimilar, the Levine true score assumptions are likely violated, which may lead an investigator to choose the Tucker method. Of course, it should be kept in mind that if forms are too dissimilar, any equating is suspect. It is virtually impossible to provide strict and all-inclusive guidelines about what characterizes forms that are "too dissimilar." However, forms that do not share common content and statistical specifications certainly are "too dissimilar" to justify a claim that their scores can be equated, as the term is used in this book, no matter what method is chosen.

The Tucker and Levine methods make linearity assumptions that are, in some cases, amenable to direct examination. For example, the regression of X on V in Population 1 can be examined directly. If it is not linear, then at least one of the assumptions of the Tucker method is false, and an alternative procedure (the Braun-Holland method) discussed in Chapter 5 might be considered.

Since the Levine γ-terms are larger than the Tucker γ-terms, under some circumstances it is possible to predict whether the mean for Form Y equivalents under Levine equating will be larger or smaller than the mean under Tucker equating. For example, when $w_1 = 1$ and $x = \mu_1(X)$, both equations (4.1) and (4.66) reduce to

$$l_Y[\mu_1(X)] = \mu_1(Y) = \mu_2(Y) + \gamma_2[\mu_1(V) - \mu_2(V)],$$

which is the Form Y equivalent of the mean score for X in Population 1 when $w_1 = 1$. Clearly, in this case, if the new group is higher achieving than the old group on the common items [i.e., $\mu_1(V) > \mu_2(V)$], then $l_Y[\mu_1(X)]$ is greater under both of the Levine methods than under the Tucker method. Of course, when the common item means are quite similar in the two groups, there will be little difference in the Form Y equivalents of $\mu_1(X)$ under the three methods.

When Levine (1955) developed his methods, he referred to the observed score method as a method for use with "equally reliable" tests, and he referred to the true score method as a method for "unequally reliable" tests. This terminology, which is also found in Angoff (1971) and other publications, is not used here for two reasons. First, as is shown in this chapter, the derivations of Levine's methods do not require any assumptions about the equality or inequality of reliabilities. (It is possible to derive Levine's methods using such assumptions, but it is not necessary to do so.) Second, this terminology seems that the two methods should give the same results if Forms X and Y are equally reliable. This conclusion does not necessarily follow, however, because it fails to explicitly take into account the facts that reliabilities are population dependent, Levine's observed score method involves a synthetic population, and Levine's true score method does not. For example, suppose that $\rho_1(X,X') = \rho_2(Y,Y')$, which means that Forms X and Y are equally reliable for Populations 1 and 2, respectively. It does not necessarily follow that $\rho_s(X,X') = \rho_s(Y,Y')$ for the particular synthetic population used in Levine's observed score method. This is evident from the fact that, even if $\sigma_1^2(X) = \sigma_2^2(Y)$, the synthetic group variances for Forms X and Y are not likely to be equal [see equations (4.19) and (4.20)]. Thus, it is quite possible for forms to be equally reliable, in some sense, without having the two Levine methods give the same Form Y equivalents.

Even though the derivations of the methods described in this chapter do not directly require assumptions about reliability, if Forms X and Y are not approximately equal in reliability then the equating will be suspect, at best. For example, suppose that Form X is very short relative to Form Y. Under these circumstances, even after "equating," it will not be a matter of indifference to examinees which form they take. Because Form X has more measurement error than Form Y, well-prepared examinees are likely to be more advantaged by taking Form Y, and poorly prepared examinees are likely to be more advantaged by taking Form X. Probably the most favorable characteristic that such an equating might possess is first-order equity.

4.4.6 Scale Scores

In most testing programs, equated raw scores (e.g., Form Y equivalents) are not reported to examinees and users of scores. Rather, scale scores are reported, where the scale is defined as a transformation of the raw scores for the initial form of the test, as was discussed in Chapter 1. In principle, the scale scores could be either a linear or nonlinear transformation of the raw scores. This section extends the discussion of linear conversions in Chapter 2.

Let sc represent scale scores. If Form Y is the initial test form and the raw-to-scale score transformation is linear, then

$$sc(y) = B_{Y|sc} + A_{Y|sc}(y). \tag{4.86}$$

The linear equation for equating raw scores on Form X to the raw score scale of Form Y can be represented as

$$l_Y(x) = y = B_{X|Y} + A_{X|Y}(x). \tag{4.87}$$

Therefore, to obtain scale scores associated with the Form X raw scores, y in equation (4.87) is replaced in equation (4.86), giving

$$\begin{aligned} sc(x) &= B_{Y|sc} + A_{Y|sc}[B_{X|Y} + A_{X|Y}(x)] \\ &= (B_{Y|sc} + A_{Y|sc}B_{X|Y}) + A_{Y|sc}A_{X|Y}(x) \quad (4.88) \\ &= B_{X|sc} + A_{X|sc}(x), \quad (4.89) \end{aligned}$$

where the intercept and slope are, respectively,

$$B_{X|sc} = B_{Y|sc} + A_{Y|sc}B_{X|Y} \text{ and } A_{X|sc} = A_{Y|sc}A_{X|Y}.$$

Suppose that $A_{Y|sc} = 2$ and $B_{Y|sc} = 100$. Then, for the illustrative example, assuming Tucker equating with $w_1 = .5$ (see Table 4.4), equation (4.88) gives

$$\begin{aligned}sc(x) &= [100 + 2(.5378)] + 2(1.0291)(x) \\ &= 101.08 + 2.06(x).\end{aligned}$$

For example, if $x = 25$,

$$sc(x = 25) = 101.08 + 2.06(25) = 152.58.$$

[Alternatively, the Form Y equivalent of $x = 25$ could be obtained first and then used as y in equation (4.86).]

The same process can be used for obtaining scale scores for scores on a subsequent form, say Z, that is equated to Form X. The transformation has the same form as equations (4.88) and (4.89):

$$\begin{aligned}sc(z) &= (B_{X|sc} + A_{X|sc}B_{Z|X}) + A_{X|sc}A_{Z|X}(z) \\ &= B_{Z|sc} + A_{Z|sc}(z).\end{aligned}$$

If the transformation of raw scores on the initial form to scale scores is nonlinear, then equation (4.86) is not valid and the process described in this section will not work. In that case, the scale score intercepts and slopes for each form [e.g., equation (4.89)] are replaced by a conversion table that maps the raw score on each form to a scale score, as was discussed in Chapter 1 and illustrated in Chapter 2.

4.5 Appendix: Proof $\sigma_s^2(T_X) = \gamma_1^2 \sigma_s^2(T_V)$ Under Classical Congeneric Model

The true score analogue of equation (4.4) (see also Exercise 4.1) is

$$\sigma_s^2(T_X) = w_1\sigma_1^2(T_X) + w_2\sigma_2^2(T_X) + w_1w_2[\mu_1(T_X) - \mu_2(T_X)]^2.$$

For the classical congeneric model, $\mu_1(T_X) = \mu_1(X), \mu_2(T_X) = \mu_2(X)$ and, from equation (4.34),

$$\mu_2(X) = \mu_1(X) - [\sigma_1(T_X)/\sigma_1(T_V)][\mu_1(V) - \mu_2(V)].$$

It follows that

$$\begin{aligned}\sigma_s^2(T_X) &= w_1\sigma_1^2(T_X) + w_2\sigma_2^2(T_X) + w_1w_2[\sigma_1^2(T_X)/\sigma_1^2(T_V)][\mu_1(V) - \mu_2(V)]^2 \\ &= \frac{\sigma_1^2(T_X)}{\sigma_1^2(T_V)}\left\{w_1\sigma_1^2(T_V) + w_2\frac{\sigma_1^2(T_V)}{\sigma_1^2(T_X)}\sigma_2^2(T_X) + w_1w_2[\mu_1(V) - \mu_2(V)]^2\right\}.\end{aligned}$$

Under the Levine assumptions, the slope of the linear regression of T_X on T_V in both Populations 1 and 2 is given by equation (4.28):

$$\sigma_1(T_X)/\sigma_1(T_V) = \sigma_2(T_X)/\sigma_2(T_V).$$

Applying this equation to the second term in braces in the previous equation gives

$$\sigma_s^2(T_X) = \frac{\sigma_1^2(T_X)}{\sigma_1^2(T_V)} \left\{ w_1 \sigma_1^2(T_V) + w_2 \sigma_2^2(T_V) + w_1 w_2 [\mu_1(V) - \mu_2(V)]^2 \right\}.$$

The term in braces is $\sigma_s^2(T_V)$ and, by equation (4.38), $\sigma_1^2(T_X)/\sigma_1^2(T_V) = \gamma_1^2$. Thus,

$$\sigma_s^2(T_X) = \gamma_1^2 \sigma_s^2(T_V),$$

as was to be proved.

4.6 Exercises

4.1. Prove equation (4.4). [Hint:

$$\sigma_s^2(X) = w_1 \operatorname*{E}_{1}[X - \mu_s(X)]^2 + w_2 \operatorname*{E}_{2}[X - \mu_s(X)]^2,$$

where $\operatorname*{E}_{i}$ means the expected value in Population i ($i = 1$ or 2)].

4.2. Using the notation of this chapter, Angoff (1971, p. 580) provides the following equations for the synthetic group means and variances under Tucker assumptions:

$$\mu_s(X) = \mu_1(X) + \alpha_1(X|V)[\mu_s(V) - \mu_1(V)],$$
$$\mu_s(Y) = \mu_2(Y) + \alpha_2(Y|V)[\mu_s(V) - \mu_2(V)],$$
$$\sigma_s^2(X) = \sigma_1^2(X) + \alpha_1^2(X|V)[\sigma_s^2(V) - \sigma_1^2(V)],$$

and

$$\sigma_s^2(Y) = \sigma_2^2(Y) + \alpha_2^2(Y|V)[\sigma_s^2(V) - \sigma_2^2(V)].$$

Show that Angoff's equations give results identical to equations (4.17)–(4.20), using equations (4.21) for γ_1 and (4.22) for γ_2. (Strictly speaking, Angoff refers to a "total" group rather than a synthetic group with the notion of a total group being all examinees used for equating, which implies that Angoff's weights are proportional to sample sizes for the two groups.)

4.3. Verify the results in Table 4.4 when $w_1 = .5$ and $w_1 = .5026$.

4.4. Suppose the data in Table 4.3 were for an external anchor of 12 items, and X and Y both contain 36 items. If $w_1 = .5$, what are the linear equations for the Tucker and Levine observed score methods?

4.5. Under classical congeneric model, what are the reliabilities $\rho_1(X, X')$ and $\rho_2(Y, Y')$ for the illustrative example?

4.6. Suppose the Levine assumptions are invoked and X, Y, and V are assumed to satisfy the classical test theory model assumptions for both populations, such that $\sigma_1(T_X) = (K_X/K_V)\sigma_1(T_V)$ and $\sigma_2(T_Y) = (K_Y/K_V)\sigma_2(T_V)$.

   a. Under these circumstances, what are the γ's given by equations (4.38) and (4.39)?

   b. Provide a brief verbal interpretation of these γ's as contrasted with the γ's under the classical congeneric model.

4.7. If $w_1 = 1$ and the common-item means for the two groups are identical, how much of the difference $\mu_1(X) - \mu_2(Y)$ is attributable to forms?

4.8. Jessica is a test development specialist for a program in which test forms are equated. She has been taught in an introductory measurement course that good items are highly discriminating items. Therefore, in developing a new form of a test, she satisfies the content requirements using more highly discriminating items than were used in constructing previous forms. From an equating perspective, is this good practice? Why? [Hint: If p_i is the difficulty level for item i and r_i is the point-biserial discrimination index for item i, then the standard deviation of total test scores is $\sum_i r_i \sqrt{p_i(1-p_i)}$.]

4.9. Given equation set (4.70), show that the external anchor γ_2 given by equation (4.59) is λ_Y/λ_V.

4.10. Let V be an internal anchor such that $X = A + V$ and assume that $0 < \rho_1(X, V) < 1$. Show that

   a. $\sigma_1^2(V) < \sigma_1(X, V) < \sigma_1^2(X)$ and

   b. $1 < \gamma_{1T} < \gamma_{1L}$, where T stands for Tucker equating and L stands for Levine observed score equating under the classical congeneric model.

   c. Name one condition under which the result in (a) would not hold if V were an external anchor.

5
Nonequivalent Groups—Equipercentile Methods

Equipercentile equating methods have been developed for the common-item nonequivalent groups design. These methods are similar to the equipercentile methods for random groups described in Chapter 2. Equipercentile methods with nonequivalent groups consider the distributions of total score and scores on the common items, rather than only the means, standard deviations, and covariances that were considered in Chapter 4. As has been indicated previously, equipercentile equating is an observed score equating procedure that is developed from the perspective of the observed score equating property described in Chapter 1. Thus, equipercentile equating with the common-item nonequivalent groups design requires that a synthetic population, as defined in Chapter 4, be considered. In this chapter, we present an equipercentile method that we show to be closely allied to the Tucker linear method of Chapter 4. We also describe how smoothing methods, such as those described in Chapter 3, can be used when conducting equipercentile equating with nonequivalent groups. The methods described in this chapter are illustrated using the same data that were used in Chapter 4, and the results are compared to the linear results from Chapter 4.

5.1 Frequency Estimation Equipercentile Equating

The *frequency estimation method* described by Angoff (1971) and Braun and Holland (1982) provides a means for estimating the cumulative distributions of scores on Form X and Form Y for a synthetic population from data that are collected using the common-item nonequivalent groups design. Percentile ranks are then obtained from the cumulative distributions and the forms equated by equipercentile methods, as was done in Chapter 2.

5.1.1 Conditional Distributions

Conditional score distributions are required in order to use these statistical methods. Two identities are particularly useful, and they are presented here. The use of these identities is illustrated later, in connection with the frequency estimation method.

Define $f(x,v)$ as the joint distribution of total score and common-item score, so that $f(x,v)$ represents the probability of earning a score of x on Form X and a score of v on the common items. Specifically, $f(x,v)$ is the probability that $X = x$ and $V = v$. Define $f(x)$ as the *marginal distribution* of scores on Form X, so that $f(x)$ represents the probability of earning a score of x on Form X. That is, $f(x)$ represents the probability that $X = x$. Also define $h(v)$ as the marginal distribution of scores on the common items, so that $h(v)$ represents the probability that $V = v$, and define $f(x|v)$ as the conditional distribution of scores on Form X for examinees earning a particular score on the common items. Thus, $f(x|v)$ represents the probability that $X = x$ given that $V = v$. Using standard results from conditional expectations, it can be shown that

$$f(x|v) = \frac{f(x,v)}{h(v)}. \tag{5.1}$$

From equation (5.1), it follows that

$$f(x,v) = f(x|v)h(v). \tag{5.2}$$

These identities are used to develop the frequency estimation method.

5.1.2 Frequency Estimation Method

To conduct *frequency estimation equipercentile equating*, it is necessary to express the distributions for the synthetic population. These distributions are considered to be a weighted combination of the distributions for each population. Specifically, for Form X and Form Y,

$$f_s(x) = w_1 f_1(x) + w_2 f_2(x) \tag{5.3}$$

and

$$g_s(y) = w_1 g_1(y) + w_2 g_2(y),$$

where the subscript s refers to the synthetic population, the subscript 1 refers to the population administered Form X, and the subscript 2 refers to the population administered Form Y. As before, f and g refer to distributions for Form X and Form Y, respectively, and w_1 and $w_2 (w_1 + w_2 = 1)$ are used to weight Populations 1 and 2 to form the synthetic population.

From the data that are collected in the nonequivalent groups design, direct estimates of $f_1(x)$ and $g_2(y)$ may be obtained. Because Form X is not administered to examinees from Population 2, a direct estimate of $f_2(x)$ is unavailable. Also, because Form Y is not administered to examinees from Population 1, a direct estimate of $g_1(y)$ is unavailable. Statistical assumptions need to be invoked to obtain expressions for these functions using quantities for which direct estimates are available from data that are collected.

The assumption made in the frequency estimation method is that, for both Form X and Form Y, the conditional distribution of total score given each score, $V = v$, is the same in both populations. The same assumption is made whether the common items are internal or external. This assumption is stated as follows:

$$f_1(x|v) = f_2(x|v), \quad \text{for all } v \quad \text{and} \quad g_1(y|v) = g_2(y|v), \quad \text{for all } v. \quad (5.4)$$

For example, $f_1(x|v)$ represents the probability that total score $X = x$, given that $V = v$ in Population 1. The other conditional distributions are interpreted similarly. Equation (5.2) can be used to obtain expressions for these functions using quantities for which direct estimates are available from data that are collected.

The following discussion describes how the assumptions presented in equation (5.4) can be used to find expressions for $f_2(x)$ and $g_1(y)$ using quantities for which direct estimates are available.

From equation (5.2), the following equalities hold:

$$f_2(x, v) = f_2(x|v)h_2(v) \quad \text{and} \quad g_1(y, v) = g_1(y|v)h_1(v). \quad (5.5)$$

For Population 2, $f_2(x, v)$ represents the joint distribution of total scores and common–item scores. Specifically, $f_2(x, v)$ represents the probability that $X = x$ and $V = v$ in Population 2. For Population 2, $h_2(v)$ represents the distribution of scores on the common items. Thus, $h_2(v)$ represents the probability that $V = v$ in Population 2. The expressions $g_1(y, v)$ and $h_1(v)$ are similarly defined for Population 1.

Combining the equalities in equation (5.5) with the assumptions in equation (5.4), $f_2(x, v)$ and $g_1(y, v)$ can be expressed using quantities for which direct estimates are available from data that are collected as follows:

$$f_2(x, v) = f_1(x|v)h_2(v) \quad \text{and} \quad g_1(y|v) = g_2(y|v)h_1(v). \quad (5.6)$$

For the first equality, $f_1(x|v)$ can be estimated directly from the Population 1 examinees who take Form X. The quantity $h_2(v)$ can be estimated directly from the Population 2 examinees who take Form Y. For the second equality,

$g_2(y|v)$ can be estimated directly from the Population 2 examinees who take Form Y, and $h_1(v)$ can be estimated directly from the Population 1 examinees who take Form X.

The associated marginal distributions can be found by summing over common-item scores as follows:

$$f_2(x) = \sum_v f_2(x,v) = \sum_v f_1(x|v)h_2(v) \quad \text{and}$$

$$g_1(y) = \sum_v g_1(y,v) = \sum_v g_2(y|v)h_1(v). \tag{5.7}$$

In this equation, $f_2(x)$ represents the probability that $X = x$ in Population 2, and $g_1(y)$ represents the probability that $Y = y$ in Population 1.

All of the terms in equation (5.7) use quantities for which direct estimates are available from data. The expressions in equation (5.7) can be substituted into equation (5.3) to provide expressions for the synthetic population as follows:

$$f_s(x) = w_1 f_1(x) + w_2 \sum_v f_1(x|v)h_2(v) \quad \text{and}$$

$$g_s(y) = w_1 \sum_v g_2(y|v)h_1(v) + w_2 g_2(y). \tag{5.8}$$

Equation (5.8) uses quantities for which direct estimates are available from data.

For the synthetic population, $f_s(x)$ can be cumulated over values of x to produce the cumulative distribution $F_s(x)$. The cumulative distribution $G_s(y)$ is similarly derived. Define P_s as the percentile rank function for Form X and Q_s as the percentile rank function for Form Y, using the definitions for percentile ranks that were developed in Chapter 2. Similarly, P_s^{-1} and Q_s^{-1} are the percentile functions.

The equipercentile function for the synthetic population is

$$e_{Ys}(x) = Q_s^{-1}[P_s(x)], \tag{5.9}$$

which is analogous to the equipercentile relationship for random groups equipercentile equating in equation (2.17).

5.1.3 Evaluating the Frequency Estimation Assumption

The frequency estimation assumption of equation (5.4) cannot be tested using data collected using the common-item nonequivalent groups design. To test this assumption, a representative group of examinees from Population 1 would need to take Form Y, and a representative group of examinees from Population 2 would need to take Form X. Unfortunately, these data are not available in practice. If Populations 1 and 2 were identical, then

TABLE 5.1. Form X and Common-Item Distributions for Population 1 in a Hypothetical Example.

x	\multicolumn{4}{c}{v}	$f_1(x)$	$F_1(x)$
	0	1	2	3		
0	.04	.04	.02	.00	.10	.10
1	.04	.08	.02	.01	.15	.25
2	.06	.12	.05	.02	.25	.50
3	.03	.12	.05	.05	.25	.75
4	.02	.03	.04	.06	.15	.90
5	.01	.01	.02	.06	.10	1.00
$h_1(v)$	.20	.40	.20	.20		

Note: Values shown in the body of table are for $f_1(x,v)$.

the assumption in equation (5.4) would be met. Logically, then, the more similar Populations 1 and 2 are to one another, the more likely it is that this assumption will hold. Thus, frequency estimation equating should be conducted only when the two populations are reasonably similar to one another. How similar "reasonably similar" is depends on the context of the equating and on empirical evidence of the degree of similarity required. When the populations differ considerably, methods based on true score models, such as the Levine linear method described in Chapter 4 or item response theory methods described in Chapter 6, should be considered, although adequate equating might not be possible when populations differ considerably. This problem will be considered further in Chapter 8.

5.1.4 Numerical Example

A numerical example based on synthetic data is used here to aid in the understanding of this method. In this example, Form X has 5 items, Form Y has 5 items, and there are 3 common items. Assume that the common items are external.

Table 5.1 presents the data for Population 1 for the hypothetical example. The values in the body of the table represent the joint distribution, $f_1(x,v)$. For example, the upper left-hand value is .04. This value represents the probability that an examinee from Population 1 would earn a score of 0 on Form X *and* a score of 0 on the common items. The values in the body of Table 5.1 sum to 1. The values at the bottom of the table are for the marginal distribution on the common items for Population 1, $h_1(v)$. For example, the table indicates that the probability of earning a common-item score of 0 is .20 over all examinees in Population 1. The values listed under the column labeled $f_1(x)$ represent the marginal distribution for total score on Form X. The sum of the values in each row in the body of the

TABLE 5.2. Form Y and Common-Item Distributions for Population 2 in a Hypothetical Example.

y	\multicolumn{4}{c}{v}	$g_2(y)$	$G_2(y)$
	0	1	2	3		
0	.04	.03	.01	.00	.08	.08
1	.07	.05	.07	.01	.20	.28
2	.03	.05	.12	.02	.22	.50
3	.03	.04	.13	.05	.25	.75
4	.02	.02	.05	.06	.15	.90
5	.01	.01	.02	.06	.10	1.00
$h_2(v)$	.20	.20	.40	.20		

Note: Values shown in the body of table are for $g_2(y,v)$.

table equals the value for the marginal shown for $f_1(x)$ and the sum of the marginal distribution values for $f_1(x)$ equals 1. The rightmost column is the cumulative distribution for Form X scores, $F_1(x)$. The values in this column are obtained by cumulating the probabilities shown in the $f_1(x)$ column. Table 5.2 presents the joint and marginal distributions for Form Y and common-item scores in Population 2.

Estimates of the distributions presented in Tables 5.1 and 5.2 would be available from the common-item nonequivalent groups design. Estimates of the distribution for Form X in Population 2 would be unavailable, because Form X is not administered in Population 2. Similarly, estimates of the distribution for Form Y in Population 1 would be unavailable. However, equating still can proceed by making the frequency estimation assumption in equation (5.4).

To simplify the example, assume that $w_1 = 1$, which results in the following simplification of equation (5.8):

$$f_s(x) = f_1(x) \quad \text{and} \quad g_s(y) = \sum_v g_2(y|v) h_1(v). \quad (5.10)$$

The first of the equations labeled (5.10) indicates that the distribution of Form X scores for the synthetic population is the same as the distribution in Population 1. Thus the rightmost column in Table 5.1 labeled $F_1(x)$ also gives $F_s(x)$ for $w_1 = 1$.

The synthetic group is Population 1, because $w_1 = 1$ in the example. Thus, the second of the equations (5.10) provides an expression for the cumulative distribution of Form Y scores for examinees in Population 1. Because Form Y was not administered in Population 1, it is necessary to use the conditional distribution of Form Y scores given common-item scores in Population 2 and assume that this conditional distribution also would hold in Population 1 at all common-item scores [see equation (5.4)].

TABLE 5.3. Conditional Distributions of Form Y Given Common-Item Scores for Population 2 in a Hypothetical Example.

	\multicolumn{4}{c}{v}			
y	0	1	2	3
0	.20	.15	.025	.00
1	.35	.25	.175	.05
2	.15	.25	.30	.10
3	.15	.20	.325	.25
4	.10	.10	.125	.30
5	.05	.05	.05	.30
$h_2(v)$	.20	.20	.40	.20

Note: Values in the body of the table are for $g_2(y|v) = \frac{g_2(y|v)}{h_2(v)}$.

Table 5.3 presents the Form Y conditional distribution for Population 2. To calculate the values in the table, take the joint probability in Table 5.2 and divide it by its associated marginal probability on the common items. Specifically,

$$g_2(y|v) = \frac{g_2(y,v)}{h_2(v)}, \qquad (5.11)$$

which follows from equation (5.1). For example, the .20 value in the upper left cell of Table 5.3 equals .04 from the upper left cell of Table 5.2 divided by .20, which is the probability of earning a score of $V = 0$ as shown in Table 5.2. Note that the conditional probabilities in each column of the body of Table 5.3 sum to 1.

To find the values to substitute into equation (5.10), at each v the conditional distribution in Population 2, $g_2(y|v)$, is multiplied by the marginal distribution for common items for Population 1, $h_1(v)$. The result is the joint distribution in Population 1 under the frequency estimation assumption of equation (5.4). The results are shown in Table 5.4.

Table 5.5 presents the cumulative distributions, percentile ranks, and equipercentile equivalents. These values can be verified using the computational procedures described in Chapter 2.

Refer to Table 5.4 to gain a conceptual understanding of what was done. In this table, the joint distribution of Form Y total scores and common-item scores was calculated for Population 1. As was indicated earlier, Population 1 did not even take Form Y. The way that the values in this table could be calculated was by making the statistical assumptions associated with frequency estimation. To estimate this joint distribution, the conditional distribution observed in Population 2 was assumed to hold for Population 1 at all common-item scores. The Population 2 conditional distribution was multiplied by the Population 1 common-item marginal distributions to

142   5. Nonequivalent Groups—Equipercentile Methods

TABLE 5.4. Calculation of Distribution of Form Y and Common-Item Scores for Population 1 Using Frequency Estimation Assumptions in a Hypothetical Example.

			v			
y	0	1	2	3	$g_1(y)$	$G_1(y)$
0	.20(.20)=.04	.15(.40)=.06	.025(.20)=.005	.00(.20)=.00	.105	.105
1	.35(.20)=.07	.25(.40)=.10	.175(.20)=.035	.05(.20)=.01	.215	.320
2	.15(.20)=.03	.25(.40)=.10	.30(.20)=.06	.10(.20)=.02	.210	.530
3	.15(.20)=.03	.20(.40)=.08	.325(.20)=.065	.25(.20)=.05	.225	.755
4	.10(.20)=.02	.10(.40)=.04	.125(.20)=.025	.30(.20)=.06	.145	.900
5	.05(.20)=.01	.05(.40)=.02	.05(.20)=.01	.30(.20)=.06	.100	1.000
$h_1(v)$	.20	.40	.20	.20		

Note: Values in the body of the table are for $g_1(y,v)=g_2(y|v)h_1(v)$.

TABLE 5.5. Cumulative Distributions and Finding Equipercentile Equivalents for $w_1 = 1$.

x	$F_1(x)$	$P_1(x)$	y	$G_1(y)$	$Q_1(y)$	x	$e_{Ys}(x)$
0	.100	5.0	0	.105	5.25	0	−.02
1	.250	17.5	1	.320	21.25	1	.83
2	.500	37.5	2	.530	42.50	2	1.76
3	.750	62.5	3	.755	64.25	3	2.92
4	.900	82.5	4	.900	82.75	4	3.98
5	1.000	95.0	5	1.000	95.00	5	5.00

form the joint probabilities shown in Table 5.4. The Population 1 marginal distribution on the common items can be viewed as providing weights that are multiplied by the Population 2 conditional distribution at each score on the common items.

5.1.5 Estimating the Distributions

Estimates of distributions can be used in place of the parameters when using frequency estimation in practice. However, a problem occurs when no examinees earn a particular common-item score in one of the groups but some examinees earn that score in the other group. When estimating the Form Y distribution in Population 1, the assumption is made in equation (5.4) that $g_1(y|v) = g_2(y|v)$, for all v. If no Population 2 examinees earn a particular score on v in a sample, then no estimate of $g_1(y|v)$ exists at that v. However, such an estimate would be needed to conduct the equating if some examinees in Population 1 earned that v. Jarjoura and Kolen (1985) recommended using the conditional distribution at a score close to that v (e.g., at $v + 1$) as an estimate for what the conditional distribution would be at v. On logical grounds, they argued that this substitution would cause insignificant bias in practice in those cases where very few examinees in one population earn a score that has a frequency of 0 in the other population. A practical solution is to use the conditional distribution for the v with nonzero frequency that is closest to the v in question as we move toward the median of the distribution of v.

Smoothing methods also can be used with the frequency estimation method. An extension of the log-linear presmoothing method was described by Holland and Thayer (1987, 1989, 2000), von Davier et al. (2003), and Rosenbaum and Thayer (1987) in the context of frequency estimation. In this extension, the joint distributions of scores on the items that are not common and scores on the common items are fit using a log-linear model. The resulting smoothed joint distributions then are used to equate forms using the frequency estimation method described in this chapter. Model fitting using this method requires the fitting of a joint distribution, which makes the moment preservation property for this method more complicated than with the random groups design. To fit the joint distribution, the number of moments for each fitted marginal distribution that are the same as those for the observed distribution need to be specified. In addition, the cross-product moments for the fitted joint distribution that are the same as those for the observed distribution need to be specified. For example, a model might be specified so that the first four moments of each marginal distribution and the covariance for the fitted and observed distributions are equal. The fit of this model could be compared to other more and other less complicated models.

Lord's (1965) beta4 method that was described in Chapter 3 also can be used to fit the joint distributions of total scores and common-item scores. In this application, the assumption is made that true score on the common items and true score on the total tests are functionally related. That is, the total test and common items are measuring precisely the same construct. Empirical research conducted by Hanson (1991c), Livingston and Feryok (1987), and Liou and Cheng (1995b) indicates that bivariate smoothing techniques can improve equating precision with the common item nonequivalent groups design.

The cubic spline postsmoothing method described by Kolen and Jarjoura (1987) is a straightforward extension of the random groups method described in Chapter 3. In this method, unsmoothed equipercentile equivalents are estimated using frequency estimation as described in this chapter. The cubic spline method described in Chapter 3 then is implemented. The only difference in methodology is that standard errors of frequency estimation equating developed by Jarjoura and Kolen (1985) are used in place of the random groups standard errors. Kolen and Jarjoura (1987) reported that the cubic spline method used with frequency estimation increased equating precision.

144   5. Nonequivalent Groups—Equipercentile Methods

5.2 Braun-Holland Linear Method

Braun and Holland (1982) presented a linear method that uses the mean and standard deviation which arise from using the frequency estimation assumptions to conduct linear equating. This method is closely related to the Tucker linear method presented in Chapter 4. Under the frequency estimation assumptions in equation (5.4), the mean and standard deviation of scores on Form X for the synthetic population can be expressed as

$$\mu_s(X) = \sum_x x f_s(x), \tag{5.12}$$

$$\sigma_s^2(X) = \sum_x [x - \mu_s(X)]^2 f_s(x), \tag{5.13}$$

where $f_s(x)$ is taken from equation (5.8). The synthetic population mean and standard deviation for Form Y are expressed similarly. The resulting means and standard deviations then can be substituted into the general form of a linear equating relationship for the common-item nonequivalent groups design that was described in Chapter 4. The resulting equation is referred to here as the Braun-Holland linear method.

Braun and Holland (1982) showed that an equating which results from using the Braun-Holland linear method is identical to the Tucker linear method described in Chapter 4 when the following conditions hold:

(1) The regressions of X on V and Y on V are linear.

(2) The regressions of X on V and Y on V are homoscedastistic. This property means that the variance of X given v is the same for all v, and the variance of Y given v is the same for all v.

Thus, the Braun-Holland method can be viewed as a generalization of the Tucker method when the regressions of total test on common items are nonlinear. Braun and Holland (1982) suggested that the regression of X on V for Population 1 and Y on V for Population 2 be examined for nonlinearity. The Braun-Holland method is more complicated computationally than the Tucker method, and it also has been used much less in practice. Still, the Braun-Holland method should be considered when nonlinear regressions are suspected.

The results of using the Braun-Holland method with the hypothetical data in the frequency estimation example with $w_1 = 1$ are presented in Table 5.6. In this table, the distribution for Form X was taken from Table 5.1. The distribution for Form Y, which was calculated using the frequency estimation assumption, was taken from Table 5.4. Means and standard deviations were calculated using equations (5.12) and (5.13). The slope and intercept were calculated from the means and standard deviations. The linear equivalents were calculated using this slope and intercept. Note that

TABLE 5.6. Computation of Equating Relationship for Braun-Holland Method in a Hypothetical Example.

From Table 5.1		From Table 5.4	
x	$f_1(x)$	y	$g_1(y)$
0	.100	0	.105
1	.150	1	.215
2	.250	2	.210
3	.250	3	.225
4	.150	4	.145
5	.100	5	.100
$\mu_1(X)$	2.5000	$\mu_1(Y)$	2.3900
$\sigma_1(X)$	1.4318	$\sigma_1(Y)$	1.4792

$slope = \dfrac{1.4792}{1.4318} = 1.0331$

$intercept = 2.3900 - 1.0331(2.5000) = -.1927$

$l_{Ys}(x=0) = -.1927, l_{Ys}(x=1) = .8404, l_{Ys}(x=2) = 1.8735,$
$l_{Ys}(x=3) = 2.9066, l_{Ys}(x=4) = 3.9397, l_{Ys}(x=5) = 4.9728$

the linear equivalents differ somewhat from the equipercentile equivalents shown in Table 5.5, indicating that the equating relationship is not linear when frequency estimation assumptions are used.

5.3 Chained Equipercentile Equating

Angoff (1971) described an alternative equipercentile method that Marco et al. (1983) referred to as the *direct equipercentile method*. Dorans (1990) and Livingston et al. (1990) referred to this method as chained equipercentile equating. In this method, Form X scores are converted to scores on the common items using examinees from Population 1. Then scores on the common items are equated to Form Y scores using examinees from Population 2. These two conversions are chained together to produce a conversion of Form X scores to Form Y scores.

More specifically, the steps are as follows:

1. Find the equipercentile equating relationship for converting scores on Form X to the common items based on examinees from Population 1 using the equipercentile method described in Chapter 2. (Note that the same examinees take Form X and the common items.) This equipercentile function is referred to as $e_{V1}(x)$.

2. Find the equipercentile equating relationship for converting scores on the common items to scores on Form Y based on examinees from Population 2. Refer to the resulting function as $e_{Y2}(v)$.

3. To equate a Form X score to a score on Form Y, first convert the Form X score to a common-item score using $e_{V1}(x)$. Then equate the resulting common-item score to Form Y using $e_{Y2}(v)$.

Specifically, to find the Form Y equipercentile equivalent of a Form X score, take

$$e_{Y(chain)} = e_{Y2}[e_{V1}(x)]. \tag{5.14}$$

This method is referred to as *chained equipercentile equating* because it involves a chain of two equipercentile equatings, one in Population 1 and another in Population 2. This chaining process is similar to the chaining process described in Chapter 2, where scores on the new form were converted to scale scores by a chain involving the old form.

Livingston et al. (1990) suggested that the chained equipercentile method sometimes can produce accurate and stable results in practice, and they suggested that smoothing methods might be used to improve the stability of the method. Livingston (1993) suggested that the log-linear smoothing method which was described previously for the frequency estimation be used for smoothing the joint distribution of total test scores and common-item scores. The resulting smoothed marginal distributions are all that would be used in chained equipercentile equating. Alternatively, only the marginal distributions of total scores and common items could be smoothed using the log-linear method described in Chapter 3 and then applying equipercentile equating. As still another alternative, the cubic spline postsmoothing method could be used to smooth estimates of $e_{V1}(x)$ and $e_{Y2}(v)$. The only modification of the cubic spline method described in Chapter 3 would be to use standard errors of single group equating rather than standard errors of random groups equating in implementing the spline method. These smoothed relationships could be used in place of the population relationships in equation (5.14).

Chained equipercentile equating does not require consideration of the joint distribution of total score and common-item score, so computationally it is much less intensive than frequency estimation equipercentile equating. However, chained equipercentile equating has theoretical shortcomings. First, this method involves equating a long test (total test) to a short test (common items). Tests of considerably unequal lengths cannot be equated in the sense that scores on the long and short tests can be used interchangeably. Second, this method does not directly incorporate a synthetic population, so it is unclear for what population the relationship holds or is intended to hold. Braun and Holland (1982, p. 42) demonstrated that chained equipercentile and frequency estimation equipercentile do not, in general, produce the same results, even when the assumptions for frequency

TABLE 5.7. Moments for Equating Form X and Form Y in the Common-item Nonequivalent Groups Design.

Group	Score	$\hat{\mu}$	$\hat{\sigma}$	$\widehat{sk}$	$\widehat{ku}$	Correlation
1	X	15.8205	6.5278	.5799	2.7217	$\hat{\rho}_1(X,V) =$
1	V	5.1063	2.3760	.4117	2.7683	.8645
2	Y	18.6728	6.8784	.2051	2.3028	$\hat{\rho}_2(Y,V) =$
2	V	5.8626	2.4515	.1072	2.5104	.8753

estimation equipercentile equating hold. Harris and Kolen (1990) demonstrated that these methods can produce equating relationships which differ from a practical perspective. However, the chained equipercentile method does not explicitly require that the two populations be very similar, so that this method might be useful in situations where the two groups differ. For example, results presented by Marco et al. (1983) and Livingston et al. (1990) suggest that chained equipercentile equating should be considered when groups differ considerably. Livingston (1996) suggested considering *chained linear equating*, which is conducted similarly to chained equipercentile, except that linear methods are used (also see Cope, 1987; Angoff, 1971).

5.4 Illustrative Example

The real data example from Chapter 4 is used to illustrate some aspects of frequency estimation equating. As was indicated in that chapter, the test used in this example is a 36-item multiple-choice test. Two forms of the test, Form X and Form Y, were used. Every third item on the test forms is a common item, and the common items are in the same position on each form. Thus, items $3, 6, 9, \ldots, 36$ on each form represent the 12 common items. Form X was administered to 1,655 examinees and Form Y to 1,639 examinees.

5.4.1 Illustrative Results

Summary statistics for this example are shown in Table 5.7 ($\widehat{sk}$ refers to estimated skewness and $\widehat{ku}$ to estimated kurtosis). The examinees who were administered Form X had a number-correct score mean of 5.1063 and a standard deviation of 2.3760 on the common items. The examinees who were administered Form Y had a number-correct score mean of 5.8626 and a standard deviation of 2.4515 on the common items. Thus, based on the common-item statistics, the group taking Form Y appears to be

148   5. Nonequivalent Groups—Equipercentile Methods

higher achieving than the group taking Form X. The statistics shown in this table were also used to calculate the Tucker and Levine equating functions described in Chapter 4. Some of the statistics shown in Table 5.7 were also presented in Table 4.3. The analyses were conducted using the $CIPE$ computer program described in Appendix B.

For frequency estimation equating, the joint distributions of total score and common-item score also need to be considered. As was indicated earlier in this chapter, the assumptions in frequency estimation equating require that the distribution of total score given common-item score be the same for both populations. However, from the data that are collected, no data are available to address this assumption directly. The linearity of the regressions of total test on common items can be addressed, however. If the regression is nonlinear, then the use of the Tucker method might be questionable, and the Braun-Holland method might be preferred.

Statistics relevant to the regression of X on V for Group 1 are shown in Table 5.8. The first column lists the possible scores on the common items. The second column lists the number of examinees in Group 1 earning each score on the common items. The third column lists the mean total score given common-item score. For example, the mean total score on Form X for the 14 examinees earning a common-item score of zero is 6.2143. Note that, as expected, the means increase as v increases. The fourth column presents the standard deviation, and the fifth column is based on estimating the mean on Form X given v using standard linear regression. The slope and intercept of the regression equation can be estimated directly from the data in Table 5.7 as follows:

$$\begin{aligned}
\text{regression slope} &= \hat{\rho}_1(X,V)\frac{\hat{\sigma}(X)}{\hat{\sigma}_1(V)} = .8645\frac{6.5278}{2.3760} = 2.3751. \\
\text{regression intercept} &= \hat{\mu}_1(X) - (\text{regression slope})\,\hat{\mu}_1(V) \\
&= 15.8205 - (2.3751)\,5.1063 = 3.6923,
\end{aligned}$$

apart from the effects of rounding. The slope and intercept can be used to produce the values in the fifth column, The residual mean equals the third column minus the fifth column. The residual mean indicates the extent to which the mean predicted using linear regression differs from the mean that was observed. The mean residuals for Form X are plotted in Figure 5.1.

If the regression was truly linear, then the mean residuals would vary randomly around 0. However, the residual means are positive for low and high scores on v and are negative for scores from 3 through 6. This pattern suggests that the regression is not linear. More sophisticated methods for testing hypotheses about the linearity of regression could also be used (e.g., see Draper and Smith, 1998). The regression of Y on V for Group 2 is shown in Table 5.9, and the mean residuals are plotted in Figure 5.2.

TABLE 5.8. Analysis of Residuals from the Linear Regression of Total Score on Common-Item Score For Group 1.

v	Number of Examinees	Mean X Given v	Standard Deviation X Given v	Mean X Given v, Linear Regression	Residual Mean
0	14	6.2143	2.2097	3.6923	2.5220
1	54	7.5741	2.2657	6.0674	1.5067
2	142	9.1901	2.6429	8.4425	.7476
3	249	10.8032	2.9243	10.8177	−.0145
4	274	12.7628	3.1701	13.1928	−.4300
5	247	15.1377	3.3302	15.5680	−.4303
6	232	16.9957	3.6982	17.9431	−.9474
7	173	20.5260	3.5654	20.3182	.2078
8	118	23.1610	3.5150	22.6934	.4676
9	75	25.6533	2.8542	25.0685	.5848
10	42	28.5000	3.4658	27.4436	1.0564
11	27	31.1852	2.1780	29.8188	1.3664
12	8	33.2500	1.6394	32.1939	1.0561

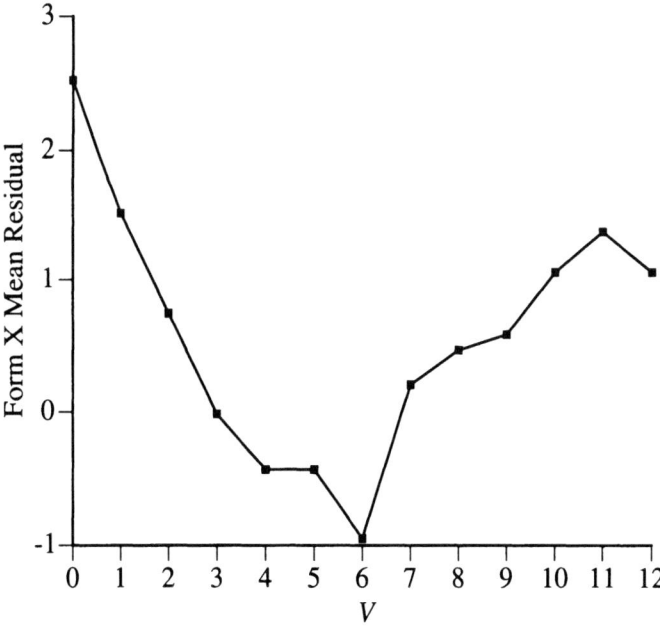

FIGURE 5.1. Form X mean residual plot.

150   5. Nonequivalent Groups—Equipercentile Methods

TABLE 5.9. Analysis of Residuals from the Linear Regression of Total Score on Common-Item Score For Group 2.

v	Number of Examinees	Mean Y Given v	Standard Deviation Y Given v	Mean Y Given v, Linear Regression	Residual Mean
0	11	6.2727	2.1780	4.2740	1.9988
1	36	8.0000	2.2361	6.7300	1.2700
2	88	9.6023	3.0359	9.1860	.4162
3	159	12.1195	3.2435	11.6421	.4774
4	213	13.9202	3.3929	14.0991	−.1779
5	240	16.0750	3.4234	16.5541	−.4791
6	232	18.3147	1.5623	19.0101	−.6955
7	246	21.2073	3.4854	21.4662	−.2588
8	161	24.1801	3.3731	23.9222	.2579
9	120	27.3333	2.9533	26.3782	.9551
10	85	29.1294	2.8811	28.8343	.2952
11	34	31.8235	1.8396	31.2903	.5332
12	13	33.6154	1.7338	33.7463	−.1309

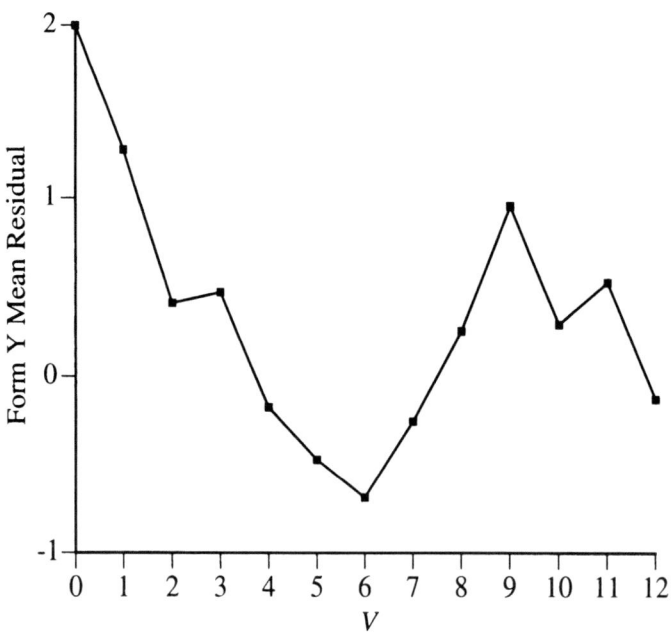

FIGURE 5.2. Form Y mean residual plot.

TABLE 5.10. Moments of Form X Scores Converted to Form Y Scores Using Various Methods for Examinees from Population 1.

Method	$\hat{\mu}$	$\hat{\sigma}$	$\widehat{sk}$	$\widehat{ku}$
Tucker linear	16.8153	6.7168	.5799	2.7217
Levine linear	16.2485	6.6007	.5799	2.7217
Braun-Holland linear	16.8329	6.6017	.5799	2.7217
Equipercentile				
Unsmoothed	16.8329	6.6017	.4622	2.6229
$S = .10$	16.8334	6.5983	.4617	2.6234
$S = .25$	16.8333	6.5947	.4674	2.6249
$S = .50$	16.8192	6.5904	.4983	2.6255
$S = .75$	16.8033	6.5858	.5286	2.6503
$S = 1.00$	16.7928	6.5821	.5501	2.6745

This regression also appears to be somewhat nonlinear. These nonlinear regressions suggest that the Braun-Holland method might be preferable to the Tucker method.

5.4.2 Comparison Among Methods

The Tucker and Braun-Holland linear methods and frequency estimation equipercentile equating with cubic spline smoothing were all applied to these data. The Levine observed score method under a congeneric model was also applied. The resulting moments are shown in Table 5.10, and the equating relationships are shown in Figure 5.3.

First, refer to Figure 5.3. The Levine relationship seems to differ from the others. As was indicated in Chapter 4, the Levine method is based on assumptions about true scores, whereas the other methods make assumptions about observed scores. The differences in assumptions are likely the reason for the discrepancy. Unfortunately, data are not available that allow a judgment about whether the Levine method assumptions (other than possibly linearity of regression) are more or less preferable than the assumptions for the other methods in this example.

The Tucker, Braun-Holland, and frequency estimation methods all require assumptions about characteristics of the observed relationship between total score and score on the common items being the same for the two populations. These methods differ with respect to which characteristics of the relationship are assumed to be the same.

First consider the Tucker and Braun-Holland methods. The major difference between these methods is in the assumption of linearity of regression. Thus, the relatively small differences between the two methods in the exam-

152   5. Nonequivalent Groups—Equipercentile Methods

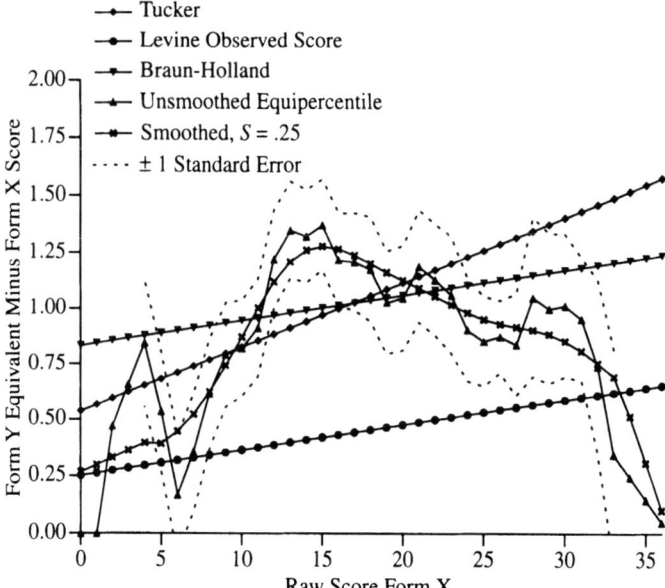

FIGURE 5.3. Equating relationships for frequency estimation equipercentile equating and linear methods.

ple are due to the differences in assumptions. The Braun-Holland method might be preferred, because the regression was judged to be nonlinear.

Next compare the Braun-Holland and frequency estimation method, referred to as unsmoothed, in Table 5.10 and Figure 5.3. The relationship appears to be nonlinear. The Braun-Holland relationship falls outside the standard error band for the frequency estimation method over parts of the score range. Thus, the frequency estimation method (labeled unsmoothed) appears to more accurately reflect the equipercentile relationship between the forms than does the Braun-Holland method in this example.

Table 5.10 presents the results for various degrees of cubic spline smoothing. The moments for values of S that are greater than .25 seem to differ more than would be desired from those for the unsmoothed equating. For this reason, the relationship for $S = .25$ is plotted in Figure 5.3. This relationship stays within the standard error bands and seems to be smooth without deviating too far from the unsmoothed values.

5.4.3 Practical Issues in Equipercentile Equating with Common Items

A series of additional practical issues should be considered when deciding on which method to use when equating is conducted in practice. First, scale score moments and conversions should be considered, as was done in Chapter 2. Second, the reasonableness of the frequency estimation assumptions should be evaluated. Third, practical considerations might dictate that a linear method would need to be used with a particular testing program. For example, suppose that the major focus of the testing program was on deciding whether examinees were above or below a cutting score that was near the mean. Then a linear equating method (or even a mean equating method) might be considered adequate, because the results for the Tucker and Braun-Holland linear methods are typically similar to those for frequency estimation equipercentile equating near the mean, and linear methods are less complicated computationally. Practical issues in choosing among methods are considered further in Chapter 8.

Sometimes it is possible to equate forms that have items in common when using the random groups design. Such a design is referred to as the *common-item random groups design*. In this design, the use of the common items can lead to greater precision than would be attained using the random groups design without considering the common items. Computationally, equipercentile equating would proceed in the same way as it would for frequency estimation equating. The linear methods described in Chapter 4 also could be applied in this design. The increase in equating precision that is achieved by using common items is discussed briefly in Chapter 7.

5.5 Exercises

5.1. Using the data in Table 5.1, find the conditional distribution of X given v, and display the results in a format similar to Table 5.3.

5.2. Using frequency estimation assumptions, find the joint distribution of X and V in Population 2 and display the results in a format similar to Table 5.4. Also display the marginal distributions.

5.3. Using the data in Tables 5.1 and 5.4, the results shown in Table 5.4, the results from Exercise 5.2, and assuming that $w_1 = w_2 = .5$, find the Form Y equipercentile equivalents of Form X integer scores 0, 1, 2, 3, 4, and 5.

5.4. Find the Braun-Holland and Tucker linear equations for the equating relationship for the data in the example associated with Tables 5.1 and 5.2 for $w_1 = w_2 = .5$.

5.5. Do the relationships between X and V and Y and V in Tables 5.1 and 5.2 appear to be linear? How can you tell? How would you explain the difference in results for the Braun-Holland and Tucker methods in Exercise 5.4?

5.6. Use chained equipercentile equating to find the Form Y equivalents of Form X integer scores 1 and 3 using the data in Tables 5.1 and 5.2.

6
Item Response Theory Methods

Item response theory (IRT) methods are used in many testing applications, and the use of IRT has been reinforced by many book-length treatments (e.g., Baker, 1992a; Hambleton and Swaminathan, 1985; Hambleton et al., 1991; Lord, 1980; van der Linden and Hambleton, 1997; Wright and Stone, 1979). Applications of IRT include test development, item banking, differential item functioning, adaptive testing, test equating, and test scaling. A major appeal of IRT is that it provides an integrated psychometric framework for developing and scoring tests. Much of the power of IRT results from the fact that it explicitly models examinee responses at the item level, whereas, for example, the focus of classical test models and strong true score models is on responses at the level of test scores.

Unidimensional IRT models have been developed for tests that are intended to measure a single dimension, and *multidimensional IRT models* have been developed for tests that are intended to measure simultaneously along multiple dimensions. IRT models have been developed for tests whose items are scored dichotomously (0/1) as well as for tests whose items are scored polytomously (e.g., a short answer test in which examinees can earn a score of 0, 1, or 2 on each item). See Thissen and Steinberg (1986) for a taxonomy of IRT models.

Many testing programs use unidimensional IRT models to assemble tests. In these testing programs, the use of IRT equating methods often seems natural. Also, IRT methods can be used for equating in some situations in which traditional methods typically are not used, such as equating to an item pool. Thus, IRT methods are an important component of equating methodology. However, IRT models gain their flexibility by making strong statistical assumptions, which likely do not hold precisely in real testing situations. For this reason, studying the robustness of the models to violations of the assumptions, as well as studying the fit of the IRT model, is a crucial aspect of IRT applications. See Hambleton and Swaminathan (1985) and Hambleton et al. (1991) for general discussions of testing model fit.

The initial focus of this chapter is on equating dichotomously (0/1) scored test forms using the unidimensional IRT model referred to as the *three-parameter logistic model* (Lord, 1980). This model, which is described more fully later in this chapter, is the most general unidimensional model for dichotomously scored tests that is in widespread use. The *Rasch model* (Rasch, 1960; Wright and Stone, 1979) also is discussed briefly. In this chapter, after an introduction to IRT, methods of transforming IRT scales are discussed. Then IRT true score equating and IRT observed score equating are treated. The methods are illustrated using the same data that were used in Chapters 4 and 5. Equating using IRT-based item pools also is discussed. Equating with polytomous IRT models is considered near the end of this chapter. Issues in equating computer administered and computer adaptive tests are considered in Chapter 8.

As will be described more fully later in this chapter, equating using IRT typically is a three-step process. First, item parameters are estimated using a computer program such as BILOG 3 (Mislevy and Bock, 1990) or LOGIST (Wingersky et al., 1982). Second, parameter estimates are scaled to a base IRT scale using a linear transformation. Third, if number-correct scoring is used, number-correct scores on the new form are converted to the number-correct scale on an old form and then to scale scores.

6.1 Some Necessary IRT Concepts

A description of some necessary concepts in IRT is presented here to provide a basis for understanding unidimensional IRT equating of dichotomously scored tests. References cited earlier provide a much more complete presentation of IRT. Instructional modules on IRT by Harris (1989) and on IRT equating by Cook and Eignor (1991) can be used as supplements to the material presented here.

6.1.1 Unidimensionality and Local Independence Assumptions

Unidimensional item response theory (IRT) models for dichotomously (0/1) scored tests assume that *examinee ability* is described by a single latent variable, referred to as θ, defined so that $-\infty < \theta < \infty$. The use of a single latent variable implies that the construct being measured by the test is *unidimensional*. In practical terms, the unidimensionality assumption in IRT requires that tests measure only one ability. For example, a mathematics test that contains some items that are strictly computational and other items that involve verbal material likely is not unidimensional.

The *item characteristic curve* for each item relates the probability of correctly answering the item to examinee ability. The item characteristic curve for item j is symbolized by $p_j(\theta)$, which represents the probability of correctly answering item j for examinees with ability θ. For example, if 50% of the examinees with ability $\theta = 1.5$ can be expected to answer item 1 correctly, then the probability can be symbolized as $p_1(\theta = 1.5) = .5$. Note that p_j is written as a function of the variable θ. IRT models typically assume a specified functional form for the item characteristic curve, which is what distinguishes IRT models from one another.

An assumption of *local independence* is made in applying IRT models. Local independence means that, after taking into account examinee ability, examinee responses to the items are statistically independent. Under local independence, the probability that examinees of ability θ correctly answer *both* item 1 *and* item 2 equals the product of the probability of correctly answering item 1 and the probability of correctly answering item 2. For example, if examinees of ability $\theta = 1.5$ have a .5 probability of answering item 1 correctly and a .6 probability of answering item 2 correctly, for such examinees the probability of correctly answering *both* items correctly under local independence is $.30 = .50(.60)$.

The local independence assumption implies that there are no dependencies among items other than those that are attributable to latent ability. One example where local independence likely would not hold is when tests are composed of sets of items that are based on common stimuli, such as reading passages or charts. In this case, local independence probably would be violated because items associated with one stimulus are likely to be more related to one another than to items associated with another stimulus.

Although the IRT unidimensionality and local independence assumptions might not hold strictly, they might hold closely enough for IRT to be used advantageously in many practical situations. In using IRT equating, it is important to choose an equating design that minimizes the effects of violations of model assumptions.

6.1.2 IRT Models

Various IRT models are in use that differ in the functional form of the item characteristic curve. Among unidimensional models, the three-parameter logistic model is the most general of the forms in widespread use. In this model, the functional form for an item characteristic curve is characterized by three item parameters. Under the three-parameter logistic model, the probability that persons of ability equal to the ability of person i correctly

158   6. Item Response Theory Methods

TABLE 6.1. Item and Person Parameters on Two Scales for a Hypothetical Test.

	Scale I			Scale J		
Item Parameters						
Item	a_{Ij}	b_{Ij}	c_{Ij}	a_{Jj}	b_{Jj}	c_{Jj}
$j=1$	1.30	-1.30	.10	2.60	-1.15	.10
$j=2$	.60	$-.10$	.17	1.20	$-.55$	.17
$j=3$	1.70	.90	.18	3.40	$-.05$	.18

Person Abilities

Person	θ_{Ii}			θ_{Ji}		
$i=1$	-2.00			-1.50		
$i=2$	1.00			.00		

Scale Transformation Constants

$A = .5 \qquad B = -.5$

Probability of Correctly Answering Items

	$p_{ij}(\theta_{Ii}; a_{Ij}, b_{Ij}, c_{Ij})$			$p_{ij}(\theta_{Ji}; a_{Jj}, b_{Jj}, c_{Jj})$	
	Person			Person	
Item	$i=1$	$i=2$		$i=1$	$i=2$
$j=1$	.26	.99		.26	.99
$j=2$	.27	.80		.27	.80
$j=3$	.18	.65		.18	.65

answer item j is defined as

$$p_{ij} = p_{ij}(\theta_i; a_j, b_j, c_j) = c_j + (1 - c_j) \frac{\exp[Da_j(\theta_i - b_j)]}{1 + \exp[Da_j(\theta_i - b_j)]}. \qquad (6.1)$$

In this equation, θ_i is the ability parameter for person i. Ability, θ, is defined over the range $-\infty < \theta < \infty$ and often is scaled to be normally distributed with a mean of 0 and standard deviation of 1. In this case, nearly all of the persons have θ values in the range -3 to $+3$. The expression "exp" in equation (6.1) stands for the natural exponential function. That is, the quantity in brackets after exp is the exponent of $e = 2.71828\ldots$. The constant D typically is set to 1.7 so that the logistic item response curve and the normal ogive differ by no more than .01 for all values of θ.

The item parameters a_j, b_j, and c_j are associated with item j. The meanings of these parameters are illustrated in the portion of Table 6.1 labeled "Item Parameters" and in Figure 6.1. For now, consider only the item parameters for the three items listed below the labeled portion "Scale I" on the left-hand side of the table. Also ignore the I subscript for the present. The item parameter c_j is the *lower asymptote or pseudo-chance level parameter* for item j. The parameter c_j represents the probability that

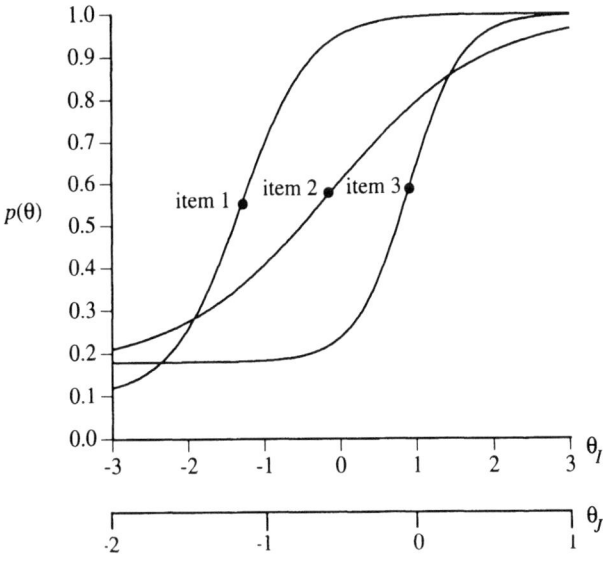

FIGURE 6.1. Hypothetical example of scale transformations.

an examinee with very low ability (actually, $\theta = -\infty$) correctly answers the item. For example, for low ability examinees, the curve for item 3 in Figure 6.1 appears to be leveling off (have a lower asymptote) at a probability of .18, which corresponds to the c-parameter for this item listed in Table 6.1. If the horizontal axis in Figure 6.1 were extended beyond $\theta = -3$, items 1 and 2 would appear to have the lower asymptotes of .10 and .17 shown in Table 6.1. The c-parameter for an item must be in the range 0 to 1. Typically, the c-parameter for an item is somewhere in the range of 0 to the probability of correctly answering an item by random guessing (1 divided by the number of options).

The item parameter b_j is referred to as the *difficulty* or *location parameter* for item j. The logistic curve has an inflexion point at $\theta = b$. When $c = 0$, b is the level of ability where the probability of a correct answer is .5. Otherwise, b is the ability level where the probability of a correct response is halfway between c and 1.0. The inflexion point of each curve is indicated by the circular symbol on each item characteristic curve in Figure 6.1. Typically, b is in the range -3 to $+3$. Higher values of b are associated with more difficult items. As an illustration, item 3 has the highest b-parameter in Table 6.1. Of the three items in Figure 6.1, the item characteristic curve for item 3 tends to be shifted the farthest to the right.

The item parameter a_j is referred to as the *discrimination parameter* for item j. The a-parameter is proportional to the slope of the item characteristic curve at the inflexion point. As can be seen in Table 6.1, item 3 has the highest a-parameter (1.7) and item 3 also has the steepest item characteristic curve in Figure 6.1.

The abilities for two persons are shown in the middle of Table 6.1 under the heading "Person Abilities." The probabilities of correctly answering each of the three items for examinees of ability $\theta = -2.00$ and $\theta = 1.00$ are shown at the bottom of Table 6.1 under the heading "Probability of Correctly Answering Items." For example, the probability of person $i = 1$ with ability $\theta_{Ii} = -2.00$ correctly answering the first item can be calculated as follows using equation (6.1):

$$p_{ij} = .10 + (1 - .10) \frac{\exp\{1.7(1.30)[-2.00 - (-1.30)]\}}{1 + \exp\{1.7(1.30)[-2.00 - (-1.30)]\}} = .26.$$

The reader should verify the computation of the other probabilities by substituting the abilities and item parameters into equation (6.1).

Various simplifications of the three-parameter logistic model have been used. One variation can be obtained by setting c_j equal to a constant other than 0. The *two-parameter logistic model* is obtained from equation (6.1) by setting c_j equal to 0. This model does not explicitly accommodate examinee guessing. The Rasch model is obtained from equation (6.1) by setting c_j equal to 0, a_j equal to 1, and D equal to 1. The Rasch model, therefore, requires all items to be equally discriminating, and it does not explicitly accommodate guessing. Other models exist that use a normal ogive to model p_{ij}.

The three-parameter logistic model is the only one of the three models presented that explicitly accommodates items which vary in difficulty, which vary in discrimination, and for which there is a nonzero probability of obtaining the correct answer by guessing. Because of its generality, the three-parameter model is the focus of this chapter. However, the assumed form of the relationship between ability and the probability of a correct response (e.g., the three-parameter logistic curve) is chosen primarily for reasons of mathematical tractability. No reason exists for this relationship to hold, precisely, for actual test items.

6.1.3 IRT Parameter Estimation

IRT parameters need to be estimated when using IRT methods in practice. LOGIST (Wingersky et al., 1982) and BILOG 3 (Mislevy and Bock, 1990) are two computer programs for the three-parameter logistic model that often are used to estimate ability and item parameters. An IRT parameter estimation computer program, such as BILOG or LOGIST, is necessary if the concepts and methodologies described in this chapter are to be applied to equating tests other than those used in the examples. Mislevy and Stocking (1989) compared these two programs, and Baker (1992a) wrote extensively about IRT estimation. The basic input for these programs is

0/1 (wrong or right) scores of examinees at the item level. These programs use different estimation methods, have various options for estimating parameters, and produce somewhat different results. Unless the user chooses to do otherwise, the scaling of ability in LOGIST removes persons with extreme ability estimates before the ability estimates are scaled to have a mean of 0 and a standard deviation of 1. Extreme ability estimates are not included in the computation of the mean and standard deviation. These estimates are considered to be poor because they are likely to have considerable estimation error. Unless the user chooses otherwise, the ability scaling in BILOG also results in abilities with means of approximately 0 and standard deviations of approximately 1. Baker (1984, 1990) discussed the implication of scaling of the ability distributions with these programs.

One important characteristic of ability estimation that arises from either of these programs is that the ability estimates depend on the pattern of item responses, rather than just on the number of items an examinee answers correctly (except for the Rasch model). That is, examinees who earn the same number-correct score would likely earn different estimated θ's if some of the items that they correctly answered were different. The use of such *pattern scoring* in IRT increases the precision of the IRT ability estimates over using the number-correct score if the IRT model holds. However, for many practical reasons, including equating, number-correct scoring often is used.

6.2 Transformations of IRT Scales

When conducting equating with nonequivalent groups, the parameters from different test forms need to be on the same IRT scale. However, the parameter estimates that result from IRT parameter estimation procedures are often on different IRT scales. For example, assume that the parameters for the IRT model are estimated for Form X based on a sample of examinees from Population 1 and separately for Form Y based on a sample of examinees from Population 2, where the two populations are not equivalent. As was already indicated, computer programs often define the θ-scale as having a mean of 0 and a standard deviation of 1 for the set of data being analyzed. In this case, the abilities for each group would be scaled to have a mean of 0 and a standard deviation of 1, even though the groups differed in ability. Thus, a transformation of IRT scales is needed.

As will be demonstrated later in this section, if an IRT model fits a set of data, then any linear transformation of the θ-scale also fits the set of data, provided that the item parameters also are transformed. When the IRT model holds, the parameter estimates from different computer runs are on linearly related θ-scales. Thus, a linear equation can be used to convert IRT parameter estimates to the same scale. After conversion, the means and standard deviations of the abilities for the two groups on the common scale would be expected to differ. The resulting transformed parameter estimates, which sometimes are referred to as being *calibrated*, then can be used to establish score equivalents between number-correct scores on Form X and Form Y, and then to scale scores.

6.2.1 Transformation Equations

Define Scale I and Scale J as three-parameter logistic IRT scales that differ by a linear transformation. Then the θ-values for the two scales are related as follows:

$$\theta_{Ji} = A\theta_{Ii} + B, \tag{6.2}$$

where A and B are constants in the linear equation and θ_{Ji} and θ_{Ii} are values of θ for individual i on Scale J and Scale I. The item parameters on the two scales are related as follows:

$$a_{Jj} = \frac{a_{Ij}}{A}, \tag{6.3}$$

$$b_{Jj} = Ab_{Ij} + B, \tag{6.4}$$

and

$$c_{Jj} = c_{Ij}, \tag{6.5}$$

where a_{Jj}, b_{Jj}, and c_{Jj} are the item parameters for item j on Scale J and a_{Ij}, b_{Ij}, and c_{Ij} are the item parameters for item j on Scale I. The lower asymptote parameter is independent of the scale transformation, as is indicated by equation (6.5).

6.2.2 Demonstrating the Appropriateness of Scale Transformations

To demonstrate that there is an A and a B which result in the scale transformation that correctly transforms parameters from Scale I to Scale J, note that the right-hand side of equation (6.1) for Scale J equals

$$c_{Jj} + (1 - c_{Jj}) \frac{\exp[Da_{Jj}(\theta_{Ji} - b_{Jj})]}{1 + \exp[Da_{Jj}(\theta_{Ji} - b_{Jj})]}.$$

Now replace θ_{Ji}, a_{Jj}, b_{Jj}, c_{Jj} with the expressions from equations (6.2)–(6.5) as follows:

$$c_{Ij} + (1 - c_{Ij}) \frac{\exp\left\{D\frac{a_{Ij}}{A}[A\theta_{Ii} + B - (Ab_{Ij} + B)]\right\}}{1 + \exp\left\{D\frac{a_{Ij}}{A}[A\theta_{Ii} + B - (Ab_{Ij} + B)]\right\}}$$

$$= c_{Ij} + (1 - c_{Ij}) \frac{\exp[Da_{Ij}(\theta_{Ii} - b_{Ij})]}{1 + \exp[Da_{Ij}(\theta_{Ii} - b_{Ij})]}.$$

This resulting expression is the right-hand portion of equation (6.1) for Scale I, which demonstrates that A and B in equations (6.2)-(6.5) provide the scale transformation.

6.2.3 Expressing A and B Constants

One way to express the constants A and B is as follows. For any two individuals, i and i^*, or any two items, j and j^*, A and B in equations (6.2)-(6.5) can be expressed as

$$A = \frac{\theta_{Ji} - \theta_{Ji^*}}{\theta_{Ii} - \theta_{Ii^*}} = \frac{b_{Jj} - b_{Jj^*}}{b_{Ij} - b_{Ij^*}} = \frac{a_{Ij}}{a_{Jj}} \qquad (6.6)$$

and

$$B = b_{Jj} - Ab_{Ij} = \theta_{Ji} - A\theta_{Ii}. \qquad (6.7)$$

To illustrate these equalities, refer back to Table 6.1 and Figure 6.1 for a hypothetical example of scale transformations. Parameters for three items are presented in the portion of Table 6.1 labeled "Item Parameters." Parameters for these items are given for Scale I and for Scale J. The item characteristic curves for these three items are presented in Figure 6.1. Note that horizontal scales are presented in this figure for Scale I and Scale J, and these are labeled θ_I and θ_J. As is evident from this figure, the item characteristic curves are the same shape on either scale. To calculate A from equation (6.6) using the difficulty parameters for items 1 and 2 ($j = 1$ and $j^* = 2$), take

$$A = \frac{(-1.15) - (-.55)}{(-1.30) - (-.10)} = \frac{-.6}{-1.2} = .5.$$

Alternatively, using the slope parameters for item 1,

$$A = \frac{1.3}{2.6} = .5.$$

Using equation (6.7) with the difficulty parameters for item 1,

$$B = (-1.15) - (.5)(-1.30) = -.5.$$

These values agree with those in the section labeled "Scale Transformation Constants" in Table 6.1. Equations (6.6) and (6.7) also can be used to calculate A and B using the θ-values for Persons 1 and 2. These A and B values can be used to transform parameters from Scale I to Scale J using equations (6.2)–(6.5). For example, to transform the ability of Person 1 from Scale I to Scale J using equation (6.2), take

$$\theta_{J1} = A\theta_{I1} + B = .5(-2.00) + (-.5) = -1.5,$$

which is the value for Person 1 shown under "Person Abilities" in Table 6.1. To convert the parameters for item 3 from Scale I to Scale J using equations (6.3)–(6.5), take

$$a_{J3} = \frac{a_{I3}}{A} = \frac{1.7}{.5} = 3.4,$$
$$b_{J3} = Ab_{I3} + B = .5(.90) - .5 = -.05,$$

and
$$c_{J3} = c_{I3} = .18.$$

These values agree with the Scale J values in the portion of Table 6.1 labeled "Item Parameters."

The p_{ij} values based on equation (6.1) are presented in the portion of Table 6.1 labeled "Probability of Correctly Answering Items." These values can be calculated from the item and person parameters presented in Table 6.1; they are the same for Scales I and J, and the p_{ij} values will be identical for any linearly related scales. This property often is referred to as *indeterminacy of scale location and spread.*

6.2.4 Expressing A and B Constants in Terms of Groups of Items and/or Persons

So far, the relationships between scales have been expressed by two abilities and two items. Often, it is more useful to express the relationships in terms of groups of items or people. From equations (6.6) and (6.7) it follows that (see Exercise 6.3)

$$A = \frac{\sigma(b_J)}{\sigma(b_I)}, \tag{6.8a}$$
$$= \frac{\mu(a_I)}{\mu(a_J)}, \tag{6.8b}$$
$$= \frac{\sigma(\theta_J)}{\sigma(\theta_I)}, \tag{6.8c}$$

$$B = \mu(b_J) - A\mu(b_I), \quad \text{and} \tag{6.9a}$$
$$= \mu(\theta_J) - A\mu(\theta_I). \tag{6.9b}$$

The means $\mu(b_J)$, $\mu(b_I)$, $\mu(a_I)$, and $\mu(a_J)$ in these equations are defined over one or more items with parameters that are expressed on both Scale I and Scale J. The standard deviations $\sigma(b_J)$ and $\sigma(b_I)$ are defined over two or more items with parameters that are expressed on both Scale I and Scale J. The means $\mu(\theta_J)$ and $\mu(\theta_I)$ are defined over one or more examinees with ability parameters that are expressed on both Scale I and

Scale J. The standard deviations $\sigma(\theta_J)$ and $\sigma(\theta_I)$ are defined over two or more examinees with parameters that are expressed on both Scale I and Scale J.

To illustrate the use of equations (6.8a), (6.8b), and (6.9a), the following quantities can be calculated for the three items from the example in Table 6.1: $\mu(b_I) = -.1667$, $\sigma(b_I) = .8994$, $\mu(a_I) = 1.2$, $\mu(b_J) = -.5833$, $\sigma(b_J) = .4497$, and $\mu(a_J) = 2.4$. From equations (6.8) and (6.9),

$$A = \frac{\sigma(b_J)}{\sigma(b_I)} = \frac{\mu(a_I)}{\mu(a_J)} = \frac{.4497}{.8994} = \frac{1.2000}{2.4000} = .5000,$$

and

$$B = \mu(b_J) - A\mu(b_I) = -.5833 - .5000(-.1667) = -.5000.$$

Similar calculations can be made using the mean and standard deviations for the two ability scales in Table 6.1.

In equating with nonequivalent groups, parameter estimates for the common items would be available for examinees in the two groups. The parameter estimates on the common items could be used to find the scaling constants by substituting estimates for these parameters in the preceding equations.

Consider a situation in which the mean and standard deviation of the abilities on Scale I are known for one group of examinees. Also, the mean and standard deviation of the abilities are known for a different group of examinees on Scale J. Is there any way equations (6.8c) and (6.9b) can be used to transform Scale I to Scale J? No! These equations can be used only if the parameters for the *same* group of examinees are expressed on *both* scales.

Consider a different situation, in which the mean and standard deviation of abilities on Scale I are 0 and 1, respectively. For the *same* group of examinees, the mean and standard deviation of abilities are 50 and 10, respectively, on Scale J. Can equations (6.8c) and (6.9b) be used to transform parameters from Scale I to Scale J? Yes. The resulting scaling constants calculated using equations (6.8c) and (6.9b) are as follows:

$$A = \frac{\sigma(\theta_J)}{\sigma(\theta_I)} = \frac{10}{1} = 10 \quad \text{and} \quad B = \mu(\theta_J) - A\mu(\theta_I) = 50 - 10(0) = 50.$$

These equations might be used to transform IRT parameters to a different scale when the means and standard deviations of the abilities are known.

6.3 Transforming IRT Scales When Parameters Are Estimated

The estimation of item parameters complicates the problem of transforming IRT scales. The process that needs to be followed depends on the design

166   6. Item Response Theory Methods

used for data collection. As was indicated earlier, when either LOGIST or BILOG are used for parameter estimation, unless the user chooses to do otherwise, ability estimates are scaled to have a mean of 0 and a standard deviation of 1.

6.3.1 Designs

In the *random groups equating design*, the IRT parameters for Form X can be estimated separately from the parameters for Form Y. If the same scaling convention (e.g., mean of 0 and standard deviation of 1) for ability is used in the separate estimations, then the parameter estimates for the two forms are assumed to be on the same scale without further transformation. No further transformation is assumed to be required because the groups are randomly equivalent, and the abilities are scaled to have the same mean and standard deviation in both groups. If, for some reason, different scaling conventions were used for the two forms, then estimates of the mean and standard deviations of the θ-estimates could be used in place of the mean and standard deviations of the θ-parameters in equations (6.8c) and (6.9b).

In the *single group design with counterbalancing*, the parameters for all examinees on both forms can be estimated together. Because the parameters for the two forms are estimated together on the same examinees, the parameter estimates are assumed to be on the same scale. If the parameters for the two forms are estimated separately using the same scaling conventions, the parameter estimates can be assumed to be on the same scale following the logic discussed previously for the random groups design.

In the *common-item nonequivalent groups equating design*, the Form Y item and ability parameters typically are estimated at the time Form Y is first administered. Consequently, only the Form X parameters need to be estimated when Form X is equated to Form Y. Because the examinees who took Form X are not considered to be equivalent to the examinees who took Form Y, parameter estimates for the two estimations are not on the same scale. However, there is a set of items that is common to the two forms. (See Chapter 8 for rules of thumb on the number of common items to use and a discussion of characteristics of common items.) The estimates of the item parameters for these common items can be used to estimate the scale transformation.

As an alternative, the parameters for Form X and Form Y can be estimated together. This type of estimation is often referred to as concurrent calibration (Wingersky and Lord, 1984). For example, a single run of LOGIST can be conducted using the item level data for Form X and Form Y on the two examinee groups, and indicating that the items which an examinee did not take are "not reached." [Consult the LOGIST manual (Wingersky et al., 1982) for a description of this procedure.] LOGIST parameter estimation is conducted using joint maximum likelihood (Lord, 1980). Bock and Zimowski (1997) described procedures for extending IRT estimation using marginal maximum likelihood estimation when different test questions are given to nonequivalent groups of examinees. When the estimation is conducted in this manner, the resulting estimates are all on the same scale. The computer programs BILOG-MG (Zimowski et al., 1996) and ICL (Hanson, 2002) can be used to estimate the item parameters for Form X and Form Y using concurrent calibration. BILOG 3 does not have the capability to allow for examinee groups that differ in ability, so it should not be used for estimating Form X and Form Y together in this situation. DeMars (2002) showed that item parameter estimates are biased when using marginal maximum likelihood estimation that does not take into account group differences and examinee groups taking the alternate forms differ in ability.

Parameter estimates must be on the same scale to proceed with equating number-correct scores on alternate forms and converting them to scale scores. Methods for equating number-correct scores are described later in this chapter.

6.3.2   Mean/Sigma and Mean/Mean Transformation Methods

The most straightforward way to transform the scales in the common-item nonequivalent groups design is to substitute the means and standard deviations of the item parameter estimates of the common items for the parameters in equations (6.8) and (6.9). After transformation, the item parameter estimates are often referred to as being *calibrated*. One procedure, described by Marco (1977) and referred to here as the *mean/sigma method*, uses the means and standard deviations of the b-parameter estimates from the common items in place of the parameters in equations (6.8a) and (6.9a). In another method, described by Loyd and Hoover (1980) and referred to here as the *mean/mean method*, the mean of the a-parameter estimates for the common items is used in place of the parameters in equation (6.8b) to estimate the A-constant. Then, the mean of the b-parameter estimates of the common items is used in place of the parameters in equation (6.9a) to estimate the B-constant. The values of A and B then can be substituted into equations (6.2)–(6.5) to obtain the rescaled parameter estimates.

When estimates are used in place of the parameters, or when the IRT model does not hold precisely, the equalities shown in equations (6.8) and (6.9) do not necessarily hold. So, the mean/sigma and the mean/mean methods typically produce different results. One reason that the mean/sigma method is sometimes preferred over the mean/mean method is that estimates of b-parameters are more stable than estimates of the a-parameters. However, Baker and Al-Karni (1991) pointed out that the mean/mean method might be preferable because means are typically more stable than standard deviations, and the mean/mean method uses only means. Empirical research comparing these two methods is inconclusive, so the approach suggested here is to consider both procedures, and compare the raw-to-

168   6. Item Response Theory Methods

scale score conversions that result from the application of both methods when equating is conducted.

Mislevy and Bock (1990) recommended a further variation that uses the means of the b-parameters and the geometric means of the a-parameters. Stocking and Lord (1983) also discussed procedures for using robust estimates of the means and standard deviations of estimates of the b-parameters, although they were not satisfied with the performance of these robust methods. Linn et al. (1981) described a related procedure that weights the item parameter estimates by their standard errors.

6.3.3 Characteristic Curve Transformation Methods

One potential problem with the methods considered so far arises when various combinations of a-, b-, and c-parameter estimates produce almost identical item characteristic curves over the range of ability at which most examinees score. For example, in two estimations an item with very different b-parameter estimates could have very similar item characteristic curves. In this case, the mean/sigma method could be overly influenced by the difference between the b-parameter estimates, even though the item characteristic curves for the items on the two estimations were very similar. This problem arises because the scale conversion methods described so far do not consider all of the item parameter estimates simultaneously. As a response to this problem, Haebara (1980) presented a method that considers all of the item parameters simultaneously, and Stocking and Lord (1983) developed a method similar to Haebara's. Stocking and Lord (1983) referred to both their method and the Haebara method as *characteristic curve methods*. To develop these methods, note that the indeterminacy of scale location and spread property which was described earlier implies that, for ability Scales I and J,

$$p_{ij}\left(\theta_{Ji}; a_{Jj}, b_{Jj}, c_{Jj}\right) = p_{ij}\left(A\theta_{Ii} + B; \frac{a_{Ij}}{A}, Ab_{Ij} + B, c_{Ij}\right) \quad (6.10)$$

for examinee i and item j. Equation (6.10) states that the probability that examinees of a given ability will answer a particular item correctly is the same regardless of the scale that is used to report the scores.

If estimates are used in place of the parameters in equation (6.10), then there is no guarantee that the equality will hold over all items and examinees for any A and B. This lack of equality is exploited by the characteristic curve methods.

Haebara Approach

The function used by Haebara (1980) to express the difference between the item characteristic curves is the sum of the squared difference between the item characteristic curves for each item for examinees of a particular ability. For a given θ_i, the sum, over items, of the squared difference can be displayed as

$$Hdiff(\theta_i) = \sum_{j:V} \left[p_{ij}(\theta_{Ji}; \hat{a}_{Jj}, \hat{b}_{Jj}, \hat{c}_{Jj}) - p_{ij}\left(\theta_{Ji}; \frac{\hat{a}_{Ij}}{A}, A\hat{b}_{Ij} + B, \hat{c}_{Ij}\right) \right]^2. \quad (6.11)$$

The summation is over the common items ($j:V$). In this equation, the difference between each item characteristic curve on the two scales is squared and summed.

$Hdiff$ then is cumulated over examinees. The estimation process proceeds by finding A and B that minimize the following criterion:

$$Hcrit = \sum_i Hdiff(\theta_i). \quad (6.12)$$

The summation in equation (6.12) is over examinees.

Stocking and Lord Approach

In contrast to the Haebara approach, Stocking and Lord (1983) used the sum, over items, of the squared difference,

$$SLdiff(\theta_i) = \left[\sum_{j:V} p_{ij}(\theta_{Ji}; \hat{a}_{Jj}, \hat{b}_{Jj}, \hat{c}_{Jj}) - \sum_{j:V} p_{ij}\left(\theta_{Ji}; \frac{\hat{a}_{Ij}}{A}, A\hat{b}_{Ij} + B, \hat{c}_{Ij}\right) \right]^2. \quad (6.13)$$

In the Stocking and Lord (1983) approach, the summation is taken over items for each set of parameter estimates before squaring. Note that in IRT, the function

$$\tau(\theta_i) = \sum_j p_{ij}(\theta_i) \quad (6.14)$$

is referred to as the *test characteristic curve*. So, the expression $SLdiff(\theta_i)$ is the squared difference between the test characteristic curves for a given θ_i. In contrast, the expression $Hdiff(\theta_i)$ is the sum of the squared difference between the item characteristic curves for a given θ_i, $SLdiff$ then is cumulated over examinees. The estimation proceeds by finding the combination of A and B that minimizes the following criterion:

$$SLcrit = \sum_i SLdiff(\theta_i). \quad (6.15)$$

The summation in equation (6.15) is over examinees. The approach to solving for A and B in equations (6.12) and (6.15) is a computationally intensive iterative approach.

170   6. Item Response Theory Methods

Specifying the Summation Over Examinees

In addition to differences in the function used to express the difference between the characteristic curves described in equations (6.11) and (6.13), these methods differ in how they cumulate the differences between the characteristic curves. Various ways to specify the examinees have been used in the summations in equations (6.12) and (6.15). Some of these ways are as follows:

1. Sum over estimated abilities of examinees who were administered the old form. (Stocking and Lord, 1983, used a spaced sample of 200 ability estimates.)

2. Sum over estimated abilities of examinees who were administered the new form and sum over estimated abilities of examinees who were administered the old form [used by Haebara (1980)].

3. Sum over estimated abilities that are grouped into intervals and then weight the differences by the proportion of examinees in each interval [used by Haebara (1980)].

4. Sum over a set of equally spaced values of ability [implemented by Baker and Al-Karni (1991)].

5. If a continuous distribution of ability is known or estimated, the summation over examinees could be replaced by integration over the ability distribution [see Zeng and Kolen (1994)].

A decision needs to be made about which of these options (or others) are used when implementing the characteristic curve procedures. The computer programs *ST* and *POLYST* that are listed in Appendix B can be used to implement these schemes for summation over examinees.

Hypothetical Example

A hypothetical example is presented in Table 6.2 that illustrates part of the process of scaling item parameter estimates. Assume that the three items listed are common items in a common-item nonequivalent groups equating design, and that the resulting estimates are on different linearly related ability scales. Estimates of A and B based on these parameter estimates for the mean/sigma and mean/mean methods are presented in the top portion of Table 6.2. The Scale I parameter estimates are converted to Scale J in the middle portion of the table. The results for the two methods differ somewhat. These differences likely would cause some differences in raw-to-scale score conversions, which could be studied if equating relationships subsequently were estimated.

The probability of a correct response, using equation (6.1), is shown in the bottom portion of Table 6.2 for examinees with ability $\theta_i = 0$. In this

TABLE 6.2. Hypothetical Example for Characteristic Curve Methods Using Estimated Parameters.

	Scale I			Scale J		
Item	$\hat{a}$	$\hat{b}$	$\hat{c}$	$\hat{a}$	$\hat{b}$	$\hat{c}$
1	.4000	−1.1000	.1000	.5000	−1.5000	.1000
2	1.7000	.9000	.2000	1.6000	.5000	.2000
3	1.2000	2.2000	.1000	1.0000	2.0000	.1000
Mean	1.1000	.6667	.1333	1.0333	.3333	.1333
Sd	.5354	1.3573	.0471	.4497	1.4337	.0471
	Mean/Sigma	Mean/Mean				
A	1.0563	1.0645				
B	−.3709	−.3763				
	Scale I Converted to Scale J Using Mean/Sigma Results			Scale I Converted to Scale J Using Mean mean Results		
Item	$\hat{a}$	$\hat{b}$	$\hat{c}$	$\hat{a}$	$\hat{b}$	$\hat{c}$
1	.3787	−1.5328	.1000	.3758	−1.5473	.1000
2	1.6094	.5798	.2000	1.5970	.5817	.2000
3	1.1360	1.9530	.1000	1.1273	1.9656	.1000
Mean	1.0414	.3333	.1333	1.0333	.3333	.1333
Sd	.5069	1.4337	.0471	.5030	1.4449	.0471

Estimated probability of correct response given $\theta_i = 0$

Item	Original Scale J	Mean/Sigma	Mean/Mean
1	.8034	.7556	.7559
2	.3634	.3359	.3367
3	.1291	.1202	.1203
sum	1.2959	1.2118	1.2130

example, the mean/sigma and mean/mean methods are compared using *Hdiff* and *SLdiff* as criteria. The criteria can be calculated at $\theta_i = 0$ using the estimated probabilities at the bottom of Table 6.2. To calculate $Hdiff(\theta_i)$ using equation (6.11), sum, over items, the squared difference between the estimated probabilities for the original Scale J and for the transformed scale that results from the application of one of the methods. For example, for the mean/sigma method,

$$Hdiff(\theta_i = 0) = (.8034 - .7556)^2 + (.3634 - .3359)^2 + (.1291 - .1202)^2$$
$$= .003120.$$

Similarly, for the mean/mean method,

$$Hdiff(\theta_i = 0) = (.8034 - .7559)^2 + (.3634 - .3367)^2 + (.1291 - .1203)^2$$

$$= .003047.$$

$Hdiff(\theta_i = 0)$ is smaller for the mean/mean method than it is for the mean/sigma method, indicating that the mean/mean method is somewhat "better" than the mean/sigma method at $\theta_i = 0$ based on $Hdiff(\theta_i)$.

To calculate $SLdiff(\theta_i = 0)$ using equation (6.13), the estimated probabilities are summed over items, resulting in the sums listed at the bottom of the table. These sums represent the value of the test characteristic curve at $\theta_i = 0$. For the mean/sigma method,

$$SLdiff(\theta_i = 0) = (1.2959 - 1.2118)^2 = .007073.$$

For the mean/mean method,

$$SLdiff(\theta_i = 0) = (1.2959 - 1.2130)^2 = .006872.$$

$SLdiff(\theta_i = 0)$ is smaller for the mean/mean method than it is for the mean/sigma method, indicating that the mean/mean method is somewhat "better" than the mean/sigma method at $\theta_i = 0$. Thus, the mean/mean method is "better" at $\theta_i = 0$ for both criteria. In using these methods, differences would actually need to be calculated at many values of θ_i.

If the scaling were actually done using the characteristic curve methods, $Hcrit$ and $SLcrit$ would be calculated by summing $Hdiff(\theta_i)$ and $SLdiff(\theta_i)$ over different values of θ_i. Also, the iterative minimization algorithms described by Haebara (1980) and Stocking and Lord (1983) would be used to find the A and B that minimized $Hcrit$ and $SLcrit$. Typically, the mean/mean or mean/sigma method estimates of A and B would be used as starting values in the minimization process.

Comparison of Criteria

Little empirical work has been done that compares the $Hcrit$- and $SLcrit$-based methods to each other, although Way and Tang (1991) found that methods based on the two criteria produced similar results. Theoretically, the $Hcrit$ methods might be argued to be superior to the $SLcrit$ methods for the following reason: $Hdiff(\theta_i)$ can be 0 only if the item characteristic curves are identical at θ_i, whereas $SLdiff(\theta_i)$ could be 0 even if the item characteristic curves differed. In this sense, $Hdiff(\theta_i)$ might be viewed as being more stringent than $SLdiff(\theta_i)$. On the other hand, it might be argued the $SLcrit$-based methods are preferable theoretically, because they focus on the difference between test characteristic curves.

Little empirical work has been done that compares different ways of defining the examinee group used to cumulate the differences between the item characteristic curves over examinees. If the methods were shown not to differ much from one another, then the use of an equally spaced set of abilities that covers the likely range of abilities might be easiest to implement. However, the different methods will produce somewhat different results. What would be the theoretically preferable way to define the group used to cumulate the differences? The procedure discussed by Haebara (1980), which sums over estimated abilities of examinees who were administered either the new form or the old form, seems preferable because it will produce a symmetric function. This procedure also uses data on examinees who were administered both forms. However, this procedure might be more difficult to implement. Empirical research needs to be conducted to compare these methods.

One potential limitation of the characteristic curve methods is that they do not explicitly account for the error in estimating item parameters. (See Divgi, 1985; Kim and Cohen, 1992; and Ogasawara, 2001a; for a method that takes into account such error.) The failure to take into account error in estimating item parameters, explicitly, might not be that crucial when the sample size is large and the item characteristic curves are well estimated. However, there are situations in which problems might arise. For example, if considerably larger sample sizes are used to estimate parameters for one form than for another, then ignoring the error in parameter estimates might lead to problems in estimating A and B, and in estimating equating relationships. Empirical research is needed to address this issue. Baker (1996) studied the sampling distribution of A and B for the Stocking and Lord (1983) method.

6.3.4 Comparisons Among Scale Transformation Methods

For dichotomous IRT models, research comparing the characteristic curve methods to the mean/sigma and mean/mean methods has generally found that the characteristic curve methods produce more stable results than the mean/sigma and mean/mean methods (Baker and Al-Karni, 1991; Hanson and Béguin, 2002; Hung, et al., 1991; Kim and Cohen, 1992; Ogasawara, 2001b,c; Way and Tang, 1991). In addition, Ogasawara (2000) found that the mean/mean method was more stable than the mean/sigma method. When Ogasawara (2002) estimated standard errors for item parameters and item characteristic curves, he found that the item characteristic curves could be estimated accurately, even when the item parameters were not estimated very precisely. This finding supports the finding that the test characteristic curve linking methods are more accurate than the mean/mean and mean/sigma methods. Kaskowitz and De Ayala (2001) studied the effects of error in estimating item parameters on the test characteristic curve methods. They found that the methods were robust in the presence of modest amounts of error, and that the methods were more accurate with 15 or 25 common items than with 5 common items.

Using simulation procedures in which the data fit an IRT model, Kim and Cohen (1998) compared scale linking using the Stocking and Lord (1983) test characteristic curve method to concurrent calibration using MULTILOG. They also examined concurrent calibration using BILOG, even though using concurrent calibration with this program is not strictly appropriate. The simulations were all based on data that fit the three-parameter logistic model. For small numbers of common items, Kim and Cohen (1998) found that concurrent calibration produced more accurate results than did the test characteristic curve method. Also, with small numbers of common items, concurrent calibration with MULTILOG produced more accurate results than BILOG. With large numbers of common items, they found that all of the procedures examined had similar accuracy. Also using simulation procedures in which the data fit the IRT model, Hanson and Béguin (2002) compared the mean/sigma, mean/mean, Stocking/Lord, Haebara, concurrent calibration methods using BILOG-MG, and concurrent calibration using MULTILOG. In this study, the concurrent calibration procedures produced more accurate results than the test characteristic curve methods. The mean/mean and mean/sigma methods were less accurate than the other methods. Béguin et al. (2000) and Béguin and Hanson (2001) compared the Stocking/Lord method to concurrent calibration using simulated data that purposefully did not fit the IRT model due to multidimensionality. When groups were nonequivalent and the abilities highly correlated, scaling using the Stocking/Lord method produced more accurate equating than scaling using concurrent calibration. This finding is different from what was found by Kim and Cohen (1998) and Hanson and Béguin (2002) in which the data were simulated to fit the IRT model.

As a set, these studies suggest that concurrent calibration, although more accurate than separate estimation when the data fit the IRT model, might be less robust to violations of the IRT assumptions than separate estimation using test characteristic curve methods to link the scales. One additional benefit of separate estimation is that it facilitates examining item parameter estimates for the common items, as was done in Figure 6.2. These sorts of plots can be developed only if separate estimation is used, because only one item parameter estimate for each common item is produced in concurrent calibration. In practice, separate estimation using the test characteristic curve methods seems to be safest. Concurrent calibration could be used as an adjunct to the separate estimation method.

If concurrent calibration is not used and software for implementing the test characteristic curve methods is unavailable, then the following process might produce acceptable results. Construct a scatterplot of the IRT a-parameter estimates by plotting the parameter estimates for the common items for both groups. Construct similar scatterplots for the b- and c-parameter estimates. Examine the scatterplots and identify any items that appear to be outliers. The identification of outliers is necessarily a subjective process. Estimate the A- and B-constants with the mean/sigma and mean/mean methods both with and without including the item or items with parameter estimates that appear to be outliers. If the mean/sigma and mean/mean procedures give very different results with the outliers included but similar results with the outliers removed, then consider removing these items. If the results from this procedure are not clear, then the use of the characteristic curve procedure might be the best alternative. Note that even when the characteristic curve procedures are used, it is best to use more than one method, and to examine scatterplots to consider eliminating items with very different parameter estimates. In practice, it might be best to implement each of the methods and evaluate the effects of the differences between the methods on equating relationships and on resulting scale scores. Procedures for choosing among equating results are considered in Chapter 8.

6.4 Equating and Scaling

When a test is scored using estimated IRT abilities, there is no further need to develop a relationship between scores on Form X and Form Y. Still, the estimated abilities can be converted to scale scores. The ability estimates can be converted so that the reported scores are positive integers, which are presumably easier for examinees to interpret than are scores that may be negative and noninteger, as is the case with estimated IRT abilities. This conversion might involve a linear conversion of estimated abilities, followed by truncating the converted scores so that they are in a specified range of positive numbers, and then rounding the scores to integers for reporting purposes.

However, using estimated IRT abilities results in several practical problems, which might be why they are not used that often. One issue is that, to use estimated abilities with the three-parameter logistic model, the whole 0/1 response string, rather than the number-correct score, is used to estimate θ. Thus, examinees with the same number-correct score often receive different estimated abilities, which can be difficult to explain to examinees. In addition, estimates of θ are difficult to compute (they typically cannot be computed by hand) and can be costly to obtain. Another concern is that the estimated θ-values with the three-parameter logistic model typically are subject to relatively greater amounts of measurement error for high and low ability examinees than for middle ability examinees. Lord (1980, p. 183) indicated that the measurement error variability for examinees of extreme ability could be 10 or even 100 times that of middle ability examinees, which can create problems in interpreting summary statistics such as means and standard deviations. For these practical reasons, tests are often scored number-correct, even when they are developed and equated using IRT. When tests are scored with number-correct scores, an additional step is required in the IRT equating process. The two methods that have been proposed are to equate true scores and to equate observed scores. These procedures are considered next.

6.5 Equating True Scores

After the item parameters are on the same scale, IRT true score equating can be used to relate number-correct scores on Form X and Form Y. In this process, the true score on one form associated with a given θ is considered to be equivalent to the true score on another form associated with that θ.

6.5.1 Test Characteristic Curves

In IRT, the number-correct true score on Form X that is equivalent to θ_i is defined as

$$\tau_X(\theta_i) = \sum_{j:X} p_{ij}(\theta_i; a_j, b_j, c_j), \quad (6.16)$$

where the summation $j{:}X$ is over items on Form X. The number-correct true score on Form Y that is equivalent to θ_i is defined as

$$\tau_Y(\theta_i) = \sum_{j:Y} p_{ij}(\theta_i; a_j, b_j, c_j), \quad (6.17)$$

where the summation $j{:}Y$ is over items on Form Y. Equations (6.16) and (6.17) are referred to as *test characteristic curves* for Form X and Form Y. These test characteristic curves relate IRT ability to number-correct true score.

When using the three-parameter logistic model of equation (6.1), very low true scores are not attainable with the three-parameter logistic IRT model, because as θ approaches $-\infty$ the probability of correctly answering item j approaches c_j and not 0. Therefore, true scores on Forms X and Y are associated with a value of θ only over the following ranges (recall that K_X and K_Y are the numbers of items on Form X and Form Y, respectively):

$$\sum_{j:X} c_j < \tau_X < K_X \quad \text{and} \quad \sum_{j:Y} c_j < \tau_Y < K_Y. \quad (6.18)$$

6.5.2 True Score Equating Process

In IRT true score equating, for a given θ_i, true scores $\tau_X(\theta_i)$ and $\tau_Y(\theta_i)$ are considered to be equivalent. The Form Y true score equivalent of a given true score on Form X is

$$irt_Y(\tau_X) = \tau_Y(\tau_X^{-1}), \quad \sum_{j:X} c_j < \tau_X < K_X, \quad (6.19)$$

where τ_X^{-1} is defined as the θ_i corresponding to true score τ_X. Equation (6.19) implies that true score equating is a three-step process:

1. Specify a true score τ_X on Form X (typically an integer $\sum_{j:X} c_j < \tau_X < K_X$).

Equating True Scores   177

2. Find the θ_i that corresponds to that true score (τ_X^{-1}).

3. Find the true score on Form Y, τ_Y, that corresponds to that θ_i.

Form Y equivalents of Form X integer number-correct scores typically are found using these procedures.

Whereas Step 1 and Step 3 are straightforward, Step 2 requires the use of an iterative procedure. For example, suppose that the Form Y equivalent of a Form X score of 5 is to be found. Implementation of Step 2 requires finding the θ_i that results in the right-hand side of equation (6.16) equaling 5. Finding this value of θ_i requires the solution of a nonlinear equation using an iterative process. This process is described in the next section.

6.5.3 The Newton-Raphson Method

The Newton-Raphson method is a general method for finding the roots of nonlinear functions. To use this method, begin with a function that is set to 0. Refer to that function as $func(\theta)$, which is a function of the variable θ. Refer to the first derivative of the function with respect to θ as $func'(\theta)$. To apply the Newton-Raphson method, an initial value is chosen for θ, which is referred to as θ^-. A new value for θ is calculated as

$$\theta^+ = \theta^- - \frac{func(\theta)}{func'(\theta)}. \qquad (6.20)$$

Typically, θ^+ will be closer to the root of the equation than θ^-. The new value then is redefined as θ^-, and the process is repeated until θ^+ and θ^- are equal at a specified level of precision or until the value of $func$ is close to 0 at a specified level of precision.

When using the Newton-Raphson method, the choice of the initial value is an important consideration, because a poor choice can lead to an erroneous solution. Press et al. (1989) describe modifications to the Newton-Raphson method that are more robust than the Newton-Raphson method to the choice of poor initial values.

Using the Newton-Raphson Method in IRT Equating

To apply this method to IRT true score equating, let τ_X be the true score whose equivalent is to be found. From equation (6.16) it follows that θ_i is to be found such that the expression

$$func(\theta_i) = \tau_X - \sum_{j:X} p_{ij}(\theta_i; a_j, b_j, c_j) \qquad (6.21)$$

equals 0. The Newton-Raphson method can be employed to find this θ_i using the first derivative of $func(\theta_i)$ with respect to θ_i, which is

$$func'(\theta_i) = -\sum_{j:X} p'_{ij}(\theta_i; a_j, b_j, c_j) \qquad (6.22)$$

178   6. Item Response Theory Methods

where $p'_{ij}(\theta_i; a_j, b_j, c_j)$ is defined as the first derivative of $p_{ij}(\theta_i; a_j, b_j, c_j)$ with respect to θ_i, Lord (1980, p. 61) provided this first derivative:

$$p'_{ij}(\theta_i; a_j, b_j, c_j) = \frac{1.7 a_j (1 - p_{ij})(p_{ij} - c_j)}{(1 - c_j)}, \quad (6.23)$$

where $p_{ij} = p_{ij}(\theta_i; a_j, b_j, c_j)$. The resulting expressions for $func(\theta_i)$ and $func'(\theta_i)$ are substituted into equation (6.20).

A Hypothetical Example

A hypothetical example using this procedure is presented in Table 6.3. In this example, a five-item Form X is to be equated to a five-item Form Y. Parameters (not estimates) are given, and assume that the parameters for the two forms are on the same scale. Table 6.3 shows how to find a Form Y equivalent of a Form X score of 2. The item parameters for Form X are presented in the top portion of the table. To find the Form Y equivalent, the θ_i must be found that corresponds to a Form X score of 2. That is, the θ_i must be found such that, when it is substituted into the right-hand side of equation (6.16), it results in a 2 on the left-hand side. The second portion of Table 6.3 illustrates how to find θ_i using the Newton-Raphson method. First, a starting value of $\theta_i^- = -2$ is chosen (this value is an initial guess). Using $\theta_i^- = -2$, the item characteristic curve value from equation (6.1) is calculated for each item. For example, the probability of an examinee with an ability of -2 correctly answering item 1 is .5393. The first derivative is also calculated. For example, for the first item, the first derivative of this item evaluated at an ability of -2 can be calculated using equation (6.23) as

$$p'_{ij} = \frac{1.7(.60)(1 - .5393)(.5393 - .20)}{(1 - .20)} = .1993,$$

which is also presented in the table.

Next, $func(\theta_i^-)$ from equation (6.21) is calculated using 2 for τ_X and the tabled value of 1.5405 as the sum of the item characteristic curves at an ability of -2. So, $func(\theta_i^-) = 2 - 1.5405$. Then, the negative of the sum of the first derivatives is $func'(\theta_i^-) = -.3811$ from equation (6.22). Finally, using equation (6.20), the updated ability is

$$\theta_i^+ = \theta_i^- - \frac{func(\theta_i^-)}{func'(\theta_i^-)} = -2 - \frac{2 - 1.5405}{-.3811} = -.7943.$$

The value of $-.7943$ differs in the fourth decimal place from the tabled value because of rounding error; the tabled value is more accurate. The value of $-.7941$ then is used as θ_i^- in the next iteration. The iterations continue until the values of θ stabilize. Note that after the fourth iteration, θ_i^+ equals θ_i^+ after the third iteration, to four decimal places. Also, the sum of the p_{ij} is 2.0000 when $\theta_i = -1.1308$. Thus, a true score of 2 on Form X corresponds to a θ_i of -1.1308.

TABLE 6.3. Hypothetical Example for IRT True Score Equating.

Form X Item Parameters

Item Parameter	Item 1	Item 2	Item 3	Item 4	Item 5
a_j	.60	1.20	1.00	1.40	1.00
b_j	−1.70	−1.00	.80	1.30	1.40
c_j	.20	.20	.25	.25	.20

Solve for $\tau_X = 2$ Using Starting Value $\theta_i = -2$

Iteration		Item 1	Item 2	Item 3	Item 4	Item 5	sum	θ_i^+
1	p_{ij}	.5393	.2921	.2564	.2503	.2025	1.5405	−.7941
	p'_{ij}	.1993	.1662	.0107	.0007	.0042	.3811	
2	p_{ij}	.7727	.6828	.2968	.2551	.2187	2.2261	−1.1295
	p'_{ij}	.1660	.3905	.0746	.0121	.0311	.6743	
3	p_{ij}	.7132	.5475	.2772	.2523	.2107	2.0009	−1.1308
	p'_{ij}	.1877	.4010	.0446	.0055	.0180	.6566	
4	p_{ij}	.7130	.5469	.2771	.2523	.2107	2.0000	−1.1308
	p'_{ij}	.1877	.4008	.0445	.0055	.0179	.6564	

Therefore, $\tau_X = 2$ corresponds to $\theta_i = -1.1308$.

Form Y Item Parameters

Item Parameter	Item 1	Item 2	Item 3	Item 4	Item 5
a_j	.70	.80	1.30	.90	1.10
b_j	−1.50	−1.20	.00	1.40	1.50
c_j	.20	.25	.20	.25	.20

Form Y True Score Equivalent of $\theta_i = -1.1308$

	Item 1	Item 2	Item 3	Item 4	Item 5	τ_Y
p_{ij}	.6865	.6426	.2607	.2653	.2058	2.0609

Therefore, $\tau_X = 2$ corresponds to $\tau_Y = 2.0609$.

The Form Y equivalent of a Form X score of 2 is found next. The Form Y item parameter estimates are needed and are shown in Table 6.3. (Note that the item parameters for Form X and Form Y must be on the same θ-scale.) To find the Form Y equivalent of a Form X score of 2, calculate the value of the item characteristic curve for each Form Y item at $\theta_i = -1.1308$ and sum these values over items. This process is illustrated at the bottom of the table. As shown, a score of 2 on Form X corresponds to a score of 2.0609 on Form Y.

Using the procedures outlined, the reader can verify that a true score of 3 on Form X corresponds to a θ_i of .3655 and a Form Y true score of 3.2586. Also, a true score of 4 on Form X corresponds to a θ_i of 1.3701 and a Form Y true score of 4.0836. Note that a Form X true score of 1 is below the sum of the c-parameters for that form, so the Form Y true score equivalent of a Form X true score of 1 cannot be calculated by the methods described so far.

Sometimes Form Y true score equivalents of all Form X integer scores that are between the sum of the c-parameters and all correct need to be found. The recommended procedure for finding these is to begin with the smallest Form X score that is greater than the sum of the c-parameters. Use a small value of θ as a starting value (e.g., $\theta_i^- = -3$), and then solve for the Form Y true score equivalent. The θ that results from this process can be used as the starting value for solving for the next highest true score. This process continues for all integer true scores on Form X that are below a score of all correct. Sometimes even this procedure can have convergence problems. In this case, the starting values might need to be modified or the modified Newton-Raphson method described by Press et al. (1989) could be tried.

6.5.4 Using True Score Equating with Observed Scores

The true score relationship is appropriate for equating true scores on Form X to true scores on Form Y. However, true scores of examinees are never known, because they are parameters. In practice, the true score equating relationship often is used to convert number-correct observed scores on Form X to number-correct observed scores on Form Y. However, no theoretical reason exists for treating scores in this way. Rather, doing so has been justified in item response theory by showing that the resulting true score conversions are similar to observed score conversions (Lord and Wingersky, 1984).

Recall from equation (6.18) that the lowest possible true score for the three-parameter IRT model is the sum of the c_j, not 0. Therefore, when using true score equating with observed scores, a procedure is needed for converting Form X scores outside the range of possible true scores on Form X. Lord (1980) and Kolen (1981) presented ad hoc procedures to handle this problem. The Kolen (1981) ad hoc procedure is as follows:

1. Set a score of 0 on Form X equal to a score of 0 on Form Y.

2. Set a score of the sum of the c_j-parameters on Form X equal to the sum of the c_j-parameters on Form Y.

3. Use linear interpolation to find equivalents between these points.

4. Set a score of K_X on Form X equal to a score of K_Y on Form Y.

To formalize this procedure, define τ_X^* as a score outside the range of possible true scores, but within the range of possible observed scores. Equivalents then are defined by the following equation:

$$irt_Y(\tau_X^*) = \frac{\sum_{j:Y} c_j}{\sum_{j:X} c_j}\tau_X^*, \qquad 0 \leq \tau_X^* \leq \sum_{j:X} c_j, \qquad (6.24)$$
$$= K_Y, \qquad \tau_X^* = K_X.$$

The use of Kolen's (1981) ad hoc procedure can be illustrated using the hypothetical example presented in Table 6.3. For the item parameters presented, the sum of the c_j-parameters is 1.1 for Form X and 1.1 for Form Y. To apply the procedure to find Form Y equivalents of Form X scores at or below 1.1, take

$$irt_Y(\tau_X^*) = \frac{\sum_{j:Y} c_j}{\sum_{j:X} c_j}\tau_X^* = \frac{1.1}{1.1}\tau_X^* = \tau_X^*.$$

Thus, for example, a score of 1 on Form X is considered to be equivalent to a score of 1 on Form Y. Note that a score of 1 on Form X would have been considered to be equivalent to a score other than 1 on Form Y if the sum of the c_j-parameters was different for the two forms.

In practice, for IRT true score equating, estimates of the item parameters are used to produce an *estimated true score relationship*. Then the estimated true score conversion is applied to the observed scores.

6.6 Equating Observed Scores

Another procedure, *IRT observed score equating*, uses the IRT model to produce an estimated distribution of observed number-correct scores on each form, which then are equated using equipercentile methods. For Form X, the *compound binomial distribution* (see Lord and Wingersky, 1984) is used to generate the distribution of observed number-correct scores for examinees of a given ability. These observed score distributions then are cumulated over a population of examinees to produce a number-correct observed score distribution for Form X. Similar procedures are followed to produce a number-correct observed score distribution for Form Y. The resulting number-correct score distributions then are equated using conventional equipercentile methods. IRT observed score equating requires explicit specification of the distribution of ability in the population of examinees.

Consider a group of examinees all of ability θ_i who have been administered a three-item test with p_{ij} defined by equation (6.1). Assuming local independence, the probability that examinees of ability equal to θ_i will incorrectly answer all three items and earn a raw score of 0 is $f(x = 0|\theta_i) = (1 - p_{i1})(1 - p_{i2})(1 - p_{i3})$. To earn a score of 1, an examinee could answer item 1 correctly and items 2 and 3 incorrectly, or the examinee could answer item 2 correctly and items 1 and 3 incorrectly, or the examinee could answer item 3 correctly and items 1 and 2 incorrectly. That is, there are three ways to earn a score of 1 on a three-item test. The probability of earning a 1 is as follows:

$$\begin{aligned}f(x=1|\theta_i) &= p_{i1}(1-p_{i2})(1-p_{i3}) + (1-p_{i1})p_{i2}(1-p_{i3})\\ &\quad + (1-p_{i1})(1-p_{i2})p_{i3}.\end{aligned}$$

The probabilities of correctly answering two and three items can be constructed similarly as follows:

$$f(x=2|\theta_i) = p_{i1}p_{i2}(1-p_{i3}) + p_{i1}(1-p_{i2})p_{i3} + (1-p_{i1})p_{i2}p_{i3},$$

and

$$f(x=3|\theta_i) = p_{i1}p_{i2}p_{i3}.$$

Based on the hypothetical example in Table 6.1, for examinees with ability equal to that of Person 1 ($\theta_{I1} = -2.0$),

$$\begin{aligned}f(x=0|\theta_1) &= (1-.26)(1-.27)(1-.18) = .4430,\\ f(x=1|\theta_1) &= (.26)(1-.27)(1-.18) + (1-.26)(.27)(1-.18)\\ &\quad + (1-.26)(1-.27)(.18)\\ &= .4167,\\ f(x=2|\theta_1) &= (.26)(.27)(1-.18) + (.26)(1-.27)(.18)\\ &\quad + (1-.26)(.27)(.18)\\ &= .1277,\\ f(x=3|\theta_1) &= (.26)(.27)(.18) = .0126.\end{aligned}$$

Note that these values sum to 1, which is consistent with their being probabilities.

A recursion formula (Lord and Wingersky, 1984) can be used to generalize this procedure to more than three items. To implement the recursion formula, define $f_r(x|\theta_i)$ as the distribution of number-correct scores over the first r items for examinees of ability θ_i. Define $f_1(x=0|\theta_i) = (1-p_{i1})$ as the probability of earning a score of 0 on the first item and $f_1(x=1|\theta_i) = p_{i1}$ as the probability of earning a score of 1 on the first item. For $r > 1$, the recursion formula is as follows:

$$\begin{aligned}f_r(x|\theta_i) &= f_{r-1}(x|\theta_i)(1-p_{ir}), & x=0\\ &= f_{r-1}(x|\theta_i)(1-p_{ir}) + f_{r-1}(x-1|\theta_i)p_{ir}, & 0<x<r, \quad (6.25)\\ &= f_{r-1}(x-1|\theta_i)p_{ir}, & x=r\end{aligned}$$

An example of the use of this recursion formula is presented in Table 6.4. An abbreviated notation is used in this table to simplify the presentation. Specifically, θ_i is dropped and p_r means p_{ir}. To find the distribution for

TABLE 6.4. IRT Observed Score Distribution Recursion Formula Example.

			Example (Using Table 6.1 test for persons with $\theta_i = -2$)		
r	x	$f_r(x)$ for $r \leq 4$			
1	0	$f_1(0) = (1 - p_1)$	$= (1 - .26)$		$= .74$
	1	$f_1(1) = p_1$			$= .26$
2	0	$f_2(0) = f_1(0)(1 - p_2)$	$= .74(1 - .27)$		$= .5402$
	1	$f_2(1) = f_1(1)(1 - p_2) + f_1(0)p_2$	$= .26(1 - .27)$	$+ .74(.27)$	$= .3896$
	2	$f_2(2) =$	$f_1(1)p_2 =$	$.26(.27)$	$= .0702$
3	0	$f_3(0) = f_2(0)(1 - p_3)$	$= .5402(1 - .18)$		$= .4430$
	1	$f_3(1) = f_2(1)(1 - p_3) + f_2(0)p_3$	$= .3896(1 - .18)$	$+ .5402(.18)$	$= .4167$
	2	$f_3(2) = f_2(2)(1 - p_3) + f_2(1)p_3$	$= .0702(1 - .18)$	$+ .3896(.18)$	$= .1277$
	3	$f_3(3) =$	$f_2(2)p_3 =$	$.0702(.18)$	$= .0126$
4	0	$f_4(0) = f_3(0)(1 - p_4)$			
	1	$f_4(1) = f_3(1)(1 - p_4) + f_3(0)p_4$			
	2	$f_4(2) = f_3(2)(1 - p_4) + f_3(1)p_4$			
	3	$f_4(3) = f_3(3)(1 - p_4) + f_3(2)p_4$			
	4	$f_4(4) =$	$f_3(3)p_4$		

a particular value of r, equation (6.25) and Table 6.4 indicate that the distribution for $r - 1$ and the probability of correctly answering item r are needed. Although expressions are only presented up to $r = 4$, the table readily generalizes to higher values of r using the recursion formula. The probabilities listed for the example under $r = 3$ (e.g., .4430, .4167, .1277, and .0126) are identical to results presented earlier.

The procedures presented thus far give the observed score distribution for examinees of a given ability. To find the observed score distribution for examinees of various abilities, the observed score distribution for examinees at each ability is found and then these are accumulated. When the ability distribution is continuous, then

$$f(x) = \int_\theta f(x|\theta)\psi(\theta)d\theta, \qquad (6.26)$$

where $\psi(\theta)$ is the distribution of θ.

To implement this procedure in practice, some method is needed to perform the integration in equation (6.26). Some form of numerical integration is one possibility. When BILOG is used, the distribution of ability typically is characterized by a discrete distribution on a finite number of equally spaced points as a method of approximating the integral. Using this characterization,

$$f(x) = \sum_i f(x|\theta_i)\psi(\theta_i). \qquad (6.27)$$

When the distribution of ability is characterized by a finite number of abilities for N examinees, then

$$f(x) = \frac{1}{N} \sum_i f(x|\theta_i). \tag{6.28}$$

This characterization can be used, for example, with a set of abilities that are estimated using LOGIST or BILOG.

To conduct observed score equating, observed score distributions are found for Form X and for Form Y. For example, assume that the characterization of the ability distribution associated with equation (6.27) is used. The following distributions could be specified using this equation:

1. $f_1(x) = \sum_i f(x|\theta_i)\psi_1(\theta_i)$ is the Form X distribution for Population 1.
2. $f_2(x) = \sum_i f(x|\theta_i)\psi_2(\theta_i)$ is the Form X distribution for Population 2.
3. $g_1(y) = \sum_i g(y|\theta_i)\psi_1(\theta_i)$ is the Form Y distribution for Population 1.
4. $g_2(y) = \sum_i g(y|\theta_i)\psi_2(\theta_i)$ is the Form Y distribution for Population 2.

These quantities then are weighted using synthetic weights described in Chapters 4 and 5 to obtain the distributions of X and Y in the synthetic population. Conventional equipercentile methods then are used to find score equivalents.

When BILOG is used, the number-correct observed score distributions can be estimated by using the estimated posterior distribution of ability in place of $\psi(\theta_i)$ in equation (6.27) along with estimates of $f(x|\theta_i)$ based on substituting estimates for parameters in equation (6.25) as suggested by Zeng and Kolen (1995). An alternative is to use the set of estimated abilities in place of the abilities in equation (6.28). However, the use of estimates of θ might create systematic distortions in the estimated distributions and lead to inaccurate equating (Han et al., 1997; Lord, 1982a). The estimation of observed score distributions using IRT models is an area for further research.

6.7 IRT True Score Versus IRT Observed Score Equating

Compared to IRT observed score equating, IRT true score equating has the advantages of (a) easier computation and (b) a conversion that does not depend on the distribution of ability. However, IRT true score equating has the disadvantage that it equates true scores, which are not available in practice. No justification exists for applying the true score relationship to observed scores. Also, with the three-parameter logistic model, equivalents are undefined at very low scores and at the top number-correct score.

IRT observed score equating has the advantage that it defines the equating relationship for observed scores. Also, assuming reasonable model fit, the distribution of Form X scores converted to the Form Y scale is approximately equal to the distribution of Form Y scores for the synthetic population of examinees. There is no theoretical reason to expect this property to hold for IRT true score equating. Also, using posterior distributions of θ from BILOG, the computational burden of IRT observed score equating is acceptable.

IRT observed score and IRT true score equating methods were found by Kolen (1981) and Han et al. (1997) to produce somewhat different results using the random groups design with achievement tests. However, Lord and Wingersky (1984) concluded that the two methods produce very similar results in a study using the common-item nonequivalent groups design in the SAT. Further research comparing these methods is need.

Larger differences between IRT true and observed score equating might be expected to occur near a number-correct score of all correct and near number-correct scores below the sum of the c-parameter estimates, because these are the regions where IRT true score equating does not produce equivalents. In practice, both methods should be applied with special attention paid to equating results near these regions. Procedures for choosing among the results from equating methods are considered in Chapter 8.

6.8 Illustrative Example

The real data example from Chapters 4 and 5 is used to illustrate some aspects of IRT equating, using the common-item nonequivalent groups design. Two forms of a 36-item multiple-choice test, Form X and Form Y, are used in this example. Every third item on the test forms is a common item, and the common items are in the same position on each form. Thus, items $3, 6, 9, \ldots, 36$ on each form represent the 12 common items. Form X was administered to 1,655 examinees and Form Y to 1,638 examinees. As was indicated in Chapters 4 and 5, the examinees who were administered Form X had a number-correct score mean of 5.11 and a standard deviation of 2.38 on the common items. The examinees who were administered Form Y had a number-correct score mean of 5.87 and a standard deviation of 2.45 on the common items. Thus, on the common items, the group taking Form Y was higher achieving than the group taking Form X.

6.8.1 Item Parameter Estimation and Scaling

Item parameters were estimated using BILOG 3 separately for each form. (Default BILOG parameter settings were used, except for the FLOAT option.) The parameter estimates are given in Table 6.5. The proportion of examinees correctly answering each item (p-value) is also presented.

TABLE 6.5. Item Parameter Estimates for Common-Item Equating.

	Form X				Form Y			
Item	p-value	$\hat{a}$	$\hat{b}$	$\hat{c}$	p-value	$\hat{a}$	$\hat{b}$	$\hat{c}$
1	.8440	.5496	−1.7960	.1751	.8527	.8704	−1.4507	.1576
2	.6669	.7891	−.4796	.1165	.6161	.4628	−.4070	.1094
3	**.7025**	**.4551**	**−.7101**	**.2087**	**.7543**	**.4416**	**−1.3349**	**.1559**
4	.5405	1.4443	.4833	.2826	.7145	.5448	−.9017	.1381
5	.6723	.9740	−.1680	.2625	.8295	.6200	−1.4865	.2114
6	**.7412**	**.5839**	**−.8567**	**.2038**	**.7946**	**.5730**	**−1.3210**	**.1913**
7	.5895	.8604	.4546	.3224	.6351	1.1752	.0691	.2947
8	.6475	1.1445	−.1301	.2209	.6094	.4450	.2324	.2723
9	**.5816**	**.7544**	**.0212**	**.1600**	**.6852**	**.5987**	**−.7098**	**.1177**
10	.5296	.9170	1.0139	.3648	.6644	.8479	−.4253	.1445
11	.4825	.9592	.7218	.2399	.7439	1.0320	−.8184	.0936
12	**.5574**	**.6633**	**.0506**	**.1240**	**.6076**	**.6041**	**−.3539**	**.0818**
13	.5411	1.2324	.4167	.2535	.5685	.8297	−.0191	.1283
14	.4051	1.0492	.7882	.1569	.6094	.7252	−3155	.0854
15	**.4770**	**1.0690**	**.9610**	**.2986**	**.5532**	**.9902**	**.5320**	**.3024**
16	.5139	.9193	.6099	.2521	.5092	.7749	.5394	.2179
17	.5175	.8935	.5128	.2273	.4786	.5942	.8987	.2299
18	**.4825**	**.9672**	**.1950**	**.0535**	**.5587**	**.8081**	**−.1156**	**.0648**
19	.4909	.6562	.3953	.1201	.6265	.9640	−.1948	.1633
20	.4081	1.0556	.9481	.2036	.4908	.7836	.3506	.1299
21	**.3404**	**.3479**	**2.2768**	**.1489**	**.3655**	**.4140**	**2.5538**	**.2410**
22	.4299	.8432	1.0601	.2332	.5905	.7618	−.1581	.1137
23	.3839	1.1142	.5826	.0644	.5092	1.1959	.5056	.2397
24	**.4063**	**1.4579**	**1.0241**	**.2453**	**.4774**	**1.3554**	**.5811**	**.2243**
25	.3706	.5137	1.3790	.1427	.4976	1.1869	.6229	.2577
26	.3077	.9194	1.0782	.0879	.5055	1.0296	.3898	.1856
27	**.2956**	**1.8811**	**1.4062**	**.1992**	**.3771**	**1.0417**	**.9392**	**.1651**
28	.2612	1.5045	1.5093	.1642	.3851	1.2055	1.1350	.2323
29	.2727	.9664	1.5443	.1431	.3894	.9697	.6976	.1070
30	**.1820**	**.7020**	**2.2401**	**.0853**	**.2231**	**.6336**	**1.8960**	**.0794**
31	.3059	1.2651	1.8759	.2443	.3166	1.0822	1.3864	.1855
32	.2146	.8567	1.7140	.0865	.3356	1.0195	.9197	.1027
33	**.1826**	**1.4080**	**1.5556**	**.0789**	**.2634**	**1.1347**	**1.0790**	**.0630**
34	.1814	.5808	3.4728	.1399	.1760	1.1948	1.8411	.0999
35	.1288	.9257	3.1202	.1090	.1424	1.1961	2.0297	.0832
36	**.1530**	**1.2993**	**2.1589**	**.1075**	**.1950**	**.9255**	**2.1337**	**.1259**

Note: Common-item numbers and parameter estimates are in **boldface** type.

TABLE 6.6. Common-Item Parameter Estimates and Scaling Constants.

	Form X				Form Y			
Item	p-value	â	b̂	ĉ	p-value	â	b̂	ĉ
3	.7025	.4551	−.7101	.2087	.7543	.4416	−1.3349	.1559
6	.7412	.5839	−.8567	.2038	.7946	.5730	−1.3210	.1913
9	.5816	.7544	.0212	.1600	.6852	.5987	−.7098	.1177
12	.5574	.6633	.0506	.1240	.6076	.6041	−.3539	.0818
15	.4770	1.0690	.9610	.2986	.5532	.9902	.5320	.3024
18	.4825	.9672	.1950	.0535	.5587	.8081	−.1156	.0648
21	.3404	.3479	2.2768	.1489	.3655	.4140	2.5538	.2410
24	.4063	1.4579	1.0241	.2453	.4774	1.3554	.5811	.2243
27	.2956	1.8826	1.4062	.1992	.3771	1.0417	.9392	.1651
30	.1820	.7020	2.2401	.0853	.2231	.6336	1.8960	.0794
33	.1826	1.4080	1.5556	.0789	.2634	1.1347	1.0790	.0630
36	.1530	1.2993	2.1589	.1075	.1950	.9255	2.1337	.1259
μ̂	.4252	.9657	.8602	.1595	.4879	.7934	.4900	.1510
σ̂	.1917	.4464	1.0658	.0707	.1960	.2837	1.2458	.0736

	Mean/Sigma	Mean/Mean	Stocking–Lord	Haebara
A =	1.1689	1.2173	1.0946	1.0678
B =	−.5156	−.5572	−.4978	−.4713

Eliminating Item #27

μ̂	.4370	.8825	.8106	.1559	.4980	.7708	.4491	.1498
σ̂	.1961	.3665	1.0999	.0728	.2019	.2858	1.2935	.0768

	Mean/Sigma	Mean/Mean	Stocking–Lord	Haebara
A =	1.1761	1.1449	1.0861	1.0638
B =	−.5042	−.4790	−.4733	−.4540

The Form X item parameter estimates need to be rescaled. The computer program ST that is described in Appendix B was used to conduct the scaling. The common items are tabulated separately in the upper portion of Table 6.6. Because the items appeared in identical positions in the two forms, item 3 on Form X is the same as item 3 on Form Y, and so forth.

The parameter estimates for the common items are plotted in Figure 6.2 to look for outliers—items with estimates that do not appear to lie on a straight line. In this figure, one item appears to be an outlier for the a-parameter estimate. This item, which is item 27, has a-parameter estimates of 1.8826 on Form X and 1.0417 on Form Y. Because item 27 appears to function differently in the two forms, this item might need to be eliminated from the common-item set. (The c-parameter estimates for item 21 might also be judged to be an outlier, so that item 21 could be considered for

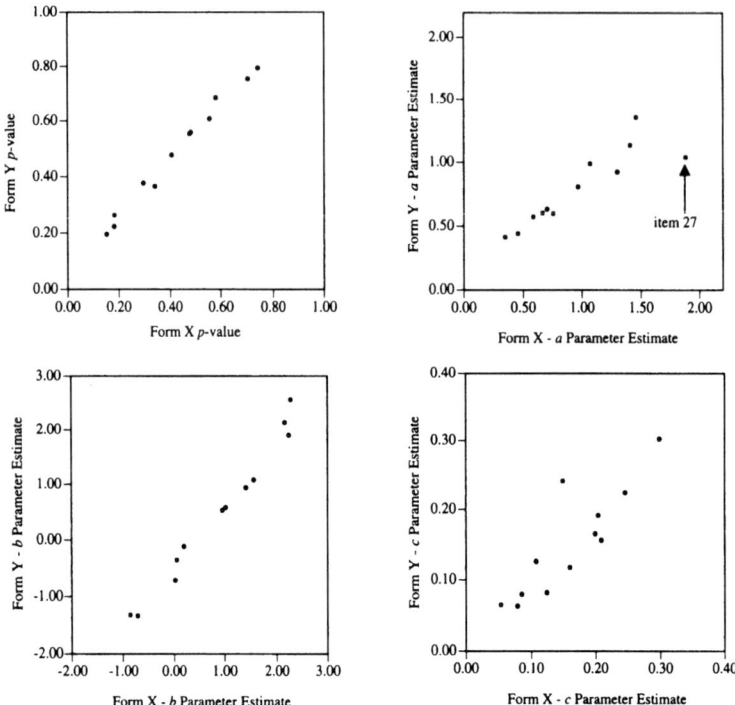

FIGURE 6.2. Plots of item parameter estimates on Form X versus Form Y.

elimination as well. This item was not considered for elimination in the present example because it does not seem to be as clearly an outlier as item 27.) Removal of items that appear to be outliers is clearly a judgmental process.

The mean and standard deviation of the item parameter estimates for the common items are shown in Table 6.6. These means and standard deviations were used to estimate the A- and B-constants for transforming the θ-scale of Form X to the θ-scale of Form Y using the mean/mean and mean/sigma methods. For example, using equations (6.8a) and (6.9a) for the mean/sigma method,

$$A = \frac{1.2458}{1.0658} = 1.1689 \quad \text{and} \quad B = .4900 - (1.1689).8602 = -.5155.$$

The B-value differs from the tabled value in the fourth decimal place because of rounding error; the tabled values are more accurate. The A- and B-constants for the Stocking and Lord and Haebara methods that are shown also were calculated using the ST computer program.

Because item 27 appeared to be an outlier, the A- and B-constants were estimated again, eliminating item 27. The means and standard deviations

TABLE 6.7. Common-Item Parameter Estimates Rescaled Using Mean/Sigma Method's A and B with All Common Items (Excluding Item 27).

	Form X				Form Y			
Item	p-value	$\hat{a}$	$\hat{b}$	$\hat{c}$	p-value	$\hat{a}$	$\hat{b}$	$\hat{c}$
3	.7025	.3870	−1.3394	.2087	.7543	.4416	−1.3349	.1559
6	.7412	.4965	−1.5118	.2038	.7946	.5730	−1.3210	.1913
9	.5816	.6414	−.4793	.1600	.6852	.5987	−.7098	.1177
12	.5574	.5640	−.4447	.1240	.6076	.6041	−.3539	.0818
15	.4770	.9089	.6260	.2986	.5532	.9902	.5320	.3024
18	.4825	.8224	−.2749	.0535	.5587	.8081	−.1156	.0648
21	.3404	.2958	2.1735	.1489	.3655	.4140	2.5538	.2410
24	.4063	1.2396	.7002	.2453	.4774	1.3554	.5811	.2243
30	.1820	.5969	2.1304	.0853	.2231	.6336	1.8960	.0794
33	.1826	1.1972	1.3253	.0789	.2634	1.1347	1.0790	.0630
36	.1530	1.1048	2.0349	.1075	.1950	.9255	2.1337	.1259
$\hat{\mu}$	.4370	.7504	.4491	.1559	.4980	.7708	.4491	.1498
$\hat{\sigma}$	.1961	.3116	1.2935	.0728	.2018	.2858	1.2935	.0768

after eliminating this item are shown in Table 6.6 as are the new A- and B-constants. Eliminating item 27 results in the estimates of the A- and B-constants for mean/sigma and mean/mean methods being closer to one another than when item 27 is included. The A- and B-constants for the Stocking and Lord and Haebara methods are less affected by eliminating item 27 than are the constants for the mean/sigma and mean/mean methods. In the present example, the scalings based on removing item 27 only are considered for ease of exposition. In practice, however, equating based on scalings with item 27 removed and included could be conducted and the results of the equating compared.

The rescaled Form X item parameter estimates for the common items are shown in Table 6.7. So that all of the computations in this example could be done by hand, the mean/sigma method was used, excluding item 27. Because the Form Y item parameter estimates are not being transformed, they are identical to those in Table 6.6. To verify the tabled Form X b-parameter estimate for item 3, take $1.1761(-.7101) - .5042 = -1.3393$, which differs in the fourth decimal place because of rounding. To find the tabled Form X a-parameter estimate for this item, take $.4551/1.1761 = .3870$.

The means and standard deviations of the rescaled parameter estimates for the common items are shown at the bottom of Table 6.7. Because the mean/sigma method was used, the mean and standard deviation of the rescaled b-parameter estimates for Form X are equal to those for Form Y. Note, however, that the mean of the a-parameter estimates for Form

190   6. Item Response Theory Methods

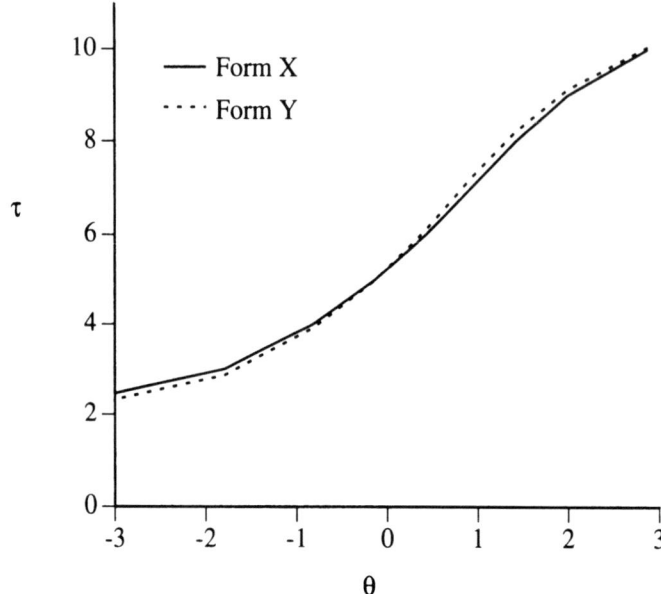

FIGURE 6.3. Estimated test characteristic curves for common items.

X differs from the mean for Form Y. These two means would have been the same if the mean/mean method was used. How would the means and standard deviations of the parameter estimates compare if a characteristic curve method was used? All of these statistics would likely differ from Form X to Form Y. These results illustrate that the different methods of scaling using parameter estimates can produce different results, which in turn would affect the equating.

Test characteristic curves for the common items after the common-item parameter estimates were placed on the same θ-scale using the mean/sigma method are shown in Figure 6.3. The Form X curve is the test characteristic curve for the 11 common items (excluding item 27) estimated using BILOG on the examinees who took Form X. The Form Y curve is the test characteristic curve for these same items estimated using BILOG on the examinees who took Form Y. In general, the test characteristic curves appear to be similar. However, if the Stocking-Lord method had been used, then these test characteristic curves likely would have been even closer, because the Stocking-Lord procedure finds the A- and B-constants that minimize the difference between these characteristic curves. However, if the Stocking-Lord method had been used, then the means and standard deviations of both the a-parameter and the b-parameter estimates for the common items would have differed from Form X to Form Y.

Even after transformation to a common scale, however, the common items have different parameter estimates on Form X than they do on Form

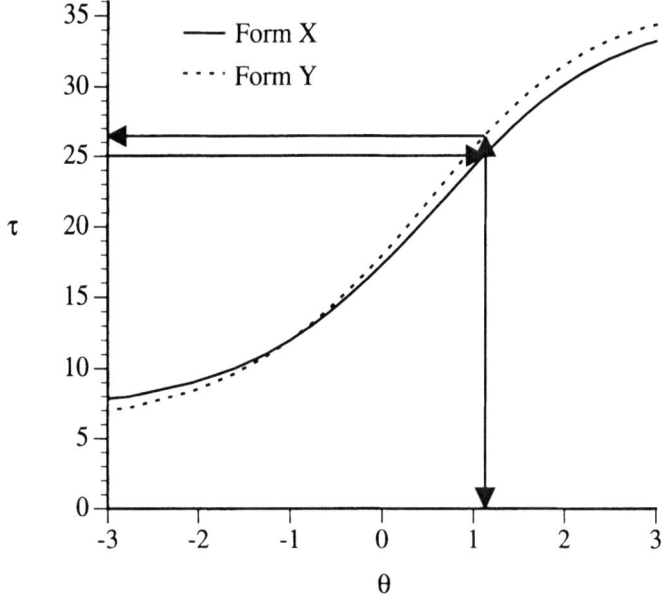

FIGURE 6.4. Estimated test characteristic curves for Form X and Form Y.

Y. These differences must be due to error in estimating the item parameters or failure of the IRT model to hold, because the items are identical on the two forms. McKinley (1988) described various methods for dealing with different parameter estimates.

The rescaled Form X item parameter estimates for all of the items are shown in Table 6.8. The same transformation that is used for the common items on Form X is also used for the other items.

6.8.2 IRT True Score Equating

The rescaled item parameter estimates then are used to estimate the true score equating function; this process is illustrated in Table 6.9 and Figure 6.4. Figure 6.4 presents the test characteristic curves for Form X and Form Y, and Table 6.9 presents the conversion table. The equating was conducted using the *PIE* computer program described in Appendix B. Suppose, for example, interest focuses on finding the Form Y equivalent of a Form X score of 25. First, find the θ that is associated with a true score of 25. In Figure 6.4, begin at a vertical axis value of 25 and go over to the Form X curve. Going down to the horizontal axis, the score of 25 is associated with a θ of approximately 1.1. With greater precision, from Table 6.9, this θ is 1.1022. This tabled value was found using the Newton-Raphson procedure that was described earlier. Next, find the Form Y true score that is associated with a θ of 1.1022. Graphically, this Form Y score is

TABLE 6.8. Form X Item Parameter Estimates Resealed with the Mean/Sigma Method's A and B Using All Common Items Except Item 27.

		Form X				Form Y		
Item	p-value	$\hat{a}$	$\hat{b}$	$\hat{c}$	p-value	$\hat{a}$	$\hat{b}$	$\hat{c}$
1	.8440	.4673	−2.6165	.1751	.8527	.8704	−1.4507	.1576
2	.6669	.6709	−1.0683	.1165	.6161	.4628	−.4070	.1094
3	**.7025**	**.3870**	**−1.3394**	**.2087**	**.7543**	**.4416**	**−1.3349**	**.1559**
4	.5405	1.2280	.0641	.2826	.7145	.5448	−.9017	.1381
5	.6723	.8282	−.7018	.2625	.8295	.6200	−1.4865	.2114
6	**.7412**	**.4965**	**−1.5118**	**.2038**	**.7946**	**.5730**	**−1.3210**	**.1913**
7	.5895	.7316	.0304	.3224	.6351	1.1752	.0691	.2947
8	.6475	.9731	−.6572	.2209	.6094	.4450	.2324	.2723
9	**.5816**	**.6414**	**−.4793**	**.1600**	**.6852**	**.5987**	**−.7098**	**.1177**
10	.5296	.7797	.6882	.3648	.6644	.8479	−.4253	.1445
11	.4825	.8156	.3446	.2399	.7439	1.0320	−.8184	.0936
12	**.5574**	**.5640**	**−.4447**	**.1240**	**.6076**	**.6041**	**−.3539**	**.0818**
13	.5411	1.0479	−.0141	.2535	.5685	.8297	−.0191	.1283
14	.4051	.8921	.4228	.1569	.6094	.7252	−.3155	.0854
15	**.4770**	**.9089**	**.6260**	**.2986**	**.5532**	**.9902**	**.5320**	**.3024**
16	.5139	.7817	.2130	.2521	.5092	.7749	.5394	.2179
17	.5175	.7598	.0989	.2273	.4786	.5942	.8987	.2299
18	**.4825**	**.8224**	**−.2749**	**.0535**	**.5587**	**.8081**	**−.1156**	**.0648**
19	.4909	.5580	−.0511	.1201	.6265	.9640	−.1948	.1633
20	.4081	.8976	.6109	.2036	.4908	.7836	.3506	.1299
21	**.3404**	**.2958**	**2.1735**	**.1489**	**.3655**	**.4140**	**2.5538**	**.2410**
22	.4299	.7169	.7425	.2332	.5905	.7618	−.1591	.1137
23	.3839	.9473	.1809	.0644	.5092	1.1959	.5056	.2397
24	**.4063**	**1.2396**	**.7002**	**.2453**	**.4774**	**1.3554**	**.5811**	**.2243**
25	.3706	.4368	1.1176	.1427	.4976	1.1869	.6229	.2577
26	.3077	.7917	.7639	.0879	.5055	1.0296	.3898	.1856
27	.2956	1.5995	1.1495	.1992	.3771	1.0417	.9392	.1651
28	.2612	1.2792	1.2708	.1642	.3851	1.2055	1.1350	.2323
29	.2727	.8217	1.3120	.1431	.3894	.9697	.6976	.1070
30	**.1820**	**.5969**	**2.1304**	**.0853**	**.2231**	**.6336**	**1.8960**	**.0794**
31	.3059	1.0757	1.7020	.2443	.3166	1.0822	1.3864	.1855
32	.2146	.7285	1.5115	.0865	.3356	1.0195	.9197	.1027
33	**.1826**	**1.1972**	**1.3253**	**.0789**	**.2634**	**1.1347**	**1.0790**	**.0630**
34	.1814	.4939	3.5801	.1399	.1760	1.1948	1.8411	.0999
35	.1288	.7871	3.1654	.1090	.1424	1.1961	2.0297	.0832
36	**.1530**	**1.1048**	**2.0349**	**.1075**	**.1950**	**.9255**	**2.1337**	**.1259**

Note: Common-item numbers and parameter estimates are in **boldface** type.

TABLE 6.9. Form Y Equivalents of Form X Scores Using IRT Estimated True Score Equating.

Form X Score	θ-Equivalent	Form Y Equivalent
0		.0000
1		.8890
2		1.7760
3		2.6641
4		3.5521
5		4.4401
6		5.3282
7	−4.3361	6.1340
8	−2.7701	7.1859
9	−2.0633	8.3950
10	−1.6072	9.6217
11	−1.2682	10.8256
12	−.9951	12.0002
13	−.7633	13.1495
14	−.5593	14.2803
15	−.3747	15.3995
16	−.2043	16.5135
17	−.0440	17.6271
18	.1088	18.7429
19	.2562	19.8612
20	.3998	20.9793
21	.5409	22.0926
22	.6805	23.1950
23	.8197	24.2806
24	.9598	25.3452
25	1.1022	26.3874
26	1.2490	27.4088
27	1.4031	28.4138
28	1.5681	29.4083
29	1.7491	30.3977
30	1.9533	31.3844
31	2.1916	32.3637
32	2.4824	33.3179
33	2.8604	34.2096
34	3.3992	34.9799
35	4.3214	35.5756
36		36.0000

194   6. Item Response Theory Methods

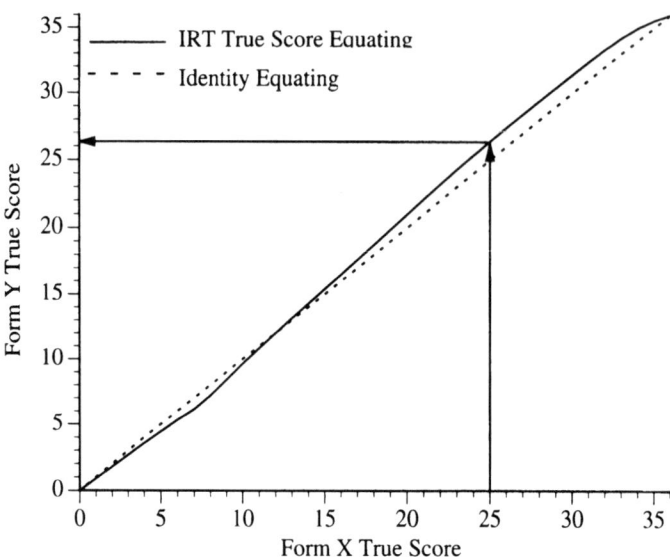

FIGURE 6.5. Estimated Form Y true score equivalents of Form X true scores using IRT true score equating.

approximately 26.4. With greater precision, from Table 6.9, this true score is 26.3874. These procedures are repeated with each of the Form X integer scores, and the resulting equivalents are plotted in Figure 6.5.

The arrows in this figure illustrate that a Form X score of 25 corresponds to a Form Y score of 26.4 (26.3874 with greater precision). Based on this graph, Form Y is easier than Form X, except at the lower scores, because the curve for true score equating is higher than the line for identity equating at all but the low scores.

In Table 6.9 θ equivalents are not given for very low Form X scores or for a Form X score of 36. The sum of the c-parameter estimates on Form X equals 6.5271, so that true score equivalents for Form X integer scores at or below a score of 6 are undefined. Kolen's (1981) ad hoc method was used to find the Form Y equivalents for these scores.

6.8.3   IRT Observed Score Equating

Estimates of the distribution of θ are needed to conduct observed score equating in this example. The posterior distributions of θ that were estimated using BILOG are presented in Table 6.10. As was noted earlier, BILOG treats the posterior distribution as a discrete distribution on a finite number (10 in this example) of points. For Form X, the posterior distribution of θ needs to be converted to the ability scale of the group that took Form Y. Because the distribution is discrete, the scale conversion can be accomplished by using equation (6.2) linearly to trans-

TABLE 6.10. Distributions of θ Estimated Using BILOG.

Group Taking Form X		Group Taking Form X Converted to Form Y Scale		Group Taking Form Y	
θ_I	$\hat{\psi}_1(\theta_I)$	θ_J	$\hat{\psi}_1(\theta_J)$	θ_J	$\hat{\psi}_1(\theta_J)$
−4.0000	.000101	−5.2086	.000101	−4.0000	.000117
−3.1110	.002760	−4.1630	.002760	−3.1110	.003242
−2.2220	.030210	−3.1175	.030210	−2.2220	.034490
−1.3330	.142000	−2.0720	.142000	−1.3330	.147100
−.4444	.314900	−1.0269	.314900	−.4444	.314800
.4444	.315800	.0184	.315800	.4444	.311000
1.3330	.154200	1.0635	.154200	1.3330	.152600
2.2220	.035960	2.1090	.035960	2.2220	.034060
3.1110	.003925	3.1546	.003925	3.1110	.002510
4.0000	.000186	4.2001	.000186	4.0000	.000112

form the θ-values using the A- and B-constants that were estimated earlier using the mean/sigma methods. For example, to transform the first tabled θ-value using the constants from the mean/sigma method, take $1.1761(-4.0000) - .5042 = -5.2086$, which is the tabled value. The discrete densities (ψ) do not need to be transformed.

To continue the equating process, the number-correct observed score distributions need to be estimated for the synthetic group. To simplify the presentation, the synthetic group is chosen to be the group taking Form X, so that $w_1 = 1$. In this case, estimates of $f_1(x)$ and $f_1(y)$ are needed.

The distribution of Form X number-correct scores for Group 1 can be estimated directly from the data. However, equation (6.27) can be used to obtain a smoothed estimate of the distribution of $f_1(x)$ by using (a) the item parameter estimates for Form X converted to the Form Y scale shown in Table 6.8 and (b) the distribution of θ for the group taking Form X converted to the Form Y scale shown in Table 6.10. (In Table 6.10, the distribution of θ is approximated using 10 points, which is the number produced by BILOG if the user does not specify a different number. The use of 10 points reduces the computational time when running BILOG and makes it easier to display the distribution in the present example. However, the distribution of θ can be more accurately represented by 20 or even 40 points.)

The distribution of Form Y number-correct scores in Group 1 is not observed directly. To estimate this distribution use (a) the item parameter estimates for Form Y shown in Table 6.8 and (b) the distribution of θ for the group taking Form X converted to the Form Y scale shown in Table 6.10.

TABLE 6.11. IRT Observed Score Results Using $w_1 = 1$.

Score	$\hat{f}_1(x)$	$\hat{g}_1(y)$	$\hat{e}_Y(x)$
0	.0000	.0000	−.3429
1	.0001	.0002	.6178
2	.0005	.0011	1.5800
3	.0018	.0034	2.5457
4	.0050	.0081	3.5182
5	.0110	.0155	4.5021
6	.0201	.0248	5.5042
7	.0315	.0349	6.5309
8	.0437	.0446	7.5848
9	.0548	.0527	8.6604
10	.0626	.0595	9.7464
11	.0660	.0606	10.8345
12	.0651	.0589	11.9282
13	.0615	.0545	13.0431
14	.0579	.0501	14.1945
15	.0560	.0480	15.3672
16	.0555	.0488	16.5109
17	.0541	.0505	17.5953
18	.0498	.0502	18.6416
19	.0424	.0459	19.6766
20	.0338	.0379	20.7364
21	.0271	.0290	21.8756
22	.0240	.0221	23.1020
23	.0245	.0195	24.2897
24	.0261	.0209	25.3624
25	.0262	.0242	26.3651
26	.0233	.0264	27.3440
27	.0182	.0251	28.3226
28	.0132	.0205	29.3203
29	.0102	.0147	30.3521
30	.0092	.0106	31.3787
31	.0087	.0093	32.3473
32	.0072	.0092	33.2818
33	.0049	.0083	34.2001
34	.0027	.0060	35.0759
35	.0012	.0035	35.8527
36	.0003	.0014	36.3904

TABLE 6.12. Moments for Equating Form X and Form Y.

Group	Score	$\hat{\mu}$	$\hat{\sigma}$	$\widehat{sk}$	$\widehat{ku}$
Actual					
1	X	15.8205	6.5278	.5799	2.7217
2	Y	18.6728	6.8784	.2051	2.3028
Estimated Using IRT Observed Score Methods					
1	X	15.8177	6.5248	.5841	2.7235
1	Y	16.1753	7.1238	.5374	2.5750
2	X	18.0311	6.3583	.2843	2.4038
2	Y	18.6659	6.8788	.2270	2.3056
Group 1 Form X Converted to Form Y Scale Using IRT True,					
IRT Observed, and Frequency Estimation Methods					
1	$\hat{\tau}_Y(x)$	16.1784	7.2038	.4956	2.5194
1	$\hat{e}_Y(x)$ IRT	16.1794	7.1122	.5423	2.5761
1	$\hat{e}_Y(x)$ Freq. Est.	16.8329	6.6017	.4622	2.6229

The distributions estimated using the IRT model are shown in Table 6.11 along with the equipercentile equivalents that are obtained using these distributions. The equivalents were calculated using the *PIE* computer program described in Appendix B. (These smoothed distributions are still somewhat irregular, which might be due to the use of only 10 quadrature points in BILOG. For example, modes are present at Form X scores of 11 and 25 and at Form Y scores of 11, 17, and 26.) Moments for these distributions are shown in Table 6.12, where the moments labeled "Actual" are those that came from the data without any IRT estimation. These moments were presented in Chapters 4 and 5. The moments in the next section of Table 6.12 are for the distributions estimated using the IRT model. For example, the mean of 15.8177 for Group 1 on Form X is the mean of the distribution for Group 1 on Form X shown in the second column of Table 6.11. The Group 1 Form X moments from the two sources are quite similar. The actual mean, without any IRT estimation, was 15.8205, whereas the mean for the estimate of the distribution using the IRT model was 15.8177. Similarly, the moments for Group 2 Form Y from the two sources are similar.

Because $w_1 = 1$, the moments for Group 1 are the only ones needed. In Group 1, for example, Form X is $16.1753 - 15.8177 = .3576$ points more difficult than Form Y.

The bottom portion of Table 6.12 shows the moments of converted scores for Group 1 examinees for IRT true score, IRT observed score, and frequency estimation (from Chapter 5) equating. For example, the mean of the Form X scores converted to the Form Y scale using IRT true score equating is 16.1784; using IRT observed score equating the mean is 16.1794. The mean for frequency estimation equating is 16.8329, which was given in Ta-

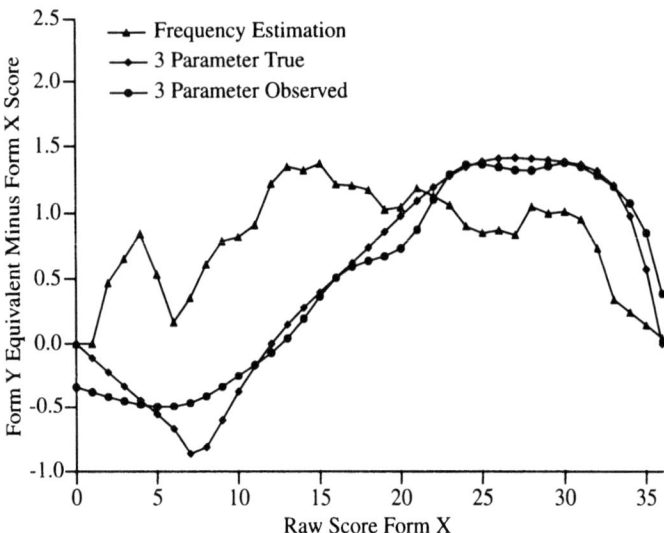

FIGURE 6.6. Estimated equating relationships for IRT true and IRT observed score equating.

ble 5.10. The moments of converted scores are very similar for the two IRT methods, although the moments differ noticeably from those for frequency estimation. Note that frequency estimation included item 27 as a common item, whereas item 27 was not included as a common item for the IRT equating. This difference, and the different statistical assumptions made for frequency estimation compared to the IRT methods, likely contributed to the differences in moments that were observed.

The conversions are plotted in Figure 6.6. In this plot, the relationship for both IRT methods differs noticeably from the frequency estimation relationship. This difference is likely a result of the very different statistical assumptions used in frequency estimation as compared to IRT. Also, the true and observed score methods relationships are similar over most of the score range. The largest differences occur around the sum of the c-parameter estimates and at the very high scores, which are near the regions of the score scale where true scores are undefined. This figure illustrates that if interest is in accurately estimating equivalents at very high scores or near the sum of the c-parameter estimates, such as when a passing score is at a point in one of these score scale regions, then distinctions between the IRT true and observed score methods need to be considered.

6.8.4 Rasch Equating

The fit of the Rasch model to these data might not be good because these multiple-choice items are possibly subject to the effects of guessing, and

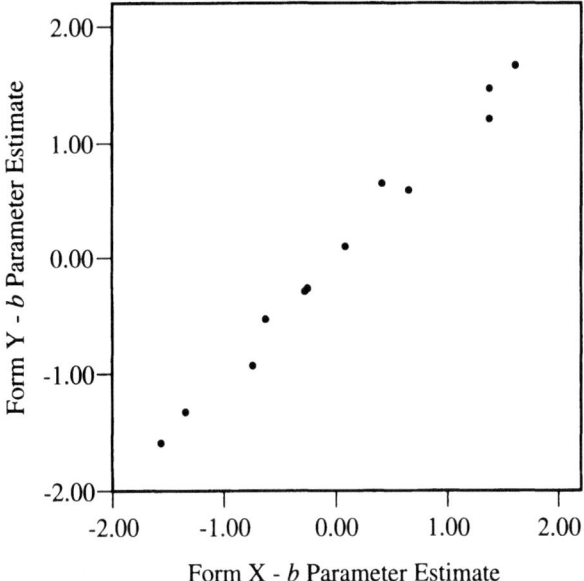

FIGURE 6.7. Plots of Rasch difficulty estimates on Form X versus Form Y.

the items on these forms are not built to be equally discriminating. Still, these data can be used to examine equating with the Rasch model. As was described earlier in this chapter, the Rasch model can be viewed as a special case of the three-parameter logistic model, where $D = 1.0$, all $a_j = 1$, and all $c_j = 0$.

BILOG was used to estimate the item parameters and posterior distributions of θ using the Rasch model. After being placed on a common scale, the Rasch item difficulty parameter estimates are shown in Table 6.13. The item difficulty estimates for the common items (after scaling) are shown in Figure 6.7. There appear to be no outliers.

Rasch true score and observed score (with $w_1 = 1$) equating results are shown in Table 6.14, and moments are shown in Table 6.15. The equating relationships for the Rasch and three-parameter model are plotted in Figure 6.8.

Overall, the Rasch results appear to differ from the three-parameter model results shown earlier. The Rasch observed score and true score results differ slightly at the lower scores.

These results demonstrate that Rasch observed score equating and Rasch true score equating methods are distinct. Even though Rasch true score equating is typically used in practice, Rasch observed score equating also should be considered, especially when interest is in ensuring comparability of observed score distributions. Issues in choosing among results when conducting equating in practice are discussed in Chapter 8. Because the Rasch

TABLE 6.13. Rasch Item Difficulty Estimates.

Item	Form X	Form Y
1	−2.2593	−2.0388
2	−1.1559	−.5748
3	**−1.3429**	**−1.3275**
4	−.5455	−1.0935
5	−1.1838	−1.8460
6	**−1.5596**	**−1.5901**
7	−.7757	−.6703
8	−1.0582	−.5412
9	**−.7384**	**−.9317**
10	−.4947	−.8215
11	−.2756	−1.2651
12	**−.6246**	**−.5325**
13	−.5484	−.3414
14	.0903	−.5417
15	**−.2502**	**−.2675**
16	−.4217	−.0569
17	−.4386	.0893
18	**−.2757**	**−.2943**
19	−.3150	−.6273
20	.0757	.0306
21	**.4129**	**.6461**
22	−.0285	−.4484
23	.1936	−.0570
24	**.0844**	**.0948**
25	.2594	−.0015
26	.5861	−.0396
27	**.6525**	**.5864**
28	.8508	.5463
29	.7831	.5246
30	**1.3792**	**1.4673**
31	.5958	.9051
32	1.1458	.8025
33	**1.3750**	**1.2106**
34	1.3835	1.8085
35	1.8361	2.0944
36	**1.6137**	**1.6644**

Note: Common-item numbers and parameter estimates are in **boldface** type.

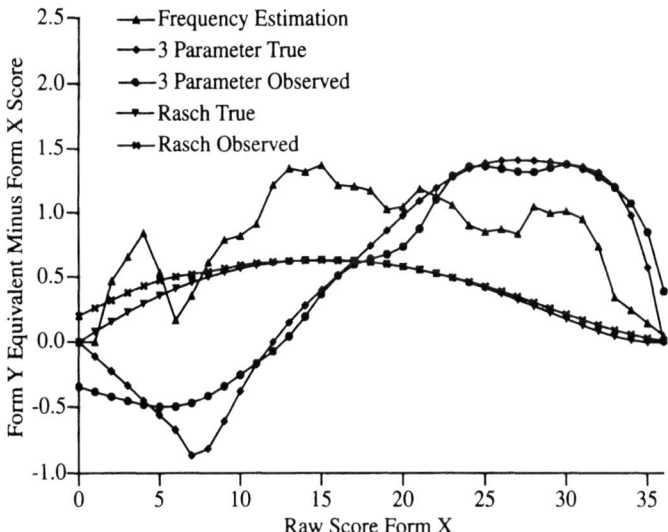

FIGURE 6.8. Estimated equating relationships for three-parameter and Rasch true and observed score equating.

model has relatively modest sample size requirements, this model might be considered when the sample size is small.

6.9 Using IRT Calibrated Item Pools

A *calibrated item pool* (Lord, 1980; Vale, 1986) is a group of items that have item parameter estimates which have all been placed on the same θ-scale. One potential benefit of using IRT is that calibrated item pools can be constructed, and the item parameter estimates can be used directly in equating. Equating designs that use calibrated item pools often allow for greater flexibility in constructing test forms than the other designs that have been described previously. In this section, the development of IRT calibrated item pools, and how they are used in equating, are described.

6.9.1 Common-Item Equating to a Calibrated Pool

Consider the following simplified example of how an IRT calibrated item pool might evolve. Form Y is constructed and then administered. A transformation is developed to convert scores on Form Y to scale scores, and the item parameters for Form Y also are estimated. So far, equating has not been considered, because there is only a single form.

Form X_1 is constructed next. Form X_1 contains some new items and some items in common with Form Y. Form X_1 is administered to a new group of

TABLE 6.14. Rasch True and Observed Score Equating Results.

x	$\hat{t}_Y(x)$	$\hat{e}_Y(x)$
0	.0000	.6995
1	1.0780	1.2612
2	2.1550	2.3202
3	3.2280	3.3782
4	4.2953	4.4318
5	5.3563	5.4739
6	6.4107	6.5024
7	7.4586	7.5207
8	8.5002	8.5419
9	9.5358	9.5670
10	10.5655	10.5914
11	11.5896	11.6098
12	12.6083	12.6206
13	13.6218	13.6257
14	14.6302	14.6275
15	15.6336	15.6280
16	16.6322	16.6274
17	17.6260	17.6239
18	18.6150	18.6153
19	19.5994	19.6010
20	20.5793	20.5809
21	21.5546	21.5560
22	22.5257	22.5272
23	23.4925	23.4956
24	24.4554	24.4628
25	25.4147	25.4269
26	26.3707	26.3891
27	27.3241	27.3486
28	28.2754	28.3047
29	29.2255	29.2587
30	30.1757	30.2137
31	31.1275	31.1711
32	32.0827	32.1302
33	33.0439	33.0914
34	34.0142	34.0572
35	34.9978	35.0302
36	36.0000	36.0113

TABLE 6.15. Moments for Equating Form X and Form Y Using Rasch Equating.

Group	Score	$\hat{\mu}$	$\hat{\sigma}$	$\widehat{sk}$	$\widehat{ku}$
Actual					
1	X	15.8205	6.5278	.5799	2.7217
2	Y	18.6728	6.8784	.2051	2.3028
Estimated Using Rasch Observed Score Methods					
1	X	15.8307	6.4805	.3658	2.5974
1	Y	16.3808	6.4388	.3107	2.5542
2	X	18.1342	6.9291	.1328	2.3458
2	Y	18.6553	6.8406	.0810	2.3438
Group 1 Form X Converted to Form Y Scale Using Rasch					
True, Rasch Observed, and Frequency Estimation Methods					
1	$\hat{\tau}_Y(x)$	16.3554	6.4685	.5212	2.6521
1	$\hat{e}_Y(x)$ Rasch	16.3830	6.4266	.3156	2.5559
1	$\hat{e}_Y(x)$ Freq. Est.	16.8329	6.6017	.4622	2.6229

examinees, and the item parameters are estimated for the new form. Form X_1 can be equated to Form Y using the common-item equating procedures described earlier in this chapter. Along with a conversion table for Form X_1 scores, this common-item equating procedure results in item parameter estimates for Form X_1 which are on the ability scale that was established with Form Y. Actually, there is now a calibrated pool of items, some of which were in Form Y only, some of which were in Form X_1 only, and some of which were in both forms. Refer to Table 6.8. The item parameter estimates in this table are all on the same θ-scale. The items in this table could be considered to be an IRT calibrated item pool.

The use of an IRT calibrated item pool makes possible the use of an equating design that is similar to the common-item nonequivalent groups design. However, in this new design, the common items are drawn from the pool rather than from a single old form. This new design is referred to here as *common-item equating to a calibrated pool*.

To describe this design, suppose that another new form, Form X_2, is constructed. This form consists of a set of common items from the IRT calibrated item pool and some new items. Assume that Form X_2 is administered to a group of examinees. Procedures described earlier can be used to transform the IRT scale that results from estimating Form X_2 item parameters to the scale that was established for the pool. To implement these procedures, the item parameter estimates from the calibrated pool for the common items are considered to be on Scale J, and the item parameter estimates from the calibration of Form X_2 are considered to be on Scale I.

After the new form item parameter estimates are transformed to the θ-scale for the calibrated pool, IRT estimated true score or observed score equating could be conducted. Estimated true score equating for Form X_2

204   6. Item Response Theory Methods

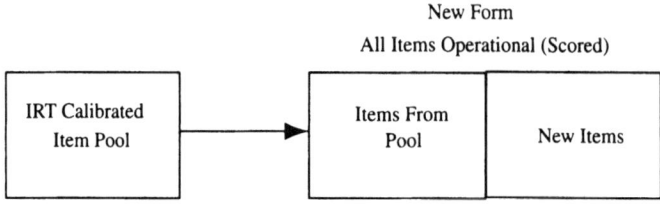

FIGURE 6.9. Equating designs that use an IRT calibrated item pool.

could be implemented as follows. First, find the θ that corresponds to each Form X_2 integer number-correct score. Finding these θ values requires an iterative procedure as described earlier. Second, find the Form Y true score equivalent of each of the θ-values. Following this step results in a true score equating of Form X_2 to Form Y. Use the Form Y scale score transformation to convert the Form X_2 integer number-correct scores to scale scores. These procedures are very similar to what is done in common-item equating, with the major difference being that the common items are taken from a calibrated item pool rather than from a single previously equated form.

After the equating is completed, the new Form X_2 items have item parameter estimates on the θ-scale that was established for the pool. These new items can be added to the IRT calibrated item pool. In this way, the pool can be continually expanded. The common-item sets for new forms are constructed from a continually increasing IRT calibrated item pool. A diagram representing common-item equating to a calibrated pool is presented in the top portion of Figure 6.9.

Many practical issues affect the implementation of IRT calibrated item pools in practice. For example, items might be removed from a pool because their content becomes dated or for test security purposes. Also, when items are used more than once, procedures need to be considered for updating the parameter estimates that are associated with each item in the pool. (For example, two sets of item parameter estimates exist for each common item in Table 6.8.) These are among the issues that are considered when using item pools in a testing program.

Common-item equating to a calibrated pool is more flexible than the common-item nonequivalent groups design, because it allows the common-item set to be chosen from many previous test forms rather than from a single test form. The effects of violations of IRT assumptions need to be considered, however, when using this design. For example, the position of items can affect their performance. For this reason, the position of each common item on the new form should be as close as possible to its position on the form in which it appeared previously.

Also, real tests are typically not strictly unidimensional. To guard against multidimensionality's causing problems with equating, as with traditional equating, the set of common items should be built to the same content specifications, proportionally, as the total test. In this way, the violations of assumptions might affect the common items in the same way that they affect the total scores. Also, a large enough number of common items should be chosen to represent fully the content of the total test.

IRT might be the only procedure that could be used when equating using common-item equating with a calibrated item pool. What if the IRT assumptions are severely violated? Then adequate equating might be impossible with this design. For this reason, if common-item equating to a calibrated item pool is being considered for use, the common-item nonequivalent groups design should be used for a few administrations. The results for the IRT method and traditional methods could be compared and the effects of multidimensionality could be assessed. Switching to common-item equating with a calibrated item pool should be done only if no problems are found with that procedure.

6.9.2 Item Preequating

The use of IRT calibrated item pools also makes an *item preequating design* possible. The goal of item preequating is to be able to produce raw-to-scale score conversion tables *before* a form is administered intact. If a conversion table is produced before the test form is administered, then scores can be reported to examinees without the need to wait for equating to be conducted. Item preequating is possible if the items that contribute to examinees' scores have been previously administered and calibrated.

Consider the following example of how an item preequating design might evolve. Form Y is developed. Form Y contains *operational items*, which are items that contribute to examinees' scores. Form Y also contains *nonoperational items*, which are items that do not contribute to examinees' scores. A conversion of Form Y number-correct scores on the operational items to scale scores is constructed. (The scale could be defined either before or after administration of Form Y.) Form Y is administered and item parameters of the operational and nonoperational items are estimated. At this point, the

IRT calibrated item pool consists of the operational and the nonoperational Form Y items that have parameter estimates on the same IRT scale. So far, equating has not been considered, because there is only a single form.

The operational component of a new form, Form X_1, could be constructed from this calibrated pool of items. If so, the operational component of Form X_1 would consist of some combination of Form Y operational and Form Y nonoperational items. Because the operational items in Form X_1 already have estimated item parameters, a conversion table could be constructed for the operational component of Form X_1 before Form X_1 was ever administered intact. That is, the operational portion of Form X_1 could be "preequated." Form X_1 also would contain nonoperational items, which would be newly written items that were not yet part of the item pool. After Form X_1 was administered, the item parameters for all Form X_1 items (operational and nonoperational) could be estimated. The operational Form X_1 items then could be used as the set of common items for transforming the item parameter estimates for the nonoperational items to the θ-scale that was established with Form Y. These nonoperational Form X_1 items then would be added to the calibrated item pool. The operational portion of subsequent test forms would be constructed from the calibrated pool. The nonoperational portion of subsequent test forms would consist of new items, and would be used to expand the item pool continually.

A diagram representing the item preequating design is presented in the bottom portion of Figure 6.9. The item preequating design and common-item designs differ as to whether or not scores on the new items contribute to examinee scores. These designs also differ in whether or not conversion tables can be produced before the new form is administered.

A variety of issues need to be considered when using item preequating in practice. Suppose it is found that the answer key for an operational item needs to be modified (e.g., an item needs to be double-keyed) after the test is administered. Then the preequating would need to be modified.

In addition, to ensure that items will behave the same on each administration, items should appear in contexts and positions when they appear operationally that are similar to those used when they appear nonoperationally. Although item preequating has been found to produce acceptable results (Bejar and Wingersky, 1982), problems can occur when the nonoperational items are presented in a separate section. For example, Eignor (1985), Eignor and Stocking (1986), and Stocking and Eignor (1986) conducted a series of studies that suggested problems with item preequating if it were used with the SAT. Kolen and Harris (1990) found similar problems with item preequating if it was used with the ACT tests. Context effects and multidimensionality were suggested as reasons for these problems. In situations where the context and positions of items cannot be fixed from one testing to the next, formal studies need to be conducted to make sure that the resulting data will produce fairly robust parameter estimates and equated scores.

The use of item preequating can cause difficulties in estimating the item parameters for the nonoperational items. For example, assume that a test is not strictly unidimensional. In this case, IRT estimation procedures will estimate some composite of multidimensional abilities. The appropriate composite for a test will be the composite for forms that are all built to the test specifications. Estimates that are based only on considering the operational items would estimate this composite. Consider a situation in which the nonoperational items do not represent well the test content specifications. What would happen if the nonoperational item parameters were estimated in the same run of an IRT computer program as the operational items? The composite that is estimated might differ from the composite that would result if only the operational items were used. The use of a different composite might lead to bias in the estimation of item parameters. Although it might be possible to handle estimation problems in practice, the scenario just described suggests that estimation can be quite complicated when estimating parameters for nonoperational items. The problems just described can affect parameter estimates whenever nonoperational items are used in tests that are equated using IRT methods under any of the equating designs described in this book, such as whenever items are tried out (pretested) for inclusion in future forms.

On the surface, item preequating seems straightforward. However, its implementation can be quite complicated. Context effects and dimensionality issues need to be carefully considered, or misleading results will be likely.

Many variations on designs for equating using IRT calibrated item pools exist. For example, new forms might consist of items in common with the pool, new operational items, and nonoperational items. Such pools can be used to produce computer administered and computer adaptive tests (see Chapter 8 for a brief discussion). No attempt will be made here to enumerate all of these variations. However, context effects and dimensionality issues that arise with each variation need to be carefully considered when using item pools in operational testing programs.

6.9.3 Robustness to Violations of IRT Assumptions

A unidimensionality assumption is required to use the IRT methods discussed in this chapter. Research suggests that IRT equating is fairly robust to violations of the unidimensionality assumption when equating alternate forms of a test, as long as the violation of the unidimensionality assumption is not too severe (Bolt, 1999; Camilli et al., 1995; Cook et al., 1985; De Champlain, 1996; Dorans and Kingston, 1985; Yen, 1984). Some investigators have suggested using multidimensional IRT models for tests that violate the unidimensionality assumption. In such cases, methods must be used to link the multidimensional IRT parameter estimates (Davey et al., 1996; Hirsch, 1989; Li and Lissitz, 2000; Oshima et al., 2000). Violations of the local independence assumption might create problems for IRT equating methods. The next section of this chapter considers a procedure that can be used to address violations of the local independence assumption.

6.10 Equating with Polytomous IRT

For the IRT models discussed so far, it has been assumed the items are scored dichotomously. When items are scored in more than two categories, dichotomous models are not appropriate, and polytomous IRT models can be used. In this section, the focus is on equating with polytomously scored items in which the responses are ordered. Typically, the responses are ordered so that responses to higher categories are associated with better performance on the item, although it is possible for the ordering to be in the other direction.

One situation where polytomous IRT models can be used is when writing samples are collected from students and are scored holistically by raters, say, on a scale from 1 to 5. A second situation occurs when multiple items are associated with a common stimulus block, as often occurs in reading comprehension tests. Because there could be some dependency among items associated with a particular stimulus, violations of local independence might make the use of dichotomous IRT questionable. To address this problem, items associated with a common stimulus could be scored as a block, with scores on the block of items ranging from 0 to the number of items in the block. For analysis purposes, a block of items could be treated as a single polytomous item. For example, a 15-dichotomous item reading test containing 3 passages with 5 items each could be treated as a test with 3 polytomous items (blocks), with scores on each polytomous item ranging from 0 to 5. These blocks of items are sometimes referred to as testlets (Thissen et al., 1989). Lee et al. (2001) compared equating based on polytomous and dichotomous IRT models in the testlet situation and found that the polytomous models produced more accurate equating.

Many of the same considerations associated with dichotomous models come into play when IRT equating is conducted with polytomous models. With polytomous models, scales can be linked using generalizations of the item characteristic curve linking methods, and generalizations of IRT true and IRT observed score equating methods can be used to equate total scores.

In the polytomous models considered here, each item is scored in two or more ordered categories. As with dichotomous models, examinee ability is described by a single variable, θ, defined so that $-\infty < \theta < \infty$. The category response curve for each category of an item relates the probability of earning the category score to examinee ability. The category response curve for category k of item j is symbolized as $p_{jk}(\theta)$, which represents the probability that an examinee of ability θ receives a score in category k. For example, if 10% of the examinees with ability 1.5 can be expected to earn a score in category 3 on item 1, then $p_{13}(\theta = 1.5) = .10$. Each category of the item has a category response curve.

As with dichotomous models, local independence for polytomous IRT models means that after taking into account examinee ability, examinee responses to the items are statistically independent. So, for example, if examinees with $\theta = 1.5$ have a .1 probability of earning a score in category 3 for item 1 *and* a .4 probability of earning a score in category 4 for item 2, their probability of earning a score in category 3 for item 1 and a score in category 4 for item 2 equals $.04 = .1(.4)$.

6.10.1 Polytomous IRT Models for Ordered Responses

Various polytomous IRT models have been developed that can be used to model items that are scored polytomously using ordered categories. These include models suggested by Samejima (1969) and Bock (1972), and more recently described by Samejima (1997) and Bock (1997). Samejima designated the categories of each item with consecutive integers beginning with 0. Bock designated categories with consecutive integers beginning with 1. In this section, Bock's designation is used, even in describing Samejima's model, for consistency sake. However, as described later in this section, a scoring function is also introduced, that might differ from the category designator. This scoring function is used to accommodate the scores as used by Samejima as well as other item scoring schemes.

Samejima's Graded Response Model

Although originally developed as a normal ogive model, Samejima's (1969) graded response model also has been presented in the logistic form that is considered here. The graded response model directly models the cumulative category response function. The cumulative category response function for category k of item j is the probability of earning a score at or above category k on that item. For this model, the probability that persons of ability equal to that of person i will earn a score on item j at or above category k can be expressed as

$$p^*_{ijk}(\theta_i; a_j, b_{j_2}, \cdots, b_{jm_j}) = 1, \qquad k = 1,$$
$$p^*_{ijk}(\theta_i; a_j, b_{j_2}, \cdots, b_{jm_j}) = \frac{\exp[Da_j(\theta_i - b_{jk})]}{1 + \exp[Da_j(\theta_i - b_{jk})]}, k = 2, \ldots, m_j. \quad (6.29)$$

For the first category, the cumulative category response function is 1, because the probability is 1 that any examinee, regardless of their θ, will earn a score at or above the first category. In this equation, D is a scaling factor (usually 1.7 so that the logistic is similar to the cumulative normal) and a_j

is the item slope parameter. The item has m_j categories, and b_{jk} are item difficulty parameters for categories 2 through m_j. The first category does not have a difficulty parameter. For categories 2 through m_j, the expression is essentially the item characteristic function for the two-parameter logistic model.

The category response function is calculated by taking the difference between the cumulative category response functions as follows:

$$\begin{aligned} p_{ijk}(\theta_i; a_j, b_{j_2}, \cdots, b_{jm_j}) &= p^*_{ijk}(\theta_i; a_j, b_{j_2}, \cdots, b_{jm_j}) \\ &\quad - p^*_{ij(k+1)}(\theta_i; a_j, b_{j_2}, \cdots, b_{jm_j}), \quad k = 1, \cdots, m_{j-1}, \\ p_{ijk}(\theta_i; a_j, b_{j_2}, \cdots, b_{jm_j}) &= p^*_{ijk}(\theta_i; a_j, b_{j_2}, \cdots, b_{jm_j}), \qquad k = m_j. \end{aligned} \quad (6.30)$$

As an example, consider a 5-category item with parameters $a = 1.2$, $b_2 = -.5$, $b_3 = .6$, $b_4 = 1.1$, $b_5 = 1.3$. Using equation (6.29), the cumulative category response function for this item at $\theta = 1.0$ can be shown to be .964, 684, .452, and .359 for categories 2 through 5. Then from equation (6.30), the category response function is $.036 = (1 - .964)$ for the first category, $0.28 = (.964 - .684)$ for the second category, $0.232 = (.684 - .452)$ for the third category, and $0.093 = (.452 - .359)$ for the fourth category. As is always the case, the category response function for the last category is equal to the cumulative category response function for the last category. For this item, this probability is .359.

The cumulative category response functions for this item, which represent the probability of earning a score at or above a particular category, are graphed in Figure 6.10. Note that the cumulative category response functions are parallel, which is always the case for Samejima's graded response model. Also note that the curves are farther apart when the differences between adjacent b-parameters are large. For example, the difference between the b-parameters for category 2 and 3 is 1.1 units [.6−(−.5)], which is the largest difference between adjacent b-parameters.

The category response functions for this item are graphed in Figure 6.11. The category response function for the first category decreases as θ increases. The category response function for the last category increases as θ increases. The first and last categories can be expected to have this pattern with polytomous models for items with ordered categories, as long as higher category designations tend to be associated higher θ. The intermediate categories have category response functions that all begin with probability near 0, increase to their maximum probability, and then decrease to a probability near zero. Intermediate categories for polytomous models for items with ordered response items typically have curves of this form. The highest point for an intermediate curve is greater when the differences between adjacent b-parameters are large. Thus, for example, the curve for the second category is the highest among the intermediate curves in Figure 6.11.

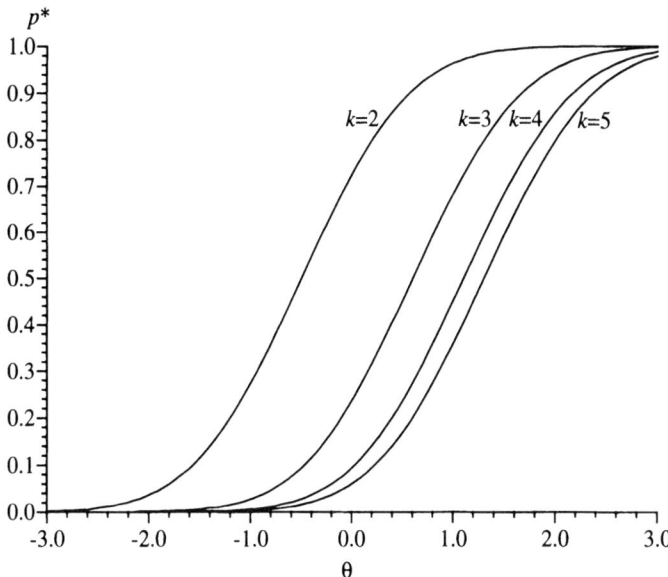

FIGURE 6.10. Cumulative category response functions for a graded response model item.

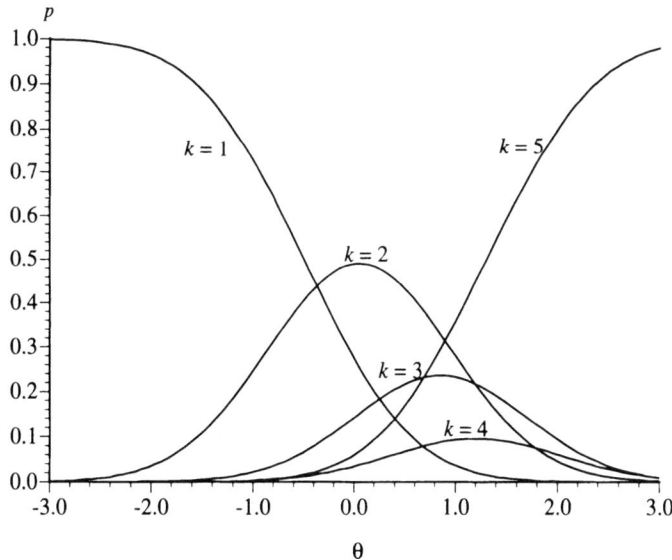

FIGURE 6.11. Category response functions for a graded response model item.

212   6. Item Response Theory Methods

Bock's Nominal Model

Bock's (1972) nominal model can be used to model polytomous items that have ordered or unordered categories. The category response function for this model is

$$p_{ijk}(\theta_i; a_{j1}, a_{j2}, \cdots, a_{jm_j}, c_{j1}, c_{j2}, \cdots, c_{jm_j}) = \frac{\exp(a_{jk}\theta_i + c_{jk})}{\sum_{h=1}^{m_j} \exp(a_{jh}\theta_i + c_{jh})}.$$

(6.31)

Each category for an item has a slope parameter, a_{jk}, and an intercept parameter, c_{jk}. This model is very general. It can be shown that if the slope parameters, a_{jk}, increase from one category to the next, such that $a_{j1} < a_{j2} < \cdots < a_{jm_j}$, then this model can be used to represent items with ordered categories (Bock, 1997; Samejima, 1972; Wainer et al., 1991). Thissen et al. (1989) described how to fit this model when responses are ordered using polynomial contrasts on the slope parameters.

As an example, consider an item with four categories with a_{jk} parameters of 1.7, 3.4, 5.1, 6.8, and c_{jk} parameters of 0.0, 2.55, -.85, -2.55. Note that the a_{jk} parameters increase as category increases, consistent with this item's having ordered categories. For this item, for example, the reader can verify that the probability of an examinee with $\theta = 1$ earning a score in category 1 is 0.010; and in categories 2–4, the probabilities are 0.725, 0.132, and 0.132, respectively. The category response function for this item is shown in Figure 6.12. As can be seen in this figure, the general shapes of the functions for the first and last categories are similar to those for the Samejima graded response model item discussed previously. The general shapes of intermediate curves are also similar for the two models.

Various other models can be viewed as being special cases of the nominal categories model. Muraki's (1992, 1997) generalized partial credit model is one of these. In this model,

$$p_{ijk}(\theta_i; a_j^*, b_j, d_{j1}, d_{j2}, \cdots, d_{jm_j}) = \frac{\exp\left[\sum_{h=1}^{k} Da_j^*(\theta_i - b_j + d_{jh})\right]}{\sum_{g=1}^{m_j} \exp\left[\sum_{h=1}^{g} Da_j^*(\theta_i - b_j + d_{jh})\right]}.$$

(6.32)

In this equation, D is a scaling constant (typically 1.7), item parameters are the discrimination parameter a_j^* and the difficulty parameter, b_j. There are also difficulty parameters for each category, $d_{j1}, d_{j2}, \cdots, d_{jm_j}$. This model is overparameterized as stated, and sometimes the parameters are set as follows: $b_j = 0$ and $d_{j1} = 0$. An alternative parameterization is sometimes used in which a category difficulty parameter is used that is the difference

6.10 Equating with Polytomous IRT

between b_j and d_{jk}. In this section, the parameterization shown in equation (6.32) is used.

The form of this equation, with the single summation in the numerator and double summation in the denominator, is more complicated than the other IRT models discussed so far. As an example of how this equation would be implemented for a three category item the numerator is

$\exp[Da_j^*(\theta_i - b_j + d_{j1})]$, for category 1,

$\exp[Da_j^*(\theta_i - b_j + d_{j1}) + Da_j^*(\theta_i - b_j + d_{j2})]$, for category 2, and

$\exp[Da_j^*(\theta_i - b_j + d_{j1}) + Da_j^*(\theta_i - b_j + d_{j2}) + Da_j^*(\theta_i - b_j + d_{j3})]$, for category 3.

The denominator is the sum of these three numerators.

As an example, consider an item with four categories with $D = 1.7$, $a_j^* = 1$, $b_j = 0$, and d_{jk} of 0, 1.5, –2, and 1 for the four categories. For this item, the reader can verify that the probability of an examinee with $\theta = 1$ earning a score in category 1 is 0.010, and in categories 2–4, respectively, the probabilities are 0.725, 0.132, and 0.132. Note that these four probabilities are the same as the probabilities for Bock's nominal model example discussed earlier. In addition, the category response function for this item is the same as that for Bock's nominal model item shown in Figure 6.12. Because Muraki's generalized partial credit model is a special case of Bock's nominal model, there are Bock's nominal model parameters that correspond to the generalized partial credit model parameters. This Muraki's generalized partial credit model example was purposefully chosen to have the same model parameters as Bock's nominal model example.

The relationship between the parameters for the two models is expressed as follows:

$$a_{jk} = Dka_j^*, \text{ and}$$

$$c_{jk} = -Dka_j^*b_j + Da_j^* \sum_{h=1}^{k} d_{jh}. \quad (6.33)$$

If Muraki's generalized partial credit model parameters for the example are substituted in this equation, Bock's nominal model parameters in the earlier example are obtained.

The relationship between the parameters of these two models and the appearance of the category response functions is much less clear than the relationships for dichotomous items or for Samejima's graded response models. For the purposes of this chapter, it is primarily important to note that these models can be used with test items that have ordered categories. These models provide descriptions of the category response functions for these types of items. In addition, there are other models discussed by Bock (1997) and Muraki (1997) that can be viewed as special cases of Muraki's generalized partial credit model.

214   6. Item Response Theory Methods

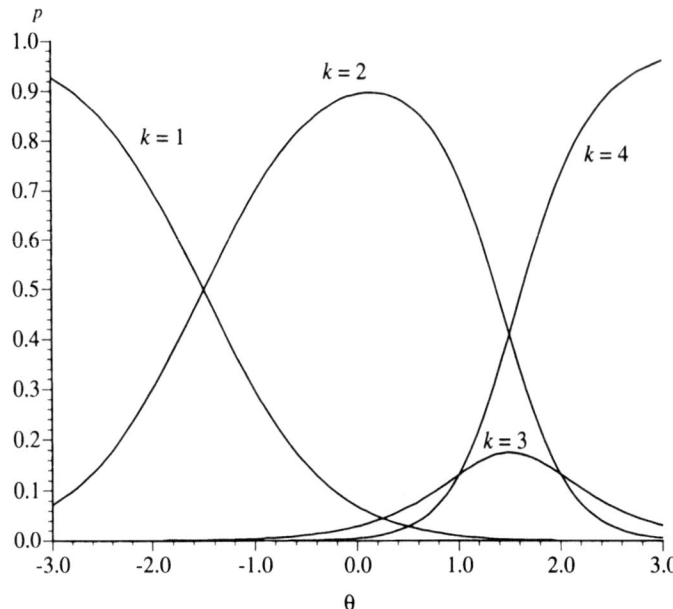

FIGURE 6.12. Category response functions for a generalized partial credit model item.

6.10.2 Scoring Function, Item Response Function, and Test Characteristic Curve

Often, total scores are used with test items that are polytomously scored. A scoring function is used to associate the scores with the categories. Let W_{jk} refer to the integer score associated with category k. Often a scoring function of $W_{jk} = k$ is used. In this case, a response associated with the first category earns a score of 1, a response associated with the second category earns a score of 2, and so forth. Another scoring function that is often used is $W_{jk} = k - 1$. For this function, a response associated with the first category earns a 0, a response associated with the second category earns a score of 1, and so forth.

Based on a scoring function, the minimum and maximum scores on test Form X can be calculated as

$$\min_X = \sum_{j:X} W_{j1},$$

$$\max_X = \sum_{j:X} W_{jm_j}. \quad (6.34)$$

Thus, to obtain the minimum, the minimum scores for items are summed over items on Form X. To obtain the maximum, the maximum scores for items are summed. Note that if all items are scored using a minimum for each item as zero, then the minimum score is zero. If the minimum score for each item is 1, then the minimum score for Form X equals the number of items.

The item response function relates total score on an item to θ. This function is expressed as

$$\tau_j(\theta_i) = \sum_{k=1}^{m_j} W_{jk} p_{ijk}(\theta_i), \qquad (6.35)$$

where $p_{ijk}(\theta_i)$ is the category response function for item j for a polytomous IRT model.

For polytomous IRT models, the test characteristic curve for Form X is calculated as

$$\tau_X(\theta_i) = \sum_{j:X} \tau_j(\theta_i). \qquad (6.36)$$

Similar to dichotomous IRT models, the test characteristic curve relates IRT ability to true total scores.

6.10.3 Parameter Estimation and Scale Transformation with Polytomous IRT Models

Item and ability parameters for Samejima's graded response model and Bock's nominal model can be estimated using the computer program MULTILOG (Thissen, 1991). PARSCALE (Muraki and Bock, 1997) can be used to estimate parameters for Samejima's graded response model and for the generalized partial credit model. ICL (Hanson, 2002) can be used for the generalized partial credit model. As with dichotomous IRT models, for the random groups or single group designs, as long as the item parameters are estimated using the same scaling conventions (e.g., mean ability of 0 and standard deviation of ability 1), then the estimates from separate runs on Form X and Form Y are on the same scale. For the single group design, the item and ability parameters for Samejima's graded response model and Bock's nominal model can be estimated with MULTILOG in a single computer run.

For the common item non-equivalent groups design, ICL can be used to simultaneously estimate parameters for the old and new form. In this case, a single data file is created that contains the data for Group 1 and Group 2 examinees on all of the items on Form X and Form Y. Responses for Group 1 on Form Y items are coded as "not reached." Similarly, responses for Group 2 on Form X are treated as "not reached." A single run of the computer program is used to estimate the parameters for both forms.

Alternatively, when test forms are administered to nonequivalent groups, scale transformation methods can be used with the polytomous IRT models that are analogous to those for dichotomous IRT models. Methods using

216   6. Item Response Theory Methods

moments of item parameter estimates are given first followed by characteristic curve methods.

Mean/Sigma and Mean/Mean Methods

Mean/mean and mean/sigma methods were suggested by Cohen and Kim (1998) for the graded response model. For the mean/sigma method, the mean and standard deviation of the b-parameter estimates are found over all items and all categories. The mean and standard deviation of the b-parameter estimates for the common items are calculated separately for the old form and new form calibration. For example, if there are 5 common items with 4 score categories each, then there are 15 b-parameter estimates in the common item set (5 items times $4 - 1 = 3$ b-parameter estimates per item in each calibration). The resulting means and standard deviations are substituted for the parameters in equations (6.8a) and (6.9a) to obtain the slope and intercept of the transformation equation. Equations (6.2), (6.3), and (6.4) are used to transform the θ-, a-, and b-parameters. The mean/mean method uses the mean of the b-parameter estimates as calculated for the mean/sigma method as well as the mean of the a-parameter estimates over the common items. Equations (6.8b) and (6.9a) are used to obtain the slope and intercept of the transformation function.

A similar process can be followed for scale linking using the mean/mean and mean/sigma method with Muraki's generalized partial credit model shown in equation (6.32). For the mean/sigma method, the mean and standard deviation of the estimates of $b_j - d_{jh}$ are found over all items and categories for each calibration. These standard deviations are substituted for the standard deviations in equation (6.8a) to calculate the slope and the means substituted in equation (6.9a) to find the intercept of the transformation equation. The mean/mean method uses the means of the a^* parameter estimates and the means of the estimates of $b_j - d_{jh}$. Equations (6.8b) and (6.9a) are used to obtain the slope and intercept of the transformation function. The a^* parameter estimates are transformed using equation (6.3). The b parameter estimates are transformed using equation (6.4). The d parameter estimates are transformed by multiplying them by the slope computed using equation (6.8a). The θ-estimates are transformed using equation (6.2). Masters (1984) described linking procedures for the partial credit model, a special case of the generalized partial credit model, which involve only adding a constant for this model.

Test Characteristic Curve Methods

Test characteristic curve methods can be used with polytomous IRT models. For polytomous IRT models, it is necessary to establish the criteria over categories within item as well as over items. The Haebara difference for the graded response model is

$$Hdiff(\theta_i) = \sum_{j:V} \sum_{k:j} \left[\begin{array}{l} p_{ijk}(\theta_{Ji}; \hat{a}_{Jj}, \hat{b}_{Jj2}, \cdots, \hat{b}_{Jjk}, \cdots, \hat{b}_{Jjm_j}) - \\ p_{ijk} \left(\begin{array}{l} \theta_{Ji}; \dfrac{\hat{a}_{Ij}}{A}, A\hat{b}_{Ij2} + B, \cdots, \\ A\hat{b}_{Ijk} + B, \cdots, A\hat{b}_{Ijm_j} + B \end{array} \right) \end{array} \right]^2. \tag{6.37}$$

The first summation is over items and the second is over categories within item. Thus this function is the sum of squared differences between category response curves over all categories and items. *Hcrit* is found by substituting equation (6.37) in equation (6.12). This criterion is minimized by summing over examinees as discussed with the dichotomous model.

The Stocking and Lord difference for the graded response model is

$$SLdiff(\theta_i) = \left[\begin{array}{l} \sum_{j:V} \sum_{k:j} W_{jk} p_{ijk}(\theta_{Ji}; \hat{a}_{Jj}, \hat{b}_{Jj2}, \cdots, \hat{b}_{Jjk}, \cdots, \hat{b}_{Jjm_j}) - \\ \sum_{j:V} \sum_{k:j} W_{jk} p_{ijk} \left(\begin{array}{l} \theta_{Ji}; \dfrac{\hat{a}_{Ij}}{A}, A\hat{b}_{Ij2} + B, \cdots, \\ A\hat{b}_{Ijk} + B, \cdots, A\hat{b}_{Ijm_j} + B \end{array} \right) \end{array} \right]^2. \tag{6.38}$$

Recall that the Stocking and Lord approach was based on the squared difference between the test characteristic curves expressed on the two scales. Referring to equation (6.35) and equation (6.36), it can be seen that this equation is the squared difference between test characteristic curves. Note that the scoring function (W_{jk}) is used in *SLdiff* but not in *Hdiff*. *SLcrit* is found by substituting equation (6.38) in equation (6.15). This criterion is minimized by summing over examinees as discussed with the dichotomous model.

Baker (1992b) developed a Stocking and Lord related method for the graded response model. Baker's (1993a) EQUATE 2.0 program can be used with the Stocking and Lord approach, using a fixed set of abilities to cumulate over abilities. Other ways of cumulating over ability for the Stocking and Lord method are implemented in *POLYST* listed in Appendix B. Baker (1993b, pp. 249,250) described a procedure for minimizing *Hcrit* for this model, which is also implemented in *POLYST*.

Hdiff and *SLdiff* are defined similarly for the generalized partial credit model. With this model, though, it is necessary to also transform the *d*-parameter estimates.

For Bock's nominal model,

218   6. Item Response Theory Methods

$$Hdiff(\theta_i) = \sum_{j:V} \sum_{k:j} \left[p_{ijk} \begin{pmatrix} \theta_{Ji}; \hat{a}_{Jj1}, \cdots, \hat{a}_{Jjk}, \cdots, \hat{a}_{Jjm_j}, \\ \hat{c}_{Jj1}, \cdots, \hat{c}_{Jjk}, \cdots, \hat{c}_{Jjm_j} \end{pmatrix} - p_{ijk} \begin{pmatrix} \theta_{Ji}; \dfrac{\hat{a}_{Ij1}}{A}, \cdots, \dfrac{\hat{a}_{Ijk}}{A}, \cdots, \dfrac{\hat{a}_{Ijm_j}}{A}, \\ \hat{c}_{Ij1} - \dfrac{B}{A}\hat{a}_{Ij1}, \cdots, \hat{c}_{Ijk} - \dfrac{B}{A}\hat{a}_{Ijk}, \cdots, \\ \hat{c}_{Ijm_j} - \dfrac{B}{A}\hat{a}_{Ijm_j} \end{pmatrix} \right]^2 .$$

(6.39)

$Hcrit$ is found by substituting equation (6.39) in equation (6.12). This criterion is minimized by summing over examinees as discussed with the dichotomous model. Baker (1993b) described this method summing over equally spaced points and it is implemented in his EQUATE 2.0 computer program (Baker, 1993a). Kim and Hanson (2002) provided a correction to one of Baker's (1993b) equations. Generalizations of these methods are implemented in *POLYST*.

The Stocking and Lord procedure can be implement for this model in situations when modeling graded response data. For Bock's nominal model,

$$SLdiff(\theta_i) = \left[\sum_{j:V}\sum_{k:j} W_{jk} p_{ijk} \begin{pmatrix} \theta_{Ji}; \hat{a}_{Jj1}, \cdots, \hat{a}_{Jjk}, \cdots, \hat{a}_{Jjm_j}, \\ \hat{c}_{Jj1}, \cdots, \hat{c}_{Jjk}, \cdots, \hat{c}_{Jjm_j} \end{pmatrix} - \sum_{j:V}\sum_{k:j} W_{jk} p_{ijk} \begin{pmatrix} \theta_{Ji}; \dfrac{\hat{a}_{Ij1}}{A}, \cdots, \dfrac{\hat{a}_{Ijk}}{A}, \cdots, A\hat{a}_{Ijm_j}, \\ \hat{c}_{Ij1} - \dfrac{B}{A}\hat{a}_{Ij1}, \cdots, \hat{c}_{Ijk} - \dfrac{B}{A}\hat{a}_{Ijk}, \cdots, \\ \hat{c}_{Ijm_j} - \dfrac{B}{A}\hat{a}_{Ijm_j} \end{pmatrix} \right]^2 .$$

(6.40)

As pointed out by Baker (1993b), this procedure is not appropriate when items are nominally scored, because in this case scoring weights would not typically be available. Thus, this procedure can be used only with items scored in ordered categories. This method is implemented in *POLYST*.

Research on Scale Linking in Polytomous IRT

In a simulation study, Cohen and Kim (1998) compared the mean/mean, mean/sigma, weighted mean/sigma, Stocking and Lord (1983) extension, and an extension of Divgi's (1985) method that Kim and Cohen (1995) developed for linking scales under the graded response model. They concluded that the methods produced similar results. Baker (1997) studied the empirical sampling distributions of the linking coefficients under the graded response model. Kim and Cohen (2002) compared linking using the Stocking and Lord method and concurrent calibration for data that were simulated to fit the graded response model. They found that concurrent calibration was slightly more accurate. Clearly, more research on linking

6.10.4 True Score Equating

Using equation (6.36) to calculate IRT true scores, the true score equating process described for dichotomous models in conjunction with equation (6.19) is used, except that typically there is no lower asymptote parameter in the polytomous models.

6.10.5 Observed Score Equating

IRT observed score equating for polytomous IRT models is very similar to that for dichotomous IRT models. The major difference is that the distribution of observed score given IRT ability is modeled using a compound multinomial distribution, which is a generalization of the compound binomial distribution described earlier. A recursion formula that was described by Thissen et al. (1995) can be used to perform the calculations.

Define $f_1(x = W_{11}|\theta_i) = p_{i11}(\theta_i)$ as the probability of earning a score in the first category of item 1, $f_1(x = W_{12}|\theta_i) = p_{i12}(\theta_i)$ as the probability of earning a score in the second category of item 1, and so forth up to the last category of item 1. Then for $r > 1$, the recursion formula for finding the probability of earning score x after the r-th item added is,

$$f_r(x|\theta_i) = \sum_{k=1}^{m_j} f_{r-1}(x - W_{jk}) p_{ijk}(\theta_i) \text{ for } x \text{ between } \min_r \text{ and } \max_r, \quad (6.41)$$

where $\min_r$ and $\max_r$ are the minimum and maximum scores after adding the r-th item. Note that when $x - W_{jk} < \min_{r-1}$ or $x - W_{jk} > \max_{r-1}$, then $f_{r-1}(x - W_{jk}) = 0$, by definition.

An example using the recursive formula is given in Table 6.16. This example is for a three-item test, where each item has a scoring function that consists of consecutive integers beginning with 1. The first and second items have four categories each. The third item has three categories. In this table, the i subscript for ability is dropped to simplify the table. To use the recursion formula, it is important to identify the maximum and minimum score after each new item is added. For the first item ($r = 1$) the minimum score is 1 and the maximum is 4. When the second item is added ($r = 2$), the minimum is 2 and the maximum is 8. After the third item is added ($r = 3$), the minimum is 3 and the maximum is 11. In Table 6.16, a zero is displayed whenever $x - W_{jk}$ is less than the minimum score or greater than the maximum score.

A computational example that goes along with the recursive example in Table 6.16 is given in Table 6.17. Assume that $\theta = 1$. For this example, the first item is Bock's nominal model item used as an example earlier. The

220   6. Item Response Theory Methods

TABLE 6.16. Polytomous IRT Recursive Formula Example.

r	x	$f_r(x)$				
1	1	$f_1(1)$	$= p_{11}$			
	2	$f_1(2)$	$= p_{12}$			
	3	$f_1(3)$	$= p_{13}$			
	4	$f_1(4)$	$= p_{14}$			
2	2	$f_2(2)$	$= f_1(1)p_{21}$	$+0$	$+0$	$+0$
	3	$f_2(3)$	$= f_1(2)p_{21}$	$+f_1(1)p_{22}$	$+0$	$+0$
	4	$f_2(4)$	$= f_1(3)p_{21}$	$+f_1(2)p_{22}$	$+f_1(1)p_{23}$	$+0$
	5	$f_2(5)$	$= f_1(4)p_{21}$	$+f_1(3)p_{22}$	$+f_1(2)p_{23}$	$+f_1(1)p_{24}$
	6	$f_2(6)$	$= 0$	$+f_1(4)p_{22}$	$+f_1(3)p_{23}$	$+f_1(2)p_{24}$
	7	$f_2(7)$	$= 0$	$+0$	$+f_1(4)p_{23}$	$+f_1(3)p_{24}$
	8	$f_2(8)$	$= 0$	$+0$	$+0$	$+f_1(4)p_{24}$
3	3	$f_3(3)$	$= f_2(2)p_{31}$	$+0$	$+0$	
	4	$f_3(4)$	$= f_2(3)p_{31}$	$+f_2(2)p_{32}$	$+0$	
	5	$f_3(5)$	$= f_2(4)p_{31}$	$+f_2(3)p_{32}$	$f_2(2)p_{33}$	
	6	$f_3(6)$	$= f_2(5)p_{31}$	$+f_2(4)p_{32}$	$f_2(3)p_{33}$	
	7	$f_3(7)$	$= f_2(6)p_{31}$	$+f_2(5)p_{32}$	$f_2(4)p_{33}$	
	8	$f_3(8)$	$= f_2(7)p_{31}$	$+f_2(6)p_{32}$	$f_2(5)p_{33}$	
	9	$f_3(9)$	$= f_2(8)p_{31}$	$+f_2(7)p_{32}$	$f_2(6)p_{33}$	
	10	$f_3(10)$	$= 0$	$+f_2(8)p_{32}$	$f_2(7)p_{33}$	
	11	$f_3(11)$	$= 0$	$+0$	$f_2(8)p_{33}$	

probabilities for this item as well as the other two items, conditional on $\theta = 1$, are given at the bottom of the table. The outcome of applying the recursion formula in this example is a distribution of total scores on this three-item test for examinees with $\theta = 1$. Note that the total scores range from 3 to 11.

For IRT observed score equating, the recursion formula, along with a quadrature distribution for θ, is used to find the marginal distribution for Form X using equation (6.26) and implemented using equation (6.26) or (6.27). Similar procedures are used for Form Y. These distributions are then equated using equipercentile methods in the same way that the scores were equated in observed score equating with dichotomous IRT; the main difference is that the total scores range between, rather than between 0 and K_X.

6.10.6 Example Using the Graded Response Model

A new real data example is used to illustrate use of the graded response model in equating. The test in this example is Level 9 of the Maps and Diagrams of the Iowa Tests of Basic Skills (ITBS). Two forms of this test (Form L and Form K) were administered using a random groups design. Each form contains 24 items. There are 5 stimuli on each form of the test.

TABLE 6.17. Polytomous IRT Recursive Formula Computational Example.

r	x	$f_r(x)$					
1	1	$f_1(1)$	$= .010$				
	2	$f_1(2)$	$= .725$				
	3	$f_1(3)$	$= .132$				
	4	$f_1(4)$	$= .132$				
2	2	$f_2(2)$	$= .010(.15)$	$+0$	$+0$	$+0$	$= .0015$
	3	$f_2(3)$	$= .725(.15)$	$+.010(.25)$	$+0$	$+0$	$= .1112$
	4	$f_2(4)$	$= .132(.15)$	$+.725(.25)$	$+.010(.40)$	$+0$	$= .2050$
	5	$f_2(5)$	$= .132(.15)$	$+.132(.25)$	$+.725(.40)$	$+.010(.20)$	$= .3448$
	6	$f_2(6)$	$= 0$	$+.132(.25)$	$+.132(.40)$	$+.725(.20)$	$= .2308$
	7	$f_2(7)$	$= 0$	$+0$	$+.132(.40)$	$+.132(.20)$	$= .0792$
	8	$f_2(8)$	$= 0$	$+0$	$+0$	$+.132(.20)$	$= .0264$
3	3	$f_3(3)$	$= .0015(.05)$	$+0$	$+0$		$= .0001$
	4	$f_3(4)$	$= .1112(.05)$	$+.0015(.60)$	$+0$		$= .0065$
	5	$f_3(5)$	$= .2050(.05)$	$+.1112(.60)$	$.0015(.35)$		$= .0775$
	6	$f_3(6)$	$= .3448(.05)$	$+.2050(.60)$	$.1112(.35)$		$= .1792$
	7	$f_3(7)$	$= .2308(.05)$	$+.3448(.60)$	$.2050(.35)$		$= .2902$
	8	$f_3(8)$	$= .0792(.05)$	$+.2308(.60)$	$.3448(.35)$		$= .2631$
	9	$f_3(9)$	$= .0264(.05)$	$+.0792(.60)$	$.2308(.35)$		$= .1296$
	10	$f_3(10)$	$= 0$	$+.0264(.60)$	$.0792(.35)$		$= .0436$
	11	$f_3(11)$	$= 0$	$+0$	$.0264(.35)$		$= .0092$

Note: $p_{11} = .01$, $p_{12} = .725$, $p_{13} = .132$, $p_{14} = .132$, $p_{21} = .15$, $p_{22} = .25$, $p_{23} = .40$, $p_{24} = .20$, $p_{31} = .05$, $p_{32} = .60$, $p_{33} = .35$

TABLE 6.18. Graded Response Model Item Parameter Estimates.

Form	Testlet	a_j	b_{j2}	b_{j3}	b_{j4}	b_{j5}	b_{j6}	b_{j7}
L	1	1.197	-1.906	.103	1.713			
	2	1.029	-2.094	-.208	2.020			
	3	1.672	-2.355	-1.481	-.830	-.197	.551	1.670
	4	1.033	-2.272	-.706	.576	1.912	3.267	5.126
	5	1.048	-1.904	-.604	.567	1.683	2.944	4.346
K	1	1.407	-3.081	-1.179	.363			
	2	1.891	-1.851	-1.016	-.026			
	3	2.143	-2.476	-1.736	-1.174	-.594	.020	.961
	4	1.471	-2.286	-1.121	-.137	.795	1.717	2.840
	5	1.442	-2.043	-1.108	-.279	.519	1.312	2.475

The first two stimuli each have 3 items associated with them and the last three stimuli have 6 items associated with them. The items associated with each stimulus block were assumed to be a testlet. The testlet score was the total number correct on that testlet. Each examinee had 5 scores, one for each testlet. The range of scores for the first two testlets was 0 to 3. The range of scores for the last three testlets was 0 to 6. The total score on the test ranged from 0 to 24. Examinee testlet scores were input into the computer program MULTILOG. Defaults were used for the analyses, with the exception that 49 equally spaced quadrature points ranging from –6 to +6 were used. IRT equating was conducted using the *POLYEQUATE* computer program that is given in Appendix B.

The item parameter estimates that were obtained in two runs of MULTI-LOG are given in Table 6.18. Because the random groups design was used, the groups taking the two forms are assumed equivalent, and the item parameters from the two runs assumed to be on the same scale, without transformation. As can be seen, each item has an a_j-parameter estimate and one less b_{jk}-parameter estimate than the number of score categories.

The true score equating results are given in Table 6.19. To conduct observed score equating, it was necessary to have quadrature distributions. MULTILOG does not print out the quadrature weights. To obtain the weights, the following process was used, which produces weights that are similar to the prior weights used by BILOG. Begin with a set of quadrature points that are equally spaced and centered around zero. Find the density of the standard normal distribution at each point. Sum the weights over the points and then divide each weight by this sum, which standardizes the weights to sum to one. For the example, this process was followed with 49 quadrature points (rounded to one decimal place) ranging from –6 to +6. The results from the observed score equating are shown in Ta-

TABLE 6.19. Graded Response Model True Score Equating.

Form L Score	θ Equivalent	Form K Equivalent
0		0.0000
1	−2.8734	1.2173
2	−2.4186	2.4598
3	−2.0852	3.7232
4	−1.7878	5.0624
5	−1.5063	6.4754
6	−1.2335	7.9417
7	−0.9675	9.4249
8	−0.7093	10.8485
9	−0.4582	12.1977
10	−0.2117	13.5085
11	0.0345	14.8072
12	0.2846	16.0576
13	0.5430	17.2252
14	0.8146	18.3479
15	1.1007	19.4247
16	1.3908	20.3425
17	1.6782	21.0697
18	1.9769	21.6899
19	2.3174	22.3015
20	2.7380	22.9719
21	3.2746	23.5915
22	3.9718	23.9136
23	4.8693	23.9903
24		24.0000

224   6. Item Response Theory Methods

TABLE 6.20. Graded Response Model Observed Score Equating.

Score	Form L Relative Frequency	Form K Relative Frequency	Form K Equivalent of Form L Raw Score
0	.0032	.0015	.5120
1	.0067	.0041	1.6295
2	.0118	.0068	2.8232
3	.0191	.0102	4.0965
4	.0290	.0143	5.4718
5	.0408	.0188	6.8479
6	.0533	.0240	8.2768
7	.0649	.0296	9.6702
8	.0745	.0357	10.9918
9	.0810	.0426	12.2716
10	.0846	.0501	13.5346
11	.0863	.0572	14.7981
12	.0865	.0631	16.0148
13	.0838	.0661	17.1592
14	.0765	.0671	18.2546
15	.0643	.0693	19.3020
16	.0489	.0733	20.2601
17	.0343	.0752	21.0926
18	.0229	.0723	21.8007
19	.0144	.0657	22.3942
20	.0082	.0574	23.0970
21	.0037	.0470	23.6443
22	.0012	.0314	24.2817
23	.0002	.0134	24.4676
24	.0000	.0039	24.4981

TABLE 6.21. Moments for Graded Response Model Equating.

	$\hat{\mu}$	$\hat{\sigma}$	$\widehat{sk}$	$\widehat{ku}$
Actual				
Form L	10.8047	4.3171	0.2256	2.4343
Form K	14.0066	5.0146	−0.2638	2.2285
Estimated Using Graded Response Observed Score Method				
Form L	10.7900	4.1695	−0.0442	2.5432
Form K	14.1708	4.9801	−0.3757	2.4903
Form L Converted to Form K Using Various Methods				
Equipercentile	14.0105	5.0046	−0.2577	2.2244
IRT Obs	14.1363	5.0362	−0.1279	2.1586
IRT True	14.0504	5.1688	−0.1735	2.1276

6.10 Equating with Polytomous IRT   225

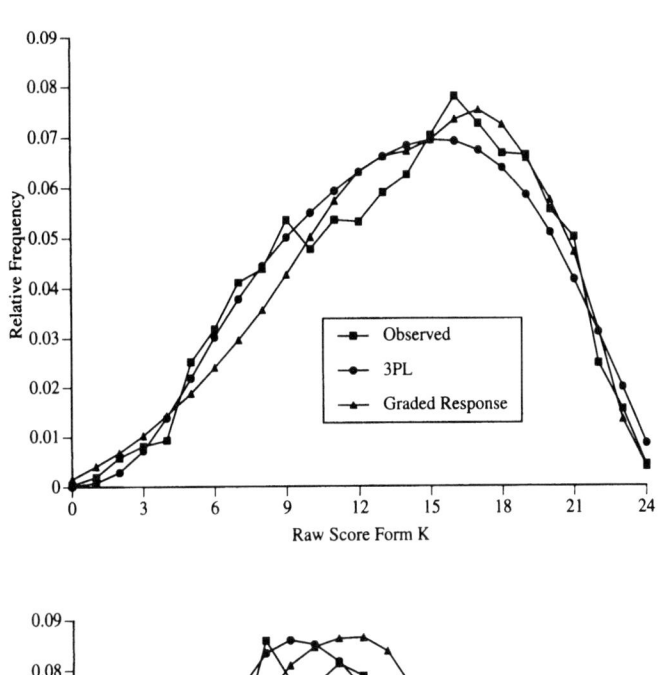

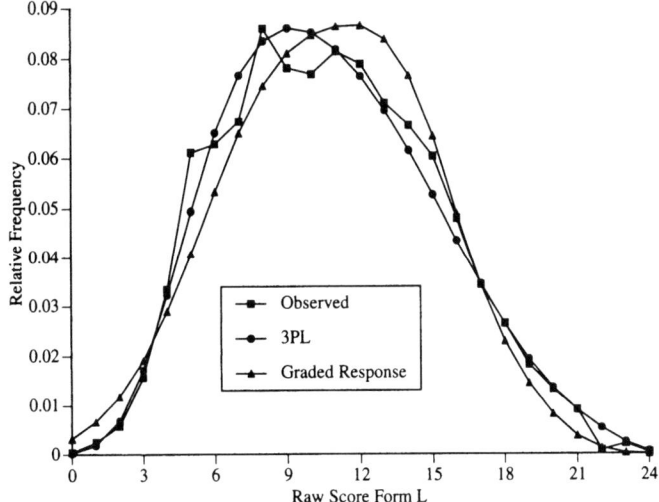

FIGURE 6.13. Observed and fitted relative frequency distributions for Form K and Form L for graded response model example.

226   6. Item Response Theory Methods

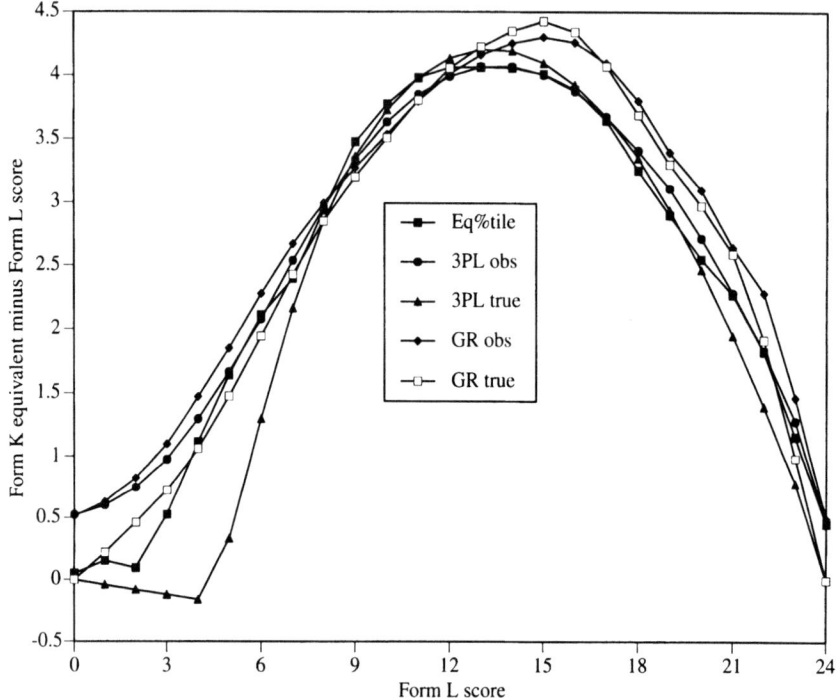

FIGURE 6.14. Equating relationships for graded response model example.

ble 6.20. In addition, the frequency distributions that were obtained from the IRT model are displayed in Table 6.20. Moments of the actual and estimated distributions and the converted scores are shown in Table 6.21 (these moments were calculated using the actual, not the smoothed, relative frequency distributions).

In addition to the graded response model, the three-parameter logistic model (3PL) was also fit to the data. In this case, each form was analyzed as having 24 dichotomously scored items. Also, unsmoothed equipercentile equating was conducted. Only final results are provided for these equatings.

The observed and fitted frequency distributions are shown in Figure 6.13. As can be seen, there appears to be a slight distortion in the fitted distribution for the graded response model, with the mode being a bit too high. This finding is consistent with the mean form Form K estimated using the graded response model (14.1708) being slightly too large compared to the actual mean (14.0066). Difference plots for all of the equatings that were conducted are shown in Figure 6.14. The three-parameter logistic model true score method produced different results at the low scores than the other methods, presumably because of the pseudo-chance level parameter.

6.11 Practical Issues and Caveat

We recommend the following when using IRT to conduct equating in practice:

1. Use both the Stocking and Lord and Haebara methods for scale transformation as well as the mean/sigma and mean/mean methods.

2. When equating number-correct scores, use both IRT true score equating and IRT observed score equating.

3. Whenever possible, conduct traditional equipercentile or linear methods on the forms that are being equated as a check.

Often all of the methods applied provide similar equating results and conversion to scale scores (where appropriate), which is reassuring. However, when the results for the different methods diverge, then a choice must be made about which results to believe. The assumptions required and the effects of poor parameter estimates need to be considered in these cases. The issue of choosing among results in equating is discussed in more detail in Chapter 8.

Unidimensional IRT methods assume that the test forms are unidimensional and that the relationship between ability and the probability of correct response follows a specified form. These requirements are difficult to justify for many educational achievement tests, although the methodology might be robust to violations in many practical situations. The general approach taken in this chapter, and in this book as a whole, is to recommend that equating studies be designed to minimize the effects of violations of assumptions. In this regard, the following advice from Cook and Petersen (1987) is especially relevant:

> Regardless of whether IRT true-score or conventional equating procedures are being used, common items should be selected that are a miniature of the tests to be equated and these items should remain in the same relative position when administered to the new- and old-form groups. It would also seem prudent to evaluate the differential difficulty of the common items administered to the equating samples, particularly when equating samples come from different administration dates. (p. 242)

6.12 Exercises

6.1 For the test in Table 6.1, find the probability of correctly answering each of the three items for examinees with ability $\theta_{Ii} = .5$.

6.2 For the test in Table 6.1, find the distribution of observed scores for examinees with ability $\theta_{Ii} = .5$.

6.3 Prove the following:

   a. $A = (b_{Jj} - b_{Jj*})/(b_{Ij} - b_{Ij*})$ from equation (6.6). [Hint: The proof can be done by setting up a pair of simultaneous equations for b_{Jj*} and b_{Jj} using equation (6.4) and solving for A.]

   b. $A = a_{Ij}/a_{Jj}$ from equation (6.6). [Hint: Use equation (6.3).]

   c. $A = \sigma(b_J)/\sigma(b_I)$ in equation (6.8a). [Hint: Use equation (6.4).]

   d. $A = \mu(a_I)/\mu(a_J)$ in equation (6.8b). [Hint: Use equation (6.3).]

6.4. For the test in Table 6.1, what is the value of the test characteristic curve at $\theta_{Ii} = -2.00$, .5, and 1.00? How about at $\theta_{Ji} = -1.50$ and 0.00?

6.5. For the hypothetical example in Table 6.3, conduct observed score equating for a population of examinees with equal numbers of examinees at three score levels: $\theta = -1, 0, 1$. [Hints: Use equation (6.25) to find $f(x|\theta)$ and $g(y|\theta)$ for $\theta = -1, 0,$ and 1. Then apply equation (6.26). Finally, do conventional equipercentile equating. *Warning*: This problem requires considerable computation.]

Exercises   229

6.6. For the example in Table 6.4, provide the probabilities of earning scores 0, 1, 2, 3, and 4 for $r = 4$ assuming that the probability of correctly answering the fourth item for an examinee of ability $\theta_i = -2$ equals .4.

6.7. For the example in Table 6.2, calculate $Hdiff$ and $SLdiff$ for $\theta = 1$ on Scale J using the mean/sigma and mean/mean methods.

6.8. Why is IRT equating to a particular old form important if all items are in an IRT calibrated item pool?

6.9. The following are some of the steps involved in equating (assume that number-correct scoring is used and that scale scores are reported to examinees): (a) select the design for data collection and how to implement it; (b) construct, administer, and score the test; (c) estimate equating relationships; (d) construct a conversion table of raw-to-scale scores; (e) apply the conversions to examinees; and (f) report scores to examinees. At each of these steps, what would be the differences in equating a new form using the IRT methods described in Chapter 6 versus the traditional methods described in Chapters 2–5?

6.10. Find $p^*_{ijk}(\theta_i; a_j, b_{j2}, \cdots, b_{jm_j})$ and $p_{ijk}(\theta_i; a_j, b_{j2}, \cdots, b_{jm_j})$ at $\theta_i = -.5$ for a Samejima Logistic graded response model item with the following parameters: $a_j = 1.2$, $b_{j2} = -1.1$, $b_{j3} = -1.0$, $b_{j4} = .5$, $b_{j5} = .6$, and $b_{j6} = 1.0$.

6.11. Find $p_{ijk}(\theta_i; a_{j1}, a_{j2}, \cdots, a_{jm_j}, c_{j1}, c_{j2}, \cdots, c_{jm_j})$ at $\theta_i = .5$ for a Bock's nominal model item with the following parameters: $a_{j1} = .905$, $a_{j2} = .522$, $a_{j3} = -.959$, $c_{j1} = .336$, $c_{j2} = -.206$, $b_{j3} = .126$.

6.12. Is the item in the preceding exercise consistent with being an item with ordered categories? Why or why not?

6.13. Find $p_{ijk}(\theta_i; a^*_j, b_j, d_{j1}, d_{j2}, \cdots, d_{jm_j})$ at $\theta_i = 1.0$ for a Muraki generalized partial credit model item with the following parameters: $a_j = 1$, $b_j = 0$, $d_{j1} = 0$, $d_{j2} = 1$, $d_{j3} = -1$.

6.14. For the example in Table 6.17, find the probability of earning scores of 4 through 14 if on a fourth item, the probability of earning a 1 was .3, the probability of earning a 2 was .5, and the probability of earning a 3 was .2. Use the recursive formula.

6.15. For the example in Table 6.17, what is the (conditional) expected score on item 1? On item 2? What is the (conditional) expected score on a two-item test consisting of the first two items? What relationship is there between these three expected scores? Why? In the terminology of the chapter, what are each of these (conditional) expected scores?

6.16. Show that equation (6.33) relates Muraki's generalized partial credit model parameters to Bock's nominal model parameters.

7
Standard Errors of Equating

Two general sources of error in estimating equating relationships are present whenever equating is conducted using data from an equating study: *random error* and *systematic error*. Random equating error is present when the scores of examinees who are considered to be samples from a population or populations of examinees are used to estimate equating relationships. When only random equating error is involved in estimating equating relationships, the estimated equating relationship differs from the equating relationship in the population because data were collected from a sample, rather than from the whole population. If the whole population were available, then no random equating error would be present. Thus, the amount of random error in estimating equating relationships becomes negligible as the sample size increases.

The focus of the present chapter is on estimating random error, rather than systematic error. The following examples of systematic error are intended to illustrate the concept of systematic error, and to distinguish systematic from random error. One way that systematic error can occur in estimating equating relationships is when the estimation method introduces bias in estimating the equating relationship. As was indicated in Chapter 3, smoothing techniques can introduce systematic error—a useful smoothing method results in a reduction in random error that exceeds the amount of systematic error which is introduced. Another way that systematic error in estimating equating relationships can occur is when the statistical assumptions that are made in an equating method are violated. For example, systematic error would be introduced if the Tucker method described in Chapter 4 was used in a situation in which the regression of X on V differed from Population 1 to Population 2. Similarly, systematic error would be introduced if IRT true score equating, as described in Chapter 6, was used to equate multidimensional tests. A third way that systematic error could occur is if the design used to collect the data for equating were improperly implemented. For example, suppose that in the random groups design, the test center personnel assigned Form X to examinees near the front of the room and Form Y to examinees near the back of the room. This distribution pattern likely would lead to systematic differences between examinees who were administered the forms, unless the examinees were seated randomly. As another example, suppose that in the common-item nonequivalent groups design the common items appeared near the beginning of the test in Form X and near the end of the test in Form Y. In this case, the common items might behave very differently on the two forms, because of the different placement. A fourth way that systematic error could occur is if the group(s) of examinees used to conduct equating were to differ substantially from the group who takes the equated form. It is important to note that the use of large sample sizes would not reduce the magnitude of these systematic error components. Thus, a major distinguishing factor between random and systematic error is that as the sample size increases, random error diminishes, whereas systematic error does not diminish.

Standard errors of equating index random error in estimating equating relationships only—they are not directly influenced by systematic error. Standard errors of equating approach 0 as the sample size increases, whereas systematic errors of equating are not directly influenced by the sample size of examinees. Only random error in estimating equating relationships is considered in the present chapter; systematic error is a prominent consideration in Chapter 8. In the present chapter, standard errors of equating are defined, and both bootstrap and analytic standard errors are considered. We describe procedures for estimating standard errors of equating for many of the methods described in Chapters 2 through 6, including standard errors for raw and scale scores. We show how the standard errors can be used to estimate sample size requirements and to compare the precision of different equating methods and designs.

7.1 Definition of Standard Error of Equating

The standard error of equating is a useful index of the amount of equating error. The standard error of equating is conceived of as the standard deviation of equated scores over hypothetical replications of an equating procedure in samples from a population or populations of examinees. In one hypothetical replication, specified numbers of examinees would be randomly sampled from the population(s). Then the Form Y equivalents of

Form X scores would be estimated at various score levels using a particular equating method. The standard error of equating at each score level is the standard deviation, over replications, of the Form Y equivalents at each score level on Form X. Standard errors typically differ across score levels.

To define standard errors of equating, each of the following need to be specified:

- the design for data collection (e.g., common-item nonequivalent groups);
- the definition of equivalents (e.g., equipercentile);
- the method used to estimate the equivalents (e.g., unsmoothed equipercentile);
- the population(s) of examinees;
- the sample sizes (e.g., 2,000 for the old form and 3,000 for the new form);
- the score level or score levels of interest (e.g., each integer score from 0 to K_X)

Given a particular specification, define $\widehat{eq}_Y(x_i)$ as an estimate of the Form Y equivalent of a Form X score in the sample and define $\mathbf{E}[\widehat{eq}_Y(x_i)]$ as the expected equivalent, where $\mathbf{E}$ is the expectation over random samples from the population(s). For a given sample estimate, equating error at a particular score level on Form X is defined as the difference between the sample Form Y equivalent and the expected equivalent. That is, equating error at score x_i for a given equating is

$$\widehat{eq}_Y(x_i) - \mathbf{E}[\widehat{eq}_Y(x_i)]. \tag{7.1}$$

Suppose that the equating is replicated a large number of times, such that for each replication the equating is based on random samples of examinees from the population(s) of examinees who take Form X and Form Y, respectively. The equating error variance at score point x_i is

$$var[\widehat{eq}_Y(x_i)] = \mathbf{E}\{\widehat{eq}_Y(x_i) - \mathbf{E}[\widehat{eq}_Y(x_i)]\}^2, \tag{7.2}$$

where the variance is taken over replications. The standard error of equating is defined as the square root of the error variance,

$$se[\widehat{eq}_Y(x_i)] = \sqrt{var[\widehat{eq}_Y(x_i)]} = \sqrt{\mathbf{E}\{\widehat{eq}_Y(x_i) - \mathbf{E}[\widehat{eq}_Y(x_i)]\}^2}. \tag{7.3}$$

The error indexed in equations (7.1)–(7.3) is random error that is due to the sampling of examinees to estimate the population quantity, $\widehat{eq}_Y(x_i) = \mathbf{E}[\widehat{eq}_Y(x_i)]$.

Standard errors can be considered for specific data collection designs. In a random groups design, a single population of examinees is considered. A random sample of size N_X is drawn from the population and administered Form X, another random sample of size N_Y is drawn from the population and administered Form Y, and equating is conducted using these data. Conceptually, the hypothetical sampling and equating process is repeated a large number of times, and the variability at each score point is tabulated to obtain standard errors for this design. Recall from Chapter 3 that a conceptual scheme for considering standard errors of equipercentile equating using the random groups design was presented in Figure 3.1.

How would this hypothetical sampling/equating process proceed for the common-item nonequivalent groups design? In this design, on each replication N_X examinees from Population 1 who took Form X and N_Y examinees from Population 2 who took Form Y would be sampled. On each replication, the equivalents would be found using an equating method appropriate for this design, such as the frequency estimation method. The standard error at a particular Form X score would be the standard deviation of the Form Y equivalents over replications.

In the present chapter, the population of examinees is assumed to be infinite (or at least very large) in size. Often it makes sense to conceive of the population as being infinite in size, such as when the population is conceived of as all potential past, current, and future examinees. The examinees in a current sample could be considered as a sample from this population. Although not the approach taken here, it might be argued that the group of examinees *is* the whole population. In this case, there can be no random error in estimating equating relationships because no sampling of examinees is involved.

In practice, data are available from a single sample or pair of samples of examinees. Two general types of procedures have been developed for estimating the standard errors from such data collection designs. The first type is computationally intensive resampling procedures. In these procedures, many samples are drawn from the data at hand and the equating functions estimated on each sampling. Standard errors are calculated using the data from these many resamplings. The resampling method that is considered in this chapter is the bootstrap. The second type is analytic in that the procedures result in an equation that can be used to estimate the standard errors using sample statistics. The development of the equations in these analytic methods can be very time-consuming, and the resulting equations can be very complicated. The analytic method that is described in this chapter is referred to as the delta method. Both types of methods are useful, depending on the information desired and the uses to be made of the standard errors.

7.2 The Bootstrap

The *bootstrap method* (Efron, 1982; Efron and Tibshirani, 1993) is a method for estimating standard errors of a wide variety of statistics that is computer-intensive. As is described subsequently in more detail, the bootstrap involves taking multiple random samples with replacement from the sample data at hand. A computer is used to draw random samples using a pseudo-random number generator when applying the bootstrap in practice. Refer to Press et al. (1989) for a discussion of pseudo-random number generation. To introduce the bootstrap method, a simple example is used in which the standard error of a sample mean is estimated. Then applications to equating are described.

7.2.1 Standard Errors Using the Bootstrap

The steps in estimating standard errors of a statistic using the bootstrap from a single sample are as follows:

1. Begin with a sample of size N.

2. Draw a random sample, *with replacement*, of size N from this sample data. Refer to this sample as a *bootstrap sample*.

3. Calculate the statistic of interest for the bootstrap sample.

4. Repeat steps 2 and 3 R times.

5. Calculate the standard deviation of the statistic of interest over the R bootstrap samples. This standard deviation is the estimated bootstrap standard error of the statistic.

Of special importance is that the random sample in step 2 is drawn *with replacement*.

Consider a simple hypothetical example for illustrative purposes. Suppose that an investigator is interested in estimating the standard error of a mean using the bootstrap method. Assume that a sample of size $N = 4$ is drawn from the population and the sample values are 1, 3, 5, and 6. To estimate the standard error of the mean using the bootstrap, bootstrap samples would be drawn with replacement from these four sample values and the mean calculated for each bootstrap sample. Suppose that the following four random bootstrap samples were drawn with replacement from the sample values 1, 3, 5, and 6:

$$\begin{aligned}
&\text{Sample 1: 6 3 6 1} \quad Mean = 4.00\\
&\text{Sample 2: 1 6 1 3} \quad Mean = 2.75\\
&\text{Sample 3: 5 6 1 5} \quad Mean = 4.25\\
&\text{Sample 4: 5 1 6 1} \quad Mean = 3.25
\end{aligned}$$

The same sample value may be chosen more than once because bootstrap sampling is done *with replacement*. For example, the score of 6 was chosen twice in bootstrap Sample 1, even though there was only one 6 in the data. The bootstrap estimate of the standard error of the mean is the standard deviation of the means over the four bootstrap samples. To calculate the standard deviation, note that the mean of the four means is $(4.00 + 2.75 + 4.25 + 3.25)/4 = 3.5625$. Using $R - 1 = 3$ as the divisor, the standard deviation of the four means is

$$\sqrt{\frac{(4.00 - 3.5625)^2 + (2.75 - 3.5625)^2 + (4.25 - 3.5625)^2 + (3.25 - 3.5625)^2}{3}}$$

$$= .6884.$$

Thus, using these four bootstrap samples, the estimated standard error of the mean is .6884. In practice, many more than four samples would be chosen. Efron and Tibshirani (1993) recommended using between 25 and 200 bootstrap samples for estimating standard errors. In practice, however, as many 1,000 bootstrap replications are common.

In this situation, standard statistical theory would have been easier to implement than the bootstrap. Noting that the sample standard deviation (using $N-1$ in the denominator) of the original sample values (1, 3, 5, 6) is 2.2174, the estimated standard error of the mean using standard procedures is $2.2174/\sqrt{4} = 1.1087$. The bootstrap estimate would likely be similar to this value if a large number of bootstrap replications were used for estimating the standard error for the population.

In equating, analytic procedures are not always available for estimating standard errors, or the analytic procedures that are available might make assumptions that are thought to be questionable. The bootstrap can be used in such cases. Although computationally intensive, the bootstrap can be readily implemented using a computer, often with much less effort than it would take to derive analytic standard errors.

7.2.2 Standard Errors of Equating

Now consider using the bootstrap to equate two forms using the random groups design. To implement this method, begin with sample data. For equipercentile equating with the random groups design, the samples would consist of N_X examinees with scores on Form X and N_Y examinees with scores on Form Y. To estimate the $se[\hat{e}_Y(x_i)]$:

1. Draw a random bootstrap sample with replacement of size N_X from the sample of N_X examinees.

2. Draw a random bootstrap sample with replacement of size N_Y from the sample of N_Y examinees.

3. Estimate the equipercentile equivalent at x_i using the data from the random bootstrap samples drawn in steps 1 and 2, and refer to this estimate as $\hat{e}_{Yr}(x_i)$.

4. Repeat steps 1 through 3 R times, obtaining bootstrap estimates $\hat{e}_{Y_1}(x_i), \hat{e}_{Y2}(x_i), \ldots, \hat{e}_{YR}(x_i)$.

5. The standard error is estimated by

$$\widehat{se}_{boot}[\hat{e}_Y(x_i)] = \sqrt{\frac{\sum_r [\hat{e}_{Yr}(x_i) - \hat{e}_{Y.}(x_i)]^2}{R-1}}, \qquad (7.4)$$

where

$$\hat{e}_{Y.}(x_i) = \frac{\sum_r \hat{e}_{Yr}(x_i)}{R}. \qquad (7.5)$$

These procedures can be applied at any x_i. Typically, the same R bootstrap samples are used to estimate standard errors for all integer values of x_i between 0 and K_X, because the interest is in estimating standard errors for the whole range of scores.

The equipercentile equating of the ACT Mathematics test forms that was described in Chapter 2 is used to illustrate the computation of bootstrap standard errors. In this example, Form X and Form Y of the 40-item test were equated using equipercentile methods. The sample sizes were 4,329 for Form X and 4,152 for Form Y. Unsmoothed equipercentile results were presented in Table 2.7.

To compute bootstrap standard errors in this example, 4,329 Form X scores and 4,152 Form Y scores were sampled with replacement from their respective distributions. Form Y equipercentile equivalents at each Form X integer score were found. $R = 500$ bootstrap replications were used, and the estimated standard errors were calculated at each score point using equation (7.4). The computer program *Equating Error* listed in Appendix B was used to conduct these and the subsequent bootstrap analyses described in this chapter.

The resulting bootstrap standard errors are graphed in Figure 7.1. For comparison purposes, the estimated analytic standard errors that were presented in Table 3.2 also are graphed. [These analytic standard errors were calculated using equation (7.12), which is presented later in the present chapter.] In this figure, the standard errors tend to be smallest around Form X scores in the range of 8 to 12. These scores tend to be the most frequently occurring Form X scores, as can be seen in Figure 2.8. Also, the analytic and bootstrap standard errors are very similar. Empirical studies have found that the two methods produce very similar results in both linear and equipercentile equating of number-correct scores when a large number of bootstrap replications are used (e.g., Kolen, 1985; Jarjoura and Kolen, 1985). Finally, the graph of the standard errors is irregular in appearance,

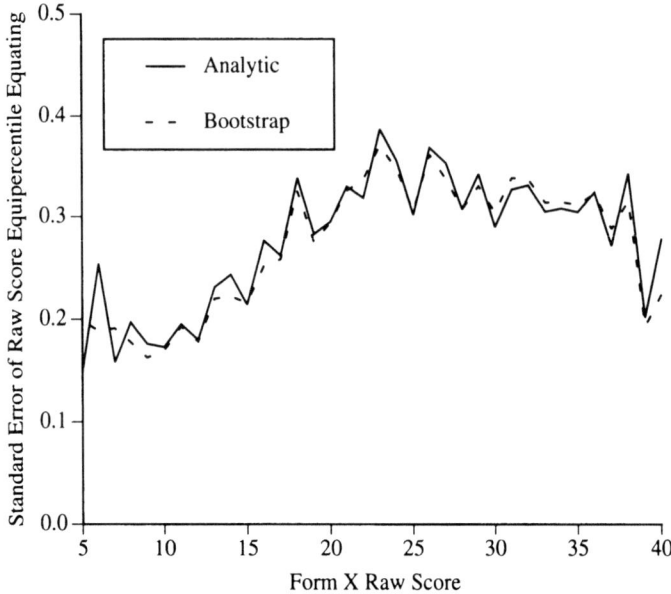

FIGURE 7.1. Bootstrap and analytic standard errors of equipercentile equating for raw scores.

which is presumably due to the relatively small numbers of examinees earning each score.

The bootstrap can be readily applied in the common-item nonequivalent groups design. In this design, a sample of N_X examinees would be drawn from the examinees who were administered Form X, and a sample of N_Y examinees would be drawn from among the examinees who were administered Form Y. An appropriate method, such as the Tucker linear method or the frequency estimation equipercentile method, then would be used to find the equivalents. The sampling process would be repeated a large number of times, and the standard error again would be the standard deviation of the estimates over samples.

7.2.3 Parametric Bootstrap

One problem that can be encountered in estimating standard errors in equipercentile equating is that estimates of standard errors might not be very accurate, especially at score points with very small frequencies, as was illustrated by the irregular graphs in Figure 7.1. Efron and Tibshirani (1993) suggested using the *parametric bootstrap* in these situations. In the parametric bootstrap, a parametric model is fit to the data. The standard errors are estimated by treating the fitted parametric model as if it appropriately described the population and simulating standard errors by sampling from the fitted model. Because populations are assumed to be infinite in size, sampling with or without replacement is considered to be the same. As an example, the following steps could be used to apply the parametric bootstrap to estimate the standard errors of equipercentile equating using the random groups design:

1. Fit the Form X empirical distribution using the log-linear method. Choose C using the techniques described in Chapter 3.

2. Fit the Form Y empirical distribution using the log-linear method, Choose C using the techniques described in Chapter 3.

3. Using the fitted distribution from step 1 as the population distribution for Form X, randomly select N_X scores from this population distribution. The distribution of these scores is the parametric bootstrap sample distribution of scores on Form X.

4. Using the fitted distribution from step 2 as the population distribution for Form Y, randomly select N_Y scores from this population distribution. The distribution of these scores is the parametric bootstrap sample distribution of scores on Form Y.

5. Conduct equipercentile equating using the sampled parametric bootstrap distributions from steps 3 and 4, and tabulate the equipercentile equivalent at score x_i.

6. Repeat steps 3 through 5 a large number of times. The estimated standard error is the standard deviation of the equivalents at x_i over samples.

In the parametric bootstrap, samples are taken from fitted distributions. In the bootstrap, samples are taken from the empirical distribution. The parametric bootstrap leads to more stable estimates of standard errors than the bootstrap. However, the parametric bootstrap can produce biased estimates of the standard errors if the fitted parametric model is not an accurate estimate of the population distribution. Very little research has been conducted on the parametric bootstrap in equating. More research would be required for the parametric bootstrap to be recommended as a general procedure, although it seems promising.

Results from the use of the parametric bootstrap are shown in Figure 7.2. The bootstrap standard errors are the same as those shown in Figure 7.1. To calculate the parametric bootstrap standard errors in Figure 7.2, a log-linear model with $C = 6$ was fit to the Form X and Form Y distributions. Each parametric bootstrap replication involved drawing a random sample from the fitted distributions and conducting unsmoothed equipercentile equating. As can be seen in Figure 7.2, the parametric bootstrap results in a more regular graph of the standard errors than the bootstrap. In addition, the parametric bootstrap results are more regular than the analytic results shown in Figure 7.1

240   7. Standard Errors of Equating

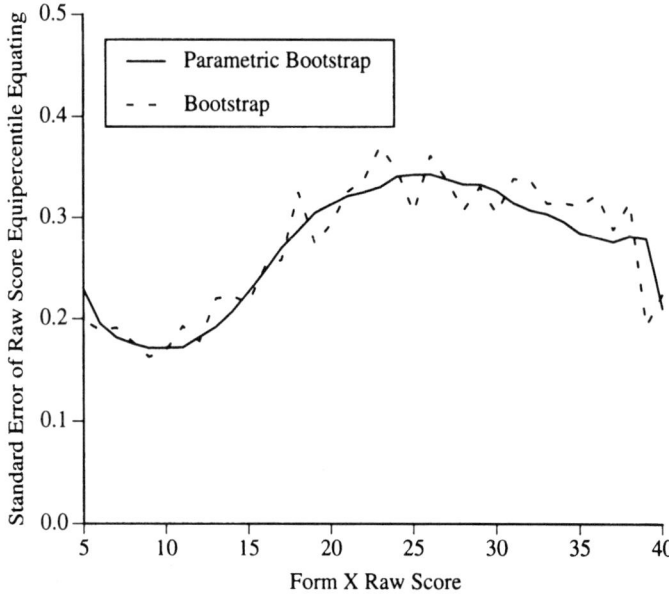

FIGURE 7.2. Bootstrap and parametric bootstrap standard errors of equipercentile equating for raw scores.

7.2.4 Standard Errors of Equipercentile Equating with Smoothing

Smoothed equivalents can be used in place of the unsmoothed equivalents in the preceding procedures to estimate standard errors of smoothed equipercentile equating. A comparison of standard errors of smoothed and unsmoothed equipercentile equating is presented in Figure 7.3. The parametric bootstrap was used in these comparisons. (The regular bootstrap could have been used here also.) The standard errors of unsmoothed equipercentile equating shown in Figure 7.3 are identical to those shown in Figure 7.2 for the parametric bootstrap. To calculate the standard errors for smoothed equating, the distributions on each parametric bootstrap replication were smoothed using the log-linear model with $C = 6$. The smoothed distributions on each replication then were equated using equipercentile methods. Over most of the score range the standard errors for smoothed equipercentile equating were less than those for unsmoothed, indicating that smoothing reduces the standard error of equating. Note, however, that the standard errors only take into account random error; systematic error is not indexed. Thus, as was stressed in Chapter 3, a smoothing method that results in lower standard errors still could produce more total error than unsmoothed equipercentile equating.

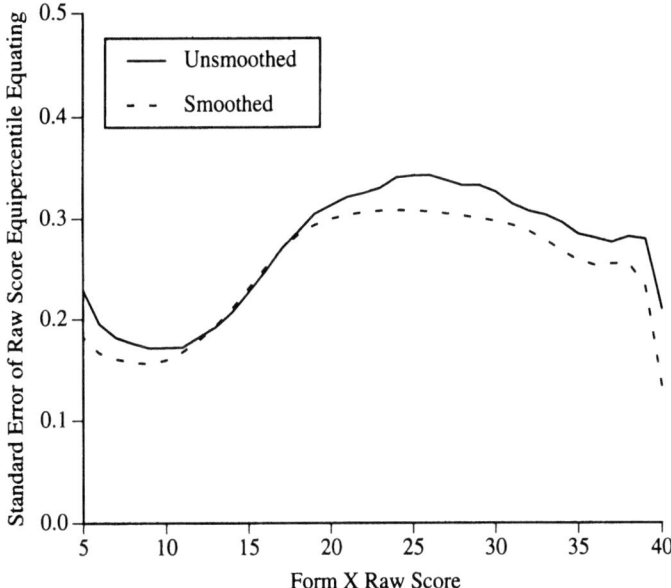

FIGURE 7.3. Parametric bootstrap standard errors of equipercentile equating for raw scores.

7.2.5 Standard Errors of Scale Scores

So far, the bootstrap has been presented using equated raw scores. The bootstrap can be readily applied to scale scores, as well, by transforming the raw score equivalents to scale score equivalents on each replication. The standard error is the standard deviation of the scale score equivalents over replications. Standard errors of both unrounded and rounded scale score equivalents can be estimated using the bootstrap procedure.

Scale score standard errors of equipercentile equating are shown in Figure 7.4. First consider the standard errors for unrounded scale scores. The standard errors tend to be relatively large in the range of raw scores of 36 to 39, which results because the raw-to-scale score transformation is steeper than at other ranges. (The raw-to-scale score transformation for equipercentile equating is shown in Table 2.8.)

Next consider the standard errors for rounded scale scores. These standard errors tend to be greater than those for the unrounded scores, because the rounding process introduces error. When the decimal portion of the unrounded scale scores is close to 1/2, there tends to be a larger difference between the unrounded and rounded standard errors. For example, from Table 2.8, the unrounded scale score at a Form X score of 22 is 20.5533, and the standard error for rounded scale scores for a Form X score is much larger than the standard error for unrounded scale scores. When the deci-

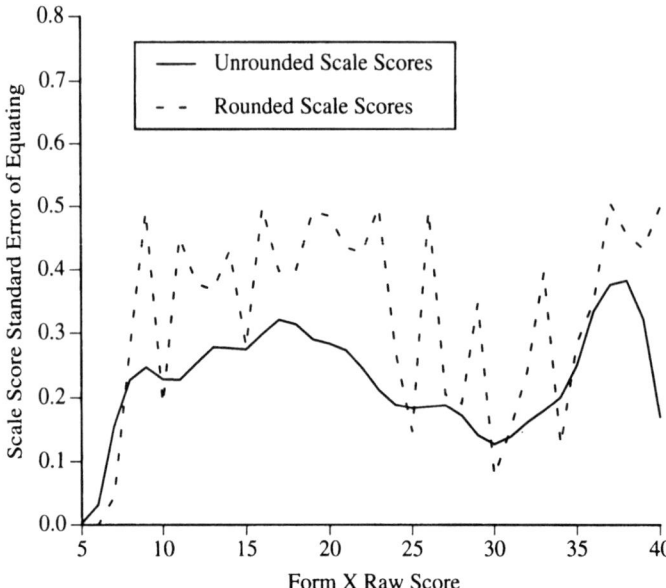

FIGURE 7.4. Parametric bootstrap standard errors of equipercentile equating for scale scores.

mal portion of the unrounded scale score is close to 0, the standard errors for the rounded and unrounded scale scores tend to be similar.

7.2.6 Standard Errors of Equating Chains

Often equating involves a chain of equating so that scores can be reported on the scale of an earlier form or in terms of scale scores. For example, in ACT Assessment (ACT, 1997) equating, new forms are equated to the score scale using a chain of equating which goes to the score scale which was developed for use in 1989. This chain could include numerous test forms. (Also refer to the discussion of the scaling and equating process described with Table 1.1.) Error in a chain of equating can be estimated using the bootstrap.

Consider an example where Form X_2 is to be equated to Form Y through Form X_1. The chaining process involves equating Form X_2 to Form X_1, which can be symbolized as $eq_{X1}(X_2)$, and equating Form X_1 to Form Y, which can be symbolized as $eq_y(X_1)$. The chain can be symbolized as $eq_{Y(\text{chain}:X1)}(X_2) = eq_Y[eq_{X1}(X_2)]$. The notation "chain:X1" in the subscript is used to indicate that the equating function is for a chain that involves Form X_1. The equating chain expression implies that to convert a Form X_2 score to Form Y, the Form X_2 score first is converted to the Form X_1 scale using $eq_{X1}(X_2)$. Then take this converted score and convert it to the Form Y scale using $eq_Y(X_1)$. In practice, estimates of the equating relationships would be available. In the example, each of the two equatings that need to be estimated has error which needs to be incorporated into an estimate of the standard error of the equating chain.

To develop the example further, assume the following: (a) the equating relationships are to be estimated using the random groups design; (b) Form X_1 and Form Y are spiraled in Administration A, and the resulting data are used to equate these forms; and (c) Form X_2 and Form X_1 are spiraled in Administration B, and the resulting data are used to equate these forms. Given this situation, the following steps could be used to estimate bootstrap standard errors of the equating chain:

1. Take a bootstrap sample of the examinees from Administration A who were administered Form X_1. Take a bootstrap sample of examinees from Administration A who were administered Form Y. Equate Form X_1 to Form Y using these bootstrap samples. Refer to the estimated equating relationship from bootstrap samples r as $\hat{eq}_{Yr}(X_1)$.

2. Take a bootstrap sample of the examinees from Administration B who were administered Form X_2. Take a bootstrap sample of examinees from Administration B who were administered Form X_1. Equate Form X_2 to Form X_1 using these bootstrap samples. Refer to the estimated equating relationship from bootstrap samples r as $\hat{eq}_{X_1 r}(X_2)$.

3. Find the conversion of Form X_2 scores to Form Y scores through the equating chain using the equating relationships developed in steps 2 and 3. Refer to the estimated equating chain from bootstrap samples r as $\hat{eq}_{Yr(\text{chain}:X1)}(X_2)$.

4. Repeat steps 1–3 a large number of times. The standard deviation of the converted scores from step 3 at a particular Form X_2 score is the bootstrap standard error of the equating chain at that score.

This procedure could be generalized to longer chains, although the process can become extremely computationally intensive as the length of the chain increases. This process also could be adapted to the single group and common-item nonequivalent groups designs, and to other equating methods, such as linear methods.

7.2.7 Mean Standard Error of Equating

Sometimes it is useful to have an aggregate value for the standard error of equating, such as when an index of the overall effect of smoothing is desired. One way to get an aggregate value is to find the square root of the average equating error variance over examinees from the population that was administered Form X. In this way, the average standard error of

TABLE 7.1. Average Standard Errors of Equipercentile Equating.

Score	Bootstrap	Parametric Bootstrap	Analytic
Raw Score			
Unsmoothed	.2713	.2674	.2767
Smoothed	.2536	.2519	
Unrounded Scale Score			
Unsmoothed	.2549	.2501	
Smoothed	.2373	.2385	
Rounded Scale Score			
Unsmoothed	.3636	.3632	
Smoothed	.3526	.3494	

equipercentile equating is defined as

$$\sqrt{\sum_i f(x_i) se^2[\hat{e}_Y(x_i)]}.$$

In this equation, the error variance at each score point is weighted by its density, $f(x_i)$, and then summed over score points. Weighting by the density is done so that the error variance for each examinee in the population is weighted equally.

For the equipercentile equating example, the average standard errors estimated by substituting estimates for the parameters are shown in Table 7.1. Average analytic standard errors were calculated only for raw scores without smoothing. The averages for the bootstrap and parametric bootstrap are very similar. For raw scores, the average standard error is somewhat lower for smoothed equating than for unsmoothed equating. The same is true for scale scores and rounded scale scores. The average standard error for rounded scale scores is considerably larger than the average for unrounded scale scores in this example.

7.2.8 Caveat

A major concern in using the bootstrap is that it is computationally very intensive. If, for example, 500 bootstrap replications are to be conducted, then samples need to be drawn and equating needs to be conducted 500 times. Stable standard error estimates might require using 1,000 or more replications. However, with modern computer equipment, this many replications often can be accomplished without great expense, at least for the mean, linear, and equipercentile methods considered in Chapters 2–5.

Bootstrap standard errors of equating also can be used with item response theory methods. However, to use the bootstrap with IRT methods, random samples would need to be drawn *and* item parameters estimated many times. Although possible, as shown by Tsai, et al. (2001), the computation of boostrap standard errors of IRT equating are difficult due to extensive computation requirements.

7.3 The Delta Method

Equations for estimating standard errors can be useful when computational time needs to be minimized or when estimating the desired sample sizes for an equating study. The *delta method* is a commonly used statistical method for deriving standard error expressions. The delta method is used to derive the approximate standard error of a statistic that is a function of statistics for which expressions for the standard errors already exist. As a simple example, the standard error of the sample mean squared could be estimated using the delta method, because an expression for the standard error of a sample mean is known. For the mean, linear, and equipercentile equating methods that were considered in Chapters 2 through 5, the estimated equating relationships are functions of sample moments and cumulative probabilities that have standard errors which can be estimated directly. Thus, the delta method can be used to estimate standard errors of scores equated using mean, linear, and equipercentile equating methods.

The delta method (Kendall and Stuart, 1977) is based on a Taylor series expansion. Define for the population $eq_Y(x_i; \Theta_1, \Theta_2, \ldots, \Theta_t)$ as an equating function of test score x_i and parameters $\Theta_1, \Theta_2, \ldots, \Theta_t$. In linear equating, $\Theta_1, \Theta_2, \ldots, \Theta_t$ are moments. In equipercentile equating, $\Theta_1, \Theta_2, \ldots, \Theta_t$ are cumulative probabilities. By the delta method, an approximate expression for the sampling variance is

$$var[\widehat{eq}_Y(x_i)] \cong \sum_j eq_{Yj}'^2 \, var(\hat{\Theta}_j) + \sum_{j \neq k} \sum eq_{Yj}' eq_{Yk}' \, cov(\hat{\Theta}_j, \hat{\Theta}_k). \quad (7.6)$$

In this equation, $\hat{\Theta}_j$ is a sample estimate of Θ_j and eq_{Yj}' is the partial derivative of eq_{Yj} with respect to Θ_j and evaluated at $x_i, \Theta_1, \Theta_2, \ldots, \Theta_t$. This equation requires that expressions for the sampling variances (*var*) and sampling covariances (*cov*) of the $\hat{\Theta}_j$ be available. The standard error is the square root of *var* in equation (7.6).

The following steps are used to apply the delta method:

1. Specify the error variances and covariances for each $\hat{\Theta}_j$.

2. Find the partial derivative of the equating equation with respect to each Θ_j.

3. Substitute the variances and partial derivatives into equation (7.6).

246   7. Standard Errors of Equating

The resulting standard errors are expressed in terms of parameters. Estimates of the parameters are used in place of the parameters to obtain the estimated standard errors.

7.3.1 Mean Equating Using Single Group and Random Groups Designs

For illustrative purposes, consider a simple example using mean equating in the single group design with no counterbalancing (use of counterbalancing would make this example more complicated). In this design, for the population,

$$m_Y(x_i) = x_i - \mu(X) + \mu(Y),$$

which is estimated by

$$\hat{m}_Y(x_i) = x_i - \hat{\mu}(X) + \hat{\mu}(Y).$$

To apply the delta method, note that from standard statistical theory,

$$var[\hat{\mu}(X)] = \sigma^2(X)/N, \, var[\hat{\mu}(Y)] = \sigma^2(Y)/N, \quad \text{and}$$
$$cov[\hat{\mu}(X), \hat{\mu}(Y)] = \sigma(X,Y)/N.$$

Also, the required partial derivatives are as follows:

$$\partial \hat{m}/\partial \hat{\mu}(X) = -1, \qquad \partial \hat{m}/\partial \hat{\mu}(Y) = 1.$$

Define Θ_1 as $\mu(X)$ and Θ_2 as $\mu(Y)$. Substituting the sampling variances and covariances and partial derivatives into equation (7.6) results in

$$\begin{aligned} var[\hat{m}_Y(x_i)] &\cong (-1)^2 \sigma^2(X)/N + (1)^2 \sigma^2(Y)/N + 2(-1)(1)\sigma(X,Y)/N \\ &= [\sigma^2(X) + \sigma^2(Y) - 2\sigma(X,Y)]/N, \end{aligned} \quad (7.7)$$

for the single group design without counterbalancing.

What if a random groups design were used for mean equating with $N_X = N_Y = N$? In this case, the covariance between X and Y is 0 because independent samples of examinees are administered the two forms. Thus, for random groups,

$$var[\hat{m}_Y(x_i)] \cong [\sigma^2(X) + \sigma^2(Y)]/N. \quad (7.8)$$

As can be seen by comparing equations (7.7) and (7.8), if scores on Form X and Form Y have a positive covariance for the single group design, then the error variance for the single group design will be smaller than the error variance for the random groups design.

7.3.2 Linear Equating Using the Random Groups Design

In implementing the delta method for linear equating with the random groups design, $\mu(X)$, $\sigma(X)$, $\mu(Y)$, and $\sigma(Y)$ need to be estimated. Because Form X and Form Y are given to independent random samples, estimates of the moments for Form X are independent of estimates of the moments for Form Y.

Braun and Holland (1982, p. 33) presented the necessary partial derivatives and standard errors and covariances between the moments to apply the delta method. They showed that

$$var[\hat{l}_Y(x_i)] \cong \sigma^2(Y)\left\{\frac{1}{N_X} + \frac{1}{N_Y} + \left[\frac{sk(X)}{N_X} + \frac{sk(Y)}{N_Y}\right]\left[\frac{x_i - \mu(X)}{\sigma(X)}\right]\right.$$
$$\left. + \left[\frac{ku(X) - 1}{4N_X} + \frac{ku(Y) - 1}{4N_Y}\right]\left[\frac{x_i - \mu(X)}{\sigma(X)}\right]^2\right\}. \quad (7.9)$$

This equation indicates that the standard error of equating depends on the skewness and kurtosis of the population distribution.

Inspection of this equation leads to some observations about the standard errors for the random groups design. First, as the sample sizes increase, the error variance decreases. In this equation, this observation is made by noting that the sample sizes are always in the denominators of the expressions. Second, error variance tends to be smallest near the mean. This observation is based on noting that the term

$$\left[\frac{x_i - \mu(X)}{\sigma(X)}\right]^2$$

becomes larger as x_i moves farther from the mean, and this term is multiplied by a term that is almost always positive (because kurtosis is positive as defined here). Third, error variance tends to be larger in the direction that a distribution is skewed. This observation follows because, if both distributions are positively skewed, then the term

$$\left[\frac{sk(X)}{N_X} + \frac{sk(Y)}{N_Y}\right]\left[\frac{x_i - \mu(X)}{\sigma(X)}\right]$$

is positive for all x_i that are above the mean and negative for all x_i that are below the mean. The reverse is true for negatively skewed distributions.

As can be seen, the error variance expression in equation (7.9) is fairly complicated, even in the simple situation in which linear equating is used with the random groups design. Also, this expression requires computing skewness and kurtosis terms. Equation (7.9) can be simplified. If X and Y are assumed to be normally distributed, then skewness is 0 and kurtosis is 3. In this case, equation (7.9) simplifies to

$$var[\hat{l}_Y(x_i)] \cong \frac{\sigma^2(Y)}{2}\left[\frac{1}{N_X} + \frac{1}{N_Y}\right]\left\{2 + \left[\frac{x_i - \mu(X)}{\sigma(X)}\right]^2\right\}. \quad (7.10)$$

This expression is presented in Petersen et al. (1989) and is similar to the one presented by Angoff (1971).

A further simplification is possible if sample sizes for the two forms are assumed to be equal. if $N_{tot} = N_X + N_Y = 2N_X = 2N_Y$, then equation (7.10) further simplifies to

$$var[\hat{l}_Y(x_i)] \cong \frac{2\sigma^2(Y)}{N_{tot}} \left\{ 2 + \left[\frac{x_i - \mu(X)}{\sigma(X)} \right]^2 \right\}. \tag{7.11}$$

From equation (7.11) it can readily be seen that error variance becomes larger as x_i departs farther from the mean.

As Braun and Holland (1982) pointed out, if equation (7.10) or (7.11) for error variance is used with nonnormal distributions, then the estimates of the standard errors will be biased to some extent. However, the expressions that assume normality are easier to calculate and might be useful as approximations in some situations. For example, when planning sample size requirements for equating studies, data are unavailable on the forms that are to be equated. In this case, the approximations might provide sufficiently accurate estimates of equating error. Procedures for estimating sample size requirements are described later in this chapter.

7.3.3 Equipercentile Equating Using the Random Groups Design

Lord (1982b) used the delta method to develop expressions for the standard error of equipercentile equating under the random groups design. Using the notation developed in Chapter 2, this error variance can be expressed as

$$var[\hat{e}_Y(x_i)] \cong \frac{1}{[G(y_U^*) - G(y_U^* - 1)]^2} \left\{ \frac{[P(x_i)/100][1 - P(x_i)/100](N_X + N_Y)}{N_X N_Y} \right.$$
$$\left. - \frac{[G(y_U^*) - P(x_i)/100][P(x_i)/100 - G(y_U^* - 1)]}{N_Y[G(y_U^*) - G(y_U^* - 1)]} \right\}. \tag{7.12}$$

To estimate the error variances, sample values can be substituted in place of the parameters in equation (7.12). The error variance depends on the proportion of examinees at scores on Form Y, as symbolized by $G(y_U^*) - G(y_U^* - 1)$. If this quantity were 0, then the error variance would be undefined because of a 0 term in the denominator. As an alternative to using sample values, the Form X and Form Y distributions could be smoothed using the log-linear method and the smoothed distribution values used in place of the parameters in equation (7.12). The use of smoothed distribution values in equation (7.12) would be similar to using the parametric bootstrap that was described earlier.

Lord (1982b) also presented an approximation to equation (7.12). Petersen et al. (1989) used Lord's approximation and made a normality assumption to provide the following approximation to the standard error of equipercentile equating under the random groups design:

$$var[\hat{e}_Y(x_i)] \cong \sigma^2(Y)\frac{[P(x_i)/100][1-P(x_i)/100]}{\phi^2}\left(\frac{1}{N_X}+\frac{1}{N_Y}\right), \quad (7.13)$$

where ϕ is the ordinate of the standard normal density at the unit-normal score, z, below which $P(x_i)/100$ of the cases fall. If the sample sizes are equal, such that $N_{tot} = N_X + N_Y = 2N_X = 2N_Y$, then equation (7.13) simplifies to

$$var[\hat{e}_Y(x_i)] \cong \frac{4\sigma^2(Y)}{N_{tot}}\frac{[P(x_i)/100][1-P(x_i)/100]}{\phi^2}. \quad (7.14)$$

7.3.4 Standard Errors for Other Designs

The derivations of standard errors of equating using the delta method can be very complicated, and the expression of the results can be particularly cumbersome. For example, Kolen (1985) derived the standard errors of Tucker equating. The presentation of the required partial derivatives took one full page in the article and the presentation of the sampling errors for the moments took another full page. The presentation of standard errors of frequency estimation equating by Jarjoura and Kolen (1985) took even more space to present. For this reason, a comprehensive presentation of standard errors is not provided in this book.

Table 7.2 contains references to articles that provide standard errors of equating for many of the methods and designs discussed in this book. These articles should be consulted for the standard error equations. See Lord (1975) and Zeng (1993) for descriptions of the use of numerical derivatives in using the delta method. Also, Angoff (1971), Lord (1950), and Petersen et al. (1989) provide standard errors using normality assumptions. Liou and Cheng (1995a) used statistical procedures different from the delta method to derive analytic standard errors for equipercentile equating.

Note that standard errors for IRT methods provided in Table 7.2 are only for dichotomous IRT models. For IRT equating, standard errors were given by Lord (1982c) and Ogasawara (2001b) for chained true score equating in which scores on Form X are "equated" to the common items, the common items are "equated" to Form Y, and the Form X is equated to Form Y by a chaining process. Standard errors for IRT equating that are not chained were derived by Ogasawara (2001b, 2003a). Tsai et al. (2001) examined bootstrap standard errors of common item equating using both IRT true and observed score equating with Stocking and Lord scale linking, chained IRT equating, and concurrent estimation. Ogasawara (2000, 2001c,d) estimated standard errors of A- and B- constants for various IRT scaling methods. Baker (1996) examined the sampling distribution of the slope and intercept for IRT scaling methods in dichotomous IRT models. Also, Baker (1997) conducted a similar study for polytomous models.

TABLE 7.2. References[a] to Analytic Standard Errors.

Design and Method	Reference
Single Group	
Linear	Zeng and Cope (1995)
Equipercentile	Lord (1982b), Liou and Cheng (1995a)
Random Groups	
Linear	Braun and Holland (1982)
Equipercentile	Lord (1982b), Liou and Cheng (1995a)
Smoothed Equipercentile	Holland et al. (1989)
Common-Item	
Nonequivalent Groups	
Linear-Tucker	Kolen (1985)
Linear-Levine Observed Score	Hanson et al. (1993)
Linear-Levine True Score	Hanson et al. (1993)
Frequency Estimation	Jarjoura and Kolen (1985)
	Liou and Cheng (1995a)
Chained Equipercentile	Liou and Cheng (1995a)
Smoothed Equipercentile	Holland et al. (1989)
	Liou et al. (1997)
IRT A- and B- Constants	Ogasawara (2000, 2001c,d)
IRT True Score-Chained	Lord (1982c), Ogasawara (2001a)
IRT True Score	Ogasawara (2001a)
IRT Observed Score	Ogasawara (2003a)

[a]Lord (1950) and Angoff (1971) provided standard errors for linear methods based on a normality assumption. Petersen et al. (1989) also provided standard error expressions.

Computer subroutines for calculating standard errors of some IRT equating methods are available from Ogasawara (2003b). Also, standard errors of equating have not been derived for polytomous IRT models. Additional empirical work is needed to assess the accuracy of the IRT standard errors that have been derived.

For comparative purposes, estimated standard errors of equating for the real data example presented in Chapters 4 and 5 are presented in Table 7.3. In this example, Form X and Form Y were equated using the common-item nonequivalent groups design. These standard errors were calculated using the *CIPE* computer program listed in Appendix B. The synthetic population weight $w_1 = 1$ is used in this example. Estimated standard errors for the Tucker method, the Levine observed score method, and the frequency estimation equipercentile method are presented. Average standard errors also were calculated. As can be seen from this example, the estimated standard errors are smaller near the middle of the distribution than at the extremes. Also, of the three methods, the Tucker method produced the smallest estimated standard errors. The Levine observed score method produced smaller estimated standard errors than the frequency estimation equipercentile method at most score points. Recall that standard errors account for random error only. Just because the Tucker method has smaller standard errors than the Levine method in this case does not necessarily mean that the Tucker method is preferable. More systematic error might be present with the Tucker method than with the Levine method in this case, although it is impossible to know for sure. In practice, a choice of method involves assessing the reasonableness of the statistical assumptions described in Chapter 4 for the equating at hand, as well as other practical issues that are described in Chapter 8.

7.3.5 Approximations

Approximations to standard error expressions that are less complicated than the expressions in the Table 7.2 references are useful in some situations. In this section, two approximations are considered which are useful for comparing designs and equating methods.

One approximation for the single group design was presented by Angoff (1971). This approximation ignores counterbalancing and assumes that X and Y have a bivariate normal distribution. Note also that N refers to the number of examinees who take both forms:

$$var[\hat{l}_Y(x_i)] \cong \frac{\sigma^2(Y)[1-\rho(X,Y)]}{N} \left\{ 2 + [1+\rho(X,Y)] \left[\frac{x_i - \mu(X)}{\sigma(X)}\right]^2 \right\}. \tag{7.15}$$

In this equation, $\rho(X,Y)$ is the correlation between scores on X and Y.

Another approximation was presented by Angoff (1971) for the common-item random groups design mentioned in Chapter 5, in which randomly equivalent groups of examinees are administered two forms that contain common items. This equation assumes that the populations taking X and Y are equivalent, that X and V are bivariate normally distributed in the population, that Y and V are bivariate normally distributed in the population, that the correlation between X and V is equal to the correlation between Y and V, and that the sample sizes for examinees taking the old and new forms are equal. This equation is

$$var[\hat{l}_Y(x_i)] \cong \frac{\sigma^2(Y)[1-\rho^2(X,V)]}{N_{tot}} \left\{ 2 + [1+\rho^2(X,V)] \left[\frac{x_i - \mu(X)}{\sigma(X)}\right]^2 \right\}. \tag{7.16}$$

In this equation, $\rho(X,V)$ is the correlation between common items and total score, and N_{tot} is the total number of examinees taking the forms (i.e., twice the number of examinees taking any one form).

TABLE 7.3. Standard Errors of Equating for the Common-Item Nonequivalent Groups Example.

			Standard Error	
x	$\hat{F}_1(x)$	Tucker	Levine Observed Score	Frequency Estimation Equipercentile
0	.0000	.2643	.3615	
1	.0000	.2518	.3437	
2	.0006	.2395	.3261	
3	.0036	.2273	.3087	
4	.0091	.2154	.2915	.2880
5	.0169	.2038	.2746	.2665
6	.0387	.1925	.2580	.2592
7	.0695	.1816	.2419	.2603
8	.1160	.1712	.2262	.2499
9	.1680	.1613	.2111	.2351
10	.2236	.1521	.1967	.2172
11	.2918	.1437	.1832	.2199
12	.3692	.1363	.1709	.2188
13	.4236	.1300	.1598	.2123
14	.4918	.1250	.1505	.2041
15	.5402	.1214	.1432	.1995
16	.5952	.1193	.1381	.2072
17	.6477	.1190	.1357	.2160
18	.6918	.1203	.1359	.2336
19	.7221	.1232	.1388	.2308
20	.7662	.1276	.1443	.2349
21	.7988	.1334	.1520	.2506
22	.8314	.1404	.1617	.2487
23	.8562	.1484	.1730	.2614
24	.8773	.1572	.1855	.2321
25	.9027	.1668	.1992	.2022
26	.9215	.1770	.2137	.1639
27	.9402	.1877	.2289	.2299
28	.9541	.1988	.2447	.3578
29	.9674	.2103	.2610	.3377
30	.9776	.2221	.2776	.3207
31	.9825	.2341	.2946	.2777
32	.9909	.2464	.3118	.3864
33	.9952	.2589	.3292	.4707
34	.9988	.2715	.3468	
35	.9994	.2942	.3646	
36	1.0000	.2971	.3826	
Average		.1480	.1819	.2302

The error variance in equation (7.16) can be rewritten as follows:

$$var[\hat{l}_Y(x_i)] \cong \frac{\sigma^2(Y)}{N_{tot}} \left\{ 2[1 - \rho^2(X,V)] + [1 - \rho^4(X,V)] \left[\frac{x_i - \mu(X)}{\sigma(X)}\right]^2 \right\}.$$
(7.17)

From equation (7.17), it can readily be seen that, as positive values of $\rho(X,V)$ increase, the error variance decreases. That is, the greater the correlation between the total score and the common-item score, the smaller the error variance. Equations (7.16) and (7.17) provide an approximation to the Kolen (1985) result for the Tucker method that might be useful when estimating sample size requirements for linear equating in the common-item nonequivalent groups design. However, the standard errors presented by Hanson et al. (1993) should be used whenever possible, and especially when documenting the amount of error in an equating.

7.3.6 Standard Errors for Scale Scores

Standard errors of equating for scale scores can be approximated based on the delta method standard errors for raw scores. A variation of the delta method can be used to estimate the scale score standard errors. To develop this variation, consider a situation in which a parameter Θ is being estimated, where the estimate is symbolized by $\hat{\Theta}$. Also assume that the error variance in estimating the parameter is known, which is symbolized by $var(\hat{\Theta})$. Finally, assume that the estimate is to be transformed using the function f. In this situation, Kendall and Stuart (1977) showed that, approximately,

$$var[f(\hat{\Theta})] \cong f'^2(\Theta) var(\hat{\Theta}),$$

where f' is the first derivative of f. That is, the error variance of the function of a random variable can be approximated by the product of the square of the derivative of the function at the parameter value and the error variance of the random variable.

This formulation can be applied to equating by substituting $eq_Y(x_i)$ for the parameter Θ, $\widehat{eq}_Y(x_i)$ for $\hat{\Theta}$, and the Form Y raw-to-scale score transformation s for the function f. To apply this equation directly, the first derivative of the Form Y raw-to-scale score transformation is needed at $eq_Y(x_i)$.

If the Form Y raw-to-scale score transformation is linear, then the derivative of the raw-to-scale score transformation is equal to the slope of the Form Y raw-to-scale score linear transformation, which is a constant at all $eq_Y(x_i)$. In this case, the scale score error variance can be approximated by taking the product of the raw score error variance and the squared slope of the Form Y raw-to-scale score transformation. If the Form Y raw-to-scale score transformation is nonlinear but continuous, then the scale score error variance can be approximated by taking the product of the squared first derivative of the estimated Form Y raw-to-scale score transformation at $eq_Y(x_i)$ and the estimated raw score error variance.

The Form Y raw-to-scale score transformation is often nonlinear and not continuous. In this case, the derivative of the Form Y raw-to-scale score conversion near $eq_Y(x_i)$ needs to be approximated. To approximate this derivative, the Form Y raw-to-scale score conversion can be viewed as a set of points connected by straight lines. The slope of the line near $\widehat{eq}_Y(x_i)$ can be used as an approximation of the derivative. For example, in the numerical example presented in Chapter 2 (see Table 2.7), under equipercentile equating a Form X raw score of 24 was estimated to be equivalent to a Form Y raw score of 23.9157. The slope of the Form Y raw-to-scale score conversion at a Form Y raw score of 23.9157 can be found by taking the difference between the Form Y scale score equivalents at Form Y raw scores of 24 and 23. From Table 2.8, these equivalents are 22.3220 and 21.7000. The difference between these equivalents is .6220, which can be taken as the slope of the raw-to-scale score conversion at a Form Y raw score of 23.9157. From Table 3.2, the estimated raw score standard error of unsmoothed equipercentile equating at a Form X score of 24 is .3555. Thus, the scale score error variance for unsmoothed equipercentile equating is approximately $.6220^2(.3555^2) = .0489$, and the scale score standard error is approximately $.6220(.3555) = .2211$. This process can be used to approximate scale score standard errors of equating at other score points as well. Because these standard errors are designed only for unrounded scale scores, the bootstrap or a similar procedure should be used to estimate standard errors for rounded scale scores.

7.3.7 Standard Errors of Equating Chains

Delta method standard errors can be used to estimate standard errors of equating chains. When the equatings are independent, as is typically the case with the random groups design, a delta method variant suggested by Braun and Holland (1982, p. 36) can be used. Suppose that in the equating chain, Form X_2 is equated to Form Y by equating Form X_2 to Form X_1 and Form X_1 to Form Y. The error variance of converted scores for an equating chain can be approximated as follows:

$$var[\widehat{eq}_{Y(\text{chain}:X1)}(x_2)] \cong var[\widehat{eq}_Y(x_1^*)] + eq'^2_{X1}(x_2) \cdot var[\widehat{eq}_{X1}(x_2)],$$

where $x_1^* = eq_{X1}(x_2)$ and $eq'^2_{X1}(x_2)$ is the squared first derivative of the function for equating Form X_2 to Form X_1. The standard error is the square root of this expression. If the equating function is not continuous, then an approximation to the derivative (e.g., the slope of the conversion at x_2) could be used in its place. Braun and Holland (1982) pointed out that when forms which are constructed to be parallel are equated, this derivative is generally close to 1. In this case, the derivative can be set equal to 1 and

TABLE 7.4. Selected Equating Error Variance Equations Assuming Normality and Equal Sample Sizes Per Test Form.

Random Groups Linear
$$var[\hat{l}_Y(x_i)] \cong \frac{2\sigma^2(Y)}{N_{tot}} \left\{ 2 + \left[\frac{x_i - \mu(X)}{\sigma(X)} \right]^2 \right\} \quad (7.11)$$

Random Groups Equipercentile
$$var[\hat{e}_Y(x_i)] \cong \frac{4\sigma^2(Y)}{N_{tot}} \frac{[P(x_i)/100][1 - P(x_i)/100]}{\phi^2} \quad (7.14)$$

Single Group Linear
$$var[\hat{l}_Y(x_i)] \cong \frac{\sigma^2(Y)[1 - \rho(X,Y)]}{N} \left\{ 2 + [1 + \rho(X,Y)] \left[\frac{x_i - \mu(X)}{\sigma(X)} \right]^2 \right\} \quad (7.15)$$

the error variance of the chain can be approximated by summing the error variances of the two component equatings.

The procedure just described is appropriate only when the equatings are independent, such as in a chain of equatings conducted using the random groups design. When using the common-item nonequivalent groups design, Zeng et al. (1994) suggested that equatings are dependent. As an example of this dependency in a chain, examinees who were administered Form X_1 would be involved in equating Form X_2 to Form X_1, and Form X_1 to Form Y. In this case, the dependency needs to be incorporated into the estimation. See Lord (1975) and Zeng et al. (1994) for details on how the effects of the dependency can be incorporated into the process of estimating standard errors.

7.3.8 Using Delta Method Standard Errors

The standard error expressions are useful for comparing the precision of equating designs and equating methods, and for estimating sample sizes. Because comparisons can become exceedingly complicated, in this section only an idealized situation is examined in which normal distributions are assumed. Also, only the random groups and single group designs are studied, although the approach described can be generalized to other designs. Equipercentile equating is examined only for the random groups design. Lord (1950) and Crouse (1991) provided comparisons in addition to the ones presented here. For ease of reference, Table 7.4 lists the equations that are used in this section.

TABLE 7.5. Comparison of Relative Magnitudes of Random Groups Linear and Equipercentile Error Variances.

z	P^{**}	$1-P^{**}$	ϕ	$\dfrac{2P^{**}(1-P^{**})}{\phi^2}$	$2+z^2$	$\dfrac{2P^{**}(1-P^{**})}{\phi^2(2+z^2)}$
.0	.5000	.5000	.3989	3.14	2.00	1.57
.5	.6915	.3085	.3521	3.44	2.25	1.52
1.0	.8413	.1587	.2420	4.56	3.00	1.52
1.5	.9332	.0668	.1295	7.43	4.25	1.75
2.0	.9772	.0228	.0540	15.28	6.00	2.54
2.5	.9938	.0062	.0175	40.23	8.25	4.88
3.0	.9987	.0013	.0044	134.12	11.00	12.19

Random Groups Linear Versus Random Groups Equipercentile

One question that might be asked is how precise is equipercentile equating relative to linear equating when using the random groups design? This question can be addressed readily if the sample size is equal and a normality assumption is made. Under these assumptions, the linear error variances are given in equation (7.11), the equipercentile error variances are given in equation (7.14), and

$$z = \frac{x_i - \mu(X)}{\sigma(X)}$$

is a unit-normal score, To compare the error variances note that both equations have $2\sigma^2(Y)/N_{tot}$ as multipliers, so these terms can be ignored when comparing the *relative* magnitudes of the error variances by taking the ratio of one error variance to the other.

A comparison of the relative magnitudes is made in Table 7.5 at selected z-scores. The z-scores are used so that the table can be used with any test by converting the number-correct scores to z-scores. In this table, $P^{**} = P/100$. The rightmost column of the table presents the ratio of the error variances at selected z-scores. For scores near the mean, the values around 1.5 indicate that the error variance for equipercentile equating is approximately 1.5 times that of linear equating. The ratio becomes much larger farther away from the mean; for example, for a z-score of 2.5, the ratio is nearly 5.

The ratios in the table can be used to make statements about the relative sample sizes required in linear and equipercentile equating to achieve the same equating precision. For example, to achieve the equating precision near the mean that is achieved with a sample size of 1,000 with linear equating, a sample size of 1,570 $(1,000 \times 1.57)$ would be needed with equipercentile equating. As another example, to achieve the equating precision at a z-score of 2.5 that is achieved with a sample size of 1,000 with

TABLE 7.6. Ratio of Linear Method Random Groups Equating Error Variance to Single Group Equating Error Variance.

	$\rho = .0$	$\rho = .2$	$\rho = .5$	$\rho = .7$	$\rho = .9$
$z = .0$	2.00	2.50	4.00	6.67	20.00
$z = .5$	2.00	2.45	3.79	6.19	18.18
$z = 1.0$	2.00	2.34	3.43	5.41	15.38
$z = 1.5$	2.00	2.26	3.16	4.86	13.55
$z = 2.0$	2.00	2.21	3.00	4.55	12.50
$z = 2.5$	2.00	2.17	2.90	4.36	11.89
$z = 3.0$	2.00	2.15	2.84	4.24	11.52

linear equating, a sample size of 4,880 (1,000 × 4.88) would be needed with equipercentile equating.

Do smaller standard errors for the linear method mean that the linear method is better than the equipercentile method? Not necessarily. Recall that standard errors account only for random error in equating. If the relationship is nonlinear, then equipercentile equating might provide a more accurate estimate of the population equivalent, even when it has a much larger standard error than the linear method, because of systematic error that could be introduced by using the linear method.

Random Groups Linear Versus Single Group Linear

Table 7.6 presents the ratio of random groups to single group equating error variance for the linear method. Normal distributions are assumed. The values in this table were calculated by taking the ratio of equation (7.11) to equation (7.15) for selected values of z and $\rho(X,Y)$, where ρ is used to symbolize $\rho(X,Y)$ in the single group design. In taking the ratio, the total number of examinees for the single group design (N) cancels out the total number of examinees for the random groups design (N_{tot}).

These ratios indicate the relative precision of linear equating in the two designs. These ratios also indicate the relative number of examinees needed to achieve a given level of precision. For example, in the unlikely event that the correlation between X and Y is 0, the tabled ratio of 2.00 indicates that twice as many examinees are needed in random groups design to get the same precision that is achieved with the single group design. Thus, for example, if $\rho(X,Y) = 0$, then 2,000 examinees would be required in the random groups design to achieve the same level of precision that could be attained with 1,000 examinees using the single group design.

In the single group design, however, each examinee takes Form X and Form Y. In the random groups design, different examinees take Form X and Form Y. Thus, in the preceding example, the 1,000 examinees in the single group design would take 2,000 test forms (1,000 Form X and 1,000

Form Y). That is, if $\rho(X,Y) = 0$, then the same number of forms would need to be administered under the two designs to achieve a given level of precision. This example illustrates that, if interest is in estimating the relative number of test forms that need to be taken, rather than the relative number of examinees that need to be tested, the values in Table 7.6 should be divided by 2.

The quantity $\rho(X,Y)$ in the single group design is an alternate forms reliability coefficient. Of the tabled values, $\rho(X,Y) = .7$ or .9 are the most realistic, because alternate forms to be equated can be expected to be positively correlated when administered to the same examinees. For $\rho = .70$ and $z = 0$, depending on the level of z, between 4.24 and 6.67 times as many examinees would be needed for the random groups design to achieve the same level of precision as for the single group design. For example, for $\rho = .70$, a total of 6,670 examinees would be needed with the random groups design to achieve the same level of precision as would be achieved with 1,000 examinees in the single group design. For $\rho = .90$ and $z = 0$, a total of 20,000 examinees would be needed with the random groups design to achieve the same level of precision as would be achieved with 1,000 examinees in the single group design. Therefore, for highly reliable tests, the sample size requirements for the single group design can be considerably less than those for the random groups design. Of course, it is possible that either of these sample sizes would lead to considerably more precision than would be necessary in an equating. (Estimating sample size requirements is considered in the next section.)

Counterbalancing issues and context effects, such as practice and fatigue, can introduce systematic error with the single group design. These issues are effectively ignored in Table 7.6. Using counterbalancing can lead to greater sample size requirements. Also, recall from Chapter 2 that when differential order effects are present in the single group with counterbalancing design, the data from the test taken second might need to be disregarded. In this case, the data that can actually be used to equate Form X and Form Y are from the form taken first, and the random groups standard errors would need to be used.

Estimating Sample Size for Random Groups Linear Equating

In addition to comparing equating error associated with different designs and methods, standard errors of equating also can be useful in specifying the sample size required to achieve a given level of equating precision for a particular equating design and method. In order to use standard errors in the process of estimating sample size requirements, the desired level of precision needs to be stated. Ideally, equating error should be small and not make a significant contribution to error in reported test scores. In practical situations, the significance of this contribution needs to be operationalized.

Consider the following example. Suppose that linear equating with the random groups design is to be used. Also suppose that, for a particular equating, a standard error of equating that is less than .1 standard deviation unit is judged not to make a significant contribution to error in reported scores. In this situation, what sample size would be required?

Equation (7.11) presents the error variance for this situation. Let u refer to the maximum proportion of standard deviation units that is judged to be appropriate for the standard error of equating. The value of N_{tot} is found that gives a specified value for $u\sigma(Y)$ for the standard error of equating. In the example just presented, $u = .1$ standard deviation unit. Based on this specification, from equation (7.11),

$$u^2\sigma^2(Y) \cong \frac{2\sigma^2(Y)}{N_{tot}}\left\{2 + \left[\frac{x_i - \mu(X)}{\sigma(X)}\right]^2\right\}.$$

Solving for N_{tot},

$$N_{tot} \cong \frac{2}{u^2}\left\{2 + \left[\frac{x_i - \mu(X)}{\sigma(X)}\right]^2\right\}, \qquad (7.18)$$

which represents the total sample size required for the standard error of equating to be equal to u standard deviation units on the old form. For example, if $u = .1$, then the sample size needed for a Form X unit-normal (z) score of 0 is

$$N_{tot} \cong \frac{2}{.1^2}(2+0) = 400.$$

Thus, a total of 400 examinees (200 per form) would be required at a unit normal score of 0. How about at a z-score of 2? Using formula (7.18), $N_{tot} = 1,200$ (600 per form).

What can be concluded? Over the range of Form X z-scores between -2 and $+2$, the standard error of equating will be less than .1 Form Y standard deviation unit if the total sample size is at least 1,200. This specification requires a normality assumption, so it should be viewed as an approximation. In addition, the range of scores is stated in z-score units, which could be transformed to reported score units when describing how the necessary sample size was estimated.

Estimating Sample Size for Random Groups Equipercentile Equating

A similar question could be asked about equipercentile equating with the random groups design. Using the same logic that was used with linear equating, an expression for N_{tot} can be derived from equation (7.14) as

$$N_{tot} \cong \frac{4[P(x_i)/100][1 - P(x_i)/100]}{u^2\phi^2}. \qquad (7.19)$$

Recall that this equation assumes that the scores on Form X are normally distributed. Consequently, $z = 0$ when $P(x_i) = 50$, and $z = 2$ when $P(x_i) = 97.72$ (see Table 7.5).

For example, if u is set at .1 for a Form X z-score of 0, this equation results in $N_{tot} = 628.45$. For a Form X z-score of 2, this equation results in $N_{tot} = 3,056.26$. So, over the range of Form X z-scores between -2 and $+2$, the standard error of equating will be less than .1 Form Y standard deviation unit if the total sample size is at least 3,057 (by rounding up) using equipercentile equating. No smoothing is assumed in deriving this result.

Refer to Table 7.5. The ratio of sample sizes for equipercentile and linear equating equals (within rounding error) the ratios given in Table 7.6. For example, for $z = 2$, the ratio of sample sizes is $3,056.26/1,200 = 2.55$, which is the value shown in Table 7.6, apart from rounding error.

Estimating Sample Size for Single Group Linear Equating

Sample size requirements also can be estimated for linear equating using the single group design. Using equation (7.15) and a process similar to that used to derive equation (7.18),

$$N \cong \frac{[1 - \rho(X,Y)]}{u^2} \left\{ 2 + [1 + \rho(X,Y)] \left[\frac{x_i - \mu(X)}{\sigma(X)} \right]^2 \right\}. \quad (7.20)$$

To use equation (7.20) it is necessary to specify $\rho(X,Y)$.

To continue the example considered earlier, what sample size is required with linear equating for the single group design so that the standard error of equating is less than .1 Form Y standard deviation unit over the range of z-scores from -2 to $+2$? Assume that $\rho(X,Y) = .7$. In this case, application of equation (7.20) indicates that a sample size of $N = 60$ is required at $z = 0$ and a sample size of $N = 264$ is required at $z = 2$. At $z = 0$, the ratio of sample sizes for the linear random groups design to the linear single group design is 6.67 (400/60), which is the ratio shown for $z = 0$ and $\rho = .7$ in Table 7.6. Similarly, the ratio for $z = 2.0$ is 4.55 (1,200/264), which also is shown in Table 7.6.

Specifying Precision in sem Units

Sometimes, equating error is specified in terms of the standard error of measurement (*sem*) rather than the standard deviation, especially when the focus of test use is on individual examinees' scores. For example, an investigator might ask what sample size would be needed for the random groups design if the standard error of equating is to be less than .1 of the standard error of measurement? Using $\rho(X,Y)$ as alternate forms reliability, the standard error of measurement is

$$sem = \sigma(Y)\sqrt{1 - \rho(X,Y)}.$$

To use equations (7.18)–(7.20) to estimate sample size, it is necessary to relate error specified in terms of *sem* units to standard deviation units. Let u_{sem} represent sem units. Then, multiplying both sides of the preceding equation by u_{sem} results in

$$u_{sem}\,sem = u_{sem}\sigma(Y)\sqrt{1-\rho(X,Y)}.$$

Because u was defined earlier as a multiplier for $\sigma(Y)$,

$$u = u_{sem}\sqrt{1-\rho(X,Y)}.$$

In the example, assume that $\rho(X,Y) = .7$, as was done earlier. If the standard error of equating is to be less than .1 of the standard error of measurement, then

$$u = u_{sem}\sqrt{1-\rho(X,Y)} \cong .1\sqrt{1-.7} = .055.$$

In the example, finding the sample size for which the standard error of equating is .1 standard error of measurement unit is the same as finding the sample size for which the standard error of equating is .055 standard deviation unit. What would be the required sample size for the random groups design at $z = 2$? Applying equation (7.18),

$$N_{tot} \cong \frac{2}{.055^2}(2+2^2) \cong 3966.94.$$

For the single group design, applying equation (7.20) gives

$$N \cong \frac{1-.7}{.055^2}[2 + (1+.7)2^2] \cong 872.73.$$

The ratio of these two sample sizes is approximately the value of 4.55 shown in Table 7.6 for $z = 2.0$ and $\rho = .7$.

7.4 Using Standard Errors in Practice

Standard errors of equating are used as indices of random error in equating. As was discussed earlier in this chapter, the delta method standard errors of equating can be used to compare the amount of equating error variability in different designs and methods, and to estimate sample size requirements. In this process, the degree of precision needs to be stated, which is necessarily situation-specific. In some situations it is necessary to have considerable precision. For example, with the ACT Assessment (AAP, 1989), important decisions are made over most of the score range; this test is used to track educational trends, and small changes in the national mean from one year to the next make front-page news; and large samples can be made available

262   7. Standard Errors of Equating

for equating, so that high equating precision can be obtained. For tests where the decisions are viewed to be less critical, more equating error (as well as measurement error) might be judged to be acceptable. Or, it might be impossible to obtain large samples for equating, and more equating error might need to be present. For many certification and licensure tests, interest is primarily in deciding whether examinees exceed a passing score. Often with these tests, a passing score is set on one test form, and the primary purpose of equating is to ensure that an equivalent passing score is used on other test forms. In this case, scores near the passing score are of primary interest, and the focus would be on equating error near the passing score when comparing designs and estimating sample size requirements. For example, in finding the sample size, the standard error of equating at the passing score that would be desirable to achieve might be no more than .1 standard deviation unit.

In using equating error variability to compare different designs and methods, and to estimate sample size requirements, the delta method standard errors with the most restrictive assumptions (e.g., normality) were used in this chapter to provide reasonable approximations. The simplicity of these approximations facilitates these comparisons and sample size estimation. Also, more specific information about distributions, such as precise estimates of skewness and kurtosis, often is not available, providing further justification for using the approximations. However, these approximations should be used cautiously because they can be inaccurate, especially when the distributions are not normal or when the other simplifications used in these derivations are unrealistic.

Equating is a statistical procedure, and, as such, the amount of random error that is present in estimating equating relationships should be documented. Like measurement error, which is often indexed by the standard error of measurement, random equating error is potentially a significant source of error in scores that are reported to examinees. Therefore, it is important to have reasonable estimates of random equating error, and to be able to tell whether random equating error adds substantially to the amount of error in test scores. Bootstrap standard errors are useful for documentation purposes, and, as was indicated earlier in this chapter, bootstrap standard errors can be calculated for rounded scale scores. If available, delta method standard errors provide an analytic expression for the standard errors, although delta method standard errors have not been developed for rounded scale scores. When using delta method standard errors for documentation purposes, standard errors derived under the least restrictive assumptions (e.g., without a normality assumption) should, in general, be used unless the sample size is very small. With small samples, the standard errors derived under the least restrictive assumptions might be inaccurately estimated. For example, estimates of skewness and kurtosis are needed to apply the standard errors of linear equating derived under the least restrictive assumptions. Large samples are needed to estimate skewness and kurtosis precisely. In one simulation, Kolen (1985) found that the delta method standard errors with the normality assumption were preferable for estimating the standard errors of Tucker equating with a sample size of 100 examinees per form. In simulations with larger sample sizes conducted by Kolen (1985), the delta method standard errors without the normality assumption were more accurate. Parshall, et al. (1995) also used bootstrap standard errors of linear equating with small sample sizes. Standard errors also can be useful in the process of choosing among methods of equating. For example, in Chapter 3, standard errors were used to help choose between different degrees of smoothing in equipercentile equating.

The lack of availability of computer programs for estimating standard errors of IRT equating limits the usefulness of IRT equating. Although bootstrap procedures might be used, such as those by Tsai et al. (2001), these procedures are computationally intensive. In addition, the development of approximations to standard errors of IRT equating could be very useful for planning sample sizes for IRT equating.

7.5 Exercises

7.1. Assume that the four bootstrap samples of size $N_X = 4$ shown near the beginning of the chapter (see the section titled "Standard Errors Using the Bootstrap") and listed below were for Form X of a test. Also assume that, for Form Y, $N_Y = 3$ with values 1, 4, and 5 and that the following four bootstrap samples were drawn (use $N - 1$ to calculate sample variances):

Form X	Form Y
Sample 1: 6 3 6 1	Sample 1: 1 4 4
Sample 2: 1 6 1 3	Sample 2: 4 5 5
Sample 3: 5 6 1 5	Sample 3: 1 5 5
Sample 4: 5 1 6 1	Sample 4: 1 1 4

Also assume that Form X and Form Y were administered using the random groups design.

   a. What is the bootstrap estimated standard error of linear equating at Form X raw scores of 3 and 5?

   b. Assume that the following raw-to-scale score conversion equation for Form Y has already been developed: $s(y) = .4y + 10$. What is the bootstrap estimated standard error of linear equating of unrounded scale scores for Form X raw scores of 3 and 5?

   c. For the situation described in (b), what is the bootstrap estimated standard error of linear equating of scale scores, rounded to integers, for Form X raw scores of 3 and 5?

d. What is the delta method (assume normality) estimated standard error of linear equating of raw scores for Form X raw scores of 3 and 5?

7.2. Verify that the standard error of equipercentile equating at a Form X raw score of 25 is approximately .30 for the data shown in Table 2.5. Use equation (7.12). How does this value compare to the value calculated using (7.13)? What possible factors would cause these values to differ?

7.3. A standard setting study was conducted on Form Y of a test, and the passing score was set at a score on Form Y that was approximately 1 standard deviation below the mean in a group of examinees who took the test earlier. Assume that the group of examinees to be used in an equating study is similar to the group of examinees that was administered Form Y earlier. What sample size would be needed in random groups linear equating to achieve a standard error of equating less than .2 standard deviation unit near the passing score? Use equation (7.18). What sample size would be needed to achieve comparable precision near the passing score using random groups equipercentile equating? Use equation (7.19). Suppose that the population equating relationship was truly linear. Which method would be preferable? Why?

7.4. Suppose that Form X scores and Form Y scores each had a population mean equal to 0 and standard deviation equal to 1. Also assume that, for the population, the Form Y equipercentile equivalent of a score of 1 on Form X was 1.2 and that the linear equivalent was 1.3. For estimating the equipercentile equivalent of a Form X score of 1, would it be better to use linear or equipercentile equating in this situation if the sample size was 100 examinees per form? How about if the sample size was 1,000 examinees per form? What are the implications of your answers? [Use equations (7.11) and (7.14) as a means to simplify this situation. Hint: It is necessary to incorporate the notion of equating bias and provide an expression for mean squared equating error as discussed in Chapter 3 to answer this question. In this exercise, assume that equipercentile has no bias and that linear has bias of $.1 = 1.3 - 1.2$.]

7.5. For Form X and Form Y of a 50-item test, assume that $\mu(X) = 25$, $\mu(Y) = 27$, $\sigma(X) = 5$, and $\sigma(Y) = 4$.

   a. Assume that a random groups design was used with $N_X = N_Y = 500$. Find the standard error of linear equating for $x = 23$ and 35. (Use normal distribution assumptions.)

b. Assume that a single group design was used with $N = 500$ and that $\rho(X,Y) = .75$. Find the standard error of linear equating for $x = 23$ and 35. (Use normal distribution assumptions.)

c. Assume that a random groups design was used with $N_X = N_Y = 500$. Find the standard error of equipercentile equating for $x = 23$ and 35. (Use normal distribution assumptions.)

d. Assuming that the reliability of the test is .75, what sample size would be needed for the standard error of random groups linear equating to be less than .3 standard errors of measurement on the Form Y scale for $x = 23$ and 35? (Use normal distribution assumptions.)

7.6. How would you estimate the standard error of the identity equating? What are the implications of your answer for using this method in practice?

8
Practical Issues in Equating

Many of the practical issues that are involved in conducting equating are described in this chapter. We describe major issues and provide references that consider these issues in more depth. The early portions of this chapter focus on equating dichotomously scored paper-and-pencil tests. In later portions, the focus broadens to include practical issues in other contexts, including computerized testing and performance assessments. Various articles have been written that review practical issues in equating (Brennan and Kolen, 1987b; Cook and Petersen, 1987; Harris, 1993; Harris and Crouse, 1993; Skaggs, 1990a; and Skaggs and Lissitz, 1986b) in greater depth than those provided in this chapter.

The practical issues described in this chapter follow from the discussion of equating in Chapter 1. Chapter 1 indicated that equating should be considered when alternate forms of tests exist, scores on the alternate forms are to be compared, and the alternate forms are built to the same detailed specifications so that they are similar to one another in content and statistical characteristics. It was stressed that, under appropriate conditions, equating can be used to improve the accuracy of test scores used in making important individual level, institutional level, or public policy level decisions. When decisions might be made along the entire range of scores, equating at all score points is important. if only pass-fail decisions are to be made, then the accuracy of equating might be of concern mainly near the passing score.

Also, as was indicated in Chapter 1, a major consideration in designing and conducting equating is to minimize equating error. Although the purpose of equating is to decrease error, under some circumstances implementing an equating method can increase equating error, in which case it might be best not to equate, As was described in Chapter 7, random error is error due to sampling of examinees from a population of examinees. The use of large sample sizes, smoothing in equipercentile equating, and a judicious choice of an equating design can help control random error.

Systematic error results from violations of the conditions of equating or the statistical assumptions required; it is more difficult to control than random error. Some examples of situations where systematic error might be a problem include (1) the use of a regression method (refer to Chapter 2 for a discussion of the lack of symmetry of regression methods) to conduct equating, (2) the use of linear equating to estimate an equipercentile relationship when the linear relationship does not hold, (3) the use of the Levine observed score method when true scores on the common items are not perfectly correlated with true scores on the total test, and (4) *item context effects*, in which, for example, a common item appears as the first item in Form X and as the last item in Form Y, with consequent changes in the performance of that common item. Systematic error is difficult to quantify. In practice, whether or not equating reduces systematic error can be difficult to determine, and often no clear-cut criterion for evaluating the extent of the error exists. Systematic error can best be controlled through careful test development, adequate implementation of an equating design, and use of appropriate statistical techniques.

When conducting equating, judgments must be made that go beyond the statistical and design issues described in Chapters 2 through 7. Equating requires judgments about issues in test development, designing the data collection, implementing the design, analyzing the resulting data, and evaluating the results. As is discussed later in this chapter, sometimes practical constraints do not allow sound equating to be conducted, in which case it might be better not to equate. When equating is judged to be useful, many decisions need to be made. Prior to collecting data or applying statistical equating methods, choices need to be made, such as which data collection design to use, which form(s) to use as old form(s), and how many common items to use. Other choices about how to analyze the data need to be made as well, such as which operational definition(s) of equating to use and which statistical estimation method(s) to apply. Other decisions are made after the data are collected, such as which examinees to include in the equating process, which common items to retain, and which equating result to use. Clear-cut criteria and rules for making these decisions do not exist: The specific context of equating in the particular testing program dictates how these issues are handled. Equating involves compromises among various competing practical constraints. In this sense, an ideal equating likely has never occurred in practice.

Even when an equating study is well designed and statistical assumptions are met, an otherwise acceptable equating can be destroyed because of inadequate quality control procedures. Serious problems can result, for example, if an item is incorrectly keyed, if a common item differs from one form to another, or if a mistake is made in communicating the correct conversion table. In our experience, quality control procedures deserve considerable emphasis, because problems with quality control have serious consequences. If quality control procedures fail, then the data gathered in an equating study can lead to erroneous conclusions about the comparability of test forms. In major testing programs, quality control procedures often require considerably more effort than that expended in actually conducting the statistical equating.

The practical issues in equating described in this chapter are organized by topics in roughly the order that they might need to be considered: test development, equating designs, statistical procedures, evaluating results, and quality control and standardization procedures. Then, issues in speical circumstances, including comparability for computer-based tests and performance assessments, are discussed.

8.1 Equating and the Test Development Process

According to Mislevy (1992),

> Test construction and equating are inseparable. When they are applied in concert, equated scores from parallel test forms provide virtually exchangeable evidence about students' behavior on the same general domain of tasks, under the same specified standardized conditions. When equating works, it is because of the way the *tests are constructed* ... (p. 37)

Thus, systematic test development procedures are vital to producing adequate equating. (See Millman and Greene, 1989, for a general discussion of test development procedures.)

8.1.1 Test Specifications

Equated scores on alternate forms can be used interchangeably only if the alternate forms are built to carefully designed *content and statistical specifications*. Developing tests in this way can result in forms that are very similar in what they measure, with the only major difference being the particular items that appear on the alternate forms. No matter how careful the test construction process is, however, the forms that result will differ somewhat in difficulty. Equating is intended to adjust for these statistical differences.

When test construction procedures are functioning well in large-scale testing programs, considerable effort is made to ensure that alternate forms are similar. The content and statistical test specifications are detailed and forms are constructed to meet these specifications. Equating can be successful only if the test specifications are well defined and stable.

The content specifications are developed by considering the purposes of testing, and they provide an operational definition of the content that the test is intended to measure. The content specifications typically include the content areas to be measured and the item types to be used, with the numbers of items per content area and item types specified precisely. The content specifications are crucial for developing alternate forms that can be equated. A test form must be sufficiently long to be able to achieve the purposes of the test, and it must provide a large enough sample of the domain for the alternate forms to be similar. For example, a 10-item test that covers a content domain consisting of 20 areas could not be expected to sample the domain adequately. If each form is an inadequate sample, then the forms can differ considerably in what they measure, and scores on alternate forms might not be interchangeable, even after equating is attempted. One useful rule of thumb is that test length should be at least 30–40 items when equating educational tests with tables of specifications that reflect multiple areas of content, although the length of a test required depends on the purposes of testing, the heterogeneity of the content measured, and the nature of the test specifications.

Although not as crucial as content specifications, statistical specifications are also important. Statistical specifications often are based on classical statistics such as the target mean, standard deviation, and distribution of item difficulties and discriminations for a particular group of examinees. Correlations of items with other tests in a test battery also might be checked to maintain the same degree of association among tests in the new forms of the battery. Statistical specifications based on IRT often are used, such as target test characteristic curves and target information curves.

For previously used items, the statistics are based on previous administrations. Statistics for new items often are estimated using *pretesting* procedures. Another benefit of pretesting is that previously undetected item flaws might be discovered before an item is used operationally. Often item statistics are adjusted to estimate the item characteristics for a particular group of examinees under operational testing conditions. When a large pool of items with item statistics exist, procedures described by van der Linden and Adema (1998) and van der Linden and Luecht (1998) can be used to assemble test forms that meet prespecified statistical characteristics.

In situations where new items cannot be pretested, tests might need to be constructed without the benefit of item statistics, which can make it difficult to control the statistical characteristics of the test. In these situations methodology described by Mislevy et al. (1993) might be useful for estimating item statistics from characteristics of items including item content, item format, and expert judgment about the items.

8.1.2 Characteristics of Common-Item Sets

When using the common-item nonequivalent groups design, common-item sets should be built to the same specifications, proportionally, as the total test if they are to reflect group differences adequately. In constructing common-item sections, the sections should be long enough to represent test content adequately.

The number of common items to use should be considered on both content and statistical grounds. Statistically, larger numbers of common items lead to less random equating error (Budescu, 1985; Wingersky et al., 1987). Petersen et al. (1983) indicated that too few items could lead to equating problems. Very small numbers of items were suggested as adequate in some of the studies reviewed by Harris (1993), although in most of the studies that supported the use of very few common items the recommendations were based on simulating data from a unidimensional model. Because educational tests tend to be heterogeneous, larger numbers of common items are likely required for equating to be adequate in practice. Experience suggests the rule of thumb that a common item set should be at least 20% of the length of a total test containing 40 or more items, unless the test is very long, in which case 30 common items might suffice. (Angoff, 1971, suggested a very similar rule of thumb.) In considering the numbers of common items to use in a particular testing program, the heterogeneity of the test content also should be considered.

As was suggested in Chapter 6, common-item statistics can be compared across examinee groups used in the equating to help decide whether the items are functioning differently in the two groups. IRT statistics and classical statistics can be used. For example, items might be identified with classical item difficulties that differ by .1, in absolute value, for the old and new groups. These items could be inspected, and explanations for the differences could be evaluated. An item might be dropped from the common-item section if it were found to have problems: for example, an item was printed differently in the two forms, an item became easier due to many repeating examinees having been administered the item previously, an item whose key had changed because of changes in the field of study, or an item for which a preceding item provided information that helped in answering the item. Harris (1993) suggested that differential item functioning statistics also might be used to screen items.

Dropping items from the common-item set might result in the set of common items not reflecting the test specifications. In this case, additional items might be dropped from the common-item set (but still retained as part of the total test) to achieve proportional content balance. For this reason, the common-item set should be of sufficient length to be able to tolerate removal of some items and still remain content and statistically representative. As an alternative to dropping items to achieve proportional content balance, Harris (1991a) suggested considering the use of statistical procedures to weight item scores statistically on the common items to help achieve such balance. In their review, Cook and Petersen (1987) reported that inadequate content representation of the common-item set creates especially serious problems when the examinee groups that take the alternate forms differ considerably in achievement level. (Refer also to Harris, 1991a; Klein and Jarjoura, 1985.) Serious problems can result if the context in which the common items appear differs from the old to the new form, as was the case with the NAEP example described in Chapter 1.

One way to help avoid having the common items function differently in the two groups is to administer common items in approximately the same position in the old and new forms (Cook and Petersen, 1987). Also, the response alternatives should appear in the same order in the old and new forms (Cizek, 1994). If a common item is associated with stimulus materials that were used with a set of items in the old form, then the entire set of items associated with those stimulus materials should be included on the new form to avoid context effects. If necessary to achieve content balance, some of these items could be treated as noncommon items for the purposes of equating. Other context effects and quality control issues (e.g., items changed from one administration to another) also should be controlled. Even after all the more obvious effects are controlled, common items might still perform differently across administrations. For example, Cook and Petersen (1987) reviewed research on a biology achievement test in which differential preparation of the groups taking the old and new forms led to differential functioning of some common items that caused serious problems with equating. In short, common items should be screened for differences in functioning across the groups taking the old and new forms.

8.1.3 Changes in Test Specifications

Test specifications often evolve over time. In a strict sense, any change in specifications leads to forms that might not be interchangeable. With minor changes, however, testing programs often continue to attempt to equate, often with only minimal problems. Sometimes the changes in the specifications are major, For example, in an achievement test, curriculum consultants might suggest that changes in instructional programs have altered the emphases in a subject matter area, thus requiring a change in the test. In professional certification examinations, the content specifications often change because of changes in the field of study. For example, a particular content area might become obsolete and be replaced by a new area. It is even possible for the answer key for an item to change, say, because of a change in law or a change in standard procedures.

When the test specifications are modified significantly, scores obtained before the test was modified cannot be considered interchangeable with scores obtained after the test was modified, even if an "equating" process is attempted. Indeed, in these situations it is better to refer to this process as *linking* or *scaling to achieve comparability*. Instead of scaling to achieve comparability, the changes in content are often judged to be severe enough that the tests are rescaled. For example, when the SAT was revised, various technical issues associated with implications of changes in the test and the score scale were studied intensively (Lawrence et al., 1994; Dorans, 1994a,b, 2002). When the ACT Assessment was rescaled (Brennan, 1989) concordance tables were developed that related scores on the new test to scores on the old test. In both of these cases, the ranges of scale scores stayed the same for political reasons, although choosing a distinct new score scale might have avoided confusion between the old and new scores. In practice, changes in specifications come in varying degrees, and the chosen approach should be tailored to the situation.

8.2 Data Collection: Design and Implementation

To conduct equating, a choice must be made about which equating design to use (see Chapters 1 and 6). Choices also need to be made about which previously administered form(s) are to be the old form(s) and what sample size to use. Adequate equating depends on having well-constructed tests, as was described earlier, and well-developed statistical and quality control procedures, as is described later in this chapter.

8.2.1 Choosing Among Equating Designs

The random groups, single group, single group with counterbalancing, and common-item nonequivalent groups designs were discussed in Chapter 1 and in subsequent chapters. In addition, designs that involve equating to an IRT calibrated item pool were described in Chapter 6.

The choice of an equating design involves a number of practical considerations that include test administration complications, test development complications, and statistical assumptions required to achieve the desired degree of equating precision. The relationship of these considerations to each of these designs is summarized in Table 8.1. As can be seen from this summary, the choice of a design requires making a series of trade-offs.

The random groups design typically results in the fewest test development complications, because there is no need to develop common-item sets that are representative of the content of the total test. (However, alternate forms still should be built to the same content and statistical specifications, and the forms must be developed in time to be equated in a special study.) Also, because group differences are handled by randomly assigning forms to examinees, and because there is no problem with order effects, this design results in the fewest problems with statistical assumptions.

TABLE 8.1. Comparison of Equating Designs.

Design	Test Administration Complications	Test Development Complications	Statistical Assumptions Required
Random Groups	Moderate—more than one form needs to be spiraled	None	Minimal—that random assignment to forms is effective
Single Group with Counterbalancing	Major—each examinee must take two forms and order must be counterbalanced	None	Moderate—that order effects cancel out and random assignment is effective
Common-Item Nonequivalent Groups	None—forms can be administered in typical manner	Representative common-item sets need to be constructed	Stringent—that common items measure the same construct in both groups, the examinee groups are similar, and required statistical assumptions hold
Common Item to an IRT-Calibrated Item Pool	None—forms can be administered in typical manner	Representative common-item sets need to be constructed	Stringent—that common items measure the same construct in both groups, the examinee groups are similar, and the IRT model assumptions hold

Many equating situations exist, however, for which the random groups design cannot be used. If not enough examinees are available for using the random groups design, then the single group design might be preferable, provided that a study can be undertaken in which two forms can be administered to each examinee and order can be counterbalanced effectively.

One situation that is often encountered in which the random groups and single group designs cannot be used is when only a single test form can be administered on a test date. Many of the reasons for using a single form revolve around test security. For example, administering a single form exposes fewer items than administering more than one form. Also, administering a form that is composed mainly of new items minimizes the chances that examinees previously would have been exposed to the test items and minimizes the chances of a security breach in which items become known to examinees.

When only a single form can be administered on a test date and equating is to be conducted, the choice of equating design is restricted to a design that uses common items. When using these designs, representative common-item sets must be developed. Constructing representative common-item sets and incorporating them into the forms requires considerable effort during the test development process.

Test disclosure legislation also can complicate the choice of design (Marco, 1981). Such legislation often requires that all items which contribute directly to an examinee's score be released to the examinee soon after the test. When the items are released in this way, they cannot be used in future test forms because they are considered to be nonsecure. The typical legislation provides test developers with a way to conduct equating by not requiring that an unscored portion of a test be provided to examinees. Equating could be conducted, therefore, using the common-item nonequivalent groups design with external sets of common items, as is done with the SAT (Donlon, 1984). As was pointed out in Chapter 1, external common-item sets do not contribute directly to an examinee's raw score. Thus, these sections do not need to be released to examinees, even though the scored portion would be released to examinees.

Preequating methods also can be considered in test disclosure situations. In item preequating (see Chapter 6), an IRT-calibrated item pool is developed. A new form is constructed from the items in this pool. Because all of the items have already been calibrated using an IRT model, the item parameter estimates for the new form are available and can be used to develop the conversion table before administering the new form intact. In using item preequating, new items are introduced by including some new items on the operational form, but not including these new items in the computation of examinees' scores. Research reviewed in Chapter 6 suggests that various context effects need to be controlled with item preequating. To minimize context effects, items should appear in a position and context when they are operational that is similar to the position and context in which they appeared when they were preequated.

Section preequating is another type of preequating methodology. In section preequating the operational portion of the test consists of sections of items that have been previously administered, with necessary item or section parameters estimated using data from the previous administrations. Using these results, the conversion table for the operational portion is estimated before it is ever administered as an intact form. Other sections administered to examinees are unscored, and are used to build up the pool of sections with estimated item or section parameters for use in subsequent forms. Linear methods, as well as IRT methods, can be used in section preequating. Linear methods can accommodate sections that measure different abilities. Petersen et al. (1989) provided a summary of section preequating procedures. Holland and Wightman (1982) empirically studied section preequating. Brennan (1992) illustrated that context effects involving the positioning of sections of items need to be controlled in section preequating designs. Harris (1993) presented a discussion, with many references, of practical issues in preequating.

Some situations require that tests be equated before being administered intact in a standard operational setting, such as when scores need to be reported to examinees immediately after they are administered a test. In this case, a conversion table needs to be available before the test administration, Preequating can be used in these situations.

Another way conversion tables could be made available prior to administering the test operationally is to use nonoperational administrations to conduct equating, so conversion tables will be available later for operational administrations. The equating results then are used when the form is used operationally. For example, a random groups design is used initially to equate new forms to an old form of the *Armed Services Vocational Aptitude Battery* (ASVAB) (Thomasson et al., 1994) based on examinees who are already in the military. In a second random groups equating study, these new forms, along with a form that was equated previously, are administered operationally to examinees who want to be accepted into the military. Scores on the new forms for examinees in the second equating study are based on the initial equating. The conversion tables from the second equating are used subsequently, because the examinees in the second equating, as compared to examinees in the first equating, are likely to be more motivated and more similar to the examinees who are to be tested subsequently.

Another variation is used for equating the ACT Assessment (ACT, 1997). On most national test dates, the items on the ACT tests are released to examinees, in part, to meet test legislation requirements. However, on certain test dates the items are not released. On one of these test dates, one or more previously administered unreleased forms along with the new forms to be equated are administered using a random groups design. These

TABLE 8.2. A Random Groups Equating Linkage Plan that Uses a Different Old Form at Each Administration.

Process	Administration	Forms		
Construct Score Scale	1	A		
Equate Using Spiraling	2	[A]	B	C
Equate Using Spiraling	3	[C]	D	E
Equate Using Spiraling	4	[E]	F	G
Equate Using Spiraling	5	[G]	H	I

forms are equated following this administration, and scores are reported to examinees who were administered the new forms. The conversion tables developed in the equating administration also are used when the new forms are administered later on.

Although not a comprehensive set of possibilities, the SAT, ASVAB, and ACT equating designs illustrate the use of the random groups design and the common-item nonequivalent groups design in situations that might suggest the need for an item or section preequating design.

8.2.2 Developing Equating Linkage Plans

When conducting equating, a choice is made about which old form or forms are to be used for equating a new form or forms. The choice of the old form or forms has a significant effect on how random and systematic equating error affects score comparisons across forms.

Random Groups Design

Consider the following example of a simple equating linkage plan. For the ACT Assessment (ACT, 1997), new forms are equated each year using a random groups design in which the new forms are spiraled along with one form that was equated in a previous year. This process allows the new form raw scores to be converted to scale scores by first equating raw scores on the new forms to raw scores on the old form. The raw-to-scale score conversion that was developed previously for the old form then is used to estimate raw-to-scale score conversions for the new forms.

A hypothetical example that displays a linkage plan which is similar to the ACT plan is shown in Table 8.2, where the old form is listed in a box. In Administration 1, the raw-to-scale score transformation for Form A establishes the score scale. In Administration 2, new Forms B and C are administered with Form A in a spiral administration. The data collected from this administration are used to develop the conversion that trans-

TABLE 8.3. A Random Groups Equating Linkage Plan that Uses the Same Old Form at Each Administration.

Process	Administration	Forms		
Construct Score Scale	1	A		
Equate Using Spiraling	2	[A]	B	C
Equate Using Spiraling	3	[A]	D	E
Equate Using Spiraling	4	[A]	F	G
Equate Using Spiraling	5	[A]	H	I

forms Form B and Form C raw scores to scale scores through Form A. In Administration 3, Form C serves as the old form and Forms D and E as the new forms. The general plan is to spiral new forms along with an old form that was equated previously.

ASVAB (Thomasson et al., 1994) also is equated using the random groups design. However, in the ASVAB program, the form that was used to conduct the original scaling is always the old form that is spiraled with the new forms. A hypothetical example that displays a linkage plan similar to the ASVAB plan is shown in Table 8.3. Note that the major difference between the plans shown in Tables 8.2 and 8.3 is the old form that is used in the spiraling process. In Table 8.2, the old form is a form that was equated in the previous year. In Table 8.3, the old form is a form that was used initially in the scaling process. Both plans can be used to produce raw-to-scale score conversions. Is one plan preferable to the other? The answer depends on various practical issues having to do with the context of the equating.

One of these issues has to do with error in equating. As was suggested earlier, each time an equating is conducted, equating error is introduced. Error might accumulate over equatings. In Table 8.2, how many equatings separate Form I from Form A?

Equating 1: Form I is equated to Form G.
Equating 2: Form G is equated to Form E.
Equating 3: Form E is equated to Form C.
Equating 4: Form C is equated to Form A.

Thus, four equatings separate Form I and Form A. Equating error from four different equatings would influence the comparison of scores between examinees who took Form A and those who took Form I.

How many equatings separate Form I from Form A in the example in Table 8.3? Just one. That is, error sources from only one equating influence the comparison of scores between examinees who took Form A and those who took Form I in the Table 8.3 plan. At least from this perspective, the plan in Table 8.3 is preferable.

However, there are at least two potential problems with the plan in Table 8.3. First, this plan requires Form A to be administered repeatedly. If the items became known to some examinees because of security breaches (e.g., test booklets stolen or students memorizing items and supplying them to coaching schools) or because many repeating examinees had seen the items in an earlier administration, then the equating could be severely compromised. Second, the content of Form A might become dated. For example, reading passages might become less relevant, causing examinee groups to respond differently to the passages over time. Also, an accumulation of minor changes in the way test specifications are applied over time might make Form A somewhat different from later forms. For these reasons, a plan like the one displayed in Table 8.3 must be used cautiously. Whether to use a plan like the one in Table 8.2 or one like that in Table 8.3 depends on weighing the problems associated with each of the plans and deciding which problems are more serious for the testing program at hand.

Compromise plans also could be constructed. For example, in the plan in Table 8.3, Form A could be used as the old form in Administrations 2 and 3. Then Form E could be used as the old form in Administrations 4 and 5. Compared to the plan in Table 8.3, this compromise plan would reduce the usage of Form A. Compared to the plan in Table 8.2, this compromise plan would lead to fewer equating error sources in comparing scores on Form A to scores on Form I.

In practice, constructing equating plans can be much more complicated than what has been considered in these hypothetical examples. A particular form might need to be ruled out as an old form because of security concerns or because many of the examinees to be included in the equating were administered the old form on a previous occasion. Also, an old form might be found to have bad items (e.g., items that are ambiguous, multiply keyed, or negatively discriminating), which could rule out its use in equating. These sorts of practical concerns often make it impossible to develop equating plans that are actually used very far into the future.

Double Linking with Random Groups

One procedure that is often used to help solve the problems associated with developing linkage plans is to use two old forms to equate new forms. This process is referred to as *double linking*. As an example of double linking, the scheme in Table 8.2 could be modified by also administering Form B in Administration 4 and Form D in Administration 5. The resulting plan is shown in Table 8.4. In applying double linking, the new forms are equated separately to each of the old forms. The resulting equating relationships could then be averaged. For example, in Administration 5, one equating relationship could be developed to equate Form H to scale scores using

280   8. Practical Issues in Equating

TABLE 8.4. A Random Groups Equating Linkage Plan that Uses Double Linking.

Process	Administration	Forms			
Construct Score Scale	1	A			
Equate Using Spiraling	2	[A]	B	C	
Equate Using Spiraling	3	[C]	D	E	
Equate Using Spiraling	4	[B]	E	F	G
Equate Using Spiraling	5	[D]	G	H	I

Form D as the old form. A second equating relationship could be developed for equating Form H to scale scores using Form G as the old form. These two relationships likely would differ because of equating error. The two conversions could be averaged to produce a single conversion. (Braun and Holland, 1982, suggested using bisection instead of averaging when linear equating is used. Averaging and bisection produce very similar results, and averaging is simpler.)

The process of double linking has much to recommend it. It provides a built-in stability check on the equating process. Two conversions that differ more than would be expected by chance might suggest problems with statistical assumptions, quality control (e.g., scores incorrectly computed), administration (e.g., spiraling was not properly performed), or security (e.g., a security breach led to many examinees' having access to one of the old forms). If such problems are suspected, then one of the links could be eliminated without destroying the ability to equate in the testing program. (Note, however, that if a security breach led to many examinees having had access to one of the old forms, then the scores of the examinees who took that old form might not be valid.) In addition, the use of double linking can provide for greater equating stability than the use of a single link, especially when the two old forms are chosen from different administrations, as was done in Administrations 4 and 5 in Table 8.4.

The average of two links also can be shown to contain less random equating error than the use of a single link. Consider the following situation. In one equating, Form C is equated directly to Form A; and in a second equating, Form C is equated first to Form B and then to Form A. For simplicity, assume that the error variance in equating is the same for any single equating. The equating of Form C to Form A contains the same amount of equating error variance as the equating of Form B to Form A. Refer to the error variance at a particular score point on Form C as var. Also assume that all equatings are independent.

In this case, the equating error in equating Form C to Form A equals *var*. Equating error variance in equating Form C to Form A through Form B equals 2*var*. The average of the equivalents of the two equatings equals the sum of the equivalents divided by 2. In this case, equating error variance for the average can be shown to equal

$$\frac{1}{2^2}var + \frac{1}{2^2}(2)var = \frac{3}{4}var.$$

In this example, equating error variance for the average of the two links, 3/4*var*, is less than the equating error variance for either link taken by itself. This relationship illustrates that the use of double linking can reduce random equating error. See Hanson et al. (1997) for an empirical demonstration that random equating error is reduced when two links are averaged.

In practice, the double links might not be equally weighted. If one link is considered to have more error than another link, the first link might be weighted less than 1/2. If substantial problems are present with one of the links, that link can be weighted 0.

Double linking does introduce complications into equating. More than one old form must be included in the study, which assumes the availability of another form and requires exposing more forms in the study, which might lead to security concerns. Using additional forms also requires that the overall sample size be larger, which in some cases might not be possible. For example, if the sample size needs to be 2,000 examinees per form and 4,000 examinees are available to do equating, then only one old form could be used when equating one new form. Even though there are complications in using two old forms, we recommend using double linking when feasible.

Common-Item Nonequivalent Groups Design

Additional complications are present when developing equating plans with the common-item nonequivalent groups design. Group differences across administrations sometimes are substantial. As was suggested earlier, the similarity between examinee groups that are administered the old and new forms significantly affects the quality of equating: The more similar the groups, in general, the more adequate the equating.

The following situation illustrates some of these complications. A test is administered in the spring and in the fall every year, with a different form administered on each occasion. The group of examinees that tests in the spring tends to be different in its overall level of achievement than the group that tests in the fall. This difference in group level achievement suggests greater equating stability when a new form is equated to a form from the same time of year than to a form from a different time of year. A single section of common items is used to equate a new form.

Single Link Plan 1 in Figure 8.1 presents one possible single link pattern for this situation over a 5-year period. In this example, assume that the

282   8. Practical Issues in Equating

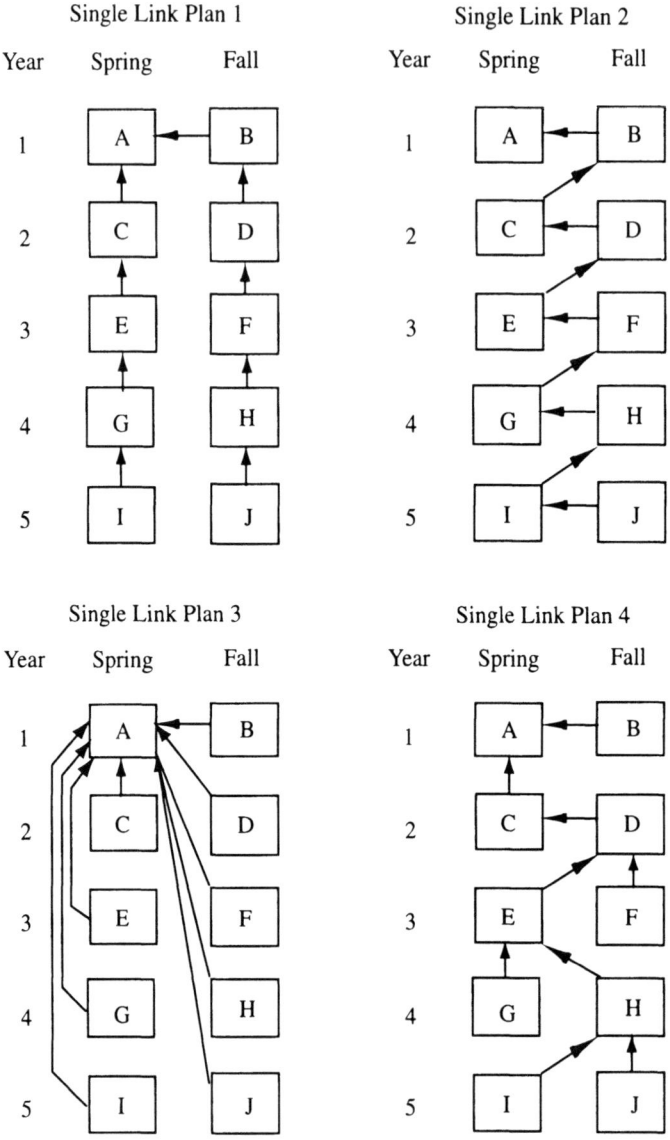

FIGURE 8.1. Four hypothetical single link plans.

score scale was established on Form A. The arrows indicate which old form has items shared with the new form. For example, Form J is equated to the score scale using items that are in common with Form H. In this plan, spring forms are always equated to spring forms and fall forms are always equated to fall forms, with the exception of Form B. Note that in setting up equating patterns, all forms must link back to a single old form through an equating chain, so scores on all forms can be converted to scale scores. For this reason, Form B must be equated to Form A in the Figure 8.1 example.

This equating plan can be used to equate all forms to the score scale, because all forms eventually link back to Form A. This pattern makes as extensive use as possible of linking to forms that were previously administered in the same time of year, thus maximizing the similarity of groups used in the equatings. From the perspective of using similar groups, this plan is nearly ideal.

However, this plan has significant problems. Suppose that examinees tested in the fall of Year 5 were to be compared to examinees tested in the spring of Year 5. How many links would affect this comparison? Another way to ask this question is, how many arrows does it take to go from Form J to Form I in the linkage plan? By going from J to H, H to F, F to D, D to B, B to A, A to C, C to E, E to G, and G to I, there are nine of these arrows. Thus, nine links affect the comparison of scores on Form I and Form J. If this pattern were extended, the number of links for comparisons between forms administered in a given year increases by two each year. This linkage plan illustrates the development of what is sometimes referred to as an *equating strain*. Equating strains can lead to a situation in which examinees earn higher scale scores on one form than on another form. In developing equating linkage plans, equating strains should be avoided.

The random groups and common-item nonequivalent groups examples considered so far illustrate the following four rules that can be used to construct equating linkage plans for the common-item nonequivalent groups design with internal common items:

Rule 1. Avoid equating strains by minimizing the number of links that affect the comparison of scores on forms given at succesive times. (Single Link Plan 1 in Figure 8.1 violates this rule.)

Rule 2. Use links to the same time of the year as often as possible. (Single Link Plan 1 in Figure 8.1 is an example of a plan that follows this rule.)

Rule 3. Minimize the number of links connecting each form back to the initial form. (The plan in Table 8.3, for the random groups design, is an example of a plan that follows this rule.)

Rule 4. Avoid linking back to the same form too often. (The plan in Table 8.2, for the random groups design, is an example of a plan that follows this rule.)

Obviously, all of these rules cannot be followed simultaneously when constructing a plan that uses single links. Choosing a plan involves a series of compromises that must be made in the context of the testing program under consideration. For example, Rule 3 might be considered important when following trends in scores over time, but not otherwise.

Some additional examples can be used to explore these four rules more fully. Refer to Single Link Plan 2 in Figure 8.1. Rule 1 is followed as closely as possible, because forms are equated directly to the adjacent form. Rule 2 is violated as much as possible, because forms are always equated to a form from the other month. Rule 3 also is violated, in that the number of links back to Form A is as large as possible. Rule 4 is followed.

The Single Link Plan 3 in Figure 8.1 follows Rules 1 and 3. Rules 2 and 4 are not followed.

In the Single Link Plan 4 in Figure 8.1, Rule 1 is followed reasonably closely, in that there are no more than two links (arrows) separating adjacent forms. Rule 2 is followed for nearly 1/2 of the forms. Rule 3 is followed more closely for this plan than for Single Link Plan 2 in Figure 8.1, but less closely than for Single Link Plan 3 in Figure 8.1. Rule 4 is followed reasonably closely, although nearly 1/2 of the forms are equated back to twice. Although Single Link Plan 4 in Figure 8.1 is less than ideal, this plan might be a reasonable compromise.

The linkage plans in Figure 8.1 are presented for illustrative purposes only. Often, practical constraints make plans like these unworkable. For example, if many examinees repeat the test, a form that was administered within the last year or two might not be a good choice to use as a link form. The examinees who repeat the test could be unfairly advantaged by being administered the same items a second time. In other situations, scores might need to be comparable over a long period, in which case it probably would be desirable for at least one of the link forms to be a form that was originally administered in the more distant past. Sometimes problems exist with a potential old form which suggest that the form not be used as a link form. For example, the sample size for a potential link might have been very small when that form was equated, a potential link form might have had security problems, or a potential link form might have been found to have not been well constructed. Many testing programs have more than two test dates per year, which also complicates the design of equating plans. For an example, refer to the SAT linkage plan that is presented in Donlon (1984, pp. 16,17). Of necessity, linkage plans should be tailored to the particular testing program. However, the principles discussed here can be useful in designing and evaluating these plans.

Double Linking with the Common-Item Nonequivalent Groups Design

Double linking is useful in the common-item nonequivalent groups design because, as with the random groups design, it provides a built-in check on the equating process leading to greater equating stability, and it can be used to avoid equating strains. In addition, with two links, a second link still is available to be used for equating even if the strong statistical assumptions required under the common-item nonequivalent design are violated for one of the links. Also, if a significant number of common items on one link are found to have problems, or if security problems are discovered with one of the old forms, then a second link still exists that can be used to conduct the equating.

Double linking requires greater effort in test development and in equating than does equating using a single link. When using the common-item nonequivalent groups design, double linking requires that two sets of common items which are content representative be used in the development of new forms, which sometimes can be difficult. Using two links also creates a greater exposure of old forms in the random groups design and of common items with the common-item nonequivalent groups design. Double linking is most desirable in situations where form-to-form comparability is important over a long time, and might be less important in situations where periodic changes in test content require that the test be rescaled every few years. It is strongly recommended that double linking be used when feasible.

To capitalize on the benefits associated with double linking, the use of triple links has been suggested (McKinley and Schaeffer, 1989). However, triple linking can be difficult, practically, because it requires building three sets of common items that are content representative, and it can create even more exposure of forms and items than double linking does.

One beneficial way to use double linking in IRT equating to an item pool is for one link to be to a single old form and the other link to be to the overall pool. In this way, one of the links is an equating using the common-item nonequivalent groups design. This double linking process allows for use of the traditional methods as a check on the IRT methods.

8.2.3 Examinee Groups Used in Equating

Equating relationships typically are group dependent, so the group or groups of examinees used in equating affect the estimated equating relationship. For this reason, more adequate equating is expected when the examinees used in the equating study are as similar as possible to the entire group that is tested (Harris, 1993). Problems might occur when equating is conducted in a special study in which the groups are very different from the examinees who are to be tested later. In addition to differences in group characteristics, differences in examinee motivation between special studies and operational testing can affect equating. The ASVAB example presented in Chapter 1, in which the examinees were more motivated on the old form than the new form, is an extreme example of how motivation differences can cause significant problems.

The effect of the group used for equating depends on the data collection design. When carefully constructed alternate forms are equated using large samples in the random groups design, the equating relationship seems not to be too dependent on the group of examinees used to conduct the equating (Angoff and Cowell, 1986; Harris and Kolen, 1986). In the common-item nonequivalent groups design, however, large differences between the old and the new groups can cause significant problems in estimating equating relationships, both for traditional and IRT equating methods (for reviews of relevant research see Cook and Petersen, 1987; Harris, 1993; Skaggs, 1990a; Skaggs and Lissitz, 1986b). Large group differences can lead to failure of the statistical assumptions for any equating method to hold. The research in the Dorans (1990) special issue of *Applied Measurement in Education* (Eignor et al., 1990b; Kolen, 1990; Lawrence and Dorans, 1990; Livingston et al, 1990; Schmitt et al, 1990; Skaggs, 1990a) and Eignor et al. (1990a) assessed the use of matching procedures to make otherwise disparate groups more similar, but found that the procedures studied were not satisfactory. However, the results found by Wright and Dorans (1993) suggest that matching might be worthwhile to consider in certain situations. Liou et al. (1999,2001) suggested using variables other than common items as a means for adjusting for group differences.

The various statistical methods handle group differences differently. The Tucker, Braun-Holland and frequency estimation equipercentile methods require assumptions about the same regression holding across the different populations. These assumptions cannot be expected to hold when groups differ substantially. The IRT and Levine methods require that the common items and total scores measure the same construct in the two groups, in the sense that true scores are functionally related. This requirement places considerable emphasis on test development procedures, so that the same construct is measured in precisely the same way across alternate forms and common-item sets. If this requirement is met precisely, then the Levine and IRT methods might function more adequately than the other methods when there are large group differences. However, when the group differences become too large, no method likely will function well (see Cook and Petersen, 1987).

In our experience with the common-item nonequivalent groups design, mean differences between the two groups of approximately .1 or less standard deviation unit on the common items seem to cause few problems for any of the equating methods. Mean group differences of around .3 or more standard deviation unit can result in substantial differences among methods, and differences larger than .5 standard deviation unit can be especially troublesome. In addition, ratios of group standard deviations on the common items of less than .8 or greater than 1.2 tend to be associated with substantial differences among methods. Differences in group standard deviations have the potential to lead to differences among methods that are at least as great as those caused by differences in means. These rules of thumb are necessarily situation specific.

Repeating Examinees

A consideration when conducting equating is whether or not to eliminate examinees who have taken the test previously. One argument for removing examinees who are repeating the test is that they might have seen the old form or common items, which could bias the equating. However, repeating examinees might not be identifiable in the time allowed for conducting equating. Also, excluding repeating examinees reduces sample size, which might lead to inadequate equating precision. Excluding repeaters might also cause the group being included in the equating not to be representative of the group tested, especially if many examinees repeat the test. Research on the effects of repeating examinees on equating (Andrulis et al., 1978; Cope, 1986) produced mixed results. Decisions about whether or not to include repeating examinees in equating in a particular testing program depend on assessing how likely it is that examinees would have seen previously administered items or forms and whether or not it is possible to identify repeating examinees.

Editing Rules

Another consideration is whether to delete examinees whose scores are very low or who omitted many items. For example, examinees who omit all the items on a test or earn a number-correct score of 0 often are excluded from equating, These are likely to be examinees who did not attempt the test and might have been erroneously included in the data. Editing rules should be tailored to the particular testing program.

Less conservative rules might negatively affect equating. Suppose that in a random groups design a sizable number of examinees typically earn scores below "chance" (number of multiple-choice items divided by the number of alternatives per item) on a test, and that more examinees scored below chance on the more difficult of the two forms. Eliminating these below "chance" examinees from the equating process could destroy the random equivalence between the samples taking Form X and Form Y, and it would result in the loss of all data in the lower tail of the distributions. We recommend using conservative editing rules whenever possible.

Another consideration is whether to eliminate test centers or testing sessions that had administration problems. For example, in the random groups design, each of the forms to be equated would be expected to be administered to approximately the same number of examinees in each test session. Numbers that are grossly unequal suggest administrative problems. In this case, elimination of the data for a test center or session can be considered. Elimination of data from test centers or test sessions with significant irregularities, such as a power failure that disrupted testing, also can be considered.

8.2.4 Sample Size Requirements

Sample size has a direct effect on random equating error. Livingston (1993), Kolen and Whitney (1982), and Parshall et al. (1995) conducted empirical research on the use of equating with small samples. Harris (1993) reviewed research on sample size in equating and suggested that larger samples lead to better equating. In this section, schemes for estimating sample size requirements are considered that are mainly based on considerations in estimating random error in equating.

Rules of Thumb Using Standard Deviation Units as a Criterion

In Chapter 7, procedures were provided for estimating the sample size required to achieve a given level of equating precision. For the random groups design under normality assumptions, the standard error of equating between z-scores of -2 and $+2$ was shown to be less than .1 raw score standard deviation unit when the sample size was 400 per form for linear equating and slightly over 1,500 per form for equipercentile equating. In any given situation, however, the shapes of the distributions, the degree of equating precision required, and the effects of smoothing if equipercentile equating is used (see the sample size discussion in Chapter 3) can be taken into account when developing sample size requirements. In addition, if a passing score is to be used in the testing program, then the precision at that passing score might be of primary concern (see Brennan and Kolen, 1987b, pp. 285,286).

Our experience suggests that these figures are also useful rules of thumb for sample size requirements for linear and equipercentile equating in the common-item nonequivalent groups design. Sample size considerations under this design, however, are complicated in that the degree of relationship between the total score and common-item score (see Budescu, 1985), along with the distribution shapes, have a strong influence on the standard errors.

Standard error of equating expressions that can be readily used to estimate sample sizes have yet to be developed for IRT equating procedures. The procedure used to estimate item parameters will likely affect the sample sizes required. A rule of thumb that is loosely based on the literature surveyed by Harris (1993) would be to require the same number of examinees for the three-parameter model as for equipercentile equating (approximately 1,500 per form) and to require the same number of examinees for the Rasch (one-parameter) model as for the linear methods (400 per form).

Rules of Thumb Based on Comparisons with the Identity Equating

The rules of thumb just developed for the traditional methods were based on using a conservative criterion (standard errors of equating being less than .1 raw score standard deviation unit). The sample size issue can be addressed by asking a different question: What is the smallest sample size that would be expected to reduce equating error as compared to identity equating?

If identity equating is used, the Form Y equivalent of a Form X score is set to equal to the Form X score. That is, the Form Y equivalent of a Form X score of x_i is x_i. If equipercentile equating is the most appropriate method, then the bias incorporated by using identity equating is $x_i - e_Y(x_i)$. As was indicated in Chapter 3, the sum of random equating error variance and squared bias equals mean squared error in equating. Based on this relationship, *the identity equating is preferable to equipercentile equating if the squared bias associated with the identity equating is less than the random equating error variance associated with using equipercentile equating.*

The following example illustrates the application of this principle. In developing the rules of thumb mentioned earlier, a sample size of approximately 1,500 per form was found to be required for the standard error of equating at any score to be less than .1 raw score standard deviation unit over the z-score range of -2 to $+2$. *Assume* that the largest absolute difference in equivalents between identity equating and equipercentile equating, $|x_i - e_Y(x_i)|$, is .1 standard deviation unit over the z-score range of -2 to $+2$. Thus, over this range, the maximum absolute equating bias associated with identity equating is *assumed* to be .1 standard deviation unit. Because squared bias and squared standard errors contribute equally to mean squared error, the same maximum level of mean squared error will accrue over the z-score range of -2 to $+2$ through the use of identity equating or equipercentile equating with a sample size of approximately 1,500. Thus, in this situation, a sample size over 1,500 would be required for equipercentile equating to result in less mean squared error than identity equating.

What if the largest difference in equivalents between using identity equating and equipercentile equating was *assumed* to be .2 standard deviation unit over the z-score range -2 to $+2$? Using equation (7.19) with $u = .2$, the sample size per form is approximately 382. Assuming a maximum difference in equivalents of .2 standard deviation unit, a sample size of over 382 would be required for equipercentile equating to produce less mean squared error than identity equating.

As was just demonstrated, this scheme is very sensitive to the extent that the forms are assumed to differ. Assuming that the forms are similar enough to be equated, *the larger the anticipated difference between forms, the smaller the sample size needed for equating to be useful.* However, larger representative samples lead to less random error. This scheme depends on the distributions of the scores (normal distributions were assumed here). However, if reasonable approximations to the distribution shapes can be found, and if reasonable assumptions about the degree of difference between forms can be made, then this scheme can be used to decide whether identity equating is preferable to another equating method.

8.3 Choosing from Among the Statistical Procedures

Various statistical methods for equating have been presented. For any of these methods to be used appropriately, the test specifications, the data collected, and the standardization and quality control procedures should be adequate. Otherwise, not equating (or using identity equating) might be the preferred option. Although it might be possible to implement all of the methods that have been discussed in a particular testing program, practical circumstances often rule out implementing some methods and suggest ruling out others.

8.3.1 Equating Criteria in Research Studies

Considerable research has been conducted that can be consulted when deciding which procedures to use. Studies by Marco et al. (1979) and Petersen et al. (1982, 1983) are among the most extensive. The reviews of research that have been done (Brennan and Kolen, 1987b; Cook and Petersen, 1987; Harris, 1993; Harris and Crouse, 1993; Skaggs, 1990a; Skaggs and Lissitz, 1986b) should be consulted for more comprehensive summaries of research. Conducting research on equating and using the results from research on similar tests can help in deciding which statistical procedures to implement when equating a test. Consider the following questions:

1. In what situations do each of the equating methods perform adequately, and in what situations do each of the equating methods perform inadequately?

2. In a particular testing program, which equating method(s) should be applied?

Equating criteria are useful for addressing these questions.

Harris and Crouse (1993) conducted an exhaustive survey of criteria for comparing equating methods and results that have been used to address these questions. Some criteria for addressing these questions have been discussed previously in this book. In this section, some criteria are considered that have been used to address Question 1. Refer to Harris and Crouse (1993) for a more complete discussion.

One of the criteria identified by Harris and Crouse (1993) that has been used in research studies is *equating in a circle*. To use this paradigm in a situation with three forms, Form X is equated to Form Y, Form Y is equated to Form Z, and Form Z is equated back to Form X. Following through this chain, Form X is equated to itself. In this paradigm, equating is adequate to the extent that a Form X raw score of 1 converts to a score of 1, a raw score of 2 to a score of 2, etc. This paradigm can be used if Forms X, Y, and Z are equated using a random groups design. This paradigm also can be used with the common-item nonequivalent groups design if there are items in common between Forms X and Y, between Forms Y and Z, and between Forms Z and X. Angoff (1987) considered this criterion to be useful because "it provides advance knowledge of what the errorless result should be ..." (p. 298). This criterion has been used in various equating and linking studies (e.g., Cope 1987; Gafni and Melamed, 1990; Klein and Jarjoura, 1985; Lord and Wingersky, 1984; Marco et al., 1979; Petersen et al., 1983; Phillips, 1985).

Although equating in a circle might appear to be sensible, Brennan and Kolen (1987a,b) pointed out concerns with this paradigm. First, they indicated that identity equating will always be preferable to equating when using this paradigm. They demonstrated that equating methods which estimate fewer parameters (e.g., linear equating) tend to perform better than methods that estimate more parameters (e.g., equipercentile equating). They also demonstrated that, under the common-item nonequivalent groups design, the results of the comparison depend on the form used to start the circle. That is, different results are found when Form X is equated to itself through Forms Y and Z than when Form Z is equated to itself through Forms X and Y. Wang et al. (2000) reinforced many of the concerns discussed by Brennan and Kolen (1987a,b) through a set of simulation and real data studies. These problems suggest cautious use of the equating in a circle paradigm. However, this procedure could be useful in identifying methods that produce poor equating results, in that if a method does not work well when equating a form to itself, it might not work well when equating alternate forms.

Another criterion reported by Harris and Crouse (1993) involves using *simulated equating* by defining true equating using a psychometric model and then generating data to fit the model. In this way, the true equating is known and can be used as the criterion equating. They pointed out, however, that the particular model used to generate the data might tend to favor certain methods over others, and that the usefulness of this approach depends on how well the generated data mimic data from real testing programs.

Harris and Crouse (1993) also discussed *large sample criteria*, in which data from a large sample of examinees are used to represent the population relationship. Smaller samples are drawn and the results are compared to the large sample results. For example, Livingston et al. (1990) used SAT forms from a spiral administration in which approximately 250,000 examinees were tested. The equating relationship based on the random groups design was used as the "true" equating relationship. The forms also had common-item sections. Nonequivalent examinee groups were formed from the available random groups. Various procedures were used to equate the forms using the common-item nonequivalent groups design. The results for the different procedures were compared to the random groups equating based on all 250,000 examinees. Harris and Crouse (1993) pointed out that this criterion is limited in its usefulness, because large groups of examinees typically are not available. In addition, the results are meaningful only to the extent that the examinee groups are formed in a manner that is similar to how groups occur in practice.

Based on their review of these criteria and others, Harris and Crouse (1993) concluded that "... no definitive criterion for evaluating equating exists ..." (p. 230). They went on to say that

> Given the controversy regarding which criterion is best, whether certain criteria are useful, and whether a criterion is needed at all, much work needs to be done in the area of equating criteria. As long as equating is performed, equating criteria will be needed to evaluate the results ... The fact that equating results appear to be so situation specific demands that studies be replicated and that some method of comparing results across studies be developed. (p. 232)

This discussion of criteria suggests that research can provide information about which method to use. However, it is unlikely that such research will lead to an unambiguous choice of an equating method, in part because different criteria might lead to the choice of different methods (see Harris and Crouse, 1993, for examples and additional references).

8.3.2 Characteristics of Equating Situations

Table 8.5 presents a list of characteristics of equating situations for which each of the methods is most appropriate. Mean and linear equating are most useful to consider when the sample size is small, the test forms are not too dissimilar, and a great degree of accuracy is needed only at scores that are not too far from the mean. The conversions for these methods are easy to express (a linear equation, with rounding and truncation rules), the analyses are relatively easy to conduct (summary statistics such as means, variances, and covariances are all that are needed), and the methods are relatively easy to explain to individuals who do not routinely conduct equating. Many applied situations exist in which these methods are adequate.

For example, many certification testing programs are concerned only that equating be accurate near a single passing score. In some programs,

TABLE 8.5. Testing Situations in Which Various Equating Methods Are Most Appropriate.

Method	Situation
Identity	Random Groups and Common-Item Nonequivalent Groups Designs 1. Poor quality control or standardization conditions. 2. Very small samples, or no data at all. 3. Similar test form difficulties. 4. Simplicity in conversion tables or equations, in conducting analyses, and in describing procedures to non-psychometricians is desirable. 5. Possibly inaccurate results can be tolerated. Common-Item Nonequivalent Groups Design 6. Assumptions used to disconfound group and form differences do not hold reasonably well. Likely causes of problems are common item sets that are not representative of the full length test or examinee groups that differ considerably in overall achievement level.
Mean	Random Groups and Common-Item Nonequivalent Groups Designs 1. Adequate quality control and standardization conditions. Alternate forms built to same specifications. 2. Very small samples. 3. Similar test form difficulties. 4. Simplicity in conversion tables or equations, in conducting analyses, and in describing procedures to non-psychometricians is desirable. 5. Accuracy of results is most important near the mean. Common-Item Nonequivalent Groups Design 6. Assumptions used to disconfound group and form differences hold reasonably well. For these assumptions to hold, common items need to be representative, and examinee groups cannot differ too much in overall achievement level.
Linear	Random Groups and Common-Item Nonequivalent Groups Designs 1. Adequate quality control or standardization conditions. Alternate forms built to same specifications. 2. Small samples. 3. Similar test form difficulties. 4. Simplicity in conversion tables or equations, in conducting analyses, and in describing procedures to non-psychometricians is desirable. 5. Accuracy of results is most important near the mean. Common-Item Nonequivalent Groups Design 6. Assumptions used to disconfound group and form differences hold reasonably well. For these assumptions to hold, common items need to be representative, and examinee groups cannot differ too much in overall achievement level.

294   8. Practical Issues in Equating

TABLE 8.5. (continued)

Method	Situation
Equi-percentile	Random Groups and Common-Item Nonequivalent Groups Designs 1. Adequate quality control and standardization conditions. Alternate forms built to same specifications. 2. Large samples. 3. Test forms can differ in difficulty level more than for a linear method. 4. Complexity in conversion tables or equations, in conducting analyses, and in describing procedures to non-psychometricians can be tolerated. 5. Accuracy of results is important all along the score scale. Common-Item Nonequivalent Groups Design 6. Assumptions used to disconfound group and form differences hold reasonably well. For these assumptions to hold, common items need to be representative, and examinee groups cannot differ too much in overall achievement level.
Rasch	Random Groups and Common-Item Nonequivalent Groups Designs 1. Adequate quality control and standardization conditions. Alternate forms built to same specifications. 2. Small samples. 3. Similar test form difficulties. 4. Complexity in conversion tables, in parameter estimation, in conducting analyses, and in describing procedures to nonpsychometricians can be tolerated. 5. Accuracy of results is most important in area that is not very far from the mean. 6. IRT model assumptions hold reasonably well. Common-Item Nonequivalent Groups Design 7. Assumptions used to disconfound group and form differences hold reasonably well. For these assumptions to hold, common items need to be representative, and examinee groups cannot differ too much in overall achievement level.
Three-Parameter IRT	Random Groups and Common-Item Nonequivalent Groups Designs 1. Adequate quality control and standardization conditions. Alternate forms built to same specifications. 2. Large samples. 3. Test forms can differ in difficulty level more than for a linear method. 4. Complexity in conversion tables, in parameter estimation, in conducting analyses, and in describing procedures to nonpsychometricians can be tolerated. 5. Can tolerate computationally intensive item parameter estimation procedure. This problem is mitigated if item parameter estimates are needed for other purposes, such as for test construction. 6. Accuracy of results is important all along the score scale. 7. IRT model assumptions hold reasonably well. Common-Item Nonequivalent Groups Design 8. Assumptions used to disconfound group and form differences hold reasonably well. For these assumptions to hold, common items need to be representative, and examinee groups cannot differ too much in overall achievement level.

the equating might be used only to ensure that the passing score indicates the same level of achievement from administration to administration. If the passing score is not too far from the mean, then linear equating could be the most complex equating method that should be considered.

As another example, small samples of examinees often are administered tests on test dates in which equating is conducted. In these small sample situations, mean or linear equating might be the most complicated method that would be needed, especially if the interest is in accuracy near the mean.

Assuming that the equating relationship is not linear, nonlinear methods (equipercentile and IRT) are most often required when the sample sizes are large and accuracy is required all along the score scale. For example, the ACT Assessment (1997) uses equipercentile equating with large sample sizes because decisions are made at points all along the score scale. The SAT (Donlon, 1984) uses equipercentile and three-parameter IRT methods, along with linear methods, for similar reasons.

For any equating design, the use of IRT methods requires making strong assumptions. Research should be conducted in the context of the testing program to make sure that the methods are robust to the violations of these assumptions which are likely to occur in practice. Because Rasch equating is an IRT method, it requires strong statistical assumptions. However, Rasch equating has considerably smaller sample size requirements than do the three-parameter model methods.

For any equating method, the assumptions required for the common-item nonequivalent groups design (or common-item equating to an IRT calibrated item pool) are very strong. These assumptions can be especially problematic when examinee groups differ substantially, when alternate forms differ substantially, or when the specifications of the common-item sets differ from the specifications for the total test. In these situations, perhaps none of the equating methods would work well. Because of the strong assumptions that are required, methods based on different assumptions can be implemented and the results compared to each other and to results from previous test dates.

Situations can arise in which none of the methods produces an adequate equating. Suppose that (a) high equating accuracy is required at all points along the score scale, (b) the forms are expected to differ more than a little in difficulty, and (c) the sample size is small. In this situation, the objective of high equating accuracy might not be achieved by any of the equating methods. Other similar situations sometimes arise in practice.

8.4 Choosing from Among Equating Results

When various equating methods are applied in a particular situation, a process should be developed to choose from among the results. The use of double linking increases the choices that should be considered. Various statistical indices, procedures, and criteria can be used for comparing results from different equatings. Harris (1993) and Harris and Crouse (1993) reviewed many of these indices, criteria, and procedures.

8.4.1 Equating Versus Not Equating

Assuming that the test specifications, design, data collection, and quality control procedures are adequate, it is still possible that using the identity function will lead to less equating error than using one of the other equating methods. Hanson (1992) developed an approach that can be used to help decide whether to equate or use the identity function when using the random groups design. This approach includes using a significance test with the null hypothesis that the distribution of raw scores on alternate forms is the same in the relevant population of examinees. If the null hypothesis is rejected, it is concluded that the distributions differ in the population and that equating should be considered. If the null hypothesis is retained, identity equating is used. Only random error is considered in Hanson's (1992) approach. However, systematic error can be even more problematic than random error. (See Dorans and Lawrence, 1990, for a similar procedure that considers only the mean and standard deviation.)

In small sample situations it is recommended that Hanson's (1992) procedure be used to help decide whether identity equating is preferable to another equating. If the significance test suggests that the distributions are the same, then identity equating could be used. Otherwise, the procedure described previously in this chapter can be used to estimate whether equating would result in more or less error than identity equating. Only if equating is expected to add in less error than identity equating, should an equating other than identity equating be considered.

8.4.2 Use of Robustness Checks

Many procedures have been suggested for estimating the equating relationship for a population using data from a sample. In any equating situation, a relevant question is: How robust is the estimation to the choice of method or procedure? To address this question of *robustness*, various methods and procedures can be applied, and if all of the results are similar, then the results are said to be robust with respect to the choice of method. If the results differ, then the results are not robust with respect to the choice of method. In this case, the choice of method is crucial, although a clear-cut basis for making the choice typically is not available.

In addition, equating can be conducted for various subgroups of examinees (e.g., males versus females). To the extent that the equating is robust, the equating should be similar in the various subgroups. For a particular method, substantial differences in equating results for different subgroups are suggestive of problems with that method.

8.4.3 Choosing from Among Results in the Random Groups Design

A general scheme for choosing from among different equipercentile smoothing results was presented in Chapter 3. Identity equating, mean equating, and linear equating can be considered as more drastic smoothing, and can be compared with unsmoothed equipercentile equating and with each other. In the discussion of postsmoothing in Chapter 3, it was suggested that a method be chosen which results in a smooth relationship without departing more than necessary (based on standard error bands) from the unsmoothed relationship. A process for choosing from among the different degrees of smoothing was described. Statistical tests were incorporated in the choice of presmoothing method. The methods that were presented depend on judgment at various stages in the process.

Statistical procedures other than those described so far in this book have been suggested for choosing from among results. Budescu (1987) and Jaeger (1981) considered statistical indices that could help in choosing between linear and equipercentile equating. Zeng (1995) developed a computerized expert system that chooses between postsmoothing results in a manner intended to mimic the procedures used by psychometricians.

Thomasson et al. (1994) presented a detailed set of heuristics for choosing among different smoothed equatings in the ASVAB program. In these procedures, statistical summary indices between the smoothed and unsmoothed relationships for different degrees of smoothing are calculated. Heuristics lead to a single relationship being chosen, based on the similarity of smoothed equating with unsmoothed equating. Graphic inspection and other judgmental procedures are used to make sure that the relationship chosen results in an apparently reasonable conversion which is consistent with previous experience.

Heuristics should be developed within the context of the testing program. Also, heuristics should not be applied blindly or followed rigidly. New wrinkles constantly are occurring. Therefore, the procedures should be flexible.

When double linking is used, a method must be chosen for combining the results from the two links. The results might be combined by first conducting the equating separately for the two links. After each equating is conducted, the results could be combined using a weighted average, and properties of this weighted average studied. If problems are detected, different combinations of results from the two links can be tried. Again, procedures should be tailored to the specific testing program.

8.4.4 Choosing from Among Results in the Common-Item Nonequivalent Groups Design

The choice among results in the common-item nonequivalent groups design is complicated further because so many sets of assumptions can be used to disconfound group and form differences. For example, in linear equating, results based on Tucker and Levine observed score method assumptions could be compared. If nonlinear methods are to be considered, IRT observed score (Chapter 6) and frequency estimation (Chapter 5) results (with various smoothing degrees and smoothing methods) can enter into the decision process. In theory, the choice of synthetic population weights is also of some concern, as was indicated in Chapter 4.

Some of the assumptions required for methods can be assessed. For example, the linearity of the regression of X on V that is required for the Tucker method could be checked (Braun and Holland, 1982, p. 25). If the regression were found to be nonlinear, the Braun-Holland (see Chapter 5) method might be used. The disattenuated correlation between X and V could be estimated. A disattenuated correlation substantially less than 1 would suggest problems with assumptions for the Levine method. IRT assumptions could be tested (see Hambleton et al., 1991).

A major problem with this design is that it is impossible to test some of the crucial assumptions. For example, no direct way exists to assess the Tucker method assumption that the regression of X on V in Population 2 is the same as the regression of X on V in Population 1. Similarly, no direct way exists to assess the Levine method assumption that the correlation between true scores for X and V equals 1 in Population 2.

The assumptions required for the methods might lead to a preference of one method over another. For example, Tucker and frequency estimation equipercentile equating might be preferred when groups are similar. When groups are very different, the Levine observed score or IRT methods might be preferred, if the assumptions for these methods hold well enough. Sample size might also affect which method would perform better in a situation. Only general guidelines can be given here: The choice among results should be made in the context of the testing program.

8.4.5 Use of Consistency Checks

When conducting equating, the consistency of current results with past results is often the most informative data for choosing a method. For example, consider the scale score means and standard deviations in Table 8.6 for Years 1 through 4. Over the period from Year 1 to Year 4, the tested

TABLE 8.6. Scale Score Means and Standard Deviations for a Hypothetical Example.

Year	Number Tested	Mean	Standard Deviation
1	1005	33.8	5.4
2	1051	33.1	5.6
3	1161	33.0	5.7
4	1192	32.8	5.8
5 (Tucker)	1210	32.5	5.9
5 (Levine Obs. Score)	1210	33.4	5.7

group became larger, overall lower achieving, and more variable. Assume that we are in Year 5. Equating has been conducted, and the scale score means and standard deviations that resulted from applying Tucker and Levine observed score equating are shown in Table 8.6. Which method gives results that appear more sensible assuming that the past results were accurate? In this case, the sample size is increasing, which is consistent with the past 4 years. Scale scores using the Tucker method have a lower mean than the previous year and a higher standard deviation that is consistent with trends over the past 4 years. The mean and standard deviation for the Levine observed score method are not consistent with this trend. Thus, the Tucker results are more consistent with past trends than are the Levine observed score results. The greater consistency of the Tucker method might lead to the choice of the Tucker method results in this situation, although the method that actually produced the most accurate results would never be known for sure.

The example in Table 8.6 is based on comparing means and standard deviations. Examining the consistency of entire score distributions can be useful, too, especially when accuracy is important all along the score scale. Also, examining the consistency of pass rates or consistency at particular important score points also can be helpful. Suppose that approximately 40% of the examinees have passed a test on previous test dates. In a current equating, 41% would pass using the Levine observed score method and 32% would pass using the Tucker method. In this case, the Levine observed score results might be preferred for consistency reasons, especially if the major uses of the test involve a passing score.

Large unexpected differences in consistency checks might suggest either quality control problems or problems with the assumptions of a particular method. When these differences are found, the implementation of the equating should be checked including the functioning of the common items (if appropriate), the execution of the equating design, and other quality control issues. Problems might have existed with past equatings, suggesting that they should be checked as well. These potential sources of problems should be examined before accepting the results from an equating.

8.4.6 Equating and Score Scales

As was indicated in Chapter 1, equating is part of a scaling and equating process. Score scales are discussed in detail in Chapter 9 where we indicate that the score scale often is chosen to facilitate score interpretation. The choice of score scale is especially important for tests in which decisions are made along a range of scores. The particular score scale is much less important if a test is used only in making pass-fail decisions, where decision consistency is crucial.

The choice of score scale affects equating. For example, in Chapter 2, rounding scale scores to integers was shown to have a significant effect on the similarity, across forms, of the scale score means, standard deviations, and other moments. Also, in Chapter 9 we discuss problems that can result when raw scores on a form are used as the score scale—in particular, raw scores become easily confused with scale scores.

Typically, rounded scale scores are reported to examinees. These rounded scores might have some properties that appear to be undesirable. For example, in ACT Assessment (ACT, 1997) equating, a conversion table might result in many number-correct scores converting to a single scale score. Also, gaps can occur in conversion tables, in which no raw score converts to a particular scale score. These occurrences can be viewed as problematic by examinees. If the scale score increment is 1 point, an examinee might justifiably question why earning 1 number-correct score less than someone else would result in a 2- or 3-point difference in scale scores. Under the assumption that gaps, and too many raw scores converting to a single scale score, would not occur except for sampling error, results for a method or degree of smoothing might be chosen that minimize these problems.

In testing programs, such as the ACT Assessment (ACT, 1997) and the SAT (Donlon, 1984, pp. 19,20), for practical reasons a number-correct score of all correct is forced to convert to the highest possible scale score, even if the equating suggests that some other score would be more appropriate. This process is used with the SAT and the ACT to ensure that the highest possible scale score can be earned on any form. However, doing so makes it easier to earn a top score on some forms than on others. For this reason, other testing programs allow the top score to differ depending on the difficulty of the form for high-scoring examinees. The effects of adjustments to the score scale and choosing methods to avoid gaps in the conversion should be evaluated on a case-by-case basis. The effects on moments and on score distributions should be carefully monitored.

8.4.7 Assessing First- and Second-Order Equity for Scale Scores

Kolen et al. (1992) described procedures that can be used to find the conditional means and standard errors of measurement using strong true score models. Kolen et al. (1996) described similar procedures that can be used with dichotomous IRT models, and Wang et al. (2000) presented procedures that can be used with polytomous IRT models. These procedures can be used to assess first- and second-order equity properties for equated scores earned on alternate forms for raw, scale, and rounded scale scores.

To apply these methods, it is necessary to assume that a particular test theory model (either strong true score model or IRT model) holds and that the model has been fit to the equated forms. The model is then used to calculate expected scores, conditional on true score (or IRT ability). The conditional expected scores, after equating, are compared across alternate forms. First-order equity is said to hold to the extent that these conditional expected scale scores are similar for the alternate forms. The model also is used to calculate standard errors of measurement, conditional on true score (or IRT ability). Second-order equity is said to hold to the extent that the conditional standard errors of measurement, after equating, are similar for the alternate forms.

Some of the necessary theory needed for the version of this approach was already presented in Chapter 6. For dichotomous IRT models, the recursion formula given in equation (6.25) can be used to find the conditional distribution of observed scores given IRT ability, which is symbolized $f(x|\theta_i)$. The mean of this distribution can calculated as

$$K\tau = \sum_{j=0}^{K} j f(X = j|\theta_i). \tag{8.1}$$

Note that this value is the true number-correct score on Form X and could have been calculated from the test characteristic curve. The conditional error variance of number-correct scores is

$$var(X|\theta_i) = \sum_{j=0}^{K} (j - k\tau)^2 f(X = j|\theta_i). \tag{8.2}$$

The square root of this variance represents the standard error of measurement of number-correct scores.

Also, assume that the transformation sc is used to transform raw scores to scale scores. The mean of the conditional distribution of scale scores given θ_i is

$$\xi(\theta_i) = \sum_{j=0}^{K} sc(j) f(X = j|\theta_i), \tag{8.3}$$

which is the true scale score for examinees with ability θ_i. By considering various values of θ_i, this equation relates true scale score to IRT ability.

Conditional measurement error variance of scale scores given θ_i is

$$var[sc(j)|\theta_i] = \sum_{j=0}^{K}[sc(j) - \xi(\theta_i)]^2 f(X=j|\theta_i). \tag{8.4}$$

The square root of this variance represents the conditional standard error of measurement of scale scores.

Equation (8.3) can be used to assess first-order equity for scale scores on alternate forms. If first-order equity holds, then the conditional scale score means would be the same on Form X and Form Y. The extent to which these conditional scale score means differ indicates the extent to which first-order equity fails to hold. Equation (8.4) can be used to assess second-order equity on alternate forms. If second-order equity holds, then the conditional scale score standard errors of measurement would be the same on Form X and Form Y. The extent to which these conditional scale score standard deviations differ indicates the extent to which second-order equity fails to hold.

Average error variance can be calculated as

$$var(E_s) = \int_\theta var[sc(j)|\theta]g(\theta)d\theta, \tag{8.5}$$

where $g(\theta)$ is the distribution of θ in the population. If this distribution is expressed using quadrature points and weights, then the integration can be accomplished by summation, as was done in Chapter 6.

Letting $\sigma^2[sc(X)]$ represent the variance of observed scale scores, an index of test reliability can be defined as

$$\rho(X, X')_{scale} = 1 - \frac{var(E_s)}{\sigma^2[sc(X)]}. \tag{8.6}$$

Reliability is defined as 1 minus the ratio of scale score error variance to scale score observed variance.

As an example of how to apply equations (8.1) through (8.4), consider the hypothetical example of the use of the recursion formula presented in Table 6.4. Given $\theta_i = -2$, the distribution of number correct scores on a three item multiple-choice test was calculated in the example. The number-correct scores of 0 to 3 are given in the first column of Table 8.7. The probabilities of earning each of these scores from Table 6.4 are given in the second column of Table 8.7. In the third column, the conditional mean is found to be .71 using equation (8.1). In the fourth column, the conditional variance is calculated as .5370 using equation (8.2).

A hypothetical raw-to-scale score conversion is given in the fifth column. In this conversion, a number-correct score of 0 is converted to a scale score

TABLE 8.7. Example Calculating Scale Score Conditional Means and Error Variances using Data From the Example in Table 6.4.

x	$f(x\|\theta_i)$	$x \times f(x\|\theta_i)$	$(x - k\tau)^2$ $\times f(x\|\theta_i)$	$sc(x)$	$sc(x)$ $\times f(x\|\theta_i)$	$[sc(x) - \xi(\theta_i)]^2$ $\times f(x\|\theta_i)$
0	.4430	0(.4430)	$(0 - .71)^2$ $\times(.4430)$	1	1(.4430)	$(1 - 2.2921)^2$ $\times(.4430)$
1	.4167	1(.4167)	$(1 - .71)^2$ $\times(.4167)$	3	3(.4167)	$(3 - 2.2921)^2$ $\times(.4167)$
2	.1277	2(.1277)	$(2 - .71)^2$ $\times(.1277)$	4	4(.1277)	$(4 - 2.2921)^2$ $\times(.1277)$
3	.0126	3(.0126)	$(3 - .71)^2$ $\times(.0126)$	7	7(.0126)	$(7 - 2.2921)^2$ $\times(.0126)$
Sum		$K\tau =$ .71	$\text{var}(X\|\theta_i) =$ .5370		$\xi(\theta_i) =$ 2.2921	$\text{var}[sc(X)\|\theta_i] =$ 1.6002

of 1, a number-correct score of 1 is converted to a scale score of 3, and so on. In the sixth column, equation (8.3) is used to calculate the mean of this conditional scale score distribution. As can be seen, each scale score is multiplied by the probability of earning that score and then summed over scale scores. In the last column, equation (8.4) is used to calculate the conditional error variance. Each scale score is subtracted from the conditional mean, the difference is squared and multiplied by the probability of earning that scale score, and the quantities are summed over scale scores. Note that the conditional standard error of measurement of scale scores is 1.2650, which is the square root of the variance given at the bottom of the last column.

As an example of an application of this methodology to real data, consider the ITBS Maps and Diagrams example from Chapter 6. The raw score distributions for this example were shown in Figure 6.13. As can be seen, Form L is more difficult than Form K. This observation suggests that Form L discriminates among examinees better at higher scores and Form L discriminates better at lower scores.

Raw-to-scale score conversions that are used operationally with Forms K and L are shown in Figure 8.2. Equipercentile equating was used to equate these forms. Consistent with Form K's being the easier form, to earn a given scale score, examinees need to earn a higher raw score on Form K than on Form L. The mean scale score is 176.6 for Form K and 176.9 for form L. The scale score standard deviations are 21.8 for Form K and 21.7 for Form L.

The computer program *POLYCSEM*, listed in Appendix B, was used to examine first- and second-order equity for these two forms using the methodology described by Kolen et al. (1996). Three-parameter logistic IRT model parameters were fit to the forms. Conditional on a set of θ-

304   8. Practical Issues in Equating

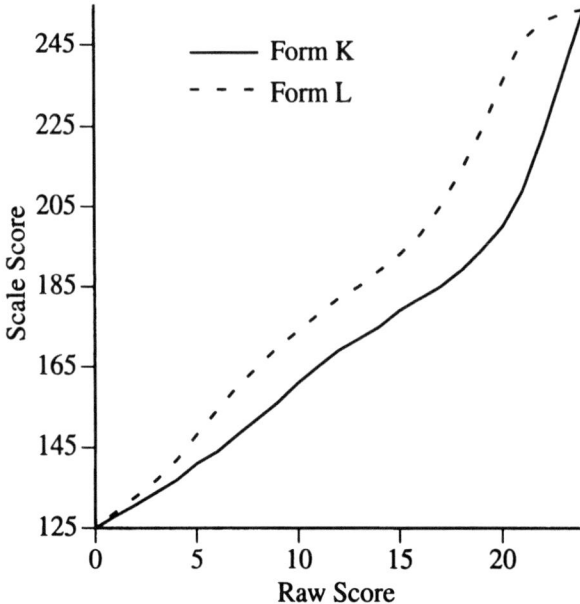

FIGURE 8.2. Raw-to-scale score conversions for Form K and Form L.

values, true scale scores were calculated for Form K using equation (8.3). Conditional on the same set of θ-values, true scale scores were calculated for Form L also using equation (8.3). In Figure 8.3, the Form K true scale scores are given along the horizontal axis and Form K true scale scores minus Form L true scale scores are given along the vertical axis. If first-order equity held perfectly, the relationship would be a line at a vertical axis value of zero. As can be seen, Form K has slightly higher true scale scores (positive vertical axis values) in the middle scores and Form L has higher true scale scores (negative vertical axis values) at the very high and low scores. Note that most of the differences are small relative to the scale score standard deviation of 21.8 for Form K and 21.7 for Form L.

Conditional scale score standard errors of measurement were calculated for each of the forms using equation (8.4) to evaluate second-order equity. These conditional standard errors of measurement are plotted in Figure 8.4. The conditional standard errors of measurement tend to be larger for Form K at the high scores, which is consistent with Form K being an easier form, and not discriminating as well as Form L at the high scores. The conditional standard errors of measurement tend to be larger for Form L at the low scores, which is consistent with Form L's being a more difficult form, and not discriminating as well as Form K at the low scores. The conditional standard errors of measurement are similar for the two forms at the middle scores. In general, these results suggest that first- and second-order equity were not well achieved with these forms.

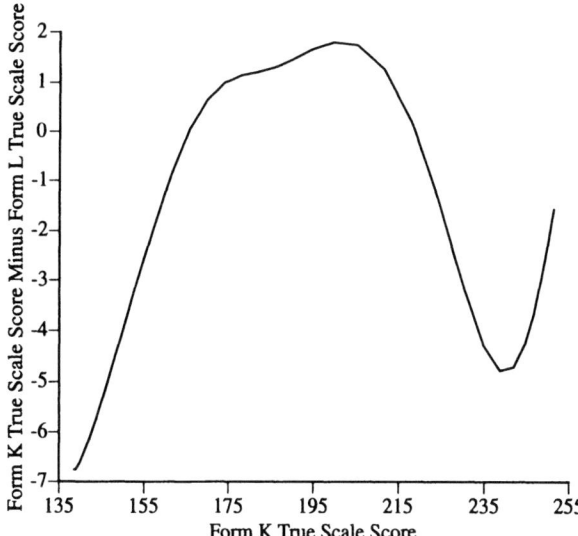

FIGURE 8.3. First-order equity plot for Forms K and L.

Given that equipercentile procedures were used, it must be the case that the scale score distributions for the two forms are similar to one another. However, as illustrated in Figure 8.3, for example, examinees with true scale scores around 195 are expected to earn scale scores on Form K that are nearly 2 points higher than those expected on Form L. Examinees with true scale scores around 150 or around 240 are expected to earn scores that are around 5 points higher on Form L than on Form K. Based on the results in Figure 8.4, examinees are measured more precisely with Form L at higher scores and more precisely with Form K at the lower scores. These observations suggest that, depending on an examinee's scale score and the purposes of the testing, certain examinees would prefer taking one test form over the other.

The large difference in raw score means between the two forms likely contributed to the finding that first- and second-order equity were not well achieved for these forms. Tong (2002) examined the first- and second-order equity properties for a number of equatings. She found that the first- and second-order equity properties held reasonably well, except when the score distributions for the forms to be equated differed markedly, as is the case with the example given in this section. Thus, first- and second-order equity can be expected to hold reasonably well when the score distributions for forms to be equated are similar to one another.

In an illustrative example, Kolen et al. (1992) examined second-order equity for ACT Assessment equatings. In one of the examples considered for the English test, they found that at high scale scores, the conditional standard errors of measurement were elevated for three of the five forms

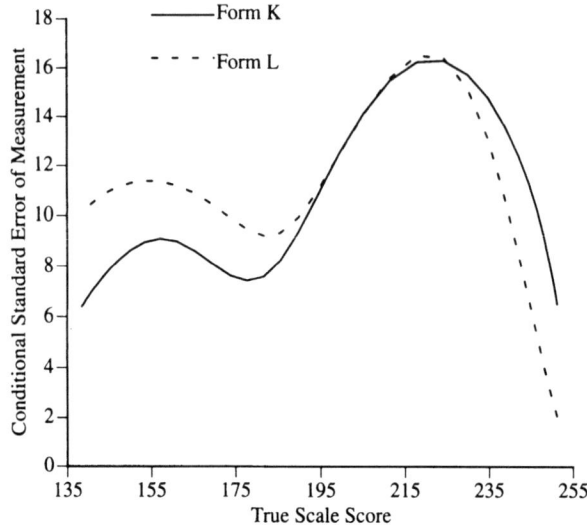

FIGURE 8.4. Second-order equity plot for Forms K and L.

examined. On reviewing the test forms, they found that these three test forms were noticeably less difficult than the other two forms. The difficulty differences resulted in gaps in the conversion tables. As a result, the concluded that "these three English forms are less capable of distinguishing among high-achieving students than the other forms" (p. 303).

As the examples considered in this section suggest, examination of first- and second-order equity provide evidence of the quality of equatings. Such an examination can provide evidence of problems in equating when the forms that are equated are significantly different from one another. For this reason, we recommend that an evaluation of first- and second-order equity be part of the equating process.

8.5 Importance of Standardization Conditions and Quality Control Procedures

For equating to be adequate, testing conditions should be standardized and quality control procedures should be followed. Otherwise, identity equating, rescaling, or scaling to achieve comparability might be the best options. Quality control procedures are vital to adequate equating, and they often take more effort than other aspects of the equating process.

8.5.1 Test Development

The following is a list of changes in how the test forms are developed that can cause problems for equating:

1. *Test specifications change.* (See Chapter 1 and previous portions of this chapter.)

2. *In a common-item nonequivalent groups design or an item preequating design, the context of the common-items changes.* For example, it could be problematic if common items appear in considerably different positions on the two forms, such as a common item appearing near the beginning of the old form and near the end of the new form (Cook and Petersen, 1987; Eignor, 1985; Kolen and Harris, 1990). Another example involves items associated with a common stimulus (such as a reading passage) that have interdependencies. If one item associated with the passage is removed from the test, other items associated with that passage might be affected. To be safe, when items associated with a common stimulus are used as common items, the set of items associated with the common stimulus on the new form should be exactly the same set of items as the items that were associated with the common stimulus on the old form. For example, the context in which common items were administered resulted in a significant scaling problem for NAEP (Zwick, 1991), as was described in Chapter 1.

3. *In a common-item nonequivalent groups design or an item preequating design, the text of the common items changes.* The text should be *exactly* the same in the old and new forms. Otherwise, the items might function differently. Minor editorial changes and rearranging of answer choices (Cizek, 1994) in items should be avoided.

8.5.2 Test Administration and Standardization Conditions

The conditions under which a test is administered should be standardized in order for tests administered at different locations and at different times to be comparable to one another. Some issues related to standardization that could have significant effects on scaling and equating include the following:

1. *Changes in the number of items on the test.* (Harris, 1987, 1988; Linn and Hambleton, 1991; Way et al., 1989).

2. *Changes in timing of the test.* Changes in timing can have a significant effect on the scores of examinees. For example, Hanson (1989) reported a study in which scores on a test were compared with scores on a lengthened version of the same test, with the testing time extended accordingly. The lengthening was accomplished by appending unscored items to the original (unlengthened) test. In this study,

scores on the lengthened test (excluding the appended items) were substantially higher than scores on the unlengthened test. (Also see Brennan, 1992, for a discussion of this study.)

3. *Changes in motivation conditions.* Studies in which a new version of a test is administered under different motivation conditions than the old version of the test. This problem occurred in the ASVAB scaling example described in Chapter 1 (see Maier, 1993). Also see Kiplinger and Linn (1996) and O'Neil et al. (1996) for discussions of how motivation affects NAEP scores.

4. *Security breaches.* Examinees are found to have had prior exposure to test forms or items that appear in the forms involved in the equating, which suggests that a security breach occurred.

5. *Changes in the answer sheet design.* These changes can affect test performance (Bloxom et al., 1993; Burke et al., 1989; Harris, 1986).

6. *Scrambling of test items for security purposes.* Sometimes, test items within forms are scrambled to discourage examinee copying. However, scrambling can affect score distributions (e.g., Harris, 1991b,d; Leary and Dorans, 1982, 1985; Kingston and Dorans, 1984). Dorans and Lawrence (1990) and Hanson (1992) developed procedures for testing whether score distributions on scrambled forms differ.

7. *Changes in the font used in printing the test or in the pagination used.* These changes can affect scores.

8. *Section preequating in which preequating and operational sections appear in different positions in different forms* (e.g., Brennan, 1992).

9. *Use of calculators.* If calculators are allowed in some administrations and not in others, then scores from administrations that allow calculators are not directly comparable to scores from administrations that do not allow calculators. In these cases, separate calculator and noncalculator norms and scales might be needed. Loyd (1991) and Morgan and Stevens (1991), for example, investigated the effects of calculators. Other similar changes in standardization conditions that might affect scores include allowing students to use dictionaries or word processors.

10. *Administration under nonstandard conditions,* such as large type, Braille, or extra time for handicapping conditions (Tenopyr et al., 1993; Abedi et al., 2000; Camara et al. 1998; Camara and Schneider, 2000; Pitoniak and Royer, 2001; Willingham et al. , 1988; Ziomek and Andrews, 1996, 1998).

Variations in standardization conditions can affect scores. The research cited suggests that such variations might lead to scores that are not comparable. The effects of variations in standardization procedures, and how to deal with them, should be considered in the context of the testing program.

8.5.3 Quality Control

Quality control checks are vital to adequate equating. They can be quite elaborate and extraordinarily time-consuming. Some of the quality control checks that can be made are as follows:

1. *Check that the test administration conditions are followed properly.* Some examples of problematic circumstances include test administrators giving examinees extra time to take the test, examinees found to be copying from one another, test administrators not spiraling the tests properly in a random groups design, and noise in test centers.

2. *The answer keys are correctly specified.* The correct key should be applied when scoring examinee records. Correctly applying answer keys requires special care when more than one form is administered and when different versions of a form exist, such as when items are scrambled for security purposes.

3. *The items appear as intended.* The text of the items, and especially the common items, should be checked.

4. *The equating procedures that are specified are followed correctly.* Typically, equating involves many interrelated steps, often necessitating the involvement of many people and the use of multiple computer programs. Without careful checking, an important step can be forgotten.

5. *The score distributions and score statistics are consistent with those observed in the past.* These consistency checks sometimes can suggest problems in scoring or data processing.

6. *The correct conversion table or equation is used with the operational scoring.* In general, the result of equating is an equation or conversion table that is supplied to whomever is to do the operational scoring. Usually, a few steps occur between the choice of the conversion and the creation of the table to be supplied. In our experience, it is vitally important to check the table or equation that is supplied against the one that was developed when the conversion was chosen.

8.5.4 Reequating

Consider a situation in which a form of a test has been administered and equated, and subsequently it is discovered that an item possesses some type of ambiguity that makes the keyed alternative technically incorrect, or that the keyed alternative is only one of two or more technically correct answers.[1] After reconsidering such an item, suppose that content matter specialists decide that the originally keyed alternative (say, a) is indeed correct, but the other alternatives (say, b, c, and d) also can be defended as correct, based on an obscure fact or facts. Clearly, decisions must be made about whether to give all examinees credit for the item and whether to reequate the form with that item scored correct for all examinees. (For the sake of this discussion, assume that even examinees who omitted the item would be given credit for it.)

Suppose that a firm decision on these matters is postponed until the form is reequated with all examinees being given credit for the item. There are then four conceivable ways to arrive at examinee "equated" scores:

1. original key applied with original equating relationship;

2. original key applied with revised equating relationship;

3. revised key applied with original equating relationship; and

4. revised key applied with revised equating relationship.

Applying the first option produces the scores that were originally reported to examinees, and essentially means acting as if the item is *not* flawed. The examinee who discovered the flaw may well consider this option to be unfair, and, in all likelihood, the public will share the examinee's concern. However, an examinee who is insightful enough to recognize such a flaw is also often insightful enough to choose the alternative that was intended as the correct answer. If so, the first option does not really treat that particular examinee unfairly, although it would be unfair for some other unidentified examinee who chose one of the other alternatives *for a correct reason*.

The second option, using the original key with the revised equating relationship, is difficult to defend under any reasonable scenario.

The third option, using the revised key with the original equating relationship, may appear to be an option that is generous to examinees. In effect, all examinees who selected alternatives b, c, or d (or omitted the item) will receive a higher "equated" score, whatever the reason for selecting that alternative. However, those examinees who are given credit unjustifiably (e.g., those who had misinformation or no information about the item) will fare better than their equally achieving counterparts, especially in a quota-based decision process. Thus, while this option is generous

---

[1] This section is largely from Brennan and Kolen (1987b, pp. 286,287).

for some examinees, that very generosity may create a potential disservice to other examinees. In evaluating the fairness or reasonableness of any of these options, it is necessary to consider the consequences for not only examinees who are directly affected, but also examinees who are indirectly affected by the decision.

The fourth option, using the revised key with the revised equating relationship, essentially avoids the problems mentioned above with the third option, and the fourth option has considerable face validity. Indeed, this appearance of face validity is almost always judged to be an overwhelming argument in favor of the fourth option.

However, under some circumstances it can be argued that the first option may well be preferable *psychometrically* to the fourth if the goal is to be as fair as possible to *all* examinees, not just those who voice a legitimate complaint. For example, when all examinees are given credit for an item, the effective test length is reduced by one item, which, on average, benefits lower achieving examinees and works to the disadvantage of higher achieving examinees. To put it another way, when all alternatives are keyed correct because an item possesses an obscure ambiguity, it is likely that many examinees will be given credit for the item who would not otherwise have answered the item correctly. This fact will cause these examinees to appear higher achieving than they actually are, and other examinees will appear lower achieving by comparison. Indeed, examinees who selected alternative a (the response originally keyed as correct) will receive a *lower* equated score under the fourth option than under the first option. Reequating cannot really eradicate these problems., Indeed, reequating can never completely remove a test development flaw; the best it can do is mitigate the impact of such a flaw.

The above points are not intended to be interpreted as arguments in favor of never rescoring or reequating when a flawed item is discovered. Even if the psychometric arguments were compelling, arguments from other perspectives could be even more compelling. Nor are these points to be interpreted as arguments about the differential utility of benefiting lower achieving examinees versus disadvantaging higher achieving examinees. When such judgments need to be made, they should be based on a much broader set of considerations than merely psychometrics. The point here is that the issues involved in rescoring and reequating are quite complex, and certain unintended negative consequences are easily overlooked. (These problems become even more complex when the flawed item is in a common-item equating section.)

If reequating is judged necessary and scores have already been reported to examinees, then questions arise about what the effects of the reequating will be on examinees' scores. Specifically, how many scores will increase, how many will decrease, and how many will stay the same? Other practical questions arise, such as should scores be reissued for examinees whose scores would decrease after reequating? In addition, what is the effect on the test specifications and on the technical properties of the test when an item is removed? Can the test with the item removed be considered to be equated? These questions often can be very difficult to answer. Brennan and Kolen (1987b) and Dorans (1986) have addressed some of these questions. Reequating also sometimes needs to be considered when a security breach occurs, in which examinees obtain answers or questions prior to a test administration. Brennan and Kolen (1987b) and Gilmer (1989) illustrated some of the consequences of security breaches on equating relationships and on examinee scores.

8.6 Conditions Conducive to Satisfactory Equating

Conditions that are conducive to a satisfactory equating can be distilled from the various practical issues in equating which have been considered in this chapter. A list of some of these conditions, which is a modified version of the list provided by Brennan and Kolen (1987b), is given in Table 8.8. This table lists many of the characteristics of testing programs that are conducive to a satisfactory equating. Satisfactory equating does not require that all of these conditions hold. However, it might be best not to equate when some of these do not hold. For example, equating could not be conducted if the tests were built to different content specifications.

8.7 Comparability Issues in Special Circumstances

Various special issues affect equating and how the results are used. In addition, situations arise that are similar to equating situations, but in which it is questionable whether or not equating can be accomplished. Some of these situations are discussed in this section.

As has been stressed, scores on alternate forms of a test can be used interchangeably only if the forms are built carefully to well-defined test specifications and adequate test equating procedures are used. The test development process is crucial to being able to use scores on test forms interchangeably. After equating, examinees are expected to earn the same scale score and be measured with the same precision, regardless of the form taken. In addition, accurate equating relationships are symmetric and approximately the same across subgroups of examinees.

Various other linking processes are used with educational tests that are not built to common specifications. These processes, which do not lead to score interchangeability, are considered in Chapter 10.

TABLE 8.8. Conditions Conducive to a Satisfactory Equating.[a]

A. General
1. The goals of equating, such as equating accuracy and the extent to which scores are to be comparable over long time periods, are clearly specified.
2. The design for data collection, the equating linkage plan, the statistical methods used, and the procedures for choosing among results, are appropriate for achieving the goals in the particular practical context in which equating is conducted.
3. Adequate quality control procedures are followed.

B. Test Development—All designs
1. Test content and statistical specifications are well defined and stable over time.
2. When the test form is constructed, statistics on all or most of the items are available from pretesting or previous use.
3. The test is reasonably long (e.g., 30 items, and preferably longer).
4. Scoring keys are stable when items or forms are used on multiple occasions.

C. Test Development—Common-Item Nonequivalent Groups Design
1. Each common item set is representative of the total test in content and statistical characteristics.
2. Each common-item set is of sufficient length (e.g., at least 20% of the test for tests of 40 items or more; at least 30 items for long tests).
3. Each common item is in approximately the same position in the old and new forms. Common-item stems, alternatives, and stimulus materials (if applicable) are identical in the old and new forms. Other item level context effects are controlled.
4. Double linking is used. One old form was administered during the same time of year as the form to be equated. One old form was administered within the last year or so.

D. Examinee Groups
1. Examinee groups are representative of operationally tested examinees.
2. Examinee groups are stable over time.
3. Examinee groups are relatively large.
4. In the common-item nonequivalent groups design, the groups taking the old and new forms are not extremely different.

E. Administration
1. The test and test items are secure.
2. The test is administered under carefully controlled standardized conditions that are the same each time the test is administered.

F. Field of Study/Training
1. The curriculum, training materials, and/or field of study are stable.

[a] Adapted from Brennan and Kolen (1987b).

8.7.1 Comparability Issues with Computer-Based Tests

Recently considerable effort has been devoted to researching, developing, and implementing computer-based tests as is reflected by the recent book length treatments of computer-based testing (Drasgow and Olson-Buchanan, 1999; Mills et al., 2002; Parshall et al., 2002; Wainer, 2000; Sands et al., 1997; van der Linden and Glas, 2000b). In this section comparability issues for computer-based fixed tests and computer adaptive tests are discussed.

Computer-Based Fixed and Randomized Tests

The computer-based test that most closely resembles traditional paper-and-pencil testing is the *computer-based fixed test*. The major difference between a computer-based fixed test and a traditional test is the administration of the test questions on computer rather than using paper-and-pencil. The basic equating designs and methods that have been described previously can be used to equate alternate test forms of these types of test. In *computer-based randomized tests*, items are randomly (sometimes stratified) from a large set of items. Equating can be conducted by IRT methods if items are precalibrated. Sometimes no equating is conducted with such tests. In this case, it is assumed that the tests are comparable because the items were randomly chosen.

Computer Adaptive Tests

Computer adaptive tests create additional equating and comparability issues. An *item pool* for a computer adaptive test is a set of items that is available to be administered to an examinee. Item pools typically are built to detailed content and statistical specifications, much in the same way that test forms have detailed content and statistical specifications in paper-and-pencil tests. In a computer adaptive test administration, an examinee is administered items that are chosen from the item pool. The choice of items to administer to an examinee is adaptive, in that the choice is made based on the examinees responses to previously administered questions. A particular examinee typically is administered only a subset of the items in the item pool. IRT typically is used as a psychometric foundation for computer adaptive testing.

The choice of items to administer to an examinee often is constrained by content and test security considerations. As a simple example of *content balancing*, consider a test that contains items from two content areas. To ensure that both content areas are represented equally on a test, the items administered to an examinee might be forced to alternate between the two content areas. To facilitate test security, item administration might also be constrained by *exposure control*, which is used to ensure that individual items are administered too often. Various procedures have been developed for content balancing and exposure control.

For test security reasons and so that examinees can be tested more than once, item pools for computer adaptive tests can be periodically replaced with alternate item pools (Drasgow, 2002; Mills and Stocking, 1996; Mills, 1999; Mills and Steffen, 2000; Stocking, 1994; Way, 1998; Way et al., 2002). Wang and Kolen (2001) addressed the question of whether scores from alternate item pools can be used interchangeably through simulation studies. They found that when pools differed systematically, such as in the number of items in the pool, scores on the resulting adaptive test were not interchangeable. For example, when the pool size was cut in half, scores from the smaller pool had more measurement error than scores on the larger pool leading to the second-order equity property not being achieved. In addition, they found that the same distributions property was not achieved when the pool size was cut in half. Wang and Kolen (2001) also found scores from item pools administered with different degrees of exposure controls were not interchangeable. Their study suggested that for scores to be interchangeable from one alternate item pool to another, the item pools should be built to the same content and statistical specifications. In addition, administration conditions, including content balancing, exposure control, and how the examinee responses are converted to scale scores, should be the same from one item pool to another for the scores are to be interchangeable.

Even when the alternate item pools are built to be as similar as possible, a subsequent equating process might be used to improve score comparability across item pools. For example, in adaptive testing with the ASVAB (Segall, 1997), two distinct item pools were developed. The pools were randomly assigned to examinees and scale scores found. Even though the IRT item parameter estimates for the two pools were on the same scale, the resulting IRT ability estimates were found to have different distributions, presumably because of differences in the items in the pools. In the ASVAB program, the differences in distributions were eliminated by using an equipercentile equating of the ability estimates on the forms. This finding illustrates that a need might exist for equating alternate adaptive test forms, even when the pools are on the same IRT scale.

With computer adaptive tests, over time new test items often need to be calibrated so that new pools can be created. Wainer and Mislevy (2000) considered a process of *on-line calibration* of new, uncalibrated items in an adaptive test, in which uncalibrated items are introduced into the pool by embedding them in operational adaptive tests. These uncalibrated items do not contribute to an examinee's score. Responses are tabulated over a sufficient number of examinees, and these responses are used to estimate item parameters. These new items then are added to the pool. An issue with adaptive testing is that, typically, examinees are administered items that are close to their ability level. In conducting on-line calibration, examinees might be administered items that are far from their ability level. The quality of the item parameter estimates from on-line calibration (or from other sources) can affect the scale scores from operational item pools that contain

316   8. Practical Issues in Equating

these items (van der Linden and Glas, 2000a). Error in estimating item parameters can affect the comparability of scores across alternate pools.

Item context effects can be a particularly difficult problem to handle in adaptive tests. Whereas with paper-and-pencil tests, item position within a test can be fixed, with adaptive tests items position can vary from one examinee to the next. These item position effects can lead to an uncontrolled source of error in test scores from computer-adaptive tests. Structuring an adaptive test by adapting by blocks of items, rather than by individual items, has been suggested as one means for helping to control position effects. In addition, the amount of review of previous responses can affect scores on adaptive tests (e.g., Lunz and Bergstrom, 1994; Stone and Lunz, 1994; Stocking, 1997; Vispoel, 1998).

In summary, comparability of scores from alternate item pools for computer adaptive tests depends on having detailed item pool specifications, administration rules that are the same from one item pool to another, and developing pools so that failure to control context effects and item parameter estimation error has similar effects across all pools. Given that most current computer adaptive tests have been operational for a short period of time, it may be that few testing programs have been able to fully develop procedures for ensuring that scores from alternate item pools are comparable. For this reason, it is important to review testing ongoing computer adaptive testing programs for threats to comparability using an outline such as the one suggested by Kolen (1999).

Comparability of Computer-Based and Paper-and-Pencil Tests

Test developers are often interest in administering operational multiple-choice tests on computers that previously had been administered in paper-and-pencil format (e.g., Eignor and Schaeffer, 1995; Lunz and Bergstrom, 1995; Segall, 1997). Wainer (1993a, 2000) discussed many of the practical issues that are involved in making this transition. Often, when such a transition is made, the tests are used operationally in both modes for some period of time. Some of the issues that should be considered are discussed below.

Test content. When scores from computer adaptive tests are used operationally along with scores from paper-and-pencil tests, differences in test content could threaten the comparability of scores from the two modes of administration. Content balancing procedures with the computer adaptive tests have been used to help ensure that the content of the paper-and-pencil and computer adaptive tests are similar (Eignor et al., 1994; Eignor and Schaeffer, 1995; Kingsbury and Zara, 1989, 1991; Luecht et al., 1996; Lunz and Bergstrom, 1995; Schaeffer et al., 1995, Segall, 1997; Stocking and Swanson, 1993; Wainer, 2000).

Test administration. Taking a test on computer can be quite a different experience for examinees than taking a paper-and-pencil test. Some of these differences are (a) ease of reading passages; (b) ease of reviewing or changing answers to previous questions; (c) speed in taking the test, and the effects of time limits on test speededness; (d) clarity of figures and diagrams; and (e) responding on a keyboard vs. responding on an answer sheet. Computer adaptive tests might lead to different test-taking strategies on the part of examinees than on paper-and-pencil tests.

In their review of computer and paper-and-pencil testing, Mazzeo and Harvey (1988) concluded that "...it is clear that test publishers need to perform separate equatings and/or norming studies when computer-administered versions of standardized tests are introduced" (p. 26), which is consistent with the standards presented in APA (1986). Some of the studies that they reviewed indicated that computer administration favors certain subgroups over others. Along these lines, Segall (1997) reported that relative to the paper-and-pencil test, the computer based ASVAB increased differences between men and women on at least one of the tests. Gallagher et al. (2000) and Parshall and Kromrey (1993) also found mode effects that had a differential effect on examinee subgroups.

Various studies have found mode of administration effects for computer-based and paper-and-pencil tests (e.g., Lee et al., 1986; Mazzeo et al., 1991; Schaeffer et al., 1993; Sukigara, 1996; van de Vivjer and Harsveldt, 1994; Vispoel et al., 1994, 1997). Other studies and reviews concluded that the constructs measured by paper-and-pencil and computer-based measures are similar (Donovan et al., 2000; Finger and Ones, 1999; Hetter et al., 1997; Mead and Drasgow, 1993; Neuman and Baydoun, 1998; Spray et al., 1989; Vispoel et al., 2001). Overall, it appears that the specific findings from these studies and reviews might depend on the aspects of mode of administration effects that were investigated and the content area of the instruments.

Mode of administration effects appear to be very complex, and likely depend on the particular testing program. For this reason, the comparability of scores should be investigated whenever scores from the two modes are to be used together. Given the mixed results of the studies of equivalence cited, the advice by Green et al. (1984) should be followed: "When a CAT [computer-administered test] is intended to be equivalent to a corresponding conventional test, the two tests are equally valid only if they have been demonstrated to yield equivalent measures" (p. 357).

Test Scoring. In adaptive testing, items typically are chosen because they are highly discriminating around provisional estimates of the examinees ability. In addition, the raw score (ability estimate) often is based on a weighted sum of the item responses. In paper-and-pencil tests, item responses typically are equally weighted in forming the raw scores. This difference in test scoring might threaten the comparability of scores between test administration modes, especially if the weighting schemes are affected by test multidimensionality.

318   8. Practical Issues in Equating

In computer adaptive testing, rules are used to estimate scores of examinees that do not complete the test. Schaeffer et al. (1998) conducted a study of the GRE in which examinees were randomly assigned to take the computer based GRE or the paper-and-pencil GRE. They found that, on average, students scored higher on the computer based GRE. They concluded that the procedure used for calculating scores for students who did not complete the computer based GRE was responsible for this difference.

Psychometric properties. The comparability of scores from the two modes of administration also are affected to the extent that their psychometric properties differ. Various procedures have been developed that can be used to help evaluate the extent to which computer based tests have similar psychometric properties (such as equity and same distribution properties) as their paper-and-pencil counterparts (e.g., Davey and Thomas, 1996; Stocking, 1994; Thomasson, 1997; Wang and Kolen, 2001).

In some testing programs, the adaptive test is constructed so the conditional standard errors of measurement are the same for the adaptive and nonadaptive version as was done with the GRE (Mills et al., 1994). However, a further equipercentile transformation was needed with the GRE Analytical test. Wang and Kolen (2001) demonstrated violations of first-order, second-order equity, cut-score equity, and same distributions properties when comparing computer adaptive and paper-and-pencil tests. The composition of the item pool and the type of scoring (number-correct versus pattern scoring) influenced the lack of comparability between the two modes of testing. van der Linden (2001) described a process in which number-correct scoring is used and the computer adaptive tests are constructed and designed so that the scores are comparable, psychometrically, to a paper-and-pencil test.

Studies used to establish score comparability. Establishing comparability of scores on computer adaptive and paper-and-pencil tests is accomplished through data collection. Statistical assumptions are made in the process of establishing comparability, and the effect of the violations on score comparability often can be checked.

The study for establishing comparability between ASVAB computer adaptive tests and paper-and-pencil tests reported by Segall (1997) used a random groups design in which large samples of examinees (over 3,000 per mode) were randomly assigned to take computer adaptive or paper-and-pencil versions. Equipercentile procedures were used to convert scores on the computer adaptive version to the paper-and-pencil scale. Potential problems with this design might occur if the tests measured different constructs or if one mode of administration favored certain subgroups over others.

The single group design in which the same examinees take both the computer adaptive and paper-and-pencil versions with order counterbalanced across examinees was used by Eignor (1993) and Eignor and Schaeffer (1995), In these studies, the single group design was used with the SAT.

A differential order effect was found. That is, the effect of first taking the computer adaptive test on the paper-and-pencil test was different than the effect of first taking paper-and-pencil test on the computer adaptive test. The same type of effects were also found in a comparability study for a licensure examination (Sykes and Ito, 1997). Differential order effects, such as these, violate the assumption of the single group design that no differential order effects exist (see Chapter 1). For these reasons, Eignor (1993) and Eignor and Schaeffer (1995) strongly recommended that the single group design not be used when studying the comparability of paper-and-pencil and computer adaptive tests. However, it seems that at least some examinees need to take the test in both modes in order to fully examine whether or not the computer adaptive and paper-and-pencil test are measuring the same construct, so that correlations can be calculated.

A variation of common item equating to an IRT calibrated item pool (see Chapter 6) has also been used. In this type of study, IRT item parameters are typically estimated based on paper-and-pencil administrations. These paper-and-pencil item parameters are then used as item parameter estimates for the item pool in the computer adaptive test. A major assumption is that the items behave the same way in a computer adaptive test as in a paper-and-pencil test. This assumption seems exceptionally strong, given the research on the effects of mode of administration on items cited earlier. This design also relies heavily on the fit of the IRT model to the data in establishing score comparability. This design was used to establish comparability for the GRE. However, because of concerns with the statistical assumptions required, Schaeffer et al. (1993, 1995) reported extensive studies of the effects of this assumption using a random groups design. In these studies, the random groups results were used to adjust the GRE Analytical score conversions that were obtained by making the assumption that the items behaved the same in the two modes. These studies also suggested that the GRE Quantitative scores based on the assumption that common items behaved the same way in the two modes were somewhat inaccurate, but not enough to warrant an adjustment. Similar studies on the National Council of State Boards of Nursing Licensure Examinations reported by Eignor et al. (1994) and Eignor and Schaeffer (1995) indicated that no adjustments were needed. A study reported by Lunz and Bergstrom (1995) also indicated that no adjustments were needed to keep pass rates the same for a professional certification test; adjustments would have been required, however, if scores were reported all along the scale.

A computer adaptive version of the SAT was linked to the paper-and-pencil SAT in a study described by Lawrence and Feigenbaum (1997). A group of examinees who had taken the paper-and-pencil operational SAT at a single administration were identified. Of those examinees who agreed to be part of the study, in a subsequent administration that took place one month later, half were assigned to take a paper-and-pencil SAT and half were assigned to take a computer adaptive SAT. The operational SAT was used as an external set of common items to link the CAT and paper-and-pencil versions that were administered in the subsequent administration. Lawrence and Feigenbaum (1997) indicated that this study had serious limitations including a lack of representativeness of the examinee groups included in the study, motivation differences, differential motivation between the CAT and paper-and-pencil examinees in the subsequent administration, and possible differential order effects, and violations of statistical assumptions used in the linking.

Overall, the research reviewed here suggests that sufficient differences between computer adaptive and paper-and-pencil tests exist that the construct measured could be affected and that various subgroups might favor one mode over another. To evaluate these threats fully, the equity properties and the equal distribution property should be checked by randomly assigning examinees to take computer adaptive and paper-and-pencil versions. In addition, when the purpose of a test is classification of examinees, classification consistency should be examined. Such data can also be used to check on the comparability of relationships with other variables and to compare subgroups. Refer to Eignor et al. (1994), Eignor and Schaeffer (1995), Lunz and Bergstrom (1995), and Segall (1997) for examples of how these properties have been checked in operational testing programs. A second data collection effort often is needed, in which the tests are administered in both modes to the same examinees, to check whether the same construct is being measured by the two modes. Analyses such as computation of disattenuated correlations can be undertaken. In addition, statistical properties of composites (e.g., Segall, 1997) can be compared across modes, and scores on tests from the two modes can be related to other measures (e.g., Gorham and Bontempo, 1996; Segall, 1997). Similar relationships would be expected to be found if the tests in the two modes are functioning similarly.

8.7.2 Comparability of Performance Assessments

From the perspective of equating, at least three characteristics distinguish performance and other alternative assessments from multiple-choice assessments. First, judges are used to score these assessments, which leads to an additional source of error. Second, often very few tasks are administered to each examinee. Third, many of the typical equating designs cannot be used. As described in this section, these characteristics greatly complicate equating of performance assessments, and in many cases make equating impossible.

Use of judges to score assessments. Whereas the scoring of multiple-choice questions is relatively straightforward, the scoring of performance assessments is subject to error by judges. Training is probably the best way to control differences in scoring among judges. In addition, various statistical procedures for adjusting for judge leniency have been developed (e.g., Braun, 1988; Congdon and McQueen, 2000; Engelhard, 1992, 1994, 1996; Fitzpatrick et al., 1998; Houston et al., 1991; Linacre, 1988; Longford, 1994; Lunz et al., 1994, Raymond and Viswesaran, 1993; Tate, 1999, 2000).

Small numbers of tasks. Often very few tasks are administered to examinees with performance and other alternative assessments, because of lengthy per-task administration times. Many authors (e.g., Baxter et al., 1992; Dunbar et al., 1991; Haertel and Linn, 1996; Linn, 1995; Wainer, 1993b) have indicated that the use of a small number of tasks results in an inadequate sample of the domain of interest. If the domain is sampled inadequately, then it is likely to have been sampled differently on alternate forms. The result of the inadequate sampling is that scores on one form cannot be used interchangeably with scores on another form, even if equating is attempted. With inadequate domain specification, certain examinee subgroups would favor certain forms and other examinee subgroups would favor other test forms (Ferrara, 1993).

For some performance assessments, the use of small numbers of tasks leads to assessments with very few raw score points being available (Ferrara, 1993; Harris et al., 1994). In studies using a test with small numbers of score points, Harris and Welch (1993) and Harris et al. (1994) found few differences between the identity function, equipercentile methods, and Rasch methods.

Equating designs. The commonly used equating designs might not be able to be used with performance and other alternative assessments. A random groups design might be difficult to implement when forms cannot be spiraled within test centers due to administration constraints. A common-item nonequivalent groups design might not be able to be implemented, either, if a content balanced common-item set cannot be developed because the tests contain too few items or if the performance assessment items cannot be reused. If two forms cannot be administered to examinees, then even the single group design cannot be used.

Equating methods. For situations where differences among judge leniency can be adequately controlled, alternate forms adequately represent the content domain, and the equating designs can be properly implemented, equating methods can be implemented. Otherwise, it might be best not to attempt to equate performance assessments.

Traditional equating methods have been used to equate performance assessments. For example, if feasible, the random groups design could be applied by randomly assigning forms to examinees. If a content representative set of common items can be developed, then the common-item nonequivalent groups design also can be used. Linear or equipercentile methods can be applied in these situations (see Harris et al., 1994; Huynh and Ferrara, 1994, for some examples).

IRT methods might also be applied using polytomous models such as those described in Chapter 6. These models, however, might require use of more test questions per examinee for stable estimation than is feasible.

For example, Fitzpatrick and Yen (2001) showed that equating is inaccurate when too few performance assessment items are included on the assessment. When using IRT methods, strategies should be developed for managing local item dependence (Ferrara et al., 1997; Yen, 1993) and assessing model fit. Harris et al. (1994) and Huynh and Ferrara (1994) compared traditional and IRT equating methods for performance. See Muraki et al. (2000) for a review of equating methods for performance assessments that emphasizes IRT methodology.

Tests that contain multiple-choice and performance assessment items. Sometimes tests contain both multiple-choice and performance assessment questions. In these situations, it is tempting to use only multiple-choice items as common items when conducting equating with a common-item nonequivalent groups design. However, such a procedure can provide an inadequate representation of group differences, especially when the group differences are not appropriately reflected by the multiple-choice items.

Mixed IRT models have been used to scale tests that contain both performance assessment (e.g., use the generalized partial credit model) and multiple-choice items (e.g., use the three-parameter logistic model) (Muraki et al., 2000). Although these models can be fit by assuming that the same dimension underlies both item types, this assumption might not hold in practice (e.g., Thissen et al., 1994; Wainer et al., 1993). Using a model in which the multiple-choice and performance assessment items measure different constructs would greatly complicate the analyses. Even if a single dimension is assumed to underlie both item types, the use of only multiple-choice items in a set of common items could lead to inadequate equating as suggested previously.

Using an external measure to adjust scores on performance assessments. For test security reasons, sometimes forms of performance and other alternative assessments cannot be administered in special equating administrations and forms cannot be reused. One approach that might be considered is to use a measure that is not constructed to be parallel to the assessment as an external set of common items. DeMauro (1992) used an external measure containing multiple-choice items to adjust scores on a performance assessment and found the procedure to be inadequate. Along these same lines, Hanson (1993) attempted to use multiple-choice items as an external common-item set and apply equating procedures. He found that the results were sensitive to the assumptions made about the relationship between the multiple-choice and performance assessments, and he concluded that the identity equating would be preferable to any of the other equatings in the situation studied. More research is needed to address the question of when external measures can be used to adjust scores. The strength of the relationship between the available measure and the performance or other alternative assessment and the extent to which the groups are nonequivalent should be investigated regarding how they affect the adjustment procedures that are developed.

Summary and future directions. Currently, there is much activity in the development of performance and other alternative assessments. Many unresolved issues exist in equating and scaling such assessments (e.g., Baker et al., 1993; Ferrara, 1993; Fitzpatrick et al., 1998; Gordon et al., 1993; Harris et al., 1994; Loyd et al., 1996; Muraki et al., 2000; Yen and Ferrara, 1997), in combining scores from performance and other alternative assessments and multiple-choice tests (Ercikan et al., 1998; Kennedy and Walsted; 1997; Rosa et al., 2001; Sykes and Yen, 2000; Thissen et al., 2001; Wilson and Wang, 1995; Wainer and Thissen, 1993), in equating when using automated essay scoring (Shermis and Burstein, 2003), and there is still some question about the conditions under which such assessments can be equated. When equating cannot be conducted, other score adjustment methods could be investigated. Methodology and procedures for addressing the comparability of alternate forms of performance and other alternative assessments are continuing to emerge.

8.7.3 Score Comparability with Optional Test Sections

On some tests, examinees can choose which sets of items they are going to take. For these tests, some of the items are taken by all of the examinees and the rest are in optional sections. Examinees choose which optional section to take, and the examinee groups that take the alternate forms typically differ in performance on the common portion. What if some optional sections are more difficult, in some sense, than other optional sections? A major issue in this situation is whether scores for examinees taking different optional sections can be equated.

If the optional sections measure different content, then the scores for examinees who take one optional section cannot be said to be equivalent to scores for examinees who take a different optional section, even after some score adjustment is attempted. The comparability problems are even more severe if examinee choice of optional sections is related to their overall level of skill or to their area of expertise.

Bradlow and Thomas (1998) outlined statistical assumptions necessary for optional sections to be consistent with IRT assumptions. They pointed out that consistency requires that the item characteristic curves for choice items be the same for examinees who choose an item as it would have been for who examinees who did not choose the item. Wang et al. (1995) had examinees respond to pairs of multiple-choice items and asked the examinees which of the items in each pair they would choose to have scored. They found that examinee choice on multiple-choice items was related to item difficulty. They also found item characteristic curves for items that students chose differed from those that students did not choose. These results suggest that choice is related to item characteristics.

In general, it seems impossible in most practical situations for scores on optional sections to be treated interchangeably. Wainer and Thissen (1994) provided a discussion of these and related issues, and concluded that choice is inconsistent with the notion of standardized testing, "unless those aspects that characterize the choice are irrelevant to what is being tested" (p. 191).

Even if it is impossible to make scores on tests involving choice interchangeable through equating, it might be possible to improve the comparability of scores using score adjustment procedures. Livingston (1988) suggested adjusting scores by linking them to the common portion of the test. Wainer et al. (1994) attempted to use a unidimensional IRT to adjust scores and encountered some serious problems. Gabrielson et al. (1995) found a relationship between task choice and student characteristics that might result in problems with adjustment procedures. However, they also concluded that these differences were not very large. In another study, Fitzpatrick and Yen (1995) concluded that IRT adjustment procedures worked well. Bridgeman et al. (1997) suggested that when choice is used it is important to adjust scores for differential difficulty of the choice items, and they provide practical guidelines that can be followed to minimize the effects of violations of assumptions for the adjustment. Allen et al. (1994a,b) showed how the results from adjustment procedures can vary depending on the assumptions made about the relationship between the common and the optional sections.

8.8 Conclusion

Equating is now an established part of the development of many tests. When conditions allow, scores from equated test forms can be used interchangeably. Equated scores for examinees can be compared even when the examinees are administered different test forms. Equating facilitates the charting of trends. Without equating, we might be unable to tell whether or not there have been trends in student achievement over time. Without equating, examinees could be advantaged by happening to be administered an easier form. Other examinees could be disadvantaged by happening to be administered a more difficult form. Effective equating results in tests being more useful for making many decisions and for making the process of testing more equitable.

As has been discussed in this chapter, equating requires that many practical issues be considered by the individual conducting the equating. How these issues are handled can have profound effects on the quality of the equating. The test construction process that is followed and how the equating study is designed are crucial to adequate equating. If problems exist with the test construction or with the data, then no amount of statistical manipulation can lead to adequate equating results. In this sense, the design of tests and the design of data collection are of central concern. In addition, thorough quality control procedures need to be implemented for the equating to be successful. Even though the ideal equating likely has never been conducted in practice, adequate equating requires that practical issues be effectively handled. Otherwise, it might be best not to even attempt to conduct equating. The diversity of practical issues, and deciding how to address them, is what makes the practice of equating so challenging.

As we have seen in Chapters 2–7, the statistical and psychometric techniques involved in equating are diverse and require considerable statistical sophistication to understand. These techniques have evolved considerably in recent years, and likely will continue to do so. From a psychometric perspective, equating is a rich area because it draws from a wide variety of psychometric theories, such as congeneric test theory, strong true score theory, and IRT. Equating provides for an application of these theories to an important practical problem.

The field of testing currently is undergoing significant change. Many major testing programs are incorporating alternatives to the paper-and-pencil multiple-choice tests that have dominated much of standardized testing for the past 50 years or so. One set of alternatives includes tests that require examinees to produce written and verbal responses to tasks. These responses often are scored by judges, although procedures also are being developed for machine scoring. In addition, many testing programs are implementing testing in which examinees can take a test at almost any time, rather than having to take the test on one of a few test dates. Often, this type of testing involves computer administration. Such on-demand testing creates new issues in test security, development, quality control, equating, and score comparability. All of these changes in testing are causing psychometricians to reevaluate the concepts of equating and score comparability.

8.9 Exercises

8.1. Assume that scores on Forms X and Y are normally distributed and that the forms were administered using a random groups design. Also assume that the forms differed by .1 standard deviation unit at a z-score of .5.

   a. What sample size would be required for linear equating to be preferable to the identity equating at this z-score?

   b. What sample size would have been required for linear equating to be preferable to the identity equating at this z-score if the forms had differed by .2 standard deviation unit at a z-score of .5?

   c. Describe a practical situation where it would make sense to ask these questions.

8.2. The single link plans in Figure 8.1 each have a definable pattern that could be used to extend the pattern indefinitely. For example, consider Single Link Plan 1. For Form C and following, forms are linked to the form that was administered in the same time of the preceding year.

   a. Provide a verbal description for Single Link Plan 4 in Figure 8.1. (Hints: Different statements are needed for even-numbered and odd-numbered years. Begin the description with Form D.)

   b. Using this description, indicate to which form each of Forms K, L, M, and N would link.

8.3. Suppose that a psychometrician recommended Single Link Plan 4 in Figure 8.1 for equating in a testing program and subsequently found out that it was not possible to link to a form from the previous administration. In particular, suppose that in Single Link Plan 4, Form E could not link to Form D, and Form I could not link to Form H. The psychometrician developed two modified plans. In Modified Plan 1, Form E linked to Form B and Form I linked to Form F. In Modified Plan 2, Form E linked to Form C and Form I linked to Form G.

   a. Provide verbal descriptions for Modified Plan 1 and Modified Plan 2.

   b. Indicate to which forms Forms K, L, M, and N would link to in the two modified plans. (Try drawing a figure illustrating the plan.)

   c. Evaluate Modified Plans 1 and 2 with regard to the four rules for developing equating plans.

8.4. Consider the example using consistency checks in Table 8.6. Based on consistency checks the results for which method should be chosen if the number tested had been 1,050 instead of 1,210? Why?

8.5. A test has been previously administered in a paper-and-pencil mode. The test now is to be administered by computer. The computer version is built to exactly the same content specifications as the paper-and-pencil test. All items that were administered in the paper-and-pencil mode have item parameters that have been estimated using an IRT model. The computerized version is constructed using some items that had been previously administered in the paper-and-pencil mode and some items that are new. Suppose the paper-and-pencil and computerized versions are being equated.

   a. How could a random groups design be implemented in this situation?

b. How could a common-item equating to an IRT calibrated item pool design be implemented?

c. What are the limitations of each design?

d. How might context effects influence the common-item equating to an IRT calibrated item pool design in this situation?

e. Which design is preferable?

8.6. List as many causes as you can think of for common items to function differently on two testing occasions. Be sure to consider causes having to do with changes in the items themselves, changes in the examinees, and changes in the administration conditions.

8.7. Assume you are creating an equating design for a testing program. Some of the characteristics of the program are as follows:

   I. Form A was the first form of the test and was scaled previously. Form B is to be equated to Form A. For practical reasons, the equating must be conducted during an operational administration. Each examinee can take only one form.

   II. The test to be equated is a reading test. Each test form consists of three reading passages, with each passage being from a different content area (science, humanities, and social studies). There are 15 items associated with each passage. Testing time is 45 minutes.

   III. It will be easy to get large numbers of examinees to participate in the study.

   IV. Various different decisions are made using this test, so it is important that equating be accurate all along the score scale.

   Which equating design should be used—single group with counterbalancing, random groups, or common-item nonequivalent groups? Why? Which equating method should be used—equipercentile, or linear? Why?

8.8. Show that the conditional number-correct score mean in Table 8.8 could also be calculated using the test characteristic curve by Equation 6.16 as the sum of the probabilities of correctly answering each of the 3 items. (Hint: obtain the probabilities from Table 6.4.) Why does this work?

8.9. Note that the conditional variance of number-correct scores is the variance of a compound binomial distribution, which can also be calculated as $\sum_{j=1}^{K} p_{ij}(1-p_{ij})$, where p_{ij} is the probability of an examinee with ability θ_i correctly answering item j. Show that the conditional variance using this formula for the example in Table 8.7

gives conditional variance of number-correct scores. (Hint: obtain the probabilities from Table 6.4.) Why does this work?

9
Score Scales

As discussed briefly in Chapter 1, *scaling* is the process of associating numbers or other ordered indicators with the performance of examinees. These numbers and ordered indicators are intended to reflect increasing levels of achievement or ability. The process of scaling results in a *score scale*. The scores that are used to reflect examinee performance are referred to as *scale scores*. The term *primary score scale* is used here to describe the scale that is used to underly all psychometric operations. In testing programs that equate alternate forms, scores typically are reported on the primary score scale and equating is used to ensure that scores have the same meaning regardless of the test form taken. As suggested in Chapter 1, the primary score scale is typically developed for an initial form. Subsequently developed forms are equated to an earlier form and then linked to the primary score scale.

Many testing programs also use what Petersen et al. (1989) referred to as *auxiliary score scales* to enhance the meaning of the primary scale scores. Auxiliary score scales provide information to test users about examinee performance that goes beyond information incorporated in the primary score scale. Percentile ranks for various groups of examinees are widely used auxiliary score scales. Other types of auxiliary score scales include performance levels (e.g., basic, proficient, and advanced), normal curve equivalents, and percentage correct scores. Score scales that are used with a test can influence the usefulness of the resulting scores.

By using an equating process, score scales enable the comparison of individuals who take different forms of a test. Score scales can be developed so that the performance of an examinee can be readily compared to examinees nationwide. For example, by setting the nationwide mean scale score equal to 60, the scale score reported to an examinee indicates whether that examinee is above or below the nationwide mean. Alternatively, the score reported to an examinee might directly indicate that the examinee is above the level of *proficient* that was set by a panel of subject matter experts. The use of score scales along with an equating process also allows the tracking of trend in group performance over time.

In some situations, a test is part of a *test battery* – a set of tests developed together. In these cases, score scales can be developed that allow statements about an individual's strengths and weaknesses across these tests. Suppose, the national mean is set to 60 for all of the tests in a battery. Relative to the national norm group, an examinee who scores substantially above 60 in mathematics and substantially below 60 in English could be said to be stronger in mathematics than in English as measured by the tests in the battery. Also, scales for a battery can facilitate computation of composite scores across tests.

In some testing programs, such as *elementary achievement test batteries*, interest is in tracking growth of individuals, say, from one grade to another. In these situations, a *developmental score scale* can be constructed to allow for comparisons of scores earned on test levels differing in difficulty.

When developing score scales, procedures are used to associate examinee performance on the test with the scale scores reported to examinees. Typically, raw scores, such as the number-correct scores on a test consisting of dichotomously scored items, are calculated. Then these raw scores are transformed to scale scores. For some scales, linear transformations are used. For other scales, the transformations are nonlinear. In either case, test developers make decisions about the particular numbers to use and the form of the transformation of raw scores to scale scores.

In this chapter, the development of score scales on a single test and for test batteries is discussed. The section begins by considering different perspectives on constructing score scales. Linear and non-linear transformation are considered, including normalizing scores. Procedures for incorporating information from norming and standard setting studies into a score scale are discussed. Also, procedures for using score precision information to help decide on the number of scale score points and the form of the raw-to-scale score transformation are described. Issues associated with maintaining score scales over time and scales for batteries and composites are discussed. The chapter concludes with a lengthy consideration of developmental vertical scaling. Numerical examples are used to illustrate most of the methodology that is introduced.

9.1 Scaling Perspectives

A variety of score scales and methods for constructing them have been used. The choice of score scale can significantly influence the meaning attached to scores and the types of interpretations made.

Attempts have been made to use a psychometric model to drive the development and scaling of measurement instruments. Thurstone (1925) developed one of the first psychometric scaling models. The use of his psychometric model led to a process for choosing items as well as a process for assigning scale scores to individuals. In later work, Thurstone (1928) made claims about the equality of units of measurement. Guttman's (1944) model for scaling attitude items and individuals led to the choice of items and the assignment of scale scores to individuals. His method included criteria to determine whether a scale could be constructed, and it focused on appropriately rank ordering examinees and placing individuals and items on the same scale.

The Rasch (1960) model has been used to scale achievement test data. In discussing scaling from the perspective of the Rasch model, Wright (1977) stated,

> When a person tries to answer a test item the situation is potentially complicated. Many forces might influence the outcome—too many to be named in a workable theory of the person's response. To arrive at a workable position, we must invent a simple conception of what we are willing to suppose happens, do our best to write items and test persons so that their interaction is governed by this conception, and then impose its statistical consequences upon the data to see if the invention can be made useful. (p. 97)

As suggested by this statement and by the brief discussion of the Thurstone and Guttman models, the focus of instrument development and scaling in this approach is on fitting a model, with the benefit that the model can be used to make various predictions about the behavior of individuals. With this approach, the use of the scale to facilitate interpretation of scale scores occurs only after a scale is developed that adequately fits the model.

Stevens' (1946, 1951) well-known theory of scaling provides a framework for understanding scales. Stevens (1946, 1951) classified scales as being nominal, ordinal, interval, or ratio. Suppes and Zinnes (1963) further developed the scaling theory described by Stevens, and a summary of their theory is provided by Coombs et al. (1970, pp. 7–19). This theory requires that relationships among individuals on the attribute be clearly and unambiguously defined. The scaling process is used to associate numbers to appropriately reflect levels of the attribute.

The attributes being measured by educational and psychological tests, however, are not well enough defined to be scaled using this theory. In discussing intelligence tests, Coombs et al. (1970, p. 17) stated that, because "no measurement theory [of this type] for intelligence is available ... no meaning [from the perspective of this measurement theory] can be given" to the scores from intelligence tests. From this point of view, until the educational and psychological constructs that are measured by tests are better defined, the scales that are used with these constructs cannot be classified according to this scaling theory.

Fitting psychometric models like those of Thurstone (1925), Guttman (1944), and Rasch (1960) to test data is not sufficient to make claims about the scale properties (e.g., ordinal or interval) based on this scaling theory. There is no reason to believe, for example, that scores that arise from fitting a Rasch model to achievement test data are on an interval scale based on the scaling theory of Stevens (1946) and Suppes and Zinnes (1963).

If the scaling models do not lead to scores that have particular scale properties in terms of this scaling theory, then how can a decision be made about what scale to use? In discussing this issue, Angoff (1971) stated that score scales have been "defined to have approximately equal units in some special sense. For example, they have been defined in terms of a particular group of individuals, either with or without a transformation of distribution shape" (p. 510). He cited the following 1950 personal communication with Frederic Lord:

> The claim for equality of score units can no longer be justified on an external operational basis. Such score scales can be said to have equal units of ability only if we are willing arbitrarily to define the ability in terms of the scale itself. However, such a definition of ability, while not indefensible, cannot hope to be generally accepted since the units of ability would vary with the group tested as well as with the choice of the measuring instrument. (p. 510)

Angoff (1971) provided another 1950 personal communication from Lord:

> Problems arise in mental measurements either because (a) experts cannot agree on a clear operational definition of the ability to be measured or (b) the ability is defined in terms of operations for which the symbolic processes of addition or multiplication can be given no useful operational meaning. Any set of measurements can be expressed in terms of a scale with equal units, in some sense, if only we can agree on a definition in operational terms of what is meant by equality. (p. 511)

Thus, given the current state of knowledge about educational and psychological attributes, scales can be developed and treated as if the scores are "equal interval" in "some sense." However, from the perspective of scaling theory, there is little that can be done to help decide whether one scale is more "equal interval" than another scale.

Individuals writing from an IRT perspective have made similar points. As stated by Yen (1986),

> It is important for educators and test developers to acknowledge that until the achievement traits are much more adequately defined, it is not possible to develop measurement scales that are linearly related to such traits. In fact, it appears impossible to provide such trait definition. Test users are therefore left to use other criteria to choose the best scale for a particular application; choosing the *right* scale is not an option. It is important that any choice of scale be made consciously and that the reasons for the choice be carefully considered. (p. 314)

Yen (1986) also stated that, "IRT does not offer a simple answer to the question of what is the best method for scaling educational achievement tests" (p. 322).

When IRT methods are used as a psychometric foundation for test analysis, scales other than the IRT θ-scale are often found to be more useful for score reporting. In considering scores to report in a testing program that uses IRT, Bock et al. (1997) stated,

> Educational measurement, insofar as it refers to measuring the extent to which a student or group of students, has mastered some area of content or skill, does not fit comfortably within the trait concept. Measurement in this context is better conceived of as testing student performance on a sample of tasks from the area for the purposes of predicting the extent of satisfactory performance in the area as a whole. The concept is that of domain mastery, and the domain score, expressed as a percentage, is the index of the proportion of the domain mastered. (p. 197)

They also discussed how it might be advantageous to convert the IRT θ-scale to an index of the proportion of the domain mastered (also see Pommerich et al., 1999). Similarly, Lord (1975) stated, "the θ scale seems inadequate for many tests" (p. 216).

Lord (1980, p. 84) demonstrated that even if a three-parameter logistic model fits a particular set of test data, a nonlinear transformation of the θ scale also fits the data. In certain situations, the nonlinear transformation can be argued to be a more realistic metric for expressing proficiency than the θ scale. A somewhat simplified version of Lord's demonstration follows.

Let θ be the proficiency scale for the three-parameter logistic model. From equation (6.1), the probability that person i will correctly answer item j is

$$p_{ij} = p_{ij}(\theta_i, a_j, b_j, c_j) = c_j + (1 - c_j)\frac{\exp[Da_j(\theta_i - b_j)]}{1 + \exp[Da_j(\theta_i - b_j)]},$$

where the terms in the equation were defined in Chapter 6. Define a transformed variable $\theta^* = g(\theta) = \exp(\theta)$ and define a transformed item difficulty $b^* = \exp(b)$. From the laws of exponents and a substitution, note that

$$\exp[Da_j(\theta_i - b_j)] = \{\exp[\theta_i - b_j]\}^{Da_j} = \left\{\frac{\exp[\theta_i]}{\exp[bj]}\right\}^{Da_j} = \left\{\frac{\theta_i^*}{b_j^*}\right\}^{Da_j}.$$

Substituting this expression into equation (6.1),

$$p_{ij}(\theta_i^*; a_j, b_j, c_j) = c_j + (1 - c_j)\frac{\left\{\frac{\theta_i^*}{b_j^*}\right\}^{Da_j}}{1 + \left\{\frac{\theta_i^*}{b_j^*}\right\}^{Da_j}}.$$

As Lord (1980) pointed out, there is no compelling psychometric reason to prefer the θ parameterization to the θ^* parameterization. Zwick (1992, p. 209) and Mislevy (1987, p. 248) made similar observations.

Thus, even if a psychometric model holds in a particular test area, developing tests from the perspective of the psychometric model cannot provide an answer to the following question: What scale should be used for reporting scores? Even if the model holds, nonlinear transformations of the scale that is produced by the model may be preferable to the original scale.

Petersen et al. (1989) suggested that the "the usefulness of a primary score scale depends in its fulfilling two important goals: facilitating meaningful inferences and minimizing misinterpretations and unwarranted inferences" (p. 222). Following this reasoning, a score scale should be used that best facilitates the primary uses to which the scale is to be put. In constructing a test, its major purposes are considered, it is constructed to achieve these purposes as well as possible, and a scale is developed to help support these purposes.

In constructing a test, it is important that the scaling process support the test purposes rather than drive its development. According to Lindquist (1953),

A good educational achievement test must itself define the objective measured. This means that the method of scaling an educational achievement test should not be permitted to determine the content of the test or to alter the definition of objectives implied in the test. From the point of view of the tester, the definition of the objective is sacrosanct; he has no business monkeying with that definition. The objective is handed down to him by those agents of society who are responsible for decisions concerning educational objectives, and what the test constructor must do is to attempt to incorporate that definition as clearly and as exactly as possible into the examination that he builds. (p. 35)

Thus, scaling methods that involve removing items from an achievement test that do not fit a particular statistical model would go against the perspective of Lindquist (1953).

When developing score scales, normative or content-related information is often built into the scale. For example, the mean scale score might be set at a score of 60 for a nationally representative group of examinees. In discussing the incorporation of normative information, Flanagan (1951) noted that "if much information is built into the score itself, continual use makes its interpretation more and more direct and immediate" (p. 743). Gardner (1962) also made a strong case for incorporating normative information into score scales as a means of aiding interpretation of the scores, and Ebel (1962) advocated incorporating content meaning.

Angoff (1962) pointed out, however, that the normative meaning incorporated at the time a score scale is constructed becomes obsolete over time for two reasons. First, after the passage of time, the norm group that was used to set the scale becomes of little interest. Suppose the mean test score increases over time on a test originally normed to have a mean of 60. Test users might be tempted to interpret a score of 61 as being "above average," even if the current mean was, say, 63.5. Thus, building normative information into the scale might result in confusion among test users. According to Angoff (1962), "what is suggested here is a non-normative scale—a scale that has no normative meaning at all" (p. 30). Based on this reasoning, Angoff (1962) stated that, "these principles can be stated here: *One*, that the meaning that is invested in a scale at the time of its definition is not lasting; indeed, there is some question whether it is useful. *Two*, that a scale has a reasonable chance of being meaningful to a user if it does not change" (p. 32). In discussing these issues, Lindquist (1953) presented many of the points made by Angoff (1962), but indicated that "this point of view is not my own, it is not one by which I would abide in practice" (p. 38).

The perspective followed in the present chapter is consistent with that taken by Petersen et al. (1989), who stated that "the main purpose of scaling is to aid users in interpreting test results" (p. 222). They stressed "the importance of incorporating meaning into score scales as a primary means of enhancing score interpretability" (p. 222). Following this perspective, meaning is incorporated into the primary score scale to the greatest extent possible, with auxiliary score scales incorporating additional meaning not incorporated into the primary score scale. In addition to being used to incorporate meaning, the primary score scale is used as a reference scale for the purposes of equating alternate forms and for displaying the auxiliary score scales.

9.2 Score Transformations

Raw scores, such as number-correct scores, proportion correct, or percent correct, are often calculated in the process of calculating an individual's score on a test. Although raw scores may be easy to calculate, often they have serious limitations as primary scale scores for a test. One problem with raw scores is that they depend on the items in a particular form of a test. As discussed in Chapter 1, if raw scores are used for reporting scores on alternate forms, then examinees who are administered an easier form of the test will tend to earn higher scores than examinees who are administered a more difficult form. The use of raw scores as primary scale scores can lead to confusion on tests when scores on alternate forms are equated. Table 1.1 illustrates hypothetical conversion tables for three test forms. Suppose raw scores on Form Y were used as the primary score scale, rather than the scale scores that are shown. In this case, after equating, a raw score of 27 on Form X_1 would be converted to a Form Y raw score of 26. An examinee who was administered Form X_1 and scored 27 might wonder why 1 point was being subtracted from the raw score of 27. This sort of confusion is bound to occur whenever raw scores are used as primary scale scores when there are alternate forms of a test. Scale scores other than raw scores need to be chosen to prevent this sort of misinterpretation.

Sometimes the test construction process is viewed as sampling items from a well-defined domain of items (Ebel, 1962; Nitko, 1984), especially for tests that are curriculum based. In this case, a proportion-correct raw score might be viewed as a reasonable estimate of an examinee's proportion correct in that domain. Such scores are often useful as auxiliary score scales when the domain of items can be clearly represented to test users. However, these scores can cause confusion as primary score scales when alternate forms of a test exist and proportion-correct scores might be confused with percentile ranks.

Because of the limitations of raw scores as primary scale scores, typically raw scores are transformed to scale scores that are different from raw scores on any particular form. Sometimes the conversions used are linear in form. More often, the transformations are nonlinear. In the process of developing a score scale, typically, the transformation is chosen to make it easier for test users to interpret test scores. Test use can be facilitated by incorporating normative, score precision, and content information into the score scale.

9.3 Incorporating Normative Information

Normative information can be used to enhance the interpretability of scale scores (Flanagan, 1951; Gardner, 1962; Lindquist, 1953). The process of incorporating normative information begins with administering the test to a group of examinees, referred to as the *norm group*. Summary statistics from the administration are used to help set the score points for an initial form of the test. The raw scores can be transformed using linear or nonlinear transformations.

9.3.1 Linear Transformations

As discussed in Chapter 2, a linear raw-to-scale score transformation can be used if the mean and standard deviation of the scale scores are specified and the mean and standard deviation of the raw scores are calculated for the norm group. In this case, the transformation was given as

$$sc(y) = \frac{\sigma(sc)}{\sigma(Y)} y + \left[\mu(sc) - \frac{\sigma(sc)}{\sigma(Y)} \mu(Y) \right],$$

where $\mu(Y)$ and $\sigma(Y)$ are the mean and standard deviations of raw scores in the norm group and $\mu(sc)$ and $\sigma(sc)$ are the desired mean and standard deviation of the scale scores. In the example given in Chapter 2, $\mu(Y) = 70$ and $\sigma(Y) = 10$ for a national norm group. The desired scale score mean is $\mu(sc) = 20$ and the desired scale score standard deviation is $\sigma(sc) = 5$, so

$$sc(y) = \frac{5}{10} y + \left[20 - \frac{5}{10} 70 \right] = .5y - 15.$$

For example, an examinee with a raw score of 50 would receive a scale score of 10 using this equation. If an equating process was followed with subsequent test forms, any examinee with a scale score above 20 would be above the mean of the national norm group.

Instead of specifying the mean and standard deviation of scale scores, specification of scale score equivalents of two raw score points also can define a line. Defining y_1 and y_2 as two raw score points and $sc(y_1)$ and $sc(y_2)$ as the desired scale score equivalents of these two points,

$$sc(y) = \left[\frac{sc(y_2) - sc(y_1)}{y_2 - y_1} \right] y + \left\{ (sc(y_1)) - \left[\frac{sc(y_2) - sc(y_1)}{y_2 - y_1} \right] y_1 \right\}, \quad (9.1)$$

defines a linear raw-to-scale score equivalent. For example, suppose that for the norm group just considered, the mean scale score is intended to be 20, and a raw score of 0 is intended to equal a scale score of 1. In this case,

$$sc(y) = \left[\frac{20-1}{70-0}\right] y + \left\{1 - \left[\frac{20-1}{70-0}\right] 0\right\} = .2714y + 1.$$

For example, an examinee with a raw score of 50 would receive a scale score of 14.57.

At times, it might be desirable to specify one scale score equivalent and the standard deviation of the scale scores. In this case, let y_1 be a raw score and $sc(y_1)$ be its scale score equivalent. Taking $\sigma(sc)$ as the desired scale score standard deviation,

$$sc(y) = \frac{\sigma(sc)}{\sigma(Y)} y + \left[sc(y_1) - \frac{\sigma(sc)}{\sigma(Y)} y_1\right]. \tag{9.2}$$

For example, suppose that for the norm group just considered, a raw score of 50 is intended to convert to a scale score of 20, and the scale score standard deviation is intended to be 5 points. In this case,

$$sc(y) = \frac{5}{10} y + \left[20 - \frac{5}{10} 50\right] = .5y - 5.$$

9.3.2 Nonlinear Transformations

To aid score interpretation, the scores that result from the linear transformation procedures just described often are rounded to integers, as was discussed in Chapter 2. The rounded scale scores are symbolized as $sc_{int}(y)$. In the example described earlier where $sc(y = 50) = 14.57$, $sc_{int}(y = 50) = 15$. Sometimes, scale scores are rounded to values other than integers, such as to the 10's place. For example, SAT scores are reported with a 0 in the units place. Another fairly simple linear transformation is to truncate the raw-to-scale score transformation at a specified point. Truncation was discussed in Chapter 2. In the earlier example where $sc(y) = .5y - 15$, it might be desirable to truncate the transformation so that scale scores below 1 are set to 1. So, for example, the scale score equivalent of a Form Y score of 10 would be set to 1.

Sometimes, more complex nonlinear transformations are used. One often-used nonlinear transformation involves transforming scores so that they have a particular distributional shape, at least approximately. The normal distribution is one commonly used distributional shape. Traditionally, normalized scores were constructed graphically using procedures such as those described by Angoff (1971, pp. 515 – 519). However, the process for normalizing scores can be accomplished using more modern techniques, as follows, based on data from a sample of examinees:

1. Find the relative frequency distribution of scores, $\hat{g}(y)$.

2. As an optional step, smooth the relative frequency distribution using a smoothing method such as the polynomial log-linear method described in Chapter 3.

3. Find the percentile ranks of the smoothed distribution, and refer to these as $\hat{Q}(y)$.

4. Find the particular score in a unit normal distribution for which the proportion $\hat{Q}(y)/100$ of the scores lie below the particular score. Refer to this score as z. That is, find z such that

$$\Phi(z) = \hat{Q}(y)/100 = \frac{1}{\sqrt{2\pi}} \int_{-\infty}^{z} e^{-w^2/2} dw. \qquad (9.3)$$

5. Transform z to have a particular mean and standard deviation for the sample using a linear transformation, $sc(y) = \sigma(sc)z + \mu(sc)$, where $\mu(sc)$ is the desired mean and $\sigma(sc)$ is the desired standard deviation.

6. Round the resulting scale scores to integers, producing $sc_{int}(y)$.

Following these steps leads to scale scores that are approximately normal with a specified mean and standard deviation. McCall (1939) suggested using what he referred to as T-scores, which are approximately normally distributed integer scores with mean of 50 and standard deviation 10. Intelligence test scores (IQ scores) typically are normalized scores with a mean of 100 and a standard deviation of 15 or 16 for a national norm group (Angoff, 1971, pp. 525,526). Stanines (Flanagan, 1951, p. 747) are normalized integer scores that range from 1 to 9 with an approximate mean of 5 and a standard deviation of 2 for the reference group. Normal curve equivalents (NCE scores) are normalized scores reported as integers with an approximate mean of 50 and standard deviation of 21.06 for a nationally representative norm group (Petersen et al., 1989, p. 227). NCE scores are often used in evaluations of federally funded educational programs.

As pointed out by Petersen et al. (1989), "usually there is no good theoretical reason for normalizing scores. Observed scores are not usually normally distributed ..., and there is often reason to expect test score distributions to be nonsymmetric (pp. 226,227). According to Petersen et al. (1989), "the advantage of normalized scores is that they can be interpreted by using facts about the normal distribution. For example, a scale score that is one standard deviation above the mean has a percentile rank of approximately 84 in the reference group" (p. 227).

Percentile ranks for various examinee groups are nonlinear transformations that are often used as auxiliary score scales. For example, percentile ranks might be reported for an entire national norm group. Separate percentile ranks might be reported for a national group of males, a national group of females, national groups of examinees from various racial/ethnic classifications, and groups from various geographical regions. In addition, percentile ranks might be reported for different groups of examinees who take a test. Each of these sets of percentile ranks can be viewed as auxiliary score scales that can be used to enhance the meaning of the information reported.

9.3.3 Example: Normalized Scale Scores

An example of how to normalize scores to create a primary score scale is presented in Table 9.1. The data for this example are the Form K ITBS Maps and Diagrams data used in Chapter 6. The first column of Table 9.1 gives the raw scores, ranging from 0 to 24; the second column, the frequencies observed in the sample; and the third column, the relative frequencies. As suggested in the steps for normalizing, the data were smoothed. Smoothing was conducted using the log-linear method of Chapter 3 using a C-parameter of 4. The fourth column gives the relative frequencies of the smoothed distribution; the fifth column, the relative cumulative frequencies of the smoothed distribution; and the sixth column, the percentile ranks of the smoothed distribution.

To normalize the distribution, scores were transformed using equation (9.3). The z-scores are shown in the seventh column. For example, a raw score of 14 has a percentile rank in the smoothed distribution of 46.82, as can be seen in Table 9.1. Using equation (9.3), or a normal curve table, the z-score with a percentile rank of 46.82 is $-.0797$, which is the value shown in seventh column in the table. All of the values in the column labeled z can be found similarly. The effect of this transformation is to make the transformed distribution approximately normal.

Refer to Figure 9.1, which is the smoothed raw score distribution. This distribution is negatively skewed. The distribution of z-scores is shown in Figure 9.2. Note that the relative frequency values are all the same in Figure 9.2 and Figure 9.1. The effect of the transformation is to compress the distance between the score points in the middle of the distribution and expand the distances at the upper and lower scores. This expansion is greater at the upper scores than at the lower scores, resulting in a transformed distribution in Figure 9.2 that is more nearly symmetric than the original raw score distribution in Figure 9.1.

Summary statistics for the raw and transformed scores are shown in the first two rows of Table 9.2. The skewness index for the raw scores was negative and the kurtosis index is well below the kurtosis for a normal distribution, which is 3. Note that for the z-scores, the skewness is near 0 and the kurtosis near 3, which is to be expected for scores that are approximately normally distributed. Note also that the mean of the z-scores is near 0 and the standard deviation near 1, also as expected for z-scores. The discreteness of the score distribution causes the z-scores to

TABLE 9.1. Calculating Normalized Scores.

Y	$N\hat{f}(y)$	$\hat{f}(y)$	$\hat{f}(y)$ Smooth	$\hat{F}(y)$ Smooth	$\hat{P}(y)$ Smooth	z
0	1	.0004	.0004	.0004	.02	−3.5617
1	5	.0019	.0014	.0018	.11	−3.0691
2	15	.0058	.0040	.0058	.38	−2.6723
3	21	.0081	.0087	.0145	1.01	−2.3219
4	24	.0093	.0156	.0301	2.23	−2.0088
5	65	.0252	.0236	.0537	4.19	−1.7291
6	82	.0318	.0316	.0853	6.95	−1.4794
7	106	.0411	.0384	.1237	1.45	−1.2561
8	113	.0438	.0438	.1675	14.56	−1.0553
9	138	.0535	.0478	.2153	19.14	−.8727
10	123	.0477	.0509	.2662	24.07	−.7039
11	138	.0535	.0537	.3199	29.30	−.5446
12	137	.0531	.0566	.3764	34.82	−.3903
13	152	.0589	.0599	.4364	40.64	−.2368
14	161	.0624	.0637	.5001	46.82	−.0797
15	181	.0702	.0678	.5679	53.40	.0853
16	201	.0779	.0714	.6393	60.36	.2626
17	187	.0725	.0736	.7129	67.61	.4568
18	172	.0667	.0728	.7857	74.93	.6722
19	171	.0663	.0675	.8531	81.94	.9131
20	143	.0554	.0571	.9102	88.17	1.1835
21	129	.0500	.0427	.9529	93.16	1.4878
22	64	.0248	.0272	.9801	96.65	1.8321
23	40	.0155	.0141	.9943	98.72	2.2321
24	11	.0043	.0057	1.0000	99.71	2.7625

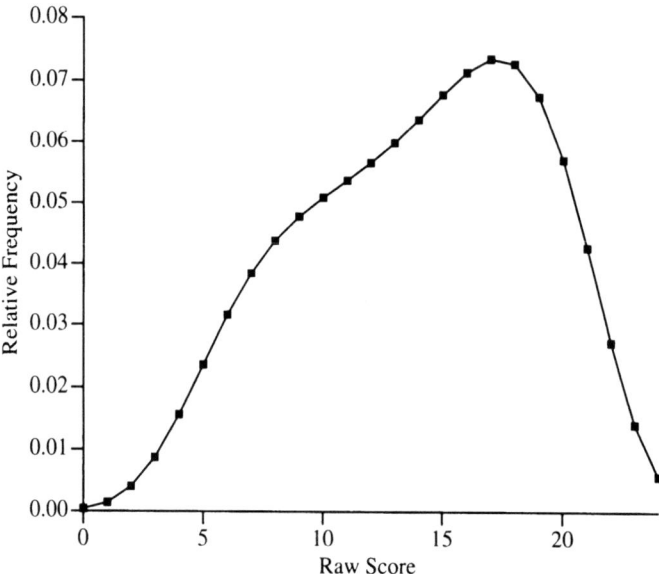

FIGURE 9.1. Raw score distribution for normalization example.

have moments that are slightly different from those expected for scores that are normally distributed with mean of 0 and standard deviation of 1.

T-scores are presented in the column labeled T in Table 9.3. These scores are calculated by multiplying the z-scores in Table 9.1 by 10 and adding 50. The scores labeled T_{int} are calculated by rounding the T-scores to integers. The stanines (st) shown are calculated by multiplying the z-scores by 2 and adding 5. In the next column, the stanines are rounded to integers (st_{int}). In addition, the stanines are truncated to be in the range 1 to 9. NCE scores shown are calculated by multiplying the z-scores by 21.06 and adding 50. In the last column, the NCE scores are rounded to integers and truncated to be in the range 1 to 99.

TABLE 9.2. Moments of Normalized Scores.

	$\hat{\mu}$	$\hat{\sigma}$	$\widehat{sk}$	$\widehat{ku}$
Y	14.0066	5.0146	−.2638	2.2285
z	−.0012	.9922	−.0396	2.9218
T	49.9881	9.9215	−.0396	2.9218
T_{int}	50.0512	9.9895	−.0745	2.8656
st	4.9976	1.9843	−.0396	2.9218
st_{int}	5.0434	1.9237	−.0430	2.4712
NCE	49.9750	20.8948	−.0396	2.9218
NCE_{int}	50.1430	20.4823	−.0010	2.6704

TABLE 9.3. Calculating T-Scores and Stanines.

X	T	T_{int}	st	st_{int}	NCE	NCE_{int}
0	14.38	14	−2.12	1	−25.01	1
1	19.31	19	−1.14	1	−14.64	1
2	23.28	23	−.34	1	−6.28	1
3	26.78	27	.36	1	1.10	1
4	29.91	30	.98	1	7.69	8
5	32.71	33	1.54	2	13.58	14
6	35.21	35	2.04	2	18.84	19
7	37.44	37	2.49	2	23.55	24
8	39.45	39	2.89	3	27.77	28
9	41.27	41	3.25	3	31.62	32
10	42.96	43	3.59	4	35.18	35
11	44.55	45	3.91	4	38.53	39
12	46.10	46	4.22	4	41.78	42
13	47.63	48	4.53	5	45.01	45
14	49.20	49	4.84	5	48.32	48
15	50.85	51	5.17	5	51.80	52
16	52.63	53	5.53	6	55.53	56
17	54.57	55	5.91	6	59.62	60
18	56.72	57	6.34	6	64.16	64
19	59.13	59	6.83	7	69.23	69
20	61.84	62	7.37	7	74.92	75
21	64.88	65	7.98	8	81.33	81
22	68.32	68	8.66	9	88.58	89
23	72.32	72	9.46	9	97.01	97
24	77.62	78	10.52	9	108.18	99

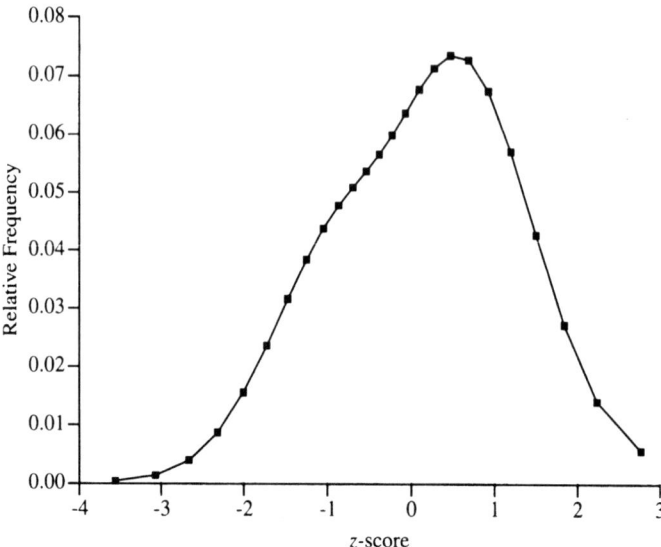

FIGURE 9.2. Normalized score distribution.

The summary statistics for the T and the T_{int} scores shown in Table 9.2 indicate that the first four moments are close to those that would be expected for a normal distribution with mean of 50 and standard deviation of 10. The first three moments for the stanines are close to what would be expected for a normal distribution with a mean of 5 and standard deviation of 2. However, the st_{int} scores have a kurtosis index well below the value of 3 expected for a normal distribution; this finding likely occurred because of the score truncation at the very high and very low scores. The first three moments for the NCE scores are reasonably close to what would be expected for a normal distribution with mean of 50 and standard deviation of 21.06. However, the NCE_{int} scores have a kurtosis index that is lower than that for a normal distribution, although not as low as the kurtosis for the st_{int} scores. This difference again appears to be due to the truncation of the score scale.

9.3.4 Importance of Norm Group in Setting the Score Scale

When the score scale is set by incorporating normative information, the choice of the group used to set the norms influences the usefulness of the score scale. For some testing programs, such as the ITBS (Hoover et al., 2003), norms used in the scaling are based on nationally representative samples of examinees at each grade level. For example, the average scale score for fourth-grade students on the ITBS was set at 200. Because of the scaling, a test user would know that if a fourth-grade student earned a score above 200, that student would be above the average for a nationally representative sample of fourth-grade students. As another example, the ACT Assessment used a nationally representative group of twelfth-grade college-bound high-school seniors to establish the score scale (Brennan, 1989). For the SAT, the score scale was based on a reference group of all students who graduated high school in 1990 and who took the SAT in either their junior or senior year (Dorans, 2002). In each of these cases, the test developers carefully chose the norm group in order to facilitate score interpretation.

Sometimes the norm group used to set a score scale is chosen, for convenience, to be a group of individuals who happen to take a test at a particular time. Little useful information is provided when a student scores above the mean in a group of convenience. Thus, in this case the score scale does little to help test users interpret test scores.

9.4 Incorporating Score Precision Information

The number of distinct score points that is used in a score scale can affect score interpretability. As pointed out by Flanagan (1951), score scale units should "be of an order of magnitude most appropriate to express their accuracy of measurement" (p. 746). If too few distinct scale score points are used, precision will be lost. For example, Flanagan (1951) stated that although being simple and easy to interpret, stanines "in general are too coarse to preserve all of the information contained in raw scores" (p. 747). If very many score points are used, then test users might attach significance to score differences that are small relative to the standard error of measurement. When a new testing program is started, sometimes few data exist that can be used to decide on the number of distinct score points to use. In these situations, Flanagan's (1951) general notions might suggest choosing a scale that has fewer score points than the number of test items, but that has more than a few score points. Even when few data exist, a rough estimate for reliability often can be obtained from a convenience sample or from a similar test. The rough estimate of reliability can be used along with rules of thumb described in the next section for choosing the number of score points to use. In many testing programs, an operational scaling is conducted using data from a representative sample of test takers. When such representative data exist, procedures that are described following the rules of thumb provide a more comprehensive framework for choosing the numbers of score points to use.

9.4.1 Rules of Thumb for Number of Distinct Score Points

Rules of thumb have been developed to help choose the number of distinct integer score points. These rules are designed to lead to a number of score points that is not so small that score precision is lost, but not so large that test users will be tempted to interpret small differences in scale scores as being significant.

One rule of thumb was used in developing the *Iowa Tests of Educational Development* (ITED, 1958). The scales for the ITED were constructed in 1942, using integer scores with the property that an approximate 50% confidence interval for true scores could be found by adding 1 scale score point to and subtracting 1 scale score point from an examinee's scale score. Similarly, Truman L. Kelley (W. H. Angoff, personal communication, February 17, 1987) suggested constructing scale scores so that an approximate 68% confidence interval could be constructed by adding 3 scale score points to and subtracting 3 scale score points from each examinees scale score. These confidence interval statements can be translated into the number of discrete score points.

To implement these rules of thumb, a range of integer scores is found that is consistent with the confidence interval properties as stated. The outcome is the number of scale score points that is consistent with the integer scores covering a range of 6 standard deviation (σ) units, under the assumption that a 6 standard deviation unit range covers nearly all of the observed scores. For example, if the rule of thumb produces scale scores with a desired standard deviation of 5, then the rule suggests that 30 (6 × 5) integer score points should be used.

To proceed, assume that only linear transformations of raw to scale scores are being considered, measurement errors are normally distributed, the standard error of measurement (sem) is constant along the score scale, and the range of scores of interest covers 6σ units (from -3σ to $+3\sigma$). In general, the rules suggest that interest is in developing a score scale such that

$$sc \pm h. \qquad (9.4)$$

is a $100\gamma\%$ confidence interval, where the developer of the scale chooses h and γ. Let z_γ be the unit-normal score used to form a $100\gamma\%$ confidence interval. Note that a confidence interval is

$$sc \pm z_\gamma sem. \qquad (9.5)$$

Setting the right-hand portions of equations (9.4) and (9.5) equal to one another, $h = z_\gamma sem$, which implies that

$$sem = \frac{h}{z_\gamma}. \qquad (9.6)$$

That is, the desired sem can be calculated from the values of h and γ that are specified by the investigator. Because $sem = \sigma(Y)\sqrt{1 - \rho(Y, Y')}$, where $\rho(Y, Y')$ is reliability, it follows that

$$\sigma(Y) = \frac{sem}{\sqrt{1 - \rho(Y, Y')}}.$$

TABLE 9.4. Numbers of Scale Score Points Using Rules of Thumb.

$\rho(Y,Y')$	$h=1, \gamma=.5$	$h=3, \gamma=.68$
.95	40	80
.91	30	60
.84	22	45
.75	18	36
.50	13	25

Combining this equation with equation (9.6),

$$\sigma(Y) = \frac{h}{z_\gamma \sqrt{1-\rho(Y,Y')}}. \qquad (9.7)$$

The number of score points is then 6σ units.

To implement the rule used with the ITED, for example, $h = 1$ and $\gamma = .50$. The reader can verify using a normal curve table that when $\gamma = .50$, $z_\gamma = .6745$. Assume that $\rho(Y,Y') = .91$. Applying equation (9.7),

$$\sigma(Y) = \frac{1}{.6745\sqrt{1-.91}} = 4.94.$$

Rounding this value of 4.94 to 5 and multiplying by 6, the rule of thumb suggests that 30 scale score points should be used.

Applying equation (9.7) for a test with $\rho(X,X') = .91$, using Kelley's rule of thumb, $h = 3$ and $z_\gamma = 1$, so

$$\sigma(Y) = \frac{3}{1\sqrt{1-.91}} = 10,$$

suggesting 60 score points should be used to cover the range of 6σ units.

Applying these rules of thumb, the results, rounded to integers, are given in Table 9.4 for selected reliabilities. The test lengths calculated for a reliability of .91 (30 and 60 items) are consistent with those calculated in the preceding examples. For other reliabilities, the number of score points can be seen to decrease as reliability decreases. Also, Kelley's rule of thumb leads to approximately twice as many score points as the rule of thumb used with the ITED for tests of a particular reliability.

To use these rules of thumb in developing a score scale, the desired confidence interval properties are stated and the associated number of distinct score points is found. A raw-to-scale score transformation is then found that leads to scale scores with an integer score range consistent with the number of distinct score points associated with the rule. Using the rule of thumb for the ITED, assuming $\rho(Y,Y')=.91$, the ITED score scale was constructed using 30 distinct integer scores ranging from 1 to 30. Consistent with Kelley's rule, the SAT score scale (Donlon, 1984) ranges from 200 to 800, with the last digit always being zero. Thus, there are 61 distinct score points which is very close to the 60 distinct score points suggested by Kelley's rule of thumb. Note that these rules of thumb lead only to a desired number of distinct score points. The rule of thumb leaves open the form of the raw-to-scale score transformation (e.g., linear or nonlinear) and the specific set of distinct scores that are to be used.

9.4.2 Linearly Transformed Score Scales with a Given Standard Error of Measurement

Raw scores can be transformed to scale scores using a linear transformation, where the average standard error of measurement is specified along with one score equivalent. In this case, equation (9.2) can be modified by replacing the standard deviations with standard errors of measurement as follows,

$$sc(y) = \frac{sem_{sc}}{sem_y} y + \left[sc(y_1) - \frac{sem_{sc}}{sem_y} y_1 \right], \qquad (9.8)$$

where sem_{sc} is the desired average scale score standard error of measurement, sem_y is the average raw score standard error of measurement, and the other terms have been previously defined.

The average raw score standard error of measurement can be calculated from a reliability coefficient from the relationship $sem = \sigma(Y)\sqrt{1 - \rho(Y, Y')}$. A variety of reliability coefficients (Feldt and Brennan, 1989) could be used. In this chapter, two classical coefficients, KR-20 and KR-21 are considered explicitly as is an IRT-based coefficient described by Kolen et al. (1996).

9.4.3 Score Scales with Approximately Equal Conditional Standard Errors of Measurement

For the confidence interval properties associated with equation (9.5) to hold conditional on score level, the conditional standard error of measurement should be approximately constant along the score scale. However, the conditional standard error of measurement for raw scores on tests is, in general, not expected to be constant (Feldt and Brennan, 1989). For number-correct scores, the standard errors of measurement tend to be larger in middle and smaller for low and high scores. However, nonlinear transformations of raw scores can lead to a pattern of conditional standard errors of measurement that is quite different from that of raw scores (see, for example, Kolen et al., 1992).

In situations where the conditional standard error of measurement varies along the score scale, Standard 2.14 of the *Test Standards* (American Educational Research Association et al., 1999) states that "conditional standard errors of measurement should be reported at several score levels if

9.4 Incorporating Score Precision Information

constancy cannot be assumed" (p. 35). To follow this standard, test developers should, in general, report standard errors at various score levels when the standard errors of measurement vary.

In an attempt to simplify score interpretation, Kolen (1988) suggested using a nonlinear transformation that stabilizes the magnitude of the conditional standard error of measurement. The result of applying the transformation is to make the conditional standard errors of measurement approximately equal along the score scale. With equal conditional standard errors of measurement, test developers would need only report a single standard error of measurement, and test users would be able use a single standard error of measurement when interpreting test scores.

Freeman and Tukey (1950) used the arcsine transformation to stabilize the variance of binomially distributed variables. The variance of the transformed variable is nearly equal for a given sample size, over a wide range of binomial parameters. The transformation suggested by Freeman and Tukey (1950) is

$$g = g(y|K) = .5 \left\{ sin^{-1}\left[\left(\frac{y}{K+1}\right)^{\frac{1}{2}}\right] + sin^{-1}\left[\left(\frac{y+1}{K+1}\right)^{\frac{1}{2}}\right] \right\}. \quad (9.9)$$

In this equation, K is the number of binomial trials, y is the number of successes in the K trials, and sin^{-1} is the arcsine function with its arguments expressed in radians.

This arcsine transformation was used by Jarjoura (1985) and Wilcox (1981) to stabilize conditional error variance using strong true score models discussed in Chapter 3. Recall that in these models (and in IRT) the distribution of number-correct score given true score is binomial or compound binomial. Equation (9.9) can be used to stabilize error variance by replacing y with the number-correct score and K with the number of items on the test. Under strong true score models, scores transformed in this way can be expected to have approximately equal conditional standard errors of measurement along the score scale.

To use equation (9.9) to develop a score scale that equalizes the conditional standard error of measurement along the score scale, it is necessary to have an estimate of the average conditional standard error of measurement for the arcsine transformed scores. If a strong true score model or an IRT model is fit to the data, equation (8.5) (which was introduced in Chapter 8 to evaluate second-order equity) can be used to calculate the average standard error and equation (8.6) to calculate the associated reliability of these arcsine transformed scores by treating them as preliminary scale scores.

For the strong true score models described in Chapter 3, Jarjoura (1985) provided the following expressions for the standard error of measurement of the scores transformed using equation (9.9), which is much more direct computationally than equation (8.5):

$$sem_{b|g} = \frac{1}{\sqrt{4K+2}}, \quad (9.10)$$

under the binomial error model, and

$$sem_{c|g} = \sqrt{\frac{K-2k}{4K^2+2K}}, \quad (9.11)$$

under the beta4 model, where k is Lord's k term discussed in Chapter 3. For $k > 0$, it can be shown that $sem_{c|g} < sem_{b|g}$. Lord (1965) suggested using a value of k that leads to the average standard error of measurement for number-correct scores being equal to the average standard error of measurement associated with the KR-20 reliability coefficient. Kolen et al. (1992, equations 14 and 15) showed that if $sem^2_{y|KR-20}$ is set equal to the average error variance using KR-20 as the reliability coefficient, this value of k can be calculated as

$$k = \frac{K\{(K-1)[\sigma^2(Y) - sem^2_{y|KR-20}] - K\sigma^2(Y) + \mu(Y)[K - \mu(Y)]\}}{2\{\mu(Y)[K - \mu(Y)] - [\sigma^2(Y) - sem^2_{y|KR-20}]\}}, \quad (9.12)$$

where $\mu(Y)$ and $\sigma^2(Y)$ are the mean and variance of observed scores. They also indicated that $sem^2_{y|KR-20}$ could be replaced by an error variance consistent with other reliability coefficients. Taking sem^2_y as the error variance and noting that $\sigma^2(Y) - sem^2_y = $ *true score variance* and that *true score variance* $= \rho(Y,Y')\sigma^2(Y)$, equation (9.12) can be rewritten as

$$k = \frac{K\{(K-1)\rho(Y,Y')\sigma^2(Y) - K\sigma^2(Y) + \mu(Y)[K - \mu(Y)]\}}{2\{\mu(Y)[K - \mu(Y)] - \rho(Y,Y')\sigma^2(Y)\}}. \quad (9.13)$$

Lord (1965) showed that if k is set equal to 0, then the resulting standard error of measurement is consistent with KR-21. So, if KR-21 were substituted for $\rho(Y,Y')$ in equation (9.13), the resulting value of k would equal zero.

To stabilize the conditional standard errors of measurement using the arcsine transformation, the number-correct scores are transformed using equation (9.9). If a particular standard error of measurement of scale scores is desired, based on equation (9.2) scale scores can be found by linearly transforming the arcsine transformed scores as

$$sc[g(y)] = \frac{sem_{sc}}{sem_g}g(y) + \left\{sc[g(y_1)] - \frac{sem_{sc}}{sem_g}g(y_1)\right\}, \quad (9.14)$$

where g is the arcsine transformed score from equation (9.9), sem_g is the standard error of measurement of the transformed scores calculated from equations (8.5), (9.10), or (9.11), $sc[g(y_1)]$ is the scale score equivalent

9.4 Incorporating Score Precision Information

TABLE 9.5. Summary Statistics.

Statistic	Value
N	2580
K	24
$\mu(Y)$	14.0066
$\sigma(Y)$	5.0146
$\sigma^2(Y)$	25.1461
$\rho(Y,Y')_{IRT}$	.8338
KR-20	.8307
KR-21	.8015
$sem_{y|IRT}$	2.0443
$sem_{y|KR-20}$	2.0632
$sem_{y|KR-21}$	2.2344
Lord's k (Equation 9.13)	1.7051
$sem_{IRT|g}$	.0907
$sem_{c|g}$ (Equation 9.11)	.0936
$sem_{b|g}$ (Equation 9.10)	.1010

associated with a prespecified number-correct score on Form Y (y_1), and sem_{sc} is the desired scale score standard error of measurement.

Alternatively, scale scores with stabilized conditional standard errors of measurement can be calculated to have a particular mean and standard deviation. To do so, the number-correct scores are transformed using equation (9.9), and the mean and standard deviation of the transformed scores are calculated. Equation (9.2) is used to linearly transform the scores from equation (9.9), using the calculated mean and standard deviation of the scores from equation (9.9) in place of the mean and standard deviation of raw scores in equation (9.2).

9.4.4 Example: Incorporating Score Precision

The data for this example are again the Form K ITBS Maps and Diagrams data. Relevant summary statistics for these data are presented in Table 9.5. In this table, the IRT reliability coefficient calculated from equation (8.6) is .8338 with an associated raw score standard error of measurement of 2.0443. The KR-20 reliability coefficient is .8307 with an associated raw score standard error of measurement of 2.0632. Consistent with the empirical results presented by Kolen et al. (1996), the IRT-based reliability coefficient is slightly larger than KR-20. As expected from classical test theory, KR-21 is somewhat lower and the associated standard error of measurement somewhat higher than that for KR-20.

The rules of thumb for number of score points can be applied with these data. Using Kelley's rule of thumb, $h = 3$ and $z_\gamma = 1$, with the IRT-based reliability coefficient, the desired number of score points can be calculated using equation (9.7) as,

$$6\sigma(Y) = 6\frac{3}{1\sqrt{1-.8338}} = 44.$$

The reader should verify that using this rule of thumb, the desired number of score points is 44 with KR-20 and 40 with KR-21.

Suppose, for example, that interest is in creating a score scale for this test where a score of 12 corresponds to a scale score of 50 and, consistent with Kelley's rule of thumb, the standard error of measurement is 3. Using a linear transformation and the IRT-based reliability, equation (9.8) produces a raw-to-scale score transformation of

$$sc(y) = \frac{3}{2.0443}y + \left[50 - \frac{3}{2.0443}12\right] = 1.46y + 32.39.$$

The linear transformations using standard errors of measurement associated with KR-20 and KR-21 as the reliability coefficient can be calculated similarly. After rounding to integers, the conversion tables resulting from applying these equations are shown in the second, third, and fourth columns of Table 9.6. Note that because the IRT-based reliability coefficient is greater than KR-20, the conversion table based on the IRT reliability coefficient covers more scale score points than that for KR-20. For similar reasons, the conversion table based on the KR-21 coefficient covers even fewer scale score points.

Now suppose that interest is in creating a score scale for this test such that a score of 12 corresponds to a scale score of 50, and consistent with Kelley's rule of thumb, the standard error of measurement is 3. Suppose also that it is desired that the conditional standard error of measurement be approximately constant along the score scale. To create this score scale, first the raw scores are transformed using the arcsine transformation in equation (9.9). The arcsine transformed scores (g) are shown in the fifth column of Table 9.6. The arcsine transformed scores are then linearly transformed using equation (9.14). Using the standard error of measurement associated with the IRT-based reliability coefficient ($sem_{IRT|g}$) this transformation is

$$sc[g(y)] = \frac{3}{.0907}g(y) + \left[50 - \frac{3}{.0907}.79\right] = 33.08g(y) + 23.87.$$

The transformations using the standard errors of measurement associated with KR-20 ($sem_{c|g}$) and KR-21 ($sem_{b|g}$) as reliability coefficients can be similarly calculated. After rounding to integers, the conversion tables resulting from applying these equations are shown in the last three columns of Table 9.6. Because the IRT-based reliability coefficient is greater than KR-20, the conversion table based on the IRT reliability covers more scale

9.4 Incorporating Score Precision Information

TABLE 9.6. Scale Score Conversions for $sem = 3$.

	Linear				Nonlinear		
Y	IRT	KR-20	KR-21	g	IRT	KR-20	KR-21
0	32	33	34	.10	27	28	30
1	34	34	35	.24	32	33	34
2	35	35	37	.32	34	35	36
3	37	37	38	.38	37	37	38
4	38	38	39	.44	38	39	40
5	40	40	41	.49	40	40	41
6	41	41	42	.53	42	42	43
7	43	43	43	.58	43	43	44
8	44	44	45	.62	45	45	45
9	46	46	46	.66	46	46	46
10	47	47	47	.70	47	47	48
11	49	49	49	.75	49	49	49
12	50	50	50	.79	50	50	50
13	51	51	51	.83	51	51	51
14	53	53	53	.87	53	53	52
15	54	54	54	.91	54	54	54
16	56	56	55	.95	55	55	55
17	57	57	57	.99	57	57	56
18	59	59	58	1.04	58	58	57
19	60	60	59	1.08	60	60	59
20	62	62	61	1.13	62	61	60
21	63	63	62	1.19	63	63	62
22	65	65	63	1.25	66	65	64
23	66	66	65	1.33	68	67	66
24	68	67	66	1.47	73	72	70

score points than that using KR-20. For similar reasons, the conversion table based on the KR-21 coefficient covers even fewer scale score points.

The nonlinear transformations in Table 9.6 cover more score points than the linear transformations. This additional coverage occurs because the arcsine transformation effectively stretches the ends of the score scale so that the conditional standard errors of measurement can be made nearly equal. Note that for the IRT-based reliability coefficient, the range of scale score points is 47, which is close to the 44 points suggested by Kelley's rule of thumb calculated earlier in this section. For KR-20 and the nonlinear transformation, the range of scale scores is 45 points, which is even closer to that suggested by Kelley's rule of thumb.

Also, note that there are large gaps in the conversion tables for the nonlinear methods. For example, for the nonlinear conversion table based on KR-20, there are no raw scores that convert to scale scores of 68, 69, 70, or 71. This large gap might be unacceptable in operational testing programs, because test users might complain that it is unfair that earning a raw score of 24 instead of 23 leads to a 5-point increase in scale score. For this reason, the scales that arise often are truncated. In the example just given, it might be decided that a raw score of 23 would convert to a scale score of 69. Truncating the score scale in this way, however, could cause the conditional standard errors of measurement to be unequal along the score scale.

9.4.5 Evaluating Psychometric Properties of Scale Scores

Psychometric properties of scale scores, such as reliability and conditional standard errors of measurement, are influenced by the scale score transformation. Kolen et al. (1992) demonstrated that test reliability is influenced by the scale transformation, and that test reliability can be lowered substantially when very few distinct scale score points are used. They also demonstrated that the form of the raw-to-scale score distribution influences the pattern of the conditional standard errors of measurement. For example, for a particular situation in which conditional standard errors of measurement for number-correct scores were highest for scores near the middle, conditional standard errors of measurement for scale scores were highest for the high and low scale scores.

When comparing the pattern of scale score conditional standard errors of measurement for different scales, the analyses presented by Kolen et al. (1992) suggested that the pattern of conditional standard errors of measurement depends on where the score scale is compressed and stretched, relative to the number-correct score scale. For linear transformations, the pattern of conditional standard errors of measurement for scale scores is the same as that for raw scores. For nonlinear transformations, however, the stretching and compressing of the score scale influences the pattern.

For example, refer to the linear IRT and nonlinear IRT score scales in Table 9.6. Recall that the IRT linear scale was constructed by linearly transforming the number-correct scores, and then rounding to integers. The pattern of conditional standard errors for the IRT linear scale is expected to be the same as that for the number-correct scores (apart from rounding). Relative to the IRT linear scale, the ends of the scale for the IRT nonlinear scale are stretched. This stretching can be seen by noting that the raw-to-scale score equivalents for both scales are similar for scores near the middle; however, at the upper and lower ends, the IRT nonlinear scale scores are more extreme. For example, at the upper end, a raw score of 24 converts to a scale score of 68 for the IRT linear scale and to a 73 for the IRT nonlinear scale. Because the ends of the IRT nonlinear scale are stretched, conditional standard errors of measurement are expected to be larger at the extreme scores for the IRT nonlinear than for the IRT linear scale.

Methodologies for evaluating reliability of scale scores and conditional standard errors of measurement for scale scores were described by Kolen et al. (1992) using strong true score theory as a psychometric model and by Kolen et al. (1996) using IRT as a psychometric model. Wang et al. (2000) generalized the IRT method to polytomously scored items. Other related methods have also been discussed and evaluated for tests consisting of dichtomously scored items (Brennan and Lee, 1999; Lee et al., 2000) and for polytomously scored items (Lee, 2001). Feldt and Qualls (1998) developed a general methodology that allows for calculation of conditional standard errors of measurement of scale scores from raw-score conditional standard errors of measurement and a conversion table. Their method does not take into account error introduced by rounding.

The Kolen et al. (1996) methodology for estimating reliability of scale scores and conditional standard errors of measurement for scale scores was described in Chapter 8 in association with equations (8.1) through (8.5), and it is implemented in the computer program *POLYCSEM*. The computer program requires input of item parameter estimates for the items on the test, a number-correct to scale score conversion table, and a distribution of θ, provided in quadrature form.

As an example, this methodology was applied to some of the scales constructed in the present chapter. In Table 9.5, the IRT-based reliability for Form K of the ITBS Maps and Diagrams test was .8338. The IRT-based reliability for scale scores that are linear transformations of raw scores would necessarily be .8338, also. Using the Kolen et al. (1996) methodology as implemented in *POLYCSEM*, the IRT-based reliability of the IRT linear scores obtained using the conversion in the second column of Table 9.6 was .8323. The slight decrease in reliability is due to rounding scale scores to integers in Table 9.6. The IRT-based reliability for the IRT linear scores obtained using the sixth column of Table 9.6 was .8285. The use of a nonlinear transformation in this case led to a slight decrease in the reliability coefficient.

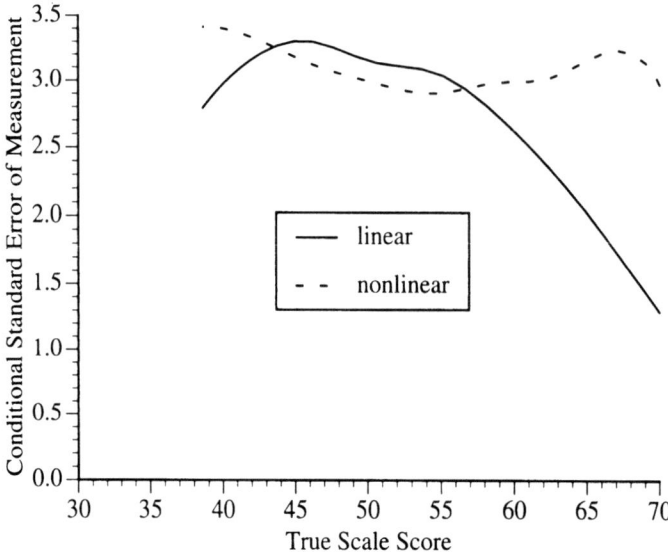

FIGURE 9.3. Conditional standard errors of measurement for linear and nonlinear scale scores.

Conditional standard errors of measurement are shown in Figure 9.3 for the linear and nonlinear IRT-based scales from Table 9.6. For the linear scale, the conditional standard errors of measurement are highest for the middle scores and lower at extreme scores. The pattern for the nonlinear scale suggests nearly equal conditional standard errors of measurement along the entire score scale. This finding is as expected, because the nonlinear transformation that was used was intended to equalize the conditional standard errors of measurement along the score scale. The stretching of the ends of the scale mentioned earlier caused the pattern of conditional standard errors of measurement for the nonlinear scale to be different from the pattern for the linear scale.

As another example, this methodology was applied to the T-scores shown in Table 9.3. The IRT-based reliability for these scores was .8251, again only slightly below that for the number-correct scores. The conditional standard errors of measurement for scale scores using this transformation are shown in Figure 9.4. For this transformation, the pattern is that the conditional standard errors of measurement are smaller for the middle scores and larger at the extreme scores. This pattern is completely opposite of that for the raw scores. The reason is that normalized scores stretch the ends of the score scale, relative to the middle, more than does, say, the arcsine transformation.

As this demonstration illustrates, the pattern of the conditional standard errors of measurement depends heavily on the form of the raw-to-scale score transformation. Even when the pattern of conditional standard

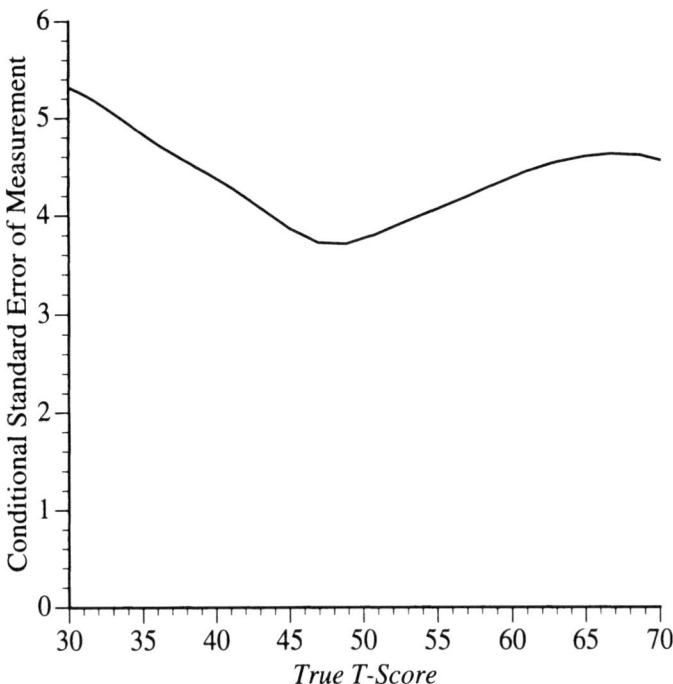

FIGURE 9.4. Conditional standard errors of measurement for T-scores.

errors of measurement for raw scores is concave down, the pattern for scale scores can be nearly flat (arcsine transformation) or concave up (normalization). Kolen et al. (1992) also showed that the transformation to θ that is typically used in IRT also produces concave up patterns for the examples investigated. When, relative to raw scores, the transformation compresses the scale in the middle and stretches it at the end, the pattern of the conditional standard errors of measurement will be concave up, even though the pattern for the raw scores was concave down.

The linear transformation procedures described in the previous section can lead to a score scale that has a prespecified average standard error of measurement. The nonlinear procedures described in that section can lead to a score scale with a prespecified average standard error of measurement and conditional standard errors of measurement that are approximately equal along the score scale. The scales that are created using these procedures typically are rounded to integers, and the scale may be truncated. In addition, the arcsine transformation leads only to *approximately* equal conditional standard errors of measurement along the score scale. The methodology described here is useful for evaluating psychometric properties of scale scores following the rounding and truncation processes.

9.4.6 The IRT θ-Scale as a Score Scale

The IRT θ-scale, or a linear transformation of that scale, could be used as the score scale for a test. However, for paper-and-pencil tests, Petersen et al. (1989) pointed out that the standard errors of measurement for extreme scores are considerably larger than for scores near the middle. This discrepancy in standard errors can be much greater than the discrepancy for T-scores shown in Figure 9.4. As Petersen et al. (1989) indicated, "measurement error variance for examinees of extreme ability could easily be 10 or even 100 times that for more typical examinees" (p. 228). Lord (1980, p. 183) gave a relevant illustrative example. He suggested that the greater amount of measurement variability associated with using estimates of θ creates problems in interpreting summary statistics such as means and correlations. In addition, the large discrepancies in standard errors of measurement can create problems when test users interpret scores for individuals. For these reasons, scales other than the θ-scale typically are preferable for paper-and-pencil tests, and often for computer adaptive tests.

9.5 Incorporating Content Information

According to Ebel (1962), "to be meaningful any test scores must be related to test content as well as to the scores of other examinees" (p. 18). However, when score scales are constructed, the direct relationship of the scores to the test content might be lost. Ebel (1962) suggested that efforts be made to provide content information along with the scale scores to aid in score interpretation. He suggested constructing content standard scores, which relate the content of the test to scale scores. Various efforts have been made to provide content meaning with scale scores. Three types of procedures are considered here and are referred to as *item mapping, scale anchoring*, and *standard setting*. Each of these methods is intended to help test users understand what examinees who earn particular scale scores know and are able to do.

9.5.1 Item Mapping

In item mapping, a primary score scale is constructed using one of the methods already discussed. To enhance the meaning of the scale scores, items are found that represent various scale score points, and these representative items are reported to test users. This type of procedure was suggested by Bock et al. (1982) for use in NAEP. Item mapping, as used in NAEP, is discussed by Beaton and Allen (1992). Recently, Zwick et al. (2001) reviewed and studied item mapping procedures.

One choice made in item mapping is the *response probability* (*RP*) *level*, which is the probability of a correct response that is associated with mastery for *all* items on a test, expressed as a percentage. The *mastery level* for a specific item is defined as the scale score for which the probability times 100 of correctly answering the item equals the RP level. Given the overall RP level, the mastery level for each item in a set of items can be found. Each item is mapped to a particular point on the score scale that represents the item's mastery level. The mastery level for items can be found by regressing probability of correct response on scale score, using procedures such as logistic or cubic spline regression, or by using an IRT model.

Additional criteria are often used when choosing which items to report in item maps. Item discrimination is one such criterion, where items are chosen only if they discriminate well between examinees who score above and below the score. Item content is a second often used criterion, where subject matter experts review the content of each item to make sure that the item appears to be an adequate representation of test content. The outcome of the item mapping procedure is the specification of test questions that represent various scale score points.

For some tests a set of items is chosen and used to represent various score points. For other tests, a sentence or phrase describing each item is presented instead of the entire item.

As reported by Zwick et al. (2001), the RP level can have a substantial effect on the item mapping results. According to Zwick et al. (2001) values of RP ranging from .50 to .80 have been used for this NAEP application. See Huynh (1998) for a discussion of psychometric justifications for choosing RP. The procedures for item mapping described here apply to dichotomously scored items. Generalizations for polytomously scored items have been discussed by Donoghue (1996) and Huynh (1998).

Item maps are reported for the main NAEP assessments. Figure 9.5 provides selected portions of an item map that was reported for the 1996 NAEP 4th grade Science Assessment by O'Sullivan et al. (1997) for multiple-choice items. Methodology for constructing the item map was discussed by Allen et al. (1999). The NAEP score scale ranges from 0 to 300. An RP value of 74% was used for multiple-choice items for this NAEP item mapping. Complications in NAEP item mapping include the use of polytomous items and the use of a scale score that is a composite of subject area scale scores. In NAEP item mapping, a phrase describing what an examinee can do who correctly answers an item is presented, rather than the item itself. For example, for the item in Figure 9.5 that is associated with a scale score of 185, a total of 74% of the examinees who earn a scale score of 185 can be expected to answer the item correctly that measures whether an examinee can "identify patterns of ripples." The short-hand description that might be used for test users is that an examinee who earns a score of 185 can "identify patterns of ripples." Or, as another example, an examinee who earns a score of 117 can "recognize a graph that corresponds to data."

360   9. Score Scales

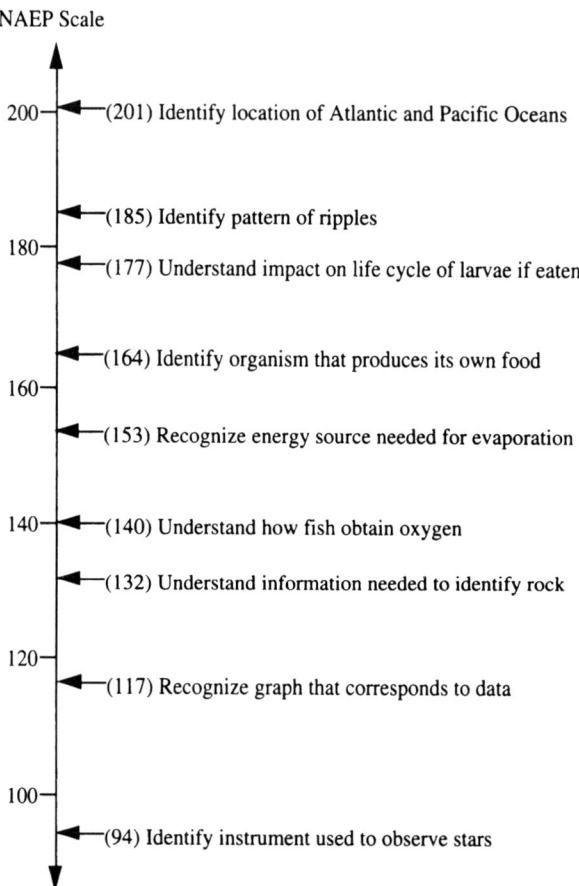

FIGURE 9.5. Selected portions of an item map for the 1996 NAEP fourth-grade Science Assessment.

9.5.2 Scale Anchoring

The goal of scale anchoring is to provide general statements of what students who score at each of a selected set of scale score points know and are able to do. The scale anchoring process used with NAEP was described by Allen et al. (1999). In scale anchoring, a set of scale score points is chosen. Typically, these points are either equally spaced along the score scale or are selected to be a set of percentiles, such as the 10th, 25th, 50th, 75th, and 90th percentiles. Item maps are created for a set of items. Items that map at or near these points are chosen to represent the points. Criteria are also used that require the items to discriminate well around the point (Beaton and Allen, 1992). Subject matter experts review the items that map near each point and attempt to develop general statements that represent the skills of examinees scoring at these points. In scale anchoring, it is assumed that examinees know and are able to do all of the skills in the statements at or below a given score level.

A scale anchoring process was used to create the ACT *Standards for Transition* for EXPLORE, PLAN, and the ACT Assessment (ACT, 2001). Item mapping procedures were used to associate items with various score ranges. Based on the items that mapped at each score range, content specialists developed statements of skills and knowledge demonstrated by students scoring in each range.

A scale anchoring approach also was suggested by Ebel (1962), although he used scores on a subset of items rather than statements to display performance at each of the levels. Ebel (1962) selected the most discriminating item from each of 10 content categories on a Preliminary Scholastic Aptitude Test (PSAT) mathematics test form to create what he referred to as a *scale book*. This scale book was used to represent the test content to test users with a small number of test items. For examinees with PSAT scores at a selected set of score intervals, the most frequently occurring raw score on the 10-item set was found. For example, examinees with a PSAT score of 550 would be expected to have a "most probable raw score" of 6 on the 10 item test. Ebel suggested providing to test users this information relating PSAT scale scores to raw scores on the 10 items along with the 10 items. In this way, the standard set of 10 items could be used by test users as a statement of what examinees could do who earned each score.

9.5.3 Standard Setting

Standard setting begins with a statement of what competent examinees know and are able to do. Standard setting methods are an attempt to find the score point that divides those examinees who know and are able to do what is stated from the other examinees. Standard setting methods have been used to set passing scores for professional certification examinations. In these situations, judgmental techniques are used to find the score point that differentiates those who are minimally competent to practice in the profession from those who are less than minimally competent. In achievement testing situations, various achievement levels often are stated, such as *basic*, *proficient*, and *advanced*. Statements are created indicating what students who score at each of these levels know and are able to do. Judgmental techniques are used to find the score points that differentiate among these different levels. Standard setting methods have been widely researched and discussed. In this chapter, standard setting is briefly discussed. Refer to Livingston and Zieky (1982) for an extensive discussion of many of the standard setting methods that are used and to the book edited by Cizek (2001) for a recent discussion. Kane (1994) provided a conceptual framework for validating performance standards.

Typically, in standard setting techniques, judges are provided with statements about what subjects know and are able to do, and who might be described in a particular way (e.g., "proficient"). The judges are also provided with a set of test questions. A systematic procedure is used to collect information from judges. They are asked to consider examinees who score just at the score point which divides one level from the next level. In one often used standard setting method, the so-called Angoff method, the judges are asked to indicate the proportion of examinees scoring at this point who would be expected to correctly answer each item. Procedures are used to aggregate the judgments over items and judges. The outcome of these procedures typically is a number-correct score on the set of items that represents the cut-point. Various methods can be used to collect data, to provide feedback to the judges, to provide normative information to judges, and to aggregate data.

Descriptions of what examinees know and are able to do can be developed as part of the standard setting process; at other times, NAEP provided expanded descriptions. For example, with NAEP, the standard setting process is initiated using "policy definitions," such as those shown in Table 9.7 (Bourque, 1999a). During the standard setting process, more specific content-based descriptions sometimes were developed by the judges to help guide the process; at other times the judges were provided expanded descriptions. Following the standard setting process, sometimes item maps and other procedures were used by subject matter experts to develop more refined statements about what students know and are able to do who score at various levels. Summary content statements for the 1996 NAEP Science Assessment in 4th grade are shown in Table 9.8. More detailed statements are provided by Bourque (1999b). See Reckase (1998) for a description of the process used to set achievement levels for the 1996 NAEP Science Assessment; see Reckase (2000) for a history of standard setting in NAEP.

TABLE 9.7. NAEP Policy Definitions[a].

Level	Policy Definition
Basic	This level, below proficient, denotes partial mastery of the knowledge, and skills that are fundamental for proficient work at each grade–4, 8, and 12.
Proficient	This central level represents solid academic performance for each grade tested–4, 8, and 12. Students reaching this level have demonstrated competency over challenging subject matter and are well prepared for the next level of schooling.
Advanced	This higher level signifies superior performance beyond proficient grade-level mastery at grades 4, 8, and 12.

[a]From Bourque (1999a, p. 739).

TABLE 9.8. 1996 NAEP Science Summary Achievement Level Descriptions at Grade 4[a].

Level	Description
Basic	Students performing at the Basic level demonstrate some of the knowledge and reasoning required for understanding of the earth, physical, and life sciences at a level appropriate to Grade 4. For example, they can carry out simple investigations and read uncomplicated graphs and diagrams. Students at this level also show a beginning understanding of classification, simple relationships, and energy.
Proficient	Students performing at the Proficient level demonstrate the knowledge and reasoning required for understanding of the earth, physical, and life sciences at a level appropriate to Grade 4. For example, they understand concepts relating to the Earths features, physical properties, and structure and function. In addition, students can formulate solutions to familiar problems as well as show a beginning awareness of issues associated with technology.
Advanced	Students performing at the Advanced level demonstrate a solid understanding of the earth, physical, and life sciences as well as the ability to apply their understanding to practical situations at a level appropriate to Grade 4. For example, they can perform and critique simple investigations, make connections from one or more of the sciences to predict or conclude, and apply fundamental concepts to practical applications.

[a]From Bourque (1999b, p. 763).

9.5.4 Numerical Example

A numerical example of how to construct item maps is provided in Table 9.9 for data based on Form K of the ITBS Maps and Diagrams test that was used in earlier examples. This example uses the three-parameter logistic IRT model. The mapping could have been accomplished using non-IRT procedures or a different IRT model. For this item mapping, the item parameters were estimated as in Chapter 6. Based on these item parameter estimates, the item mastery level on the θ-scale for a particular RP-level on item j can be found from the three-parameter logistic model equation, assuming the probability $(RP/100)$ is known, by solving for θ using the following equation:

$$\theta_j(RP) = b_j - \frac{1}{Da_j} \ln\left(\frac{1 - c_j}{RP/100 - c_j} - 1\right). \qquad (9.15)$$

The mastery levels on the θ-scale calculated using this equation are shown in the second column of Table 9.9. Note that the items are sorted by their mastery level. In the third column, the mastery level on the true number-correct score scale was calculated by finding the value of the test characteristic curve (see equation (6.16)) at the mastery level. The true scale score was calculated using the methodology described in Chapter 8.

Assuming that scores are to be reported as scale scores, the mastery levels on this scale are of principal interest. An item map, like that shown in Figure 9.5, could be constructed for these items on the score scale. Such a map might show item 5 at a scale score level of 166, item 7 at 167, item 9 at 169, etc.

Note that if a different RP value had been used, the items would have mapped to different score points. Note also that with the three-parameter logistic model, the order of the items in the item mapping depends on the RP value as well. For example, the item ordering would be different in this example if an RP value of .65 had been used.

These data might also be used for scale anchoring. Suppose it was desired to anchor the scale at score levels 170, 190, and 210. In this case, subject matter experts might be given the items near 170 (e.g., that map within 5 points of 170), maybe items 5, 7, 9, 8, and 4, and asked to develop a statement of what examinees who correctly answer these items know and can do. For a score of 190, a similar process could be followed using items 19, 20, 2, and 15. For a score of 210, items 24, 14, and 17 would be used.

As another example, suppose that a standard setting process had been used for this test to distinguish mastery from non-mastery. In this case, a score would have been identified as the minimum cut-score. Suppose the standard setting study indicated that a true score of 15 or higher constituted mastery. In this case, the IRT ability corresponding to a true score of 15 would be found using the iterative process described as part of the IRT true score equating procedures in equation (6.19). The true scale score

TABLE 9.9. Example of Item Mapping (Items Sorted By Mastery Level).

Item	θ-Mastery Level for $RP = 75\%$	True Number-Correct Score	True Scale Score
1	−1.21	7.89	151.93
5	−.50	11.39	165.83
7	−.42	11.81	167.43
9	−.35	12.21	168.93
8	−.34	12.26	169.08
13	−.29	12.54	170.13
4	−.19	13.10	172.14
11	.00	14.12	175.71
6	.18	15.12	179.22
3	.30	15.75	181.48
23	.50	16.77	185.34
10	.51	16.78	185.42
19	.52	16.87	185.76
20	.59	17.20	187.14
2	.66	17.53	188.61
15	.73	17.83	189.99
22	1.09	19.33	198.50
12	1.25	19.92	202.75
24	1.42	20.48	207.59
14	1.45	20.59	208.58
17	1.64	21.19	214.70
18	1.92	21.90	223.16
16	2.13	22.36	229.19
21	2.95	23.37	244.12

corresponding to the theta value could be found using the methodology described in Chapter 8. In the example, a true number-correct score of 15.12 corresponds to a true scale of 179.22. A scale score of around 179 would be used as the minimum score to pass the test.

9.5.5 Practical Usefulness

Although much effort has been expended in developing procedures for interpreting scale scores in terms of what students know and are able to do, investigators have questioned the usefulness of the resulting statements. Forsyth (1991), in considering whether the content information provided on NAEP meets the goal of accurately describing what examinees can and cannot do, argued that "NAEP, despite its claims, has not achieved this goal to any reasonable extent" (p. 9). He further argued that unless the content domains are very well defined, providing useful content-based information in terms of item mapping or scale anchoring may be unattainable. His argument was based on a detailed analysis of NAEP scale anchoring and item mapping results. Pellegrino et al. (1999) argued that the current process for setting NAEP achievement levels is flawed, in part because they believe that the process is overly subjective and the judges are given a difficult and confusing task. Hambleton et al. (2000) disputed the arguments made by Pellegrino et al. (1999). In any case, Ebel's (1962) goal of attaching content meaning to scale scores is an important one. As Forsyth (1991) stated regarding being able to describe what examinees can and cannot do, "teachers have pleaded for such measures for decades" (p. 9).

9.6 Maintaining Score Scales

Equating methods are used to maintain score scales as new forms are developed. Over time, however, the normative, score precision, or content information that was originally incorporated into a score scale can become less relevant. The norm group that was central to score interpretation initially might be of less interest. Also, the content of a test might slowly evolve, with the cumulative effect being that forms used in one year might have somewhat different content than forms used a few years later.

As Petersen et al. (1989) suggested, professional certification tests are especially affected by the evolution of test content. With these types of test, a passing score is often set using standard setting methods with an initial test form. Over time, the profession might change in its emphases, knowledge bases, and legal context. Due to these changes, some items and content become less relevant. It is even possible for the keyed answer to an item to change due to changes in relevant laws. Although an equating process can be used to maintain the score scale over time, the cumulative effects of changes might make the scores from one form have different meaning from scores on earlier forms. These changes also can lead the testing agency to question the relevance of the standards that were set initially. When it is judged that these changes have caused the standards to lose their meaning, a study can be conducted to set new standards.

Changes in norm groups also can contribute to score misinterpretation. For example, when the SAT scale was established in 1941, the mean Verbal and Mathematical scores were set at 500 for the group of examinees who took the test that year. This scale was maintained through the mid-1990s. In the early 1990s, the mean Mathematical score was lower than 500, due in part to changes in the composition of the group of examinees who take the SAT (Dorans, 2002). A test user, thinking that the mean in, say, 1992 was 500, might erroneously conclude that an examinee scoring 490 was below average, when, in reality, this student was above average among the 1992 examinees. In addition, the content of the SAT had changed subtly over time. As indicated by Cook (1994, April), due to changes in test content, "it is difficult to think of scores on the current SAT as comparable to scores on the version of the SAT that was administered in 1941, even with the effective equating plan that has been used over the years to maintain score comparability" (p. 3). Concern about possible score misinterpretation led the Educational Testing Service to rescale the SAT, which was referred to as "recentering." The new scale was set at a mean of 500 for students who graduated high school in 1990 and who took the SAT in either their junior or senior year in high school (Dorans, 2002), and was first used in the April 1995 administration. For similar reasons, the ACT Assessment was rescaled in 1989 (Brennan, 1989).

Some testing programs periodically adjust the scaling of their tests. For example, new editions of the the ITBS are released approximately every seven years. For each new edition, the developmental scale scores are based on scores for examinees in a national norming study. By periodically adjusting the scale scores, the ITBS scale scores are always referenced to a recent norm group.

Rescaling a test (or setting new standards) makes it difficult to compare scores from before and after the rescaling. Often a study is conducted to link the two scales to help test users make the transition. Because the development of a new score scale causes complexities in score interpretation, the decision about whether to rescale can be difficult. The decision involves weighing possible score misinterpretations associated with the old scale against the possible complexities associated with adopting a new scale. The effect of the changes on test users often is a prime consideration in making this choice. As the examples considered suggest, the decision on when to rescale depends on the context in which the testing program operates.

9.7 Scales for Test Batteries and Composites

Test batteries consist of tests in various areas, and separate scores are provided for each area. Sometimes *composite scores* are calculated, which are combinations of scores from some or all tests in the battery. When the processes of test construction, scaling, and norming are handled similarly for each of the tests in the battery, the comparison of examinee scores across tests in the battery and the computation of meaningful composite scores are facilitated.

9.7.1 Test Batteries

When norms are used to scale a test, typically the same norm group is used for all of the tests in the battery. Often the scale is constructed so that the scale score distributions on the tests in the battery are identical for the norm group. In this case, relative strengths and weaknesses of examinees can be found directly by comparing scores on the different tests. For example, when the SAT was rescaled, the Verbal and Mathematics scores were normalized and the scale on each test set to have a mean of 500 and standard deviations of 110 as discussed previously (Dorans, 2002). Because the score distributions are nearly the same on the two tests, an examinee's score on the Verbal test can be compared directly to his or her score on the Mathematics test. For example, consider an examinee scoring 500 on the Verbal test and 610 on the Mathematics test. Because the scores were normalized with a mean of 500 and a standard deviation of 110, this student's score is near the 50th percentile on the Verbal test and near the 84th percentile on the Mathematics test. Relative to the norm group of those who graduated high school in 1990 and who took the SAT in either their junior or senior year in high school, this examinee ranks higher on the Mathematics test than on the Verbal test.

Some primary score scales for batteries are constructed by emphasizing characteristics other than identical score distributions across the tests. For example, in the ACT Assessment rescaling (Brennan, 1989), the score scale was set to have a mean of 18 for each test, with constant standard errors of measurement across the score scale. This process led to the standard deviations being unequal across tests. In addition, the distributions were not normalized. Because of the way this test was scaled, scores on different tests cannot be directly compared to each other. Consider an examinee who scores 22 on the English Usage test and 25 on the Mathematics test. This examinee is above the mean on both tests. However, relative to the norm group, there is no way to be sure on which test the examinee ranks higher.

For tests like the ACT Assessment, percentile ranks on each of the tests in a relevant norm group often are presented. These percentile ranks function as auxiliary score scales. When the norms across tests in a battery are based on the same norm group, then the percentile ranks can be used to assess relative strengths and weaknesses. For example, based on a 1995 norming study, the percentile rank of a score of 22 on English Usage was 75 among college-bound high school students (ACT, 1997); the percentile rank of a score of 25 on Mathematics was 90. From these percentile ranks, the examinee who scored 22 on English Usage and 25 on Mathematics ranked higher in this norm group in Mathematics than in English Usage.

9.7.2 Composite Scores

Composite scores reflecting performance on two or more tests are often reported. Composite scores typically are a linear combination of either raw or scale scores on the different tests. For example, on the ACT Assessment, the Composite score is the average of the English Usage, Mathematics, Reading, and Science Reasoning scale scores. The Composite score for the ACT Assessment is intended to reflect general educational development over the four areas measured by the ACT Assessment.

The contribution of individual tests to a composite score can be defined based on data from a group of examinees. Wang and Stanley (1970) distinguished *nominal weights* from *effective weights*. The nominal weight is the weight by which a score on a test is multiplied when forming a composite. The effective weight is the statistical contribution of the test to the variance of a particular composite. Defining w_i as the nominal weight for test i, the proportional effective weight is

$$ew_i = \frac{w_i^2 \sigma_i^2 + w_i \sum_{j \neq i} w_j \sigma_{ij}}{\sum_i \left[w_i^2 \sigma_i^2 + w_i \sum_{j \neq i} w_j \sigma_{ij} \right]}, \qquad (9.16)$$

where σ_i^2 is the variance of scale scores on test i, and σ_{ij} is the covariance between scale scores on tests i and j. The summation in the numerator is over all of the tests used to form the composite, except test i. The denominator sums up the numerator values for all of the tests, and it is used to standardize the numerator so that the proportional effective weights sum to 1. A special case of equation (9.16) involves using equal weights for the tests. Without loss of generality, the equal weights can be assumed to equal 1. In this case, equation (9.16) simplifies to

$$ew_i = \frac{\sigma_i^2 + \sum_{j \neq i} \sigma_{ij}}{\sum_i \left[\sigma_i^2 + \sum_{j \neq i} \sigma_{ij} \right]}. \qquad (9.17)$$

TABLE 9.10. ACT Assessment Effective Weights Calculation.

	Variance-Covariance Matrix			
	English	Math	Reading	Science Reasoning
English	27.7	17.0	25.6	15.8
Mathematics	17.0	20.8	18.2	13.1
Reading	25.6	18.2	41.8	21.0
Science Reasoning	15.8	13.1	21.0	19.5
Column Sum	86.1	69.1	106.6	69.4
Proportional Effective Weight	.26	.21	.32	.21

The numerator of equation (9.17) sums a column of the variance-covariance matrix among the scale scores on the tests. The denominator sums all of the elements in the variance-covariance matrix. Note that large effective weights tend to be associated with a test having a large variance, since the variance is in the numerator. Large effective weights also tend to be associated with large covariances with the other tests.

An example of equation (9.17) is given in Table 9.10. This table is based on data from the 1988 ACT norming study reported by Kolen and Hanson (1989, p. 53). The ACT Assessment Composite is calculated as the sum of the four scores divided by 4. Because the weights are equal, equation (9.17) can be used. The body of the table contains the variance-covariance matrix for scale scores. The row labeled column sum calculates the value in the numerator of equation (9.17). The denominator equals 331.2, which is the sum of the 4 column sums. The last row of the table gives the proportional effective weights, which are calculated by dividing the column sum by 331.2.

The proportional effective weight for Reading is .32, which is larger than the other effective weights. The main reason that Reading has a larger effective weight is that it has a variance of 41.8, which is greater than the variances of the other tests: 27.7, 20.8, and 19.5. This finding suggests that the Reading test contributes more to the Composite variance than do any of the other tests. The larger weight for Reading is primarily a result of the scaling process used for the ACT test battery that led to a higher standard deviation for Reading.

When tests are scaled to have the same variances and tests have equal nominal weights, the nominal and effective weights differ only due to the covariances. In these cases, as long as the correlations (and hence covariances) among the tests are similar to one another, the nominal and effective weights will be similar.

When the individual tests are scaled to have the same mean, variance, and score distribution, the distributional form of scores for the composite likely will be different from that of the tests. In such cases, the composites might be rescaled to have the same distribution as the test scores.

9.7.3 Maintaining Scales for Batteries and Composites

Over time, the scale scores for tests in a test battery become less comparable. One of the reasons that the SAT was rescaled was because the mean Verbal and Mathematics scores differed considerably for the groups who took the test (Dorans, 2002). The rescaling was conducted to ensure that the score distributions for both tests were the same for a recent group of test users. As the user groups change, however, the score distributions for Verbal and Mathematics will likely diverge. At some point, the score distributions will differ enough that scores on the two tests will not be comparable. At that point, either test users will need to be cautioned against comparing scores, or another rescaling will be needed. However, even if the Verbal and Mathematics scores cannot be compared, percentile ranks in a relevant norm group could be used to compare Verbal and Mathematics scores.

When new forms are introduced, the test scores are equated to maintain the score scale. Typically, the composite scores are not separately equated. However, equating the test scores does not ensure that the composite scores are equated. If the correlations between scores on a new form differ from those on the old form, then the composites likely will not have identical score distributions on the old and new forms, regardless of the equating method used.

Thomasson et al. (1994) encountered this issue when equating new forms of the ASVAB. Table 9.11 presents some of their results for equating ASVAB Form 21a to Form 15h. Three tests are considered, Mechanical Comprehension (MC), General Science (GS), and Auto-Shop (AS). The forms for these tests were equated using equipercentile methods, and the resulting scale score means and standard deviations are shown in the first six rows of the table. The means and standard deviations differed by no more than .1 from Form 15h to Form 21a, suggesting the equating of the tests worked well. The next three rows of the table provide correlations between the tests. The correlations between the tests in all cases were higher for Form 15h than for Form 21a. The Air Force M composite, which is one of many composites used by the military, is calculated by adding MC, GS, and 2 times AS and then rounding the result to an integer. As can be seen, the standard deviation for Form 15h is more than 1 point larger than the standard deviation for Form 21a. Thomasson et al. (1994) suggested that a difference of this magnitude could have practical implications for use of the Air Force M composite. This example illustrates that even when tests are equated, composite scores might not be comparable. The difference in standard deviations for the composite on the two forms can be traced directly to the differences in correlations between the pairs of tests. When composites are created for tests in a battery, it is important to check whether the composites are also comparable. Although equating

TABLE 9.11. Summary Statistics for ASVAB Forms 15h and 21a.

Statistic	Form 15h	Form 21a
MC-Mean	51.90	52.00
GS-Mean	50.80	50.90
AS-Mean	50.90	50.90
MC-SD	9.30	9.30
GS-SD	8.60	8.60
AS-SD	8.90	9.00
r(MC,AS)	.65	.58
r(MC,GS)	.67	.60
r(AC,GS)	.58	.36
Air Force M-SD	26.00	24.90

procedures could be applied to composite scores, this process typically is not followed.

9.8 Vertical Scaling and Developmental Score Scales

In vertical scaling, tests that differ in difficulty, but that are intended to measure similar constructs are placed on the same scale. Vertical scaling is used with elementary school achievement tests, which is the primary use considered in this section.

When assessing educational achievement or aptitude for grade-school students, it is often important to be able to estimate the extent to which students grow from one year to the next and over the course of their schooling. Growth might be assessed by administering alternate forms of the same test each year, and charting growth in test scores from year-to-year and over multi-year periods. Students learn so much during their grade school years, however, that using a single set of test questions over a wide range of educational levels can be problematic. Such a test would contain many items that are too advanced for students at the early educational levels and too elementary for students at the later educational levels. Administering items that are too advanced for students in the early grades could cause the students to be overwhelmed. Administering many items that are too elementary for students in the upper grades could cause the students to be careless or inattentive. In addition, administering many items that are too advanced or too elementary is not an efficient use of testing time.

To address these problems, educational achievement and aptitude batteries typically are constructed using multiple test levels. Each test level is constructed to be appropriate for examinees at a particular point in their education, often defined by grade or age. To measure student growth, performance on each of the test levels is related to a single score scale. The process used for associating performance on each test level to a single score scale is *vertical scaling* and the resulting scale is a *developmental score scale*.

Equating cannot be used to conduct vertical scaling. Recall that the goal of equating is to be able to use scores on alternate forms interchangeably. Because of differences in content and difficulty for test levels, it is unlikely that scores on different test levels could be used interchangeably. For example, in an achievement test, the questions on a test level appropriate for eighth graders are designed to be more difficult than the questions on a test level appropriate for third graders. So, eighth graders would be measured more precisely on the test level appropriate for eighth graders than on the test level appropriate for third graders. In addition, the content of a test level appropriate for eighth graders would be more appropriate for eighth graders than for third graders. Thus, equating is not appropriate, because scores earned on different test levels would not be able to be used interchangeably.

In this section, vertical scaling methods and designs are discussed. The type of domain being measured and the definition of growth are considered. Methodology is presented for three data collection designs. Three types of statistical procedures are considered. The methodology used in vertical scaling is much more complicated than that used in equating. In addition, there are a large number of decisions that must be made in the process of conducting the scaling. Because of the large number of possibilities in implementing vertical scaling methods, this section will only be able to provide a general framework and discuss the types of decisions that are made.

This section concludes with a survey of research on vertical scaling. Unfortunately, the research is quite sparse and provides minimal guidance for making many of the required decisions. A framework for vertical scaling is presented. This framework is intended to help future researchers fill in many of the gaps in the research so that decisions about designs and statistical methods can be made based on a stronger research foundation.

9.8.1 Structure of Batteries

Vertical scaling procedures are often used with elementary achievement test batteries, such as the ITBS (Hoover et al., 2003). They are also used with elementary aptitude batteries such as the Cognitive Abilities Test (CogAT) (Lohman and Hagen, 2002). These batteries contain tests in a number of areas, and they are used with students in a range of grades.

For achievement batteries, students at each grade level are administered test questions designed to assess achievement over content that is relevant for that grade level. Moving from assessments that are used at earlier grades

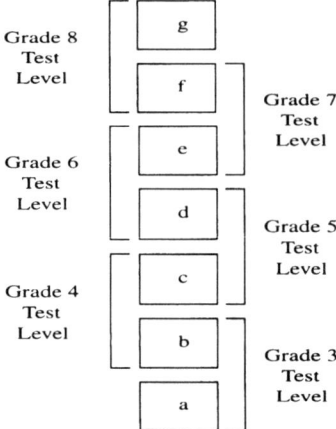

FIGURE 9.6. Illustrative structure of a grade level test.

to those used at later grades, the test questions become more difficult, and the content becomes more advanced. In some cases, the content covered at later levels is quite different from the content covered at earlier levels.

Often, there is overlap of test questions from one test level to the next. The primary reason for the overlap is that the content is taught across grades. Also, doing so reduces the test development burden, because the same items are used on adjacent test levels.

Figure 9.6 illustrates this overlap, showing the structure of a test such as the ITBS. The test illustrated in Figure 9.6 covers grades 3 through 8. This test contains 7 blocks of items, labeled a–g. Blocks a and b are administered as part of the grade 3 test level, blocks b and c as part of the grade 4 test level, blocks c and d as part of the grade 5 test level, and so on. Beginning with the grade 4 test level, each test level has a block of items in common with the previous level. For example, block b contains the more advanced content on the grade 3 test level and the less advanced content on the grade 4 level.

At least two alternate forms of these tests typically are constructed and used so that individuals do not receive the same items in consecutive years. For example, if Forms A and B were constructed, Form A might be administered in year 1 and Form B in year 2. A third grader in year 1 would receive Form A. When that third grader becomes a fourth grader in year 2, he or she would receive Form B. Assuming Forms A and B contain none of the same items, this examinee would receive different items in the third and the fourth grades. Thus, alternate forms avoid the problem of the examinee being administered some of the same items in two years, which would have happened if Form A had been administered in years 1 and 2.

9.8.2 Type of Domain Being Measured

The extent to which the subject matter covered by a test is tied to the school curriculum can influence the choice of methodology for vertical scaling. Most areas included on aptitude tests, and some areas tested on educational achievement tests, are not closely tied to the educational curriculum. For example, vocabulary, which is often assessed on aptitude and achievement batteries, tends not to be taught systematically by grade level—at least not throughout the country.

Other achievement test areas are closely tied to the curriculum in schools. For such tests, students tend to score better on the new subject matter near the end of the year in which the subject matter is emphasized than they do at the end of the previous year. For this reason, the amount of growth shown on the new subject matter is greater than the amount of growth shown in subject matter introduced in previous years.

For example, in the mathematics computation area, "division with whole numbers" is typically covered in grades 3 and 4. "Addition with decimals" is typically covered in grades 5 and 6. Thus, based on what students are studying in school, students in grades 3 and 4 are expected to show considerable growth on test items covering "division with whole numbers." Less growth is expected on these test items in grades 5 and 6. Students in grades 3 and 4 are expected to do poorly on items covering "addition with decimals" and show little growth from previous years. More growth is expected on items covering "addition with decimals" in grades 5 and 6.

Refer to Figure 9.7 for an illustration of how, in an area such as mathematics computation, growth might be shown in the different subject matter areas. In this figure, item blocks from Figure 9.6 are shown along with grade 3 through grade 6. A "+" indicates those blocks administered at each grade. A "0" indicates which blocks are not administered. As shown in Figure 9.7, "division with whole numbers" items are administered to third- and fourth-grade students as part of block b. "Addition with decimals" items are administered to fifth- and sixth-grade students as part of block d. This figure illustrates that for subject matter areas like mathematics computation, students are administered items that closely relate to what they have been studying in school.

For example, a student who is tested at the beginning of fifth grade with the appropriate test level will show growth based on the material studied during fifth grade, including "addition with decimals." What if this fifth-grade student was tested using the fourth-grade level? In this case, the student would not have the opportunity to show growth based on what was learned about "addition with decimals," since these items were not included on the fourth-grade level. Thus, this fifth-grade student might be expected to demonstrate less growth on the fourth-grade level than on the fifth-grade level. Conceptually, this example suggests that students will tend to show different amounts of growth depending on which level they

		Grade 3	Grade 4	Grade 5	Grade 6	Grade 7	Grade 8
	g	0	0	0	0	0	+
	f	0	0	0	0	+	+
	e	0	0	0	+	+	0
Item Block	d (Includes "addition with decimals")	0	0	+	+	0	0
	c	0	+	+	0	0	0
	b (Includes "division with whole numbers")	+	+	0	0	0	0
	a	+	0	0	0	0	0

FIGURE 9.7. Illustration of the structure of a grade level mathematics test.

are administered when a test area is closely tied to the curriculum. Thus, the amount of growth shown by students in a particular grade is expected to vary across sub-content areas within the test area. By contrast, when an achievement test area is not closely tied to the curriculum, the amount of growth shown by students in a particular grade is expected to be similar across sub-content areas.

9.8.3 Definition of Growth

One crucial component in constructing a vertical scale is to develop a conceptual definition of growth, especially for test areas that are closely related to the school curriculum. Under what is referred to here as the *domain definition*, growth is defined over the entire range of test content covered by the battery, or the *domain* of content. Defined in this way, the domain includes content that is typically taught during a given grade as well as content that is typically taught in other grades. Thus, grade-to-grade growth is defined over all of the content in the domain.

One way to operationalize the domain definition involves administering all levels of the test battery to examinees in each grade. So, for example, in Figure 9.7 all item blocks (blocks *a* through *g*) are administered to students in each grade. Raw scores over all levels are calculated and transformed to a score scale to be used for score reporting. Following this process allows students from all grades to be ordered on the same scale. Grade-to-grade growth is defined as the change in scores from one grade to the next over the entire domain of content.

As suggested earlier, however, operationalizing growth in this way is difficult to implement in practice, because the test is too long and many questions are too difficult for some examinees and too easy for others. As discussed in the next section, more practical procedures can be used to operationalize growth under the domain definition.

Under what is referred to here as the *grade-to-grade definition*, growth is defined over the content that is on a test level appropriate for typical students at a particular grade. Growth from the beginning of grade 3 to the end of grade 3 might be assessed using only the content on the third-grade level of a test, which is item blocks a and b in Figure 9.7.

One way to operationalize the grade-to-grade definition is to administer the level of the test designed for each grade at the beginning of that grade and at the beginning of the next grade. Using the common items to link the levels together, these data are used to transform scores on each level to a score scale used for score reporting. Grade-to-grade growth is defined as the change from one grade to the next over the content taught in a particular grade.

The grade-to-grade definition of growth defines growth over content that is part of the curriculum in a particular grade. Under the domain definition of growth, average growth is defined over the content that is covered across all of the grades. For subject matter areas that are closely related to the school curriculum, growth observed between adjacent grades will tend to be different under the grade-to-grade definition from under the domain definition. If the content area of the test is closely tied to the curriculum, then the two definitions are expected to lead to different scaling results. Otherwise, the scaling results are expected to be similar.

The actual situation is even more complex than the preceding discussion suggests. When conducting scaling, the observed average grade-to-grade growth depends on the nature of the area to be assessed, the definition of growth that is used, how the data are collected, on the characteristics of the score scale that is used, and on the statistical methods that are used to conduct the scaling.

9.8.4 Designs for Data Collection for Vertical Scaling

Taking advantage of the overlapping structure of elementary achievement and aptitude test batteries, a *common item design* can be used to conduct the scaling. Following this design, each test level is administered to examinees at the appropriate grade. Examinee performance on the items that are common to adjacent test levels are used to indicate the amount of growth that occurs from one grade to the next. The data from this design can be used to place scores from all of the test levels on a common scale.

This design is illustrated in Figure 9.8. Note that the grades are now given as rows in the figure, and item blocks as columns. To implement this design, one test level is considered as the base level. The item blocks that are common between adjacent levels are used to link scores from the adjacent levels. A chaining process is used to place scores from all of the levels on the base level. For example, if the grade 3 level is chosen as the

378   9. Score Scales

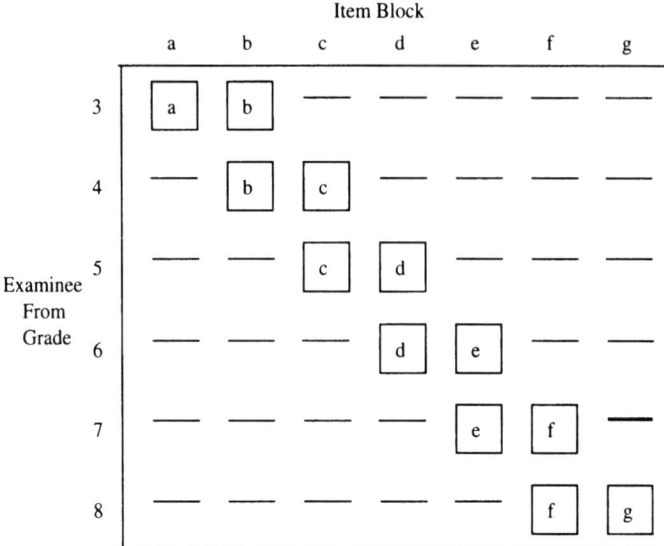

FIGURE 9.8. Illustration of a common-item design.

base level, the grade 4 level is linked to the grade 3 level using item block b. The grade 5 level is linked to the grade 4 level using item block c. The grade 5 level is linked to the grade 3 through the grade 4 level using a linking chain. A similar process is used to link the grade 6, 7, and 8 levels to the base level.

In the *equivalent groups design*, examinees in each grade are randomly assigned to take either the test level designed for their grade or the test level designed for adjacent grades. In one variant of this design, to avoid administering test questions that are too difficult, examinees in each grade (except the lowest) are randomly assigned to take the test level designed for their grade or the test level designed for one grade below their grade. Random assignment is often achieved using spiraling.

This variant is illustrated in Figure 9.9. Randomly equivalent groups of examinees are administered the level appropriate for their grade and the level below their grade. So, fourth graders are randomly assigned to take either the third- or the fourth-grade test level, fifth graders are randomly assigned to take either the fourth- or the fifth-grade test level, and so forth. By chaining across grades, the data from this administration also are used to place scores from all of the test levels on a common scale. Note that this design does not necessarily make use of the items that are common from one level to the next.

In the *scaling test design*, a special test is constructed that spans the content across all of the grade levels. This *scaling test* is constructed to be of a length that can be administered in a single sitting. For example,

9.8 Vertical Scaling and Developmental Score Scales 379

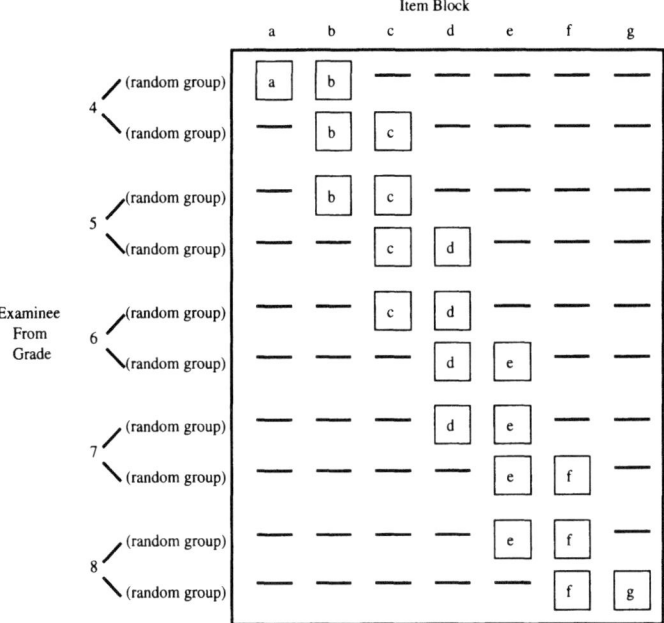

FIGURE 9.9. Illustration of an equivalent groups design.

if a scaling test is constructed for a battery that is designed for grades 3 through 8, the scaling test is constructed to represent the content covered in grades 3 through 8. Students in all of the grades are administered the same scaling test. Because many items are too difficult for students in the early grades, special instructions are given to the students telling them that there will be difficult items on the test and that they should do their best. Data from the scaling test are used to construct the score scale. Each examinee taking the scaling test also takes the test level designed for their grade. These data are used to link scores on each test level to the scale.

In the scaling test design illustrated in Figure 9.10, note that examinees in all grades are administered the scaling test (st). Each examinee is also administered the test level appropriate for her or his grade. The score scale is defined using scores on the scaling test. Scores on each test level are linked to the scaling test.

Among the designs just considered, the common-item design is the easiest to implement when the test battery contains items that are common to adjacent levels. In this case, the common-item design is implemented using standard administration conditions with the standard test battery. The equivalent groups design also uses the standard test battery, but requires a special administration in which test levels designed for adjacent grades are spiraled. Of the three designs discussed here, the scaling test design is the most difficult to implement. The scaling test design requires construction

380   9. Score Scales

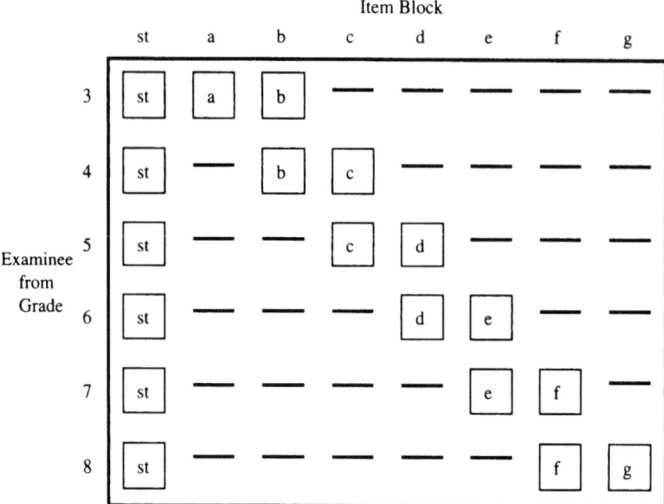

FIGURE 9.10. Illustration of a scaling test design.

of a scaling test, and requires a special administration in which the scaling test and the appropriate test level are administered to students in each grade.

One major problem with the common-item design is that it is subject to context effects. In a standard administration, the common items between adjacent levels typically are placed at the end of the test for the lower level and at the beginning of the test for the higher level. Likely items will behave differently when administered at the beginning of a testing session as opposed to at the end of a testing session. These sorts of context effects can create systematic error in the linking using the common-item design. The equivalent groups design need not be affected by this problem, because the linking of adjacent test levels can be based on random groups, rather than on common items. Similarly, the scaling test design need not be affected by the context effects associated with the common items, because the linking of each test level to the scaling test can be based on the same examinees taking the test level and the scaling test.

Although it is the most difficult to implement of the three designs, the scaling test design has the advantage of explicitly considering the domain definition of growth. As discussed earlier in this chapter, under this definition, growth is defined over the content covered across all grades. The scaling test has the advantage that it explicitly orders students from all grades on a single domain. The other two designs do not allow for an explicit ordering because examinees in all grades do not take the same test questions. Especially for content areas that are closely tied to the curriculum, the scaling test design can be expected to produce scaling results that are different from those produced by the other two designs.

9.8.5 Test Scoring

Scores on vertically scaled tests typically are calculated in two steps. In the first step, a raw score is calculated. In the second step, the raw scores are transformed to scale scores. Traditionally, the raw score has been the total number-correct score for dichotomously scored tests or the total number of points for tests that have polytomously scored items, like those containing constructed response items. For tests that are IRT-based, the raw score can be estimated ability ($\hat{\theta}$), which often must be estimated using iterative procedures, or it can be the same type of total score used with traditional methods.

The transformation of raw scores to scale scores can be linear or nonlinear. In traditional methods, a nonlinear transformation is typically used that is designed to lead to an educationally appropriate score scale. For example, when grade equivalents are constructed, the median raw score at the beginning of grade 3 might be assigned a scale score of 3.0, the median raw score at the beginning of grade 4 a scale score of 4.0, and so forth. Raw-to-scale score conversions for scores between these score points might be assigned by interpolation. A conversion resulting from this process is almost certainly nonlinear. Other traditional score scales might be constructed, with it nearly always being the case that the raw-to-scale score conversions are nonlinear.

In IRT, when raw scores are estimated abilities ($\hat{\theta}$), the raw-to-scale score transformations can be linear or nonlinear. The use of linear transformations in this case assumes that the IRT θ-scale is educationally appropriate, as suggested earlier in this chapter. Although it may be reasonable in some cases, there is no substantive reason to believe that the θ-scale, or a linear transformation of it, is educationally appropriate in general. When using IRT with the same type of total score used with traditional methods, the raw-to-scale score transformations are typically nonlinear.

When constructing the score scale, data are collected using one of the designs, and an approach for data analysis is chosen. In any approach, the first step is to relate performance on the test or tests used in the scaling study to a single *interim score scale*. The second step involves transforming the interim score scale to a scale with specified properties. The third step is to relate examinee performance on the each of the test levels to the score scale. Three statistical methods for establishing the score scale are discussed in the following sections.

9.8.6 Hieronymus Statistical Methods

Hieronymus scaling (Petersen et al., 1989) can be conducted using data from any of the data collection designs considered. In all cases, the scaling makes use of the total number-correct score for dichotomously scored tests or the total number of points for tests that have polytomously scored items.

Scaling Test Design

In Hieronymus scaling with a scaling test, raw scores on the scaling test are used as the interim score scale. The data used for conducting the scaling are the score distributions on the scaling test for students in each of the grades. Typically, the data are collected from a nationally representative sample so that the score distributions have inherent meaning.

To conduct the scaling, the median number-correct score on the scaling test for each grade level is assigned a prespecified score scale value. The remainder of the number-correct scaling test score-to-scale-score transformation is developed to meet other desired properties of scale scores.

Consider a situation in which Hieronymus scaling is used to construct grade equivalents associated with test levels appropriate for students in grades 3–8 as has been done with the ITBS (Hoover et al., 2003). Grade equivalents are normatively based scores. The school year is divided into ten months (assuming that students are on vacation for two months in the summer). The scale is defined using grade medians. At the beginning of third grade, the median scale score is set to 3.0, the median scale score at the beginning of fourth grade is set to 4.0, and so on. The median scale score for third grade students at the middle of the year is set at 3.5, the median scale score in the middle of grade 4 is set to 4.5, and so on.

Assume that a scaling test is administered in the middle of the school year. In this case, the median scaling test score for third graders is transformed to a scale score of 3.5, the median scaling test score for fourth graders is transformed to a scale score of 4.5, and so forth. These medians are used as points to define the score scale. In addition, because the authors of the test believe that for their tests, the variability of within-grade achievement should increase as grade increases, a transformation of scaling test raw scores to scale scores is sought that leads to increasing within-grade variability. Various procedures can be developed that lead to such a transformation. After the score scale is set on the scaling test, scores on each level are linked to the scores on the scaling test.

This procedure can be used to develop score scales other than grade equivalents. For example, the test developer might believe that year-to-year growth declines from one grade to the next. In this case, the grade medians might be set at values that indicate decreasing average growth over grades. For example, with the current forms of the ITBS (Hoover et al., 2003), a developmental score scale was constructed with grade medians as follows: grade 3–185, grade 4–200, grade 5–214, grade 6–227, grade 7–239, and grade 8– 250. As these values indicate, the grade-to-grade change decreases from 15 (200–185) points between grade 3 and grade 4 to 11 (250–239) points between grade 7 and grade 8.

Hieronymus scaling uses estimated true score distributions in the process of forming the score scale. By using true score distributions, the amount of growth, especially at percentiles other than the median, is defined by true score distributions rather than by observed score distributions. According to Petersen et al. (1989), regressed score estimates of true scores (Feldt and Brennan, 1989) are used when Hieronymus scaling is applied with the ITBS. The estimated true scores are found using the following equation,

$$\hat{\tau} = \sqrt{\rho(Y,Y')}\,[Y - \mu(Y)] + \mu(Y),$$

where $\rho(Y,Y')$ is test reliability for the examinee's grade group and $\mu(Y)$ is the mean for that grade group. The distributions of estimated true scores are used in the scaling process.

Some questions about this procedure which might be researched include the following: What are the effects of using true score distributions as compared to observed score distributions in the vertical scaling process? What would be the effects of estimating true score distributions using strong true score models such as those developed by Lord (1965, 1969)? What are the effects of using different types of procedures in developing the transformation of scaling test number-correct scores to scale scores?

Common-Item and Equivalent Groups Designs

In Hieronymous scaling with the common-item design, raw scores on one test level (usually one for a middle grade) are typically set as an interim scale. Through common-item linking procedures, the common items are used to transform raw scores on all of the levels on this interim score scale. In this process, plots of item difficulties for the common items can be used to help eliminate any items from the common item set that are behaving differently in adjacent grades. When the equivalent groups design is used, the randomly equivalent groups are used to transform raw scores on all of the levels to the level designated as the interim scale. Using this interim score scale in place of scores on the scaling test, the same procedures described for use with the scaling test design are then used to develop the scale using the common-item and equivalent groups designs.

9.8.7 Thurstone Statistical Methods

Thurstone (1925) described a method for scaling tests that assumes scores on an underlying scale are normally distributed within each grade group of interest. He made use of item difficulties (classical p-values) to conduct scaling. Thurstone (1938) modified this method to use total (number-correct) scores rather than item difficulties. Gulliksen (1950, p. 284) referred to this later method, which also assumes that scores are normally distributed within each grade group of interest, as Thurstone's absolute scaling method. This method has been used to scale achievement test batteries and is referred to here as Thurstone scaling.

Thurstone scaling can be conducted using data collected from any of the data collection designs introduced previously. This method makes use of the total number-correct score for dichotomously scored tests or the total number of points for tests that have polytomously scored items. Here the method is first described for two grade groups, followed by a brief discussion of the method applied to more than two grade groups.

Thurstone Scaling for Two Grade Groups–General Process

Thurstone scaling for two groups typically begins with frequency distributions of raw scores on a common set of test questions for each of two groups. To fix the score scale, the mean and standard deviation of the scale scores are specified for one of the groups. In this section, the method is developed in three steps. First, relationships between scale scores are presented for the two groups. Second, a process is developed for transforming raw scores to scale scores that are normalized within each group. Third, a process is described for converting the raw scores to the scale scores.

Step 1. Finding relationships between scale scores for two grade groups. First, consider some relationships between common scale scores that are useful for developing Thurstone scaling. Refer to the two grade groups as group 1 and group 2. Assume that the mean and standard deviation of the scale scores are fixed by the investigator for group 1. The random variable SC is used to represent these scores on the scale and sc represents a realization (particular value) of SC. Define the following terms:

$\mu_1(SC)$ is the mean scale score in group 1,

$\sigma_1(SC)$ is the standard deviation of scale scores in group 1,

$\mu_2(SC)$ is the mean scale score in group 2, and

$\sigma_2(SC)$ is the standard deviation of scale scores in group 2.

Define standardized scores within each group as follows:

$$z_1 = \frac{sc - \mu_1(SC)}{\sigma_1(SC)} \quad \text{and} \quad z_2 = \frac{sc - \mu_2(SC)}{\sigma_2(SC)}.$$

Solving each of these equations for sc,

$$sc = z_1 \sigma_1(SC) + \mu_1(SC), \text{ and} \tag{9.18}$$

$$sc = z_2 \sigma_2(SC) + \mu_2(SC). \tag{9.19}$$

Setting these equations equal to one another,

$$z_1 \sigma_1(SC) + \mu_1(SC) = z_2 \sigma_2(SC) + \mu_2(SC).$$

Solving for z_1,

$$z_1 = \frac{\sigma_2(SC)}{\sigma_1(SC)} z_2 + \frac{\mu_2(SC) - \mu_1(SC)}{\sigma_1(SC)}. \tag{9.20}$$

This equation is equivalent to equation 10 in Gulliksen (1950, p. 285) and provides the relationship between standardized scale scores for group 2 and standardized scale scores for group 1. This equation provides the foundation for Thurstone scaling.

Step 2. Transforming the raw scores. The next step is to tabulate the raw score frequency distribution for each group, and then normalize the scores within each group using equation (9.3). Refer to the raw score variable on the test as Y, and a realization (particular value) as y. Refer to a normalized score for group 1 as $z_1^*(y)$. Similarly, for group 2 refer to a normalized score as $z_2^*(y)$.

Gulliksen (1950, p. 284) recommended choosing 10 or 20 raw score points when implementing this procedure. A scatterplot is constructed for the 10 or 20 $z_1^*(y)$ and $z_2^*(y)$ pairs. Gulliksen (1950, p. 285) indicated that if the scatterplot is close to a straight line then it is said that $z_1^*(y)$ and $z_2^*(y)$ can be normalized on the same scale. Otherwise, the Thurstone scaling procedure is abandoned. Also define the following terms:

$\mu[z_1^*(y)]$ is the mean of the 10 or 20 $z_1^*(y)$ values for group 1,

$\sigma[z_1^*(y)]$ is the S.D. of the 10 or 20 $z_1^*(y)$ values for group 1,

$\mu[z_2^*(y)]$ is the mean of the 10 or 20 $z_2^*(y)$ values for group 2, and

$\sigma[z_2^*(y)]$ is the S.D. of the 10 or 20 $z_2^*(y)$ values for group 2.

The choice of score points to use in this procedure is arbitrary, but it can affect the scaling results. For example, Williams et al. (1998) compared using all score points to using all score points between the 10th and 90th percentiles for both distributions. They found quite different scaling results using these two sets of points.

Step 3. Relating the transformed raw scores to the score scale. equation (9.20) displays the relationship between a particular z_1 and z_2. Because $z_1^*(y)$ and $z_2^*(y)$ values are both normalized scores, they should satisfy the relationship in equation (9.20). Now, substitute $z_1^*(y)$ and $z_2^*(y)$ into equation (9.20). Taking the mean and standard deviation over the 10 or 20 score points gives

$$\mu[z_1^*(y)] = \frac{\sigma_2(SC)}{\sigma_1(SC)}\mu[z_2^*(y)] + \frac{\mu_2(SC) - \mu_1(SC)}{\sigma_1(SC)}, \text{ and}$$

$$\sigma[z_1^*(y)] = \frac{\sigma_2(SC)}{\sigma_1(SC)}\sigma[z_2^*(y)].$$

To find the standard deviation for group 2, rearrange terms to obtain

$$\sigma_2(SC) = \frac{\sigma[z_1^*(y)]}{\sigma[z_2^*(y)]}\sigma_1(SC). \qquad (9.21)$$

Note from the preceding equation that

$$\frac{\sigma_2(SC)}{\sigma_1(SC)} = \frac{\sigma[z_1^*(y)]}{\sigma[z_2^*(y)]}.$$

Using this result and rearranging terms, the mean for group 2 is

$$\mu_2(SC) = \sigma_1(SC)\left[\mu[z_1^*(y)] - \frac{\sigma[z_1^*(y)]}{\sigma[z_2^*(y)]}\mu[z_2^*(y)]\right] + \mu_1(SC). \qquad (9.22)$$

These expressions were presented by Williams et al. (1998, p. 97). Equation (9.18) can be used to transform any normalized score to the score scale as follows:

$$sc = z_1^*(y)\sigma_1(SC) + \mu_1(SC). \qquad (9.23)$$

To convert the $z_2^*(y)$ values to the same scale, use equation (9.21) and (9.22) in equation (9.19) to obtain

$$sc = z_2^*(y)\frac{\sigma[z_1^*(y)]}{\sigma[z_2^*(y)]}\sigma_1(SC) + \sigma_1(SC)\left[\mu[z_1^*(y)] - \frac{\sigma[z_1^*(y)]}{\sigma[z_2^*(y)]}\mu[z_2^*(y)]\right] + \mu_1(SC). \qquad (9.24)$$

To convert raw scores to scale scores (even those other than the 10 to 20 scores used in the scaling process), raw scores are normalized using equation (9.3). For group 1, equation (9.23) is used to convert the normalized scores to scale scores. To convert group 2 raw scores to scale scores, raw scores are normalized using equation (9.3). Then equation (9.24) is used to convert the normalized scores to scale scores. Because the same instrument is administered to students in both groups, any differences in the conversions of scores for group 1 and group 2 are due to sampling error or model misfit.

Note that for the special case where $\mu_1(SC) = 0$ and $\sigma_1(SC) = 1$,

$$\sigma_2(SC) = \frac{\sigma[z_1^*(y)]}{\sigma[z_2^*(y)]}, \quad \text{and}$$

$$\mu_2(SC) = \left[\mu[z_1^*(y)] - \frac{\sigma[z_1^*(y)]}{\sigma[z_2^*(x)]}\mu[z_2^*(y)]\right].$$

Thurstone Scaling for Two Groups with any of the Three Designs

The procedures just described can be used to develop a score scale for two groups. If the common-item design is used, the raw scores on the test level appropriate for a group are linked to raw scores on the common items and then to scale scores. In this process plots of item difficulties can be used to help eliminate any items from the common item set that are behaving differently in adjacent grades. If the scaling test design is used, the raw scores on the test level appropriate for a group are linked to the raw scores on the scaling test and then to scale scores. In the equivalent groups design, the scaling process provides the conversion of raw scores to scale scores on the level used in the scaling.

Thurstone Scaling for Three or More Groups

For any of the three designs, the mean and standard deviation of scale scores for one group are specified. Adjacent group raw scores on a test level are transformed to scale scores using the procedures described for two groups. A chaining process is used to convert raw scores on the other levels to the score scale.

9.8.8 IRT Statistical Methods

IRT scaling can be conducted using data from any of the three data collection designs. The scaling typically makes use of the entire set of item-level responses from the examinees to the test items.

Common-Item Design

The data used for IRT scaling under the common-item design are the item responses for students on the test level taken for students in the grades included in the scaling study. Items are in common from one level to the next, which allows for test levels to be linked to a common scale. Under the common-item design, the IRT parameters are estimated either using separate computer runs for each test level or by using a single simultaneous run for all levels.

When separate estimation is used, the IRT parameters are estimated separately at each grade. The θ-scale for one grade is chosen as the base scale, and then the common items are used to place item parameter estimates, examinee ability estimates, and estimated ability distributions on the base scale using linking methods (e.g., mean/mean, mean/sigma, or an item characteristic curve method). Plots of the item parameters can be used to help eliminate any items from the common item set that are behaving differently in adjacent grades. A chaining process is required to link estimates for levels that are not adjacent to the base level.

The following steps could be used in separate estimation runs for the example shown in Figure 9.8:

1. At each of grades 3 through 8, separately estimate IRT item parameters and ability distributions.

2. Assume that the θ-scale for grade 3 is chosen as the base scale. Using the items that are common between the test level administered to third graders and the test level administered to fourth graders, a

linear scale transformation is found (say, by using a test characteristic curve method). Items that appear to behave differently on the two levels can be eliminated from the common item set. The resulting transformation is used to place the item parameter estimates and estimated ability distributions for the test level administered to fourth graders on the θ-scale that was established for grade 3.

3. Using the items that are common between the test level administered to fourth graders and the test level administered to fifth graders, a linear scale transformation is found using a process similar to that followed in step 2 to place the item parameter estimates and estimated ability distributions on the θ-scale for fourth graders. Using a chaining process, the transformation developed in step 2 is then used to place the item parameter estimates and estimated ability distributions for the level administered to fifth graders on the θ-scale that was established for grade 3.

4. A similar process is used for the levels given to sixth, seventh, and eighth graders.

After chaining, all item parameters and estimated ability distributions are on the base scale. In addition, the mean and standard deviation of the estimated ability (quadrature) distributions transformed to the grade 3 scale can be used to compare the difference in mean ability and variability at the different grade levels.

If concurrent estimation is used with the common-item design, the item responses for all grade levels are formatted for a concurrent run. That is, an examinee item response string contains item response data for the items taken and a "not reached" code is used for the items not taken. Referring to Figure 9.8, for example, each examinee's response string would include places for responses to all items in item blocks a through g. A grade 3 examinee would have item response data for items in blocks a and b, with the "not reached" code appearing for item blocks c through g. A grade 4 examinee would have item response data for items in blocks c and d, with the "not reached" code appearing for item blocks a, b, and e through g. The resulting item parameter estimates, ability estimates, and estimated ability distributions are on the same θ-scale under the IRT assumptions

When concurrent estimation is applied, it is important to use an estimation program that allows for multiple groups, such as BILOG-MG or ICL. In these runs, the grade groups should be identified so that the program will allow for and estimate ability distributions for each grade. The regular version of BILOG does not allow for multiple groups, and should not be used. From runs using BILOG-MG or ICL, a quadrature distribution of θ is obtained along with an estimate of the mean and standard deviation of ability for each grade level.

Equivalent Groups Design

The data used for IRT scaling under the equivalent groups design are the item responses for students on the test levels taken in the grades included in the scaling study. Test levels are in common from one grade group to the next, which allows for test levels to be linked to a common scale. Under the equivalent groups design, the IRT parameters can be estimated either using separate computer runs for each test level at each grade or by using a single simultaneous run for all levels and grades.

When separate estimation is used, the IRT parameters are estimated separately for each random group at each grade. The θ-scale for one grade is chosen as the base scale, and then the level that is common between adjacent grades is used to place item parameter estimates, examinee ability estimates, and estimated ability distributions for the next grade on the base scale using linking methods (e.g., mean/mean, mean/sigma, or an item characteristic curve method). Plots of the item parameters can be used to help eliminate any items from the adjacent levels that are behaving differently in adjacent grades. A chaining process is required to link estimates for levels that are not adjacent to the base level.

The following steps can be used in separate estimation runs for the example shown in Figure 9.9:

1. At each of grades 4 through 8, separately estimate IRT item parameters and ability distributions for each of the levels given at that grade.

2. Assume that the θ-scale for grade 4 is chosen as the base scale. For the level composed of item blocks b and c, find item parameter estimates separately for fourth and fifth grade students. From these item parameter estimates, find a linear scale transformation (say, by using a test characteristic curve method) to place the item parameters and ability distributions for the grade 5 examinees on the θ-scale that was established for grade 4. Items that appear to behave differently on the two levels can be eliminated from the common item set.

3. For the level composed of item blocks c and d, find a linear scale transformation similar to that followed in step 2 to place the item parameter estimates for grade 6 on the initial grade 5 θ-scale. Using a chaining process, the transformation developed in step 2 is then used to place the grade 6 item parameter estimates and ability distributions on the θ-scale that was established for grade 4.

4. A similar process is used for the other levels.

The result is that, after chaining, all item parameters and ability distributions are on the base scale. In addition, the mean and standard deviation of the transformed ability distributions can be used to compare the difference in mean ability and variability at the different grade levels.

If concurrent estimation is used with the equivalent groups design, the item responses for all grade levels must be formatted for a concurrent run. That is, an examinee item response string contains 0/1 data for the items taken and a "not reached" code is used for the items not taken. The resulting item parameter estimates, ability estimates, and estimated ability distributions will be on the same θ-scale. With concurrent estimation, parameters for all items are estimated in a single computer run of BILOG-MG or ICL. In this run, the grade groups are identified so that ability distributions are estimated for each of the grade groups.

Scaling Test Design

When using the scaling test design, each examinee is administered the scaling test and the test level appropriate to the examinee's grade level. If separate estimation runs are used, item parameter and ability distributions are estimated for the scaling test for students in all grades. Then the item parameters and ability distributions are estimated for the test levels separately for each grade. The item parameters for the test levels are then linked to the θ-scale established using the scaling test. The following steps can be used to conduct this estimation for the example shown in Figure 9.10:

1. Use data only on the scaling test and an indicator for grade level. These data are represented in Figure 9.10 by the first column of boxes containing *st*. Estimate item parameters for the scaling test items and ability distributions for each of grades 3 through 8 using a computer program such as BILOG-MG or ICL. Set the scale to have a mean of 0 and a standard deviation of 1 for grade 3. The base θ-scale is established by this computer run.

2. Separately, for each grade, estimate the item parameters and ability distributions for the item blocks administered to that grade. Set the scale for each run to have the mean and standard deviation for that grade as estimated in step 1 (alternatively, the whole within grade quadrature distribution could be taken from step 1). Thus, six computer runs are conducted, one for students in each of grades 3 through 8.

By following steps 1 and 2, the IRT item parameter estimates for the 6 test levels and the scaling test are expressed on the base θ-scale that was established in step 1.

With concurrent estimation, parameters for scaling test items and regular items are estimated in a single computer run of BILOG-MG or ICL. In this run, the grade groups are identified so that ability distributions are estimated for each of the grade groups. Item responses must be formatted

9.8 Vertical Scaling and Developmental Score Scales

so that an examinee item response string contains 0/1 data for the scaling test items and for the items on the test level taken, and a "not reached" code is used for the items not taken. If set up properly, the resulting item parameter estimates, ability estimates, and estimated ability distributions are all on the same scale.

Separate versus Concurrent Estimation

Concurrent estimation requires only one computer run, as compared to runs for each grade with separate estimation. When using separate runs it is necessary to link the levels as described earlier. Thus, separate estimation can be more time consuming than concurrent estimation. In addition, when the IRT model holds, concurrent estimation is expected to produce more stable results because it makes use of all of the available information for parameter estimation. Thus, in theory, concurrent estimation might be preferable.

Additional considerations suggest that separate runs might be preferable in practice. With separate estimation, item parameter estimates can be compared from one grade to the next to identify items that are behaving differently in adjacent grades. Since concurrent estimation produces only one item parameter estimate for each item, it is more difficult to discover whether items are behaving differently across grades. In addition, with concurrent estimation, violation of the unidimensionality assumption might be quite severe. This assumption requires that a single ability be measured across all grades, which seems unlikely with achievement tests. Violation of the unidimensionality assumption might cause problems with concurrent estimation. With separate estimation, violation of the unidimensionality assumption might have less of an impact on the IRT parameter estimates in that parameters for only one grade level are estimated on each run. Because concurrent estimation requires an estimation run with large numbers of items and many item responses coded as "not reached," concurrent estimation runs sometimes have convergence problems and can require quite a bit of computer time. For all of these reasons, it appears that separate estimation is the safer of the two alternatives. However, additional empirical comparisons of the two procedures in vertical scaling contexts is necessary, especially when studying the robustness of estimation to violations of IRT assumptions.

Test Scoring

The IRT procedures discussed so far result in item parameter estimates and ability distributions being on the same scale. A decision must be made about how to estimate examinee proficiency. Lord (1980) and Baker (1992a) provided various estimation methods. Thissen and Orlando (2001) gave an extended discussion of proficiency estimation with many examples.

Often, when IRT methods are used IRT proficiency is estimated using the entire response string for an examinee. Maximum likelihood (ML) estimates of proficiency are unbiased (for long tests). ML estimators do not exist for scores of zero or all correct on dichotomously scored tests. Bayesian expected a posteriori (EAP) estimators are biased estimates of proficiency, but typically have smaller standard errors than ML estimators. EAP estimators are sometimes referred to as regressed or shrinkage estimators because they typically are closer to the mean proficiency than are ML estimators.

In many testing programs, number-correct scoring is used with dichotomous tests for ease of scoring and so all examinees with the same number-correct score earn the same scale score. Estimators based on the total score make less use of the information in the response string, and, thus, are typically somewhat less precise than estimators based on the entire examinee response string. One alternative with number-correct scoring is to convert number-correct scores to the θ-scale using the test characteristic curve shown in equation (6.16). To use this equation, the raw score is treated as if it were a true score in a way similar to what was done with IRT true score equating. Lord (1980, p. 60) showed that this way of estimating IRT proficiency is a ML estimator if all items are the same. This estimator also is a ML estimator under the Rasch model. Thissen and Orlando (2001) described how to calculate EAP estimators with number-correct scoring. EAP estimators with number-correct scoring are shrinkage estimators like those used with the entire response string.

Very little research has been reported that compares the different estimators in vertical scaling situations. Because EAP estimators are regressed towards the mean proficiency, a proficiency distribution is used to calculate the EAP estimator. Consider a situation in which a third-grade student and a fourth-grade student were both administered the same test level and answered the same test questions correctly. Assume that the third-grade student's EAP is calculated using the third-grade proficiency distribution and fourth-grade students EAP is calculated using the fourth-grade proficiency distribution. Because the mean proficiency for third-grade students is lower than that for fourth-grade students, the third-grade student would receive a lower EAP estimate than the fourth-grade student. This situation suggests that the use of EAP estimators might create significant practical concerns in a vertical scaling situation. Unlike EAP estimators, ML estimators for the third and fourth grader would be the same. Additional research on the practical consequences of the use of these estimators is clearly warranted.

Scale Transformations

The θ-scale is often linearly transformed to meaningful units. For example, it might be desired to set the third-grade mean to 300 and the eighth-grade mean to 800. The theta scale also can be nonlinearly transformed to provide for growth patterns that reflect the kind of patterns that are expected. Consider a situation in which a test developer believes that the variability of scale scores should increase over grades. If the variability of the θ-estimates is not found to increase over grades, a nonlinear transformation of the ability scale might be used that leads to increased variability. As Lord (1980, p. 84) has shown, there typically is no obvious theoretical reason to prefer θ to a nonlinear transformation of θ. Thus, nonlinear transformations of θ can be considered for practical reasons.

9.8.9 Thurstone Illustrative Example

Thurstone scaling is illustrated in this section based on data from the ITBS Mathematics and Data Interpretation test. The test was administered to grade 3 through grade 8 students using the scaling test design. Students from all grades were administered a 32-item scaling test that covered the content from all of the grades. Students were also administered the test level appropriate for their grade. The test contains all multiple-choice items and the raw score is the total number of items correctly answered.

Raw score frequency distributions on the scaling test are shown in Table 9.12. Sample sizes and means and standard deviations are shown, by grade, at the bottom of the table. As expected, the mean scores on the scaling test increase as grade increases. The standard deviation of the scaling test scores also increase as grade increases. The scaling test is very difficult for third graders. On average, they answer around 40% of the items correctly. The scaling test is much less difficult for eighth graders, who on average correctly answer around 68% of the items.

Percentile ranks/100 for each grade are presented in Table 9.13. To conduct Thurstone scaling, these values are converted to standard normal deviates (z-scores) using equation (9.3). A set of these deviates (recall that Gulliksen suggested using 10–20) is used in the scaling. For the purposes of this example, z-scores associated with a scaling test raw score were between -2 and $+2$ were used for all grades. This set of z-scores is given in Table 9.14, and corresponds to scaling test raw scores between 10 and 22. The means and standard deviation of these z-scores, as shown in the bottom of Table 9.14, were used to find the means and standard deviations of the scale scores. To check on the Thurstone scaling assumptions the z-scores for each pair of grades could be graphed. The relationships are expected to be approximately linear if the Thurstone assumptions hold. Although not presented here, the graphs are close to being linear.

Means and standard deviations of scale scores are shown in Table 9.15 for two scalings. In the first scaling, the mean for third grade is set equal to 0 and the standard deviation equal to 1. Equations (9.21) and (9.22) can be used to find the mean and standard deviation for grades other than

TABLE 9.12. Scaling Test Frequency Distributions.

Scaling Test Score	Frequency Distributions					
	Grade 3	Grade 4	Grade 5	Grade 6	Grade 7	Grade 8
0	0	0	0	0	0	0
1	0	0	0	0	2	0
2	2	2	1	0	0	0
3	4	3	4	1	0	2
4	5	6	4	1	4	2
5	11	13	7	1	3	3
6	24	20	11	5	1	0
7	40	27	8	10	1	2
8	47	38	13	8	2	1
9	64	43	31	20	6	3
10	51	58	43	17	15	6
11	62	80	47	42	21	2
12	58	78	60	38	22	9
13	63	101	60	50	34	7
14	58	108	88	57	38	22
15	60	120	90	77	38	19
16	48	107	99	74	38	17
17	48	102	108	85	45	31
18	38	116	100	81	64	31
19	28	100	113	100	67	25
20	18	96	111	110	67	36
21	13	74	132	101	76	26
22	12	60	120	107	70	41
23	9	61	100	114	68	37
24	5	49	83	113	74	34
25	2	35	77	91	91	38
26	0	27	68	83	67	43
27	0	16	41	51	75	29
28	0	5	25	37	52	25
29	0	4	10	22	38	20
30	0	1	6	10	21	28
31	0	2	2	5	7	13
32	0	0	1	1	6	1
N	770	1552	1663	1512	1113	553
Mean	12.9351	16.2932	18.6133	19.8505	21.1662	21.7450
S.D.	4.4522	5.1633	5.2596	5.1650	5.4407	5.5927

9.8 Vertical Scaling and Developmental Score Scales 395

TABLE 9.13. Scaling Test Percentile Ranks/100.

Scaling Test Score	Percentile Ranks/100					
	Grade 3	Grade 4	Grade 5	Grade 6	Grade 7	Grade 8
0	.0000	.0000	.0000	.0000	.0000	.0000
1	.0000	.0000	.0000	.0000	.0009	.0000
2	.0013	.0006	.0003	.0000	.0018	.0000
3	.0052	.0023	.0018	.0003	.0018	.0018
4	.0110	.0052	.0042	.0010	.0036	.0054
5	.0214	.0113	.0075	.0017	.0067	.0099
6	.0442	.0219	.0129	.0036	.0085	.0127
7	.0857	.0370	.0186	.0086	.0094	.0145
8	.1422	.0580	.0250	.0146	.0108	.0172
9	.2143	.0841	.0382	.0238	.0144	.0208
10	.2890	.1166	.0604	.0360	.0238	.0289
11	.3623	.1611	.0875	.0556	.0400	.0362
12	.4403	.2120	.1197	.0820	.0593	.0461
13	.5188	.2697	.1557	.1111	.0845	.0606
14	.5974	.3370	.2002	.1465	.1168	.0868
15	.6740	.4104	.2538	.1908	.1509	.1239
16	.7442	.4836	.3106	.2407	.1851	.1564
17	.8065	.5509	.3728	.2933	.2224	.1998
18	.8623	.6211	.4354	.3482	.2713	.2559
19	.9052	.6907	.4994	.4081	.3302	.3065
20	.9351	.7539	.5667	.4775	.3904	.3617
21	.9552	.8086	.6398	.5473	.4546	.4177
22	.9714	.8518	.7156	.6161	.5202	.4783
23	.9851	.8908	.7817	.6892	.5822	.5488
24	.9942	.9262	.8367	.7642	.6460	.6130
25	.9987	.9533	.8848	.8317	.7201	.6781
26	1.0000	.9733	.9284	.8892	.7911	.7514
27	1.0000	.9871	.9612	.9335	.8549	.8165
28	1.0000	.9939	.9811	.9626	.9119	.8653
29	1.0000	.9968	.9916	.9821	.9524	.9060
30	1.0000	.9984	.9964	.9927	.9789	.9494
31	1.0000	.9994	.9988	.9977	.9915	.9864
32	1.0000	1.0000	.9997	.9997	.9973	.9991

TABLE 9.14. Inverse Normal Transformed Scores for Scaling Test Scores from 10-22.

Scaling Test Score	z-scores					
	Grade 3	Grade 4	Grade 5	Grade 6	Grade 7	Grade 8
10	−.5564	−1.1920	−1.5511	−1.7985	−1.9808	−1.8967
11	−.3522	−.9900	−1.3564	−1.5932	−1.7509	−1.7970
12	−.1503	−.7996	−1.1767	−1.3917	−1.5607	−1.6838
13	.0472	−.6139	−1.0121	−1.2206	−1.3757	−1.5499
14	.2466	−.4207	−.8408	−1.0516	−1.1911	−1.3607
15	.4511	−.2264	−.6627	−.8749	−1.0324	−1.1559
16	.6562	−.0412	−.4942	−.7039	−.8962	−1.0093
17	.8650	.1279	−.3244	−.5437	−.7642	−.8423
18	1.0909	.3085	−.1627	−.3901	−.6088	−.6561
19	1.3117	.4979	−.0015	−.2325	−.4394	−.5058
20	1.5146	.6867	.1681	−.0564	−.2783	−.3540
21	1.6975	.8729	.3579	.1188	−.1140	−.2077
22	1.9022	1.0442	.5697	.2952	.0507	−.0544
Mean	.6711	−.0574	−.4990	−.7264	−.9186	−1.0057
S.D.	.7722	.6955	.6457	.6393	.6124	.6006

TABLE 9.15. Mean and Standard Deviation of Scale Scores for Thurstone Scaling.

Statistic	Grade 3	Grade 4	Grade 5	Grade 6	Grade 7	Grade 8
Scaled such that grade 3 Mean is 0 and S.D. is 1						
Mean	.0000	.7348	1.2678	1.5485	1.8293	1.9640
S.D.	1.0000	1.1103	1.1958	1.2078	1.2608	1.2856
Scaled such that grade 4 Mean is 200 and grade 8 Mean is 250						
Mean	170.1117	200.0000	221.6806	233.0984	244.5200	250.0000
S.D.	40.6766	45.1643	48.6413	49.1311	51.2859	52.2946

grade 3. For example, the grade 4 mean and standard deviation on this scale are

$$\mu_2(SC) = \left[\mu[z_1^*(y)] - \frac{\sigma[z_1^*(y)]}{\sigma[z_2^*(y)]}\mu[z_2^*(y)]\right] = \left[.6711 + \frac{.7722}{.6955}.0574\right] = .7348,$$

and

$$\sigma_2(SC) = \frac{\sigma[z_1^*(y)]}{\sigma[z_2^*(y)]} = \frac{.7722}{.6955} = 1.1103.$$

These are the grade 4 mean and standard deviation in Table 9.15. The other means and standard deviations for this scaling can be found similarly.

For the second scaling, the grade 4 mean is intended to be 200 and the grade 8 mean is intended to be 250. Equation (9.1) can be used to linearly

9.8 Vertical Scaling and Developmental Score Scales

transform scores for one set of units to those for another set of units when two score equivalencies are specified. This equation can be used to convert scores from the scale in which grade 3 has a mean of 0 and a standard deviation of 1 to another scale. Let y_1 be the grade 4 mean on the original scale (.7348 from Table 9.15) and $sc(y_1)=200$ be the specified scale score mean for grade 4 on the new scale. Let y_2 be the grade 8 scale score mean on the original scale (1.9640 from Table 9.15) and $sc(y_2)=250$ be the specified scale score mean for grade 8 on the new scale. Applying equation (9.1), the slope of the transformation is

$$\frac{sc(y_2) - sc(y_1)}{y_2 - y_1} = \frac{250 - 200}{1.9640 - .7348} = 40.6769,$$

and the intercept is

$$sc(y_1) - \left[\frac{sc(y_2) - sc(y_1)}{y_2 - y_1}\right] y_1 = 200 - \left[\frac{250 - 200}{1.9640 - .7348}\right].7348 = 170.1106.$$

To find the standard deviation for the new scale, multiply the standard deviation for the first scale by the slope. To find the mean for the new scale, multiply the mean for the first scale by the slope and then add the intercept. Note that the mean and standard deviation for grade 3 equal the intercept and slope, apart from rounding error.

So far, only the scaling test has been considered. The next step in the Thurstone scaling process is to develop conversions of raw scores on each level to the score scale developed using the scaling test. The examinees administered the scaling test also were administered the level appropriate for their grade. The frequency distributions for these levels are given in Table 9.16. The numbers of items per level vary from 24 items for the grade 3 level to 36 for the grade 8 level. In this table, frequencies are blank for raw scores greater than the number of items on the level. The means and standard deviations of the level scores are given at the bottom of the table. Note that the levels contained different sets of test questions, so there is no expectation that the raw score means would increase over grades. Percentile ranks/100 for these distributions are shown in Table 9.17 and the z-scores, calculated using equation (9.3), are shown in Table 9.18.

Because the z-scores have a mean of 0 and a standard deviation of 1 within grade, the easiest way to convert these z-scores to scale scores is to multiply them by the scale score standard deviation shown in Table 9.15 and add the scale score mean shown in that table. For example, to convert a grade 3 z-score for the second score scale in Table 9.15:

$$sc = 40.6766(z) + 170.1117.$$

Applying this equation to the first z-score of -3.0118 in Table 9.18 results in a scale score of 47.6019, which rounds to an integer value of 48. Integer scale

TABLE 9.16. Raw Score Frequency Distributions for Test Levels.

Level Raw Score	Frequency Distributions					
	Grade 3	Grade 4	Grade 5	Grade 6	Grade 7	Grade 8
0	0	0	0	0	0	0
1	0	0	0	0	0	0
2	2	0	2	1	1	0
3	4	3	3	1	0	0
4	7	4	4	4	0	2
5	9	9	3	6	8	0
6	15	23	12	11	12	8
7	21	31	22	25	18	10
8	26	40	27	34	17	12
9	30	30	35	38	30	28
10	22	46	39	29	46	22
11	26	52	54	41	35	33
12	29	78	39	53	41	25
13	38	65	65	54	56	21
14	39	70	60	68	65	33
15	33	85	76	75	42	25
16	48	92	73	77	42	26
17	65	87	68	86	44	38
18	57	109	85	89	54	31
19	73	129	93	78	51	24
20	81	103	73	93	58	25
21	68	116	87	79	36	21
22	45	110	91	79	47	21
23	26	104	131	85	54	20
24	6	83	113	85	48	18
25		48	108	64	50	20
26		28	113	67	43	21
27		7	71	63	38	11
28			64	49	34	11
29			36	30	48	11
30			16	30	26	11
31				11	27	8
32				7	26	11
33					11	3
34					5	3
35					0	0
36						0
N	770	1552	1663	1512	1113	553
Mean	15.9208	17.3093	19.5935	19.0754	19.4753	17.9729
S.D.	4.9878	5.1799	5.9894	6.1461	7.0596	6.7965

9.8 Vertical Scaling and Developmental Score Scales 399

TABLE 9.17. Raw Score Percentile Ranks/100 for Test Levels.

Level Raw Score	Percentile Ranks/100					
	Grade 3	Grade 4	Grade 5	Grade 6	Grade 7	Grade 8
0	.0000	.0000	.0000	.0000	.0000	.0000
1	.0000	.0000	.0000	.0000	.0000	.0000
2	.0013	.0000	.0006	.0003	.0004	.0000
3	.0052	.0010	.0021	.0010	.0009	.0000
4	.0123	.0032	.0042	.0026	.0009	.0018
5	.0227	.0074	.0063	.0060	.0045	.0036
6	.0383	.0177	.0108	.0116	.0135	.0108
7	.0617	.0351	.0210	.0235	.0270	.0271
8	.0922	.0580	.0358	.0430	.0427	.0470
9	.1286	.0805	.0544	.0668	.0638	.0832
10	.1623	.1050	.0767	.0890	.0979	.1284
11	.1935	.1366	.1046	.1121	.1343	.1781
12	.2292	.1785	.1326	.1432	.1685	.2306
13	.2727	.2245	.1639	.1786	.2120	.2722
14	.3227	.2680	.2014	.2189	.2664	.3210
15	.3695	.3180	.2423	.2662	.3145	.3734
16	.4221	.3750	.2871	.3165	.3522	.4195
17	.4955	.4327	.3295	.3704	.3908	.4774
18	.5747	.4958	.3755	.4282	.4349	.5398
19	.6591	.5725	.4290	.4835	.4820	.5895
20	.7591	.6472	.4790	.5400	.5310	.6338
21	.8558	.7178	.5271	.5969	.5732	.6754
22	.9292	.7906	.5806	.6491	.6105	.7134
23	.9753	.8595	.6473	.7034	.6559	.7505
24	.9961	.9198	.7207	.7596	.7017	.7848
25		.9620	.7871	.8089	.7457	.8192
26		.9865	.8536	.8522	.7875	.8562
27		.9977	.9089	.8952	.8239	.8852
28			.9495	.9322	.8562	.9051
29			.9796	.9583	.8931	.9250
30			.9952	.9782	.9263	.9448
31				.9917	.9501	.9620
32				.9977	.9739	.9792
33					.9906	.9919
34					.9978	.9973
35					1.0000	1.0000
36						1.0000

TABLE 9.18. z-Scores for Test Levels.

Level Raw Score	z-scores					
	Grade 3	Grade 4	Grade 5	Grade 6	Grade 7	Grade 8
0						
1						
2	−3.0118		−3.2384	−3.4051	−3.3207	
3	−2.5626	−3.1004	−2.8621	−3.0926	−3.1220	
4	−2.2465	−2.7243	−2.6348	−2.7888	−3.1220	−2.9098
5	−2.0004	−2.4368	−2.4941	−2.5150	−2.6127	−2.6859
6	−1.7706	−2.1033	−2.2965	−2.2710	−2.2122	−2.2956
7	−1.5408	−1.8104	−2.0326	−1.9867	−1.9276	−1.9248
8	−1.3273	−1.5719	−1.8019	−1.7170	−1.7204	−1.6745
9	−1.1332	−1.4014	−1.6034	−1.5001	−1.5237	−1.3840
10	−.9849	−1.2534	−1.4278	−1.3472	−1.2934	−1.1340
11	−.8650	−1.0957	−1.2556	−1.2154	−1.1062	−.9226
12	−.7414	−.9212	−1.1142	−1.0661	−.9603	−.7370
13	−.6046	−.7569	−.9787	−.9208	−.7994	−.6063
14	−.4601	−.6187	−.8365	−.7759	−.6237	−.4650
15	−.3332	−.4734	−.6988	−.6243	−.4832	−.3228
16	−.1966	−.3186	−.5618	−.4776	−.3794	−.2031
17	−.0114	−.1696	−.4412	−.3309	−.2771	−.0567
18	.1883	−.0105	−.3173	−.1809	−.1640	.0999
19	.4100	.1827	−.1788	−.0415	−.0451	.2263
20	.7034	.3779	−.0528	.1005	.0778	.3420
21	1.0618	.5763	.0679	.2453	.1846	.4549
22	1.4700	.8085	.2034	.3830	.2807	.5633
23	1.9655	1.0782	.3781	.5341	.4013	.6759
24	2.6610	1.4036	.5849	.7050	.5293	.7885
25		1.7742	.7965	.8737	.6611	.9122
26		2.2106	1.0519	1.0458	.7978	1.0636
27		2.8401	1.3340	1.2545	.9303	1.2012
28			1.6399	1.4924	1.0636	1.3110
29			2.0446	1.7317	1.2431	1.4392
30			2.5891	2.0174	1.4490	1.5968
31				2.3969	1.6462	1.7747
32				2.8317	1.9422	2.0376
33					2.3481	2.4027
34					2.8413	2.7807
35						
36						

score values calculated in this way are shown in Table 9.19. This table gives the conversions of level raw scores to scale scores using Thurstone scaling, where the mean grade 4 score is intended to be 200 and the mean grade 8 score is intended to be 250. Note that due to rounding to integers, the means shown at the bottom of the table are slightly different from these values and from the means and standard deviations shown in Table 9.15. Triple asterisks (***) are given in the table for raw scores associated with zero frequencies in Table 9.16. To use this scaling operationally, these asterisks would need to be replaced by scale score values.

A number of choices were made in this scaling, including,

1. Using the scaling test design. Instead of using the scaling test design, the scaling test could have been ignored with common items serving to link the levels.

2. Using unsmoothed frequency distributions. Smoothing methods, such as the log-linear method, could have been used to smooth the score distributions before applying the Thurstone method.

3. Using scaling test scores only in the range of 10–22. A different range of scaling test scores might have been used.

Making different choices might have had a significant impact on the scaling results.

9.8.10 IRT Illustrative Example

IRT scaling is illustrated in this section using the same scaling situation used for the Thurstone example, except that 33 items were used for the scaling test instead of the 32 items used in the Thurstone example.

The first step in the scaling was to estimate the three-parameter logistic model item parameters for the scaling test items and the ability distributions for grades 3 through 8 using the program ICL (Hanson, 2002). Grade level and item response strings for the 33 scaling test items for each examinee in each of grades 3 through 8 were input into ICL. The resulting item parameters for the scaling test items are shown in Table 9.20 for the 33 scaling test items. The estimated mean and standard deviation of the ability distributions are shown in Table 9.21. When running ICL, the grade 3 mean ability was set at 0 and the standard deviation was set at 1, corresponding to the mean and standard deviation in Table 9.21. The mean and standard deviations of estimated ability for the other grades are also shown. As expected, the means increase over grades. The standard deviation for grade 3 is the lowest standard deviation among the grade distributions.

Next, the item parameters for each grade level test were separately estimated. Item response strings for the 24 grade 3 level items for each grade 3 examinee were input into ICL, and the mean and standard deviation of

402   9. Score Scales

TABLE 9.19. Raw-to-Thurstone Scale Score Equivalents for Test Levels.

Level Raw Score	Thurstone Scale Score Equivalents					
	Grade 3	Grade 4	Grade 5	Grade 6	Grade 7	Grade 8
0	***	***	***	***	***	***
1	***	***	***	***	***	***
2	48	***	64	66	74	***
3	66	60	82	81	84	***
4	79	77	94	96	84	98
5	89	90	100	110	111	110
6	98	105	110	122	131	130
7	107	118	123	135	146	149
8	116	129	134	149	156	162
9	124	137	144	159	166	178
10	130	143	152	167	178	191
11	135	151	161	173	188	202
12	140	158	167	181	195	211
13	146	166	174	188	204	218
14	151	172	181	195	213	226
15	157	179	188	202	220	233
16	162	186	194	210	225	239
17	170	192	200	217	230	247
18	178	200	206	224	236	255
19	187	208	213	231	242	262
20	199	217	219	238	249	268
21	213	226	225	245	254	274
22	230	237	232	252	259	279
23	250	249	240	259	265	285
24	278	263	250	268	272	291
25		280	260	276	278	298
26		300	273	284	285	306
27		328	287	295	292	313
28			301	306	299	319
29			321	318	308	325
30			348	332	319	334
31				351	329	343
32				372	344	357
33					365	376
34					390	395
35					***	***
36						***
n	770	1552	1663	1512	1113	553
Mean	170.0766	199.9374	221.5979	233.0683	244.5074	250.0249
S.D.	40.2137	44.8077	48.2552	48.8389	50.9196	51.9685

9.8 Vertical Scaling and Developmental Score Scales   403

TABLE 9.20. Item Parameter Estimates for Scaling Test.

	Item Parameter Estimates		
Item	$\hat{a}$	$\hat{b}$	$\hat{c}$
1	.3554	−2.3053	.2145
2	.5481	−.9207	.0776
3	.5463	−.6806	.0463
4	.5971	−1.9165	.0606
5	.4590	−1.2700	.0920
6	.5207	−.5475	.1359
7	.6288	.2589	.0926
8	.5864	.3934	.0679
9	.6927	.2786	.1025
10	.8306	2.3457	.2342
11	1.0389	2.3496	.1944
12	.8358	1.0954	.1197
13	.6095	.2042	.1396
14	1.2019	3.0194	.2062
15	.5440	2.3563	.1766
16	2.6108	3.7035	.1318
17	.2873	−4.9715	.1833
18	.3270	−2.5100	.1352
19	.5868	−.5935	.1448
20	.3864	−.5797	.0973
21	1.0631	3.0041	.2268
22	2.9796	1.1820	.1426
23	2.9696	1.2580	.1177
24	2.0354	1.4863	.1032
25	.5321	−.3181	.3314
26	.4434	2.4119	.2021
27	1.4114	2.2739	.2858
28	.7525	2.6242	.4159
29	.6045	1.2141	.1907
30	1.4366	3.3964	.2682
31	.5942	2.1994	.1816
32	1.3261	3.0413	.1779
33	1.4910	3.2330	.2218

TABLE 9.21. Scaling Test Mean and Standard Deviation of Quadrature Distributions.

Statistic	Grade 3	Grade 4	Grade 5	Grade 6	Grade 7	Grade 8
Mean	.0000	.4766	1.0467	1.2697	1.5198	1.6294
S.D.	1.0000	1.3417	1.2376	1.1520	1.2843	1.3066

the ability estimates were set equal to their grade 3 values in Table 9.21 (mean = 0 and standard deviation = 1). Then item response strings for the 27 grade 4 level items for each grade 4 examinee were input into ICL, and the mean and standard deviation of the ability estimates were set equal to their grade 4 values in Table 9.21 (mean = .4766 and standard deviation = 1.3417). Similar runs were conducted for grades 5 through 8. The resulting item parameter estimates are shown in Table 9.22 and Table 9.23. The quadrature points and weights for each grade output by ICL are shown in Table 9.24. Note that the same set of weights are used for all grades; only the quadrature points change.

The item parameter estimates and the quadrature distributions were used to estimate IRT ability associated with each raw score. The Bayesian EAP procedures outlined by Thissen and Orlando (2001) for estimating θ from number-correct scores were used. The resulting conversions are shown in Table 9.25. The means and standard deviations of the converted scores are given at the bottom of the table. These means and standard deviations were calculated using the raw score distributions from Table 9.12. Note that, as expected, the means are very similar to the means of the ability distribution in Table 9.21. A property of Bayesian EAP estimates is that they have standard deviations that are smaller than the standard deviations of the true abilities. For this reason, the standard deviations of the estimates in Table 9.25 are smaller than those given in Table 9.21.

The scores shown in Table 9.25 were linearly transformed, in the same manner as in the Thurstone illustrative example, so that the mean for grade 4 is 200 and the mean for grade 8 is 250. The resulting scores were rounded to integers. These scale scores are shown in Table 9.26. The means and standard deviations of these rounded scale scores are shown at the bottom of Table 9.26.

Note that there are a few peculiarities in these conversion tables. For example, the minimum scale score for grade 4 is a 47, whereas the minimum for grade 3 is 71. To use this table operationally, it might be necessary to adjust some of the converted scores to remove such peculiarities.

A number of choices were made in this scaling that might have affected the results, including,

1. Using the scaling test design. Instead of using the scaling test design, the scaling test could have been ignored with common items serving to link the test levels. In this case, simultaneous estimation of all levels could have been used; alternatively, estimation could have been conducted for each level separately and then the levels linked using a characteristic curve method.

2. Using a three-parameter logistic model. Other models such as the Rasch model might have been used. Also, since some of the items are associated with common stimuli, it would have been possible to treat

TABLE 9.22. Item Parameter Estimates for Grade 3 Through Grade 5 Test Levels.

	Grade 3			Grade 4			Grade 5		
Item	$\hat{a}$	$\hat{b}$	$\hat{c}$	$\hat{a}$	$\hat{b}$	$\hat{c}$	$\hat{a}$	$\hat{b}$	$\hat{c}$
1	.6623	−1.7588	.2355	.4871	−1.7983	.2073	.7659	−.2164	.1705
2	1.8133	−.3320	.1670	.7730	−1.4807	.1709	.8027	1.7578	.3102
3	1.0046	.2879	.0903	.7361	−1.4050	.1622	.7814	−.3171	.1268
4	.8258	−.2851	.2556	.6841	−1.7446	.1682	.7791	−.3009	.1713
5	.9489	1.1444	.1398	.4099	−1.1867	.1910	1.0739	1.1705	.1960
6	1.9097	−.6433	.1749	.4510	−.6519	.1581	.9363	.6193	.2575
7	1.3385	−.2531	.1874	.7029	−.6933	.1510	.5198	−.4862	.1238
8	1.1625	−.4903	.1894	.8748	1.5770	.2270	.5710	−.5949	.1007
9	.9651	−.6715	.2068	.7201	−.6747	.1576	.5607	3.2868	.1811
10	1.1184	−.8151	.0946	.7682	−.4032	.1830	.5296	.1240	.0979
11	1.2484	−.5136	.2050	.8985	1.0518	.1653	.5125	−1.0863	.1711
12	1.0093	−.7829	.2215	.9771	.4295	.2023	.7030	−.0178	.1364
13	.6348	−.5750	.2206	.5531	−.7916	.0941	.7591	.5650	.1326
14	.9372	.0726	.2021	.6460	−.4103	.1161	.7853	1.0533	.1614
15	1.1165	−1.6683	.1819	.8562	3.2785	.1972	.8929	2.8447	.2495
16	1.3468	−1.4973	.1729	.4662	−.1358	.1443	1.0710	1.6654	.1785
17	.9986	−.0882	.1761	.2612	2.1916	.2858	1.3515	1.8801	.1878
18	.8436	−.5085	.1680	.9300	.3665	.3045	.6466	−1.1738	.2103
19	1.2548	−1.5216	.1572	.6691	1.1842	.1915	.4982	.0412	.1478
20	1.2820	−1.3700	.1436	.5153	2.7494	.2109	.5401	−.4161	.1315
21	.4834	.8896	.1818	.7163	−1.2541	.1786	.7074	−.1792	.2218
22	.7634	.2707	.2052	.4588	.4950	.2575	.6815	1.1420	.2285
23	1.1353	1.4595	.1806	.6979	−.4215	.1378	.9036	1.5563	.2301
24	.5793	2.6153	.1478	.8350	−.2601	.2124	.6498	2.0358	.1342
25				.6076	.9793	.1508	.7952	.0305	.2956
26				1.0979	1.3918	.1599	.7752	−.1035	.1993
27				.7550	2.2035	.1637	.8220	.4883	.1001
28							.5659	−.2814	.1890
29							.7807	2.0459	.2028
30							.7084	1.6909	.1638

TABLE 9.23. Item Parameter Estimates for Grade 6 Through Grade 8 Test Levels.

	Grade 6			Grade 7			Grade 8		
Item	$\hat{a}$	$\hat{b}$	$\hat{c}$	$\hat{a}$	$\hat{b}$	$\hat{c}$	$\hat{a}$	$\hat{b}$	$\hat{c}$
1	.3788	−2.0874	.2144	.5717	1.2677	.1880	.7013	−.0432	.1911
2	.5425	−.1895	.1248	.6189	.9438	.1893	.4079	2.1740	.2083
3	.6845	.2969	.2015	.8873	3.2198	.1128	.8219	2.7704	.2041
4	.6895	.7116	.1691	1.0922	.8155	.2243	.5317	.8816	.1662
5	.4618	3.0221	.1634	1.0729	1.5494	.3414	.7659	2.6665	.2087
6	.6647	1.2778	.1222	.8625	2.2878	.2121	.8440	1.9682	.2720
7	.9905	1.3662	.1211	.7801	.2487	.2100	.6961	2.0992	.2470
8	.8713	1.5638	.2649	.5304	2.8720	.1822	.7807	2.8874	.1948
9	.9681	1.1414	.2231	.7613	1.1600	.1175	.6490	2.8416	.1005
10	.8994	3.2495	.1120	.9735	2.2300	.2187	.6600	1.2002	.2116
11	1.2870	.9828	.1918	.7433	1.8170	.1939	.9251	1.2574	.1206
12	.8942	1.5167	.2380	.7179	.0274	.1282	1.0706	2.6433	.2353
13	.6193	2.5384	.2230	.4314	1.9941	.1827	.5743	3.4645	.2703
14	.8677	.6133	.2264	.9047	2.9762	.1984	1.0868	3.0774	.2903
15	.7502	2.8486	.1722	.7852	1.1199	.1569	.7693	1.0790	.1587
16	1.1630	1.5724	.2278	1.0843	2.4689	.1683	.7774	2.6013	.1993
17	1.6625	2.3451	.2247	.6478	2.3614	.2372	.7589	4.1008	.1024
18	.8360	2.0923	.2282	.7433	2.1425	.1852	.5901	3.0271	.1269
19	.6961	−.6171	.1660	.6935	2.6765	.1741	.7301	2.2874	.2945
20	.6044	−.6404	.1404	.5534	1.2748	.2649	.8756	2.8914	.1375
21	.7781	.1471	.1062	.6412	−.2945	.1793	.7575	1.9348	.1955
22	.6191	−.4619	.1627	.6609	1.8432	.2018	.6274	2.1510	.2359
23	.6340	1.8393	.1887	.6125	1.0578	.1608	1.0417	2.1051	.2666
24	.6624	1.5655	.1873	.4592	−1.3724	.2102	.5031	2.7108	.1528
25	.6153	1.1251	.2056	.4567	1.7269	.1165	.5089	−.6375	.2271
26	.8782	.2191	.1010	.5852	2.7969	.1975	.8184	3.4129	.2790
27	.5920	2.0039	.2003	.4666	1.7784	.1060	.6696	1.3210	.1409
28	.8611	1.3833	.2484	1.1759	2.2023	.1627	.5120	2.5265	.2820
29	.6332	−.5467	.2049	.8536	2.3066	.2853	.6236	1.2576	.2269
30	.4841	2.3303	.1638	.8332	2.0141	.1522	.8480	1.7921	.1765
31	.7919	2.7614	.1762	.5192	3.1862	.1676	.9586	2.7230	.2691
32	.6500	1.9298	.1210	.7271	.3043	.2082	1.1176	4.2740	.2281
33				.5015	3.5056	.1798	.6391	.9603	.2257
34				.6307	1.7738	.1999	.8493	5.8240	.1877
35				.4867	3.3887	.2488	.6978	2.9096	.2384
36							1.3649	4.1636	.2177

TABLE 9.24. Quadrature Points and Weights.

		Quadrature Points				
Grade 3	Grade 4	Grade 5	Grade 6	Grade 7	Grade 8	Weights
−4.0014	−4.8929	−3.9068	−3.3396	−3.6178	−3.6009	.0000
−3.7962	−4.6175	−3.6527	−3.1032	−3.3543	−3.3327	.0001
−3.5910	−4.3421	−3.3987	−2.8668	−3.0909	−3.0645	.0001
−3.3858	−4.0668	−3.1446	−2.6305	−2.8274	−2.7963	.0003
−3.1806	−3.7914	−2.8906	−2.3941	−2.5639	−2.5281	.0005
−2.9754	−3.5160	−2.6366	−2.1577	−2.3004	−2.2599	.0010
−2.7702	−3.2406	−2.3825	−1.9213	−2.0370	−1.9917	.0018
−2.5650	−2.9652	−2.1285	−1.6849	−1.7735	−1.7235	.0031
−2.3598	−2.6899	−1.8744	−1.4485	−1.5100	−1.4553	.0051
−2.1546	−2.4145	−1.6204	−1.2121	−1.2465	−1.1871	.0080
−1.9494	−2.1391	−1.3664	−.9757	−.9830	−.9189	.0123
−1.7442	−1.8637	−1.1123	−.7393	−.7196	−.6507	.0179
−1.5390	−1.5883	−.8583	−.5029	−.4561	−.3825	.0251
−1.3338	−1.3130	−.6043	−.2665	−.1926	−.1143	.0336
−1.1286	−1.0376	−.3502	−.0302	.0709	.1539	.0433
−.9234	−.7622	−.0962	.2062	.3344	.4221	.0534
−.7182	−.4868	.1579	.4426	.5978	.6903	.0632
−.5130	−.2114	.4119	.6790	.8613	.9585	.0718
−.3078	.0639	.6659	.9154	1.1248	1.2267	.0781
−.1026	.3393	.9200	1.1518	1.3883	1.4949	.0814
.1026	.6147	1.1740	1.3882	1.6517	1.7631	.0814
.3078	.8901	1.4281	1.6246	1.9152	2.0313	.0781
.5130	1.1654	1.6821	1.8610	2.1787	2.2995	.0718
.7182	1.4408	1.9361	2.0974	2.4422	2.5677	.0632
.9234	1.7162	2.1902	2.3338	2.7057	2.8359	.0534
1.1286	1.9916	2.4442	2.5702	2.9691	3.1041	.0433
1.3338	2.2670	2.6983	2.8065	3.2326	3.3723	.0336
1.5390	2.5423	2.9523	3.0429	3.4961	3.6405	.0251
1.7442	2.8177	3.2063	3.2793	3.7596	3.9087	.0179
1.9494	3.0931	3.4604	3.5157	4.0230	4.1769	.0123
2.1546	3.3685	3.7144	3.7521	4.2865	4.4451	.0080
2.3598	3.6439	3.9684	3.9885	4.5500	4.7133	.0051
2.5650	3.9192	4.2225	4.2249	4.8135	4.9815	.0031
2.7702	4.1946	4.4765	4.4613	5.0770	5.2497	.0018
2.9754	4.4700	4.7306	4.6977	5.3404	5.5179	.0010
3.1806	4.7454	4.9846	4.9341	5.6039	5.7861	.0005
3.3858	5.0208	5.2386	5.1705	5.8674	6.0543	.0003
3.5910	5.2961	5.4927	5.4068	6.1309	6.3225	.0001
3.7962	5.5715	5.7467	5.6432	6.3943	6.5907	.0001
4.0014	5.8469	6.0008	5.8796	6.6578	6.8589	.0000

TABLE 9.25. IRT Ability Estimated using Bayesian EAP for Raw Scores for Test Levels.

Level Raw Score	$\hat{\theta}$					
	Grade 3	Grade 4	Grade 5	Grade 6	Grade 7	Grade 8
0	−2.5068	−3.0571	−2.3031	−1.7998	−1.5994	−1.2237
1	−2.4051	−2.9248	−2.1878	−1.6799	−1.4870	−1.1216
2	−2.2911	−2.7785	−2.0615	−1.5529	−1.3680	−1.0126
3	−2.1635	−2.6174	−1.9236	−1.4179	−1.2413	−.8958
4	−2.0217	−2.4409	−1.7740	−1.2742	−1.1057	−.7704
5	−1.8668	−2.2496	−1.6131	−1.1218	−.9605	−.6355
6	−1.7020	−2.0452	−1.4420	−.9612	−.8053	−.4905
7	−1.5322	−1.8307	−1.2626	−.7934	−.6399	−.3347
8	−1.3624	−1.6099	−1.0773	−.6201	−.4654	−.1682
9	−1.1963	−1.3868	−.8890	−.4432	−.2832	.0086
10	−1.0352	−1.1646	−.7004	−.2647	−.0957	.1945
11	−.8785	−.9453	−.5136	−.0865	.0944	.3873
12	−.7242	−.7296	−.3300	.0899	.2840	.5843
13	−.5702	−.5171	−.1503	.2635	.4706	.7821
14	−.4143	−.3067	.0256	.4336	.6523	.9775
15	−.2541	−.0970	.1982	.6004	.8281	1.1681
16	−.0869	.1137	.3683	.7638	.9978	1.3521
17	.0902	.3271	.5368	.9244	1.1616	1.5291
18	.2805	.5453	.7049	1.0826	1.3204	1.6992
19	.4879	.7707	.8737	1.2393	1.4751	1.8634
20	.7171	1.0066	1.0445	1.3952	1.6266	2.0227
21	.9753	1.2569	1.2190	1.5516	1.7762	2.1784
22	1.2750	1.5260	1.3992	1.7098	1.9247	2.3318
23	1.6257	1.8190	1.5875	1.8715	2.0732	2.4840
24	1.9904	2.1415	1.7872	2.0390	2.2231	2.6363
25		2.5027	2.0026	2.2147	2.3755	2.7900
26		2.9216	2.2391	2.4012	2.5320	2.9463
27		3.4199	2.5051	2.6012	2.6943	3.1067
28			2.8136	2.8185	2.8649	3.2729
29			3.1855	3.0589	3.0467	3.4472
30			3.6397	3.3320	3.2434	3.6326
31				3.6516	3.4603	3.8336
32				4.0289	3.7042	4.0564
33					3.9844	4.3089
34					4.3130	4.6007
35					4.7015	4.9409
36						5.3332
n	770	1552	1663	1512	1113	553
Mean	.0042	.4751	1.0439	1.2665	1.5162	1.6271
S.D.	.9173	1.2136	1.1341	1.0514	1.1767	1.1745

9.8 Vertical Scaling and Developmental Score Scales   409

TABLE 9.26. Raw-to-IRT Scale Score Equivalents for Test Levels.

Level Raw Score	IRT Scale Score Equivalents					
	Grade 3	Grade 4	Grade 5	Grade 6	Grade 7	Grade 8
0	71	47	79	101	110	126
1	75	52	84	106	115	131
2	80	59	90	112	120	135
3	85	66	96	118	126	141
4	92	73	102	124	131	146
5	98	82	109	131	138	152
6	106	91	117	138	144	158
7	113	100	125	145	152	165
8	120	110	133	152	159	172
9	127	119	141	160	167	180
10	134	129	149	168	175	188
11	141	138	157	176	183	196
12	148	148	165	183	192	205
13	155	157	173	191	200	213
14	161	166	180	198	208	222
15	168	175	188	205	215	230
16	176	184	195	213	223	238
17	183	194	203	220	230	246
18	192	203	210	226	237	253
19	201	213	217	233	243	260
20	211	223	225	240	250	267
21	222	234	232	247	256	274
22	235	246	240	254	263	281
23	250	258	248	261	269	287
24	266	272	257	268	276	294
25		288	266	276	282	300
26		306	277	284	289	307
27		328	288	292	296	314
28			301	302	304	321
29			318	312	312	329
30			337	324	320	337
31				338	330	346
32				354	340	355
33					352	366
34					367	379
35					383	394
36						411
n	770	1552	1663	1512	1113	553
Mean	179.6831	200.0155	224.6356	234.4431	245.1662	249.9729
S.D.	39.9813	52.6162	49.1859	45.7063	51.0595	50.8969

the items associated with a common stimulus as a polytomous item and then use a polytomous IRT model.

3. Conducting the estimation in two steps. Instead of conducting the estimation in two steps, the item parameters for the scaling test and the grade levels could have been estimated simultaneously.

4. Using number-correct scores to estimate ability. The entire pattern of item responses could have been used, instead of using number-correct scores to estimate ability.

5. Using Bayesian EAP methods to estimate ability. Instead of using Bayesian EAP methods, other ability estimation methods might have been used.

Little research has been conducted that suggest what the effects of these, and other, choices might be on the scaling results.

9.8.11 *Statistics for Comparing Scaling Results*

The normative properties of developmental score scales have been the subject of much debate and study in the literature. Three score scale properties have been the focus of much of the debate. The first property is the amount of average *grade-to-grade growth* displayed by students in the normative sample. Grade-to-grade growth has typically been displayed as the difference between means for adjacent grades. Alternatively, medians or selected percentile points have been used.

The second property is *grade-to-grade variability*, which typically has been displayed by comparing within grade standard deviations for adjacent grades. Alternatively, other measures of variability could be used.

The third property is *separation of grade distributions*, or what Holland (2002) refers to as gaps between distributions. Hoover (1984b) and Petersen et al. (1989) referred to the related property grade-to-grade overlap. This property can be displayed by graphing the entire cumulative distribution function for adjacent age groups. Horizontal or vertical differences between the distributions (Holland, 2002) could be used as the basis for an index of separation of grade distributions. One index of separation of grade distribution suggested by Yen (1986) is the effect size as measured by the following equation:

$$\textit{effect size} = \frac{\hat{\mu}(Y)_{upper} - \hat{\mu}(Y)_{lower}}{\sqrt{(\hat{\sigma}^2(Y)_{upper} + \hat{\sigma}^2(Y)_{lower})/2}}, \qquad (9.25)$$

where $\hat{\mu}(Y)_{upper}$ is the mean for the upper grade group, $\hat{\mu}(Y)_{lower}$ is the mean for the lower grade group, $\hat{\sigma}^2(Y)_{upper}$ is the variance for the upper grade group, and $\hat{\sigma}^2(Y)_{lower}$ is the variance for the lower grade group.

9.8 Vertical Scaling and Developmental Score Scales

TABLE 9.27. Grade-to-Grade Mean Differences and Effect Sizes for Thurstone and IRT Scalings.

Statistic	Grade 4 −Grade 3	Grade 5 −Grade 4	Grade 6 −Grade 5	Grade 7 −Grade 6	Grade 8 −Grade 7
Thurstone Scaling					
Mean Difference	29.8608	21.6605	11.4704	11.4391	5.5175
Effect Size	.7426	.4834	.2377	.2342	.1084
IRT Scaling					
Mean Difference	20.3324	24.6201	9.8075	10.7231	4.8067
Effect Size	.5085	.4679	.1994	.2346	.0941

Note that the effect size standardizes the grade-to-grade difference in the means by the square root of the average of the within grade variances. This index displays the mean grade-to-grade differences in standardized units. Also, when there are differences in variability across grades, it is possible that grade-to-grade trends in effect sizes might differ from grade-to-grade changes.

The Thurstone and IRT scalings that were conducted earlier in this chapter are used to illustrate these properties. The mean differences shown in Table 9.27 are the differences between means for adjacent grades in the Thurstone and IRT scalings. For example, to calculate the mean difference of 29.8608 shown in the upper left of Table 9.27, the mean for grade 3 for the Thurstone scaling (170.0776 from Table 9.19) is subtracted from the mean for grade 4 (199.9374 from Table 9.19). Other mean differences are calculated similarly. The mean differences for IRT scaling are similarly calculated from the data in Table 9.26. The effect sizes shown in this table were calculated using equation (9.25) with the means and standard deviations given in Table 9.19 and Table 9.26.

Examining the mean differences for the Thurstone scaling in Table 9.27, the differences decline as grade level increases. This finding suggests that for the Thurstone scaling, the amount of grade-to-grade growth declines with grade. Refer to the standard deviations in Table 9.19. The standard deviations increase over grade, suggesting that the variability of scale scores increases over grade for this Thurstone scaling. Refer to the effect sizes for Thurstone scaling in Table 9.27. These effect sizes decline as grade level increases. The values suggest that the amount of grade-to-grade growth is nearly 3/4 of a standard deviation unit (.7426) from grade 3 to grade 4 and declines to around 1/10 of a standard deviation unit (.1084) from grade 7 to grade 8.

The mean differences for the IRT scaling also suggest that grade-to-grade growth declines with grade level, although there is a reversal when comparing the grade 5 to grade 6 growth with grade 6 to grade 7 growth. Refer to the standard deviations in Table 9.26. The standard deviations seem not to be as strongly related to grade level for the IRT scaling; indeed, the standard deviations appear to be somewhat erratic. Like the mean differences in Table 9.27, the effect sizes for the IRT scaling tend to decline as grade increases.

These statistics can be used to compare properties of the Thurstone and IRT scales. For the most part, the Thurstone scaling indicates greater grade-to-grade growth (based on mean differences) and greater separation of score distributions (based on effect sizes) than the IRT scaling. The differences between the two scalings are most pronounced from grade 3 to grade 4. In addition, the Thurstone scale shows increasing variability over grades, whereas for the IRT scaling the relationship between variability and grade level is irregular. Note that this example is illustrative; no general conclusions about the statistical properties of Thurstone and IRT scaling can be made.

9.8.12 Some Limitations of Vertically Scaled Tests

As indicated earlier, the different levels of vertically scaled tests purposefully differ in content and difficulty. These differences in content and difficulty limit the interpretations that can be made about scale scores from the tests.

Kolen (2001) gave an example of limitations for a vertical scaling of the PLAN Mathematics test to the score scale for the ACT Assessment Mathematics test. PLAN is designed to be administered to tenth grade students, whereas the ACT Assessment is designed to be administered to eleventh and twelfth grade students. PLAN is shorter, easier, and covers somewhat different content than the ACT Assessment. In particular, the ACT Assessment includes test questions on intermediate algebra and trigonometry, whereas these areas are not included on PLAN. The ACT Assessment score scale ranges from 1 to 36.

Based on an analysis of the expected scale scores for examinees on PLAN and the ACT Assessment, Kolen (2001) reported that the expected scale scores on PLAN and ACT were similar for examinees with true scale scores below 27. For scale scores above 27, the expected PLAN scores were too low. This finding was due to PLAN's being unable to measure well at the higher scale score region because it did not contain many difficult test questions. Thus, the psychometric comparability of scale scores on PLAN and ACT is limited to the range of scores at or below 27.

Kolen (2001) also pointed out that the content differences for the tests lead to limitations on the meaning of test scores. Because intermediate algebra and trigonometry are not included in PLAN, Kolen (2001) stated that "if a school were to initiate a program where intermediate algebra or trigonometry were taught in ninth or tenth grade, any resulting gains in achievement in these areas likely would not be reflected in PLAN scores," (p. 6) whereas they would be reflected in ACT Assessment scores.

9.8 Vertical Scaling and Developmental Score Scales 413

TABLE 9.28. Range of Scale Scores Where Root Mean Squared Error Is Less Than 25 for the IRT Scaling.

Statistic	Grade 3	Grade 4	Grade 5	Grade 6	Grade 7	Grade 8
Minimum Scale Score	90	120	133	151	163	181
Maximum Scale Score	259	284	326	338	368	393

This example illustrates that whenever tests are vertically scaled there are serious limitations to interpretability of scores, due both to psychometric properties and to content differences among the tests that are scaled. It is important to acknowledge these limitations. The range of scale scores that can be treated as comparable for different tests should be indicated. In addition, content differences on these tests should be noted so that they can be taken into account when interpreting scale scores.

The IRT illustrative example discussed previously in this chapter can be used to illustrate psychometric limitations of vertical scaling. The Bayesian EAP estimators used in this example are intended to minimize root mean squared error in estimating proficiency. Root mean squared error is made up of two components. One component is bias in the estimator, which is the difference between the true scale score and the expected estimated scale score given true scale score. The other component is the conditional standard error of measurement. Using the methodology described by Kolen et al. (1996), implemented in the computer program *POLYCSEM* listed in Appendix B, expected scale scores and conditional standard errors of measurement were estimated for the IRT vertical scaling example. Root mean squared error was estimated from these components and is plotted in Figure 9.11. Root mean squared errors greater than 50 scale score points are not shown. A separate curve is given at each grade level. The low point of each curve is somewhere in the range of root mean squared error values of 15 to 20. The root mean square error curves are relatively flat near their low points and then quickly become larger.

Using a root mean square error value of 25 as an arbitrary cut-off, values larger than this cut off are considered here to be large. Table 9.28 presents the minimum and maximum scale score that would be considered to be associated with root mean squared errors that are not large given this rule. As indicated, the minimum and maximum values increase over grade. Also, there is significant overlap of these ranges across grades. As can be seen from Table 9.28, much of the range of possible observed scale scores is encompassed for the levels. If this range were to be used in practice, individuals with observed scores outside these ranges might be cautioned that their scores contain more than an acceptable amount of measurement error.

414   9. Score Scales

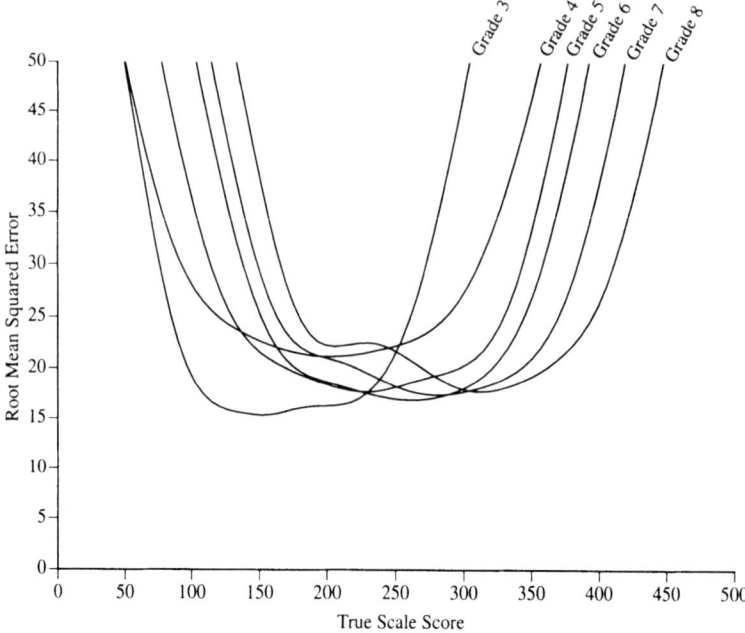

FIGURE 9.11. Root mean squared error for IRT vertical scaling example.

9.8.13   Research on Vertical Scaling

One line of research on vertical scaling has involved examining whether the results from vertical scaling methods and designs are different. Much of this research was reviewed by Skaggs and Lissitz (1986a). Research on the group dependence of vertical scaling results (Forsyth et al., 1981; Gustaffson, 1979; Harris and Hoover, 1987; Holmes, 1982; Loyd and Hoover, 1980; Slinde and Linn 1977, 1978, 1979a,b; Skaggs and Lissitz, 1988) often has found that vertical scaling is dependent on examinee groups. Vertical scaling results have been found to differ for different statistical methods (Guskey, 1981; Harris, 1991c; Kolen, 1981; Phillips, 1983, 1986; Skaggs and Lissitz, 1986b), and they have been found to be sensitive to linking design (Harris, 1991a).

In addition to studying whether general differences in the scaling results exist, methods and designs have been compared in terms of specific properties, including the pattern of grade-to-grade growth, grade-to-grade variability, and separation of grade distributions.

Hoover (1984a) reviewed norms for some of the then current elementary achievement test batteries that were scaled using Thurstone and IRT scaling methods. He found what he considered to be anomalies, including grade-to-grade growth irregularities. He observed, for example, that one set of test norms showed "that in this country average ninth graders develop over twice as much reading comprehension as average fifth graders," and he concluded that this observation "seems somewhat far-fetched" (p. 10). He also found evidence that on the then current forms of the Comprehensive Tests of Basic Skills, which were scaled with an IRT approach, the grade-to-grade differences in score variability decreased over grades. Hoover (1984a) argued that these differences should increase over grades, because on the types of tests included in elementary achievement test batteries, lower achieving students would be expected to increase at a slower rate than higher achieving students. Following similar lines of reasoning, Phillips and Clarizio (1988a) demonstrated implications of these types of scales to placement of children in special education. These assertions led to a discussion in the literature (Burket, 1984; Hoover, 1984b; Yen, 1988; Hoover, 1988; Phillips and Clarizio, 1988b; Clemans, 1993, 1996; Yen et al., 1996) about the plausibility and practical consequences of vertical scaling results.

Grade-to-Grade Growth

By definition, grade equivalent scales show equal average growth from grade-to-grade for the group of examinees used to conduct the scaling. As expected, this pattern was observed by Andrews (1995) for the grade equivalents he constructed using Hieronymus scaling. ITBS developmental score scales are constructed to display decelerating growth. Thurstone and IRT scalings also have, for the most part, produced a pattern of decelerating growth from grade to grade (Andrews, 1995; Bock, 1983; Seltzer et al., 1994; Williams et al., 1998; Yen, 1985, 1986). That is, the grade-to-grade differences in averages decrease as grade increases. However, Becker and Forsyth (1992), who only examined high-school tests, did not find evidence of decelerating growth.

Grade-to-Grade Variability

Thurstone (1925, 1927, 1928) and Thurstone and Ackerman (1929) found, using the Thurstone method of vertical scaling, that score variability increased with age. Andrews (1995), Williams et al. (1998), and Yen (1986) found evidence of increasing grade-to-grade variability in Thurstone scaling. Andrews (1995) also found increasing grade-to-grade variability with Hieronymus scaling. Williams et al. (1998) found that the extent of the increases depended on how the Thurstone method was implemented. Yen and Burket (1997) found evidence of increasing grade-to-grade variability in one implementation of the Thurstone method, but found no evidence of increasing grade-to-grade variability in another implementation. Williams et al. (1998) implemented an earlier version of the Thurstone method, which is quite different from the method that has been used in most recent Thurstone vertical scalings. With this earlier method they found evidence of decreasing grade-to-grade variability.

In examining norms tables for then current vertically scaled achievement batteries, both Hoover (1984a) and Yen (1986) found that scale score variability decreased over grades for IRT scales. Andrews (1995) documented the same finding in research for the ITBS. In simulation studies, it was found that decreases in grade-to-grade variability in IRT scaling could result from multidimensionality (Yen, 1985) and measurement error differences at different grades (Camilli, 1988). Camilli et al. (1993) speculated that problems in estimating IRT proficiency for very high and very low scoring individuals might also be the cause for decreasing grade-to-grade variability. In simulation studies, Omar (1996, 1997, 1998) found decreasing variability for various IRT estimation methods.

Other research on IRT methods did not find decreases in grade-to-grade variability in IRT scaling. Becker and Forsyth (1992) found increases in grade-to-grade variability on a high-school test battery. However, their study did not involve linking different test levels, but instead the same test level was administered in each high-school grade. Bock (1983) found fairly homogenous variances across age for an IRT scaling of the Stanford-Binet test. Seltzer et al. (1994) found no evidence of decreases in grade-to-grade variablity for a Rasch scaling of the ITBS. Little or no evidence of decreases in grade-to-grade variability has been found for IRT vertical scalings of NAEP (Camilli et al., 1993), of recent versions of the Comprehensive Tests of Basic Skills and California Achievement Tests (Yen and Burket, 1997), or of the North Carolina End-of-Grade tests (Williams et al., 1998).

Williams et al. (1998) noted that the IRT scalings of real data sets that showed substantial decreases in grade-to-grade variability used joint maximum likelihood (JML) methods, such as is used in LOGIST. However, JML was used for the recent IRT scalings of the Comprehensive Tests of Basic Skills and California Achievement Tests that did not show decreasing grade-to-grade variability, although the estimation procedures were recently revised according to Williams et al. (1998). Williams et al. (1998) speculated that the decreasing grade-to-grade variability might have resulted from using earlier JML implementations. Camilli (1999) also concluded that decreasing variability does not necessarily occur with the newer procedures for IRT parameter estimation.

Separation of Grade Distributions

For the ITBS, Andrews (1995) found less separation between distributions (more grade-to-grade overlap) for tests scaled using the scaling test design than for tests scaled using the common-item design for IRT, Thurstone, and Hieronymus scaling methods. Mittman (1958) found the opposite result for ITBS scalings using the Hieronymus method. The reasons for these contradictory results are not clear.

9.8 Vertical Scaling and Developmental Score Scales 417

Yen (1986, p. 304) illustrated how the use of effect sizes can lead to different conclusions about grade-to-grade growth compared to what is found using means. In the data presented, the year-to-year growth patterns for a test scaled using the Thurstone method and an IRT method appeared to be very different from one another. She showed that the differences in year-to-year growth patterns resulted from differences in patterns of grade-to-grade variability. When the differences were standardized using effect sizes, the IRT and Thurstone methods appeared very similar in terms of separation of grade distributions. The data provided by Yen (1986) illustrate the importance of examining both grade-to-grade growth and the separation of grade distributions.

Sensitivity of Results to Scale Transformation

As demonstrated by Zwick (1992, pp. 211–214), nonlinear monotonic increasing transformations of the score scale can change the pattern of grade-to-grade growth from increasing to decreasing, and visa versa; and transformations can change a pattern of increasing variability to decreasing variability, and visa versa. Schulz and Nicewander (1997) illustrated that when scores that show decreasing grade-to-grade growth and equal within grade variability are transformed to grade equivalents, the resulting scores have constant grade-to-grade growth and increasing within grade variability.

Some measures of the separation of grade distributions that are based on comparing percentile ranks for the two distributions are not affected by nonlinear monotonic increasing transformations of scale (see Braun, 1988). Other measures, such as the effect size discussed earlier, are affected by nonlinear scale transformations.

Factors That Might Affect Vertical Scaling Results

As Yen and Burket (1997) pointed out, and as illustrated by the preceding discussion, many characteristics of tests can affect scale characteristics. Factors that might affect scaling results for any of the methods considered include the following: the design for data collection; the complexity (dimensionality) of the subject matter area; the curriculum dependence of the subject matter area; test characteristics, including average item difficulty and discriminations, and relationships of the item characteristics to group proficiency; item types, such as multiple-choice and constructed response; grade levels; and nonlinear scale transformations following implementation of a scaling method.

For the Thurstone method, the results can depend on whether the method that involves item statistics or the method that involves score distributions is used. For the method that uses score distributions, the results can depend on the range of scores used in the process of normalizing score distributions.

The results for IRT scaling methods can depend on the IRT model used; the computer program used to conduct the parameter estimation; whether joint or marginal maximum likelihood methods are used to estimate item parameters; whether concurrent or separate estimation is used across grade groups; where needed, the procedure used to link results from different computer runs (e.g., test characteristic method vs. mean/sigma method); and the type of scoring that is used to estimate examinee proficiency (e.g., number-correct or estimated θ).

Hieronymus scaling results can depend on the scaling convention used, such as grade equivalents versus a scale defined to have decreasing grade-to-grade growth; the type of smoothing, interpolation and extrapolation procedures used; whether observed score or true score distributions are used in the scaling process; and, if true score distributions are used, the method for estimating the true score distributions.

Conclusions from Research

Research suggests that vertical scaling is a very complex process that is affected by many factors. These factors likely interact with one another to produce characteristics of a particular scale. The research record provides little guidance as to what methods and procedures work best for vertical scaling. Further research is needed to provide a clearer picture of what the effects on score scale properties are of all of the factors mentioned.

Unfortunately for practitioners, research does not provide a definitive answer concerning the characteristics of growth on educational tests. No general conclusions are possible from the research regarding whether, for example, the amount of grade-to-grade growth decreases over grades or whether the score variability increases over grades. As Yen (1986) pointed out, "choosing the right scale is not an option. It is important that any choice of scale be made consciously and that the reasons for the choice be carefully considered. In making such choices, appealing to common sense is no guarantee of unanimity of opinion or of reaching a sensible conclusion" (p. 314). As stated earlier in this chapter, the overriding justification for choosing a scale is that it facilitates score interpretation.

9.9 Exercises

9.1. Suppose that a test of fourth grade mathematics achievement is to be constructed and scaled. The test contains multiple-choice and constructed response questions. How would test development and scaling proceed using a psychometric model-based approach such as that of Wright (1977) or Thurstone (1925) as compared to the approach suggested by Lindquist (1953). Be sure to consider each of the following components: (a) creating test specifications, (b) test construction, (c) test scoring, (d) combining scores on different item types, and (e) developing score scales.

Exercises   419

9.2. Assume that a 3 parameter logistic model fits a set of data. Assume that examinees 1 through 3 have θ values of -1, 1, and 2 respectively. What would be these three examinee's θ^* values, where $\theta^* = \exp(\theta)$? Is the difference in proficiency between examinees 1 and 2 greater than the difference in proficiency between examinees 2 and 3? Why or why not?

9.3. For a test with a reliability of .70, what would be the appropriate number of score points for a scale where a 90% confidence interval is to be constructed by adding and subtracting 2 scale score points.

9.4. For the example shown in Tables 9.2 through 9.6, what is the rounded scale score equivalent of a raw score of 9 for a scale with a mean of 100 and a standard deviation of 15 if the scale is a linear transformation of observed scores? How about if the scale is a normalized transformation of observed scores?

9.5. For the example shown in Tables 9.2 through 9.6, what is the rounded scale score equivalent of a raw score of 9 for a scale with a mean of 100 and an *sem* of 3 points, if the scale is based on a nonlinear transformation designed to approximately equalize the conditional standard errors of measurement and the IRT model is used to estimate reliability?

9.6. Find the mastery level for Form X item 15 in Table 6.8 assuming that the *RP*-level is 80%.

9.7. For the data in Table 9.10, what would be the proportional effective weights of each test in a composite consisting of English, Mathematics, and Reading scores only? What would be the proportional effective weights for a composite calculated by multiplying the Math test by 3 and the other tests by 1?

9.8. Consider a situation in which there are 3 blocks of items that differ in difficulty, each of which contains 20 items. Level Q, which is made up of blocks a and b, is typically administered to third graders. Level R, which is made up of blocks b and c, is typically administered to fourth graders. Means and standard deviations for grade 3 and grade 4 for the item blocks, Level Q, Level R, and total score over all 3 item blocks are shown in Table 9.29. (Note that the standard deviations for Level R, Level Q, and Total were calculated assuming that the correlations between any pair of blocks is .5.)

   a. Suppose that as would be done in a common-item vertical scaling design, Level Q (item blocks a and b) was administered to grade 3 students and Level R (item blocks b and c) was administered to grade 4 students. Using only the data that would result from

TABLE 9.29. Means and Standard Deviations for a Hypothetical Two-Level Test.

		Item Block			Level Q	Level R	Total
		a	b	c			
Grade 3	μ	12	10	5	22	15	27
	σ	2	2	2	$\sqrt{12}$	$\sqrt{12}$	$\sqrt{24}$
Grade 4	μ	14	12	10	26	22	36
	σ	2	2	2	$\sqrt{12}$	$\sqrt{12}$	$\sqrt{24}$

this design, use chained linear methods to link scores on Level R to scores on Level Q. This procedure involves linking level R scores to block b scores for fourth graders and linking block b scores to level Q scores for third graders.

b. Find the linear equation for linking Level R scores to Level Q scores using only the third grade data.

c. Find the linear equation for linking Level R scores to Level Q scores using only the fourth grade data.

d. As might be done in a scaling test design, link Level R scores to Total scores for fourth graders. Link Total scores to Level Q scores for third graders. Use chained linear methods to combine these two linkings to arrive at a linear equation linking Level R scores to Level Q scores.

e. Why do the results of these linkings differ? How might this sort of difference occur in an actual vertical scaling?

f. Which linking is most consistent with the grade-to-grade definition of growth? Why?

g. Which linking is most consistent with the domain definition of growth? Why?

h. For linkings in parts a–d, what is the effect size of the difference between grade 3 mean on Q and the grade 4 mean on R when the means and standard deviations are expressed on the common scale (raw scores on Q) that results from applying the results from each of the linkings? What do these differences suggest about the apparent amount of growth that is found when conducting vertical scaling using the grade-to-grade definition of growth as compared to the domain definition of growth in this situation?

9.9. Refer to the data in Table 9.14.

a. What would be the grade level means and standard deviations had the scaling been done so that the mean for grade 8 was zero and the standard deviation for grade 8 was 1?

b. What would be the grade level means and standard deviations for a scale where the mean for grade 4 is 400 and the mean for grade 8 is 800?

10
Linking

Equating adjusts for differences in difficulty, not differences in content. That statement on page 3 is one of the most important sentences in the introductory chapter of this book. To a large extent this chapter considers situations in which statistical adjustments are made to scores for tests that differ in content and/or difficulty, and usually both. In some cases, these differences are relatively small; in most cases, tests clearly measure very different content/constructs. We refer generically to a relationship between scores on such tests as a *linking*.

In all cases, the goal is to put scores from two or more tests on the same scale—*in some sense*. If the tests conform to the same content and statistical specifications, then they are really test *forms*, and we are entitled to call the resulting linking an equating. Otherwise, we refrain from using the word "equating" to describe linking relationships.

Often the subject of linking is introduced with physical examples. For example, there is a well-known relationship between temperature measured on the Fahrenheit (F) and Celsius (C) scales—namely, $F = (9/5)C + 32$ or, equivalently, $C = (5/9)(F - 32)$. These equations permit a kind of linking of these two ways of measuring temperature. The first permits us to put Celsius temperatures on the Fahrenheit scale, and the second allows us to put Fahrenheit temperatures on the Celsius scale. However, this frequently-employed example is in some ways more misleading than informative for our purposes here.

First, the relationship between the two scales is functional and, in that sense, deterministic. That is, the relationship between the two scales is predefined. If any actual temperature measurements fail to conform exactly to the stated relationship, then there must be errors in the measurements, because the "construct" that we call temperature is exactly the same for both scales. Second, even if actual temperature measurements are used to "confirm" the relationship between the Fahrenheit and Celsius scales, the errors that exist are likely to be quite small for most practical purposes.

By contrast, for a linking of scores on tests administered to human beings, the tests almost always measure at least some *different* constructs, even if they have similar names. Therefore, it is virtually certain that score differences are attributable to construct differences as well as errors of measurement, either or both of which could be quite large. This does not mean that a linking of the scores on two tests cannot be determined. It can, or more correctly, a number of linkage relationships can be determined. That is a large part of the subject of this chapter. With equal force, however, the adequacy of the linking may be highly suspect depending on the nature of the decisions made based on the linking. This message will be repeated in many different ways in this chapter.

When tests measure different constructs, no linking, no matter how competently conducted, will be adequate for all purposes and all populations. Several conceptual frameworks and many statistical perspectives and indices for characterizing a linkage relationship are discussed in this chapter, but none of them can possibly provide a definitive answer about linking adequacy. There is no escaping the need for informed judgment by persons responsible for making decisions about the relationship between two tests.

This chapter is divided into four major sections: linking categorization schemes and criteria; a detailed consideration of group invariance, which is a frequently employed criterion for assessing linking adequacy; additional examples; and a discussion of other issues. Various real-data examples are discussed. (See Feuer et al., 1999, for additional examples.) Linking is a vast topic, and approaches to it are evolving at a rapid rate. This chapter is intended to provide an introduction to linking, not a definitive treatment.

10.1 Linking Categorization Schemes and Criteria

In Chapter 1, we began our introduction to equating by considering three classes of issues:

1. choosing a data collection design;

2. choosing a definition of equating, which in large part amounts to selecting one or more criteria used to judge the adequacy of equating; and

3. choosing a statistical procedure to obtain an equating result.

The same issues apply to linking, although the designs, criteria, and methodological emphases may differ. In particular, the same data collection designs

10.1 Linking Categorization Schemes and Criteria

TABLE 10.1. SAT I V+M and ACT Composite Equivalents.

SAT I V+M Equivalents		ACT Composite Equivalents	
ACT Comp	SAT I V+M	SAT I V+M	ACT Comp
36	1600	1600	36
35	1580	1560−1600	35
34	1520	1510−1550	34
33	1470	1460−1500	33
32	1420	1410−1450	32
31	1380	1360−1400	31
30	1340	1320−1350	30
29	1300	1280−1310	29
28	1260	1240−1270	28
27	1220	1210−1230	27
26	1180	1170−1200	26
25	1140	1130−1160	25
24	1110	1090−1120	24
23	1070	1060−1080	23
22	1030	1020−1050	22
21	990	980−1010	21
20	950	940−970	20
19	910	900−930	19
18	870	860−890	18
17	830	810−850	17
16	780	760−800	16
15	740	710−750	15
14	680	660−700	14
13	620	590−650	13
12	560	520−580	12
11	500	500−510	11

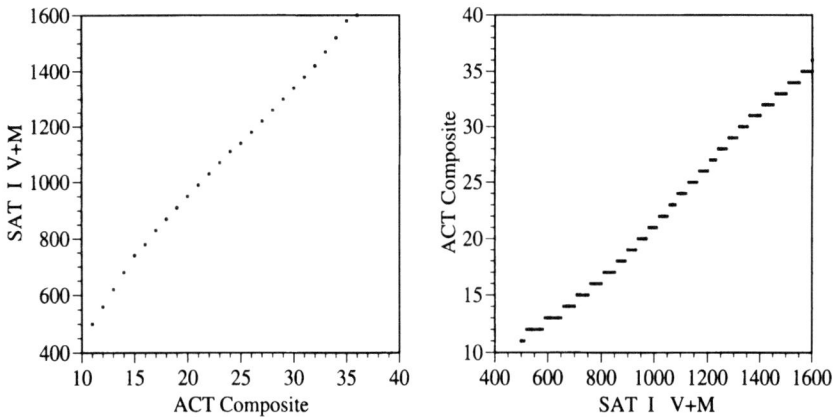

FIGURE 10.1. SAT I V+M vs. ACT Composite and ACT Composite vs. SAT I V+M equivalents.

used in equating might be used in linking, as well as others. Also, the statistical procedures used in equating might be used in linking, as well as others. Finally, many of the same criteria used in equating can be considered in linking situations, but the criteria are not likely to be met very well in most realistic circumstances, as will become particularly evident when we discuss group invariance in the next section.

Perhaps the most enduring and frequently cited example of linking is the "concordance" relationships between ACT Assessment composite scores, with a range of 1–36, and SAT I Verbal-plus-Mathematics (V+M) scores, with a range of 400–1600. Both of these testing programs are widely used for college admissions, there are similarities in the content tested, and the correlation between the ACT composite and SAT is relatively high (usually in the low .90's). Still, the forms for the two testing programs are developed according to different tables of specifications, and it is widely acknowledged that the two testing programs do not provide interchangeable scores (see Lindquist, 1964, for an old but still highly relevant statement about the problems of relating scores on non-parallel tests).

Using unsmoothed equipercentile procedures with over 100,000 examinees who took both the ACT and the SAT (i.e., the single group design[1]), Dorans et al. (1997) provided the concordance relationships in Table 10.1, which are depicted graphically in Figure 10.1.[2] How good is this ACT-SAT linking? That is a difficult question to answer, but there are some relevant statements we can make.

First, since equipercentile procedures were used, we can say with confidence that the equipercentile property was met *for the group of examinees used to do the linking.* However, this group of examinees is quite atypical in that they chose to take *both tests.* There is no a prior reason to believe that the concordance relationships in Table 10.1 would apply to examinees who chose to take only one of the tests, which is the very group of examinees for whom concordance relationships are desired.

Second, perhaps the most universally accepted criterion for an equating relationship is that it be symmetric.[3] In a sense, it is impossible for any linking of the ACT composite and SAT I V+M to be symmetric because the ACT composite and SAT I V+M have different numbers of possible score points. That is why there are two concordance tables in Table 10.1. The left-hand table (a one-to-one mapping) would be used for obtaining SAT I V+M equivalents given ACT composite scores; the right-hand table (a

---

[1] The data were counterbalanced to some unknown extent. The two testings differed by no more than 217 days. Additional, relevant information is provided in the Appendix to Dorans et al. (1997).

[2] See, also, Dorans (2000) and Dorans (in press-a).

[3] Strictly speaking, of course, it almost never happens that a reported score (usually an integer) on one form equates exactly to a reported score on another form. Symmetry may apply to continuized scores, but it seldom applys exactly to reported scores.

many-to-one mapping) would be used for obtaining ACT composite scores given SAT I V+M equivalents.[4]

Third, there is no guarantee that the concordances in Table 10.1 apply equally well for all institutions that might want to use them. Indeed, as Dorans et al. (1997) note,

> It is important to investigate how similar institution-specific concordances are across different institutions and states. Studies of the invariance of concordance tables across institutions should be guided by characteristics by which institutions differ. Preliminary results indicate some variability. (p. 30)

In other words, the concordance may not possess the property of group invariance, a topic that is discussed extensively in Section 10.2.

10.1.1 Types of Linking

In his 1997 State of the Union address, President Clinton proposed the creation of the Voluntary National Tests (VNTs) in reading and mathematics, which would provide scores for individual examinees on tests that were linked to the National Assessment of Educational Progress (NAEP) "to the maximum extent possible." The new tests were to be labeled "voluntary" to accommodate a prohibition on reporting individual-level scores for testing programs sponsored by the federal government (e.g., by law, NAEP cannot provide individual examinee scores). The VNTs were a source of considerable debate for numerous reasons, not the least of which was a concern that any linkage of the VNTs and NAEP might not be adequate for practical use. To address this concern, Congress and President Clinton asked the National Research Council (NRC) to study the matter. The resulting NRC report is entitled, *Uncommon measures: Equivalence and linkage among educational tests* (Feuer et al., 1999). Funding for the VNTs was eliminated a few years after they were proposed. Still, the *Uncommon measures* report provides very informative discussions of linking issues.

To distinguish among different types of linking, the *Uncommon measures* report focuses on three stages in test development that characterize what the authors call the "domain" of a test; namely, in their words,

- *framework definition*: a delineation of the scope and extent (e.g., specific content areas, skills, etc.) of the domain to be represented in the assessment;

- *test specification or blueprint*: specific mix of content areas and items formats, numbers of tasks/items, scoring rules, etc.; and

---

[4]Note, in addition, that a SAT I V+M score of 1600 actually has two ACT composite equivalents, 35 and 36, which constitutes a one-to-many mapping.

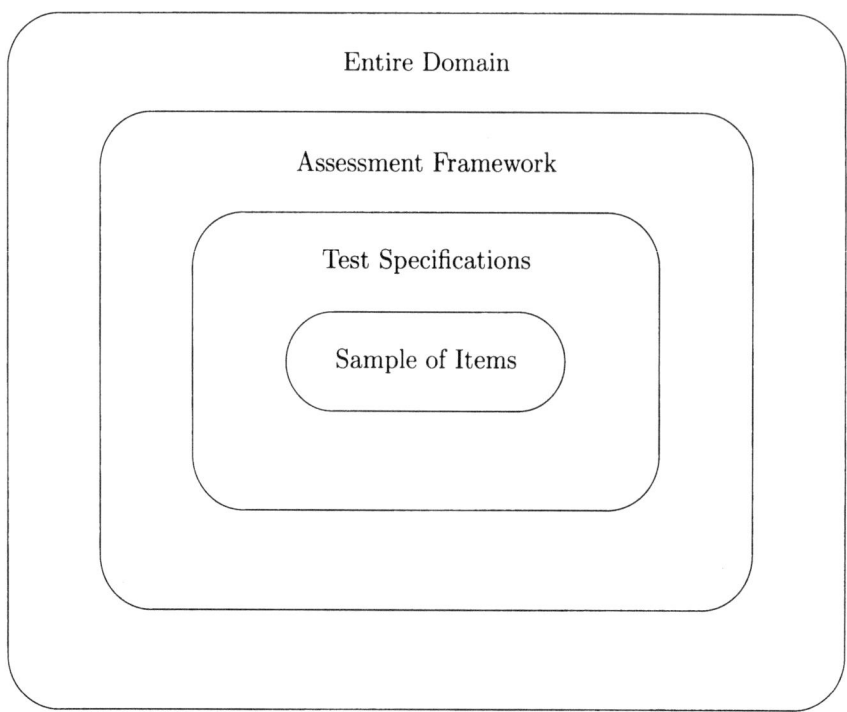

FIGURE 10.2. Feuer et al. (1999) decision stages in test development.

- *item selection*: items are selected to represent the test specifications as faithfully as possible.

Usually the framework definition is itself a subdomain of a larger domain, as indicated in Figure 10.2. For example, if fourth-grade reading is viewed as a domain, then there are many possible framework definitions.

Given this conceptualization of a test domain, Feuer et al. (1999) discuss three types of linking that adjust scores on different forms of a test that are based on

1. *the same framework and same test specifications*,

2. *the same framework and different test specifications*, or

3. *different frameworks and different test specifications*.

The first type of linking is essentially equating, as that term has been used in this book. The second type of linking is exemplified by reading tests in NAEP and the proposed VNTs, which differ in several ways, including the length of the reading passages. The word *linking* is most often associated with the third type of linking in the Feuer et al. (1999) taxonomy. Probably the most frequently cited example is the relationship between SAT-M and

ACT Math scores. For these two tests, the frameworks and test specifications are clearly different, but it is usually claimed that both tests measure developed abilities and skills in the domain of mathematics.

As another example, relationships between NAEP and the Third International Mathematics and Science Study (TIMSS) (1998) are described by Feuer et al. (1999) as follows:

> ... a given score on the NAEP grade 8 mathematics assessment is intended to measure a level of mastery of the material specified in the NAEP mathematics framework, whereas a given score on TIMSS is intended to estimate a level of mastery of the material specified by the TIMSS framework, which is overlapping, but different from the NAEP framework. Therefore, the only thing one could say with confidence is that the NAEP scores reflect mastery of the NAEP framework, and the TIMSS scores reflect mastery of the TIMSS framework. It is understandable that a student might score better on one assessment than on the other, that is, find NAEP easier than TIMSS. In practice, however, these distinctions may blur. Many users of results from a given test will interpret both scores as representing degrees of mastery of the same general domain, such as "8th-grade mathematics" and will seem perplexed at the discrepancy. It is necessary to clarify the domain to which scores should generalize in order to evaluate the quality of any linkages among tests.

10.1.2 Mislevy/Linn Taxonomy

Several years prior to the *Uncommon measures* monograph, Mislevy (1992) and Linn (1993) proposed a type of taxonomy for linking that is sometimes referred to as *forms of linking*. Their categorization system focuses in part on the methodologies used to establish linkage. More importantly, however, their four categories are largely ordered in terms of the "strength" of the resulting linkage.

1. Equating is the strongest kind of linking. When a linking relationship is truly an "equating," the relationship is invariant across different populations.

2. Calibration relationships are weaker than equating relationships. The statistical methods used in calibration may resemble those used in equating, but the resulting relationships are not likely to be invariant across different populations. There are several connotations of the word "calibration."

3. Projection is a unidirectional form of linking in which scores on one test are predicted or "projected" from another.

4. There are two types of moderation—statistical moderation and judgmental or "social" moderation. Moderation is usually considered the weakest form of linking, although arguments can be made that projection is a weaker form of linking than statistical moderation.

If the single group design is employed to collect data for a linking, then a correlation coefficient can be used to quantify the strength of the relationship between the two tests. However, the single group design is not necessarily required to obtain a linking. Each of the Mislevy/Linn types of linking methods is discussed more fully next.

Equating

Equating has been discussed extensively in previous chapters of this book. We reserve the term "equating" for a relationship between scores of different forms that are constructed according to the same content and statistical specifications. In the terminology of the *Uncommon measures* report, equating is the first type of linking, which involves the same framework and the same test specifications. Equating is successful to the extent that the form that is taken is a matter of indifference to each examinee.

Calibration

Many examples of calibration are closely related to the *Uncommon measures* second type of linking, which involves the same framework and different test specifications. However, calibration is also used to refer to the *Uncommon measures* third type of linking, which involves different frameworks and different test specifications—provided the frameworks are viewed as sharing some common features or uses.

First, calibration may refer to a relationship between test forms that share common content specifications but different statistical specifications. Perhaps the most frequently cited example is test forms that differ in length. All other things being equal, the longer form will be more reliable than the shorter form. It follows that high achieving students should prefer the longer form, and low achieving students should prefer the shorter form. Clearly, then, which form is taken is *not* a matter of indifference for examinees.

A second connotation of calibration involves test forms with somewhat difference content specifications and perhaps different statistical specifications. The quintessential example involves test forms that are designed for different grade levels, with scores on the forms put on a common scale, as discussed in Chapter 9. This type of calibration is sometimes called vertical scaling.

A third interpretation of of the term "calibration" involves the application of a methodology (almost always an item response theory model) that puts all items in a domain on a common scale. Then, if the model assumptions are met, in theory any subset of items provides examinee proficiency scores that are comparable in some sense. Of course, a long subset (i.e., form) provides more precise estimates than a short subset. Furthermore, in educational contexts, item domains are rarely unidimensional and, therefore, the manner in which the samples of items are obtained may or may not lead to forms that are optimally similar in content. It is possible that a large calibrated item pool could be used to construct forms that share the same content and statistical specifications to such a degree that scores can be truly equated; often, however, the relationship between scores on such forms is better described as calibrated.

Projection

The principal distinguishing features of projection, as opposed to equating or calibration, are (i) projection is unidirectional, (ii) the single group design is required, and (iii) there is no a prior requirement that the same constructs (or even the same domains in the terminology of the *Uncommon measures* report) are being measured. A projection relationship is almost always obtained via a regression (linear or non-linear), which is a nonsymmetric relationship. That is, the "best" projection of X on Y is not the same as the "best" projection of Y on X.

Sometimes projection involves variables that are deemed to measure at least some common constructs. For example, some of the older literature on ACT-SAT relationships provides both concordances and regressions (e.g., Houston and Sawyer, 1991). However, the predicted variable need not share much in common with the predictor(s).

Moderation

Statistical moderation is often called "distribution matching." Sometimes the distributions are matched based on data from the single group design (i.e., same examinees taking the two tests), but random groups designs and nonequivalent groups designs are possibilities, too.

For example, concordance relationships typically involve the same examinees' taking different tests, and concordance is usually placed in the statistical moderation category. (Recall the discussion of linking the ACT composite and the SAT in Section 10.1.) In older literature, concordance is sometimes called "scaling to achieve comparability." It is a type of linking in which the frameworks are different but the constructs are typically similar.

Another common example of statistical moderation with the single group design occurs when tests in a battery are taken by the same group of examinees and scaled to have a common mean and standard deviation. In this case, scores on the different tests with the same numerical value are comparable in a norm-referenced sense. However, such comparability in no way supports an inference that equal scores designate equivalent levels of knowledge or ability on different tests. Indeed, for this type of statistical moderation, the constructs are usually quite dissimilar.

Other examples of statistical moderation involve tests with different specifications that are administered to different, nonequivalent groups of examinees. The resulting distributions are matched in some manner, resulting in "score levels that are deemed comparable (Mislevy, 1992, p. 64)." For example, the original SAT Verbal test was scaled in 1941 to have a mean of 500 and a standard deviation of 100. Then, about a year later, the Mathematics test was scaled with different examinees to have approximately the same mean and standard deviation as the 1941 Verbal test.

A more complicated version of statistical moderation involves use of one or more "moderator tests" that are used to link disparate assessments taken by students in different programs or for different reasons—for example, biology tests for students who take biology and American history tests for students who take American history. Discussing this particular example in the context of the College Board Admissions Testing Program, Donlon and Livingston (1984) state

> ...If the scores are to be used for selection purposes, ...the score scales should be as comparable as possible. For example, the level of achievement in American history indicated by a score of 560 should be as similar as possible to the level of achievement in biology indicated by a score of 560 on the biology test. But what does it mean to say that one student's achievement in American history is comparable to another student's achievement in biology. The Admissions Testing Program's answer to this question, which forms the basis for scaling the achievement tests, is as follows. Suppose student A's relative standing in a group of American history students is the same as student B's relative standing in a group of biology students. Now suppose the group of American history students is equal to the group of biology students in general academic ability. Then it is meaningful to say that student A's achievement in American history is comparable to student B's achievement in biology. (p. 21)

However, the groups of students who choose to take the two tests cannot be assumed to be equal in "general academic ability." As described by Mislevy (1992), this problem is addressed using moderator tests (see, also, Donlon and Livingston, 1984).

> First, relationships among the SAT-V, SAT-M, and an Achievement Test are estimated from an actual baseline sample of students. Then, projection procedures are used to predict the distribution of a hypothetical "reference population" of students who are all "prepared" to take the special area test (i.e., have

studied biology, if we are working with the biology test) and have a mean of 500, a standard deviation of 100, and a correlation of .60 on the regular SAT sections. That is, the same relationship among the SAT tests and the Achievement Test observed in the real sample is assumed for the hypothetical sample, which could have a mean higher or lower than 500 and a standard deviation higher or lower than 100. The projected special-test raw-score distribution of the hypothetical group is transformed to have a mean of 500 and standard deviation of 100. (p. 66)

This type of statistical moderation might be called "horizontal scaling."[5] Obviously, results can differ dramatically with different samples of students and/or different moderator tests.

Judgmental or "social" moderation involves direct judgments concerning the comparability of performance levels on different assessments. Often, these judgments are obtained in one or more standard-setting studies. For example, there are generic definitions of "basic," "proficient," and "advanced" achievement levels for NAEP. These generic definitions are augmented for the various NAEP subject matter areas. Then, panels consisting of teachers, other educators, and the general public participate in an extensive, standardized rating procedure for determining cut-scores associated with these achievement levels (see Reckase, 2000). This permits comparative statements such as, "The proportion of proficient students in subject A is X, and the proportion in subject B is Y." Such statements are still value-laden, however, because they depend on judgments about what it means to be proficient in various subject matter areas. Such judgments are informed by empirical data that are incorporated in the standard setting procedure, but such data do not remove the need for value judgments.

10.1.3 Degrees of Similarity

Another way to think about linking is in terms of degrees of similarity in what we will call test "features" or "commonalities." As noted previously, it is certainly possible to link scores on any test to scores on any other test. Clearly, however, the utility and reasonableness of any linking depends upon the degree to which tests share common features. Here, we suggest consideration of at least the following four features in examining similarity:

- Inferences: To what extent are scores for the two tests used to draw similar types of inferences? This is essentially a question of whether the two tests share common measurement goals that are operationalized in scales intended to yield similar types of inferences.

---

[5]Suggested by S. A. Livingston.

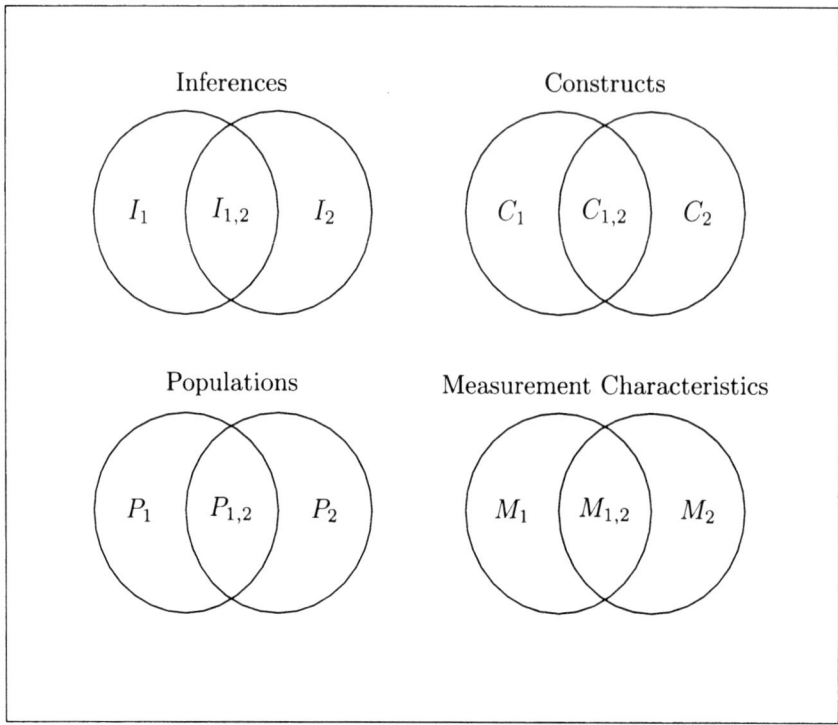

FIGURE 10.3. Degrees of similarity.

- Constructs: To what extent do the two tests measure the same constructs? This is essentially a question of whether true scores for the two tests are functionally related. In many linking contexts, the tests may share some common constructs, but they also assess unique constructs.

- Populations: To what extent are the two tests designed to be used with the same populations? Two tests might measure essentially the same construct (at least in a general sense) but not be appropriate for the same populations.

- Measurement characteristics/conditions: To what extent do the two tests share common measurement characteristics or conditions including, for example, test length, test format, administration conditions, etc. In generalizability theory (see Cronbach et al., 1972; Brennan, 2001), such measurement conditions are usually called facets, and two tests may differ with respect to numerous facets. Note that test specifications are only one part (albeit a very important part) of measurement characteristics or conditions. Typically, for example, test specifications do not make reference to stability of test scores over occasions, but this may well be a measurement condition of interest.

TABLE 10.2. Mislevy/Linn Taxonomy Categories and Degrees of Similarity.

Category	Inferences	Constructs	Populations	Meas. Char.
Equating	same	same	same	same
Vertical Scaling	same	same/similar	dissimilar	same/similar
Concordance	same	similar	same/similar	(dis)similar
Projection	(dis)similar	(dis)similar	similar	dissimilar
Stat. Moderation	(dis)similar	(dis)similar	(dis)similar	dissimilar

Also, for a performance assessment, raters are clearly a measurement condition of interest.

Figure 10.3 depicts these degrees of similarity in terms of four Venn diagrams. The extent to which each of the Venn diagrams overlap is a visual indicator of the degree of similarity in the particular test feature or commonality.

Just about any sensible discussion of a linking relationship should address these degrees of similarity (and perhaps others) in some manner. Otherwise, it is unlikely that users of linking results will be adequately informed about the extent to which the linking provides sensible results for the intended purposes.

The distinctions in the *Uncommon measures* types of linking and the Mislevy/Linn taxonomy can be couched in terms of these four degrees of similarity, at least to some extent. For example, the *Uncommon measures* "same framework" concept is essentially a question of construct similarity, and the "same test specifications" concept is a question of similarity in measurement characteristics. Also, consider the examples in Table 10.2 of some of the categories (and related terms) in the Mislevy/Linn taxonomy in terms of degrees of similarity. Clearly, the degrees of similarity for the various categories in Table 10.2 are sometimes ambiguous; i.e., the context matters, and there is not a perfect mapping of the taxonomy categories and degrees of similarity. Stated differently, the Mislevy/Linn taxonomy provides helpful but not definitive descriptions of unique categories of linking.

Clearly, there is not an unambiguous mapping of the Mislevy/Linn taxonomy categories and the degrees of similarity. Indeed, some of these categories (e.g., projection) are "wide" enough that no single specification of degrees of similarity applies to all applications. Still, it is possible to establish at least partial relationships between these two perspectives on linking.

Perhaps the most novel feature of the four degrees of similarity is its explicit incorporation of inferences. One might ask, "What would it mean for two tests to differ primarily with respect to their intended inferences?" In a general sense, this would mean that the two tests were developed and are used for different purposes.[6] Typically, inferences are partly operationalized through the choice of scoring and/or scaling procedures. So, for example, there is no distinction between a norm-referenced and criterion-referenced *test* per se; rather, the distinction is with respect to the reported scores and their interpretations—i.e., the inferences drawn based on test scores. It is certainly possible to link two different types of score scales for different tests (or even the same test). For example, sometimes achievement levels (e.g., "basic," "proficient," and "advanced") are defined relative to a norm-referenced scale such as percentile ranks.

Inferences are also tied to the "stakes" associated with a test. Even if two tests are quite similar, if one of them is used for low-stakes decisions and the other is used for high-stakes decisions, it is quite likely that any linkage will be different from what it would have been if both were used for low-stakes decisions or both were used for high-stakes decisions. Also, of course, stakes are likely to influence at least some measurement characteristics.

In this section, three perspectives on linking have been discussed: (1) the *Uncommon measures* types of linking; (2) the Mislevy/Linn taxonomy; and (3) degrees of similarity in test features or commonalities. There is no one "right" perspective, probably no "best" perspective, and uncritical acceptance of any set of linking categories is probably unwarranted. Among other things, the demarkation between categories can be very fuzzy, and differences are often matters of degree. Also, some categories, such as statistical moderation, are particularly broad. Our intent here is not to promote one perspective over another, but rather to encourage investigators who report linking relationships to provide critical discussions of them, without simply resorting to unqualified single-word category descriptions.

These perspectives on linking focus primarily on the conceptual or semantic aspects of linking; i.e., they constrain or frame how linking results can/should be interpreted. Of course, there are other important topics that must be addressed in conducting a linking study that are not always explicitly addressed by the perspectives on linking discussed in this section. Among these topics are the data collection design, the statistical methods employed and the related assumptions, and the extent to which the examinees used in a linking study faithfully represent the population(s) of interest. For the most part, these matters relate to the syntactical (psychometric/statistical) aspects of linking.

---

[6]It is likely that tests with different inferential intent will also differ with respect to some measurement characteristics or conditions, although this need not be so.

10.2 Group Invariance

As mentioned in Section 10.1, equating criteria (as well as other criteria) might be used to characterize linking relationships. Obviously, we do not expect these criteria to be satisfied nearly as well for a linking as they might be for an equating. Still, such criteria can be used as benchmarks. In the context of linking, the most frequently discussed criterion is group or population invariance. Indeed, in his review of population invariance, Kolen (in press) notes that over 50 years ago Flanagan (1951) claimed that, compared to equating, for linking "the determination of scores of comparable difficulty is ... much more definitely relative to the particular group used" (p. 759). Group invariance is a particularly attractive criterion because it can be studied empirically using relatively straightforward procedures, and the results are interpretable and useful in a reasonably direct manner.

In previous chapters, X and Y have designated new and old forms, respectively, of a test. In this chapter, the old/new designators are not used because they are seldom meaningful in a linking context (other than equating). Unless otherwise stated, in this chapter X and Y designate *different* tests that do not have the same content and statistical specifications. Furthermore, in most cases the scores under consideration are scale scores rather than raw scores. So, in this chapter $X_1, \ldots, X_I$ designate I (scale) scores associated with test X, and $Y_1, \ldots, Y_J$ designate J (scale) scores associated with test Y. In most realistic cases $I \neq J$.

Here, our focus is on the extent to which particular methods for linking X and Y give results that are invariant for $h = 1, \ldots, H$ different groups or subpopulations that partition the full population.[7] For example, if the focus is on gender groups, $H = 2$ and $h = 1, 2$. In the notational scheme used here, if the group indicator h is not present, the entire population is under consideration, which is often referred to here as the "combined group." Also, we stay with the convention of transforming scores on X to the scale of Y.[8] Group invariance is satisfied if it is a matter of indifference for all H groups of examinees whether their group-specific linking or the combined-group linking is used to obtain score equivalents.

10.2.1 Statistical Methods Using Observed Scores

There are four observed-score linking methods that will be considered here:

1. mean method,

2. linear method,

---

[7] This use of h should not be confused with the previous use of h as the discrete density for common items.

[8] Parts of this section are a revised version of Yin et al. (in press).

3. parallel-linear method, and

4. equipercentile method with and without postsmoothing.[9]

Except for the parallel-linear method, each method has been considered previously in equating contexts. The difference here is that, for each method, there is a linkage for the combined group as well as each of the subpopulations.

Mean Method

For the mean method, deviation scores from the mean are set equal:

$$x - \mu(X) = y - \mu(Y). \qquad (10.1)$$

It follows that the transformation equation for the entire population is

$$m_Y(x) = x - \mu(X) + \mu(Y), \qquad (10.2)$$

and the transformation equation for a subgroup h is

$$m_{Yh}(x) = x - \mu_h(X) + \mu_h(Y). \qquad (10.3)$$

The mean method can be useful in equating well-constructed nearly parallel forms. In linking contexts, however, unless sample sizes are very small, the mean method is not likely to be the best choice, although it has the virtue of simplicity.

Linear Method

For the linear method, standardized deviation scores (z-scores) on the two tests are set equal:

$$\frac{x - \mu(X)}{\sigma(X)} = \frac{y - \mu(Y)}{\sigma(Y)}. \qquad (10.4)$$

The transformation for the combined group can be expressed as

$$l_Y(x) = \mu(Y) + \frac{\sigma(Y)}{\sigma(X)}\left[x - \mu(X)\right], \qquad (10.5)$$

and the transformation for subgroup h is

$$l_{Yh}(x) = \mu_h(Y) + \frac{\sigma_h(Y)}{\sigma_h(X)}\left[x - \mu_h(X)\right]. \qquad (10.6)$$

It is evident from the equations for the mean and linear methods that the mean method is a special case of the linear method in which $\sigma(Y)/\sigma(X) = 1$ for the combined group and $\sigma_h(Y)/\sigma_h(X) = 1$ for each of the H subgroups.

---

[9]Although we focus here on postsmoothing with equipercentile linking, presmoothing methods can be used as well.

Parallel-Linear Method

Largely for the purpose of analytic simplicity, Dorans and Holland (2000) invented the so-called "parallel-linear" method for linking with multiple groups. The only statistical difference between the linear and parallel-linear methods is that, for the latter, the deviation scores for the subgroups are divided by the standard deviations for the *combined* group:

$$\frac{x - \mu_h(X)}{\sigma(X)} = \frac{y - \mu_h(Y)}{\sigma(Y)}. \tag{10.7}$$

It follows that the transformation equation for subgroup h is

$$pl_{Yh}(x) = \mu_h(Y) + \frac{\sigma(Y)}{\sigma(X)}\left[x - \mu_h(X)\right]. \tag{10.8}$$

When the ratios of the standard deviations from the two tests obtained from subgroup h and from the combined group are equal—i.e.,

$$\frac{\sigma_h(Y)}{\sigma_h(X)} = \frac{\sigma(Y)}{\sigma(X)},$$

the transformation equations derived from the linear and parallel-linear methods are exactly the same for subgroup h. Usually, of course, the ratios of the standard deviations are not the same, but making this assumption leads to simplification of some results.

The slope in equation (10.8) for the parallel-linear method for subgroup h is exactly the same as the slope in equation (10.5) for the linear method for the combined group. It follows that the difference between the two equations is a function of the intercepts, only

$$\begin{aligned}
l_Y(x) - pl_{Yh}(x) &= \left\{\frac{\sigma(Y)}{\sigma(X)}[x - \mu(X)] + \mu(Y)\right\} - \\
&\quad \left\{\frac{\sigma(Y)}{\sigma(X)}[x - \mu_h(X)] + \mu_h(Y)\right\} \\
&= [\mu(Y) - \mu_h(Y)] - \frac{\sigma(Y)}{\sigma(X)}[\mu(X) - \mu_h(X)]. (10.9)
\end{aligned}$$

In short, the parallel-linear method simplifies differences in subgroup transformation functions into *intercept* differences, ignoring possible slope differences.

Equipercentile Method

The equipercentile method has been discussed extensively in Chapter 2. Here, we merely summarize basic results, extend them to subgroups, and discuss them in the context of different tests rather than different forms of the same test. In doing so, some equations from Chapter 2 are duplicated here.

Under the equipercentile method, differences in difficulty between tests are described by a non-linear transformation that is defined in the following manner:
$$e_Y(x) = G^{-1}[F(x)], \qquad (10.10)$$
where F is the cumulative distribution function of X, G is the cumulative distribution function of Y, and G^{-1} is the inverse of the cumulative distribution function of Y. The net effect is that the transformed scores on X have the same distribution function as the scores on Y (neglecting the issue of discreteness).

The analytic approach to determining equipercentile equivalents with discrete data typically employs the percentile rank functions P and Q for X and Y, respectively. Using percentile rank functions, the equipercentile equivalent of score x on the Y scale for the population (i.e., the combined group) is defined as
$$\begin{aligned} e_Y(x) &= Q^{-1}[P(x)], & 0 \le P(x) < 100, \\ &= Y_J + 0.5, & P(x) = 100, \end{aligned} \qquad (10.11)$$
where Q^{-1} is the inverse of the percentile rank function for Y, and Y_J represents the highest score for Y.[10] Similarly, the transformation equation for subgroup h is
$$\begin{aligned} e_{Yh}(x) &= Q_h^{-1}[P_h(x)], & 0 \le P_h(x) < 100, \\ &= Y_J + 0.5, & P_h(x) = 100, \end{aligned} \qquad (10.12)$$
where P_h is the percentile rank function for X obtained from group h, and Q_h^{-1} is the inverse of the percentile rank function for Y based on subgroup h.

The equipercentile method has several advantages over the mean, linear and, parallel-linear methods, including the following:

- equipercentile equivalents are within the range of possible score points, which avoids the out-of-range problem that can occur with the mean, linear, and parallel-linear methods;

- for the equipercentile method, relationships between tests are not assumed to be linear;

- the cumulative distribution function of transformed scores is approximated by the cumulative distribution function of Y; and

---

[10] The primary difference between this equation and the corresponding equation in Chapter 2 is that the equation in Chapter 2 uses the number of items in a form as the highest score.

- the moments for transformed scores (e.g., mean, variance, skewness, and kurtosis) are approximately the same as those for Y.

However, difficulties are sometimes encountered using the equipercentile method in linking situations, especially when sample sizes are small. For example, Pommerich et al. (2000) found that concordance tables obtained using the equipercentile method for different institutions were not always stable, especially for smaller institutions. In such circumstances, more stable results may be obtained by presmoothing the score distributions before obtaining the equipercentile equivalents, or postsmoothing the equipercentile equivalents themselves. Even when sample sizes are quite large, smoothing is often used to obtain equivalents that have a more regular (i.e., less jagged) shape. Both types of smoothing have been discussed extensively in earlier chapters. In the linking example discussed later in Section 10.2.4, postsmoothing is used.

10.2.2 Statistics for Overall Group Invariance

Dorans and Holland (2000) introduced two statistics to summarize differences between the transformation functions obtained from subgroups and the entire population (i.e., combined group): the standardized Root Mean Square Difference, $RMSD(x)$, which is associated with a particular score on X; and the standardized Root Expected Mean Square Difference, $REMSD$, which summarizes overall differences for the entire population (i.e., combined group). Consistent with the notation used in Chapter 1, let eq denote an equivalent based on any method (e.g., mean, linear, parallel-linear, or equipercentile). Then, $eq_Y(x)$ represents transformed scores on Form X to the scale of Form Y for the entire population, and $eq_{Yh}(x)$ represents transformed scores on Form X to the scale of Form Y for subgroup h. Let N_h be the sample size for subgroup h, let N be the total number of examinees, and let $w_h = N_h/N$ be the weight for subgroup h. Then,

$$RMSD(x) = \frac{\sqrt{\sum_{h=1}^{H} w_h [eq_{Yh}(x) - eq_Y(x)]^2}}{\sigma(Y)}, \qquad (10.13)$$

and

$$REMSD = \frac{\sqrt{\sum_{h=1}^{H} w_h \mathbf{E}\{[eq_{Yh}(x) - eq_Y(x)]^2\}}}{\sigma(Y)}, \qquad (10.14)$$

where $\mathbf{E}$ is the notation for expected value introduced in Chapter 1.

A computational formula for $REMSD$ involves weighting the expected values of the squared differences in equation (10.14) by the relative frequencies of the data for X at each score point. Let $min(x)$ and $max(x)$

be the observed minimum and maximum values, respectively, of scores on Form X, let N_{xh} be the number of examinees for subgroup h with a particular score (x) on Form X, and let $v_{xh} = N_{xh}/N_h$ be a weighting factor for subgroup h and score x. Then, a computational formula for $REMSD$ is

$$REMSD = \frac{\sqrt{\sum_{h=1}^{H} w_h \sum_{min(x)}^{max(x)} v_{xh} \left[eq_{Yh}(x) - eq_Y(x)\right]^2}}{\sigma(Y)}, \quad (10.15)$$

which clearly indicates that $REMSD$ is a doubly weighted statistic. The v_{xh} weights are proportional to subgroup frequencies for score points on X; the w_h weights are proportional to subgroup sizes.

As discussed by Dorans and Holland (2000), for the parallel-linear method with $H = 2$, equation (10.15) simplifies to

$$REMSD = \sqrt{w_1 w_2} \left(\left| \frac{\mu_1(Y) - \mu_2(Y)}{\sigma(Y)} - \frac{\mu_1(X) - \mu_2(X)}{\sigma(X)} \right| \right). \quad (10.16)$$

For this special case, $REMSD$ is simply a function of the absolute value of the difference in "approximate effect sizes" for the two tests.[11] So, if the effect sizes differ substantially for the two tests, then $REMSD$ will be large.

Also, for this special case, all other things being equal, $REMSD$ will increase as the subgroup sample sizes become more similar. Indeed, the form of the general equation (10.14) for $REMSD$ indicates that if one subgroup includes most of the examinees, $REMSD$ can be quite small even when the linking for the large subgroup is quite different from the linkings for the smaller subgroups.

In equation (10.15), the squared differences between the transformed scores obtained for subgroup h and the entire population are weighted by the relative frequency at each score point on form X. Clearly, when the weights are defined in this manner, the value of $REMSD$ will depend on the specific sample of examinees used in the linking study. In most practical circumstances, however, the sample used to conduct a linking study is different from the population about whom decisions will be made based on the linking results. This suggests that an investigator might want to define the w and v weights in a manner that better reflects the likely values of these weights in the context that the linking results will be used. Alternatively, the v weights might reflect the relative importance associated with certain score points. For example, the highest weight might be around

---

[11]The denominator of an effect size is typically defined as the "common" standard deviation for the two groups, rather than the standard deviation for both groups combined. Alternatively, the v weights could be based on the combined group; i.e., for each h, the weight for $X = x$ could be set to N_x/N. These weights seem to be the ones preferred by Dorans and Holland (2000).

a certain cut score, or several cut scores. Of course, the sum of the weights must still be 1.

As a special case, consider an equally weighted $REMSD$ ($ewREMSD$), which uses the same weight—the inverse of the total number of score points—for all the score points on form X,

$$ewREMSD = \frac{\sqrt{\sum_{h=1}^{H} w_h \sum_{min(x)}^{max(x)} \frac{1}{max(x) - min(x) + 1}[eq_{Yh}(x) - eq_Y(x)]^2}}{\sigma(Y)}.$$
(10.17)

This statistic may be sensible when decisions are made throughout the range of score points. Even in other circumstances, $ewREMSD$ may be a useful statistic to compare with $REMSD$.

In equations (10.15)–(10.17), parameters [σ, μ, $eq_Y(x)$, and $eq_{Yh}(x)$] are used. In practice, of course, estimates based on observed scores [$\hat{\sigma}$, $\hat{\mu}$, $\widehat{eq}_Y(x)$, and $\widehat{eq}_{Yh}(x)$] are used instead.

10.2.3 Statistics for Pairwise Group Invariance

The $REMSD$ and $ewREMSD$ statistics discussed in the previous section consider all H groups simultaneously. As such, their advantage and their limitation is that they measure *overall* group invariance. In doing so, they can mask differences between pairs of groups that may be of interest in particular circumstances. For example, sometimes a question of interest concerning group invariance is the extent to which the linking for two particular subgroups (e.g., blacks and whites) is similar. At other times, interest may focus on the extent to which the combined group linking is similar to that for a particular subgroup. To accommodate this need, we consider the following statistics that measure invariance two groups at a time:[12]

- MD: weighted average of the differences between equivalents;

- $ewMD$: equally weighted average of the differences between equivalents;

- MAD: weighted average of the absolute value of the differences between equivalents; and

- $ewMAD$: equally weighted average of the absolute value of the differences between equivalents.

---

[12]Two-at-a-time versions of $REMSD$ and $ewREMSD$ could be defined, also, as discussed by Yang et al. (2003).

Formally, for two groups h and h' (h or h' might be the combined group),

$$MD = \sum_x \nu_{xhh'} \left[eq_{Yh}(x) - eq_{Yh'}(x)\right]. \qquad (10.18)$$

If the weights are intended to reflect the frequencies in the data used to establish the linking,

$$\nu_{xhh'} = \frac{N_{xh} + N_{xh'}}{N_h + N_{h'}}$$

if h and h' are subgroups. If one of the groups is the combined group, then $\nu_{xhh'} = N_x/N$, where N_x is the sample size for $X = x$ for the combined group. In terms of the notation introduced in equation (10.17), the equally weighted average of the differences is

$$ewMD = \sum_{min(x)}^{max(x)} \frac{1}{max(x) - min(x) + 1} \left[eq_{Yh}(x) - eq_{Yh'}(x)\right], \qquad (10.19)$$

which might also be called an "unweighted" or "simple" average. Replacing the signed differences in equations (10.18) and (10.19) with their absolute values gives formulas for MAD and $ewMAD$, respectively:

$$MAD = \sum_x \nu_{xhh'} \left|eq_{Yh}(x) - eq_{Yh'}(x)\right|, \qquad (10.20)$$

and

$$ewMAD = \sum_{min(x)}^{max(x)} \frac{1}{max(x) - min(x) + 1} \left|eq_{Yh}(x) - eq_{Yh'}(x)\right|. \qquad (10.21)$$

10.2.4 Example: ACT and ITED Science Tests

To illustrate the linking methods and statistics that have been discussed in Sections 10.2.1–10.2.3, we use data that were collected for the ACT Assessment (ACT) Science Reasoning test (ACT, 1997) and the *Iowa Tests of Educational Development* (ITED) Analysis of Science Materials test (Feldt et al., 1994). This example is hypothetical and not very realistic, because the two testing programs are not usually used for the same purpose, although they share a common history, and in several states they are taken be many of the same students.[13] In the context of this example, several "benchmarks" are considered for judging the extent to which linkage differences are large, in some sense.

---

[13]For other examples using the same testing programs, see Yin et al. (in press). For ACT-SAT examples, see Dorans (2000), Dorans and Holland (2000), and Dorans (in press-a). For examples using the Advanced Placement exams, see Dorans et al. (2003) and Dorans (in press-b).

ACT Science Reasoning

The ACT is designed to measure skills that are important for success in postsecondary education. A principal purpose of the ACT is to assist in college admissions. Content specifications for the ACT are based on curriculum and textbooks used in grades 7–12, educators' opinions about the importance of particular knowledge and skills, and college faculty members' opinions about important academic skills needed for success in college. Raw score are defined as the number of items correct, and raw scores are transformed to scale scores in the range 1–36.

The Science Reasoning test (40 multiple-choice items administered in 35 minutes) is one of four tests in the ACT battery. The test measures interpretation, analysis, evaluation, reasoning, and problem-solving skills required in the natural sciences. It is assumed that students have completed a course in earth science and/or physical science and a course in biology.

The Science Reasoning test presents seven sets of scientific information, each followed by a number of items. The scientific information is conveyed in one of three different formats: data representation (graphs, tables, and other schematic forms), research summaries (descriptions of several related experiments), or conflicting viewpoints (expressions of several related hypotheses or views that are inconsistent with one another).

ITED Analysis of Science Materials

The ITED is widely used for measuring the performance of high-school students in grades 9–12, especially for long-term goals of secondary education. The ITED can be used regardless of the particular courses students are taking or curriculum they are following. The ITED is not routinely used for college admissions purposes, although there is evidence that scores on the ITED are a good predictor of success in college (Feldt et al., 1994).

Raw score is defined as the number of items correct, and raw scores are transformed to different types of scale scores. Here we focus on the developmental standard score (DSS) scale. DSSs are used to describe the location of a student's performance on an achievement continuum. The typical performance for an 11th grade student in the spring of the school year is assigned to be 275 in DSS units (Feldt et al., 1994). DSSs range from approximately 150 to 400 for most 11th graders.

The Analysis of Science Materials test (48 multiple-choice items administered in 40 minutes) is one of seven tests in the ITED battery. The test provides information about a student's ability to interpret and evaluate information in the sciences, to recognize basic principles of scientific inquiry and measurement, and to analyze experimental procedures. Many of the items are based on reading passages/materials that provide descriptions of actual experiments and their results. Recall of specific information plays a limited role. Rather, the items require students to think critically about diverse kinds of scientific information (Feldt et al., 1994).

Data

The data used in this study were collected using a single group design; i.e., the same group of examinees took both the ACT and the ITED. Specifically, 8,628 Iowa examinees (11th graders) who took the ITED in fall 1993 and who took the ACT as 12th graders in spring 1995 were included in the study. The grouping variable used here is gender. There were 3,766 males and 4,862 females in the sample. [14]

Note that there is a year-and-a-half interval between the two testings. This time interval may be too long to be optimal, but it is a practical necessity for the reasons noted next. First, at the time the data were collected, the ITED was administered only in the fall. Second, in the state of Iowa, many high school seniors do not take the ITED, and it is reasonable to assume that many of those who do are less motivated than they were when they tested as juniors. Therefore, for the spring 1995 ACT-tested 12th graders, it was judged that the best available match was ITED-tested 11th graders who tested in the fall of 1993 (instead of fall of 1994).

Examinees first took the ITED, and then the ACT. There was no counterbalancing of the two tests. One potential problem associated with the single group design is that learning could have taken place during the period between the two testings, and the ITED-ACT order effect may be confounded with examinees' learning and growth over time. However, it was not practical to collect counterbalanced data because of the nature of the two testing programs.

The limitations in the data noted above suggest a cautious interpretation of results. However, as noted earlier, these data are used here to illustrate methodologies, not to create a linking for practical use.

Distributions and Descriptive Statistics

Tables 10.3–10.5 provide descriptive statistics, frequency distributions, and percentile ranks for Y = ACT scores, and X = ITED scores. From Table 10.3 it is evident that the ACT scores are positively skewed, whereas the ITED scores are negatively skewed (see also Figure 10.4). It is difficult to compare the means and standard deviations because scores for the two tests are on very different scales.

The observed-score ACT-ITED correlations for the combined group, males, and females were .672, .659, and .689, respectively. If we assume that reliabilities for the two tests are in the range of .8 to .9, then the corresponding disattenuated correlations are about .75–.84, .73–.82, and .77–.86. The moderate value of these disattenuated correlations suggests that, although the two tests share some common features, there is evidence

---

[14] Robert Forsyth and James Maxey were instrumental in making these data available.

TABLE 10.3. Descriptive Statistics for ACT and ITED Science Scores for Males (M), Females (F), and Combined Group (C).

Test	Gp	N	w	Min	Max	$\hat{\mu}$	$\hat{\sigma}$	$\widehat{sk}$	$\widehat{ku}$
ACT	C	8628	1.000	9	36	22.197	4.218	0.350	3.214
	M	3766	.436	10	36	22.834	4.401	0.313	3.109
	F	4862	.564	9	36	21.703	4.002	0.325	3.238
ITED	C	8628	1.000	163	382	314.191	36.186	-0.649	3.302
	M	3766	.436	163	382	315.500	39.130	-0.757	3.290
	F	4862	.564	173	382	313.177	33.694	-0.539	3.223

TABLE 10.4. Distributions for ACT Science Scores for Males $(N = 3,766)$, Females $(N = 4,862)$, and Combined Group $(N = 8628)$.

	Comb. Group		Males		Females	
y	freq	$\widehat{Q}(y)$	freq	$\widehat{Q}(y)$	freq	$\widehat{Q}(y)$
9	3	0.017	0	0.000	3	0.031
10	6	0.070	3	0.040	3	0.093
11	20	0.220	7	0.173	13	0.257
12	18	0.440	5	0.332	13	0.524
13	46	0.811	18	0.637	28	0.946
14	90	1.599	40	1.407	50	1.748
15	158	3.037	63	2.775	95	3.239
16	338	5.911	113	5.112	225	6.530
17	454	10.501	159	8.723	295	11.878
18	412	15.519	155	12.892	257	17.555
19	738	22.184	293	18.840	445	24.774
20	811	31.160	300	26.713	511	34.605
21	914	41.157	366	35.555	548	45.496
22	748	50.788	302	44.424	446	55.718
23	838	59.979	382	53.505	456	64.994
24	802	69.483	374	63.542	428	74.085
25	399	76.443	198	71.136	201	80.553
26	522	81.780	251	77.098	271	85.407
27	336	86.752	183	82.860	153	89.768
28	263	90.224	135	87.082	128	92.657
29	287	93.411	153	90.905	134	95.352
30	169	96.054	98	94.238	71	97.460
31	76	97.473	51	96.216	25	98.447
32	53	98.221	28	97.265	25	98.961
33	17	98.627	12	97.796	5	99.270
34	66	99.108	42	98.513	24	99.568
35	9	99.542	8	99.177	1	99.825
36	35	99.797	27	99.642	8	99.918

10. Linking

TABLE 10.5. Distributions for ITED Science Scores for Males ($N = 3,766$), Females ($N = 4,862$), and Combined Group ($N = 8,628$).

	Comb. Group		Males		Females	
x	freq	$\widehat{P}(x)$	freq	$\widehat{P}(x)$	freq	$\widehat{P}(x)$
163	1	0.006	1	0.013	0	0.000
169	2	0.023	2	0.053	0	0.000
173	2	0.046	1	0.093	1	0.010
177	1	0.064	0	0.106	1	0.031
181	6	0.104	3	0.146	3	0.072
186	8	0.185	4	0.239	4	0.144
192	15	0.319	9	0.412	6	0.247
199	23	0.539	16	0.743	7	0.381
207	38	0.892	27	1.314	11	0.566
216	48	1.391	29	2.058	19	0.874
225	56	1.994	34	2.894	22	1.296
234	70	2.724	43	3.917	27	1.800
242	109	3.761	50	5.151	59	2.684
249	88	4.903	41	6.360	47	3.774
255	89	5.928	42	7.461	47	4.741
260	111	7.087	44	8.603	67	5.913
264	116	8.403	51	9.865	65	7.271
268	145	9.915	56	11.285	89	8.854
272	148	11.613	68	12.931	80	10.592
275	171	13.462	67	14.724	104	12.485
278	189	15.548	67	16.503	122	14.809
282	193	17.762	79	18.441	114	17.236
285	179	19.918	65	20.353	114	19.580
288	241	22.352	95	22.477	146	22.254
290	248	25.185	100	25.066	148	25.278
293	279	28.239	111	27.868	168	28.527
297	267	31.404	109	30.789	158	31.880
301	309	34.742	114	33.749	195	35.510
305	319	38.381	116	36.803	203	39.603
309	342	42.211	121	39.950	221	43.963
314	388	46.442	157	43.640	231	48.612
319	369	50.829	155	47.783	214	53.188
323	372	55.123	155	51.899	217	57.620
328	399	59.591	159	56.067	240	62.320
333	437	64.436	158	60.276	279	67.657
337	411	69.350	186	64.843	225	72.840
342	416	74.142	186	69.782	230	77.520
347	408	78.917	190	74.774	218	82.127
351	363	83.385	175	79.620	188	86.302
355	357	87.558	174	84.254	183	90.117
360	299	91.360	150	88.555	149	93.531
364	236	94.460	131	92.286	105	96.144
368	187	96.911	122	95.645	65	97.892
372	121	98.696	66	98.141	55	99.126
377	42	99.641	29	99.403	13	99.825
382	10	99.942	8	99.894	2	99.979

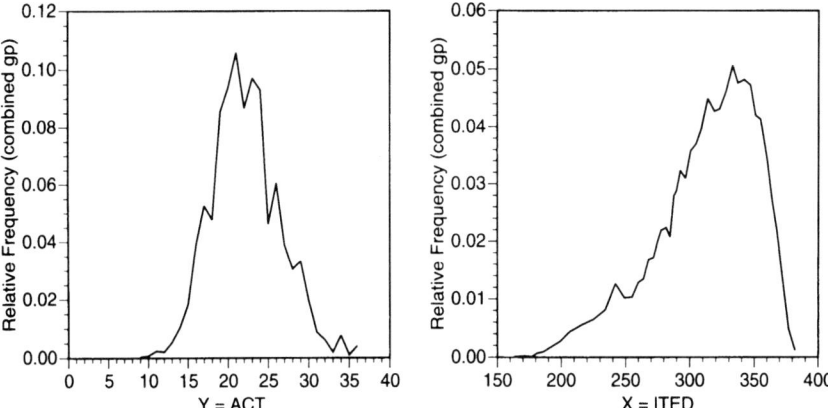

FIGURE 10.4. Combined-group relative frequencies for the ACT and the ITED.

that they are measuring something different. This evidence is somewhat stronger for males than females.

ACT scores that are reported to examinees are integers from 1 to 36, inclusive. For these data, however, no examinee got an ACT score below 9, and there were many more examinees who got a score of 36 (namely, 35 examinees) than who got a score of 35 (namely, 9 examinees).

The lowest ITED score for the sample is 163, and the highest is 382. Within this range there are $382 - 163 + 1 = 220$ possible integer scores. However, only 46 integer scores were actually obtained by examinees in the sample. This is not too surprising, given the length of the ITED test; i.e., since the ITED science test contains only 48 items, there could not be more than 49 obtained scores. The fact that there are many fewer obtained scores than possible scores is primarily attributable to the manner in which scaling is done for developmental standard scores when there are many different levels of a test (see Chapter 9).

Approximately 44% of the sample are males and 56% are females. The descriptive statistics in Table 10.3 suggest that there are some differences between males and females, but the different scales for the ACT and the ITED make it difficult to judge whether these differences are greater for the ACT or the ITED. A Standardized Mean Difference (SMD) provides a scale-independent way to quantify group mean differences (see, for example, Dorans, 2000):

$$SMD = \frac{\mu_1 - \mu_2}{\sigma}, \tag{10.22}$$

where σ is the combined-group standard deviation. Letting males be group 1 and females be group 2:

SMD for Y = ACT	SMD for X = ITED
0.27	0.06

TABLE 10.6. Mean, Linear, and Parallel-Linear Transformations.

Group	Mean[a]	Linear		Parallel-Linear	
		Intercept	Slope	Intercept	Slope
Combined	−291.99397	−14.42959	.11657	−14.42959	.11657
Males (1)	−292.66569	−12.65127	.11247	−13.94504	.11657
Females (2)	−291.47368	−15.49409	.11877	−14.80491	.11657

[a]Adjustments to observed scores on X.

In terms of the ACT scale, males score higher than females by about 27% of a combined-group standard deviation unit; in terms of the ITED scale, males score higher than females by about 6% of a combined-group standard deviation unit. In this sense, males and females score much more differently on the ACT than on the ITED. These *SMD* values suggest that transformations of ITED scores to the ACT scale are not likely to be invariant with respect to gender. This matter is considered explicitly next.

Unrounded Equivalents

Using the equations in Section 10.2.1, Table 10.6 reports the mean adjustments, slopes, and intercepts for determining the mean, linear, and parallel-linear transformations.[15] (Note that, by definition, the linear and parallel-linear methods for the combined group are the same.) These results can be used to estimate the Y = ACT equivalents. For example, for males with ITED scores of 310, using equation (10.3), the equivalent using the mean method is

$$\hat{m}_{Y1}(x = 300) = 310 - 292.66569 = 17.33;$$

using equation (10.6), the equivalent using the linear method is

$$\hat{l}_{Y1}(x = 300) = -12.65127 + .11247(310) = 22.22;$$

and using equation (10.8), the equivalent using the parallel-linear method is

$$\widehat{pl}_{Y1}(x = 300) = -13.94504 + .11657(310) = 22.19.$$

Table 10.7 provides estimated mean, linear, and parallel-linear Y = ACT equivalents for a selected sample of low, medium, and high X = ITED

---

[15]These results are reported with five decimal places of accuracy so the reader can verify the correctness of equivalents reported in subsequent tables. If only three decimal places of accuracy are used, as in Table 10.3, some computed equivalents will differ from those reported in subsequent tables.

TABLE 10.7. Unrounded and Untruncated Y = ACT Mean, Linear, and Parallel-Linear Equivalents for Males (1), Females (2), and Combined Group.

	Mean			Linear			Parallel-Linear		
x	$\widehat{m}_Y(x)$	$\widehat{m}_{Y1}(x)$	$\widehat{m}_{Y2}(x)$	$\hat{l}_Y(x)$	$\hat{l}_{Y1}(x)$	$\hat{l}_{Y2}(x)$	$\widehat{pl}_Y(x)$	$\widehat{pl}_{Y1}(x)$	$\widehat{pl}_{Y2}(x)$
163	−128.99	−129.67	−128.47	4.57	5.68	3.87	4.57	5.06	4.20
164	−127.99	−128.67	−127.47	4.69	5.79	3.98	4.69	5.17	4.31
165	−126.99	−127.67	−126.47	4.81	5.91	4.10	4.81	5.29	4.43
166	−125.99	−126.67	−125.47	4.92	6.02	4.22	4.92	5.41	4.55
167	−124.99	−125.67	−124.47	5.04	6.13	4.34	5.04	5.52	4.66
168	−123.99	−124.67	−123.47	5.15	6.24	4.46	5.15	5.64	4.78
169	−122.99	−123.67	−122.47	5.27	6.36	4.58	5.27	5.76	4.90
170	−121.99	−122.67	−121.47	5.39	6.47	4.70	5.39	5.87	5.01
171	−120.99	−121.67	−120.47	5.50	6.58	4.82	5.50	5.99	5.13
172	−119.99	−120.67	−119.47	5.62	6.69	4.94	5.62	6.11	5.25
173	−118.99	−119.67	−118.47	5.74	6.81	5.05	5.74	6.22	5.36
⋮	⋮	⋮	⋮	⋮	⋮	⋮	⋮	⋮	⋮
300	8.01	7.33	8.53	20.54	21.09	20.14	20.54	21.03	20.17
301	9.01	8.33	9.53	20.66	21.20	20.26	20.66	21.14	20.28
302	10.01	9.33	10.53	20.78	21.32	20.38	20.78	21.26	20.40
303	11.01	10.33	11.53	20.89	21.43	20.49	20.89	21.38	20.52
304	12.01	11.33	12.53	21.01	21.54	20.61	21.01	21.49	20.63
305	13.01	12.33	13.53	21.13	21.65	20.73	21.13	21.61	20.75
306	14.01	13.33	14.53	21.24	21.77	20.85	21.24	21.73	20.87
307	15.01	14.33	15.53	21.36	21.88	20.97	21.36	21.84	20.98
308	16.01	15.33	16.53	21.48	21.99	21.09	21.48	21.96	21.10
309	17.01	16.33	17.53	21.59	22.10	21.21	21.59	22.08	21.22
310	18.01	17.33	18.53	21.71	22.22	21.33	21.71	22.19	21.33
311	19.01	18.33	19.53	21.82	22.33	21.44	21.82	22.31	21.45
312	20.01	19.33	20.53	21.94	22.44	21.56	21.94	22.43	21.57
313	21.01	20.33	21.53	22.06	22.55	21.68	22.06	22.54	21.68
314	22.01	21.33	22.53	22.17	22.67	21.80	22.17	22.66	21.80
315	23.01	22.33	23.53	22.29	22.78	21.92	22.29	22.78	21.92
316	24.01	23.33	24.53	22.41	22.89	22.04	22.41	22.89	22.03
317	25.01	24.33	25.53	22.52	23.00	22.16	22.52	23.01	22.15
318	26.01	25.33	26.53	22.64	23.12	22.28	22.64	23.13	22.27
319	27.01	26.33	27.53	22.76	23.23	22.40	22.76	23.24	22.38
320	28.01	27.33	28.53	22.87	23.34	22.51	22.87	23.36	22.50
⋮	⋮	⋮	⋮	⋮	⋮	⋮	⋮	⋮	⋮
372	80.01	79.33	80.53	28.94	29.19	28.69	28.94	29.42	28.56
373	81.01	80.33	81.53	29.05	29.30	28.81	29.05	29.54	28.68
374	82.01	81.33	82.53	29.17	29.41	28.93	29.17	29.65	28.79
375	83.01	82.33	83.53	29.29	29.53	29.05	29.29	29.77	28.91
376	84.01	83.33	84.53	29.40	29.64	29.17	29.40	29.89	29.03
377	85.01	84.33	85.53	29.52	29.75	29.28	29.52	30.00	29.14
378	86.01	85.33	86.53	29.64	29.86	29.40	29.64	30.12	29.26
379	87.01	86.33	87.53	29.75	29.98	29.52	29.75	30.24	29.38
380	88.01	87.33	88.53	29.87	30.09	29.64	29.87	30.35	29.49
381	89.01	88.33	89.53	29.99	30.20	29.76	29.99	30.47	29.61
382	90.01	89.33	90.53	30.10	30.31	29.88	30.10	30.59	29.73

TABLE 10.8. Unrounded and Untruncated Y = ACT Equipercentile Equivalents for Males (1), Females (2), and Combined Group.

x	No Smoothing			$S = .30$			$S = 1.00$		
	$\hat{e}_Y(x)$	$\hat{e}_{Y1}(x)$	$\hat{e}_{Y2}(x)$	$\hat{e}_Y(x)$	$\hat{e}_{Y1}(x)$	$\hat{e}_{Y2}(x)$	$\hat{e}_Y(x)$	$\hat{e}_{Y1}(x)$	$\hat{e}_{Y2}(x)$
163	8.67	9.67	8.50	8.55	8.57	8.54	8.55	8.57	8.54
164	8.83	9.83	8.50	8.66	8.70	8.63	8.66	8.70	8.63
165	8.83	9.83	8.50	8.77	8.83	8.71	8.77	8.83	8.71
166	8.83	9.83	8.50	8.88	8.96	8.79	8.88	8.96	8.79
167	8.83	9.83	8.50	8.98	9.10	8.88	8.99	9.09	8.88
168	8.83	9.83	8.50	9.09	9.23	8.96	9.09	9.22	8.96
169	9.17	10.17	8.50	9.20	9.36	9.04	9.20	9.35	9.04
170	9.50	10.50	8.50	9.31	9.49	9.13	9.31	9.48	9.13
171	9.50	10.50	8.50	9.42	9.62	9.21	9.42	9.61	9.21
172	9.50	10.50	8.50	9.52	9.76	9.30	9.53	9.74	9.29
173	9.67	10.57	8.67	9.63	9.89	9.38	9.63	9.88	9.38
⋮	⋮	⋮	⋮	⋮	⋮	⋮	⋮	⋮	⋮
300	20.19	20.66	19.90	20.24	20.66	19.93	20.26	20.68	19.96
301	20.38	20.81	20.09	20.37	20.75	20.06	20.37	20.76	20.06
302	20.56	20.97	20.28	20.49	20.85	20.19	20.47	20.84	20.16
303	20.56	20.97	20.28	20.54	20.92	20.27	20.54	20.92	20.27
304	20.56	20.97	20.28	20.60	20.98	20.36	20.62	21.00	20.38
305	20.74	21.13	20.48	20.71	21.09	20.49	20.71	21.09	20.49
306	20.91	21.29	20.66	20.83	21.19	20.63	20.81	21.18	20.60
307	20.91	21.29	20.66	20.88	21.26	20.71	20.88	21.26	20.71
308	20.91	21.29	20.66	20.94	21.33	20.78	20.96	21.35	20.81
309	21.10	21.45	20.86	21.06	21.44	20.91	21.07	21.45	20.91
310	21.29	21.64	21.07	21.19	21.56	21.04	21.17	21.54	21.00
311	21.29	21.64	21.07	21.25	21.64	21.11	21.24	21.64	21.08
312	21.29	21.64	21.07	21.29	21.70	21.14	21.30	21.73	21.16
313	21.29	21.64	21.07	21.35	21.79	21.20	21.38	21.84	21.24
314	21.50	21.90	21.28	21.50	21.94	21.33	21.50	21.94	21.32
315	21.76	22.16	21.49	21.65	22.09	21.45	21.62	22.05	21.40
316	21.76	22.16	21.49	21.73	22.19	21.51	21.71	22.16	21.48
317	21.76	22.16	21.49	21.77	22.26	21.54	21.79	22.27	21.56
318	21.76	22.16	21.49	21.85	22.35	21.60	21.87	22.38	21.64
319	22.00	22.42	21.72	22.00	22.49	21.73	22.00	22.49	21.73
320	22.25	22.64	21.96	22.16	22.63	21.85	22.13	22.59	21.83
⋮	⋮	⋮	⋮	⋮	⋮	⋮	⋮	⋮	⋮
372	33.35	33.67	32.32	33.14	33.74	32.35	33.12	33.47	32.15
373	34.38	34.45	34.25	34.14	34.19	32.75	34.02	33.92	32.56
374	34.38	34.45	34.25	34.42	34.45	33.14	34.33	34.29	32.98
375	34.38	34.45	34.25	34.55	34.62	33.54	34.56	34.63	33.39
376	34.38	34.45	34.25	34.65	34.85	33.93	34.76	34.97	33.81
377	35.61	35.67	35.00	34.94	35.19	34.33	35.02	35.32	34.22
378	36.21	36.20	36.25	35.22	35.43	34.72	35.29	35.53	34.64
379	36.21	36.20	36.25	35.51	35.67	35.12	35.56	35.75	35.05
380	36.21	36.20	36.25	35.79	35.90	35.51	35.83	35.96	35.46
381	36.21	36.20	36.25	36.07	36.14	35.91	36.10	36.18	35.88
382	36.36	36.35	36.37	36.36	36.38	36.30	36.37	36.39	36.29

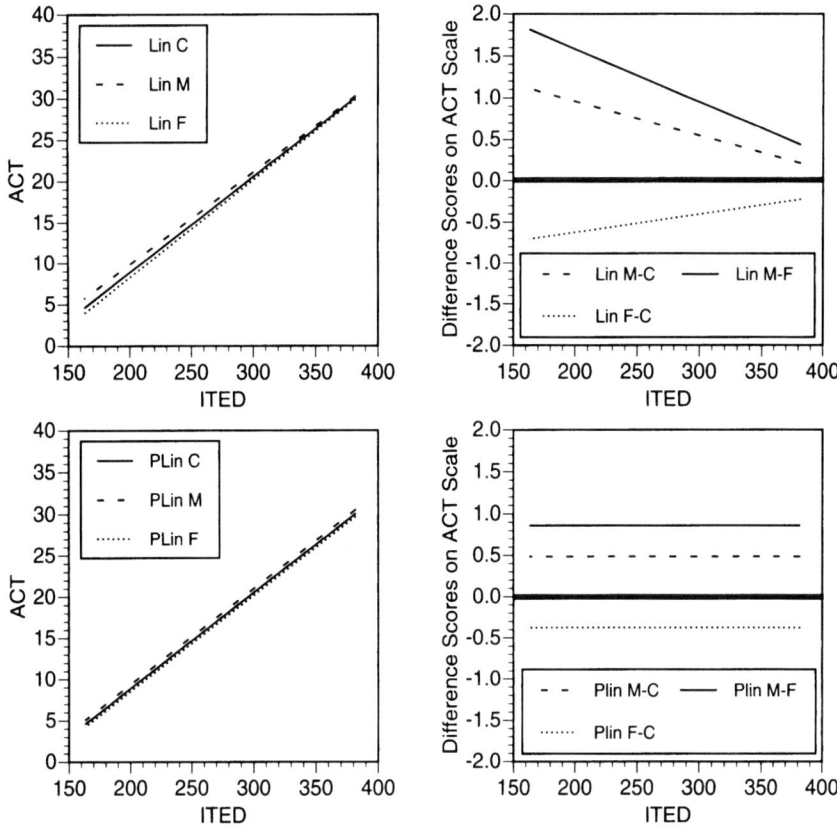

FIGURE 10.5. Linear and parallel-linear linkings.

scores. Perhaps the most striking feature of these results is that, for low and high ITED scores, the mean method gives ACT equivalents that are very much out of range. By contrast, the linear and parallel-linear results are often very similar.

Table 10.8 provides estimated unsmoothed equipercentile $Y = $ ACT equivalents, as well as postsmoothed equipercentile equivalents with $S = .30$ and $S = 1.00$, for a selected sample of low, medium, and high $X = $ ITED scores. It is evident that the equivalents for $S = .30$ and $S = 1.00$ are very similar and somewhat different from the unsmoothed results.[16]

---

[16] $S = 1.00$ would be a rather large value of S in an equating context with forms that have the same range of score points. For this linking context, however, the tests have very different ranges of score points. It follows that the unsmoothed equipercentile linkings exhibit many-to-one conversions of ITED scores to ACT scores, which give the linkings a step-function appearance (see Table 10.8). In this case, using $S = 1.00$ smooths the steps a little while preserving the moments reasonably well.

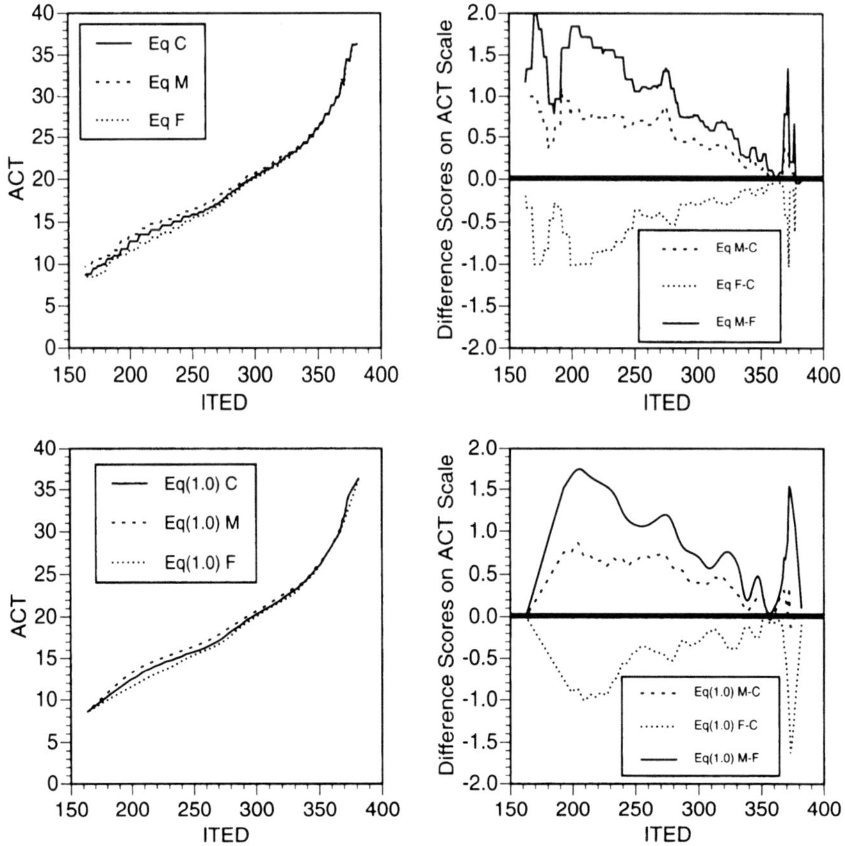

454   10. Linking

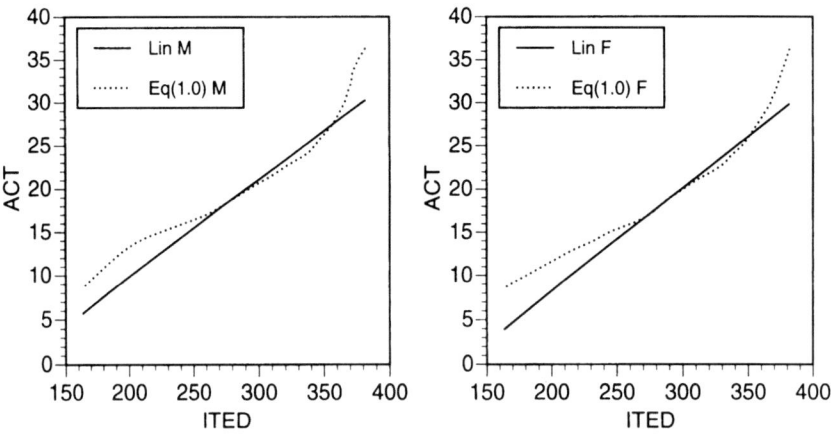

FIGURE 10.6. Equipercentile linkings without smoothing and with $S = 1.0$.

FIGURE 10.7. Male and female equivalents for linear linking and equipercentile linking with $S = 1.0$.

Graphical perspectives on differences in equivalents for the various methods are provided in Figures 10.5 and 10.6. In each of these figures, the left-hand subfigures provide the actual linkages or conversions (i.e., the ACT equivalents given ITED scores) for males (M), females (F), and the combined group (C). The right-hand subfigures provide difference plots for $M - C$, $F - C$, and $M - F$. Focusing on the $M - F$ difference plots, it is evident that

- the linear method gives equivalents that are quite different from those for the parallel-linear method, especially at the lower end of the score scale;

- there is reasonably compelling evidence that the "true" ACT equivalents are a nonlinear transformation of the ITED scores;

- smoothing seems to have its greatest effect in the lower part of the ITED score scale;

- for high ITED scores, the equipercentile equivalents seem erratic, even with smoothing; and

- the male equivalents are consistently higher than the female equivalents for all methods, with the minor exception of unsmoothed equipercentile linking for very high ITED scores.

Figure 10.7 provides the male and female equivalents for linear linking and equipercentile linking with $S = 1.00$. It is evident that the linkings are nearly linear in the 250–350 ITED score range where most examinees scored (see Table 10.5), but distinctly nonlinear outside this range.

Pairwise Statistics

For the unrounded equivalents in Tables 10.7 and 10.8, Table 10.9 provides values of MD, $ewMD$, MAD, and $ewMAD$ (see equations (10.18)–(10.21)) for $M - C$ (males minus the combined group), $F - C$ (females minus the combined group), and $M - F$ (males minus females). These three different pairs of groups (and the corresponding graphs in Figures 10.5 and 10.6) provide information for different types of decisions.

If interest focuses on $M - F$ differences in equivalents, it is evident that, for all methods, the equivalents for males are higher, on average, than those for females by approximately one ACT scale point, regardless of weighting issues. As noted previously, Figures 10.5 and 10.6 indicate that, in terms of the linear and equipercentile linkings, the differences tend to be greater at lower ITED scores.

On the other hand, interest may focus on the extent to which males and females are advantaged or disadvantaged if the equivalents for the combined group are used for all examinees. If this is the focus, then the

TABLE 10.9. Average Differences in Y = ACT Equivalents.

Groups	Method	MD	ewMD	MAD	ewMAD
$M-C$	Mean	−.672	−.672	.672	.672
	Linear	.488	.661	.488	.661
	Parallel-Linear	.485	.485	.485	.485
	Equi (unsmoothed)	.355	.521	.355	.521
	Equi ($S = .30$)	.364	.455	.364	.456
	Equi ($S = 1.00$)	.363	.451	.364	.454
$F-C$	Mean	.520	.520	.520	.520
	Linear	−.374	−.465	.374	.465
	Parallel-Linear	−.375	−.375	.375	.375
	Equi (unsmoothed)	−.276	−.454	.276	.455
	Equi ($S = .30$)	−.292	−.447	.292	.448
	Equi ($S = 1.00$)	−.295	−.457	.295	.458
$M-F$	Mean	−1.192	−1.192	1.192	1.192
	Linear	.863	1.126	.863	1.126
	Parallel-Linear	.860	.860	.860	.860
	Equi (unsmoothed)	.635	.974	.635	.976
	Equi ($S = .30$)	.660	.903	.660	.903
	Equi ($S = 1.00$)	.661	.909	.661	.909

MD and $ewMD$ statistics in the top two-thirds of Table 10.9, as well as the $M - C$ and $F - C$ graphs in Figures 10.5 and 10.6, provide relevant information. These results suggest that

- males would be assigned larger equivalents under the male transformation than under the combined-group transformation—i.e., the combined-group transformation *disadvantages* males;

- females would be assigned lower equivalents under the female transformation than under the combined-group transformation—i.e., the combined-group transformation *advantages* females;

- the disadvantage for males of using the combined group transformation is, on average, slightly larger than the advantage for females of using the combined group transformation.

Rounded Equivalents

The equivalents that have been discussed thus far are unrounded and untruncated. For overall judgments about group invariance, such equivalents seem preferable in that they do not incorporate the added "noise" that results from truncating and/or rounding scores. However, in many practical circumstances, the scores that are actually used to make decisions about examinees are rounded (almost always to integers) and truncated so that they are within some prespecified range. For the ACT Assessment the reported scores are integers in the range of 1 to 36. So, from a practical perspective, it seems sensible to examine the effects of rounding and truncation on the statistics discussed previously, even though it might be argued that, in theory, an overall evaluative judgment about group invariance is probably best made using unrounded and untruncated equivalents.

Tables 10.10 and 10.11 provide estimated rounded and truncated ACT equivalents for the mean, linear, parallel-linear, and equipercentile methods for a selected sample of low, medium, and high ITED scores. It is evident that the mean method gives equivalents that are quite different from the others, primarily because there is substantial truncation for low and high ITED scores. Also, the equipercentile methods give equivalents that are different from the linear methods at the extremes of the ITED scale and, for the equipercentile methods, there is some truncation at the very high end of the ITED scale.

Table 10.12 reports the $M - F$ difference statistics for rounded and truncated scores. As might be expected, except for the mean method, these difference statistics are similar to those for unrounded and untruncated scores in Table 10.9. A similar statement holds for the $M - C$ and $F - C$ statistics.

Overall Statistics

Table 10.13 provides $REMSD$ and $ewREMSD$ statistics for

TABLE 10.10. Rounded and Truncated Y = ACT Mean, Linear, and Parallel-Linear Equivalents for Males (1), Females (2), and Combined Group.

x	Mean			Linear			Parallel-Linear		
	$\widehat{m}_Y(x)$	$\widehat{m}_{Y1}(x)$	$\widehat{m}_{Y2}(x)$	$\hat{l}_Y(x)$	$\hat{l}_{Y1}(x)$	$\hat{l}_{Y2}(x)$	$\widehat{pl}_Y(x)$	$\widehat{pl}_{Y1}(x)$	$\widehat{pl}_{Y2}(x)$
163	1	1	1	5	6	4	5	5	4
164	1	1	1	5	6	4	5	5	4
165	1	1	1	5	6	4	5	5	4
166	1	1	1	5	6	4	5	5	5
167	1	1	1	5	6	4	5	6	5
168	1	1	1	5	6	4	5	6	5
169	1	1	1	5	6	5	5	6	5
170	1	1	1	5	6	5	5	6	5
171	1	1	1	6	7	5	6	6	5
172	1	1	1	6	7	5	6	6	5
173	1	1	1	6	7	5	6	6	5
⋮	⋮	⋮	⋮	⋮	⋮	⋮	⋮	⋮	⋮
300	8	7	9	21	21	20	21	21	20
301	9	8	10	21	21	20	21	21	20
302	10	9	11	21	21	20	21	21	20
303	11	10	12	21	21	20	21	21	21
304	12	11	13	21	22	21	21	21	21
305	13	12	14	21	22	21	21	22	21
306	14	13	15	21	22	21	21	22	21
307	15	14	16	21	22	21	21	22	21
308	16	15	17	21	22	21	21	22	21
309	17	16	18	22	22	21	22	22	21
310	18	17	19	22	22	21	22	22	21
311	19	18	20	22	22	21	22	22	21
312	20	19	21	22	22	22	22	22	22
313	21	20	22	22	23	22	22	23	22
314	22	21	23	22	23	22	22	23	22
315	23	22	24	22	23	22	22	23	22
316	24	23	25	22	23	22	22	23	22
317	25	24	26	23	23	22	23	23	22
318	26	25	27	23	23	22	23	23	22
319	27	26	28	23	23	22	23	23	22
320	28	27	29	23	23	23	23	23	22
⋮	⋮	⋮	⋮	⋮	⋮	⋮	⋮	⋮	⋮
372	36	36	36	29	29	29	29	29	29
373	36	36	36	29	29	29	29	30	29
374	36	36	36	29	29	29	29	30	29
375	36	36	36	29	30	29	29	30	29
376	36	36	36	29	30	29	29	30	29
377	36	36	36	30	30	29	30	30	29
378	36	36	36	30	30	29	30	30	29
379	36	36	36	30	30	30	30	30	29
380	36	36	36	30	30	30	30	30	29
381	36	36	36	30	30	30	30	30	30
382	36	36	36	30	30	30	30	31	30

TABLE 10.11. Rounded and Truncated Y = ACT Equipercentile Equivalents for Males (1), Females (2), and Combined Group.

	No Smoothing			$S = .30$			$S = 1.00$		
x	$\hat{e}_Y(x)$	$\hat{e}_{Y1}(x)$	$\hat{e}_{Y2}(x)$	$\hat{e}_Y(x)$	$\hat{e}_{Y1}(x)$	$\hat{e}_{Y2}(x)$	$\hat{e}_Y(x)$	$\hat{e}_{Y1}(x)$	$\hat{e}_{Y2}(x)$
163	9	10	9	9	9	9	9	9	9
164	9	10	9	9	9	9	9	9	9
165	9	10	9	9	9	9	9	9	9
166	9	10	9	9	9	9	9	9	9
167	9	10	9	9	9	9	9	9	9
168	9	10	9	9	9	9	9	9	9
169	9	10	9	9	9	9	9	9	9
170	10	11	9	9	9	9	9	9	9
171	10	11	9	9	10	9	9	10	9
172	10	11	9	10	10	9	10	10	9
173	10	11	9	10	10	9	10	10	9
⋮	⋮	⋮	⋮	⋮	⋮	⋮	⋮	⋮	⋮
300	20	21	20	20	21	20	20	21	20
301	20	21	20	20	21	20	20	21	20
302	21	21	20	20	21	20	20	21	20
303	21	21	20	21	21	20	21	21	20
304	21	21	20	21	21	20	21	21	20
305	21	21	20	21	21	20	21	21	20
306	21	21	21	21	21	21	21	21	21
307	21	21	21	21	21	21	21	21	21
308	21	21	21	21	21	21	21	21	21
309	21	21	21	21	21	21	21	21	21
310	21	22	21	21	22	21	21	22	21
311	21	22	21	21	22	21	21	22	21
312	21	22	21	21	22	21	21	22	21
313	21	22	21	21	22	21	21	22	21
314	21	22	21	21	22	21	21	22	21
315	22	22	21	22	22	21	22	22	21
316	22	22	21	22	22	22	22	22	21
317	22	22	21	22	22	22	22	22	22
318	22	22	21	22	22	22	22	22	22
319	22	22	22	22	22	22	22	22	22
320	22	23	22	22	23	22	22	23	22
⋮	⋮	⋮	⋮	⋮	⋮	⋮	⋮	⋮	⋮
372	33	34	32	33	34	32	33	33	32
373	34	34	34	34	34	33	34	34	33
374	34	34	34	34	34	33	34	34	33
375	34	34	34	35	35	34	35	35	33
376	34	34	34	35	35	34	35	35	34
377	36	36	35	35	35	34	35	35	34
378	36	36	36	35	35	35	35	36	35
379	36	36	36	36	36	35	36	36	35
380	36	36	36	36	36	36	36	36	35
381	36	36	36	36	36	36	36	36	36
382	36	36	36	36	36	36	36	36	36

TABLE 10.12. Average Male-Minus-Female Differences in Rounded and Truncated $Y =$ ACT Equivalents.

Method	MD	ewMD	MAD	ewMAD
Mean	−.627	−.318	.627	.318
Linear	.877	1.127	.877	1.127
Parallel-Linear	.881	.859	.881	.859
Equi (unsmoothed)	.707	.955	.707	.955
Equi ($S = .30$)	.717	.891	.717	.891
Equi ($S = 1.00$)	.703	.905	.703	.905

TABLE 10.13. REMSD and ewREMSD Statistics based on $Y =$ ACT Equivalents.

Statistics	Mean	Linear	Parallel-Linear	Equipercentile		
				No Smooth	$S = .30$	$S = 1.00$
Unrounded and Untruncated						
REMSD	.14015	.10500	.10109	.08719	.08894	.08921
ewREMSD	.14015	.14085	.10109	.13447	.12496	.12633
Unrounded and Truncated						
REMSD	.07757	.10500	.10109	.08719	.08894	.08921
ewREMSD	.05589	.14085	.10109	.13447	.12494	.12631
Rounded and Truncated						
REMSD	.13244	.15564	.15618	.14085	.13904	.13748
ewREMSD	.09455	.17605	.15427	.16445	.15843	.16068

1. unrounded and untruncated equivalents (see Tables 10.7 and 10.8),

2. unrounded and truncated equivalents, and

3. rounded and truncated equivalents (see Tables 10.10 and 10.11),

Comparing the statistics in the top and middle part of Table 10.13 isolates the effect of truncation, which has a dramatic effect for the mean method but very little effect for any of the other methods.[17] For the mean method, truncation alone reduces $ewREMSD$ from .14015 to .05589, which is actually smaller than $ewREMSD = .09455$ for rounded and truncated scores. Apparently, truncation lowers $ewREMSD$, whereas rounding increases it. Comparing the statistics in the top and bottom part of Table 10.13, it is evident that, except for the mean method, rounding and truncating equivalents leads to larger values of $ewREMSD$ and even larger values of $REMSD$.

The statistics in Table 10.13 also suggest that, whether or not statistics are rounded and/or truncated—

- the values of $REMSD$ for the linear and parallel-linear methods are very similar;

- the values of $ewREMSD$ for the linear method are larger than for the parallel-linear method;

- relative to the linear method, the equipercentile methods generally lead to smaller values of both $REMSD$ and $ewREMSD$;

- smoothing equipercentile equivalents has relatively little effect on $REMSD$—in fact, smoothing sometimes leads to slight increases in $REMSD$; and

- smoothed equipercentile equivalents have smaller values of $ewREMSD$ than for the unsmoothed equivalents.

$REMSD$ and $ewREMSD$ "Differences That Matter" DTM

To evaluate the relative magnitude of statistics like $RMSD(x)$, $REMSD$, and $ewREMSD$ for unrounded scores, only, Dorans et al. (2003) and Dorans (in press-b) suggest considering a score "Difference That Matters" (DTM), which is half of a reported score unit.[18] Roughly speaking, the DTM logic is that a subgroup linking that is within half a reported score unit of the

---

[17]Truncation limits the extent to which the linking results at the extremes of the score scale can differ between groups. Here, the effect is greatest for the mean method because it produces low and high scores that are considerably out of range.

[18]Strictly speaking Dorans et al. (2003) and and Dorans (in press-b) do not consider $ewREMSD$, but their logic applies to any weights, including the equal weights used for $ewREMSD$.

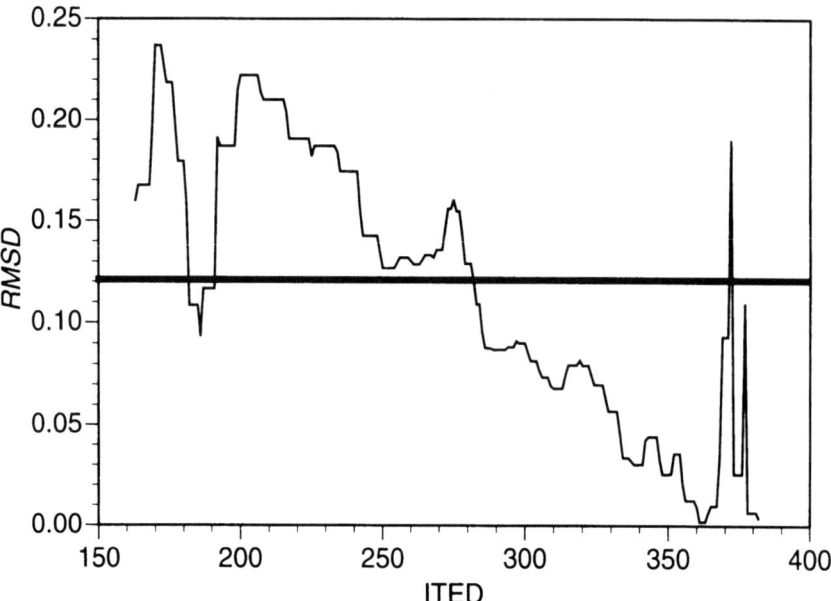

FIGURE 10.8. $RMSD(x)$ values for X = ITED relative to a standardized "Difference That Matters" (DTM) of .12.

combined group linking (at a given raw score point) is ignorable. This convention needs to be understood, however, as a convenient benchmark, not a dogmatic rule. For example, when reported scores are integers, equivalents of 15.4 and 15.6 round to *different* integers even though they differ by only .2 (*less* than a DTM). Also equivalents of 14.6 and 15.4 round to the *same* integer even though the differ by .8 (*more* than a DTM).

Recall that $RMSD(x)$, $REMSD$, and $ewREMSD$ are standardized by dividing by the standard deviation of scores on form Y. The DTM can be standardized in the same manner so that the standardized DTM can be used as a benchmark for evaluating $RMSD(x)$, $REMSD$, and $ewREMSD$. For our illustrative ACT-ITED science example, a score unit on the ACT scale is an integer, and the standard deviation of the Y = ACT scores is 4.218 for the combined group (see Table 10.3). This means that the standardized DTM is $.5/4.218 \doteq .12$. Figure 10.8 provides a visual comparison of the values of $RMSD(x)$ and this standardized DTM. It is evident that, using this benchmark, "differences that matter" occur primarily in the lower half of the score scale for X = ITED.

Revisiting the unrounded and untruncated values of $REMSD$ and $ewREMSD$ in Table 10.13, we observe that

- the $REMSD$ statistics are *smaller* than the standardized DTM of .12, except for the mean method, and

TABLE 10.14. Relationships Between ACT Science Test and Other Tests.

Test	Observed Correlations			rmsel's for Linear Linking[a]		
	Combined	Male	Female	Combined	Male	Female
ITED Science	.672	.660	.689	3.416	3.631	3.157
ACT English	.709	.727	.732	3.219	3.253	2.931
ACT Math	.697	.676	.705	3.286	3.544	3.075
ACT Reading	.736	.750	.741	3.063	3.110	2.882

[a]Linking to scale of ACT Science test.

- the $ewREMSD$ statistics are *larger* than the standardized DTM of .12, except for the parallel-linear method.

That is, for this illustrative example, it is clear that the weights used have an impact on whether the DTM benchmark is exceeded based on overall statistics. Even more importantly, from Figure 10.8 it is evident that an overall statistic may hide "differences that matter" in various regions of the score scale. In short, results such as those in Figure 10.8 are more informative than a simple comparison of a DTM value with $REMSD$ or $ewREMSD$.

The phrase "difference that matters" should not be taken too literally; it is a benchmark, not an evaluative judgment. Even when rounded differences exceed a reported score point, the extent to which such differences "matter" depends on the nature of the decisions that are made and where (along the score scale) these decisions are made.

Correlations with Other Tests as Benchmarks

A seemingly sensible benchmark for evaluating the reasonableness of a linking of two tests is to compare it to some other linking that enjoys the status of being "sensible" or suffers from the criticism of being "questionable" or even "ridiculous." To make such comparisons, we can focus on one or more statistics that are, in some sense, meaningful for both linkages. With a single group design, which was used for our example, an obvious statistic to consider is a correlation coefficient.

The top row of Table 10.14 provides the previously reported correlations between the ITED and ACT science tests for males, females, and the combined group. The subsequent rows provide correlations between the ACT Science Reasoning test and the other ACT tests in English, Mathematics, and Reading. For each of the three groups (males, females, and combined), without exception, the correlations between ACT Science Reasoning and the other ACT tests are all larger than the correlation between the ACT and ITED science tests.

It seems very unlikely that examinees, counselors, or researchers would be inclined to use ACT Science Reasoning scores interchangeably with ACT English, Mathematics, or Reading scores. If so, the correlations in Table 10.14 suggest that such persons should be even *less* inclined to use ACT Science Reasoning scores and ITED Analysis of Science Materials scores interchangeably, even if only rank-order issues are of interest. These correlations, therefore, provide another perspective on "differences that matter."

Root Mean Square Error for Linking

Correlations tell us something about how similar scores are for a pair of variables. We might also want to quantify the extent to which score equivalents based on a particular linking method reproduce the Y scores actually observed. For any linking method, we can define the root mean square error for linking ($rmsel$) as

$$rmsel[eq_Y(x)] = \sqrt{\mathbf{E}[y - eq_Y(x)]^2}, \qquad (10.23)$$

where the expectation is taken over persons.[19] For the linear method, it can be shown that

$$rmsel[l_Y(x)] = \sigma(Y)\sqrt{2[1 - \rho(Y,X)]}. \qquad (10.24)$$

These *rmsel* statistics are expressed here in terms of the combined group; corresponding equations can be defined for any subgroup.

Root mean square errors for linking are not comparable to the standard errors discussed in previous chapters, which quantified error with respect to sampling persons from a population. Rather, the *rmsel* is similar in concept to the standard error of estimate (*see*). In fact, for linear methods, the only difference between *see* and *rmsel* is that the former uses deviations from a linear regression line, whereas the latter uses deviations from a linear linking line (i.e., equations (10.5) and (10.6)).

For our illustrative example, the right-hand part of Table 10.14 provides root mean square errors for linking for the linear method. The form of equation (10.24) clearly suggests that lower correlations lead to higher values for *rmsel*, which is exactly what we observe in Table 10.14. For males, females, and the combined group, the *rmsel* values for ACT-ITED science are all larger than for ACT Science Reasoning vis-à-vis ACT English, Mathematics, or Reading scores.[20]

---

[19]The *rmsel* statistic in equation (10.23) can be computed only for the single group design in which both X and Y scores are available for each examinee, as they are for the example considered here. By contrast the statistics discussed in Sections 10.2.2 and 10.2.3 (i.e., *REMSD*, *MD*, *MAD*, and their equally weighted counterparts) can be computed for both the randomly equivalent groups design and the single group design.

[20]The *rmsel* values in Table 10.14 were computed using more decimal digits of accuracy than is reported for the correlations in Table 10.14 and the standard deviations in Table 10.3.

One might ask whether the ACT-ITED *rmsel* values for science are large or small, in some sense. One benchmark for comparison is a simple function of the standard error of measurement (*sem*) for the ACT Science Reasoning test, which is approximately 2 scale score points (see Kolen and Hanson, 1989). Specifically, a sensible benchmark is $sem \sqrt{2}$ (see Exercise 10.8), which is approximately $2\sqrt{2} = 2.828$ for Science Reasoning. The ACT-ITED *rmsel*'s are generally about 25% larger than this benchmark. In this sense, there is 25% more error in linking ITED Analysis of Science Materials scores to ACT Science Reasoning scores than there is in using scores from one form of ACT Science Reasoning as a proxy for scores on another form of the same test.

The results reported in Table 10.14 suggest that tests with similar names (i.e., science), even when they are used with similar populations, do not necessarily have enough features in common that a linking of their scores is easily defended. Or, to state it differently, the linking may have an unacceptable amount of error for the decisions to be made.

Our discussion has focused on *rmsel* for the linear method, primarily because computations are simple. We could compute *rmsel* values for the equipercentile methods using equation (10.23) directly, but, of course, computations would be more tedious.

10.3 Additional Examples

The *Uncommon measures* report (Feuer et al., 1999—see especially pp. 28–42) provides many summaries of prior linkage research. The current environment in educational testing is such that linking is likely to be a topic of considerable research in the future. Here we briefly discuss two examples that illustrate areas in which research on linking is quite difficult but may be of importance in the future.

10.3.1 Extended Time

In most large-scale testing programs, the vast majority of examinees take test forms under carefully controlled standardized conditions. However, there are often some examinees who have disabilities that are judged serious enough to justify the use of atypical testing conditions, usually called accommodations. The most frequently used accommodation is extended time. Time-and-a-half or double-time is not uncommon, and essentially unlimited time is even under discussion for some disabilities. The available evidence for many testing programs suggests that there is no compelling reason to assert that scores obtained under standard and extended time are comparable.[21] It is sometimes suggested, therefore, that scores obtained under standard and extended time should be equated.

The logic for this suggestion—and use of the word "equating" in this context—is typically stated as follows. Suppose, as is usually the case, that the form administered under standard time and the form administered under extended time are identical. Then, it is assumed that equating is appropriate because the form administered under the two timings clearly tests the same skills and content and has the same statistical characteristics. But this supposition is not necessarily true. For example, the difficulty level of items can depend on the amount of time available to examinees for responding to items. It is even possible that skills tested may differ for the same form under different timings. For example, for a form that consists of reading passages, examinees with extended time may use different strategies for responding to items than the strategies used by examinees under standard time constraints.

These differences may be especially apparent if a test is speeded under standard time conditions, but even in the absence of speededness, different timings can lead to differences in the skills tested and/or differences in statistical characteristics. Indeed, if this were not so, there should be no difference in performance under the two timings and, therefore, no need to adjust scores for extended time. Usually, however, there is at least collateral evidence to suggest that scores are not comparable under different timing conditions. The most frequently cited example is differences in predicted GPA regression equations for examinees tested under standard and extended time in admission testing programs. When this occurs, one approach to establishing comparability is to declare that a standard-time and extended-time score are comparable if they lead to the same predicted GPA.

Alternatively, a linking might be accomplished by administering the form under standard-time and extended-time conditions to randomly equivalent groups of examinees, and then determining a statistical relationship (perhaps equipercentile) between scores under the two timing conditions. Such a linking deserves to be called an "equating" only if the content, skills, and statistical characteristics are unchanged by the timing conditions. Otherwise, the relationship is probably no stronger than calibration. Even under these circumstances, however, the linking may be questionable because the data collection design does not mirror an important feature of the use of extended time in an operational setting—namely, extended time is typically provided only for examinees who have some disability. That is, in operational settings, population characteristics (non-disabled vs. disabled) are

---

[21] For the ACT Assessment, this issue is discussed by Ziomek and Andrews (1996, 1998); for the Law School Admissions Test, see Wightman (1993); and for the SAT, see Cahalan et al. (2001), Ragosta et al. (1991), and Willingham et al. (1988).

usually confounded with timing (standard vs. extended), and it is entirely possible that a standard/extended time linking for non-disabled students is different from a standard/extended time linking for disabled students.

10.3.2 Test Adaptations and Translated Tests

Translations of test forms represent one of the greatest linking challenges (see Sireci, 1997). For example, evidence exists that many translated items function differently in different languages (Allalouf, 2003; Allalouf et al., 1999; Angoff and Modu, 1973; Angoff and Cook, 1988; Sireci and Berberoglu, 2000). In current terminology, the phrase "test adaptation" is generally preferred to "test translation" because the former more correctly reflects the multitude of changes that are typically required.

Consider the situation faced by the National Institute for Testing and Evaluation (NITE) in Israel, which creates, administers, and scores the major college admissions tests used in that country (see Beller, 1994; Beller et al., in press). Among these tests are verbal and quantitative tests that are developed initially in Hebrew and then translated into Arabic, Russian, and other languages. These translated tests are necessary because many examinees are not fluent in the dominant language, Hebrew, but NITE's intent is that all examinees should be treated "fairly" in the admission's process.

Creating a linking of these translated test forms is particularly complicated for numerous reasons. For example, the populations of examinees who test in the various languages are known to differ substantially in their levels of achievement. Also, it is generally impossible to simply translate all the items in the Hebrew form into some other language and have the resulting two forms truly test the same content and skills. (This is one reason why the term "test adaptation" is preferred to "test translation.") Especially for verbal items, language and associated cultural differences make some items in one language simply not translatable into the other language—at least not in the sense the the two translations of the items measure the same thing at the same level of difficulty.[22] It is primarily for this reason that a statistical relationship between scores on translated forms probably does not merit being called an "equating."

For purposes of linking, the single group design is not possible since the vast majority of examinees are not proficient in two languages. The random groups design is not possible since the random assignment of forms

---

[22]It is often thought that an adequate way to ascertain the "correctness" of a translation is to translate the translated text back to the original language. This may be a reasonable step, but it is not likely to be a flawless approach, because not all text in one language can be translated into text that has the same meaning in another language. Hambleton (personal communication) notes that one back-translation resulted in the English phrase "out of sight, out of mind" being back-translated to "invisible, insane"!

to examinees would result in many, if not most, examinees' taking a form in a language in which they are not proficient. Since different populations of persons take different translated forms, the common-item nonequivalent groups design would seem to be an alternative. However, as discussed in Chapter 4, when populations differ substantially in ability the results may not be entirely satisfactory.

More importantly, it is usually difficult, if not impossible, to select a subset of common items that faithfully reflect the full-length test in content and statistical specifications. The problem is twofold. First, even when it appears that an item and its translated version test the same content at the same level of difficulty, the mere fact that the items do not share the same language raises doubt about their comparability. Second, the subset of items that are judged to be not translatable almost certainly test different content/constructs from the presumably translatable items. In fact, there are likely three distinctly different sets of items: those that are translatable, those that are unique to one language, and those that are unique to the other language. In short, it is often quite unlikely that an acceptable set of common items can be identified.

What, then, should be done? One alternative is no linking; simply let the quality of the translation bear the linking burden. Second, the common-item nonequivalent groups design could be used, with the linking done using the best available set of common items. (Exclude items that are non-translatable or judged to be nonequivalant when they are translated.) Third, some form of social moderation could be used. For example, bilingual experts could make judgments about which scores are comparable on the two forms. Fourth, if there is an external criterion or collateral information *that is common to examinees in both languages*, it might be used as the basis for a projection. Note that GPA may be a particularly poor criterion if examinees with different language backgrounds tend to attend different schools. None of these alternatives is likely to be entirely acceptable, and different alternatives may be more or less appropriate in different contexts.

It seems likely that any statistical relationship between scores on translated/adapted forms may be particularly fallible due to a number of intractable problems that are not amenable to psychometric solutions. To the extent that this is true, investigators should appropriately qualify any reported results so that policy makers do not draw unwarranted conclusions.

10.4 Discussion

One easily overlooked aspect of most linkages is that they are likely to change over time,[23] whereas equating relationships are likely to be invariant over reasonable time frames. Clearly, linkages between two tests will be affected if the specifications for either of the tests change. ACT-SAT concordances offer an excellent example. Prior to 1989 there were ACT-SAT concordance tables that were widely used although not well known. Then, in 1989, ACT introduced what was called the "enhanced" ACT Assessment, which had substantial differences in content with the "old" ACT, although the score scale range of 1–36 remained unchanged[24] (see Brennan, 1989). Consequently, new concordance tables had to be created (see Houston and Sawyer, 1991). Then, in the early 1990s, the SAT score scale was "recentered," which necessitated another round of new concordance tables (see Dorans et al., 1997).

Note also that, since concordance relationships generally are not group invariant, the concordances are likely to change whenever the groups tested change, even if the specifications and score scales for the two tests are unchanged. Over periods of 5–10 years, it seems likely that the populations of students who take the ACT and/or SAT change enough to cast at least some doubt on the stability of concordance relationships.

A great deal of this chapter has focused on methods for assessing the adequacy of linking through examining group invariance. But, from the perspective of an individual examinee, such a criterion has an almost inevitable ambiguity because any examinee is a member of many groups. Consider, for example, the case of a black female. Even if a study of male-female group invariance concluded that a linkage was gender invariant, that does does not necessarily mean that a study of black-white group invariance would conclude that a linkage was race invariant. So, if "fairness" for an individual is the goal, neither study alone, nor the pair of studies, provides an entirely satisfactory answer for our black female. Of course, one can conceive of a study of all four groups simultaneously (black males, black females, white males, and white females), which might provide a better answer about group invariance. However, the particular black female in our example could be characterized in terms of numerous other background characteristics, as well. Obviously, there are practical limits to what studies of group invariance can tell us about linking adequacy for individual examinees.

---

[23] An example of historical interest is the Anchor Test Study of the early 1970s (Loret et al., 1973) that put various reading tests on a common scale. Although it was a "model of linkage development (Feuer et al., 1999, p. 25)," it was obsolete by the time it was released because of changes in the various tests.

[24] This is not quite true. Some of the subtests on the old ACT did not have 36 as the highest reported score.

Group invariance has been discussed in this chapter mainly from the perspective of the single group and randomly equivalent groups design. For these designs, the computer program *LEGS* (see Appendix B) can be used to perform almost all of the analyses that have been discussed. Of course, the basic issue of group invariance is not restricted to these designs, but there has been very little research involving other designs.

A well-described linkage is almost always a *highly qualified* statement about a relationship between scores on tests. The nature of these qualifications should be specified explicitly and, whenever possible, studied with sensitivity analyses. For example, it is almost always overly simplistic to say that a linkage is or is not group invariant. Rather, it is much more likely that the linkage varies "somewhat" by group. Studies need to be conducted that operationalize what "somewhat" means in the context of the decisions made based on the linkage. It is usually unreasonable and unnecessary to require that a linkage be "group invariant" in the literal sense of that term, but, with equal force, it is usually difficult to defend linkages that are substantially different for various groups.

As noted in the introduction to this chapter, when tests measure different constructs, no linking, no matter how competently conducted, will be adequate for all purposes. This means that investigators and policy-makers cannot escape the need to make judgments about linking adequacy. Psychometrics can inform such judgments, but psychometrics alone cannot make them.

10.5 Exercises

10.1 In the introduction to this chapter it was noted that the same data collection designs used in equating might be used in linking. Although this may be true in principle, why is it unlikely that the CINEG design would be very satisfactory for establishing a linking relationship?

10.2 An administrator wants to use scores on Test A as a measure of math ability. However, not all students in the population took Test A. Some took Test B, but most took both tests. The administrator decides to use the data for the students who took both tests to obtain an equation for predicting scores on Test A from scores on Test B. The administrator plans to use the resulting prediction equation for students whose scores on Test A are missing. What are potential problems with this procedure? What might be a better procedure?[25]

---

[25] Item suggested by S. A. Livingston.

10.3 Using equation (10.16) verify the value of $REMSD$ that is reported in Table 10.13 for the parallel-linear method with unrounded and untruncated scores.

10.4 Using equation (10.6) with the statistics reported in Tables 10.3 and 10.6, verify that $MD = .863$ for the $M - F$ average difference for the linear method with unrounded and untruncated scores, as reported in Table 10.9. Similarly, verify that $ewMD = 1.126$.

10.5 For rounded and truncated equivalents in Table 10.13, $ewREMSD$ for the mean method is much lower than for any of the other methods. Provide a plausible explanation for this.

10.6 Given the answer to Exercise 10.5, why is it that $REMSD$ for the mean method with rounded and truncated equivalents is relatively large (i.e., comparable to that of the other methods).

10.7 Derive the root mean square error of linear linking, $rmsel[l_Y(x)]$, in equation (10.24).

10.8 It is suggested on page 465 that $\sqrt{2}\, sem$ be used as a benchmark for examining the size of the ACT-ITED science $rmsel$'s, where the sem is for ACT Science Reasoning. Justify this statement.

10.9 Provide a formula for the $rmsel$ for the mean method for the combined group.

11
Current and Future Challenges

In Chapter 1, we summarized the concepts of equating, scaling, and linking. In subsequent chapters, these concepts were further developed and elaborated. In Chapter 11 we focus on some current and future challenges in each of these areas.

11.1 Score Scales

A score scale is created when a test is first developed or substantially revised. Methods for creating score scales were considered in Chapter 9. In our view, a score scale should be chosen to facilitate appropriate score interpretation and minimize misinterpretation. The incorporation of content, normative, and score precision information are important vehicles for enhancing proper score interpretation.

In recent years, there has been much interest in associating test content with test scores to enable test users better to understand the meaning of scores. Some of the mechanisms for making this association were reviewed in Chapter 9, including item mapping, scale anchoring, and standard setting. The development and evaluation of new procedures for associating content with test scores is an important area for research and development, so test users can be better informed about the meaning of the test scores that they want to interpret.

11.2 Equating

An equating process is used to maintain the score scale. As we have stressed, equating is made possible by using a highly structured test development process. Through this process, test forms to be equated are constructed to be very similar in content and statistical characteristics. After equating, scale scores on alternate test forms will be comparable only to the extent that the forms are constructed to be similar. We also have stressed the importance of the design of equating studies and appropriate quality control procedures for ensuring adequate equating.

As demonstrated in Chapters 2-8, a wide array of equating procedures have been developed. Recent statistical developments include kernel equating, the use of polytomous IRT models described in Chapter 6, and procedures for estimating standard errors of equating discussed in Chapter 7. Recent developments also include procedures for evaluating equating including systematic procedures for studying population invariance described in Chapter 10 and procedures for assessing equity properties described in Chapter 8. Future challenges include evaluating kernel equating methods in operational contexts, evaluating polytomous IRT models in operational contexts, and further development and evaluation of procedures for evaluating equatings and estimating standard errors of equating.

Some of the greatest practical challenges involve linking in situations where test developers would like to be able to equate, but where the requisite conditions for equating might not be able to be met. These situations include linking paper-and-pencil and computer-based tests, linking pools for computer-adaptive tests, linking tests that contain performance assessment questions, and linking tests that contain optional sections. Are there ways that linking can reasonably approximate equating in these situations? Are there ways that linking can at least improve scores beyond doing no linking at all? Much more research is needed to address these questions.

As discussed in Chapter 8, there are many unanswered practical questions regarding equating with computer-based tests. One of the major questions is how to ensure stability of scores when item pools are updated, changed, or modified. How similar do the item pools need to be to ensure that scores from one pool to the next can be used interchangeably? How should new items be added to the item pool? What item calibration procedures work best for calibrating new items? How much linking error is present? How is comparability of scores across pools affected when unidimensional item response models are applied to multidimensional tests? General answers to these and other questions are needed as more testing programs are moving to computer-based tests.

11.3 Vertical Scaling

Vertical scaling procedures were considered in Chapter 9. Various data collection designs and statistical procedures have been developed. The designs and procedures lead to different score scales, which have different implications for how growth over grades is portrayed. Some important questions about student growth include: Does average growth remain constant or decelerate over grades? Does the variability of proficiency decrease, stay the same, or increase over grades? The answer to these questions seems to depend on the design used to collect data and on the statistical procedure used to construct the scale. As was indicated in Chapter 9, there are many decisions to be made when constructing vertical scales. The results seem to be sensitive to many of the choices made. However, the research is inconclusive as to how sensitive the results are to various choices, and how these choices interact to produce the scaling results. More research is needed to fully understand how and why vertical scaling procedures give disparate results.

Answers to these practical questions about vertical scales may be important for addressing issues that are of current concern to policy makers and educators. Scores from vertical scales are being used in processes for evaluating schools and teachers. Different scaling methods could lead to very different conclusions about the quality of schools and teachers. However, there seems to be no clear reason to prefer one data collection design or statistical method over another for constructing vertical scales. It may be that psychometrics, by itself, will be unable to provide clear answers to important questions. Educational and psychological theory about the nature of growth might be needed to address the question of which of the scaling methods produces sensible results that are consistent with what would be expected from this theory.

11.4 Linking

Chapter 10 discussed linking tests that measure different constructs and methods for evaluating linking results. For linking to be useful, the purposes for linking should be clearly stated and the linking evaluated relative to these purposes. As was stated in Chapter 10, no linking will be adequate for all purposes. As is evident from the discussion in Chapter 10, linking is a very broad area. Various schemes and criteria for linking exist. There still appears to be a clear need, however, for further development of conceptual and statistical frameworks for linking. What is needed are in-depth studies in different practical linking situations. We strongly encourage researchers to take practical linking situations and provide thorough conceptual, statistical, and psychometric analyses. Over the next few years, such analyses might be organized using a conceptual framework that can more fully highlight important issues in linking along with statistical and psychometric models for dealing with these issues.

11.5 Summary

For equating, as considered in Chapters 1–8, the purpose is clear and equating is made possible because of how tests are developed. At least in ideal situations, equating results can be expected not to depend heavily on the group used to do the equating, on the design used for data collection, or on the statistical procedure used for equating. The purposes of vertical scaling are less clear than they are for equating. In addition, the results for vertical scaling depend heavily on the examinee groups, on the data collection design, and on the statistical procedures used. Procedures for linking tests that measure different constructs are much less well defined and conceptualized than equating or vertical scaling procedures. We anticipate that over the next few years research on equating, vertical scaling, and linking will address many of the unanswered questions and issues identified.

References

Abedi, J., Lord, C., Hofstetter, C., & Baker, E. (2000). Impact of accommodation strategies on English language learners' test performance. *Educational Measurement: Issues and Practice, 19*(3), 16–26.

ACT (1997). *ACT Assessment Technical Manual.* Iowa City, IA: ACT.

ACT (2001). *Explore Technical Manual.* Iowa City, IA: ACT.

Advisory Panel on the Scholastic Aptitude Test Score Decline. (1977). *On further examination.* New York: College Entrance Examination Board.

Allalouf, A. (2003). Revising translated differential functioning items as a tool for improving cross-lingual assessment. *Applied Measurement in Education, 16*(1), 55–73.

Allalouf, A., Hambleton, R.K., & Sireci, S.G. (1999). Identifying the causes of DIF in translated verbal items. *Journal of Educational Measurement, 36,* 185–198.

Allen, N.L., Carlson, J.E., & Zelenak, C.A. (1999). *The NAEP 1996 technical report.* Washington, DC: National Center for Education Statistics.

Allen, N.S., Holland, P.W., & Thayer, D. (1994a). *A missing data approach to estimating distributions of scores for optional test sections* (Research Report 94-17). Princeton, NJ: Educational Testing Service.

Allen, N.S., Holland, P.W., & Thayer, D. (1994b). *Estimating scores for an optional section using information from a common section* (Research Report 94-18). Princeton, NJ: Educational Testing Service.

American Educational Research Association, American Psychological Association, National Council on Measurement in Education (AERA, APA, NCME) (1999) *Standards for educational and psychological testing.* Washington, DC: American Educational Research Association, American Psychological Association, National Council on Measurement in Education.

American Psychological Association (APA) (1986). *Guidelines for computer-based tests and interpretations.* Washington, DC: American Psychological Association.

Andrews, K.M. (1995). *The effects of scaling design and scaling method on the primary score scale associated with a multi-level achievement test.* Unpublished Ph. D. Dissertation, The University of Iowa.

Andrulis, R.S., Starr, L.M., & Furst, L.W. (1978). The effects of repeaters on test equating. *Educational and Psychological Measurement, 38*, 341–349.

Angoff, W.H. (1953). Test reliability and effective test length. *Psychometrika, 18*, 1–14.

Angoff, W.H. (1962). Scales with nonmeaningful origins and units of measurement. *Educational Psychological Measurement, 22*(1), 27-34.

Angoff, W.H. (1971). Scales, norms, and equivalent scores. In R.L. Thorridike (Ed.), *Educational measurement* (2nd ed., pp. 508–600). Washington, DC: American Council on Education. (Reprinted as W. A. Angoff, *Scales, norms, and equivalent scores.* Princeton, NJ: Educational Testing Service, 1984.)

Angoff, W.H. (1987). Technical and practical issues in equating: A discussion of four papers. *Applied Psychological Measurement, 11*, 291–300.

Angoff, W.H., & Cook, L.L. (1988). *Equating the scores of the "Prueba de Aptitud Academica" and the "Scholastic Aptitude Test"* (College Board Report No. 88-2). Princeton, NJ: College Board.

Angoff, W.H., & Cowell, W.R. (1986). An examination of the assumption that the equating of parallel forms is population-independent. *Journal of Educational Measurement, 23*, 327–345.

Angoff, W.H., & Modu, C.C. (1973). *Equating the scales of the Prueba de Aptitud Academica and the Scholastic Aptitude Test* (Research Report 3). New York, NY: College Entrance Examination Board.

Baker, F.B. (1984). Ability metric transformations involved in vertical equating under item response theory. *Applied Psychological Measurement, 8*(3), 261–271.

Baker, F.B. (1990). Some observations on the metric of PC-BILOG results. *Applied Psychological Measurement, 14*(2), 139–150.

Baker, F.B. (1992a). *Item response theory parameter estimation techniques.* New York: Marcel Dekker.

Baker, F.B. (1992b). Equating tests under the graded response model. *Applied Psychological Measurement, 16*, 87–96.

Baker, F.B. (1993a). Equate 2.0: A computer program for the characteristic curve method of IRT equating. *Applied Psychological Measurement, 17*(3), 20.

Baker, F.B. (1993b). Equating tests under the nominal response model. *Applied Psychological Measurement, 17*(3), 239–251.

Baker, F.B. (1996). An investigation of the sampling distributions of equating coefficients. *Applied Psychological Measurement, 20*(1), 45–57.

Baker, F.B. (1997). Empirical sampling distributions of equating coefficients for graded and nominal response instruments. *Applied Psychological Measurement, 21*(2), 157–172.

Baker, F.B., & Al-Karni, A. (1991). A comparison of two procedures for computing IRT equating coefficients. *Journal of Educational Measurement, 28*, 147–162.

Baker, E.L., O'Neil, H.F., & Linn, R.L. (1993). Policy and validity prospects for performance-based assessment. *American Psychologist, 48*, 1210–1218.

Baxter, G.P., Shavelson, R.J., Goldman, S.R., & Pine, J. (1992). Evaluation of procedure-based scoring for hands-on science assessment. *Journal of Educational Measurement, 29*, 1–17.

Beaton, A.E., & Allen, N.L. (1992). Interpreting scales through scale anchoring. *Journal of Educational Statistics, 17*(2), 191-204.

Becker, D.F., & Forsyth, R.A. (1992). An empirical investigation of Thurstone and IRT methods of scaling achievement tests. *Journal of Educational Measurement, 29*(4), 341–354.

Béguin, A.A., & Hanson, B.A. (2001, April). *Effect of noncompensatory multidimensionality on separate and concurrent estimation in IRT observed score equating*. Paper presented at the The Annual Meeting of the National Council on Measurement in Education, Seattle, WA.

Béguin, A.A., Hanson, B.A., & Glas, C.A.W. (2000, April). *Effect of multidimensionality on separate and concurrent estimation in IRT equating*. Paper presented at the American Educational Research Association, New Orleans, LA.

Bejar, I.I., & Wingersky, M.S. (1982). A study of pre-equating based on item response theory. *Applied Psychological Measurement, 6*(3), 309–325.

Beller, M. (1994). Psychometric and social issues in admissions to Israeli universities. *Educational Measurement: Issues and Practice, 13*(2), pp. 12–20.

Beller, M., Gafni, N., & Hanani, P. (in press). Constructing, adapting, and validating admissions tests in multiple languages: The Israeli case. In R. K. Hambleton, P. F. Merenda, & C. D. Spielberger (Eds)., *Adapting educational and psychological tests for cross-cultural assessment*. Hillsdale, NJ: Erlbaum.

Bishop, Y.M.M., Fienberg, S.E, & Holland, P.W. (1975). *Discrete multivariate analysis. Theory and practice.* Cambridge, MA: MIT Press.

Blommers, P.J., & Forsyth, R.A. (1977). *Elementary statistical methods in psychology and education* (2nd ed.). Boston: Houghton Mifflin.

Bloxom, B., McCully, R., Branch, R., Waters, B.K., Barnes, J., & Gribben, M. (1993). *Operational calibration of the circular-response optical-mark-reader answer sheets for the Armed Services Vocational Aptitude Battery (ASVAB)*. Monterey, CA: Defense Manpower Data Center.

Bock, R.D. (1983). The mental growth curve reexamined. In D.J. Weiss (Ed.), *New horizons in testing* (pp. 205–209). New York: Academic Press.

Bock, R.D. (1972). Estimating item parameters and latent ability when responses are scored in two or more nominal categories. *Psychometrika, 37*(1), 29–51.

Bock, R.D. (1997). The nominal categories model. In W.J. van der Linden & R.K. Hambleton (Eds.). *Handbook of modern item response theory* (pp. 34–49). New York: Springer-Verlag.

Bock, R.D., Mislevy, R., & Woodson, C. (1982). The next stage in educational assessment. *Educational Researcher, 11*(3), 4–11,16.

Bock, R.D., Thissen, D., & Zimowski, M.F. (1997). IRT estimation of domain scores. *Journal of Educational Measurement, 34*(3), 197–211.

Bock, R.D., & Zimowski, M.F. (1997). Multiple group IRT. In W.J. van der Linden & R.K. Hambleton (Eds.). *Handbook of modern item response theory* (pp. 433–448). New York: Springer-Verlag.

Bolt, D.M. (1999). Evaluating the effects of multidimensionality on IRT true-score equating. *Applied Measurement in Education, 12*(4), 383–407.

Bourque, M.L. (1999a). Appendix F. Setting the NAEP achievement levels for the 1996 Mathematics assessment. In N.L. Allen, J.E. Carlson, & C.A. Zelenak (Eds.), *The NAEP 1996 technical report*. Washington, DC: National Center for Education Statistics.

Bourque, M.L. (1999b). Appendix G. Report on developing achievement level descriptions for the 1996 NAEP Science assessment. In N. L. Allen, J. E. Carlson, & C. A. Zelenak (Eds.), *The NAEP 1996 technical report*. Washington, DC: National Center for Education Statistics.

Bradlow, E.T., & Thomas, N. (1998). Item response theory models applied to data allowing examinee choice. *Journal of Educational and Behavioral Statistics, 23*(3), 23–43.

Brandenburg, D.C., & Forsyth, R.A. (1974). Approximating standardized achievement test norms with a theoretical model. *Educational and Psychological Measurement, 34*, 3–9.

Braun, H.I. (1988). Understanding scoring reliability: Experiments in calibrating essay readers. *Journal of Educational Statistics, 13*, 1–18.

Braun, H.I., & Holland, P.W. (1982). Observed-score test equating: A mathematical analysis of some ETS equating procedures. In P.W. Holland and D.B. Rubin (Eds.), *Test equating* (pp. 9–49). New York: Academic.

Brennan, R.L. (Ed.) (1989). *Methodology used in scaling the ACT Assessment and P-ACT+*. Iowa City, IA: American College Testing.

Brennan, R.L. (1990). *Congeneric models and Levine's linear equating procedures* (ACT Research Report 90–12). Iowa City, IA: American College Testing.

Brennan, R.L. (1992). The context of context effects. *Applied Measurement in Education, 5*, 225–264.

Brennan, R. L. (2001). *Generalizability theory*. New York: Springer-Verlag.

Brennan, R.L., & Kolen, M.J. (1987a). A reply to Angoff. *Applied Psychological Measurement, 11*, 301–306.

Brennan, R.L., & Kolen, MJ. (1987b). Some practical issues in equating. *Applied Psychological Measurement, 11*, 279–290.

Brennan, R.L., & Lee, W.-C. (1999). Conditional scale-score standard errors of measurement under binomial and compound binomial assumptions. *Educational and Psychological Measurement, 59*(1), 5-24.

Bridgeman, B., Morgan, R., & Wang, M. M. (1997). Choice among essay topics: Impact on performance and validity. *Journal of Educational Measurement, 34*(3), 273–286.

Budescu, D. (1985). Efficiency of linear equating as a function of the length of the anchor test. *Journal of Educational Measurement, 22*, 13–20.

Budescu, D. (1987). Selecting an equating method: Linear or equipercentile? *Journal of Educational Statistics, 12*, 33–43.

Burke, E.F., Hartke, D., & Shadow, L. (1989). *Print format effects on ASVAB test score performance: Literature review* (AFHRL Technical Paper 88–58). Brooks Air Force Base, TX: Air Force Human Resources Laboratory.

Burket, G. R. (1984). Response to Hoover. *Educational Measurement: Issues and Practice, 3*(4), 15–16.

Cahalan, C., Mandinach, E., & Camara, W.J. (2001). *Predictive validity of SAT I: Reasoning test for test takers with learning disabilities and extended time accommodations.* Princeton, NJ and New York: Educational Testing Service and The College Board.

Camara, W.J., Copeland, T., & Rothschild, B. (1998). *Effects of extended time on the SAT I: Reasoning test score growth for students with disabilities* (College Board Report No. 98-7). New York: College Entrance Examination Board.

Camara, W.J., & Schneider, D. (2000). *Testing with extended time on the SAT I: Effects for students with learning disabilities* (Research Notes RN-08). New York, NY: The College Board.

Camilli, G. (1988). Scale shrinkage and the estimation of latent distribution parameters. *Journal of Educational Statistics, 13*(3), 227–241.

Camilli, G. (1999). Measurement error, multidimensionality, and scale shrinkage: A reply to Yen and Burket. *Journal of Educational Measurement, 36*(1), 73–78.

Camilli, G., Yamamoto, K., & Wang, M.-m. (1993). Scale shrinkage in vertical equating. *Applied Psychological Measurement, 17*(4), 379–388.

Camilli, G., Wang, M.-m., & Fesq, J. (1995). The effects of dimensionality on equating the Law School Admission Test. *Journal of Educational Measurement, 32*(1), 79–96.

Carlin, J.B., & Rubin, D.B. (1991). Summarizing multiple-choice tests using three informative statistics. *Psychological Bulletin, 110*, 338–349.

Cizek, G.J. (1994), The effect of altering the position of options in a multiple-choice examination. *Educational and Psychological Measurement, 54*, 8–20.

Cizek, G.J. (2001). *Setting performance standards: Concepts, methods, and perspectives.* Mahwah, NJ: Erlbaum.

Clemans, W.V. (1993). Item response theory, vertical scaling, and something's awry in the state of test mark. *Educational Assessment, 1*(4), 329–347.

Clemans, W.V. (1996). Reply to Yen, Burket, and Fitzpatrick. *Educational Assessment, 3*(2), 192–206.

Cohen, A.S., & Kim, S.H. (1998). An investigation of linking methods under the graded response model. *Applied Psychological Measurement, 22*(2), 116–130.

Congdon, P.J., & McQueen, J. (2000). The stability of rater severity in large-scale assessment programs. *Journal of Educational Measurement, 37*(2), 163–178.

Congressional Budget Office. (1986). *Trends in educational achievement.* Washington, DC: Author.

Cook, L.L. (1994). *Recentering the SAT score scale: An overview and some policy considerations.* Paper presented at the annual meeting of the National Council on Measurement in Education, New Orleans.

Cook, L.L., & Eignor, D.R. (1991). An NCMF instructional module on IRT equating methods. *Educational Measurement: Issues and Practice, 10*, 37–45.

Cook, L.L., & Petersen, N.S. (1987). Problems related to the use of conventional and item response theory equating methods in less than optimal circumstances. *Applied Psychological Measurement, 11*, 225–244.

Cook, L.L., Dorans, N.J., Eignor, D.R., & Petersen, N.S. (1985). *An assessment of the relationship between the assumption of unidimensionality and the quality of IRT true-score equating* (Research Report 85-30). Princeton, NJ: Educational Testing Service.

Coombs, C.H., Dawes, R.M., & Tversky, A. (1970). *Mathematical psychology: An elementary introduction.* Englewood Cliffs, NJ: Prentice-Hall.

Cope, R.T. (1986). *Use versus nonuse of repeater examinees in common item linear equating with nonequivalent populations* (ACT Technical Bulletin 51). Iowa City, IA: American College Testing.

Cope, R.T. (1987). How well do the Angoff Design V linear equating methods compare with the Tucker and Levine methods? *Applied Psychological Measurement, 11*(2), 143–149.

Cope, R.T., & Kolen, M.J. (1990). *A study of methods for estimating distributions of test scores* (ACT Research Report 90-5). Iowa City, IA: American College Testing.

Cronbach, L.J., Gleser, G.C., Nanda, H., & Rajaratnam, N. (1972). *The dependability of behavioral measurements: Theory of generalizability for scores and profiles.* New York: Wiley.

Crouse, J.D. (1991). *Comparing the equating accuracy from three data collection designs using bootstrap estimation methods*. Unpublished doctoral dissertation, The University of Iowa, Iowa City, IA.

Cureton, E.F., & Tukey, J.W. (1951). Smoothing frequency distributions, equating tests, and preparing norms. *American Psychologist, 6*, 404.

Darroch, J.N., & Ratcliff, D. (1972). Generalized iterative scaling for log-linear models. *Annals of Mathematical Statistics, 43*, 1470–1480.

Davey, T., Oshima, T. C., & Lee, K. (1996). Linking multidimensional item calibrations. *Applied Psychological Measurement, 20*(4), 405–416.

Davey, T., & Thomas, L. (1996, April). *Constructing adaptive tests to parallel conventional programs*. Paper presented at the Annual Meeting of the American Educational Research Association, New York, NY.

de Boor, C. (1978). *A practical guide to splines* (Applied Mathematical Sciences, Volume 27). New York: Springer-Verlag.

De Champlain, A.F. (1996). The effect of multidimensionality on IRT true-score equating for subgroups of examinees. *Journal of Educational Measurement, 33*(2), 181–201.

DeMars, C. (2002). Incomplete data and item parameter estimates under JMLE and MML estimation. *Applied Measurement in Education, 15*(1), 15–31.

DeMauro, G.E. (1992). *An investigation of the appropriateness of the TOEFL test as a matching variable to equate TWE topics* (Report 37). Princeton, NJ: Educational Testing Service.

Divgi, D.R. (1985). A minimum chi-square method for developing a common metric in item response theory. *Applied Psychological Measurement, 9*, 413–415.

Donlon, T. (Ed.) (1984). *The College Board technical handbook for the Scholastic Aptitude Test and Achievement Tests*. New York: College Entrance Examination Board.

Donlon, T.F., & Livingston, S.A. (1984). Psychometric methods used in the Admissions Testing Program. In T.F. Donlon (Ed.), *The College Board technical handbook for the Scholastic Aptitude Test and Achievement Tests*. New York: College Entrance Examination Board.

Donoghue, J.R. (1996, April). *Issues in item mapping: The maximum category information criterion and item mapping procedures for a composite scale*. Paper presented at the Annual Meeting of the American Educational Research Association, New York, NY.

Donovan, M. A., Drasgow, F., & Probst, T. M. (2000). Does computerizing paper-and-pencil job attitude scales make a difference? New IRT analyses offer insight. *Journal of Applied Psychology, 85*(2), 305–313.

Dorans, N.J. (1986). The impact of item deletion on equating conversions and reported score distributions. *Journal of Educational Measurement, 23*, 245–264.

Dorans, N.J. (1990). Equating methods and sampling designs. *Applied Measurement in Education, 3*, 3–17.

Dorans, N.J. (1994a). *Choosing and evaluating a scale transformation: Centering and realigning SAT score distributions*. Paper presented at the annual meeting of the National Council on Measurement in Education, New Orleans.

Dorans, N.J. (1994b). *Effects of scale choice on score distributions: Two views of subgroup performance on the SAT*. Paper presented at the annual meeting of the National Council on Measurement in Education, New Orleans.

Dorans, N.J. (1996). Book review. Test Equating: Methods and Practices. *Applied Psychological Measurement, 20*(2), 193–195.

Dorans, N.J. (2000). Distinctions among classes of linkages. *College Board Research Note* (RN-11). New York: The College Board.

Dorans, N.J. (2002). Recentering and realigning the SAT score distributions: How and why. *Journal of Educational Measurement, 39*(1), 59–84.

Dorans, N.J. (in press-a). Exchangeability, concordance and expectation. *Applied Psychological Measurement*.

Dorans, N.J. (in press-b). Using subpopulation invariance to assess score equity. *Journal of Educational Measurement*.

Dorans, N.J., & Holland, P.W. (2000). Population invariance and the equatability of tests: Basic theory and the linear case. *Journal of Educational Measurement, 37*, 281–306.

Dorans, N.J., Holland, P.W., Thayer, D.T., & Tateneni, K. (2003). Invariance of score linking across gender groups for three advanced placement program exams. In N.J. Dorans (Ed.), *Population invariance of score linking: Theory and applications to advanced placement program examinations* (pp. 79–118), Research Report 03-27. Princeton, NJ: Educational Testing Service.

Dorans, N.J., & Kingston, N. M. (1985). The effects of violations of unidimensionality on the estimation of item and ability parameters and on item response theory equating of the GRE verbal scale. *Journal of Educational Measurement, 22*(4), 249–262.

Dorans, N.J., & Lawrence, I.M. (1990). Checking the statistical equivalence of nearly identical test editions. *Applied Measurement in Education, 3*, 245–254.

Dorans, N.J., Lyu, C. F., Pommerich, M., & Houston, W.M. (1997). Concordance between ACT Assessment and recentered SAT I sum scores. *College and University, 73*(2), 24–32.

Draper, N.R., & Smith, H. (1998). *Applied regression analysis* (3rd ed.). New York: Wiley-Interscience.

Drasgow, F. (2002). The work ahead: A psychometric infrastructure for computerized adaptive tests. In C.N. Mills, M.T. Potenza, J.J. Fremer, & W.C. Ward (Eds.), *Computer-based testing: Building the foundation for future assessments* (pp. 1–10). Mahwah, NJ: Lawrence Erlbaum Associates.

Drasgow, F., & Olson-Buchanan, J. (Eds.). (1999). *Innovations in computerized assessment.* Mahwah, NJ: Lawrence Erlbaum Associates.

Dunbar, S.B., Koretz, D.M., & Hoover, H.D. (1991). Quality control in the development and use of performance assessments. *Applied Measurement in Education, 4,* 289–303.

Ebel, R.L. (1962). Content standard test scores. *Educational and Psychological Measurement, 22*(1), 15-25.

Ebel, R.L., & Frisbie, D.A. (1991). *Essentials of educational measurement* (5th ed.). Englewood Cliffs, NJ: Prentice-Hall.

Efron, B. (1982). *The jackknife, the bootstrap, and other resampling plans.* Philadelphia, PA: Society for Industrial and Applied Mathematics.

Efron, B., & Tibshirani, R.J. (1993). *An introduction to the bootstrap* (Monographs on Statistics and Applied Probability 57). New York: Chapman & Hall.

Eignor, D.R. (1985). *An investigation of the feasibility and practical outcomes of preequating the SAT verbal and mathematical sections* (Research Report 85-10). Princeton, NJ: Educational Testing Service.

Eignor, D. (1993). *Deriving comparable scores for computer adaptive and conventional tests: An example using the SAT* (Research Report 93-55). Princeton, NJ: Educational Testing Service.

Eignor, D.R., & Schaeffer, G.A. (1995, March). *Comparability studies for the GRE General CAT and the NCLEX using CAT.* Paper presented at the Annual Meeting of the National Council on Measurement in Education, San Francisco, CA.

Eignor, D.R., & Stocking, M.L. (1986). *An investigation of the possible causes for the inadequacy of IRT preequating* (Research Report 86-14). Princeton, NJ: Educational Testing Service.

Eignor, D.R., Stocking, M.L., & Cook, L.L. (1990a). *The effects on observed- and true-score equating procedures of matching on a fallible criterion: A simulation with test variation* (Research Report RR-90-25). Princeton, NJ: Educational Testing Service.

Eignor, D.R., Stocking, M.L., & Cook, L.L. (1990b). Simulation results of effects on linear and curvilinear observed- and true-score equating procedures of matching on a fallible criterion. *Applied Measurement in Education, 3*(1), 37–52.

Eignor, D.R., Way, W.D., & Amoss, K.E. (1994). *Establishing the comparability of the NCLEX using CAT with traditional NCLEX examinations.* Paper presented at the annual meeting of the National Council on Measurement in Education, New Orleans.

Englehard, G. (1992). The measurement of writing ability with a many-faceted Rasch model. *Applied Measurement in Education, 5,* 171–191.

Englehard, G. (1994). Examining rater errors in the assessment of written composition with a many-faceted Rasch model. *Journal of Educational Measurement, 31,* 93–112,

Engelhard, G. (1996). Evaluating rater accuracy in performance assessments. *Journal of Educational Measurement, 33*(1), 56–70.

Ercikan, K., Schwarz, R.D., Julian, M W., Burket, G.R., Weber, M.M., & Link, V. (1998). Calibration and scoring of tests with multiple-choice and constructed-response item types. *Journal of Educational Measurement, 35*(2), 137–154.

Fairbank, B.A. (1987). The use of presmoothing and postsmoothing to increase the precision of equipercentile equating. *Applied Psychological Measurement, 11*, 245–262.

Feldt, L.S., & Brennan, R.L. (1989). Reliability. In R.L. Linn (Ed.), *Educational measurement* (3rd ed., pp. 105 146). New York: Macmillan.

Feldt, L. S., Forsyth, R. A., Ansley, T. N., & Alnot, S. D. (1994). *ITED: Interpretive guide for teachers and counselors.* Chicago, IL: Riverside.

Feldt, L.S., & Qualls, A.L. (1998). Approximating scale score standard error of measurement from the raw score standard error. *Applied Measurement in Education, 11*(2), 159-177.

Ferrara, S. (1993). *Generalizability theory and scaling: Their roles in writing assessment and implications for performance assessments in other content areas.* Paper presented at the annual meeting of the National Council on Measurement in Education, Atlanta.

Ferrara, S., Huynh, H., & Baghi, H. (1997). Contextual characteristics of locally dependent open-ended item clusters in a large-scale performance assessment. *Applied Measurement in Education, 10*(2), 123-144.

Feuer, M.J., Holland, P.W., Green, B.F., Bertenthal, M.W., & Hemphill, F.C. (Eds.) (1999). *Uncommon measures: Equivalence and linkage among educational tests.* Washington, DC: National Research Council.

Finger, M.S., & Ones, D.S. (1999). Psychometric equivalence of the computer and booklet forms of the MMPI: A meta-analysis. *Psychological Assessment, 11*(1), 58–66.

Fitzpatrick, A.R., Ercikan, K., Yen, W.M., & Ferrara, S. (1998). The consistency between raters scoring in different test years. *Applied Measurement in Education, 11*(2), 195–208.

Fitzpatrick, A.R., & Yen, W.M. (1995). The psychometric characteristics of choice items. *Journal of Educational Measurement, 32*(3), 243–259.

Fitzpatrick, A.R., & Yen, W.M. (2001). The effects of test length and sample size on the reliability and equating of tests composed of constructed-response items. *Applied Measurement in Education, 14*(1), 31–57.

Flanagan, J.C. (1951). Units, scores, and norms. In E.F. Lindquist (Ed.) *Educational measurement* (pp. 695–763). Washington, DC: American Council on Education.

Forsyth, R.A. (1991). Do NAEP scales yield valid criterion-referenced interpretations? *Educational Measurement: Issues and Practice, 10*(3), 3–9, 16.

Forsyth, R., Saisangjan, U., & Gilmer, J. (1981). Some empirical results related to the robustness of the Rasch model. *Applied Psychological Measurement, 5*(2), 175–186.

Freeman, M.F., & Tukey, J.W. (1950). Transformations related to the angular and square root. *Annals of Mathematical Statistics, 21*, 607-611.

Gabrielson, S., Gordon, B., & Engelhard, G., Jr. (1995). The effects of task choice on the quality of writing obtained in a statewide assessment. *Applied Measurement in Education, 8*(4), 273–290.

Gafni, N., & Melamed, E. (1990). Using the circular equating paradigm for comparison of linear equating models. *Applied Psychological Measurement, 14*(3), 247–256.

Gallagher, A., Bridgeman, B., & Cahalan, C. (2000). *The effect of computer-based tests on racial/ethnic, gender, and language groups* (ETS Research Report RR-00-8). Princeton, NJ: Educational Testing Service.

Gardner, E.F. (1962). Normative standard scores. *Educational and Psychological Measurement, 22*(1), 7-14.

Gilmer, J.S. (1989). The effects of test disclosure on equated scores and pass rates. *Applied Psychological Measurement, 13*, 245–255.

Gordon, B., Englehard, G., Gabrielson, S., & Bernkopf, S. (1993). *Issues in equating performance assessments: Lessons from writing assessment.* Paper presented at the annual meeting of the American Educational Research Association, Atlanta.

Gorham, J.L., & Bontempo, B.D. (1996, April). *Repeater patterns on NCLEX using CAT versus NCLEX using paper-and-pencil testing.* Paper presented at the Annual Meeting of the American Educational Research Association, New York, NY.

Green, B.F., Bock, R.D., Humphreys, L.G., Linn, R.L., & Reckase, M.D. (1984). Technical guidelines for assessing computerized adaptive tests. *Journal of Educational Measurement, 21*(4), 347–360.

Gulliksen, H. (1950). *Theory of mental tests.* New York: Wiley.

Guskey, T.R. (1981). Comparison of a Rasch model scale and the grade-equivalent scale for vertical equating of test scores. *Applied Psychological Measurement, 5*(2), 187–201.

Gustafsson, J.-E. (1979). The Rasch model in vertical equating of tests: A critique of Slinde and Linn. *Journal of Educational Measurement, 16*(3), 153–158.

Guttman, L. (1944). A basis for scaling qualitative data. *American Sociological Review, 9*, 139-150.

Haberman, S.J. (1974a). *The analysis of frequency data.* Chicago: University of Chicago.

Haberman, S.J. (1974b). Log-linear models for frequency tables with ordered classifications. *Biometrics, 30*, 589–600.

Haberman, S.J. (1978). *Analysis of qualitative data. Vol. 1. Introductory topics.* New York: Academic.

Haebara, T. (1980). Equating logistic ability scales by a weighted least squares method. *Japanese Psychological Research, 22*, 144–149.

Haertel, E.H., & Linn, R.L. (1996). Comparability. In G.W. Phillips (Ed.), *Technical issues in large-scale performance assessment*. Washington, DC: National Center for Education Statistics.

Hambleton, R.K., Brennan, R.L., Brown, W., Dodd, B., Forsyth, R.A., Mehrens, W.A., Nellhaus, J., Reckase, M.D., Rindone, D., van der Linden, W.J., & Zwick, R. (2000). A response to "Setting reasonable and useful performance standards" in the National Academy of Sciences' Grading the Nation's Report Card. *Educational Measurement: Issues and Practice, 19*(2), 5–13.

Hambleton, R.K., & Swaminathan, H. (1985). *Item response theory. Principles and applications*. Boston: Kluwer.

Hambleton, R.K., Swaminathan, H., & Rogers, H.J. (1991). *Fundamentals of item response theory*. Newbury Park, CA: Sage.

Han, T., Kolen, M.J., & Pohlmann, J. (1997). A comparison among IRT true- and observed-score equatings and traditional equipercentile equating. *Applied Measurement in Education, 10*(2), 105–121.

Hanson, B.A. (1989). Scaling the P-ACT+. In R.L. Brennan (Ed.), *Methodology used in scaling the ACT Assessment and P-ACT+* (pp. 57–73). Iowa City, IA: American College Testing.

Hanson, B.A. (1990). *An investigation of methods for improving estimation of test score distributions* (ACT Research Report 90-4). Iowa City, IA: American College Testing.

Hanson, B.A. (1991a). A note on Levine's formula for equating unequally reliable tests using data from the common item nonequivalent groups design. *Journal of Educational Statistics, 16*, 93–100.

Hanson, B.A. (1991b). *Method of moments estimates for the four-parameter beta compound binomial model and the calculation of classification consistency indexes* (ACT Research Report 91-5). Iowa City, IA: American College Testing.

Hanson, B.A. (1991c). A comparison of bivariate smoothing methods in common-item equipercentile equating. *Applied Psychological Measurement, 15*, 391–408.

Hanson, B.A. (1992). *Testing for differences in test score distributions using log-linear models*. Paper presented at the annual meeting of the American Educational Research Association, San Francisco.

Hanson, B.A. (1993). *A missing data approach to adjusting writing sample scores*. Paper presented at the annual meeting of the National Council on Measurement in Education, Atlanta.

Hanson, B.A. (2002). IRT command language (Version 0.020301, March 1, 2002). Monterey, CA: Author (Available at http://www.b-a-h.com/software/irt/icl/index.html).

Hanson, B.A., & Béguin, A.A. (2002). Obtaining a common scale for item response theory item parameters using separate versus concurrent estimation in the common-item equating design. *Applied Psychological Measurement, 26*(1), 3–24.

Hanson, B.A., Harris, D.J., & Kolen, M.J. (1997, March). *A comparison of single- and multiple-linking in equipercentile equating with random groups.* Paper presented at the Annual Meeting of the American Educational Research Association, Chicago, IL.

Hanson, B.A., Zeng, L., & Kolen, M.J. (1993). Standard errors of Levine linear equating. *Applied Psychological Measurement, 17*, 225–237.

Hanson, B.A., Zeng, L., & Colton, D. (1994). *A comparison of presmoothing and postsmoothing methods in equipercentile equating* (ACT Research Report 94-4). Iowa City, IA: American College Testing.

Harnischfeger, A., & Wiley, D.E. (1975). *Achievement test score decline: Do we need to worry?* Chicago: CEMREL.

Harris, D.J. (1986). A comparison of two answer sheet formats. *Educational and Psychological Measurement, 46*, 475–478.

Harris, D.J. (1987). *Estimating examinee achievement using a customized test.* Paper presented at the annual meeting of the American Educational Research Association, Washington, DC.

Harris, D.J. (1988). *An examination of the effect of test length on customized testing using item response theory.* Paper presented at the annual meeting of the American Educational Research Association, New Orleans.

Harris, D.J. (1989). Comparison of 1-, 2-, and 3-parameter IRT models. *Educational Measurement: Issues and Practice, 8*, 35–41.

Harris, D.J. (1991a). *Equating with nonrepresentative common item sets and nonequivalent groups.* Paper presented at the annual meeting of the American Educational Research Association, Chicago.

Harris, D.J. (1991b). *Practical implications of the context effects resulting from the use of scrambled test forms.* Paper presented at the annual meeting of the American Educational Research Association, Chicago.

Harris, D.J. (1991c). A comparison of Angoff's Design I and Design II for vertical equating using traditional and IRT methodology. *Journal of Educational Measurement, 28*(3), 221–235.

Harris, D.J. (1991d). Effects of passage and item scrambling on equating relationships. *Applied Psychological Measurement, 15*(3), 247–256.

Harris, D.J. (1993). *Practical issues in equating.* Paper presented at the annual meeting of the American Educational Research Association, Atlanta.

Harris, D.J., & Crouse, J.D. (1993). A study of criteria used in equating. *Applied Measurement in Education, 6, 195–240.*

Harris, D.J., & Hoover, H. D. (1987). An application of the three-parameter IRT model to vertical equating. *Applied Psychological Measurement, 11*(2), 151–159.

Harris, D.J., & Kolen, M.J. (1986). Effect of examinee group on equating relationships. *Applied Psychological Measurement, 10*, 35–43.

Harris, D.J., & Kolen, M.J. (1990). A comparison of two equipercentile equating methods for common item equating. *Educational and Psychological Measurement, 50*, 61–71.

Harris, D.J., & Welch, C.J. (1993). *Equating writing samples.* Paper presented at the annual meeting of the National Council on Measurement in Education, Atlanta.

Harris, D.J., Welch, C.J., & Wang, T. (1994). *Issues in equating performance assessments.* Paper presented at the annual meeting of the National Council on Measurement in Education, New Orleans.

Hetter, R.D., Segall, D.O., & Bloxom, B.M. (1997). Chapter 16. Evaluating item calibration medium in computerized adaptive testing. In W.A. Sands, B.K. Waters, & J.R. McBride (Eds.), *Computerized adaptive testing: From inquiry to operation* (pp. 161–167). Washington, DC: American Psychological Association.

Hirsch, T.M. (1989). Multidimensional equating. *Journal of Educational Measurement, 26*(4), 337–349.

Holland, P.W. (2002). Two measures of change in the gaps between CDFs of test-score distributions. *Journal of Educational Behavioral Statistics, 27*(1), 3–18.

Holland, P.W., King, B.F., & Thayer, D.T. (1989). *The standard error of equating for the kernel method of equating score distributions* (Technical Report 89-83). Princeton, NJ: Educational Testing Service.

Holland, P.W., & Rubin, D.B. (1982) *Test equating.* New York: Academic.

Holland, P.W., & Thayer, D.T. (1987). *Notes on the use of log-linear models for fitting discrete probability distributions* (Technical Report 87-79). Princeton, NJ: Educational Testing Service.

Holland, P.W., & Thayer, D.T. (1989). *The kernel method of equating score distributions* (Technical Report No. 89-84). Princeton, NJ: Educational Testing Service.

Holland, P.W., & Thayer, D.T. (1990). *Kernel equating and the counterbalanced design.* Paper presented at the annual meeting of the American Educational Research Association, Boston.

Holland, P.W., & Thayer, D.T. (2000). Univariate and bivariate loglinear models for discrete test score distributions. *Journal of Educational and Behavioral Statistics, 25*(2), 133–183.

Holland, P.W., & Wightman, L.E. (1982). Section pre-equating: A preliminary investigation. In P.W. Holland & D.B. Rubin (Eds.), *Test Equating* (pp. 271–297). New York: Academic Press, Inc.

Holmes, S.E. (1982). Unidimensionality and vertical equating with the Rasch model. *Journal of Educational Measurement, 19*(2), 139–147.

Hoover, H.D. (1984a). The most appropriate scores for measuring educational development in the elementary schools: GE's. *Educational Measurement: Issues Practice, 3*(4), 8–14.

Hoover, H.D. (1984b). Rejoinder to Burket.*Educational Measurement: Issues and Practice, 3*(4), 16–18.

Hoover, H.D. (1988). Growth expectations for low-achieving students: A reply to Yen. *Educational Measurement: Issues and Practice, 7*(4), 21–23.

Hoover, H.D., Dunbar, S.D., & Frisbie, D.A. (2003). *The Iowa Tests. Guide to development and research.* Itasca, IL: Riverside Publishing.

Houston, W.M., Raymond, M.R., & Svec, J.C. (1991). Adjustments for rater effects in performance assessment. *Applied Psychological Measurement, 15*(4), 409–421.

Houston, W., & Sawyer, R. (1991). Relating scores on the Enhanced ACT Assessment and the SAT test batteries. *College and University, 67*(2), 195–200.

Hung, P., Wu, Y., & Chen, Y. (1991). *IRT item parameter linking: Relevant issues for the purpose of item banking.* Paper presented at the International Academic Symposium on Psychological Measurement, Tainan, Taiwan.

Huynh, H. (1998). On score locations of binary and partial credit items and their applications to item mapping and criterion-referenced interpretation. *Journal of Educational and Behavioral Statistics, 23*(1), 35-56.

Huynh, H., & Ferrara, S. (1994). A comparison of equal percentile and partial credit equatings for performance-based assessments composed of free-response items. *Journal of Educational Measurement, 31*, 125–141.

Iowa Tests of Educational Development. (1958). *Manual for school administrators. 1958 revision.* Iowa City, IA: University of Iowa.

Jaeger, R.M. (1981). Some exploratory indices for selection of a test equating method. *Journal of Educational Measurement, 18*, 23–38.

Jarjoura, D. (1985). Tolerance intervals for true scores. *Journal of Educational Statistics, 10*(1), 1-17.

Jarjoura, D., & Kolen, M.J. (1985). Standard errors of equipercentile equating for the common item nonequivalent populations design. *Journal of Educational Statistics, 10*, 143–160.

Kane, M. T. (1994). Validating the performance standards associated with passing scores. *Review of Educational Research, 64*, 425–461.

Kaskowitz, G.S., & De Ayala, R.J. (2001). The effect of error in item parameter estimates on the test response function method of linking. *Applied Psychological Measurement, 25*(1), 39–52.

Keats, J.A., & Lord, F.M. (1962). A theoretical distribution for mental test scores. *Psychometrika, 27*, 59–72.

Kendall, M., & Stuart, A. (1977). *The advanced theory of statistics* (4th ed., Vol. 1). New York: Macmillan.

Kennedy, P., & Walstad, W.B. (1997). Combining multiple-choice and constructed-response test scores: An economist's view. *Applied Measurement in Education, 10*(4), 359–375.

Kim, J.-S., & Hanson, B.A. (2002). Test equating under the multiple-choice model. *Applied Psychological Measurement, 26*(3), 255–270.

Kim, S.-H., & Cohen, A.S. (1992). Effects of linking methods on detection of DIF. *Journal of Educational Measurement, 29*(1), 51–66.

Kim, S.-H., & Cohen, A.S. (1995). A minimum chi-square method for equating tests under the graded response model. *Applied Psychological Measurement, 19*(2), 167–176.

Kim, S.-H., & Cohen, A.S. (1998). A comparison of linking and concurrent calibration under item response theory. *Applied Psychological Measurement, 22*(2), 131–143.

Kim, S.-H., & Cohen, A.S. (2002). A comparison of linking and concurrent calibration under the graded response model. *Applied Psychological Measurement, 26*(1), 25–41.

Kingsbury, G.G., & Zara, A.R. (1989). Procedures for selecting items for computerized adaptive tests. *Applied Measurement in Education, 2*(4), 359–375.

Kingsbury, G.G., & Zara, A.R. (1991). A comparison of procedures for content-sensitive item selection in computerized adaptive tests. *Applied Measurement in Education, 4*(3), 241–261.

Kingston, N.M., & Dorans, N.J. (1984). Item location effects and their implications for IRT equating and adaptive testing. *Applied Psychological Measurement, 8*(2), 147–154.

Kiplinger, V. L., & Linn, R. L. (1996). Raising the stakes of test administration: The impact on student performance on the National Assessment of Educational Progress. *Educational Assessment, 3*(2), 111–133.

Klein L.W., & Jarjoura, D. (1985). The importance of content representation for common-item equating with nonrandom groups. *Journal of Educational Measurement, 22*, 197–206.

Kolen, M.J. (1981). Comparison of traditional and item response theory methods for equating tests. *Journal of Educational Measurement, 18*, 1–11.

Kolen, M.J. (1984). Effectiveness of analytic smoothing in equipercentile equating. *Journal of Educational Statistics, 9*, 25–44.

Kolen, M.J. (1985). Standard errors of Tucker equating. *Applied Psychological Measurement, 9*, 209–223.

Kolen, M.J. (1988). An NCME instructional module on traditional equating methodology. *Educational Measurement: Issues and Practice, 7*, 29–36.

Kolen, M.J. (1990). Does matching in equating work? A discussion. *Applied Measurement in Education, 3*(1), 97–104.

Kolen, M.J. (1991). Smoothing methods for estimating test score distributions. *Journal of Educational Measurement, 28*, 257–282.

Kolen, M.J. (1999). Threats to score comparability with applications to performance assessments and computerized adaptive tests. *Educational Assessment, 6*(2), 73–96.

Kolen, M.J. (2001). Linking assessments effectively: Purpose and design. *Educational Measurement: Issues and Practice, 20*(1), 5–19.

Kolen, M.J. (in press). Population invariance in equating: Concept and history. *Journal of Educational Measurement.*

Kolen, M.J., & Brennan, R.L. (1987). Linear equating models for the common-item nonequivalent-populations design. *Applied Psychological Measurement, 11,* 263–277.

Kolen, M.J., & Hanson, B. A. (1989). Scaling the ACT Assessment. In R.L. Brennan (Ed.), *Methodology used in scaling the ACT Assessment and P-ACT+* (pp. 35–55). Iowa City IA: ACT, Inc.

Kolen, M.J., & Harris, D.J. (1990). Comparison of item preequating and random groups equating using IRT and equipercentile methods. *Journal of Educational Measurement, 27,* 27–39.

Kolen, M.J., & Jarjoura, D. (1987). Analytic smoothing for equipercentile equating under the common item nonequivalent populations design. *Psychometrika, 52,* 43–59.

Kolen, M.J., & Whitney, D.R. (1982). Comparison of four procedures for equating the Tests of General Educational Development. *Journal of Educational Measurement, 19*(4), 279–293.

Kolen, M.J., Hanson, B.A., & Brennan, R.L. (1992). Conditional standard errors of measurement for scale scores. *Journal of Educational Measurement, 29,* 285–307.

Kolen, M.J., Zeng, L., & Hanson, B.A. (1996). Conditional standard errors of measurement for scale scores using IRT. *Journal of Educational Measurement, 33*(2), 129–140.

Lawrence, I.M., & Dorans, N.J. (1990). Effect on equating results of matching samples on an anchor test. *Applied Measurement in Education, 3*(1), 19–36.

Lawrence, I.M., Dorans, N.J., Feigenbaum, M.D., Feryok, N.J., Schmitt, A.P., & Wright, N.K. (1994). *Technical issues related to the introduction of the new SAT and PSAT/NMSQT* (Research Memorandum 94-10). Princeton, NJ: Educational Testing Service.

Lawrence, I., & Feigenbaum, M. (1997). *Linking scores for computer-adaptive and paper-and-pencil administrations of the SAT.* Princeton, NJ: Educational Testing Service.

Leary, L.F., & Dorans, N.J. (1982). *The effects of item rearrangement on test performance: A review of the literature* (Research Report 82-30). Princeton, NJ: Educational Testing Service.

Leary, L.F., & Dorans, N.J. (1985). Implications for altering the context in which test items appear: A historical perspective on an immediate concern. *Review of Educational Research, 55*(3), 387–413.

Lee, G., Kolen, M.J., Frisbie, D.A., & Ankenmann, R.D. (2001). Comparison of dichotomous and polytomous item response models in equating scores from tests composed of testlets. *Applied Psychological Measurement, 25*(4), 3–24.

Lee, J.A., Moreno, K.E., & Sympson, J.B. (1986). The effects of mode of test administration on test performance. *Educational and Psychological Measurement, 46*(2), 467–474.

Lee, W.-C., Brennan, R.L., & Kolen, M.J. (2000). Estimators of conditional scale-score standard errors of measurement: A simulation study. *Journal of Educational Measurement, 37*(1), 1-20.

Levine, R. (1955). *Equating the score scales of alternate forms administered to samples of different ability* (Research Bulletin 55-23). Princeton, NJ: Educational Testing Service.

Li, Y.H., & Lissitz, R.W. (2000). An evaluation of the accuracy of multidimensional IRT linking. *Applied Psychological Measurement, 24*(2), 115–138.

Linacre, J.M. (1988). *Many-faceted Rasch measurement.* Chicago: MESA Press.

Lindquist, E.F. (1953). *Selecting appropriate score scales for tests.* In Proceedings of the 1952 Invitational Conference on Testing Problems (pp. 34-40). Princeton, NJ: Educational Testing Service.

Lindquist, E.F. (1964). Equating scores on non-parallel tests. *Journal of Educational Measurement, 1*, 5–9.

Linn, R.L. (1993). Linking results of distinct assessments. *Applied Measurement in Education, 6*(1), 83–102.

Linn, R.L., & Hambleton, R.K. (1991). Customized tests and customized norms. *Applied Measurement in Education, 4*, 185–207.

Linn, R.L. (1995). High-stakes uses of performance-based assessments: Rationale, examples, and problems of comparability. In T.H.R.K. Oakland (Ed.), *International perspectives on academic assessment. Evaluation in education and human services* (pp. 49-73). Boston, MA: Kluwer Academic Publishers.

Linn, R.L., Levine, M.V., Hastings, C.N., & Wardrop, J. L. (1981). Item bias in a test of reading comprehension. *Applied Psychological Measurement, 5*(2), 159–173.

Liou, M., & Cheng, P.E. (1995a). Asymptotic standard error of equipercentile equating. *Journal of Educational and Behavioral Statistics, 20*(3), 259–286.

Liou, M., & Cheng, P.E. (1995b). Equipercentile equating via data-imputation techniques. *Psychometrika, 60*(1), 119–136.

Liou, M., Cheng, P.E., & Li, M.-Y. (2001). Estimating comparable scores using surrogate variables. *Applied Psychological Measurement, 25*(2), 197–207.

Liou, M., Cheng, P.E., & Johnson, E.G. (1997). Standard errors of the kernel equating methods under the common-item design. *Applied Psychological Measurement, 21*(4), 349–369.

Liou, M., Cheng, P.E., & Wu, C.-J. (1999). Using repeaters for estimating comparable scores. *British Journal of Mathematical & Statistical Psychology, 52*(2), 273–284.

Little, R.J., & Rubin, D.B. (1994). Test equating from biased samples, with application to the Armed Services Vocational Aptitude Battery. *Journal of Educational and Behavioral Statistics, 19*(4), 309–335.

Livingston, S.A. (1988). *Adjusting scores on examinations offering a choice of essay questions* (Research Report 88-64). Princeton, NJ: Educational Testing Service.

Livingston, S.A. (1993). Small-sample equating with log-linear smoothing. *Journal of Educational Measurement, 30,* 23–39.

Livingston, S.A. (1996). Book Review of Test Equating. *Journal of Educational Measurement, 33*(3), 369–373.

Livingston, S.A., & Feryok, N.J. (1987). *Univariate vs. bivariate smoothing in frequency estimation equating* (Research Report 87-36). Princeton, NJ: Educational Testing Service.

Livingston, S.A., Dorans, N.J., & Wright, N. K. (1990). What combination of sampling and equating methods works best? *Applied Measurement in Education, 3,* 73–95.

Livingston, S.A., & Zieky, M.J. (1982). *Passing scores: A manual for setting standards of performance on educational and occupational tests.* Princeton, NJ: Educational Testing Service.

Lohman, D.F., & Hagen, E.P. (2002). *Cognitive Abilities Test. Form 6. Research Handbook.* Itasca, IL: Riverside Publishing.

Longford, N.T. (1994). Reliability of essay rating and score adjustment. *Journal of Educational and Behavioral Statistics, 19,* 171–200.

Lord, F.M. (1950). *Notes on comparable scales for test scores* (Research Bulletin 5048). Princeton, NJ: Educational Testing Service.

Lord, F.M. (1965). A strong true score theory with applications. *Psychometrika, 30,* 239–270.

Lord, F.M. (1969). Estimating true-score distributions in psychological testing. (An empirical Bayes estimation problem.) *Psychometrika, 34,* 259–299.

Lord, F.M. (1975). Automated hypothesis tests and standard errors for nonstandard problems. *The American Statistician, 29,* 56–59.

Lord, F.M. (1980). *Applications of item response theory to practical testing problems.* Hillsdale, NJ: Erlbaum.

Lord, F.M. (1982a). Item response theory and equating—A technical summary. In P.W. Holland and D.B. Rubin (Eds.), *Test equating* (pp. 141–149). New York: Academic.

Lord, F.M. (1982b). The standard error of equipercentile equating. *Journal of Educational Statistics, 7,* 165–174.

Lord, F.M. (1982c). Standard error of an equating by item response theory. *Applied Psychological Measurement, 6,* 463–471

Lord, F.M., & Novick, M.R. (1968). *Statistical theories of mental test scores.* Reading, MA: Addison Wesley.

Lord, F.M., & Wingersky, M.S. (1984). Comparison of IRT true-score and equipercentile observed-score "equatings." *Applied Psychological Measurement, 8*, 452–461.

Loret, P. G., Seder, J. C., Bianchini, J. C., & Vale, C. A. (1973). *Anchor test study final report. Project report and volumes 1 through 30.* Berkeley, CA: Educational Testing Service (ERIC Document Nos. ED 092601 through ED 092631).

Loyd, B.H. (1991). Mathematics test performance: The effects of item type and calculator use. *Applied Measurement in Education, 4*, 11–22.

Loyd, B.H., & Hoover, H.D. (1980). Vertical equating using the Rasch Model. *Journal of Educational Measurement, 17*, 179–193.

Loyd, B., Engelhard, G., Jr., & Crocker, L. (1996). Achieving form-to-form comparability: Fundamental issues and proposed strategies for equating performance assessments of teachers. *Educational Assessment, 3*(1), 99–110.

Luecht, R.M., Nungester, R.J., & Hadadi, A. (1996, April). *Heuristic-based CAT: Balancing item information, content, and exposure.* Paper presented at the Annual Meeting of the National Council on Measurement in Education, New York, NY.

Lunz, M.E., & Bergstrom, B.A. (1994). An empirical study of computerized adaptive test administration conditions. *Journal of Educational Measurement, 31*(3), 251–263.

Lunz, M.E., & Bergstrom, B.A. (1995, April). *Equating computerized adaptive certification examinations: The Board of Registry series of studies.* Paper presented at the Annual Meeting of the National Council on Measurement in Education, San Francisco, CA.

Lunz, M.E., Stahl, J.A., & Wright, B.D. (1994). Interjudge reliability and decision reproducibility. *Educational Psychological Measurement, 54*(4), 913–925.

MacCann, R.G. (1990). Derivations of observed score equating methods that cater to populations differing in ability. *Journal of Educational Statistics, 15*, 146–170.

Maier, M.H. (1993). *Military aptitude testing: The past fifty years* (DMDC Technical Report 93-007). Monterey, CA: Defense Manpower Data Center.

Marco, G.L. (1977). Item characteristic curve solutions to three intractable testing problems. *Journal of Educational Measurement, 14*, 139–160.

Marco, G.L. (1981). Equating tests in the era of test disclosure. In B.F. Green (Ed.), *New directions for testing and measurement: Issues in testing—coaching, disclosure, and ethnic bias* (pp. 105–122). San Francisco: Jossey-Bass.

Marco, G., Petersen, N., & Stewart, E. (1979). *A test of the adequacy of curvilinear score equating models.* Paper presented at the Computerized Adaptive Testing Conference, Minneapolis, MN.

Marco, G.L., Petersen, N.S., & Stewart, E.E. (1983). A test of the adequacy of curvilinear score equating models. In D. Weiss (Ed.), *New horizons in testing* (pp. 147–176). New York: Academic.

Masters, G.N. (1984). Constructing an item bank using partial credit scoring. *Journal of Educational Measurement, 21*(1), 19–32.

Mazzeo, J., & Harvey, A.L. (1988). *The equivalence of scores from automated and conventional educational and psychological tests. A review of the literature* (College Board Report 88-8). New York: College Entrance Examination Board.

Mazzeo, J., Druesne, B., Raffeld, P.C., Checketts, K.T., & Muhlstein, A. (1991). *Comparability of computer and paper-and-pencil scores for two CLEP general examinations* (College Board Report 91-5). New York: College Entrance Examination Board.

McCall, W.A. (1939). *Measurement.* New York, NY: Macmillan.

McKinley, R.L. (1988). A comparison of six methods for combining multiple IRT item parameter estimates. *Journal of Educational Measurement, 25*(3), 233–246.

McKinley, R.L., & Schaeffer, G.A. (1989). *Reducing test form overlap of the GRE subject test in mathematics using IRT triple-part equating* (Research Report 89-8). Princeton, NJ: Educational Testing Service.

Mead, A.D., & Drasgow, F. (1993). Equivalence of computerized and paper-and-pencil cognitive ability tests: A meta-analysis. *Psychological Bulletin, 114*, 449–458.

Millman, J., & Greene, J. (1989). The specification and development of tests of achievement and ability. In R.L. Linn (Ed.), *Educational measurement* (3rd ed., pp. 335–366). New York: Macmillan.

Mills, C. N. (1999). Development and introduction of a computer adaptive Graduate Record Examinations General test. In F. Drasgow & J. Olson-Buchanan (Eds.), *Innovations in computerized assessment* (pp. 117–135). Mahwah, NJ: Lawrence Erlbaum Associates.

Mills, C., Durso, R., Golub-Smith, M., Schaeffer, G., & Steffen, M. (1994). *The introduction and comparability of the computer adaptive GRE general test.* Paper presented at the annual meeting of the National Council on Measurement in Education, New Orleans.

Mills, C.N., Potenza, M.T., Fremer, J.J., & Ward, W.C. (Eds.) (2002). *Computer-based testing: Building the foundation for future assessments.* Mahwah, NJ: Lawrence Erlbaum Associates.

Mills, C.N., & Steffen, M. (2000). The GRE computer adaptive test: Operational issues. In W.J. van der Linden & C.A.W. Glas (Eds.), *Computerized adaptive testing: Theory and practice* (pp. 75–99). Dordrecht and Boston: Kluwer Academic.

Mills, C.N., & Stocking, M. (1996). Practical issues in large-scale computerized adaptive testing. *Applied Measurement in Education, 9*(4), 287–304.

Mislevy, R.J. (1987). Recent developments in item response theory with implications for teacher certification. In E.Z. Rothkopf (Ed.) *Review of*

Research in Education (Vol. 14, pp 239-275). Washington, DC: American Educational Research Association.

Mislevy, R.J. (1992). *Linking educational assessments: Concepts, issues, methods, and prospects*. Princeton, NJ: ETS Policy Information Center.

Mislevy, R.J., & Bock, R.D. (1990). *BILOG 3. Item analysis and test scoring with binary logistic models* (2nd ed.). Mooresville, IN: Scientific Software.

Mislevy, R.J., & Stocking, M.L. (1989). A consumers guide to LOGIST and BILOG. *Applied Psychological Measurement, 13*, 57–75.

Mislevy, R.J., Sheehan, K.M., & Wingersky, M.S. (1993). How to equate tests with little or no data. *Journal of Educational Measurement, 30*(1), 55–78.

Mittman, A. (1958). *An empirical study of methods of scaling achievement tests at the elementary grade level*. Unpublished Doctoral Dissertation, The University of Iowa, Iowa City.

Morgan, R., & Stevens, J. (1991). *Experimental study of the effects of calculator use in the advanced placement calculus examinations* (Research Report 91-5). Princeton, NJ: Educational Testing Service.

Morris, C.N. (1982). On the foundations of test equating. In P.W. Holland and D.B. Rubin (Eds.), *Test equating* (pp. 169–191). New York: Academic.

Muraki, E. (1992). A generalized partial credit model: Application of an EM algorithm. *Applied Psychological Measurement, 16*, 159–176.

Muraki, E. (1997). A generalized partial credit model. In W.J. van der Linden & R.K. Hambleton (Eds.), *Handbook of modern item response theory* (pp. 153–164). New York: Springer-Verlag.

Muraki, E., & Bock, R.D. (1997). *PARSCALE 3.0, IRT item analysis and test scoring for rating scale data*. Chicago, IL: Scientific Software International.

Muraki, E., Hombo, C.M., & Lee, Y.-W. (2000). Equating and linking of performance assessments. *Applied Psychological Measurement, 24*(4), 325–337.

National Center for Education Statistics (1998). *Linking the National Assessment of Educational Progress and the Third International Mathematics and Science Study: Eighth grade results*. E. Johnson and A. Siegendorf (Eds.). NCES 98-500. Washington, DC: U.S. Department of Education.

Neuman, G., & Baydoun, R. (1998). Computerization of paper-and-pencil tests: When are they equivalent? *Applied Psychological Measurement, 22*(1), 71–83.

Nitko, A.J. (1984). Defining "criterion-referenced test". In R.A. Berk (Ed.), *A guide to criterion-referenced test construction* (pp. 9-28). Baltimore, MD: Johns Hopkins.

Ogasawara, H. (2000). Asymptotic standard errors of IRT equating coefficients using moments. *Economic Review, Otaru University of Commerce, 51*(1), 1–23.
Ogasawara, H. (2001a). Item response theory true score equatings and their standard errors. *Journal of Educational and Behavioral Statistics, 26*(1), 31–50.
Ogasawara, H. (2001b). Least squares estimation of item response theory linking coefficients. *Applied Psychological Measurement, 25*(4), 3–24.
Ogasawara, H. (2001c). Marginal maximum likelihood estimation of item response theory (IRT) equating coefficients for the common-examinee design. *Japanese Psychological Research, 43*(2), 72–82.
Ogasawara, H. (2001d). Standard errors of item response theory equating/linking by response function methods. *Applied Psychological Measurement, 25*(1), 53–67.
Ogasawara, H. (2002). Stable response functions with unstable item parameter estimates. *Applied Psychological Measurement, 26*(3), 239–254.
Ogasawara, H. (2003a). Asymptotic standard errors of IRT observed-score equating methods. *Psychometrika, 68*(2), 193-211.
Ogasawara, H. (2003b, May). *EL 1.0*. Unpublished computer subroutines. (http://www.res.otaru-uc.ac.jp/ hogasa/)
Omar, M.H. (1996). *An investigation into the reasons item response theory scales show smaller variability for higher achieving groups* (Iowa Testing Programs Occasional Papers Number 39). Iowa City, IA: University of Iowa.
Omar, M.H. (1997, March). *An investigation into the reasons why IRT theta scale shrinks for higher achieving groups.* Paper presented at the Annual Meeting of the National Council on Measurement in Education, Chicago, IL.
Omar, M.H. (1998, April). *Item parameter invariance assumption and its implications on vertical scaling of multilevel achievement test data.* Paper presented at the Annual Meeting of the National Council on Measurement in Education, San Diego, CA.
O'Neil, H.F., Jr., Sugrue, B., & Baker, E.L. (1996). Effects of motivational interventions on the National Assessment of Educational Progress mathematics performance. *Educational Assessment, 3*(2), 135–157.
Oshima, T.C., Davey, T.C., & Lee, K. (2000). Multidimensional linking: Four practical approaches. *Journal of Educational Measurement, 37*(4), 357–373.
O'Sullivan, Reese, C.M., & Mazzeo, J. (1997). *NAEP 1996 science report card for the Nation and the States.* Washington, DC: National Center for Education Statistics.
Parshall, C.G., & Kromrey, J.D. (1993). *Computer testing versus paper-and-pencil testing: An analysis of examinee characteristics associated with mode effect.* Paper presented at the annual meeting of the American Educational Research Association, Atlanta.

Parshall, C.G., Houghton, P.D., & Kromrey, J.D. (1995). Equating error and statistical bias in small sample linear equating. *Journal of Educational Measurement, 32*(1), 37–54.

Parshall, C.G., Spray, J.A., Kalohn, J.C., & Davey, T. (2002). *Practical considerations in computer-based testing.* New York: Springer-Verlag.

Pellegrino, J.W., Jones, L.R., & Mitchell, K.J. (1999). *Grading the nation's report card: Evaluating NAEP and transforming the assessment of educational progress.* Washington, D.C.: National Academy Press.

Petersen, N.S., Cook, L.L., & Stocking, M.L. (1983). IRT versus conventional equating methods: A comparative study of scale stability. *Journal of Educational Statistics, 8,* 137–156.

Petersen, N.S., Kolen, M.J., & Hoover, H.D. (1989). Scaling, norming, and equating. In R.L. Linn (Ed.), *Educational measurement* (3rd ed., pp. 221–262). New York: Macmillan.

Petersen, N.S., Marco, G.L., & Stewart, E.E. (1982). A test of the adequacy of linear score equating models. In P.W. Holland & D.B. Rubin (Eds.), *Test equating* (pp. 71-135). New York: Academic Press, Inc.

Phillips, S.E. (1983). Comparison of equipercentile and item response theory equating when the scaling test method is applied to a multilevel achievement battery. *Applied Psychological Measurement, 7* (3), 267–281.

Phillips, S.E. (1985). Quantifying equating errors with item response theory methods. *Applied Psychological Measurement, 9*(1), 59–71.

Phillips, S.E. (1986). The effects of the deletion of misfitting persons on vertical equating via the Rasch model. *Journal of Educational Measurement, 23*(2), 107–118.

Phillips, S.E., & Clarizio, H.F. (1988a). Conflicting growth expectations cannot both be real: A rejoinder to Yen. *Educational Measurement: Issues and Practice, 7*(4), 18–19.

Phillips, S.E., & Clarizio, H.F. (1988b). Limitations of standard scores in individual achievement testing. *Educational Measurement: Issues and Practice, 7*(1), 8–15.

Pitoniak, M.J., & Royer, J.M. (2001). Testing accomodations for examinees with disabilities: A review of psychometric, legal, and social policy issues. *Review of Educational Research, 71*(1), 53–104.

Pommerich, M., Hanson, B.A., Harris, D.J., & Sconing, J.A. (2000). *Issues in creating and reporting concordance results based on equipercentile methods.* ACT Research Report 2000-1. Iowa City, IA: ACT.

Pommerich, M., Nicewander, W.A., & Hanson, B.A. (1999) Estimating average domain scores. *Journal of Educational Measurement, 363,* 199–216.

Press, W.H., Flannery, B.P., Teukolsky, S.A., & Vetterling, W.T. (1989). *Numerical recipes. The art of scientific computing (Fortran version).* Cambridge, UK: Cambridge University Press.

Ragosta, M., Braun, H., & Kaplan, B. (1991). *Performance and persistence: A validity study of the SAT for students with disabilities.* (College Board Report 91-3). New York: College Entrance Examination Board.

Rasch, G. (1960). *Probabilistic models for some intelligence and attainment tests.* Copenhagen: Danish Institute for Educational Research.

Raymond, M.R., & Viswesvaran, C. (1993). Least squares models to correct for rater effects in performance assessment. *Journal of Educational Measurement, 30*, 253–268.

Reckase, M.D. (1998). Converting boundaries between National Assessment Governing Board performance categories to points on the National Assessment of Educational Progress score scale: The 1996 science NAEP process. *Applied Measurement in Education, 11*(1), 9-21.

Reckase, M.D. (2000). *The evolution of the NAEP achievement levels setting process: A summary of the research and development efforts conducted by ACT.* Iowa City, IA: ACT, Inc.

Reinsch, C.H. (1967). Smoothing by spline functions. *Numerische Mathematik, 10*, 177–183.

Rosa, K., Swygert, K. A., Nelson, L., & Thissen, D. (2001). Item response theory applied to combinations of multiple-choice and constructed-response items scale scores for patterns of summed scores. In D. Thissen & H. Wainer (Eds.), *Test scoring.* Mahwah, NJ: Erlbaum.

Rosenbaum, P.R., & Thayer, D. (1987). Smoothing the joint and marginal distributions of scored two-way contingency tables in test equating. *British Journal of Mathematical and Statistical Psychology, 40*, 43–49.

Samejima, F. (1969). *Estimation of latent ability using a response pattern of graded scores.* (Psychometrika Monograph No. 17) Richmond, VA Psychometrics Society.

Samejima, F. (1972). A general model for free-response data. *Psychometrika Monograph Supplement, 37*(1, Pt. 2), 68.

Samejima, F. (1997). Graded response model. In W.J. van der Linden & R.K. Hambleton (Eds.), *Handbook of modern item response theory* (pp. 85–100). New York: Springer-Verlag.

Sands, W.A., Waters, B.K., & McBride, J.R. (Eds.). (1997). *Computerized adaptive testing: From inquiry to operation.* Washington, DC: American Psychological Association.

Schaeffer, G.A., Bridgeman, B., Golub-Smith, M.L., Lewis, C., Potenza, M.T., & Steffen, M. (1998). *Comparability of paper-and-pencil and computer adaptive test scores on the GRE General test* (ETS Research Report 98-38). Princeton, NJ: Educational Testing Service.

Schaeffer, G.A., Reese, C.M., Steffen, M., McKinley, R.L., & Mills, C.N. (1993). *Field Test of a Computer-Based GRE General Test* (Research Report 93-07). Princeton, NJ: Educational Testing Service.

Schaeffer, G.A., Steffen, M., Golub-Smith, M.L., Mills, C., & Durso, R. (1995). *The introduction and comparability of the computer adaptive*

GRE general test (ETS Research Report 95-20). Princeton, NJ: Educational Testing Service.

Schmitt, A.P., Cook, L. L., Dorans, N.J., & Eignor, D.R. (1990). Sensitivity of equating results to different sampling strategies. *Applied Measurement in Education, 3*(1), 53–71.

Schulz, E.M., & Nicewander, W.A. (1997). Grade equivalent and IRT representations of growth. *Journal of Educational Measurement, 34*(4), 315–331.

Segall, D.O. (1997). Chapter 19. Equating the CAT-ASVAB. In W.A. Sands & B.K. Waters & J.R. McBride (Eds.), *Computerized adaptive testing: From inquiry to operation* (pp. 181–198). Washington, DC: American Psychological Association.

Seltzer, M.H., Frank, K.A., & Bryk, A.S. (1994). The metric matters: The sensitivity of conclusions about growth in student achievement to choice of metric. *Educational Evaluation Policy Analysis, 16*(1), 41–49.

Shermis, M.D., & Burstein, J. (Eds.). (2003). *Automated essay scoring: A cross-disciplinary perspective.* Mahwah, NJ: Erlbaum.

Sireci, S.G. (1997). Problems and issues in linking assessments across languages. *Educational Measurement: Issues and Practice, 16*(1), pp. 12–19,29.

Sireci, S.G., & Berberoglu, G. (2000). Using bilingual respondents to evaluate translated-adapted items. *Applied Measurement in Education, 13,* 229-248.

Skaggs, G. (1990a). *Assessing the utility of item response theory models for test equating.* Paper presented at the annual meeting of the National Council on Measurement in Education, Boston.

Skaggs, G. (1990b). To match or not to match samples on ability for equating: A discussion of five articles. *Applied Measurement in Education, 3*(1), 105–113.

Skaggs, G., & Lissitz, R.W. (1986a). An exploration of the robustness of four test equating models. *Applied Psychological Measurement, 10*(3), 303–317.

Skaggs, G., Lissitz, R.W. (1986b). IRT test equating: Relevant issues and a review of recent research. *Review of Educational Research, 56*(4), 495–529.

Skaggs, G., & Lissitz, R.W. (1988). Effect of examinee ability on test equating invariance. *Applied Psychological Measurement, 12*(1), 69–82.

Slinde, J.A., & Linn, R.L. (1977). Vertically equated tests: Fact or phantom? *Journal of Educational Measurement, 14*(1), 23–32.

Slinde, J.A., & Linn, R.L. (1978). An exploration of the adequacy of the Rasch model for the problem of vertical equating. *Journal of Educational Measurement, 15*(1), 23–35.

Slinde, J.A., & Linn, R.L. (1979a). A note on vertical equating via the Rasch model for groups of quite different ability and tests of quite different difficulty. *Journal of Educational Measurement, 16*(3), 159–165.

Slinde, J.A., & Linn, R.L. (1979b). The Rasch model, objective measurement, equating, and robustness. *Applied Psychological Measurement, 3*(4), 437–452.

Spray, J.A., Ackerman, T.A., Reckase, M.D., & Carlson, J.E. (1989). Effect of medium of item presentation on examinee performance and item characteristics. *Journal of Educational Measurement, 26*, 261–271.

Stevens, S.S. (1946). On the theory of scales of measurement. *Science, 103*, 677-680.

Stevens, S.S. (1951). Mathematics, measurement and psychophysics. In S.S. Stevens (Ed.), *Handbook of experimental psychology* (pp. 1-49). New York, NY: Wiley.

Stocking, M.L. (1994). *Three practical issues for modern adaptive testing item pools* (Research Report 94-5). Princeton, NJ: Educational Testing Service.

Stocking, M.L. (1997). Revising item responses in computerized adaptive tests: A comparison of three models. *Applied Psychological Measurement, 21*(2), 129–142.

Stocking, M.L., & Eignor, D.R. (1986). *The impact of different ability distributions on IRT preequating* (Research Report 86-49). Princeton, NJ: Educational Testing Service.

Stocking, M.L., & Lord, F.M. (1983). Developing a common metric in item response theory. *Applied Psychological Measurement, 7*, 201–210.

Stocking, M.L., & Swanson, L. (1993). A method for severely constrained item selection in adaptive testing. *Applied Psychological Measurement, 17*(3), 277–292.

Stone, G.E., & Lunz, M.E. (1994). The effect of review on the psychometric characteristics of computerized adaptive tests. *Applied Measurement in Education, 7*(3), 211–222.

Sukigara, M. (1996). Equivalence between computer and booklet administrations of the new Japanese version of the MMPI. *Educational & Psychological Measurement, 56*(4), 570–584.

Suppes, P., & Zinnes, J.L. (1963). Basic measurement theory. In R.D. Luce, R.R. Bush, & E. Galanter (Eds.), *Handbook of mathematical psychology: Volume I* (pp. 1-76). New York, NY: John Wiley.

Sykes, R.C., & Ito, K. (1997). The effects of computer administration on scores and item parameter estimates of an IRT-based licensure examination. *Applied Psychological Measurement, 21*(1), 51–63.

Sykes, R.C., & Yen, W.M. (2000). The scaling of mixed-item-format tests with the one-parameter and two-parameter partial credit models. *Journal of Educational Measurement, 37*(3), 221–244.

Tate, R.L. (1999). A cautionary note on IRT-based linking of tests with polytomous items. *Journal of Educational Measurement, 36*(4), 336–346.

Tate, R.L. (2000). Performance of a proposed method for linking of mixed format tests with constructed response and multiple choice items. *Journal of Educational Measurement, 37*(4), 329–346.

Tenopyr, M.L., Angoff, W.H., Butcher, J.N., Geisinger, K.F., & Reilly, R.R. (1993). Psychometric and assessment issues raised by the Americans with Disabilities Act (ADA). *The Score, 15*, 1–15.

Thissen, D. (1991). *MULTILOG user's guide, version 6*. Chicago, IL: Scientific Software International.

Thissen, D., Nelson, L., & Swygert, K.A. (2001). Item response theory applied to combinations of multiple-choice and and constructed-response items Approximation methods for scale scores. In D. Thissen & H. Wainer (Eds.), *Test scoring*. Mahwah, NJ: Erlbaum.

Thissen, D., & Orlando, M. (2001). Item response theory for items scored in two categories. In D. Thissen & H. Wainer (Eds.), *Test scoring* (pp. 73–140). Mahwah, NJ: Erlbaum.

Thissen, D., Pommerich, M., Billeaud, K., & Williams, V.S.L. (1995). Item response theory for scores on tests including polytomous items with ordered responses. *Applied Psychological Measurement, 19*(1), 39–49.

Thissen, D., & Steinberg, L. (1986). A taxonomy of item response models. *Psychometrika, 51*, 567–577.

Thissen, D., Steinberg, L., & Mooney, J.A. (1989). Trace lines for testlets: A use of multiple-categorical-response models. *Journal of Educational Measurement, 26*(3), 247–260.

Thissen, D., Wainer, H., & Wang, X.-B. (1994). Are tests comprising both multiple-choice and free-response items necessarily less unidimensional than multiple-choice tests? An analysis of two tests. *Journal of Educational Measurement, 31*(2), 113–123.

Thomasson, G.L. (1997, March). *The goal of equity within and between computerized adaptive tests and paper and pencil forms*. Paper presented at the Annual Meeting of the National Council on Measurement in Education, Chicago, IL.

Thomasson, G.L., Bloxom, B., & Wise, L. (1994). *Initial operational test and evaluation of forms 20, 21, and 22 of the Armed Services Vocational Aptitude Battery (ASVAB)* (DMDC Technical Report 94-001). Monterey, CA: Defense Manpower Data Center.

Thurstone, L.L. (1925). A method of scaling psychological and educational tests. *The Journal of Educational Psychology, 16*(7), 433–451.

Thurstone, L.L. (1927). The unit of measurement in educational scales. *Journal of Educational Psychology, 18*, 505–524.

Thurstone, L.L. (1928). The absolute zero in intelligence measurement. *Psychological Review, 35*, 175–197.

Thurstone, L.L. (1938). Primary mental abilities. *Psychometric Monographs*. No. 1.

Thurstone, L.L., Ackerman, L. (1929). The mental growth curve for the Binet tests. *Journal of Educational Psychology, 20*, 569–583.

Tong, Y. (2002). *Assessing equating results with respect to different properties*. Unpublished MA Thesis, The University of Iowa, Iowa City, IA.

Tsai, T.-H., Hanson, B.A., Kolen, M.J., & Forsyth, R.A. (2001). A comparison of bootstrap standard errors of IRT equating methods for the common-item nonequivalent groups design. *Applied Measurement in Education, 14*(1), 17–30.

Vale, C.D. (1986). Linking item parameters onto a common scale. *Applied Psychological Measurement, 10*(4), 333–344.

van de Vijver, F.J.R., & Harsveldt, M. (1994). The incomplete equivalence of the paper-and-pencil and computerized versions of the General Aptitude Test Battery. *Journal of Applied Psychology, 79*(6), 852–859.

van der Linden, W. J. (1997). Book Review. Test Equating: Methods and Practices. *Psychometrika, 62*(2), 287–290.

van der Linden, W.J. (2000). A test-theoretic approach to observed-score equating. *Psychometrika, 65*,(4), 437–456.

van der Linden, W.J. (2001). Computerized adaptive testing with equated number-correct scoring. *Applied Psychological Measurement, 25*(4), 343-355.

van der Linden, W.J., & Adema, J.J. (1998). Simultaneous assembly of multiple test forms. *Journal of Educational Measurement, 35*(3), 185-198.

van der Linden, W.J., & Glas, C.A.W. (2000a). Capitalization on item calibration error in adaptive testing. *Applied Measurement in Education, 13*(1), 35–53.

van der Linden, W.J., & Glas, C.A.W. (Eds.). (2000b). *Computerized adaptive testing: Theory and practice.* Dordrecht, Boston: Kluwer Academic.

van der Linden, W.J., & Hambleton, R.K. (Eds.). (1997). *Handbook of modern item response theory.* New York: Springer-Verlag.

van der Linden, W.J., & Luecht, R.M. (1998). Observed-score equating as a test assembly problem. *Psychometrika, 63*(4), 401–418.

von Davier, A.A., Holland, P.W., & Thayer, D.T. (2003). *The kernel method of test equating.* New York: Springer-Verlag.

Vispoel, W.P. (1998). Reviewing and changing answers on computer-adaptive and self-adaptive vocabulary tests. *Journal of Educational Measurement, 35*(4), 328–345.

Vispoel, W.P., Boo, J., & Bleiler, T. (2001). Computerized and paper-and-pencil versions of the Rosenberg self-esteem scale: A comparison of psychometric features and respondent preferences. *Educational and Psychological Measurement, 61*(3), 461–474.

Vispoel, W.P., Rocklin, T.R., & Wang, T. (1994). Individual differences and test administration procedures: A comparison of fixed-item, computerized-adaptive, self-adapted testing. *Applied Measurement in Education, 7*(1), 53–79.

Vispoel, W.P., Wang, T., & Bleiler, T. (1997). Computerized adaptive and fixed-item testing of music listening skill: A comparison of efficiency, precision, and concurrent validity. *Journal of Educational Measurement, 34*(1), 43–63.

Wainer, H. (1993a). Some practical considerations when converting a linearly administered test to an adaptive format. *Educational Measurement: Issues and Practice, 12,* 15–20.

Wainer, H. (1993b). Measurement problems. *Journal of Educational Measurement, 30*(1), 1–21.

Wainer, H. (Ed.). (2000). *Computerized adaptive testing: A primer* (2nd ed.). Mahwah, NJ: Erlbaum.

Wainer, H., & Mislevy, R.J. (2000). Item response theory, item calibration, and proficiency estimation. In H. Wainer (Ed.), *Computerized adaptive testing: A primer* (pp. 61–100). Hillsdale, NJ: Erlbaum.

Wainer, H., Sireci, S.G., & Thissen, D. (1991). Differential testlet functioning: Definitions and detection. *Journal of Educational Measurement, 28*(3), 197–219.

Wainer, H., & Thissen, D. (1993). Combining multiple-choice and constructed-response test scores: Toward a Marxist theory of test construction. *Applied Measurement in Education, 6,* 103–118.

Wainer, H., & Thissen, D. (1994). On examinee choice in educational testing. *Review of Educational Research, 64,* 159–195.

Wainer, H., Thissen, D., & Wang, X.-B. (1993). *How unidimensional are tests comprising both multiple-choice and free-response items? An analysis of two tests* (Research Report 93-28). Princeton, NJ: Educational Testing Service.

Wainer, H., Wang, X., & Thissen, D. (1994). How well can we compare scores on test forms that are constructed by examinees choice? *Journal of Educational Measurement, 31,* 183–199.

Wang, M.W., & Stanley, J.C. (1970). Differential weighting: A review of methods and empirical studies. *Review of Educational Research, 4,* 663–704.

Wang, T., Hanson, B.A., & Harris, D.J. (2000). The effectiveness of circular equating as a criterion for evaluating equating. *Applied Psychological Measurement, 24*(3), 195–210.

Wang, T., & Kolen, M.J. (1996). A quadratic curve equating method to equate the first three moments in equipercentile equating. *Applied Psychological Measurement, 20*(1), 27–43.

Wang, T., & Kolen, M.J. (2001). Evaluating comparability in computerized adaptive testing: Issues, criteria, and an example. *Journal of Educational Measurement, 38*(1), 19–49.

Wang, T., Kolen, M.J., & Harris, D.J. (2000). Psychometric properties of scale scores and performance levels for performance assessments using polytomous IRT. *Journal of Educational Measurement, 37*(2), 141–162.

Wang, X.-B., Wainer, H., & Thissen, D. (1995). On the viability of some untestable assumptions in equating exams that allow examinee choice. *Applied Measurement in Education, 8*(3), 211–225.

Way, W.D. (1998). Protecting the integrity of computerized testing item pools. *Educational Measurement: Issues and Practices, 17*(4), 17–27.

Way, W.D., & Tang, K.L. (1991). *A comparison of four logistic model equating methods*. Paper presented at the annual meeting of the American Educational Research Association, Chicago.

Way, W.D., Forsyth, R.A., & Ansley, T.N. (1989). IRT ability estimates from customized achievement tests without representative content sampling. *Applied Measurement in Education, 2*, 15–35.

Way, W.D., Steffen, M., & Anderson, G.S. (2002). Developing, maintaining and renewing the item inventory to support CBT. In C.N. Mills, M.T. Potenza, J.J. Fremer, & W.C. Ward (Eds.), *Computer-based testing: Building the foundation for future assessments* (pp. 143–164). Mahwah, NJ: Lawrence Erlbaum Associates.

Wightman, L. (1993). *Test-takers with disabilities: A summary of data from special administrations of the LSAT*. (LSAC Research Report 93-03). Newtown, PA: Law School Admissions Council.

Wilcox, R.R. (1981). A review of the beta-binomial model and its extensions. *Journal of Educational Statistics, 6*(1), 3-32.

Williams, V.S.L., Pommerich, M., & Thissen, D. (1998). A comparison of developmental scales based on Thurstone methods and item response theory. *Journal of Educational Measurement, 35*(2), 93–107.

Willingham, W.W., Ragosta, M., Bennett, R.E., Braun, H., Rock, D.A., & Powers, D. E. (1988). *Testing handicapped people*. Boston, MA: Allyn and Bacon.

Wilson, M., & Wang, W.-C. (1995). Complex composites: Issues that arise in combining different modes of assessment. *Applied Psychological Measurement, 19*(1), 51–71.

Wingersky, M.S., Barton, M.A., & Lord, F.M. (1982). *LOGIST users guide*. Princeton, NJ: Educational Testing Service.

Wingersky, M.S., Cook, L.L., & Eignor, D.R. (1987). *Specifying the characteristics of linking items used for item response theory item calibration* (Research Report 87-24). Princeton, NJ: Educational Testing Service.

Wingersky, M.S., & Lord, F.M. (1984). An investigation of methods for reducing sampling error in certain IRT procedures. *Applied Psychological Measurement, 8*(3), 347–364.

Woodruff, D.J. (1986). Derivations of observed score linear equating methods based on test score models for the common item nonequivalent populations design. *Journal of Educational Statistics, 11*, 245–257.

Woodruff, D.J. (1989). A comparison of three linear equating methods for the common-item nonequivalent-populations design. *Applied Psychological Measurement, 13*, 257–261.

Wright, B.D. (1977). Solving measurement problems with the Rasch model. *Journal of Educational Measurement, 14*(2), 97-116.

Wright, B.D., & Stone, M.H. (1979). *Best test design*. Chicago: MESA Press.

Wright, N.K., & Dorans, N.J. (1993). *Using the selection variable for matching or equating* (RR-93-4). Princeton, NJ: Educational Testing Service.

Yang, W-L, Dorans, N. J. & Tateneni, K. (2003). Sample selection effects on AP multiple-choice score to composite score scalings. In N.J. Dorans (Ed.), *Population invariance of score linking: Theory and applications to advanced placement program examinations* (pp. 57-78), Research Report 03-27. Princeton, NJ: Educational Testing Service.

Yen, W.M. (1983). Tau-equivalence and equipercentile equating. *Psychometrika, 48*, 353–369.

Yen, W.M. (1984). Effects of local item dependence on the fit and equating performance of the three-parameter logistic model. *Applied Psychological Measurement, 8*(2), 125–145.

Yen, W.M. (1985). Increasing item complexity: A possible cause of scale shrinkage for unidimensional item response theory. *Psychometrika, 50*(4), 399-410.

Yen, W.M. (1986). The choice of scale for educational measurement: An IRT perspective. *Journal of Educational Measurement, 23*(4), 299–325.

Yen, W.M. (1988). Normative growth expectations must be realistic: A response to Phillips and Clarizio. *Educational Measurement: Issues and Practice, 7*(4), 16–17.

Yen, W.M. (1993). Scaling performance assessments: Strategies for managing local item dependence. *Journal of Educational Measurement, 30*, 187–213.

Yen, W.M., & Burket, G.R. (1997). Comparison of item response theory and Thurstone methods of vertical scaling. *Journal of Educational Measurement, 34*(4), 293–313.

Yen, W.M., Burket, G.R., & Fitzpatrick, A.R. (1996). Response to Clemans. *Educational Assessment, 3*(2), 181–190.

Yen, W.M., & Ferrara, S. (1997). The Maryland School Performance Assessment Program: Performance assessment with psychometric quality suitable for high stakes usage. *Educational Psychological Measurement, 57*(1), 60–84.

Yin, P., Brennan, R.L. & Kolen, M.J.' (in press). Concordance between ACT and ITED scores from different populations. *Applied Psychological Measurement.*

Zeng, L. (1993). A numerical approach for computing standard errors of linear equating. *Applied Psychological Measurement, 17*, 177–186.

Zeng, L. (1995). The optimal degree of smoothing in equipercentile equating with postsmoothing. *Applied Psychological Measurement, 19*, 177–190.

Zeng, L., & Cope, R.T. (1995). Standard errors of linear equating for the counterbalanced design. *Journal of Educational and Behavioral Statistics, 4*, 337–348.

Zeng, L., & Kolen, M.J. (1994). *IRT scale transformations using numerical integration.* Paper presented at the Annual Meeting of the American Educational Research Association, New Orleans.

Zeng, L., & Kolen, M.J. (1995). An alternative approach for IRT observed-score equating of number-correct scores. *Applied Psychological Measurement, 19*(3), 231–240.

Zeng, L., Hanson, B.A. & Kolen, M.J. (1994). Standard errors of a chain of linear equatings. *Applied Psychological Measurement, 18*, 369–378.

Ziomek, R., & Andrews, K. (1996). *Predicting the college grade point averages of special-tested students from their ACT assessment scores and high school grades.* Research Report 96-7. Iowa City, IA: ACT.

Ziomek, R., & Andrews, K. (1998). *ACT assessment score gains of special-tested students who tested at least twice.* Iowa City, IA: ACT.

Zimowski, M.F., Muraki, E., Mislevy, R.J., & Bock, R.D. (1996). *BILOG-MG: Multi-group IRT analysis and test maintenance for binary items.* Chicago, IL: Scientific Software International.

Zwick, R. (1991). Effects of item order and context on estimation of NAEP Reading Proficiency. *Educational Measurement: Issues and Practice, 10*, 10–16.

Zwick, R. (1992). Statistical and psychometric issues in the measurement of educational achievement trends: Examples from the National Assessment of Educational Progress. *Journal of Educational Statistics, 17*(2), 205–218.

Zwick, R., Senturk, D., Wang, J., & Loomis, S.C. (2001). An investigation of alternative methods for item mapping in the National Assessment of Educational Progress. *Educational Measurement: Issues and Practice, 20*(2), 15-25.

Appendix A: Answers to Exercises

Chapter 1

1.1.a. Because the top 1% of the examinees on a particular test date will be the same regardless of whether an equating process is used, equating likely would not affect who was awarded a scholarship.

1.1.b. In order to identify the top 1% of the examinees during the whole year, it is necessary to consider examinees who were administered two forms as one group. If the forms on the two test dates were unequally difficult, then the use of equating could result in scholarships' being awarded to different examinees as compared to just using the raw score on the form each examinee happened to be administered.

1.2. Because Form X_3 is easier than Form X_2, a raw score of 29 on Form X_3 indicates the same level of achievement as a raw score of 28 on Form X_2. From the table, a Form X_2 raw score of 28 corresponds to a scale score of 13. Thus, a raw score of 29 on Form X_3 also corresponds to a scale score of 13.

1.3. Because the test is to be secure, items that are going to be used as scored items in subsequent administrations cannot be released to examinees. Of the designs listed, the common-item nonequivalent groups design with external common items can be most easily implemented. On a particular administration, each examinee would receive a test form containing the scored items, a set of unscored items that had been administered along with a previous form, and possibly another set of unscored items to be used as a common-item section in subsequent equatings. Thus, all items that contribute to an examinee's score would be new items that would never be reused. The single group design with counterbalancing (assuming no differential order effects) and random groups design also could be implemented using examinees from other states. For example, using the random groups design, forms could be spiraled in another state which did not require that the test be released. The equated forms could be used subsequently in the state that required disclosure. The common-item nonequivalent groups design with internal common items may also be used in this way.

1.4. Random groups design. This design requires that only one form be administered to each examinee.

1.5. Only the common-item nonequivalent groups design can be used. Both the random groups and single group designs require the administration of more than one form on a given test date.

1.6. a. Group 2. b. Group 1. c. The content of the common items should be representative of the total test; otherwise, inaccurate equating might result.

1.7. Statement I is consistent with an observed score definition. Statement II is consistent with an equity definition.

1.8. Random. Systematic.

Chapter 2

2.1. $P(2.7) = 100\{.7 + [2.7 - (3 - .5)][.9 - .7]\} = 74$;
$P(.2) = 100\{0 + [.2 - (0 - .5)][.2 - 0]\} = 14$;
$P^{-1}(25) = (.25 - .2)/(.5 - .2) + (1 - .5) = .67$;
$P^{-1}(97) = (.97 - .90)/(1 - .90) + (4 - .5) = 4.2$.

2.2. $\mu(X) - 1.70$; $\sigma(X) = 1.2689$; $\mu(Y) = 2.30$; $\sigma(Y) = 1.2689$; $m(x) = x + .60$; $l(x) = x + .60$.

2.3. $\mu[e_Y(x)] = .2(.50) + .3(1.75) + .2(2.8333) + .2(3.50) + .1(4.25) = 2.3167$; $\sigma[e_Y(x)]$
$= \sqrt{[.2(.50^2) + .3(1.75^2) + .2(2.8333^2) + .2(3.50^2) + .1(4.25^2)] - 2.3167^2}$
$= 1.2098$.

2.4. Note: $\mu(X) = 6.7500$; $\sigma(X) = 1.8131$; $\mu(Y) = 5.0500$; $\sigma(Y) = 1.7284$. See Tables A.1 and A.2.

TABLE A.1. Score Distributions for Exercise 2.4.

x	$f(x)$	$F(x)$	$P(x)$	y	$g(y)$	$G(y)$	$Q(y)$
0	.00	.00	.0	0	.00	.00	.0
1	.01	.01	.5	1	.02	.02	1.0
2	.02	.03	2.0	2	.05	.07	4.5
3	.03	.06	4.5	3	.10	.17	12.0
4	.04	.10	8.0	4	.20	.37	27.0
5	.10	.20	15.0	5	.25	.62	49.5
6	.20	.40	30.0	6	.20	.82	72.0
7	.25	.65	52.5	7	.10	.92	87.0
8	.20	.85	75.0	8	.05	.97	94.5
9	.10	.95	90.0	9	.02	.99	98.0
10	.05	1.00	97.5	10	.01	1.00	99.5

TABLE A.2. Equated Scores for Exercise 2.4.

x	$m_Y(x)$	$l_Y(x)$	$e_Y(x)$
0	−1.7000	−1.3846	.0000
1	−.7000	−.4314	.7500
2	.3000	.5219	1.5000
3	1.3000	1.4752	2.0000
4	2.3000	2.4285	2.6000
5	3.3000	3.3818	3.3000
6	4.3000	4.3350	4.1500
7	5.3000	5.2883	5.1200
8	6.3000	6.2416	6.1500
9	7.3000	7.1949	7.3000
10	8.3000	8.1482	8.7500

2.5. The mean and linear methods will produce the same results. This can be seen by applying the formulas. Note that the equipercentile method will not produce the same results as the mean and linear methods under these conditions unless the higher order moments (skewness, kurtosis, etc.) are identical for the two forms.

2.6. $21.4793 + [(23.15 - 23)/(24 - 23)][22.2695 - 21.4793] = 21.5978$.

2.7. $1.1(.8x + 1.2) + 10 = .88x + 1.32 + 10 = .88x + 11.32$.

2.8. In general, the shapes will be the same under mean and linear equating. Under equipercentile equating, the shape will be the same only if the shape of the Form X and Form Y distributions are the same. Actually, the shape of the Form X scores converted to the Form Y scale will be approximately the same as the shape of the Form Y distribution.

Chapter 3

3.1. Note: $e_Y(x_i) = 28.3$; $t_Y(x_i) = 29.1$; $\hat{e}_Y(x_i) = 31.1$; $\hat{t}_Y(x_i) = 31.3$.

a. $29.1 - 28.3 = .8$. b. $31.1 - 28.3 = 2.8$. c. $31.3 - 28.3 = 3.0$. d. We cannot tell from the information given—we would need to have an indication of the variability of sample values over many replications, rather than the one replication that is given. e. Unsmoothed at $x_i = 26$. f. We cannot tell from the information given—we would need to have an indication of the variability of sample values over many replications, rather than the one replication that is given.

3.2. Mean, standard deviation, and skewness.

3.3. For Form Y, $C = 7$ is the highest value of C with a nominally significant χ^2. So, of the models evaluated, those with $C \leq 7$ would be eliminated. The model with the smallest value of C that is not eliminated using a nominal significance level of .30 is $C = 8$. For Form X, $C \leq 5$ are eliminated. $C = 6$ is the smallest value of C that is not eliminated.

3.4. Using equation (3.11), $\hat{d}_Y(28.6) = 28.0321 + 1.0557(.6) - .0075(.6)^2 + .0003(.6)^3 = 28.6629$.

3.5. Conversions for $S = .20$ and $S = .30$. Conversions for $S = .75$ and $S = 1.00$. It would matter which was chosen if Form X was used later as the old form for equating a new form, because in this process the unrounded conversion for Form X would be used.

3.6. It appears that the relationships for all S-parameters examined would fall within the ± 2 standard error bands. The identity equating relationship would fall outside the bands from 4 to 20 (refer to the standard errors in Table 3.2 to help answer this question).

3.7. For $N = 100$ on the Science Reasoning test, the identity equating was better than any of the other equating methods. Even with $N = 250$ on the Science Reasoning test, the identity equating performed as well as or better than any of the equipercentile methods. One factor that could have led to the identity equating appearing to be relatively better with small samples for the Science Reasoning test than for the English test would be if the two Science Reasoning forms were more similar to one another than were the two English forms. In the extreme case, suppose that two Science Reasoning forms were actually identical. In this case, the identity equating always would be better than any of the other equating methods.

Chapter 4

4.1. Denote $\mu_1 \equiv \mu_1(X)$, $\sigma_1 \equiv \sigma_1(X)$, etc. We want to show that $\sigma_s^2 = w_1\sigma_1^2 + w_2\sigma_2^2 + w_1w_2(\mu_1 - \mu_2)^2$. By definition, $\sigma_s^2 = w_1\mathbf{E}_1(X - \mu_s)^2 + w_2\mathbf{E}_2(X - \mu_s)^2$. Noting that $\mu_s = w_1\mu_1 + w_2\mu_2$ and $w_1 + w_2 = 1$,

$$\begin{aligned} w_1\mathbf{E}_1(X - \mu_s)^2 &= w_1\mathbf{E}_1(X - w_1\mu_1 - w_2\mu_2)^2 \\ &= w_1\mathbf{E}_1\big[(X - \mu_1) + w_2(\mu_1 - \mu_2)\big]^2 \\ &= w_1\mathbf{E}_1(X - \mu_1)^2 + w_1w_2^2(\mu_1 - \mu_2)^2 \\ &= w_1\sigma_1^2 + w_1w_2^2(\mu_1 - \mu_2)^2. \end{aligned}$$

By similar reasoning,

$$w_1\mathbf{E}_2(X - \mu_s)^2 = w_2\sigma_2^2 + w_1^2w_2(\mu_1 - \mu_2)^2.$$

Thus,

$$\begin{aligned} \sigma_s^2 &= w_1\mathbf{E}_1(X - \mu_s)^2 + w_2\mathbf{E}_2(X - \mu_s)^2 \\ &= w_1\sigma_1^2 + w_1w_2^2(\mu_1 - \mu_2)^2 + w_2\sigma_2^2 + w_1^2w_2(\mu_1 - \mu_2)^2 \\ &= w_1\sigma_1^2 + w_2\sigma_2^2 + (w_1 + w_2)w_1w_2(\mu_1 - \mu_2)^2 \\ &= w_1\sigma_1^2 + w_2\sigma_2^2 + w_1w_2(\mu_1 - \mu_2)^2. \end{aligned}$$

4.2. To prove that Angoff's $\mu_s(X)$ gives results identical to equation (4.17), note that $\mu_s(V) = w_1\mu_1(V) + w_2\mu_2(V)$, and recall that $w_1 + w_2 = 1$. Therefore, Angoff's $\mu_s(X)$ is

$$\begin{aligned} \mu_s(X) &= \mu_1(X) + \alpha_1(X\,|\,V)\big[w_1\mu_1(V) + w_2\mu_2(V) - \mu_1(V)\big] \\ &= \mu_1(X) + \alpha_1(X\,|\,V)\big[-w_2\mu_1(V) + w_2\mu_2(V)\big] \\ &= \mu_1(X) - w_2\alpha_1(X\,|\,V)\big[\mu_1(V) - \mu_2(V)\big], \end{aligned}$$

which is equation (4.17) since $\gamma_1 = \alpha_1(X\,|\,V)$.

To prove that Angoff's $\sigma_1^2(X)$ gives results identical to equation (4.19), note that

$$\sigma_s^2(V) = w_1\sigma_1^2(V) + w_2\sigma_2^2(V) + w_1w_2\big[\mu_1(V) - \mu_2(V)\big]^2.$$

(This result is analogous to the result proved in Exercise 4.1.) Therefore, Angoff's $\sigma_s^2(X)$ is

$$\begin{aligned}
\sigma_s^2(X) &= \sigma_1^2(X) + \alpha_1^2(X\,|\,V)\{w_1\sigma_1^2(V) + w_2\sigma_2^2(V) \\
&\quad + w_1w_2\big[\mu_1(V) - \mu_2(V)\big]^2 - \sigma_1^2(V)\}\\
&= \sigma_1^2(X) + \alpha_1^2(X\,|\,V)\big[-w_2\sigma_1^2(V) + w_2\sigma_2^2(V)\big]\\
&\quad + w_1w_2\alpha_1^2(X\,|\,V)\big[\mu_1(V) - \mu_2(V)\big]^2\\
&= \sigma_1^2(X) - w_2\alpha_1^2(X\,|\,V)\big[\sigma_1^2(V) - \sigma_2^2(V)\big]\\
&\quad + w_1w_2\alpha_1^2(X\,|\,V)\big[\mu_1(V) - \mu_2(V)\big]^2,
\end{aligned}$$

which is equation (4.19) since $\gamma_1 = \alpha_1(X\,|\,V)$. Similar proofs can be provided for $\mu_s(Y)$ and $\sigma_s^2(Y)$.

4.4. The Tucker results are the same as those provided in the third row of Table 4.4. For the Levine method, using equations (4.58) and (4.59), respectively,

$$\gamma_1 = \frac{6.5278^2 + 13.4088}{2.3760^2 + 13.4088} = 2.9401$$

$$\gamma_2 = \frac{6.8784^2 + 14.7603}{2.4515^2 + 14.7603} = 2.9886.$$

Note that

$$\mu_1(V) - \mu_2(V) = 5.1063 - 5.8626 = -.7563 \quad \text{and}$$
$$\sigma_1^2(V) - \sigma_2^2(V) = 2.3760^2 - 2.4515^2 = -.3645.$$

Therefore, equations (4.17)–(4.20) give

$$\begin{aligned}
\mu_s(X) &= 15.8205 - .5(2.9401)(-.7563) = 16.9323\\
\mu_s(Y) &= 18.6728 + .5(2.9886)(-.7563) = 17.5427\\
\sigma_s^2(X) &= 6.5278^2 - .5(2.9401^2)(-.3645) + .25(2.9401^2)(-.7563^2)\\
&= 45.4237\\
\sigma_s^2(Y) &= 6.9794^2 + .5(2.9886^2)(-.3645) + .25(2.9886^2)(-.7563^2)\\
&= 46.9618.
\end{aligned}$$

Using equation (4.1),

$$l_{Ys}(x) = \sqrt{46.9618/45.4237}(x - 16.9323) + 17.5427 = .33 + 1.02x.$$

4.5. Using the formula in Table 4.1,

$$\rho_1(X, X') = \frac{\gamma_1^2[\sigma_1(X,V) - \sigma_1^2(V)]}{(\gamma_1 - 1)\sigma_1^2(X)},$$

where $\gamma_1 = \sigma_1^2(X)/\sigma_1(X,V)$. For the illustrative example,

$$\gamma_1 = 6.5278^2/13.4088 = 3.1779 \quad \text{and}$$
$$\rho_1(X, X') = \frac{3.1779^2(13.4088 - 2.3760^2)}{(3.1779 - 1)6.5278^2} = .845$$

Similarly,

$$\rho_2(Y, Y') = \frac{\gamma_2^2[\sigma_2(Y,V) - \sigma_2^2(V)]}{(\gamma_2 - 1)\sigma_2^2(Y)},$$

where $\gamma_2 = \sigma_2^2(Y)/\sigma_2(Y,V)$. For the illustrative example,

$$\gamma_2 = 6.8784^2/14.7603 = 3.2054$$
$$\rho_2(Y, Y') = \frac{3.2054^2(14.7603 - 2.4515^2)}{(3.2054 - 1)6.8784^2} = .862.$$

4.6.a. From equation (4.38), the most general equation for γ_1, is $\gamma_1 = \sigma_1(T_X)/\sigma_1(T_V)$. It follows that

$$\gamma_1 = \frac{(K_X/K_V)\sigma_1(T_V)}{\sigma_1(T_V)} = \frac{K_X}{K_V}.$$

Similarly, $\gamma_2 = K_Y/K_V$.

4.6.b. Under the classical model, the γs are ratios of actual test lengths; whereas under the classical congeneric model, the γs are ratios of effective test lengths.

4.7. All of it [see equation (4.82)].

4.8. No, it is not good practice from the perspective of equating alternate forms. All other things being equal, using more highly discriminating items will cause the variance for the new form to be larger than the variance for previous forms. Consequently, form differences likely will be a large percent of the observed differences in variances, and equating becomes more suspect as forms become more different in their statistical characteristics. These and related issues are discussed in more depth in Chapter 8.

4.9. From equation (4.59),

$$\gamma_2 = \frac{\sigma_2^2(Y) + \sigma_2(Y,V)}{\sigma_2^2(V) + \sigma_2(Y,V)}.$$

Recall that, since γ_2 is for an external anchor, $\sigma_2(E_Y, E_V) = 0$. Replacing the quantities in equation (4.59) with the corresponding expressions in equation set (4.70) gives

$$\begin{aligned}\gamma_2 &= \frac{[\lambda_Y^2 \sigma_2^2(T) + \lambda_Y \sigma_2^2(E)] + \lambda_Y \lambda_V \sigma_2^2(T)}{[\lambda_V^2 \sigma_2^2(T) + \lambda_V \sigma_2^2(E)] + \lambda_Y \lambda_V \sigma_2^2(T)} \\ &= \frac{\lambda_Y[(\lambda_Y + \lambda_V)\sigma_2^2(T) + \sigma_2^2(E)]}{\lambda_V[(\lambda_V + \lambda_Y)\sigma_2^2(T) + \sigma_2^2(E)]} \\ &= \lambda_Y/\lambda_V.\end{aligned}$$

4.10.a. Since $X = A + V$,

$$\sigma_1(X, V) = \sigma_1(A + V, V) = \sigma_1^2(V) + \sigma_1(A, V).$$

The assumption that $\rho_1(X, V) > 0$ implies that $\sigma_1(X, V) > 0$. Since $\sigma_1^2(V) \geq 0$ by definition, the above equation leads to the conclusion that $\sigma_1(A, V) > 0$ and, therefore, $\sigma_1^2(V) < \sigma_1(X, V)$. Also,

$$\begin{aligned}\sigma_1^2(X) &= \sigma_1(A + V, A + V) = \sigma_1^2(A) + \sigma_1^2(V) + 2\sigma_1(A, V) \\ &= [\sigma_1^2(V) + \sigma_1(A, V)] + [\sigma_1^2(A) + \sigma_1(A, V)] \\ &= \sigma_1(X, V) + [\sigma_1^2(A) + \sigma_1(A, V)].\end{aligned}$$

Since $\sigma_1^2(A) \geq 0$ by definition and it has been shown that $\sigma_1(A, V) > 0$, it necessarily follows that $\sigma_1(X, V) < \sigma_1^2(X)$. Consequently, $\sigma_1^2(V) < \sigma_1(X, V) < \sigma_1^2(X)$.

4.10.b. $\gamma_{1T} = \sigma_1(X, V)/\sigma_1^2(V)$, which must be greater than 1 because $\sigma_1(X, V) > \sigma_1^2(V)$. Now, $\gamma_{1L} = \sigma_1^2(X)/\sigma_1(X, V)$. To show that $\gamma_{1T} < \gamma_{1L}$, it must be shown that

$$\sigma_1(X, V)/\sigma_1^2(V) < \sigma_1^2(X)/\sigma_1(X, V) \quad \text{or}$$

$$\sigma_1^2(X, V) < \sigma_1^2(X)\sigma_1^2(V) \quad \text{or} \quad \left[\frac{\sigma_1(X, V)}{\sigma_1(X)\sigma_1(V)}\right]^2 < 1,$$

which must be true because the term in brackets is $\rho_1(X, V)$, which is less than 1 by assumption.

4.10.c. Suppose that V and X measure the same construct and both satisfy the classical test theory model. If V is longer than X, then $\sigma^2(V) > \sigma^2(X)$. This, of course, cannot occur with an internal set of common items because V can be no longer than X.

Chapter 5

5.1. See Table A.3.

TABLE A.3. Conditional Distributions of Form X Given Common-Item Scores for Population 1 in Exercise 5.1.

	v			
x	0	1	2	3
0	.20	.10	.10	.00
1	.20	.20	.10	.05
2	.30	.30	.25	.10
3	.15	.30	.25	.25
4	.10	.075	.20	.30
5	.05	.025	.10	.30
$h_1(v)$	.20	.40	.20	.20

TABLE A.4. Calculation of Distribution of Form X and Common-Item Scores for Population 1 Using Frequency Estimation Assumptions in Exercise 5.2.

	v					
x	0	1	2	3	$f_2(x)$	$F_2(x)$
0	.20(.20) = .04	.10(.20) = .02	.10(.40) = .04	.00(.20) = .00	.10	.10
1	.20(.20) = .04	.20(.20) = .04	.10(.40) = .04	.05(.20) = .01	.13	.23
2	.30(.20) = .06	.30(.20) = .06	.25(.40) = .10	.10(.20) = .02	.24	.47
3	.15(.20) = .03	.30(.20) = .06	.25(.40) = .10	.25(.20) = .05	.24	.71
4	.10(.20) = .02	.075(.20) = .015	.20(.40) = .08	.30(.20) = .06	.175	.885
5	.05(.20) = .01	.025(.20) = .005	.10(.40) = .04	.30(.20) = .06	.115	1.00
$h_2(v)$	.20	.20	.40	.20		

5.2. See Table A.4.

5.3. See Table A.5.

5.4. For the Tucker method, the means and standard deviations for the synthetic group for Form X are 2.5606 and 1.4331, and for Form Y they are 2.4288 and 1.4261. The linear equation for the Tucker method is $l(x) = .9951x - .1192$. For the Braun-Holland method, the means and standard deviations for the synthetic group for Form X are 2.5525 and 1.4482, and for Form Y they are 2.4400 and 1.4531. The linear equation for the Braun-Holland method is $l(x) = 1.0034x - .1211$.

5.5. For X, V in Population 1, linear *regression slope* = .6058, and linear *regression intercept* = 1.6519. The means of X given V for $v = 0$, 1, 2, 3 are 1.9, 2.125, 2.65, 3.7. The residual means for $v = 0, 1, 2, 3$ are .2481, $-.1327$, $-.2135$, and .2308. Because the residuals tend to be negative in the middle and positive at the ends, the regression

TABLE A.5. Cumulative Distributions and Finding Equipercentile Equivalents for $w_1 = .5$ in Exercise 5.3.

x	$F_s(x)$	$P_s(x)$	y	$G_s(y)$	$Q_s(y)$	x	$e_{Ys}(x)$
0	.1000	5.00	0	.0925	4.62	0	.04
1	.2400	17.00	1	.3000	19.62	1	.87
2	.4850	36.25	2	.5150	40.75	2	1.79
3	.7300	60.75	3	.7525	63.38	3	2.89
4	.8925	81.12	4	.9000	82.62	4	3.90
5	1.0000	94.62	5	1.0000	95.00	5	4.96

of X on V for Population 1 appears to be nonlinear. Similarly, for Population 2, the mean residuals for the regression of Y on V are .2385, −.1231, −.2346, .3539, also suggesting nonlinear regression. This nonlinearity of regression would likely cause the Tucker and Braun-Holland methods to differ.

5.6. For $x = 1$; $P_1(x = 1) = 17.50$; 17.5th percentile for V in Population $1 = .375$; Percentile Rank of $v = .375$ in Population $2 = 17.5$; $Q_2^{-1}(17.5) = .975$. Thus, $x = 1$ is equivalent to $y = .975$ using chained equipercentile. For $x = 3$; $P_1(x = 3) = 62.50$; 62.5th percentile for V in Population $1 = 1.625$; Percentile Rank of $v = 1.625$ in Population $2 = 45$; $Q_2^{-1}(45) = 2.273$. Thus, $x = 3$ is equivalent to $y = 2.273$ using the chained equipercentile method.

Chapter 6

6.1. For the first item, using equation (6.1),

$$p_{ij} = .10 + (1 - .10)\frac{\exp[1.7(1.30)(.5 - -1.30)]}{1 + \exp[1.7(1.30)(.5 - -1.30)]} = .9835.$$

For the two other items, $p_{ij} = .7082$, and .3763.

6.2. For $\theta_I = .5$, $f(x = 0) = .0030$; $f(x = 1) = .1881$; $f(x = 2) = .5468$; $f(x = 3) = .2621$.

6.3.a. From equation (6.4), $b_{Jj} = Ab_{Ij} + B$ and $b_{Jj*} = Ab_{Ij*} + B$. Subtract the second equation from the first to get $b_{Jj} - b_{Jj*} = A(b_{Jj} - b_{Jj*})$, which implies that $A = (b_{Jj} - b_{Jj*})/(b_{Ij} - b_{Ij*})$.

6.3.b. From equation (6.3), $a_{Jj} = a_{Ij}/A$. Solving for A, $A = a_{Ij}/a_{Jj}$.

6.3.c. From equation (6.4), $b_{Jj} = Ab_{Ij} + B$. Taking the variance over items (j), $\sigma^2(b_J) = A^2\sigma^2(b_I)$. Solving for A and recognizing that variances must be positive, $A = \sigma(b_J)/\sigma(b_I)$.

6.3.d. From Exercise 6.3b., $A = a_{Ij}/a_{Jj}$. Taking the expectation, over items (j), $A = \mu(a_I)/\mu(a_J)$.

6.4. For $\theta_{Ii} = -2.00$, the value of the test characteristic curve is $.26 + .27 + .18 = .71$; at the other abilities, it is 2.07, 2.44, .71, and 2.44.

6.5. See Table A.6.

6.6. See Table A.7, which was constructed from Table 6.4.

6.7. See Table A.8.

6.8. Equating to a particular old form allows the use of traditional methods as a check. The traditional methods are based on different assumptions than the IRT methods, which allows for a comparison of how robust the equating is to the assumptions used. In addition, when equating to a particular old form, the common items provide direct evidence about how the new group compares to the old group for two groups of examinees that actually can be observed. In IRT equating to a calibrated pool, the only group of examinees who takes all of the common items is the new group. Thus, when equating to a pool, there is no old group with which to compare the new group on the common items, unless we rely on the assumptions of the IRT model, which is a much weaker comparison than can be made when we have two groups who actually took the common items.

6.9. Step (a) is similar, except that, with IRT, a design might be selected that involves linking to an IRT calibrated item pool. Step (b) is the same, in that the same construction, administration, and scoring procedures could be used for either type of equating method. In Step (c), IRT equating involves estimating item parameters and scaling the item parameter estimates. These steps are not needed in the traditional methods. In both types of methods, the raw scores are converted to scale scores by using statistical methods. However, traditional methods differ from the IRT methods. Also, the IRT methods might involve equating using an item pool. Steps (d), (e), and (f) are the same for the two types of methods.

6.10. $p^*_{ij1} = 1$, $p^*_{ij2} = .7728$, $p^*_{ij3} = .7350$, $p^*_{ij4} = .1151$, $p^*_{ij5} = .0959$, $p^*_{ij6} = .0448$, $p_{ij1} = .2272$, $p_{ij2} = .0378$, $p_{ij3} = .6199$, $p_{ij4} = .0192$, $p_{ij5} = .0511$, $p_{ij6} = .0448$.

6.11. $p_{ij1} = .5557$, $p_{ij2} = .2669$, $p_{ij3} = .1774$.

6.12. No. The a parameters are not increasing over categories.

6.13. $p_{ij1} = .0164$, $p_{ij2} = .4918$, $p_{ij3} = .4918$.

6.14. Probabilities of earning scores of 4 through 14 are, in order, .000022, .00198, .0265, .0938, .1922, .2599, .2258, .1305, .0505, .0133, .0018.

TABLE A.6. IRT Observed Score Equating Answer to Exercise 6.5.

Probability of Correct Answers and True Scores

θ_i	$j=1$	$j=2$	$j=3$	$j=4$	$j=5$	τ
Form X						
−1.0000	.7370	.6000	.2836	.2531	.2133	2.0871
.0000	.8799	.9079	.4032	.2825	.2678	2.7414
1.0000	.9521	.9867	.6881	.4965	.4690	3.5925
Form Y						
−1.0000	.7156	.6757	.2791	.2686	.2074	2.1464
.0000	.8851	.8773	.6000	.3288	.2456	2.9368
1.0000	.9611	.9642	.9209	.5137	.4255	3.7855

Form X Distribution

x	$f(x\,|\,\theta=-1)$	$f(x\,|\,\theta=0)$	$f(x\,|\,\theta=1)$	$f(x)$	$F(x)$	$P(x)$
0	.0443	.0035	.0001	.0159	.0159	.7966
1	.2351	.0646	.0052	.1016	.1175	6.6734
2	.3925	.3383	.0989	.2766	.3941	25.5831
3	.2524	.3990	.3443	.3319	.7260	56.0064
4	.0690	.1704	.4009	.2134	.9394	83.2720
5	.0068	.0244	.1506	.0606	1.0000	96.9718

Form Y Distribution

y	$g(y\,|\,\theta=-1)$	$g(y\,|\,\theta=0)$	$g(y\,|\,\theta=1)$	$g(y)$	$G(y)$	$Q(y)$
0	.0385	.0029	.0000	.0138	.0138	.6905
1	.2165	.0490	.0020	.0892	.1030	5.8393
2	.3953	.2594	.0425	.2324	.3354	21.9178
3	.2670	.4235	.3100	.3335	.6688	50.2114
4	.0752	.2276	.4589	.2539	.9228	79.5807
5	.0075	.0376	.1866	.0772	1.0000	96.1384

Form Y Equivalents of Form X Scores

x	$e_Y(x)$
0	.0772
1	1.0936
2	2.1577
3	3.1738
4	4.1454
5	5.1079

TABLE A.7. Answer to Exercise 6.6.

r	x	$f_r(x)$ for $r \leq 4$		Probability		
4	0	$f_4(0) = f_3(0)(1-p_4)$		$= .4430(1-.4)$		$= .2658$
	1	$f_4(1) = f_3(1)(1-p_4) +$	$f_3(0)p_4$	$= .4167(1-.4) +$	$.4430(.4)$	$= .4272$
	2	$f_4(2) = f_3(2)(1-p_4) +$	$f_3(1)p_4$	$= .1277(1-.4) +$	$.4167(.4)$	$= .2433$
	3	$f_4(3) = f_3(3)(1-p_4) +$	$f_3(2)p_4$	$= .0126(1-.4) +$	$.1277(.4)$	$= .0586$
	4	$f_4(4) =$	$f_3(3)p_4$	$=$	$.0126(.4)$	$= .0050$

TABLE A.8. Estimated Probability of Correct Response Given $\theta = 1$ for Exercise 6.7.

Item	Scale J	Mean/sigma	Mean/mean
1	.9040	.8526	.8522
2	.8366	.8076	.8055
3	.2390	.2233	.2222
sum	1.9796	1.8835	1.8799
Hdiff		.0037	.0039
SLdiff		.0092	.0099

6.15. For item 1, expected score equals $1(.01)+2(.725)+3(.132)+4(.132) = 2.384$. For item 2, the expected score equals $1(.15)+2(.25)+3(.40)+4(.20) = 2.65$. In the terminology of this chapter, these are the values examinee item response function on items 1 and 2 for examinees with the given ability. The expected score over the first two items equals $2(.0015)+3(.1112)+4(.2050)+5(.3448)+6(.2308)+7(.0792)+8(.0264) = 5.031$. In the terminology of this chapter, this is the value of the test characteristic curve for a two-item test for examinees with the given ability. Note that the sum of the expected scores over the two items is $2.384 + 2.65 = 5.034$, which agrees with the expected score over the two items, except for rounding error. This occurs because, conditional on ability, the test characteristic curve equals the sum of the item response functions.

6.16. Equations (6.31) and (6.32) will equal one another if

$$\begin{aligned}
a_{ij}\theta_i + c_{jk} &= \sum_{h=1}^{k} Da_j^*(\theta_i - b_j + d_{jh}) \\
&= \sum_{h=1}^{k} Da_j^*\theta_i - \sum_{h=1}^{k} Da_j^*b_j + \sum_{h=1}^{k} Da_j^*d_{jh} \\
&= Da_j^*k\theta_i + \left(-Dka_j^*b_j + Da_j^*\sum_{h=1}^{k} d_{jh}\right) \\
&= a_{jk}\theta_i + c_{jk}
\end{aligned}$$

as defined in equation (6.33).

Chapter 7

7.1. Answers to 7.1.a, 7.1.b, and 7.1.c are given in Table A.9. Using equation (7.10) for Exercise 7.1.d, the standard error at $x = 3$ is 1.3467. The standard error at $x = 5$ is 1.4291.

TABLE A.9. Bootstrap Standard Errors for Exercise 7.1a–c.

Statistic	Sample				$\widehat{se}_{boot}$
	1	2	3	4	
$\hat{\mu}(X)$	4.0000	2.7500	4.2500	3.2500	
$\hat{\mu}(Y)$	3.0000	4.6667	3.6667	2.0000	
$\hat{\sigma}(X)$	2.1213	2.0463	1.9203	2.2776	
$\hat{\sigma}(Y)$	1.4142	.4714	1.8856	1.4142	
$\hat{l}_Y(x=3)$	2.3333	4.7243	2.4392	1.8448	1.2856
$\hat{l}_Y(x=5)$	3.6667	5.1850	4.4031	3.0866	.9098
$sc[\hat{l}_Y(x=3)]$	10.9333	11.8897	10.9757	10.7379	.5142
$sc[\hat{l}_Y(x=5)]$	11.4667	12.0740	11.7613	11.2346	.3639
$sc_{int}[\hat{l}_Y(x=3)]$	11	12	11	11	.5000
$sc_{int}[\hat{l}_Y(x=5)]$	11	12	12	11	.5774

7.2. Using equation (7.12),

$$\hat{var}[\hat{e}_Y(x_i)] \cong \frac{1}{[.7418 - .7100]^2} \left\{ \frac{(72.68/100)(1 - 72.68/100)(4329 + 4152)}{4329(4152)} \right.$$
$$\left. - \frac{(.7418 - 72.68/100)(72.68/100 - .7100)}{4329(.7418 - .7100)} \right\} = .09084.$$

Estimated standard error equals $\sqrt{.09084} = .3014$. Using equation (7.13),

$$\hat{var}[\hat{e}_Y(x_i)] \cong 8.9393^2 \frac{(72.68/100)(1 - 72.68/100)}{.33^2} \left(\frac{1}{4329} + \frac{1}{4152} \right) = .0687.$$

Estimated standard error equals $\sqrt{.0687} = .2621$. The differences between the standard errors could be caused by the distributions' not being normal. Also, equation (7.12) assumes discrete distributions, whereas equation (7.13) assumes continuous distributions. Differences also could result from error in estimating the standard errors.

7.3. a. 150 total (75 per form). b. 228 total (114 per form). c. If the relationship was truly linear, it would be best to use linear, because linear has less random error.

7.4. Using equation (7.11), with a sample size of 100 per form, the error variance for linear equating equals .03, and the error variance for equipercentile equals .0456. The squared bias for linear is $(1.3 - 1.2)^2 = .01$. Thus, the mean squared error for linear is $.03 + .01 = .04$. Assuming no bias for equipercentile, the mean squared error for equipercentile = .0456. Therefore, linear leads to less error than equipercentile. With a sample size of 1,000 per form, the mean squared error for linear is .013 and the mean squared for equipercentile is .0046. With a sample size of 1,000, equipercentile leads to less error than linear. Thus, it appears that linear equating requires smaller sample sizes than equipercentile equating.

7.5. a. .2629 and .4382. b. .1351 and .2683. c. .3264 and .6993. d. 96 per form and 267 per form.

7.6. The identity equating does not require any estimation. Thus, the standard error for the identity equating is 0. If the population equating is similar to the identity equating, then the identity equating might be best. Otherwise, the identity equating can contain substantial systematic error (which is not reflected in the standard error). Thus, the identity equating is most attractive when the sample size is small or when there is reason to believe that the alternate forms are very similar.

Chapter 8

8.1.a. From equation (7.18), a sample size of more than $N_{tot} = (2/.1^2)(2+ .5^2) = 450$ total (225 per form) would be needed.

8.1.b. From equation (7.18), a sample size of more than $N_{tot} = (2/.2^2)(2+ .5^2) = 112.5$ total (approx. 67 per form) would be needed.

8.1.c. In a situation where a single passing score is used, the passing score is at a z-score of .5, and the equating relationship is linear in the population.

8.2.a. For Forms D and following: In even-numbered years, the spring form links to the previous spring form and the fall form links to the previous spring form. In odd-numbered years, the spring form links to the previous fall, and the fall form links to the previous fall.

8.2.b. Form K links to Form I. Form L links to Form I. Form M links to Form L. Form N links to Form L.

8.3.a. For Forms D and following in Modified Plan 1 (changes from Link Plan 4 shown in italics): In even-numbered years, the spring form links to the previous spring form and the fall form links to the previous spring form. In odd-numbered years, *the spring form links to the fall form from two years earlier* and the fall form links to the previous fall.

For Forms D and following in Modified Plan 2: In even-numbered years, the spring form links to the previous spring form and the fall form links to the previous spring form. In odd-numbered years, *the spring form links to the previous spring* and the fall form links to the previous fall.

8.3.b. In Modified Plan 1, K links to I, L links to I, *M links to J*, and N links to L. In Modified Plan 2, K links to I, L links to I, *M links to K*, and N links to L.

8.3.c. For Modified Plan 1, Rule 1 is violated (this plan results in equating strains), and Rules 2 through 4 are met as well with this plan as with Single Link Plan 4. For Modified Plan 2, Rule 1 is achieved much better than for Modified Plan 1, Rule 2 is met better than for Single Link Plan 4 or for Modified Plan 1, and Rules 3 and 4 are met as well as for Modified Plan 1 or Single Link Plan 4. Modified Plan 2 seems to be the best of the two modified plans.

8.4. In Table 8.6, for the first 4 years the decrease in mean and increase in standard deviation were accompanied by an increase in the sample size. However, now in year 5 there is a decrease in the sample size. The Levine method results are most similar to the results when the sample size was near 1,050 in year 2. For this reason, the Levine method might be considered to be preferable. However, the choice between methods is much more difficult in this situation, because a sample size decrease never happened previously. In practice, many additional issues would need to be considered.

8.5.a. Randomly assign examinees to the two modes. Convert parameter estimates for the computerized version to the base IRT scale using the random groups design. Probably two different classrooms would be needed, one for paper and pencil and one for computer.

8.5.b. Use the items that are in common between the two modes as common items in the common-item equating to an item pool design.

8.5.c. Random groups requires large sample sizes and a way to randomly assign examinees to different modes of testing. Common-item equating to an item pool requires that the common items behave the same on computerized and paper and pencil versions. This requirement likely would not be met. This design also requires that the groups taking the computerized and paper and pencil versions be reasonably similar in achievement level.

8.5.d. It is unlikely that all items will behave the same when administered by computer as when administered using paper and pencil. Therefore, the results from using this design would be suspect. At a minimum, a study should be conducted to discover the extent to which context effects affect the performance of the items.

8.5.e. The random groups design is preferable. Even with this design, it would be necessary to study whether the construct being measured by the test changes from a paper and pencil to a computerized mode. For example, there is evidence that reading tests with long reading passages can be affected greatly when they are adapted for computer administration. Note that with the random groups design, the effects of computerization could be studied for those items that had been previously administered in the paper and pencil mode.

8.6. Some causes due to changes in items include changes in item position, changes in surrounding items, changes in font, changes in wording, and rearranging alternatives. Some causes due to changes in examinees include changes in a field of study and changes in the composition of the examinee groups. For example, changes in country names, changes in laws, and new scientific discoveries might lead to changes in the functioning of an item. As another example, a vocabulary word like "exorcist" might become much more familiar after the release of a movie of the same name. Some causes due to changes in administration conditions include changes in time given to take the test, security breaches, changes in mode of administration, changes in test content, changes in test length, changes in motivation conditions, changes in calculator usage, and changes in directions given to examinees.

8.7. To consider equating, the forms must be built to the same content and statistical specifications. Assuming that they are, the single group design is eliminated because it would require that two forms be administered to each examinee, which would be difficult during an operational administration. The common-item nonequivalent groups design is eliminated because having many items associated with each reading passage would make it impossible to construct a content representative set of common items. The random groups design could be used. This design requires large samples, which would not be a problem in this example. Also, the random groups design is not affected by context, fatigue, and practice effects, and the only statistical assumption that it requires is that the process used to randomly assign forms was effective. Therefore, the random groups design is best in this situation. Equipercentile equating would be preferred because it generally provides more accuracy along the score scale (assuming that the relationship is not truly linear). Equipercentile equating also requires large sample sizes, which is not a problem in the situation described.

Chapter 9

9.1. The Wright/Thurstone procedure starts with a set of items that are believed to measure a particular construct. The questions are administered to examinees and analyzed for model fit. Items that do not fit the model are eliminated. Test scores are used that estimate the underlying variable on the "interval" scale as defined by the

528   Appendix A: Answers to Exercises

model. A generalized model might need to be considered to accommodate items of different types. The scores on different item types are combined based on the dictates of the model. A score scale is used for reporting scores that is a linear transformation of the scores that result from the scaling process.

Under Lindquist's approach, test specifications are defined based on relative importance of content based on judgment of educators. Statistical screening of items is restricted to eliminating items that are flawed in relation to the item content (e.g., item is ambiguous). The test is scored so as to reflect the educator's views of the importance of different content areas. Scores on different item types are combined to reflect the relative importance of the item types based on judgment of educators. A score scale is chosen that is judged to facilitate test use.

9.2. For $\theta = -1$, $\theta^* = .37$; for $\theta = 1$, $\theta^* = 2.72$; for $\theta = 2$, $\theta^* = 7.39$. On the θ-scale, the difference in proficiency between examinees 1 and 2 (2 points) is *greater than* the difference in proficiency between examinees 2 and 3 (1 point). On the θ^*-scale, the difference between examinees 1 and 2 (2.35) is *less than* the difference between examinees 1 and 2 (4.67). Thus, the relative magnitude of the differences depends on the scale. In general, there is no reason to believe that one of these scales is preferable to the other.

9.3. In this example, $h = 2$ and $z_\gamma = 1.645$. From equation (9.7), $\sigma = \dfrac{2}{1.645\sqrt{1 - .7}} = 2.2$. Then $6(2.2) = 13.2$. Approximately 13 scale score points.

9.4. From Table 9.2, the raw score mean is 14.0066 and the standard deviation 5.0146. Using equation (2.22) with the linear transformation

$$sc(y) = \frac{15}{5.0146}y + \left[100 - \frac{15}{5.0146}14.0066\right] = 2.99y + 58.10.$$

Then, $sc(9) = 2.99(9) + 58.10 = 85.01$, which rounds to 85.

For the normalized transformation using the smoothed distributions, $z = -.8727$. To transform to the score scale take $15(-.8727)+100=86.91$, which rounds to 87.

9.5. From Table 9.2, the raw score mean is 14.0066. Using equation (9.9), $g(14.0066) = .8661$. Using equation (9.14),

$$sc[g(y)] = g(y)\frac{3}{.0907} + \left\{100 - \frac{3}{.0907}.8661\right\} = g(y)[33.08] + 71.35.$$

Applying this equation to a raw score of 9 gives $sc[g(9)] = g(9)(33.08) + 71.35 = .66(33.08) + 71.35 = 93.18$. Rounding to integers gives 93.

Appendix A: Answers to Exercises   529

9.6. From equation (9.15)

$$\theta_j(RP) = b_j - \frac{1}{Da_j}\ln\left(\frac{1-c_j}{RP/100 - c_j} - 1\right)$$

$$= .6260 - \frac{1}{1.7(.9089)}\ln\left(\frac{1-.2986}{.8-.2986} - 1\right)$$

$$= 1.22.$$

9.7. For the first composite, the proportional effective weights are .332, .264, and .404. For the second composite, the proportional effective weights are .201, .564, and .235.

9.8.a. For grade 4, $b = \sqrt{\frac{4}{12}}R - \sqrt{\frac{4}{12}}22 + 12$. For grade 3, $Q = \sqrt{\frac{12}{4}}b - \sqrt{\frac{12}{4}}10 + 22$. Chaining, $Q = \sqrt{\frac{12}{4}}\left(\sqrt{\frac{4}{12}}R - \sqrt{\frac{4}{12}}22 + 12\right) - \sqrt{\frac{12}{4}}10 + 22 = R + 2\sqrt{3} = R + 3.46$.

9.8.b. $Q = \sqrt{\frac{12}{12}}R - \sqrt{\frac{12}{12}}15 + 22 = R + 7$.

9.8.c. $Q = \sqrt{\frac{12}{12}}R - \sqrt{\frac{12}{12}}22 + 26 = R + 4$.

9.8.d. For grade 4, $tot = \sqrt{\frac{24}{12}}R - \sqrt{\frac{24}{12}}22 + 36$. For grade 3, $Q = \sqrt{\frac{12}{24}}tot - \sqrt{\frac{12}{24}}27 + 22$. Chaining, $Q = \sqrt{\frac{12}{24}}\left(\sqrt{\frac{24}{12}}R - \sqrt{\frac{24}{12}}22 + 36\right) - \sqrt{\frac{12}{24}}27 + 22 = R + 6.36$.

9.8.e. A major reason that the results differ is that grade 3 examinees do relatively poorly on item block c compared to grade 4 examinees. If the block c mean had been 8 for grade 3 examinees, then the methods would have produced much more similar results.

9.8.f. The linking in part (a) is most consistent with the grade-to-grade definition of growth, because this linking defines growth based only on those items that would be common between the two grades on the operational test.

9.8.g. The linking in part (d) is most consistent with the domain definition of growth, because this linking defines growth based over all of the items in blocks a, b, and c.

9.8.h. The grade 3 mean on level Q is 22 and the standard deviation is 12. The grade 4 mean, transformed to the raw score scale of level Q, is for linking in part (a) is $22 + 3.46 = 25.46$. The means are 29, 26, and 28.36 for parts (b), (c), and (d), respectively. The effect

TABLE A.10. Mean and Standard Deviation of Scale Scores for Thurstone Scaling for Exercise 9.9.

Statistic	Grade 3	Grade 4	Grade 5	Grade 6	Grade 7	Grade 8
Scaled such that Grade 3 Mean is 0 and S.D. is 1						
Mean	-1.5277	-0.9561	-0.5416	-0.3233	-0.1048	0.0000
S. D.	0.7778	0.8636	0.9302	0.9395	0.9807	1.0000
Scaled such that Grade 4 Mean is 400 and Grade 8 Mean is 800						
Mean	160.8973	400.0000	573.4399	664.7582	756.1567	800.0000
S. D.	325.3851	361.2686	389.1317	393.0273	410.2912	418.3522

size for the linking in part (a) is $(25.46 - 22)/\sqrt{12} = .99$. The effect sizes are 2.02, 1.15, and 1.83 for parts (b), (c), and (d), respectively. For this example, the effect sizes are nearly twice as large for the linking in part (d) than the linking in part (a). This result suggests the grade-to-grade growth definition might lead to smaller grade-to-grade differences than does the domain definition of growth when two levels are linked in the manner described and the subject matter is curriculum dependent.

9.9. See Table A.10.

Chapter 10

10.1. As noted repeatedly in earlier chapters, for the CINEG design to work well in equating, the common items must faithfully represent the full-length forms in both content and statistical specifications. In almost all linking contexts, the tables of specifications for the two tests are different and the two tests measure at least some different constructs. Hence, it is impossible for a single set of common items to represent faithfully the content of both tests. It might be argued that two sets of common items could be used, with the two sets representing the two different tests. This might be a more satisfactory solution than using one set, but there is no compelling reason to believe that double linking with two such sets of items will somehow "balance out" the differences between the tests.

10.2. Even though most students took both tests, they are still a self-selected group that may not be comparable to the group that took Test B, only. If so, it is problematic to use the prediction equation with this group. Also, the prediction equation will involve some degree of regression of Test B scores to the mean of Test A, which may somewhat disadvantage students who score high on Test B, and advantage students who score low. Most likely, a better alternative would be a concordance of Test A and Test B scores using the students who took both tests, or perhaps a subset of these students. A subset might be better if it is possible to identify a subset that is more similar to the group that took test B, only, than the group that took both tests.

10.3. Replacing the values in Table 10.3 in equation (10.16) gives

$$\begin{aligned} REMSD &= \sqrt{w_1 w_2} \left(\left| \frac{\mu_1(Y) - \mu_2(Y)}{\sigma(Y)} - \frac{\mu_1(X) - \mu_2(X)}{\sigma(X)} \right| \right) \\ &= \sqrt{.436(.564)} \left(\left| \frac{22.834 - 21.703}{4.218} - \frac{315.500 - 313.177}{36.186} \right| \right) \\ &= .101. \end{aligned}$$

10.4. With $M = 1$ and $F = 2$,

$$\hat{l}_{Y1}(x) - \hat{l}_{Y2}(x) = [-12.65127 + .11247(x)] - [-15.49409 + .11877(x)]$$

To get $MD = .863$, x is replaced with the estimated mean for the combined group, $\hat{\mu}(X) = 314.19089$. To get $ewMD = 1.126$, x is replaced by the midpoint of the ITED score range in the data, namely, $(163 + 382)/2 = 272.5$.

10.5. Examining Table 10.10, it is evident that, for the mean method, truncation automatically causes a large number of low and high ITED scores to have ACT equivalents that are identical (1 or 36, respectively) for males and females. The "contribution" of such scores to $ewREMSD$ is zero. By contrast, truncation has only a slight effect at the upper end of the score range for some of the other methods.

10.6. In considering the magnitudes of $REMSD$ under truncation for the various methods, it is helpful to consider what is happening at the extremes of the score scale as well as in the "middle" of the scale. First, for low scores, the truncation-induced zero contributions for the mean method do not affect $REMSD$ very much because the frequencies of low scores are relatively small (see Table 10.5), but for high scores the frequencies are substantial. Therefore, for high scores, truncation tends to lower $REMSD$ for the mean method beyond what it would be without truncation. For the other methods, truncation has very little influence on $REMSD$. Second, from Tables 10.10 and 10.11, it is evident that, for the mean method, the absolute values of the differences in equivalents ($M - C$ and $F - C$) in the "middle" of the ITED score range (where frequencies are relatively high) are almost always one ACT scale-score point, whereas

532   Appendix A: Answers to Exercises

for the other methods, the differences are often zero. The first explanation tends to make *REMSD* smaller for the mean method (relative to the other method), whereas the second explanation tends to make it larger. Apparently, for these data, the second explanation is the dominant one.

10.7. Given the general definition of the *rmsel* in equation (10.23), for the linear method,

$$rmsel[l_Y(x)] = \sqrt{\mathbf{E}[y - l_Y(x)]^2}.$$

Given the definition of $l_Y(x)$ in equation (10.5),

$$\begin{aligned}
y - l_Y(x) &= y - \left\{\mu(Y) + \frac{\sigma(Y)}{\sigma(X)}[x - \mu(X)]\right\} \\
&= [y - \mu(Y)] - \frac{\sigma(Y)}{\sigma(X)}[x - \mu(X)].
\end{aligned}$$

It follows that

$$\begin{aligned}
rmsel[l_Y(x)] &= \sqrt{\sigma^2(Y) + \sigma^2(Y) - 2\frac{\sigma(Y)}{\sigma(X)}\sigma(Y, X)} \\
&= \sqrt{\sigma^2(Y) + \sigma^2(Y) - 2\frac{\sigma(Y, X)\sigma^2(Y)}{\sigma(Y)\sigma(X)}} \\
&= \sqrt{2\sigma^2(Y) - 2\sigma^2(Y)\rho(Y, X)} \\
&= \sigma(Y)\sqrt{2[1 - \rho(Y, X)]}.
\end{aligned}$$

10.8. First, since we are putting ITED scores on the ACT scale, our focus in on the $\sqrt{2}\,sem$ for the ACT science test, as opposed to the ITED science test. Second, the $\sqrt{2}\,sem$ is appropriate because it represents an approximate best case scenario. Suppose, for example, that the ITED science test were constructed according to the same specifications as the ACT science test. Then, the two tests would be classically parallel, their correlation would be the reliability for each of them, and the error in linking one to the other would be $\sigma(Y)\sqrt{2[1 - \rho(Y, Y')]} = \sqrt{2}\,sem$. (This formula is called the standard error of substitution by Gulliksen, 1950, p. 40. It can be derived by obtaining the variance of the difference between observed scores for two classically parallel forms.)

10.9. Using equation (10.2) as $eq_Y(x)$ in equation (10.23),

$$\begin{aligned}
rmsel[m_Y(x)] &= \sqrt{\mathbf{E}[y - m_Y(x)]^2} \\
&= \sqrt{\mathbf{E}\{[y - x] - [\mu(Y) - \mu(X)]\}^2} \\
&= \sigma(Y - X).
\end{aligned}$$

Appendix B: Computer Programs

Computer programs are available, free of charge, that that can be used to conduct many of the analyses in the book. Data sets from this book are included with some of the computer programs. Windows and Macintosh versions of the programs are available. These programs can be found at the following web address: http://www.uiowa.edu/~casma/.

1. **RAGE-RGEQUATE** by L. Zeng, M.J. Kolen, B.A. Hanson, Z. Cui, and Y. Chien. This program conducts linear and equipercentile equating as described in Chapter 2. The program implements the cubic spline and log-linear smoothing methods described in Chapter 3.

2. **CIPE** by M.J. Kolen and Y. Chien. This program conducts observed score equating under the common-item nonequivalent groups design as described in Chapter 4 and Chapter 5. Tucker linear (external or internal common items), Levine linear observed score (internal common items only), and frequency estimation equipercentile equating with cubic spline smoothing are implemented.

3. **ST** by L. Zeng, B.A. Hanson, and Y. Chien. This program conducts IRT scale transformations using the mean/mean, mean/sigma, Stocking and Lord, and Haebara methods described in Chapter 6.

4. **POLYST** by S. Kim and M.J. Kolen. This program conducts IRT scale transformations using the mean/mean, mean/sigma, Stocking and Lord, and Haebara methods described in Chapter 6 for both dichotomous and polytomous IRT models.

5. **PIE** by B.A. Hanson, L. Zeng, Y. Chien. This program conducts IRT true and observed score equating using the methods described in Chapter 6.

6. **POLYEQUATE** by M.J. Kolen. This program conducts IRT true and observed score equating for dichotomous and polytomous IRT models using the methods described in Chapter 6.

7. **Equating Error** by B.A. Hanson and Y. Chien. This program estimates bootstrap standard errors of equipercentile equating for the random groups design. Standard errors for both the cubic spline postsmoothing and log-linear presmoothing methods can be calculated. Uses methods described in Chapter 7.

8. **POLYCSEM** by M.J. Kolen. This programs estimates conditional standard errors of measurement and can be used for assessing first- and second-order equity properties as described in Chapters 8 and 9.

9. **LEGS** by R.L. Brennan. This program conducts linear and equipercentile linking as described in Chapter 10.

Although these programs have been tested and we believe them to be free of errors, we do not warrant, guarantee, or make any representations regarding the use or the results of this software in terms of their appropriateness, correctness, accuracy, reliability, or otherwise. The entire responsibility for the use of this software rests with the user.

Index

Adaptive tests. *See* Computer adaptive tests
Alternative assessments. *See* Performance assessments
Anchor items. *See* Common-item nonequivalent groups design
Arcsine transformation. *See* Score scales
Authentic assessments. *See* performance assessments

Beta4, 75-84, 93, 99, 143, 350
Beta-binomial, 76, 349-350
BILOG. *See* IRT
Bootstrap. *See* Standard errors of equating
Braun-Holland linear method. *See* Common-item nonequivalent groups design

Calibrated item pools. *See* IRT
Calibration. *See* Linking
Category response function. *See* IRT
Chained equipercentile. *See* Common-item nonequivalent groups design
Chained linear. *See* Common-item nonequivalent groups design

Chains of equatings. *See* Standard errors of equating
Characteristic curve scale transformation methods *See* IRT
CIPE, 121, 148, 250, 533
Classical test theory, 9, 109-115, 118-120, 128-130, 131-132, 155
Common item equating to an IRT calibrated item pool, 201, 203-205, 273-274, 285
Common item design. *See* Vertical scaling
Common-item nonequivalent groups design
  Braun-Holland linear method
    described, 144-145
    and frequency estimation method, 144, 148, 151-152
    illustrative example, 147-152
    and Levine observed score linear method, 129, 152
    and Tucker method, 144, 151-152, 298
  chained equipercentile, 145-147
  chained linear, 147
  choosing among equating designs, 273-277

Common-item nonequivalent groups design (*Cont.*)
  choosing among methods, 292-295
  choosing from among results, 296-300
  CIPE, 121, 148, 250, 533
  common items, characteristics of, 19-23, 157, 228, 271-272, 307-309, 313
  computer-based and paper-and-pencil tests, 319
  and conditions conducive to a satisfactory equating, 284
  decomposing differences in means and variances, 125-128
  described, 19-23
  examinee groups in, 125-128, 271-272, 285-287, 298, 313
  external common items, 19, 103, 108, 112-115, 117, 120, 122, 128, 137, 139, 275, 322
  frequency estimation equipercentile method
    analysis of residuals, 148-151
    assumptions, 136-139, 148-151
    and Braun-Holland linear method, 144-145, 151-152
    and chained equipercentile method, 145-147
    estimating distributions, 142-143
    and examinee group differences, 286, 298
    illustrative example, 147-151
    and IRT equating, 197-198, 201
    and Levine observed score linear method, 152
    numerical example, 139-142
    smoothing, 142-143
    standard errors, 143, 146, 152, 249-251
    and Tucker linear method, 151-152
  internal common items, 19, 103, 108, 112-115, 117, 120-124, 128, 137, 283
  and IRT, 166-173

Levine observed score linear method
  assumptions, 109-110, 268, 286, 298-299
  and Braun-Holland linear method, 129, 152
  and congeneric models, 112-115
  and consistency checks, 298-300
  decomposing differences in means and variances, 125-128
  external common items, 114-115, 122
  and frequency estimation method, 152
  illustrative example, 121-124, 147-151
  internal common items, 113-114, 122
  and Levine true score linear method, 122
  results, 111-114, 122
  standard errors, 250-252
  and test reliability, 129-130
  and Tucker linear method, 122, 128-130, 152, 298-300
Levine true score linear method
  assumptions, 115-116
  and congeneric models, 118-120
  decomposing differences in means and variances, 125-128
  first-order (weak) equity property, 118-120
  illustrative example, 121-124
  and Levine observed score linear method, 122
  observed score, use with, 117-118, 122
  results, 116-117, 122
  standard errors, 250-252
  and test reliability, 129-130
  and Tucker linear method, 122
and linkage plans, 281-285, 313
mean equating, 125
and performance assessments, 321
and repeating examinees, 287

Common-item nonequivalent groups
design (Cont.)
results, choosing among, 296-300
and sample size, 288
and scale scores, 130-131, 152-153, 300
standard errors, 249-253
synthetic population weights, 104-105, 108-109, 115-117, 120-122, 124-129, 136-138, 140, 142, 144, 184, 195, 250
and test development, 18-23, 228, 271-272, 306-307, 313
Tucker linear method
assumptions, 106-109, 298
and Braun-Holland linear method, 144, 151-152, 298
and consistency checks, 298-300
decomposing differences in means and variances, 125-128
and external common items, 108, 122
and frequency estimation equipercentile method, 151-152
illustrative example, 121-124, 147-151
and internal common items, 108, 122
and Levine linear methods, 122, 128-130, 152, 298-300
results, 107-108, 122
special cases, 108-109
standard errors, 250-253
and synthetic population weights, 108-109
Common-item random groups design
described, 153
standard errors, 253
Common items. See Common-item
nonequivalent groups design and test development
Comparability of computer-based and paper-and-pencil tests, 316-320, 474
Composite scores, 207
Compound-binomial distribution, 181-183

Computer adaptive tests, 64, 155-156, 207, 314-320, 325
Computer-based tests, 25-26, 64, 155-156, 207, 314-320, 325
Computer programs
CIPE, 121, 148, 250, 533
Equating Error, 237, 534
LEGS, 430, 534
PIE, 191, 197, 534
POLYCSEM, 303, 355, 413, 534
POLYEQUATE, 222, 533
POLYST, 170, 217-218, 533
RAGE-RGEQUATE, 51, 74, 77, 89, 533
ST, 170, 188, 533
Concordance. See Linking
Conditional standard error of measurement, 301-306
Conditions conducive to a satisfactory equating, 312-313
Congeneric models, 112-115, 117-120, 131-132, 325
Consistency checks, 24, 298-300, 309
Context effects, 15-17, 23-24, 206-207, 258, 268, 272, 276, 307-308, 316
Continuization process, 39, 46, 64, 77
Counterbalancing. See Single group design with counterbalancing
Criteria
characteristics of equating situations, 25-26, 292-295
equating in a circle, 291
large sample, 291-292
in research studies, 290-292
simulated equating, 291
Cubic spline smoothing, 73, 84-91, 143, 146, 151-152

Decomposing differences in means and variances, 125-128
Delta method. See Standard errors of equating
Designs for data collection, choosing among, 7, 268, 273-277, 285-285. See also Common-item equivalent groups design;

Common-item nonequivalent groups design; Common-item random groups design; Random groups design; Single group design; Single group design with counterbalancing

Developmental score scales. *See* Vertical scaling

"Differences that matter" (DTM). *See* Score Scales

Disclosure of tests, 21-22, 275-276

Domain scores. *See* Score scales

Double linking. *See* Linkage plans

Editing rules, 287-288

Effective weights, 369-370

Equating, definition and rationale, 1-3, 7-9

Equating error. *See* Error in equating

Equating Error, 237, 534

Equating in a circle. *See* Criteria

Equating linkage plans. *See* Linkage plans

Equating versus not equating, 290, 296. *See also* Identity equating

Equipercentile equating
 analytic procedures, 43-46
 CIPE, 121, 148, 250, 533
 in common-item nonequivalent groups design, 135-153
 continuization process in, 39, 46, 64, 77
 definition of, 36-39
 estimating relationships, 48-54
 graphical procedures, 39-43
 and identity equating, 51-55, 80, 82, 98-100, 288-291
 illustrative example, 48-54
 and IRT equating, 196-201, 219-227, 292-295
 and linear equating, 46, 51-54, 268, 292-295
 and mean equating, 46, 51-54, 292-295
 and observed score equating property, 12

percentiles
 analytic procedures, 43-46, 51-54
 continuization process in, 38
 definition, 37-38
 graphical procedures, 39-43
percentile ranks
 analytic procedures, 43-46
 continuization process in, 39
 definition, 38-39
 graphical procedures, 39-43
 and performance assessments, 321
 properties of, 12, 46-48
 RAGE-RGEQUATE, 51, 74, 77, 89, 533
 in random groups design, 29-100
 and sample size, 259-260
 and scale scores, 52-62
 and scoring of tests, 63-64
 and single group designs, 62-63
 situations when appropriate, 292-295
 standard errors, 68-72, 80-83, 86-91, 236-242
 and symmetry, 37 *See also* Common-item nonequivalent groups design; Properties of equating; Smoothing

Equipercentile linking. *See* Linking

Equity. *See* Properties of equating

Equivalent groups design. *See* Vertical scaling

Error in equating
 and form differences, 289
 and identity equating, 289
 and linkage plans, 277-285
 random, 23-24, 68-72, 231-232, 267-268, 280-281, 288-290
 and sample size. *See* sample size
 and smoothing, 68-72
 and standard errors of equating. *See* Standard errors of equating
 systematic, 23-24, 68-72, 231-232, 267-268, 288-290
 total, 68-72

Estimation methods, choosing. *See* Statistical estimation methods, choosing
Evaluating results of equating
   criteria, 24-25
   properties, 24-25
   step in equating process, 8 *See also* Criteria; Results, choosing from among
Examinee groups
   and common-item nonequivalent groups design, 125-128, 271-272, 285-287, 298, 313
   and conditions conducive to a satisfactory equating, 312-313
   and design for data collection, 285-285, 298
   editing rules, 287-288
   group invariance property, 13, 24-25, 437-465
   and moderation, 286
   and random groups design, 286
   repeating examinees, 279, 287
Extended time. *See* Linking
External common items. *See* Common-item nonequivalent groups design

First-order equity property. *See* Properties of equating
Frequency estimation equipercentile method. *See* Common-item nonequivalent groups design

Generalized partial credit model. *See* IRT
Graded response model. *See* IRT
Group invariance property. *See* Properties of equating, examinee groups
Guttman scaling, 332

Haebara approach for IRT scale transformation. *See* IRT
Heuristics, 297-298
Hieronymus scaling. *See* Vertical Scaling

ICL. *See* IRT
Identity equating
   definition of, 34-36
   and equating error, 289
   and equating in a circle, 291
   and equipercentile equating, 51-55, 80, 82, 98-100, 288-291
   and hypothesis test, 296
   and IRT equating, 194
   and linear equating, 34-36, 51-55, 65, 288-291
   and mean equating, 34-36, 51-55, 288-291
   and performance assessments, 321
   and sample size, 289-290
   significance test, 296
   situations in which most appropriate, 288-291, 306
Illustrative examples
   common-item nonequivalent groups equipercentile, 147-152
   common-item nonequivalent groups linear, 121-124, 147-151
   equipercentile equating, unsmoothed, 48-54
   equipercentile equating, smoothed, 77-85, 89-91
   IRT, 185-201, 220-227
   scale scores, 56-62
   standard errors, 237-242, 250-252
Internal common items. *See* Common-item nonequivalent groups design
Item response function. *See* IRT
IRT (item response theory)
   ability, latent, 9, 156-157
   adaptive tests, 64, 155-156, 207, 314-320, 325
   assumptions, 156-157, 208-209, 227-228, 298
   BILOG, 156, 160-161, 166-167, 173-174, 183-185, 190, 194-196, 199, 388, 390
   calibrated item pools
      common-item equating, 201-207, 274-276, 285

IRT (*Cont.*)
    computer-based tests, 25, 64, 155-156, 207, 314-320, 325, 474
    item preequating, 205-207, 274-276, 307
    category response function, 210-211, 213
    characteristic curve scale transformation methods
        comparisons among criteria, 172-173
        defined, 168
        Haebara method, 168-175, 188-189, 216-219, 227
        hypothetical example, 170-172
        ST, 170, 188, 533
        Stocking and Lord method, 168-175, 188-189, 216-217, 227
        summing over examinees, 170
    common-item nonequivalent groups design, 166-172
    computer adaptive tests, 64, 155-156, 207, 314-320, 325
    defined, 9, 155-156
    and editing rules, 287-288
    and equipercentile equating, 196-201, 219-227, 292-295
    estimation of parameters, 156, 160-161
    generalized partial credit model, 212-214, 217
    graded response model, 209-211, 217-218, 220-227
    Haebara transformation method, 168-175, 188-189, 216-219, 227
    ICL, 167, 215, 388, 390, 401
    indeterminacy of scale, 164
    item characteristic curve, 157-158
    item response function, 214-215
    and linear equating, 292-295
    local independence, 157, 181, 208
    LOGIST, 156, 160-161, 166-167, 184
    Lord and Wingersky recursion formula, 182-183, 219-220

and mean equating, 292-295
mean/mean transformation method, 167-168, 170-172, 185-191, 216, 218, 227
mean/sigma transformation method, 167-168, 170-172, 185-191, 216, 218, 227
multidimensionality, 155-156, 207, 232
MULTILOG, 173-174, 215, 222
nominal model, 212-214, 217-218
number-correct scores, 175
observed score equating
    compound-binomial distribution, 181-184
    defined, 181
    and frequency estimation equipercentile, 198
    illustrative example, 185-201
    and IRT true score equating, 184-185, 197-198
    Lord and Wingersky recursion formula, 182-183, 219-220
    observed score distributions, 180-184
    and polytomous IRT, 219-227
    Rasch illustrative example, 197-202
    synthetic population, 184
observed scores, use with IRT true score equating, 180-181
PARSCALE, 215
and performance assessments, 290
PIE, 190, 195, 323, 534
POLYEQUATE, 222, 534
POLYCSEM, 303, 534
POLYST, 170, 217-218, 533
polytomous models, 156, 208-227, 474
practical issues, 227-228
random groups design, 166
Rasch equating 197-206, 288, 22-295
Rasch model, 156, 160, 331
sample size, 288-289

IRT (Cont.)
  scale, 333-334, 358
  scale transformation of parameter estimates, 165-172, 185-191
  scale transformation of parameters, 161-165
  scoring, 161, 175
  scoring function, 214-215
  and section preequating, 276-278
  single group with counterbalancing design, 166
  situations in which appropriate, 292-295
  ST, 170, 188, 533
  standard errors of equating, 244-245, 249-250, 263, 280
  Stocking and Lord transformation method, 168-175, 188-189, 216-219, 227
  test characteristic curve, 176, 214-215
  testlet, 208, 222
  three-parameter logistic model defined, 157-160
  true score equating
    equating process, 176-177, 364
    and frequency estimation equipercentile, 196-201, 219-227
    illustrative example, 191-194, 197
    and IRT observed score equating, 184-185, 197-198
    Newton-Raphson method in, 177-180
    and observed scores, 180-181
    and polytomous IRT, 219-227
    PIE, 191, 197, 533
    Rasch illustrative example, 198-201
    test characteristic curve, 176
  two-parameter logistic model, 156, 160
  unidimensionality, 155-157, 391
  See also Vertical scaling
Item context effects. See Context effects
Item mapping, 358-360, 364-366, 473

Item preequating. See Preequating
Item response theory. See IRT

Kernel smoothing, 73, 474
Kurtosis, defined, 47

Large sample criterion. See Criteria
LEGS, 470, 534
Levine observed score linear method. See Common-item nonequivalent groups design
Levine true score linear method. See Common-item nonequivalent groups design
Linear equating
  described, 31-32
  and equipercentile equating, 46, 268, 292-295
  and identity equating, 34-36, 51-55, 288-291
  and IRT equating, 292-295
  and linear regression, 33-34
  and mean equating, 34-36, 51-54, 292-295
  and observed score equating property, 12
  properties of, 12, 32-34
  in random groups design, 31-32
  and scale scores, 56-62
  situations in which appropriate, 292-295
  standard errors, 247-248, 250-253
  and symmetry, 33 See also Common-item nonequivalent groups design
Linear linking. See Linkng
Linear regression. See Regression and equating
Linkage plans
  common-item nonequivalent groups design, 281-285
  and conditions conducive to a satisfactory equating, 313
  double linking, 279-281, 285, 297-298
  random groups design, 277-281

Linking
   categorization schemes and criteria, 424-436, 474
   and computer-based tests, 314-320
   concordance, 426, 469
   correlations with other tests as benchmarks, 463-464
   cubic spline postsmoothing, 452-461
   degrees of similarity, 433-436
   differences that matter (DTM), 461-463
   example: ACT and ITED Science Tests, 444-465
   extended time, 465-467
   group invariance, 427, 437-465, 469-470
   LEGS, 470, 534
   Mislevy/Linn Taxonomy, 429-433, 435, 468
   and optional test sections, 323-324
   and performance assessments, 320-323
   root mean square error for linking, 464-465
   rounded equivalents, 457-461
   SMD 448
   statistical methods
      mean, 437-438, 440, 450-451, 455-456
      linear, 437, 440, 450-451, 453-456
      parallel-linear, 438-439, 450-451, 453, 455-456
      equipercentile, 426, 438-441, 450, 452-456
   statistics for overall group invariance, 441-443
      $RMSD(x)$, 441, 462
      $REMSD$, 441-443, 457, 460-463
      $ewREMSD$, 443, 457, 460-463
   statistics for pairwise group invariance, 443-444
      MD, 443-444, 455-457, 460
      $ewMD$, 443-444, 455-457, 460
      MAD, 443-444, 455-457, 460
      $ewMAD$, 443-444, 455-457, 460
   symmetry, 426
   test adaptations and translated tests, 467-468
   types of linking, 427-429
   Uncommon measures categorization scheme, 427-429, 431, 435-436
   unrounded equivalents, 450-456
   See also Calibration; Projection; Moderation; Statistical moderation; Judgmental (social) moderation
Local independence, 157, 181, 208
LOGIST. *See* IRT
Log-linear smoothing. *See* Smoothing
Lord and Wingersky recursion formula, 182-183, 219-220
Lord's equity property. *See* Properties of equating

Mean equating
   in common-item nonequivalent groups design, 125
   described, 20-31
   and equipercentile equating 46, 51-54, 292-295
   and identity equating, 34-36, 51-55, 288-291
   and IRT equating, 292-295
   and linear equating, 34-36, 51-54, 292-295
   and observed score equating property, 12
   properties of, 12, 30-31
   in random groups design, 30-31
   and scale scores, 56-62
   situations in which appropriate, 292-295
   standard errors, 125, 246
Mean linking. *See* Linking
Method 20, 70
Moderation. *See* Linking
Moment preservation. *See* Smoothing
MULTILOG. *See* IRT

Negative hypergeometric, 76
Newton-Raphson method, 177-180
Nominal model. *See* IRT
Nominal weights, 369-370
Nonequivalent groups. *See* Common-item nonequivalent groups design
Normal curve equivalents (NCE), 329, 339, 342-344
Normalized scores, 330, 338-344, 385
Not equating. *See* Identity equating

Observed score, 9
Observed score equating. *See* Common-item nonequivalent groups design, equipercentile equating, linear equating, mean equating, IRT
Observed score equating property. *See* Properties of equating
On-line calibration of computer-adaptive tests, 315-316
Optional test sections, 323-324, 474

Parallel-linear linking, *See* Linking
Parametric bootstrap, 238-239
PARSCALE *See* IRT
Percentile ranks. *See* Equipercentile equating
Percentiles. *See* Equipercentile equating
Performance assessments, 25, 320-323, 474
PIE, 191, 197, 534
POLYEQUATE, 222, 534
POLYCSEM, 303, 355, 413, 534
POLYST, 170, 217-218, 533
Preequating
    item, 205-207, 274-276, 307
    section, 274-276
Pretesting. *See* Test development
Projection. *See* Linking
Properties of equating and linking
    equity, 10-11, 24, 118-120, 130, 301-306, 318, 320
    and equipercentile equating, 12, 46-48
    and evaluating results, 24-25, 301-306, 320

group invariance, 13, 24, 427, 437-465, 469-470
linear equating, 12, 31-33
mean equating, 12, 32-34
observed score, 12, 24-25
same specifications, 10, 24, 29, 269-270, 313
symmetry, 10, 24, 29, 33-34, 36, 89, 268, 426

Quality control. *See* Standardization

RAGE-RGEQUATE, 51, 74, 77, 89, 533
Random equating error. *See* Error in equating
Random groups design
    choosing among equating designs, 273-277
    choosing among methods, 292-295
    choosing from among results, 296-300
    computer-based and paper-and-pencil tests, 318
    and conditions conducive to a satisfactory equating, 313
    described, 13-15
    and examinee groups, 285-287
    and IRT, 166
    and linkage plans, 277-281
    and observed score equating, 29-101
    and performance assessments, 321
    and spiraling process, 13-15
    standard errors
        bootstrap, 236-242
        equipercentile equating, 68-72, 80-83, 86-91, 94, 236-242, 297
        linear equating, 247-248, 250-253
        mean equating, 125, 246 *See also* Equipercentile equating; Linear equating; Mean equating
Rasch model. *See* IRT

Raw-to-scale score conversions. *See* Scale scores
Reequating, 310-312
Regression and equating, 10, 32-33, 89, 268
Repeating examinees. *See* Examinee groups
Results, choosing among
　in common-item nonequivalent groups design, 296-300
　consistency checks, 24, 298-300, 309
　equating vs. not equating, 296
　in random groups design, 297-298
　robustness checks, 296-297
Robustness checks, 296-297

Same specifications property. *See* Properties of equating
Sample size
　and conditions conducive to a satisfactory equating, 313
　and IRT, 288
　and random equating error, 23-24, 268, 288-290
　rules of thumb, 288-290
　and smoothing, 98-100, 231
　and standard errors of equating, 231-232, 258-261, 288-290
Scale anchoring, 358, 361, 364, 366, 473
Scale scores
　adjusting conversions, 61-62, 83-84
　choice of, 300
　and common-item nonequivalent groups methods, 130-131, 152-153, 300
　linear conversions, 54-55
　and equity property, 301-306
　nonlinear conversions, 56-62, 83-85, 94-98
　properties, 59-62
　and smoothing, 83-85, 94-98
　standard errors of, 241-242, 253-254

truncation of linear conversions, 55-56 *See also* Scaling; Score scales; Vertical scaling
Scaling
　defined, 4
　and equating process, 4-5, 277-278
　national norm group in establishing, 4
　user norm group in establishing, 4 *See also* Scale scores; Score scales; Vertical scaling
Scaling test. *See* Vertical scaling
Scaling test design. *See* Vertical scaling
Scaling to achieve comparability. *See* Linking
Score Scales
　arcsine transformation, 349-354, 357
　auxiliary score scale, 329, 339
　beta4, 350
　binomial error, 349-350
　composite scores, 368, 371-372
　compound binomial error, 349
　content-related information, incorporating, 335, 358-366, 473
　domain score, 333, 336
　effective weights, 369-370
　equity, 301-306 349, 354-357
　Guttman scaling, 332
　IRT scale, 333-334, 358
　IRT true score equating, 364
　item mapping, 358-360, 364-366, 473
　log-linear smoothing, 340
　maintaining score scales, 330, 366-367, 371-372, 474
　mastery level, 359
　nominal weights, 369-370
　norm group, 337, 339, 344-345, 368-369
　normal curve equivalents (NCEs), 329, 339, 342-344
　normative information, incorporating, 335, 337-345, 473

Score scales (*Cont.*)
  normalized scores, 330, 338-344, 385
  numbers of distinct score points, rules of thumb, 345-357
  percentile ranks, 339
  POLYCSEM, 355
  primary score scale, 329, 334, 336
  Rasch scaling, 331
  raw scores, 336
  rescaling, 367, 371
  response probability (*RP*) level, 358-359, 364
  scale anchoring, 358, 361, 364, 366
  scale types (nominal, ordinal, interval, ratio), 331-333
  scaling perspectives, 331-336
  score precision information, incorporating, 345-357, 473
  score transformations, 336-337
    linear, 337-338
    nonlinear, 336, 338-345
  and standard error of measurement, 348-354
  standard setting, 361-363, 367, 473
  stanines, 339, 342-344
  strong true score model, 349-354
  T-scores, 339, 342-344, 356-357
  test battery, 330, 368-369, 373-374
  and test equating, 366-367, 371
  Thurstone scaling, 331 *See also* Scale scores; Scaling; Vertical scaling
Scores. *See* Scoring of tests
Scoring of tests, 25-26, 63-64, 161, 175, 300, 317-318, 320-321
Section preequating. *See* Preequating
Simulated equating. *See* Criteria
Single group design
  choosing among equating designs, 273-277
  described, 15
  estimating equivalents, 62-63

standard errors of equating, 246, 250-252, 260
Single group design with counterbalancing
  choosing among equating designs, 273-277
  computer-based and paper-and-pencil tests, 318-319
  described, 15-17
  and differential order effect, 15-17, 23
  estimating equivalents, 62-63
  and IRT, 166
  standard errors, 246, 250-252, 260
  and systematic error, 23
Skewness, defined, 47
Smoothing
  conceptual framework, 68-72
  and equating error, 68-72, 98-100, 268, 298
  and identity equating, 80, 98-100, 298
  and linear equating, 298
  presmoothing
    beta4, 75-84, 146
    beta-binomial, 76
    and chained equipercentile, 146
    defined, 68
    four parameter beta binomial, 75-84, 146
    and frequency estimation, 142-143
    illustrative example, 77-84
    kernel, 73
    log-linear, 74-75, 77-84, 93, 142, 340
    Method 20, 77
    moment preservation, 73-74, 77, 142
    negative hypergeometric, 76
    RAGE-RGEQUATE, 51, 74, 77, 89, 533
    rolling average, 73
    and scale scores, 83-85, 94-98
    strategies summary, 91-98
    strong true score, 75-84, 142
  postsmoothing
    and chained equipercentile, 147

Smoothing (*Cont.*)
  cubic spline method, 73, 84-97, 142-143, 146, 151-152
  defined, 68
  and frequency estimation, 142-143, 146
  illustrative example, 89-97, 151-152
  and linking, 452-461
  RAGE-RGEQUATE, 51, 74, 77, 89, 533
  and scale scores, 90, 92, 94-98
  strategies summary, 91, 93-94, 98
  and symmetry, 89
  properties of, 72-73
  and sample size, 98-100, 231
  and standard errors, 68-72, 80, 83, 86, 89, 98, 240, 250
  strategies, 91, 93-94, 98, 297
Specifications of tests. See Test development
Spiraling. See Random groups design
ST, 170, 187, 533
Standard errors of equating
  bootstrap
    chains of equatings, 242-243
    defined, 235-238
    Equating Error, 237, 534
    illustrative example, 237-242
    parametric bootstrap, 238-240
    scale scores, 241-242
    smoothed equipercentile, 240
    using in practice, 262
  comparing precision
    random groups linear and equipercentile, 256-257
    random groups linear and single groups linear, 257-258
  defined, 23-24, 68-72, 232-234
  delta method
    chains of equatings, 254-255
    CIPE, 121, 148, 250, 533
    in common-item nonequivalent groups design, 249-253
    in common-item random groups design, 251-253
    defined, 245
    equipercentile with random groups, 68-72, 80-83, 86-91, 236-242, 246-300
    frequency estimation equipercentile, 152, 250-252
    IRT methods, 244-245, 249-250, 263, 288
    Levine linear methods, 249-252
    linear equating with random groups design, 247-248, 260
    mean equating, 125, 246
    scale scores, 253-254
    single group design, 63, 146, 250, 252
    Tucker linear method, 250-253
    using in practice, 261-263
  and double linking, 281
  mean standard error, 243-244
  sample size estimation
    random groups, equipercentile, 259-260
    random groups, linear, 258-259
    rules of thumb, 288-290
    single group, linear, 260
  and smoothed equipercentile equating, 68-72, 80, 83, 86, 89, 98, 240, 250
  specifying precision in sem units, 260-261
  using in practice, 261-263 See also Error in equating
Standardization
  and conditions conducive to a satisfactory equating, 313
  quality control, 268-269, 280, 309, 474
  reequating, 310-312
  test administration, 7-8, 13, 22-23, 269, 273, 307-309
  test development, 269, 307, 473
Standard setting, 361-363, 473
Stanines, 339, 342-343
Statistical estimation methods, choosing 7, 290-295. See also Common-item nonequivalent groups

design; Equipercentile equating; Linear equating; Mean equating; IRT
Stocking and Lord approach to IRT scale transformation. See IRT
Symmetry. See Properties of equating
Synthetic population weights. See Common-item nonequivalent groups design
Systematic equating error. See Error in equating

T-scores, 339, 342-344, 356-357
Test adaptation and translation. See Linking
Test administration, 7-8, 13, 22, 269, 272-273, 307-308, 316-317
Test battery, 330, 368-369, 373-374
Test characteristic curve. See IRT
Test development
    changes in test specifications, 272-273, 306-309
    common items, 19-23, 157, 228, 271-272, 307-308, 313
    and computer-based tests, 316
    conditions conducive to a satisfactory equating, 313
    design for data collection, 273-277
    linkage plans, 279
    performance assessments, 320-321
    pretesting, 207, 270, 313
    reequating, 310-312
    and same specifications property, 10, 13, 24, 29, 269-270, 312
    standardization, 269, 307-308
    test forms, 2, 7
    test specifications, 2, 7, 10, 269-273, 324-325
Test disclosure, 21-22, 275
Test security, 2, 15, 19, 25, 204, 275, 279-280, 284, 308-309, 312, 314-315
Test scores. See Scoring of tests

Test specifications. See Test development
Thurstone scaling. See Vertical scaling
True score, defined, 9
True score equating
    and equity, 11, 118-120
    IRT true score equating. See IRT
    Levine true score linear method. See Common-item nonequivalent groups design
    Tucker linear method. See Common-item nonequivalent groups design

Uncommon measures categorization scheme. See Linking
Unidimensionality assumption. See IRT

Vertical scaling
    common item design, 377, 379-380, 383, 386-387, 387-388
    context effects, 380
    domains measured, 375-376
    equivalent groups design, 378, 380, 383, 386-387, 389-390
    growth, definition of
        domain definition, 376-377, 474
        grade-to-grade definition, 376-377, 474
    Hieronymus scaling, 381-383, 414-418
    interim score scale, 381
    IRT, 387-393, 401-410, 411-413, 414-418
        Bayesian EAP, 392, 404, 413
        BILOG, 388, 390
        concurrent estimation, 388, 390-391
        ICL, 388, 390, 401
        LOGIST, 416
        maximum likelihood, 392
        separate estimation, 387-388, 389-391
        scale transformations, 392-393
        unidimensionality, 391
    limitations of vertically scaled tests, 412-414

Vertical Scaling (*Cont.*)
    POLYCSEM, 413
    research on vertical scaling, 414-418, 474
    scaling test, 378-379, 382-383, 390-391
    scaling test design for data collection, 378-379, 386-387, 393, 401
    statistics for comparing results,
        effect size, 410-412, 416-417
        grade-to-grade growth, 410-412, 5
        grade-to-grade variability, 410-412, 415-416
        separation of grade distributions, 410-412, 416-417
    structure of batteries, 373-374
    test scoring, 381, 391-392
    Thurstone scaling, 331, 383-387, 393-401, 411-412, 414-418

Weak equity. *See* Properties of equating

ALSO AVAILABLE FROM SPRINGER!

THE KERNEL METHOD OF TEST EQUATING
ALINA VON DAVIER, PAUL W. HOLLAND, and **DOROTHY T. THAYER**

Kernel Equating (KE) is a powerful, modern and unified approach to test equating. It is based on a flexible family of equipercentile-like equating functions and contains the linear equating function as a special case. This book will be an important reference for statisticians interested in the theory behind equating methods and the use of model-based statistical methods for data smoothing in applied work: practitioners who need to equate tests, and instructors in psychometric and measurement programs.

2003/256 PP./HARDCOVER/ISBN 0-387-01985-5
STATISTICS FOR SOCIAL SCIENCE AND PUBLIC POLICY

EXPLORATORY ITEM RESPONSE MODELS
A Generalized Linear and Nonlinear Approach
PAUL DE BOECK and **MARK WILSON** (Eds.)

This volume gives a new and integrated introduction to item response models (predominantly used in measurement applications in psychology, education, and other social science areas) from the viewpoint of the statistical theory of generalized linear and nonlinear mixed models. This new framework allows the domain of item response models to be co-ordinated and broadened to emphasize their explanatory uses beyond their standard descriptive uses.

A unified approach to notation and model description is followed throughout the chapters, and a single data set is used in most examples. SAS code is included.

2004/350 PP./HARDCOVER/ISBN 0-387-40275-6
STATISTICS FOR SOCIAL SCIENCE AND PUBLIC POLICY

USING SPSS 12.0 FOR WINDOWS
Data Analysis and Graphics
Second Edition
SUSAN B. GERBER and **KRISTIN VOELKL FINN**

The second edition of this popular guide demonstrates the process of entering and analyzing data using the latest version of SPSS (12.0), and is also appropriate for those using earlier versions of SPSS. The book is easy to follow because all procedures are outlined in a step-by-step format designed for the novice user. Students are introduced to the rationale of statistical tests and detailed explanations of results are given through clearly annotated examples of SPSS output. Topics covered range from descriptive statistics through multiple regression analysis. In addition, this guide includes topics not typically covered in other books such as probability theory, interaction effects in analysis of variance, factor analysis, and scale reliability.

2004/248 PP./SOFTCOVER/ISBN 0-387-40083-4

To Order or for Information:

In the Americas: **CALL:** 1-800-SPRINGER or **FAX:** (201) 348-4505 • **WRITE:** Springer-Verlag New York, Inc., Dept. S7818, PO Box 2485, Secaucus, NJ 07096-2485 • **VISIT:** Your local technical bookstore • **E-MAIL:** orders@springer-ny.com

Outside the Americas: **CALL:** +49 (0) 6221 345-217/8 • **FAX:** + 49 (0) 6221 345-229 • **WRITE:** Springer Customer Service, Haberstrasse 7, 69126 Heidelberg, Germany • **E-MAIL:** orders@springer.de

PROMOTION: S7818